# 1 MONTH OF
# FREE
# READING

## at

## www.ForgottenBooks.com

By purchasing this book you are eligible for one month membership to ForgottenBooks.com, giving you unlimited access to our entire collection of over 1,000,000 titles via our web site and mobile apps.

To claim your free month visit:

www.forgottenbooks.com/free875383

ISBN 978-0-266-61014-4
PIBN 10875383

This book is a reproduction of an important historical work. Forgotten Books uses
state-of-the-art technology to digitally reconstruct the work, preserving the original format
whilst repairing imperfections present in the aged copy. In rare cases, an imperfection in
the original, such as a blemish or missing page, may be replicated in our edition. We do,
however, repair the vast majority of imperfections successfully; any imperfections that
remain are intentionally left to preserve the state of such historical works.

# COLBURN'S

# UNITED SERVICE

# MAGAZINE,

AND

## NAVAL AND MILITARY JOURNAL.

1863, PART II.

LONDON :

HURST AND BLACKETT, PUBLISHERS,

*SUCCESSORS TO HENRY COLBURN,*

*13, GREAT MARLBOROUGH STREET.*

Army Ordnance

COLBURN'S

# UNITED SERVICE

# MAGAZINE,

AND

NAVAL AND MILITARY JOURNAL.

1863, PART II.

LONDON:
HURST AND BLACKETT, PUBLISHERS,
SUCCESSORS TO HENRY COLBURN,
13, GREAT MARLBOROUGH STREET.

SOLD BY ALL BOOKSELLERS.

LONDON:

Printed by A. Schulze, 13, Poland Street.

# INDEX

TO THE

# SECOND PART FOR 1863.

---

# CONTENTS

OF THE

# SECOND PART FOR 1863.

# COLBURN'S
# UNITED SERVICE MAGAZINE

AND

## NAVAL AND MILITARY JOURNAL.

### No. CCCCXVI.—JULY, 1863.

## CONTENTS.

### To CORRESPONDENTS.

We beg to thank "H. (Athenæum)" for his communication. "Steamship Ventilator" under consideration.

### LONDON:

## HURST AND BLACKETT, PUBLISHERS,
### SUCCESSORS TO HENRY COLBURN,
### 13, GREAT MARLBOROUGH STREET.
SOLD ALSO BY BELL AND BRADFUTE, EDINBURGH; M'GLASHAN AND GILL, DUBLIN; AND ALL BOOKSELLERS.

## FRANCE AND MEXICO.

The curtain has fallen upon the first act of the Mexican war. The news of the capture of Puebla, which was even doubted by the Ministers of the French Emperor, has been officially confirmed. We have General Forey's despatches before us. The capitulation of General Ortega, with 12,000 men, after so gallant a defence, every inch of ground having been manfully contested, borders on the marvellous. The Emperor Napoleon III. breathes again more freely. Forey is made a Marshal of France and the political barometer has risen again in favour of the second Empire. The result of the recent elections at Paris distinctly pointed out that a great crisis was impending. The French nation were getting tired of the Mexican campaign. Thousands of Frenchmen had fallen victims, either to the yellow fever or the bullets of the enemy; re-inforcements were sent out almost daily, yet the Mexicans held out, and refused to submit to the sway of a foreigner. The Mexican campaign has been a greater source of anxiety to Louis Napoleon than anything which has occurred during his successful reign. If a proof were needed, the delight of the Emperor, as expressed in his letter to General Forey, on receiving the news of the surrender of Puebla, would alone suffice to show that he is glad that he can now withdraw with some semblance of victory from a war which cannot lead to any substantial results. A peace, and an indemnity will follow. Our object in this article is to give to our readers a correct insight into the causes which led to the Mexican campaign, and to explain why England and Spain, who at first joined in the expedition, withdrew from it, and left France to herself. We shall also endeavour to give a connected narrative of the events which have taken place in Mexico since the first landing of the French troops at Vera Cruz. We must go back as far as November, 1861. Sir Charles Wyke, our minister at Mexico, sent in towards the end of that month an *ultimatum* for certain claims due to British subjects. M. de Saligny, the French minister, did the same as regarded French subjects, but the *ultimatum*, was rejected by the Mexican government. The Spanish government also sent in claims, but in consequence of the refusal of the Mexican government to take notice of them, the three Powers resolved to have recourse to arms. In December, 1861, a French squadron, under the orders of Admiral Jurien de la Gravière sailed for Vera Cruz. General Serrano, Captain-General of Cuba, was ordered by the Spanish government to send a squadron to Vera Cruz. Serrano, on the 8th December, 1861, took possession of San Juan d'Ulloa without firing a shot. The Mexican troops evacuated Vera Cruz, and fell back upon Puebla. The Spanish naval expedition appeared off Vera Cruz on the morning of the 8th December. It consisted of two frigates and nine steam transports. On the morning of the

10th, the second Spanish division composed of thirteen ships of war and sailing transports came to join those which were lying at anchor at Anton Lizardo. The Spanish Admiral Rulealcaba demanded the surrender of San Juan d'Ulloa within twenty-four hours. The demand was complied with. On the 17th M. de Saligny, the French minister at Mexico, arrived at Vera Cruz, and immediately embarked on board the Foudre. We shall quickly pass over the arrival of an English division of marines, the negotiations which ensued and terminated with the treaty of Soledad, the retirement of the English and Spanish contingents, and come at once to the narrative of the war in which France has been engaged single-handed with Mexico.

The French army laid formal siege to Puebla in the month of March last. The resistance offered by the Mexicans was quite unexpected. After thirteen days siege, on the 29th March, one of the exterior forts, Fort St. Xavier was taken by assault, and the Mexicans abandoned the redans of the Parral or Morelos. The defence of Puebla was entrusted to General Ortega, who was in constant communication with General Comonfort at the capital, Mexico. On the 29th of April, General Ortega thus sums up the state of the siege to that date :—

" The French have made eight assaults, succeeding only in two. We have lost nothing, save our abandoned forts and one line of defences. For the last thirty-one days we have not lost a foot of ground. The French continue to throw their bombs into the city, and are cutting ditches, and covered ways for an attack on Santa Anita."

General Ortega's despatches to General Comonfort state that on the night of the 24th of April the French exploded a mine on the block called Stemino, occupied by Mexican troops. A number of the Mexicans were buried in the ruins, but the remainder resisted the French all night, fighting desperately. On the morning of the 25th both parties were reinforced, and continued the fight with the greatest determination, the Mexicans at its close holding their original position. During the contest the French exploded another mine, in the Santa Jesu, and another fight ensued here, lasting seven hours, the Mexicans remaining masters of the field, and capturing 130 prisoners from the First Regiment of French Zouaves. The French left 400 dead on the field. Since these fights the French have kept up the bombardment of the city, though less vigorously than before. On the 1st of May President Juarez left the city of Mexico for General Comonfort's camp, near Puebla, for the purpose of urging immediate offensive operations against the French.

As the siege advanced, the resistance became more desperate. Even the Emperor of the French became anxious, and found it necessary to make an official announcement in the "Moniteur."

" *The prolongation* of the military operations before Puebla," says the official writer, "and the resistance which the French troops encounter, disturb the public mind.   The greater the confidence in the rapid success of the expedition, the greater was the impatience to see the troops triumphant over the unforeseen obstacles against which the courage of the soldiers and the skill and devotedness of the officers so energetically struggle.

To those pre-occupations is naturally added the question of supplies, both of food and ammunition, which have, however, never ceased to be amply provided.   Thus, at the date of the last official news, 19th April, the troops before Puebla were provided with rations for fifty days, the renewal of which was being effected with facility.   In addition, a reserve of three millions of complete rations, sufficient for the whole expeditionary corps for three months, was concentrated at Vera Cruz.

As to the ammunition for infantry and artillery successively shipped, added to what the different fractions of the expeditionary corps had taken with them, it consists, to mention only the principal articles, of 12,800,000 cartridges for infantry, being an average of 600 for each man : 42,348 cartridges for rifled cannon, being 675 rounds for each mountain gun ; 1,120 each field-piece ; 1,021 for each gun of the reserve ; and 1,000 for each siege gun.

"To those stores, and the supply of cannon, powder, and ammunition found at Vera Cruz, or supplied by the navy, will shortly be added a million of cartridges, 19,800 rounds for rifled cannon, 9,000 bombs, and 55,000 kilogrammes of gunpowder, now leaving St. Nazaire and Toulon.

"With a view to keep the supplies of every kind adequate to the consumption, the Minister of Marine, independently of the departures from St. Nazaire by the Transatlantic steamers, organised as early as March last, a regular line of transports sailing on the 23rd of every month, either from Toulon or Cherbourg, for Vera Cruz ; which will, on their return, bring back the men whose wounds or impaired health render necessary their native air or the attentions which can only be obtained at home."

The following are the clauses of the Convention of London and the instructions on which M. de Saligny and Vice-Admiral Jurien de la Gravière acted upon in renouncing negociations with the plenipotentiaries of President Juarez, and in ordering the French troops to advance on Mexico.

The preamble of the Convention of the 31st of October, which indicates the double object assigned to the common action of France, Great Britain, and Spain :

"The Emperor of the French, the Queen of Spain, and the Queen of Great Britain and Ireland, finding themselves placed, by the arbitrary and vexatious conduct of the authorities of the Republic of Mexico, under the necessity of exacting from them a more effectual protection for the persons and properties of their subjects, as well as the execution of the obligations contracted to-

wards them by the Republic of Mexico, have come to an understanding to conclude a Convention for the object of combining their
common action, and for that purpose have named as their plenipotentiaries, &c."

The first article of this Convention simply specifies a combined
action on the part of the allies. The second article is more important. It runs thus :

"The high contracting powers engage not to seek for themselves, in the employment of the coercive measures provided for by
the present Convention, any acquisition of territory, or any particular advantage, and not to exercise, in the internal affairs of
Mexico, any influence of a nature to attack the right of the Mexican
nation to freely choose and constitute the form of its Government."

On the 17th of April (1862) the French commanders issued a
proclamation to the Mexican people, in which it is said :—" Between your Government and ours war is now declared ; however,
we do not confound the Mexican people with an oppressive and
violent minority ; the Mexican people has ever been entitled to our
warmest sympathies ; it remains that they should show themselves
worthy of them. * * * * Let all men, so long divided by quarrels,
at present without an object, hasten to join us ; they hold in their
hands the destinies of Mexico ; the flag of France has been planted
in the Mexican soil—that flag will never flinch. Let all honourable men receive it as a friendly flag ! Let madmen dare to
fight it."

Despite the above appeal, the Mexicans came to the resolution
not to submit to a foreign ruler, whether Prince Napoleon or the
Archduke Maximilian of Austria. The negociations which were
opened, were broken off, England and Spain withdrew, and France
and Mexico have fought it out between them, with the only result, as yet—the capture of Puebla.

The following is a brief summary of the events which have taken
place since April last year :

In April last year the French Commissioners in Mexico,
M. Dubois de Saligny and Admiral Jurien de la Gravière, issued
a proclamation to the Mexicans setting forth the object and scope
of the French intervention. On the 20th of the same month
the expeditionary force quitted Cordova, and, after a successful
affair with Mexican cavalry, entered Orizaba, thirty-five leagues
distant from Vera Cruz. On the 28th, General Lorencez, who
then commanded, attacked the fortified heights of Cumbres, defended by 5,000 men and 18 guns belonging to the corps of Saragossa, drove them from their position and captured two mortars
and 20 men. On the 5th of May the French army came in sight
of Puebla. Whether owing to want of accurate information as to
the strength of the position, or to the excessive ardour of his troops,
*it was, in spite* of the most desperate efforts, repulsed from the

heights of Guadaloupe, and, with a loss of 177 men and officers killed, and 305 wounded or missing, forced to retire. This seems to have acted upon the Mexicans as Baylen did upon the Spaniards in 1808. They thought themselves invincible; and Barriozabal, the Mexican General, announced, in a boastful order of the day, that 'the Eagles had come across the ocean to fling down before the Mexican flag the laurels they had won at Sebastopol, Magenta, and Solferino.' Vain-glorious as he was, Barriozabal was too prudent to face the French in the open field, or to attempt to harass their retreat. They returned unmolested to their encampment, where they reposed three days. On the 8th they fell back on Orizaba, to get up their reinforcements and secure their communications with Vera Cruz. On the march occurred the brilliant affair of Acalcingo, when a battalion of the 99th Regiment greatly distinguished itself. The Mexican chief Marquez, who had been gained over by the French, was attacked by Saragossa. His position was most critical, when the officer who commanded the battalion in question hastened to his relief with 500 men, and completely routed the Mexicans, who left on the ground 150 killed, a flag, and 1,200 prisoners. Once more, at Orizaba, the French fortified themselves, throwing up works, which made a *coup de main* impossible. But, though safe against the enemy, they suffered greatly from want of provisions. Supplies came up very slowly from Vera Cruz, and in the beginning of June a large convoy was attacked and captured by the Mexican guerillas. The rations of officers and men had to be reduced to the lowest point ; and, in his report of the 17th of November, the French Minister of War, Marshal Randon, described the sufferings and the constancy of this handful of men in what he termed their 'unprecedented condition.' Mount Borrego, close to Orizaba, was essential to the complete security of the French position, and it was held by Ortega. A company of the 99th was sent to take it. After a short and vigorous attack it was taken, and the enemy driven from it with the loss of 200 killed and wounded, three mortars, and two flags. On the 28th of August the first instalment of the reinforcements, sent from France under General Forey, landed at Vera Cruz. A few weeks later the General himself arrived, and issued a proclamation declaring that 'it was not against the Mexican people that he was making war, but against a band of unscrupulous men, who were not ashamed to sell to foreigners the territory of their country.' He also said that the nation, when liberated by the French, would be free to choose the Government they thought proper, and that the part of France would be to aid Mexico in forming herself into a powerful, independent, rich, and free State.

On the 13th of November the unhealthy season passed away, and operations were resumed. Five companies of the 1st Regiment of Zouaves, and a party of the 5th Hussars attacked and took Omeaculpa; and on the 22nd a regiment of the line, 300 Marines, and a battery of artillery occupied Tampico, which, however, they soon after evacuated. On the 4th of December the French drove the enemy from Palma and St. Andres, and established themselves on the plateau of Anahuac. From that plateau the army began to manœuvre on its way to Puebla, so as to invest the place and cut off the retreat of the garrison. Puebla was invested on the 18th of March; the trenches were opened on the 23rd, and an entrance effected on the 29th, and, after a vigorous attack, the French made themselves masters of the Fort of San Xavier, with a loss of five officers, including a General, killed, 30 officers wounded, 56 non-commissioned officers and privates killed, and 443 wounded. The siege was continued with great energy, while the besieged made a desperate resistance. One block of houses after another was attacked and carried amid a storm of balls from innumerable loopholes, terraces, doors, windows, and church-steeples. The streets were covered with barricades, which the Mexicans defended inch by inch, while General Bazaine's corps, which had turned the place and intercepted the road to Mexico, watched Comonfort's army, and prevented it from succouring the besieged with men or provisions. The besieged suffered the greatest privations, and a body of Indians, who had made a last attempt to introduce a supply of flour into the town, were taken by the French. On the 1st of May Juarez left Mexico for the camp of Comonfort, to persuade him to attack the French and relieve Ortega from his desperate position in Puebla. Comonfort, however, did not venture to risk an engagement, the result of which would have been the destruction of his own corps without saving Ortega. Being thus reduced by famine, the defenders had no choice but to capitulate. The check at Guadaloupe has now been avenged. Comonfort's army, which consisted of about 20,000 men, has been dispersed, and there is no other corps capable of opposing the French on their march to the capital. In his letter of the 3rd of July last year, the Emperor ordered General Forey to establish a Provisional Government in Mexico, summon an Assembly under the laws of the country, and try to restore order in the administration and the finances. The events that have taken place in Poland since then may induce the Emperor to modify these instructions, and recall his troops before the period originally intended for the occupation of Mexico.

The political side of the " Mexican Question " seems to have been now quite cast into the back-ground. France no longer pretends to force a foreign Prince upon Mexico, and, with the fall of Puebla, probably, the war will terminate. The following are the circumstances which led to the departure of the Spanish and English troops.

The Commissioners of England, France and Spain had agreed to meet, on the 19th of April (1862), the Mexican Ministers at Orizaba, for the purpose of conducting negociations there, and bringing them to a conclusion. The forces of the Allies were allowed to advance on the understanding that if, after the Conference of the 19th the Commissioners of the three European Powers could not agree with the Mexican Government, they were again to withdraw their troops to Vera Cruz. The French Minister did not make his appearance. General Prim showed great impatience, and rode to the French quarters to ascertain the cause of the delay. To his surprise he met the French army advancing in military array. The French Admiral, Renier, informed him that he had received orders from France which absolved him from all former treaties; moreover, that he was informed that there was a conspiracy on foot to murder the sick. General Prim rode back to Orizaba and consulted Commodore Drummond. As he could not find any corroboration of the plot, General Prim waited upon the Mexican Minister and told him that he should urge the fulfilment of the stipulations. Admiral Renier declined compliance, and General Prim returned to Vera Cruz in disgust. On the 25th of April the English hauled down their flag, and saluted the Mexican flag with twenty-one guns. In a few days Spaniards and English reimbarked, and left the shores of Mexico.

The withdrawal of the Spaniards is thus explained by General Prim himself, in a letter dated Orizaba, 14th of April.—"Inflexible destiny is stronger than the will of man. Could I have doubted it, what has just occurred here would have convinced me. The triple alliance no longer exists. The soldiers of the Emperor remain in this country to establish a throne for the Archduke Maximilian—what madness!—while the soldiers of England and Spain withdraw from the Mexican soil. * * * * The Allies came here bound by the Convention of London, and we could not depart from it without placing ourselves in the wrong. I withdraw, then, with my troops, and go to Havannah to await the orders of my Government."

In the House of Lords, on the 19th June, Earl Russell explained why the English contingent had been withdrawn, which statement gave great satisfaction. It had never been the intention of England to invade Mexico. A convention had been signed between Sir Charles Wyke, Commodore Dunlop, and General Doblado, which satisfied the demands of England.

Since then, as already stated, France has carried on the war single-handed, and the last event, the fall of Puebla is thus described by General Forey in his despatch to the French Minister of War :—

"Puebla, May 18, 1863.

"M. le Maréchal,—Puebla is in our hands!

"The combat of San Lorenzo having dispersed the *corps d'armée* of Comonfort, which sought to force our line of investment and to throw supplies into Puebla, where the garrison was already suffering from hunger, although it had taken possession of everything available; on the other hand, a trench having been opened before the Fort of Téotimé-huacan, and our batteries of 30 guns, of various calibre, having opened their fire on the 16th against that fort, and in two hours completely destroyed its works, two vigorous attacks were made upon the place. General Ortega, at this juncture, made an offer of capitulation. But he had the presumption to ask to leave with all the honours of war, with arms, baggage, and artillery, to withdraw to Mexico. I declined all these strange proposals, telling him he might leave with all the honours of war, but that his army must march past the French army, lay down their arms, and remain prisoners of war, promising to him all those concessions which are customary among civilised people when a garrison has bravely performed its duty.

"These proposals were not accepted by General Ortega, who, in the night between the 16th and 17th, disbanded his army, destroyed the weapons, spiked his guns, blew up the powder magazines, and sent me an envoy to say that the garrison had completed its defence and surrendered at discretion.

"It was scarcely daylight when 12,000 men, most of them without arms or uniforms, which they had cast away in the streets, surrendered as prisoners, and the officers, numbering from 1,000 to 1,200, of whom 26 generals and 200 superior officers, informed me that they awaited my orders at the Palace of the Government.

"All the *matériel* of the place is in our hands, and has not been so much damaged as was supposed.

"I hasten to forward this dispatch to your Excellency, with instructions to Vera Cruz to send a fast steamer to the Havannah, so that the news should reach Europe, viâ New York, before the English steamer which would leave Vera Cruz on the 1st of June, and will bring you a detailed account of our situation.

"The army is in high spirits, and will advance in a few days on Mexico.

"I am, with respect, &c.,
"GENERAL FOREY."

Full and impartial details of the capitulation can scarcely be expected before the 2nd of July.

General Forey's official reports, which have now arrived, give ample details respecting the operations of the siege of Puebla, and the fall of that city. They testify to the determined resistance shown by the Mexicans, which General Forey attributes to the fact that the defence was organized by European demagogues. The first of General Forey's reports is anterior to the surrender, and bears date the 3rd May :—

"Monsieur le Maréchal,—I have the honour to make known to your Excellency the result of the operations of the siege of Puebla since the 19th of April, the date of my last report.

"On the night of the 19-20th the two islets 29 and 31, which had been put in a position of defence, were brilliantly carried—on the 19th by Colonel Mangin, of the 3rd Zouaves, and on the morning of the 20th islet No. 30 was taken possession of.

"On the 20th I wished to see our brave soldiers on the very theatre of their exploits during the night in the squares, or islets 29, 30, and 31, where I immediately gave the Cross of the Legion of Honour to a serjeant-major of the 18th battalion of Chasseurs, who was pointed out to me as having signalised himself in an extraordinary manner. The fact is that it would be necessary to see the incredible defences accumulated by the enemy in those squares to form an idea of, and appreciate all that has been done by our soldiers, who displayed boldness, energy, and patience in capturing these forts, which were much more difficult to carry than regular forts. I have already written to your Excellency that the defence of Puebla, organised by European demagogues, proves that they are masters in the art of making barricades. No one can compare anything to be seen in France with the disposition of Puebla—a disposition similar to what is found in all the cities of Mexico, which have almost as many churches as houses, and where all the houses are placed on terraces commanding one another. In the square, or block of buildings, No. 29, among others, there is a manufactory in the court, of which the Mexicans had made a species of Redan, of which the two faces were supported on two sides of the court by crenelated houses. This Redan had in front an enormous ditch, from four to five yards broad, and as many deep. The parapet was more than four yards thick, and the interior talus was formed of enormous planks of oak. Behind this Redan all the buildings were crenelated, and the issues were carefully protected. From one square to another the communication was maintained by a subterranean gallery. Our soldiers would never have been able to carry this work if an inhabitant had not indicated a passage in the stables of the manufactory, through a species of vaulted cellars parallel with the great face of the Redan. Upon our soldiers entering these cellars, a complete rout of the Mexicans took place, and they, by their flight through the subterranean gallery, showed a road to our soldiers from square 31, and the latter followed the Mexicans, and killed a great number, taking 200 prisoners.

"Our losses were very small owing to the dash of our Chasseurs of the 18th battalion, and the Zouaves of the 3rd Regiment, who acted admirably. By a happy providence not a single officer of the troops was wounded. M. de Galiffet alone, of my staff, was severely wounded by the bursting of a bomb or hand grenade, but I am in hopes he will not die.

"I visited also, in the afternoon of the 20th, the elevated battery which the marines had constructed on the church of St. Ildefonso, and the three islets recently captured. On the same day the column sent to Atlisco having terminated its labours, returned to the camp of San Juan.

"On the 21st the enemy evacuated the islets 26, 27, and 28, and set them on fire. This fire was very destructive, and lasted all the morning."

[The General then states that he visited other points, and the ambulances of head-quarters, and was satisfied with the treatment of the wounded soldiers.]

"On the 21st two sorties of the enemy took place against our positions of San Francisco and San Baltazar, which were repulsed.

"On the 22nd I went to Cholula, where we had established an hospital. I wished at the same time to visit that establishment, and to distribute some rewards among the Chasseurs d'Afrique of the squadron of Commandant de Tiné, of the 3rd Regiment, who had distinguished himself in the brilliant affair at Atlisco on the 14th instant. To Colonel de la Pena I gave the Cross of the Legion of Honour in the presence of the people of Cholula, who greatly applauded the act. The effect of this proceeding was very good. On the same day preparations were carried on for the attack on Santa Inez, and the islets 26, 27, and 28 were occupied and put in a defensive state, and two sorties which were made were repulsed, in which Captain Audin of the 62nd was killed in a charge on the enemy at the point of the bayonet."

[The General then details some affairs with the enemy, but they were of small account.]

"Everything being ready for attacking Santa Inez during the 25th, it was determined to carry the square or islet 52, in which the convent and the church of Santa Inez are situated. The engineers had formed under the street two galleries, in which were placed 250 kilogrammes of powder. The artillery had brought into the square 30 a battery of four 12-pounders in order to make a breach, and batter the interior of the square and the convent. Nothing was neglected to ensure the success of this attack. Unfortunately, on the 24th a violent storm took place, and floods of water invaded the galleries. General Douay then ordered the mines to be fired, and they produced the expected effect. On the 25th the battery in breach was unmasked; fire was opened, and when the breach was practicable a battalion of the 1st Zouaves charged into the square. But unforeseen obstacles presented themselves—such as a fierce fire in front and rear from entrenchments like those we encountered in our attacks on preceding days. More in arrear still there were terraces from which our soldiers were exposed to a heavy fire. The head of the column bravely bore this terrible fusillade; they succeeded even in effecting a lodgment in a house in the square; but the rest of the battalion, which followed, impeded by the rubbish and a converging fire from all the houses directed on them, was separated from the head of the column, which remained alone in the middle of the entrenchments which they had entered. Our loss was 5 officers and 27 soldiers killed, and 11 officers and 27 soldiers wounded."

[The General then says that the army was no way discouraged by this check, and mentions that he had received news of the departure of a large supply of artillery and munitions of war from Vera Cruz, for the service of the army. The General also gives details of proceedings up to the 28th, but nothing of importance occurred.]

" On the 29th a redan was established in front of San Miguelite to disturb the fort of Santa Anita. Two batteries were constructed, intended to batter the terraces of the town from Belen to Santa Inez, and on the 30th these batteries were armed, and ambuscades made to approach Santa Anita. General Bazaine completed by degrees the closing up of the line of investment above Puebla by means of trenches, fortified points, and works relieved by ambuscades. This line extended to Amazoc.

" On the 1st of May a sortie of cavalry of the enemy took place in the morning, on the side of Manzanilla, but it could not force our lines."

[A suspension of hostilities took place in order that the dead might be interred, and an exchange of prisoners effected. The General then continues as follows :—]

" The sanitary state of the expeditionary corps is very good ; the yellow fever has not yet appeared at Vera Cruz. All our wounded, whom I frequently see, go on well, and of those who have lost limbs two only have died up to the present time."

[The General concludes his report by giving an account of the progress made in constructing the intended railway.]

A despatch from the Commander of the " Darien," dated from Vera Cruz on the 22nd May, and addressed to the French Minister of Marine and of the Colonies, gives the following particulars of the surrender.

On Saturday, 16th May, the French troops had opened a parallel at 180 metres from Fort Téotimé-huacan and opened a heavy cannonade against it with the greatest effect. On the following day a sufficient breach was made to attempt the assault. General Mendoza at this juncture proceeded to General Forey's camp, offering to surrender Puebla if the Mexican troops were allowed to leave with their arms and a portion of their artillery. This General Forey formally declined to accede to. At five o'clock a messenger arrived with a letter from General Gonzales Ortega announcing to General Forey that he was willing to surrender unconditionally with the garrison. Colonel Manèque, second in command of the staff, was sent to occupy the city with the 1st battalions of foot Chasseurs, under the orders of Commandant du Courcy, and a squadron of hussars, which was quickly done. The French troops continued to enter on the 17th, 18th, and on the 19th General Forey made his entrance into Puebla. A salvo of 101 guns was immediately fired. General Ortega, 25 generals, 900 officers, 15,000 to 17,000 men with their arms, artillery and

baggage, surrendered prisoners of war.  On the 20th General
Bazaine, at the head of a division, advanced on the road towards
Mexico.

## DEPOT BATTALIONS.

Some disappointment is felt that the Depot Battalion System has
been allowed to survive another period of discussion on Military
affairs.  Although we may have reason to feel satisfied that no ill-
considered steps have been taken, for the subject is a difficult one, it
is certainly to be regretted that an opportunity has been lost of
urging Government to inquire into the working of the system, with
the view of testing the accuracy of the unfavourable opinions so
generally expressed regarding it.

When we consider how closely connected the system is with every
part of our military economy, we cannot but feel that the criticism
it has hitherto undergone has been founded on observation made
from restricted points of view, and that considerations of great
general importance have yet to be studied before we can say confidently that a change is desirable.  I propose to consider the practical
working of the depot battalion system in its bearing on the several
parts of our military organization.  In treating the subject I mean to
weigh the merits not only of the existing system, but of the various
substitutes that have been proposed in its place.  I shall endeavour to
do so with impartiality, pointing out what appears to me the peculiar recommendations which each plan possesses, as well as its defects.
It will be seen that I lean to one of these substitutes as possessing,
in my judgment, a larger amount of excellence than any other; but
my object is rather to draw attention to this important subject, and
to provoke discussion, than to insist on the adoption of any particular change as expedient.

Before we proceed, it will be well to determine what objects are
or ought to be contemplated in a system such as that of Depot
Battalions.  We shall probably find that these are not only important in themselves, but that their proper attainment is essential to
the efficiency of the service, and cannot be secured by our present
regimental organization without the aid of a depot, or reserve system
of some sort.

The first of these objects is to provide for the thorough training
of our recruits in establishments at a distance from the regiments to
which they belong, so that the efficiency of our forces, if called suddenly into the field, may not be marred by the presence of untrained
men.  These establishments require also to be so constituted that
the disciplining of reinforcements may not be disturbed by any
emergency of war, arising either at home or abroad.  It may be said,
perhaps, that it is needless to provide for the disciplining of rein-

forcements in case of war upon our own soil, inasmuch as any such war would be so sudden and short as to oblige us to rely solely upon forces actually prepared to take the field on the instant. I cannot agree in this view. No such emergency can occur without some warning, and even a few weeks, if our training establishments are organized upon sound principles, might be turned to useful account.

The next object is to provide an efficient organization for purposes of home defence of a considerable body of men, whom it is not possible in some cases, and not expedient in others, to employ on such duty with the service companies of their regiments. This body consists of trained recruits belonging to regiments abroad, who happen to be still in the United Kingdom, and of soldiers temporarily or permanently incapacitated by bodily infirmity for general service abroad, but whose cases (admitting of home duty) are not such as are held to necessitate discharge. A number of men of the latter class are to be found even in the regiments on the home establishment, and, as it is necessary that the service companies of these should be at all times prepared for immediate service, it is not expedient that such men should continue on their strength. In regiments on the foreign establishment the number is, of course, greater as the hardship and exposure incidental to our foreign service necessitate invaliding to England, in very many cases annually. Besides finding employment for men temporarily incapacitated for such service, it is necessary to keep the door open for their return to duty when fit for it.

Another object is to provide a satisfactory system of home training for young officers whose regiments are stationed abroad. However desirable it may appear, from some points of view, that all young officers should join their regiments direct, we find that it is quite indispensable that previous to joining the service companies, at all events if abroad, some home training should be provided. We cannot allow untrained officers to do duty with troops proceeding abroad, as our young officers must occasionally do, and we cannot send untrained officers to join a regiment which on their arrival may be employed on active service in the field. In the one case, complete inexperience might lead to results not only prejudicial to the service, but disastrous to the young men themselves; and in the other, the officers' services would be entirely useless to the country at the time, of all others, when they would be most wanted. All that we can do, therefore, is to endeavour to secure that, whilst the young officer is undergoing the indispensable preparatory training, he shall be placed under the most favourable conditions possible for the acquirement, not merely of professional knowledge, but of habits of steadiness and self-control.

The last object I need refer to is, that of arranging for the proper custody of regimental records and attestations. In this respect, all that is required is, that the documents shall not be exposed to risk of loss when regiments are on active service in the field.

Such, I believe, are the chief objects which the Depot Battalion organization is intended to attain for us, and it requires no argument to prove that very important public interests are involved in the issue. An impression, however, prevails very generally that these objects are attained not only imperfectly, but in a way that operates mischievously in many important respects. I will detail shortly the principal items of the charge against the Depot Battalion System, and I propose that we should consider, as we proceed, the validity of the grounds on which they are founded.

It is asserted that, as a school for recruits, a Depot Battalion is ill-adapted for either physical or moral training. Arguments of considerable force are adduced in support of this assertion. Each battalion being composed generally of six depots, the progress and conduct of any one recruit are matters, if not of entire indifference, at least of little interest to five-sixths of the officers and non-commissioned officers of the battalion. When it is borne in mind that the officers and non-commissioned officers are required to instruct and do duty with men chosen indiscriminately from the six depots, the force of the objection is apparent. Let us take a case of constant occurrence as an illustration. One of the depots happens to stand weaker on parade than the others, but its officers and non-commissioned officers are all present. When the battalion is equalized for drill, the officers and non-commissioned officers are necessarily sent to command men of other depots, none of whom they know or feel an interest in. Hence habits of careless indifference too often take the place of zeal, and the entire weight of instruction and supervision is thrown on the battalion staff. The men on their part feel that this is the case, and, as might be expected under such conditions, the objects of the instruction are often very imperfectly attained. Now, if this state of things is mischievous as regards drill, what, it is asked, must be its effects in more important matters—duty, discipline, and conduct?

Again, it is urged that many of the officers actually doing duty with each depot battalion are, from their inexperience, the last who should be selected to officer a body of recruits. It is scarcely possible to dispute this, when we consider that the young officers of no less than six regiments are frequently attached to one battalion and remain with it, sometimes for the greater part of a year, until the annual drafts embark, and that each after a short noviciate varying from two to three months, enters on his regular duties with the men. Much of the responsibility of the instruction and supervision requisite to convert recruits into disciplined soldiers thus falls into the hands of lads who are necessarily without either the knowledge which qualifies for instruction, or the tact and experience which are so essential in the management of men.

It is said, further, that recruits on joining a depot battalion, are not placed under favourable conditions for acquiring habits of steadiness and good conduct. This assertion is founded on the belief that the home service men, of whom there are a large number in every battalion, who never leave their depots, are not good companions in general for young soldiers. The lengthened stay of these men at one station, and constant intercourse with raw young recruits who have bounties to spend, is apt to have a demoralizing effect on them, which of course re-acts on the young soldiers as these pass in a continuous stream through the battalion. They live under constant temptation to make the young soldier minister to their vices whilst his money lasts, and their numbers and long association together constitute them a powerful clique, against which the well-disposed recruit may struggle in vain.

So much for the depot battalion as a training school for recruits in time of peace; let us now see what would become of it as a school for reinforcements in time of war. If the war should be in some foreign country, the system would remain undisturbed in its operation, but if war threatened us on our own soil, the case, it is asserted, would be different. In anticipation of such an emergency, the twenty-three depot battalions, no inconsiderable portion, be it remembered, of our available forces, would be called into the field and become involved in the excitement and movement incidental to preparations for defence. Their functions as training schools and depots for arming and clothing reinforcements would necessarily cease at the time when, from the impetus given to recruiting, they would be most wanted. In short, the depot battalion system does not contemplate this extreme case. Yet it is one which might occur.

Let us now turn to the next point—the efficiency for purposes of home defence of the depot battalion, considered as an individual fighting corps. The assailants of the system urge that this is the point in which, of all others, it fails most signally. They maintain that all the arguments we have noticed against the composition of the battalions apply with ten-fold force, when we contemplate the possibility of their taking the field. It would certainly be extremely difficult to find any answer to this charge. It is scarcely possible to conceive that a battalion composed of individuals belonging to six different regiments, whose connection with it is generally temporary and often distasteful, can be relied on as an effective force. With the exception of its staff, we cannot expect that any of its officers or men should feel such attachment or real interest in its reputation as to ensure its efficiency.

The next objection—and it is one on which great stress is laid—is, that the depot battalion is a bad school for young officers. The grounds on which this statement is based are, to some extent, similar to those on which the depot battalion is condemned as a school for recruits. The young officer's general duty at that critical time, when his professional habits, so to speak, are being formed, is superintended by officers to the majority of whom it is, or least may be, a matter of indifference how he performs it. Moreover, he feels from the first that his duty is performed not on behalf of his own regiment, but on behalf of an establishment in which his regiment is interested only to a small degree, and with which his own connection is temporary.  He may do conscientiously all that he believes is required of him, but without effectual supervision or *esprit de corps*, he will not do his work efficiently.  The consequence, it is alleged, is, that the young officers do not in general take sufficient interest in their work, and in many cases fall into lax habits of performing it when out of sight of the staff officers, who alone interfere actively in matters of general battalion duty.  I desire to guard myself from being misunderstood on this point.  It is not intended by those who are hostile to the system to convey the impression that the duty of depot battalions is throughout loosely conducted—quite the contrary—but it is believed that the efficiency to which these battalions often attain, notwithstanding these adverse circumstances, is due chiefly to the exertions of the battalion staff and depot commanders, and to the interest which some of the senior regimental officers and non-commissioned officers take in their own depots.

When we consider that the absence of effectual superintendence affects not only the performance of professional duty, but far more important matters, the formation of the character and habits of life, it is impossible to shut out altogether the uncomfortable suspicion, that our present arrangements in regard to young officers may result in much mischief to them and to the service generally.

It is asserted further, that the feeling of attachment of a young officer towards his own regiment is checked, or at least not sufficiently encouraged during a sojourn at a depot battalion, and that this operates injuriously on the service generally.  It is difficult to estimate aright the weight to which this assertion is entitled as an argument against the system ; but it is easy enough to see that a depot battalion is not a favourable place for the growth of attachment to a corps which may be many thousand miles distant.  The necessity which the very peculiar composition of a depot battalion imposes on its commander and staff of trying to stifle every little regimental prejudice or peculiarity, in order that the individuality of the battalion, as a distinct corps, may be established, certainly constitutes an unfavourable condition for the development of regimental *esprit de corps*.  But is any general or permanent injury the result ? I cannot think so.  It appears to me that the growth of the feeling in question is merely postponed until the youth joins his regiment. I am afraid, however, that even if this last argument is not admitted, enough remains to shake our faith in depot battalions as the best places for the training of young officers.

Another complaint against the system is, that it gives rise to endless jealousy between commanders of battalions and commanders of regiments.  The latter complain that their most promising men are intercepted at the depot for employment in various capacities, and *that when* they apply for particular soldiers, whose services are wanted at the regiment, there is an adverse interest to be attended to, and the application is often successfully resisted.   The former, on the other hand, complain that the interests of the depots are not sufficiently considered in the selection of non-commissioned officers for service with them, and that a man no sooner becomes useful at a depot than the commander of his regiment applies for his transfer.

All this, it appears to me, is rather the result of abuse than of any inherent defect in the system.   If Her Majesty's regulations regarding the selection of men for drafts, as well as of those for depot service, were more literally obeyed, these causes of quarrel would be removed, and it is difficult to conceive what others can arise.

The sum of the whole case against depot battalions appears to be this, that they are objectionable as training establishments, and fail to provide a satisfactory organization for an important branch of our defensive forces.

Having now considered in detail the case against depot battalions, and it certainly is a grave one, let us turn our attention for a little to the other side, and see what can be said for them.

First: they supply a want in our military system, although in a way that is open to serious objections.

Second: they give us an organization which is convenient, manageable, and easily controled; which saves us much correspondence and official labour, simplifies the business of regiments with each other and with departments, facilitates the operations of recruiting, invaliding and discharging, provides satisfactorily for the care of records and attestations, and to some extent ensures uniformity of detail throughout the service.

Third: no good substitute for them has yet been shown to be practicable.

Such, briefly stated, is the case in favour of the depot battalion organization.   It is admitted, even by those who most strongly condemn it on the grounds we have stated, that some of the objects it secures for us are of great practical value.   Without it, or some other auxiliary organization fulfilling at least the same acquirements, our military system would be exposed to constant derangement. Moreover, it possesses in itself features which entitle it to at least partial approval.   Efficient means of control, simplicity of detail, and uniformity of system, as far as they go, are unquestionable recommendations.   When we consider the number and variety of the subordinate depot arrangements necessary to maintain the strength and efficiency of our one hundred and forty-three regiments, we can understand that a system which enables twenty-three officers to become responsible to the central authority for the whole of them is extremely convenient. By simplifying the troublesome, but unavoidable business connected with the depot service of the Army, the depot battalion system greatly lightens the labour of the supreme command.

These considerations not only render the present system attractive to the executive, but to some extent recommend it to the army and the public. Whilst we fully recognize this, however, we do not lose sight of the arguments on the other side, which still remain unanswered. If, as I believe is the case, the arguments on both sides are generally admitted, it only remains for us to weigh the relative importance of the issues involved in order to arrive at a conclusion.

On the one hand, we find that the system is convenient; on the other, that it weakens our means of defence, and exposes our young officers and recruits to a. vicious system of training. Convenience is undoubtedly an immediate and tangible gain, but if it is obtained by means which affect our safety, and poison the source of the supply on which our forces depend for healthy support, it is clear we pay too much for it.

I trust that those who have had the patience to accompany me thus far will assent to the conclusion which appears to me inevitable—that the defects of the. depot battalion system are, on the whole, such as greatly outweigh its merits; and that, therefore, the only reasons which can be held sufficient to justify its continuance for a time lie in the difficulty of finding a suitable substitute for it.

This conclusion, if well founded, reduces the question within narrow limits. I purpose, if permitted, to discuss in another paper some of the substitutes that have been proposed.

## SIR MORTON PETO ON NAVAL AND MILITARY EXPENDITURE.

There is a peculiar tendency in the minds of several of the Members of Parliament who are elected by commercial constituencies, and who are themselves employed in mercantile pursuits, to misquote official statements, and to use the valuable statistics which are published at considerable expense under Government authority, for their own purposes rather than the public benefit.

Thus it frequently happens that whenever the representatives of the commercial or manufacturing classes attempt to grapple with the important question of national expenditure, or venture on publishing their ideas on matters connected with the naval or military professions, they base their arguments on figures which are incorrect, or draw their deductions from statements which are altogether wrong. This arises partly from a want of knowledge of the subject, partly from an innate feeling of dislike to everything connected with Government. It is also caused by an absence of that discriminating power which is requisite to enable men, who have not been trained to official pursuits, to rightly understand the various details of which all accounts rendered by the great departments of the State are necessarily composed—a power which is seldom found amongst persons accustomed to view all things in their own light, and never to look beyond their own limited business sphere.

Nothing is easier than to declaim in general terms against the wasteful extravagance of the various public departments—nothing is more difficult than to show in what manner any particular expense might be avoided, or any special vote might be reduced. Every one knows that of the seventy millions spent annually for the public service, several thousands, or, to speak more correctly, several hundreds of thousands might, with proper management, be saved; but very few persons are sufficiently acquainted with the intricacies of the voluminous accounts in which those seventy millions are shown, to place their fingers on any of the figures and convince us that those figures might be reduced without detriment to the service. There are those, however, who are bold enough to attempt this plan of effecting a reduction of the public expenditure. That they have not been successful in their work must be attributed principally to the causes adverted to above, rather than to any want of desire on their part to bring about the object they have in view. Since the death of Mr. Hume, the leadership of the economy and retrenchment party in the House of Commons has been vacant. For some years Mr. Williams made a point of asking questions, raising discussions, and calling for "divisions" on some or other of the votes contained in the Army and Navy Estimates, but it was evident that he did not possess the knowledge or ability of the great economist whose mantle he wished to wear; and, after vainly struggling against fearful odds, he gave up the contest and retired from his self-assumed post.

Mr. Bright and Mr. Cobden used occasionally to attempt to cut down the Estimates; but they have lately adopted the extraordinary course of first allowing the sums to be voted, and afterwards calling attention to the subject by stating that the money was not needed for the purposes to which it was intended to be applied.

The latter gentleman especially, seems to take delight in that course; he seldom or ever takes any part in the mild debates to which the discussion of the Estimates in Committee of Supply usually give rise, and his name is rarely found in the division lists on financial questions; but he generally indulges the House during the dog-days with a long statement of his views on things in general, and on the Navy and Army in particular, and, as a rule, he quotes figures and produces statistics which, as we have constantly shown in the pages of the United Service Magazine, are not even approximately correct. It is easy enough to say that the navy ought not to cost more than ten millions, and that twelve instead of sixteen millions are sufficient for the army; that the Duke of Somerset has wasted twelve millions in building useless ships; or that Lord Palmerston has cost the country upwards of a hundred millions; but it is very difficult to produce details showing correctly in what manner these sums are composed, or how these reductions might be effected; and until

z 2

those who are so fond of *playing* with the question show themselves
to be *in earnest* in the matter by descending to particulars, we must
withhold our confidence in their statistics, and disagree from the
conclusions they draw therefrom.

Our views on this subject have been greatly strengthened on
examining the work on Taxation and Expenditure which has recently
been published by Sir Morton Peto, the member for Finsbury.   In
our last Number we brought under consideration several of the
various items of taxation to which he adverts; our purpose at present is to call attention to his remarks on the Army and Navy; but,
before doing so, we will offer a few observations on the chapters
which Sir Morton Peto devotes to the remaining heads of Taxation.
Next to the duties levied by the Board of Customs, those raised
under the head of excise are the largest—having amounted during
the last financial year to upwards of seventeen millions.   Modern
legislation has made almost as many and as important changes in
the number and description of the articles chargeable with excise
duty, as with those liable to duty of Customs.   Free trade has
effected as great a revolution in some of the branches of trade and
manufactures placed under the cognizance of the Board of Inland
Revenue at Somerset House as in those superintended by the Commissioners of Customs in Thames Street.   Glass, soap, bricks, and
paper, which were heavily taxed when Sir Robert Peel began his
great commercial reforms, rather more than twenty years ago, are
now free from duty; and the stimulus which has consequently been
given to the manufacture of those articles has been immense.   Instead of our importing large quantities of glass from Bohemia and
other foreign countries, we now furnish supplies to other nations;
and, at the great International Exhibition, the productions of the
English in glass shone conspicuous above those of every other country
in the world.   Had not the duty on this article been repealed it
would not have been possible to have erected the Crystal Palace
of 1851 in Hyde Park, or the large building which crowns the hill
at Sydenham.

To the repeal of the duty on bricks may be attributed very much
of the vast improvement which has been made in the style and appearance of the edifices and buildings erected during the last ten
years, and the immense increase in the number of houses in the
suburbs of many of the principal towns.   By discontinuing the tax
upon soap, less difficulty was placed in the way of the humbler classes
availing themselves of the facilities for cleanliness which their
wealthier neighbours were desirous of affording them; and by removing the restrictions which were imposed upon the manufacture
of paper, encouragement has been afforded for making vast improvements in the construction of an article which is in such general use.
Whether the predictions of the Chancellor of the Exchequer, that
when the duty was taken off paper we should have houses and car-
*riages,* and many other things, built of paper; or whether, what

Sir. M. Peto styles " the recent attempt to introduce paper collars and paper cuffs" will prove successful, and the movement in this direction will be extended to other articles of attire, we will not now stop to inquire; suffice it to say that the ingenuity of those interested in enlarging the demand for articles made of paper will no doubt turn it to the best account, and that the public are sure to purchase anything in which usefulness and elegance are combined.

Sir Morton Peto very naturally approves of the measures adopted with regard to abolishing the excise duty on glass, bricks, and everything else required for building purposes, and most people will agree with him in the remark that " fever has abated since air has been admitted to our dwellings by the repeal of the window tax, light by the repeal of the glass duty, and cleanliness by the repeal of the tax upon soap "—few will, however, go with him in his views on the existing sources of revenue from the excise. At present, the principal articles subject to duty are spirits, malt, licenses, railways, and hackney and stage carriages ; of these the amount paid into the Exchequer for spirits is larger than that received from all the other articles. The arguments used by the Member for Finsbury, in support of his theory, that the consumption of spirits is not checked by high rates of duty, may be very good, and his deductions may be very correct, his figures will not, however, bear the test of close examination with official returns. Without wearying our readers with the uninteresting details, and the long statements with which the work before us abounds, we will merely point out a few of the errors into which the author has fallen. In the table by which he shows the periods at which the changes in the rate of duty on English spirits were made, he gives the year 1856 as that in which the rate was raised from seven shillings and tenpence to eight shillings per gallon, the number of gallons consumed as 9,343,549, and the amount of duty received as £3,737,419, whereas the duty was really increased to eight shillings in 1855, the quantity on which duty was paid that year being 10,384,100 gallons, and the duty received amounting to £4,090,530. Again, Sir Morton Peto shows that the tax was raised to ten shillings in 1861, although the official returns show that the advance took place in the previous year ; and he gives the consumption as 9,508,002 instead of 8,952,174 gallons, with the revenue as £4,469,749 in lieu of £4,476,093. Similar mistakes occur in his statements with regard to Scotch and Irish spirits. We have now before us a return furnished from the Inland Revenue Office in April last, showing the number of distillers in England, Scotland, and Ireland on the 31st day of December in each year from 1822 down to 1862, the quantity of spirits entered for home consumption during the same period, the rate of duty charged thereon, and the amount of revenue derived therefrom ; and we are unable to find in it several of the figures produced by Sir M. Peto. In the following table are placed side by side the figures given in the worthy Baronet's book and those contained in the Parliamentary return,—for the year 1861 :—

| | | No. of Gallons. | Amount of duty. |
|---|---|---|---|
| Scotland. | { Sir M. Peto's figures . . | £5,816,835 | £2,750,781 |
| | { Official Return . . . | £6,070,091 | £3,035,042 |
| Ireland | { Sir M. Peto's figures . . | £4,822,987 | £2,269,860 |
| | { Official Return . . . | £5,022,894 | £2,511,423 |

The privilege of distilling spirits for the people of England appears to be limited to only ten firms, being exactly the same number as existed in 1822. Like the brewing trade in London, the distilling business in England is a monopoly, and the sooner it is put an end to the more chance there will be of the consumer obtaining spirits lower in price and better in quality. In Scotland the number of distillers is much larger, being 119; and even in Ireland, where the quantity made is only about one half of what it is in England, there are twenty-seven firms engaged in this lucrative trade.

We will not follow Sir Morton Peto into all the difficulties which surround the malt duty, nor into the question of whether there should or should not be a railway-passenger tax; neither will we discuss the propriety of taxing hackney-carriages, or of getting up an agitation for the repeal of that tax; but, before proceeding to consider his remarks on the expenditure incurred for Naval and Military purposes, we must not omit to notice some of the inaccuracies into which he has fallen in his statements with regard to the cost of collecting the revenue, and which are so glaring that they were recently pointed out in a publication which is circulated principally amongst commercial men, and which generally supports writers of the Peto, Cobden, and Bright school.

Sir Morton Peto asserts that the cost of collecting the revenue increases out of all proportion to the revenue itself; an examination of the following figures will show how very incorrect is that statement :—

| | Sir M. Peto's Statement. | | Official Reports. | |
|---|---|---|---|---|
| | Gross. Receipts. | Charges of. Collection. | Gross. Receipts. | Charges of. Collection. |
| 1826 . | £54,839,685 | £4,030,337 | £58,138,843 | £4,030,337 |
| 1846 . | £64,774,438 | £7,004,438 | £58,860,472 | £3,877,446 |
| 1861 . | £70,671,020 | £8,061,338 | £67,584,335 | £5,599,633 |

It also shows that Sir Morton Peto's figures are not so reliable as might reasonably be expected in a work of such pretensions as his "Taxation, its Levy and Expenditure."

That the expenditure of the country has greatly increased during the last few years is a fact so well known that it was scarcely necessary for any one in the position of the Right Honourable Baronet, the Member for Finsbury, to devote a whole chapter to this subject, except to raise hopes which cannot be realised. He pretends to show us the manner in which the expenditure may, without disadvantage, be speedily reduced. Our readers will not be surprised at learning that his pruning knife is to be applied principally to the *Army and Navy;* the Civil List, the various items of Miscellaneous expenses, and many other things, are all capable of reduction, but great mercy is shown to them in comparison with the Military departments. Many of the arguments adduced have been so often repeated by others of the same school, and have been so frequently confuted, that we do not consider it necessary to waste the time either of our readers or of ourselves in showing them to be false, defective, and weak; we will, therefore, content ourselves with merely drawing attention to some of the principal mistakes.

As a matter of course the favourite year 1835 is taken as the starting point for all comparisons as regards the Army as well as the Navy. The military force employed at that happy period was under 70,000 men—why should not that number suffice at present? We then spent about four millions on our Navy—why should we now require nearly eleven millions? In reply, we would ask, are the circumstances in which we are placed with reference to our possessions abroad, our commerce, and our relations with foreign countries the same as they were in 1835? Is there any sensible man, calling himself a Briton, desirous of seeing the Army in the same want of organization as it was at the period referred to? or the Navy reduced to so low a condition that our ships were only partially manned, and in anything but an efficient state? The constitution of "the Services" was at that time, and during several succeeding years, brought so low that it has been absolutely necessary to administer medicine of a most expensive and very stimulating nature ever since.

After the experience gained during the last two years from the events which have occurred in America, it is hardly credible that any one endowed with an ordinary amount of common sense should attempt to show that "in time of peace a standing army, with all its vast attendant charges, and its disposition for active duty, always must be a source of weakness"—that the "very preparations for war, in time of peace, excite war, either by engendering acrimonious feelings abroad, or exciting a thirst for martial exploits abroad,"— that "all the trouble and all the cost of military preparations for war in time of peace will be thrown away,"—and that as "the facilities for the preparations for war are far greater than they were some years ago, inasmuch as arms can be manufactured, and ammunition can be supplied in much less time than formerly," we can now do with very less number of trained men than we could formerly have done. It would have been far better for the Americans if they had paid several millions annually for the last ten years in warlike preparations; they might then have prevented such sad destruction of life and property, and have saved themselves from the expenditure of hundreds of millions of money, rendered necessary since the civil war broke out, in consequence of their having to raise three or four large armies in the course of a few months.

It may be quite true that, "considering our army expenditure as a whole, there can be little doubt that there is ample room for revision and reduction,"—such is the case with all large establishments, whether public or private,—but it is simply absurd to say that "the military estimates of this country ought to be based, in time of peace, on the principle simply of maintaining military efficiency; there should be no such thing as preparation for war until the outbreak of war is obvious and inevitable"—or that the formation of the Chobham camp "brought upon us that thirst for active military service which led to the expedition to Varna, and then to the invasion of the Crimea and the leaguer of Sebastopol." It is equally puerile to assert that "what is most to be feared from a standing army is that the cost it entails on the people will lead to discontents, and that the bayonets intended for self-defence may be employed and directed against the bosoms of the people."

Sir Morton Peto sets out by stating that in 1790 the expenditure on the Army and Ordnance was only £2,200,000—that immediately on the outbreak of war it was greatly increased—that it was increased still more when the war was at its height—and that it was considerably diminished in the course of a few years after the restoration of peace. He gives nearly the same account of the expenditure for the Navy during the same period. "Prior to the war of 1793," he says, "the Navy of England cost about £2,000,000 a year. Our Navy Estimates rose in 1804 to £12,000,000, at the conclusion of the war in 1815 they amounted to £16,000,000, but in 1817 they were reduced to £6,500,000." And yet he tells us that a war expenditure once increased cannot be brought back to the scale of the original peace establishment. "If we consider the matter calmly we shall see," he writes, "that there are several causes for this. When an addition is once made to an establishment, it is difficult, if not impossible, suddenly to cut it down. Every man clings to the post to which he has been appointed, pleads his services, and, instead of expecting to retire when those services are no longer needed, urges them as a claim for promotion and additional emolument. Then, as the army is officered from amongst those who move in the upper ranks of society, the Government are afraid of the unpopularity which might result from reduction, and consequently do not propose it." All this twaddle may be very interesting and convincing to "my constituents whose interests are affected by the subject" and to whom his book is dedicated, but it will only raise a smile with those who are conversant with and have really calmly considered the subject.

To a certain extent, the number of men voted by Parliament governs every other item of expense for the army—it does not, however, do so altogether, for the grand total of the force employed may be increased or diminished without altering the numbers of battalions, and consequently the numbers of officers; neither need it affect the staff. According, however, to the author of "Taxation," the numbers increase in a sort of arithmetical progression. "Soldiers," he very truly says, "must be commanded; and," he adds, "therefore, every additional body of men entails additional commanding officers; additional commanding officers entail additional staffs and additional commands; additional commands require additions to the departments of the Secretary of State for War and and the General Commanding-in-Chief." It is a pity the climax is not completed by multiplying the Secretaries of State and the Commanders-in-Chief. The extent of "the staff" appears to be very objectionable in the eyes of Sir Morton Peto. According to him it consists of 1,354 officers; and, although it is popularly supposed only to relate to the Commander-in-Chief, or some great general of division, the present practice is to have "a staff" everywhere. If, however, he will turn to page 32 of the valuable little work on "The Organization, Composition, and Strength of the Army of Great Britain," printed by order of the Secretary of State for War, he will find that the composition and distribution at home and abroad of the real "staff" are as follows, viz.:—

| | |
|---|---:|
| At head-quarters | 21 |
| In Great Britain | 89 |
| In Ireland | 34 |
| At stations in the Mediterranean | 30 |
| At other stations abroad | 116 |
| Total | 290 |

Having made up his mind that the military expenditure of the country must be considerably reduced—that it must be brought down from the fifteen millions of the present year to the ten millions of 1853—he proceeds to show in what manner this desirable object is to be effected. It should always be borne in mind that the Estimates are composed of an immense number of details, which details make up the great total, and that, therefore, any reduction must be made in the several details. Sir Morton Peto, however, does not appear to be of this opinion, for he proposes to take the "bull by the horns." "There is one broad way in which reduction of these estimates can be enforced. It is by limiting the amount of money to be expended." One might as well say you should limit the sum to be raised by taxes, and then distribute it amongst the several departments entrusted with expending it. A very slight examination of the budget speeches of Mr. Gladstone and other Chancellors of the Exchequer, will soon convince even the most ardent advocate for retrenchment and economy that this is not a business-like or practical mode of proceeding. We firmly believe that any sensible reduction of the public expenditure can only be effected by every person belonging to the service, in whatever position he may be, doing his utmost to save every penny of the public money which he has the power of spending either wholly or in part; acting, in fact, in every case as though he had a personal interest in the matter; but before this can be done, those who are in the service of Her Majesty must have the same inducement to do the best for

the interest of the Crown and of the public that those have who are
in private employ.

Having shown to his own satisfaction that the present "excessive
expenditure" for army purposes ought to be considerably reduced, Sir
Morton Peto proceeds to demonstrate the manner in which his views
may be carried out; and, knowing that any attempt to bring down
the force maintained at home would be sure to fail, he joins in the
cry which has been raised against the Colonies, adopting entirely
the view taken by the members of the Committee on Colonial Military
expenditure, and producing many of the statements contained in the
Blue Book.  He compares the number of troops stationed in the
Mediterranean in 1851 and 1861, and innocently asks in what the
circumstances of the world in 1861 differ so entirely from those
of 1851 as to have rendered it necessary almost to double the troops
of the line in each of those fortresses? as though he was not fully
aware that the circumstances are entirely different.  Fortifications
he would altogether dispense with, and he would defend the colonies
by our fleets, yet he strangely enough proposes to dismantle
nearly all our ships and to sell the bulk of them out of the service.
As with the Army, so with the Navy; economy and retrenchment
must be enforced, even if the best interests of the country must be
sacrificed.   We are often surprised to find what ignorance of facts
is generally displayed by commercial writers in dealing with the
great question of our Naval requirements, and how perseveringly they
insist on mis-stating the cost of the fleet.   They do not appear to
comprehend the difference between the sums wanted for Military
from those asked for Naval purposes, but because they are voted on
the same Estimates, they immediately set them down as expended for
Naval service.   Thus we are told, that "on the outbreak of the
Crimean war, the Navy estimate was immediately doubled, and in
the very next year, 1855, it was raised to a point exceeding that of
the year in which we fought the battle of Trafalgar," and then we
are favored with the annexed table, which is evidently taken (like
those which follow) from Mr. Cobden's pamphlet, "The Three
Panics," and which is at variance with the accounts presented to
Parliament :—

| | |
|---|---|
| 1854 . . . . . | £12,182,769 |
| 1855 . . . . . | 19,014,708 |
| 1856 . . . . . | 16,013,995 |

What are the facts?  The *total* sums expended under the votes
contained in the Navy Estimates were, in—

| | |
|---|---|
| 1853 . . . . . | 7,197,804 |
| 1854 . . . . . | 15,017,591 |
| 1855 . . . . . | 19,590,833 |
| 1856 . . . . . | 14,664,514 |

but, as of these sums there were required for services unconnected
with the Navy, viz., for the Army and Ordnance Department (conveyance of troops), for prisoners of war, and for the Post Office
Department (Packet Service), in

$$1853 \quad . \quad . \quad . \quad . \quad . \quad . \quad £1,034,051$$
$$1854 \quad . \quad . \quad , \quad . \quad . \quad . \quad 4,291,379$$
$$1855 \quad . \quad . \quad . \quad . \quad . \quad . \quad 7,277,789$$
$$1856 \quad . \quad . \quad . \quad . \quad . \quad . \quad 3,758,137$$

it follows that the expenditure on the Navy in those years was, in

$$1853 \quad . \quad . \quad . \quad . \quad . \quad . \quad 6,163,753$$
$$1854 \quad . \quad . \quad . \quad . \quad . \quad . \quad 10,726,212$$
$$1855 \quad . \quad . \quad . \quad . \quad . \quad . \quad 12,813,044$$
$$1856 \quad . \quad . \quad . \quad , \quad . \quad . \quad 10,906,377$$

So that it was not nearly doubled on the commencement of hostilities with Russia in 1854; neither was it raised in 1855 to an amount exceeding that of the Navy Estimates for the year in which Trafalgar was won, which was (exclusive of the expenses for the transport service and the maintenance of prisoners of war), £13,478,680. Very few of the figures inserted in the chapter of this work on Taxation devoted to the Navy are correct, and consequently many of the arguments drawn from the statements of which they are formed are valueless. " The great outlay of the Navy," he says, " is not on seamen. The great expenditure is upon the naval establishments, the wages of artificers employed in them—dockyard improvements and repairs, and naval stores, &c., for the building of the fleet. Out of the sum expended on the Navy in 1861 the yards and the works carried on therein were estimated to cost *almost the moiety.*" We have now before us the annual account of Naval receipt and expenditure for the year ended the 31st March, 1862 (1861-62), printed by order of the House of Commons on the 13th February last, and we find that, of the total sum of £12,092,564 spent for Navy services £5,485,847 was for Her Majesty's establishments at home and abroad, wages to artificers, &c., naval stores for the building, repair, &c., of the fleet, steam machinery, and ships built by contract, new works, improvements, and repairs in the yards, &c., while £6,606,717 (considerably more than half) was for wages to seamen and marines, and other purposes.

As a matter of course, the dockyards come in for a liberal share of abuse, and the most is made of the opinions expressed by the Commissioners appointed to inquire into the management of those establishments. Everything that they reported in favour of contractors is placed boldly in front, while all that they said in favour of the Government authorities is carefully kept in the back-ground. The statements which are so constantly paraded before the public on every available opportunity, to the effect that work performed in private yards is better and cheaper than that done in the Royal Naval Arsenals, are repeated over and over again. " The dockyards are not adapted for iron ship-building. They do not contain the necessary machinery, nor do they command the sort of labour that is required. The best and by far the cheapest mode of obtaining iron hulls, is to contract for their construction with builders of unquestioned reputation, at fixed and certain prices."

Since Sir Morton Peto's work was published, the statement prepared by the Controller of the Navy relating to the advantages of iron and wood, and the relative cost of those materials, in the construction of ships for Her Majesty's Navy, has been laid before Parliament, and it contains the best reply that could be given to many of the off-hand assertions of the Member for Finsbury. It also shows how absurd are some of the opinions advanced by him with regard to the construction of men-of-war. If Sir Morton Peto were to have his own way he would forthwith reduce the Navy to the few iron vessels which we possess; the others would be at once consigned to the auctioneer's hammer; we should not even have any iron-*plated* ships. "Wooden vessels plated with iron are," he says, "so shaken by the action of a heavy sea, and by their own machinery, as speedily to become unseaworthy. A wooden frame only, in fact, weakens an iron plate." "I have expressed my opinion that this arrangement will be found to be an error." "That which it seems desirable principally to aim at, is the construction of a few large and powerful iron vessels, of sufficient size to mount the largest guns in central batteries, and fitted to act as rams, by the aid of powerful machinery." If Sir Morton Peto has since read the account of the attack on Charleston by the Federal iron-clads, he may perhaps have changed his opinion on this subject, and if he were responsible for the efficiency of the Navy, and for the money voted by Parliament being spent in the manner most advantageous for the interests of the Crown and of the public, he would come, we have no doubt, to the conclusion at which Admiral Robinson arrived in March last—"in every way the system of building by contract armour-plated iron ships would be more expensive than building armour-plated ships of wood in our dockyards."

---

## THE INTERNAL ORGANIZATION OF THE FRENCH NAVY.

The fact of France being our only great rival upon that element the dominion of which we almost believe to be exclusively our own is, apart from other causes, enough to make us regard all that concerns her Navy with much interest. The manner in which of late years that Navy has increased in numbers and efficiency is now well known in this country; so well known, indeed, that it has become almost an invariable custom to accompany demands to Parliament for the increase of our own sea-forces by statements of the powerful condition of those of our neighbours and allies. Acknowledging, therefore, as per-force we must, the almost regeneration (since its practical annihilation by our own Navy during the old war) of the maritime power of France, it will be interesting and instructive to inquire how it has been brought about. British

Naval officers who have chanced to serve in the company of their French brethren-in-arms, and in the presence of the ships and squadrons of that nation, have often been struck by the remarkable regularity of the organization which seems to act as the life-blood of their whole service.

It is this organization, so complete and symmetrical, which has raised the Naval power of the French from the depths into which the disasters of the Revolutionary Wars had plunged it, to that admirable height of efficiency at which we see it now. It may seem yielding over-much to mere theorizing to declare that the manifest superiority as seamen of the British nation over the French is such that the latter can scarcely hope to equal us on our own element—the Sea. Still there is a great deal of truth in such an assertion, and the Government of France seems to have acknowledged it in the eager desire it has from time to time expressed to compensate by artificial means, such as improved organization, for the lack of that natural aptitude for the sea in which they are so far behind ourselves. The genius of the French people too is eminently that which loves to regulate and symmetrize, which is abundantly manifest in all their institutions and undertakings from the Code Napoléon to the at-present proceeding reconstruction of Paris.

With regard to their Navy, the fact may be stated to be this:— With a raw material inferior to ours, they have constructed a force of which the discipline and organization are the admiration of all who impartially contemplate them. We ourselves have paid their efforts in this particular a silent tribute of admiration in various imitations of their system.

To form some idea of the completeness of the organization of the French Navy, and the manner in which it pervades its every branch, we have only to examine two small works, which together answer to our own "Queen's Regulations and Admiralty Instructions," and which are called—" Décret sur le service à bord des bâtiments de la flotte," and " Réglement sur le service intérieur à bord des bâtiments de la flotte." These two volumes are small 16mos., of 365 and 460 pages respectively, capable of being carried separately in the pocket with ease, and when bound together closely resembling in size one of those commonly-seen volumes called a "Church Service." The first of these books relates exclusively to the more general regulations of the Navy, and the particular duties of each separate branch and rank of officers; the second is devoted to the details of the interior economy of each individual ship, and also of fleets and squadrons, and the special duties of the warrant and petty officers, and even of the private seamen particularly employed. Each publication is divided into titles, chapters, and articles, of which last the "Décret" contains 777, and the "Réglement" 1584, besides forms of reports and official papers.

To the former work is affixed a very interesting "Rapport," drawn up and presented to the head of the Government in 1851, by the then Minister of Marine, M. De Chasseloup-Laubat, which traces the history of the Regulations of the French Navy from the reign of Louis XIV. downwards. "At the commencement of the reign of that monarch," says the minister in his report, "the Navy, which had already considerably increased, required a more complete system of regulation," a system which he goes on to say was given to the service by Colbert, and his son who succeeded him. This was in 1689, for even at that distant period the organization of the French Navy had reached a stage of completeness, at which we at the present day cannot but feel surprised. In the history of the French Navy appended to Père Daniel's "Histoire de la Milice Française," various extracts from the regulations are given, and they show a minuteness of detail to which we can present no equal in our own. In fact the ordinance of 1689 has, the minister declares, remained the basis of all which have since succeeded it; and it has undergone revision, and alteration in 1765, 1786, 1827, and at the date of the publication of the work from which we have just been quoting.

The immense and numerous changes in Naval science having rendered this latter revision necessary, a commission was appointed to prepare it. The constitution of this commission shows us the manner in which the French Government applied itself to the attainment of perfection in the object which they had in view; it consisted of a Vice-Admiral as president; and as members, two Captains, three Commanders, one Engineer of Naval Constructions, one Comptroller of the Navy, one Medical Officer, and one Lieutenant as Secretary. All classes being thus represented in the preparation of a code by which all classes were to be governed, the result of the labours of the commission in its accuracy and minuteness does ample justice to the enlightened foresight which led to its peculiar constitution, and affords a clear example of the benefits to be derived from entrusting a like work to a body so composed. Indeed, so minutely is every course of proceeding laid down, that it would seem as though little were left to the individual discretion (though it is in reality to be believed that such is not the case) of officers who may be placed in positions of command; but the commission and the Government acknowledged the necessity of guarding against the ignorance of the many, instead of allowing for the possible ability of the few.

The first "Title" of the Décret treats of the different duties assigned to the various ranks of officers, and answers, to a great extent, to the chapter of our own Regulations, entitled "Officers in General." Commencing with the flag-officers, it explains with great minuteness the command and functions assigned to each; for instance, of the Rear-Admiral we read—

1st. That he *can* command (in-chief) a squadron.

2nd. He commands (in-chief) a division.

3rd. He is employed subordinately in a fleet, squadron or division, *according to its* importance.

Of the Captain we find that—

1st. He *can* command (in-chief) a division.

2nd. In this case he holds the temporary rank of Commodore.

3rd. He can be employed (subordinately) as a Commodore in a large Naval force.

4th. He commands ships (steam or sailing) of the line-of-battle or frigate classes, and sailing corvettes with a main-deck battery.

The Commander by section 4—

Is declared to fulfil the duties of second-in-command on board every ship commanded by a Captain.

The Lieutenant and Ensign fill the same position in all ships commanded by Commanders and Lieutenants respectively.

Art. 12 states the titles borne by officers in command; the senior officer is called "*commandant-supérieur.*"

The Flag-officer commanding (in-chief) a fleet, division, or Naval station, is called "*commandant-en-chef.*"

The Flag-officer commanding a detached or subordinate division receives the title of "*commandant-en-sous-ordre.*"

Captains and Commanders when in command of ships are entitled "Commandants," and Lieutenants commanding "Capitaines."

The second "Title," treats of flags and ensigns.

Several Flag-officers meeting are ordered to hoist flags containing their numbers on the Seniority List.

Senior-officers present, when Captains, hoist a broad pendant, and when Commanders a triangular flag. When of the rank of Lieutenant, the senior-officer hoists a triangular flag at the Fore. When more officers than one entitled to fly these broad pendants are in company, that of the senior flies at the Main, those of the others at the Fore.

The position of the officer whom we generally designate as commanding officer, that is, the First Lieutenant or Commander, under a Captain, is acknowledged in the French Instructions, and his duties are specified under the different headings of "Fitting out," and "At Sea," with such minuteness, that his quarters in action, and the division of boarders which he commands, are especially stated. Next follow the instructions for the Officer of the Watch at Sea, for the same officer in harbour, and for the various subordinate officers who also keep watch under a superior. Nor are the duties of the different officers, as attached to quarters and divisions, overlooked, but they are laid down at considerable length in some fifteen Articles.

Title XII. regulates the duties of officers of the Paymaster's department (*de l'administration*), who are, we find, divided into the ranks of Commissary of Fleets, Commissary of Squadrons, and Commissary of Divisions, to whom their subordinates in each particular ship report and send in returns.

The seventeenth and last Title treats of the salutes, honours, and visits of various Naval functionaries, native and foreign, and extends even to compliments paid by tossing of oars, piping and manning the side, and disposing lanterns at the gangway at night. Sentries are ordered to salute officers of either service, and of *all nations*, coming on board, or passing near in boats. When hailed at night, persons coming on board are to answer, if of the rank of Flag-officer, " *Officier général*," if Captains or Commanders, " *Officier supérieur*," if officers of any other rank, " *Officier*," and if below the rank of officer, " *Abord.*"

But if the " Décret" is remarkable for minuteness of detail, the "Réglement," which is said in the report prefixed to it, to be its "indispensible complement," is still more so, and gives the clearest possible insight into the interior economy of a French ship of war.

The first portion of it explains the system of numbering the members of a ship's company, and of distributing them in what we may call Watch and Quarter-Bills. Properly speaking, there is no watch-bill in the French Navy ; all stations and distributions of the crew of a ship depend upon the quarter-bill alone, and each man's number is based upon that of the guns arming a single broadside. These guns have, beside their number on each particular deck, one comprised in a general enumeration commencing with the foremost gun on the lower deck, and ending with the after gun, on the main deck in three-deckers, and on the quarter deck in smaller vessels.

In this enumeration each battery is presumed to be armed with sixteen pieces; so that the first gun of the middle deck is No. 17, and the first of the main deck No. 33, and the last No. 48. The seventeenth guns on the main and middle decks of ships of the line are numbered 49 and 50. The upper deck guns of three-decked ships are not numbered in this scheme.

The ship's company is divided into as many fractions, called series, as there are guns in this enumeration. Each series is composed of the *gun-numbers* who work the gun giving a No. to the series, and other men employed at different stations.

These last, who fulfil the duties of magazine-men, &c., are called "*servants fictifs*." Each captain of a gun is also " leading-hand" of a series, and his No. is the same as that of the series itself. The men on the right of each gun have for their Nos. the No. of their series augmented by the No. indicating their rank in the gun's crew; that is to say, the first man on the right of a gun has for his No. 100 plus the No. of his gun or series, the second man 200 plus the same No. Thus, 420 is the fourth man on the right of the twentieth gun. The men on the left have the same Nos. increased by fifty. Thus, 476 is the fourth man on the left of the twenty-sixth gun. Each series, and in many cases particular men, are appointed to special stations, and the system of numbering tells an officer at a glance where any individual is quartered, and what duties he has to perform. The odd numbers and series belong to the starboard watch, and the even numbered to the port watch; and each watch is divided into two divisions composed of alternate series. Each series messes, sleeps, and cleans the deck at the gun from which its No. is derived. The duties of every individual are so minutely specified in this "Réglement," that the particular objects to be cleaned by certain men, even the man-ropes which some have to scrub, are mentioned in its various articles. But what may strike an English officer as still more extraordinary, is the fact that the words of command of the various nautical evolutions, such as tacking, wearing, fidding top-gallant masts, and shifting sails and spars, are given at full length, and are accompanied by a detailed explanation, as are the words of command, in a book of gunnery or musket drill. Orders, we are told, are always to be given in the plural, and the word "*envoyez!*" is to be used on all occasions, such as swaying across yards, when several different things are to be done together.

But perhaps what chiefly merits our attention in these regulations, is the care that is taken that the *routine* shall be made intelligible to all who have to see it carried out. Each separate item is accompanied by a sort of commentary describing very closely what is expected to be done; and this part of the Instructions alone occupies more than fifty-six pages.

The duties of sentries, too, according to their different posts, are stated at length; and, even in this small particular, much trouble must be saved the commanding officer who has to fit out a ship, when he finds that he has only to transfer copies of these to the various order-boards.

It is not to be doubted that so penetrating a system of organization is repulsive to the character of British seamen in general, and that its adoption into our own Navy, in any but a very partial form, would be fraught with the greatest difficulty. Still we cannot but admire the cleverness with which the Government of France has supplemented, by an improved organization, that ability for maritime affairs in which the French seamen are so far behind our own. Discipline has almost invariably prevailed over simple valour, however great; and that discipline is undoubtedly the highest which rests upon the most perfect system of organizing a force that can be devised.

## OCEAN STATIONS—A VOYAGE IN 1862.

### COASTING—SINGAPORE.

The Cochin China coast soon loomed boldly on our starboard bow and the weather continued fine. Our chart was from a survey made by the French in 1798, and I was assured that there was none of a later date. On the 8th of November we experienced some heavy squalls accompanied by thunder and lightning, but they were very transient, and left the atmosphere cool and balmy. A few days more and at sunset we were in sight of a group of no fewer than seventeen islands, all more or less of considerable size, and generally lofty, but apparently barren. Passing the lighthouse on the rocks of Pedra Branca we soon came in sight of Singapore, which is about thirty miles off. It was a humid, squally morning. The low-lying, richly-wooded coast of the Malay peninsula seemed, as no doubt it is, a fine retreat for beasts of prey.

This being my second visit to the grand *entrepôt* of Eastern Asia within a few months, I had little to expect in the way of novelty. There was still the pretty anchorage—the same wooded heights above the town; the old story of the disparity of one hundred and twenty to one between the combined Chinese, Malays, and Madrasees, and the heroic band of three hundred European officials and merchants.

Madras seems to have stamped its peculiarities upon this creation of Sir S. Raffles, not only as regards the style of the houses and laying out of the gardens, but likewise in the mode of living. A Madras regiment is generally in garrison, but this does not seem to allay the inquietude felt on account of the overwhelming Chinese population, a member of which—originally a Coolie—it has been deemed expedient to raise to the magisterial bench ; and this functionary, besides bearing his faculties as meekly as might be expected, has, I believe on emergencies, justified the liberality of the local government, by proving himself a most politic mediator between his own countrymen and the former. The Chinese, when removed from the contagion of bad example, are by no means unfitted to govern in a subordinate capacity with integrity and ability ; and it, perhaps, only requires time to develope their higher qualities in a larger field. Another cause of apprehension, in the event of an European war, would certainly be the proximity of the military (for commercial it surely is not) station, which our Gallic allies have established at Saigon.

The plan of the town of Singapore seems at first irregular, but after a few drives in the convenient little palkee garries of the place, one perceives that the various races of the population keep as distinct from each other as practicable, the Malays occupying the one extremity, and the Chinese the other ; the intermediate space being appropriated by the English. The landing-place is protected by a weak battery occupying the angle formed by a small estuary, which further up is spanned by light bridges connecting the villa quarter with the mercantile. In the former of these, and skirting the shore, there are several excellent hotels, a cathedral, court-house, and on a green eminence behind, the Government House.

The hotels of Singapore are commodious and inexpensive; the attendance excellent, as indeed it always is, where there are Madrasee servants ; and the living is of the best description. The gardens which surround these agreeable places of resort are well kept, and contain many rare plants in addition to those which are common to this zone, but vegetation here seems rather to be characterised by the beauty of the trees, than of the flowers. The climate is humid, and in consequence of the soapy red clay of the soil, the effects of a heavy fall of rain are experienced for many days after. I cannot say that I should like to make Singapore my place of residence. There is an oppressive monotony in its physical aspect. So long as the sun is shining, one may find sources of amusement and interest in the natural features and productions of the soil, but when good things of day begin to droop and drowse, and the harsh croaking of the frog is only relieved by the voices of countless insect tribes, and no breath of air can force itself into the damp lanes gloomy with sombre foliage matted together, one must be in robust health and buoyant spirits to endure such a locality.

The best index to the climate is the appearance of the European children. These poor little fleshless mites with pale cheeks, wan eyes, and feeble querulous voices, do not seem to make the same impression on their parents that they do upon strangers, who are able to contrast their blighted infancy with the rosy cheeks of England. I should imagine the soil of Singapore to be well adapted for the cultivation of coffee, but I confess to having serious doubts in respect of cotton, for which, I venture to surmise, that there is a nearer and better field in the waste lands of our Indian possessions.

The Malay boats are exceedingly elegant in their lines and are generally kept scrupulously clean—at least, those that ply for passengers. A mat shed in the centre, affords shelter from sun and rain; the fiery-eyed, wiry Malay in his picturesque costume of bright colours, chiefly red, is not a little proud of his personal appearance and of the skill with which he feathers his light oar; these boats are, however, unfitted for rough and squally weather. I have seen one of our crew obliged to swing himself backwards over the windward gunwale and hold on by a stay rope, to prevent the wind capsizing us as our snowy lateen sailed swelled before it. The Chinese have also their small crab-like shampans, generally sculled by one man, who stands up and works with two long oars so vigorously, that he is a serious competitor for the Malay, who, in consequence, has no word too bad for him; he works harder and charges less than the natives, and thus prevents an extortionate monopoly.

During our stay in this port, the ship was daily surrounded at daybreak by bumboats filled with golden bananas, in their chandelier whorls, shaddocks, mangosteens, "creepy"-looking ramostans, and green oranges. I know that there is a strong prejudice against allowing soldiers and sailors to purchase fruit on such occasions, but various circumstances that have come under my notice have led me to believe that this, like the mania with some of excluding the night air, is a snare and a delusion. Judiciously eaten, a fruit diet is, after a voyage, often attended with the best results; if unnecessary apprehensions do not interfere with the practice of nature.

Manias are peculiar to localities, as well as to certain seasons; and accordingly we, who had suffered so terribly from the Chinese and Japanese "curio" (endemics), now found ourselves rapidly succumbing to the "cockatoo" phrensy, which seemed at first to make its ravages amongst the sailors, each of whom boldly invested two or three dollars in the purchase of one of these noisy lemon-crested denizens of Golden-Chersonesian forests, or their cousins in various degrees—the red, the purple, and the green parrots.

I observed a curious evidence of something above ordinary instinct, in a small monkey belonging to one of the sailors. The little animal was sitting pensively scratching his ear, in a way peculiar to his race, when I brought him a piece of bread; he nibbled it carelessly, and finding it not much to his liking, dropped it. I then gave him a banana, which he seized with avidity and began to eat with great gusto, when I again returned with a sprig of bread pills stuck on small wires, so as to represent rudely a cluster of berries. Instantly was the banana abandoned, and one by one with the greatest satisfaction were the fictitious berries transferred to his jaw pouches. Here was imagination—perhaps even a sense of the beautiful! In the meantime a more practical dog quietly walked off with the half-eaten banana.

Malacca canes as well as fine matting were also in demand; but it was in vain that the eager Chinese offered his Japanese cabinets at lower prices than they fetch in Hong Kong. That passion had decayed, and the elegant trifles by which so recently it had been gratified, had now to be reserved for the outward bound.

All the ordinary "curios" of the country which we had just left are to be had in this town, except ancient pictures and that matchless imperial porcelain only procurable in Northern China, and even there becoming scarce.

A Madrasee, who had attended on me at the *table d'hôte* of the Esperanza Hotel, received as an acknowledgment of his attention, a "chit" or recommendation, for which he appeared grateful. I asked him if he would accompany me to England, and he seemed pleased at the idea; but when I added, that he must be prepared to start next day, he excused himself: "I cannot go, Sir," said he, "so soon, because my mother stop with me; and before I could go to England I. must put her back to the Madras." By a strange coincidence I had known the relations of this man many years before, at Poonamalee.

### THE STRAITS OF RHIO, BANCA AND SUNDA.

Having waited until the last available moment for the outward English mail, we were obliged to say farewell to Singapore without it, and the same night we entered the southern hemisphere. The weather was cool and pleasant, and our course lay through the Rhio Straits, so called from a small Dutch settlement of that name, which may be observed, and barely observed, about seven miles off, and seemingly perfectly oppressed by the plethora of vegetation, from which its scattered houses struggle into outer light.

These straits lie between the islands of Pulo Battam and Pulo Bintang, whose shores are magnificently wooded apparently to the water's edge, with here and there verdant satellite islets along their coasts.   On the latter of these islands two isolated mountains, densely wooded to their summits, reach the altitudes respectively of 759 and 1,212 feet.   In the absence of any evidences of human habitations, the scenery reminded me sometimes of the wider branches of the Sunderbunds, and at other times of the solitudes along the shores of the Gulf of Paria.   The waters of this channel are comparatively shallow, for although between ten and twenty fathoms occur, our lead occasionally shewed only five and a half. There were several very elegant two-masted boats cruising about.

We had frequent light and picturesque squalls, which broke into the dense green forests and opened a passage for the gleams of sunshine, that often slanted forth at such moments with the most beautiful effect, and which forced from me an involuntary tribute to the genius of Poussin ; although, by the way, I am privately of opinion that he has more than one successful rival amongst our living artists.

The following day we were slowly and cautiously feeling our way through the difficult straits of Banca, with wooded uplands on our left and long sandy spits on the opposite side.   It was hereabouts, I believe, that the Transit was lost in 1857.   Some of the detached mountain peaks of Pulo Banca are as high as fourteen hundred feet, but these interminable forests and isolated mountains soon become monotonous.

We observed two English barques hugging the low coasts of Sumatra, but as the navigation is a matter of some nicety, all three came to an anchor at dusk, and waited for daylight to resume progress.   The scenery continued much the same.   We were in nine fathoms when we observed a Dutch barque making signals of distress.   She was to appearance, judging by our charts, in about four fathoms.   We afforded such assistance as was in our power, and left her.   After losing sight of land for about eight hours, it again loomed in bold outlines on our starboard bow.

We were now five days out from Singapore.   Land was in sight all morning.   Sunbeams were coursing over the mountain forests of Sumatra, while fierce squalls were ravaging the partially cultivated uplands of the fine Island of Java ; far in the distance faintly loomed through the shower-streaked space, the bold island cone of Krakatoa, whose apex is 2,600 feet above the sea level.   Almost in mid-channel we passed the romantic islet called " the Button."

The scenery of the Straits of Sunda is exceedingly bold and picturesque, and in some respects resembles that on the coast of Trinidad in the West Indies.   Some of the Sumatran mountains are of considerable height; that known as Raja Bassa attaining an altitude of 4,398 feet.   I have already alluded to the characteristic of these mountains—wooded isolation—the single blessedness of the passive world! Now occasional groves of cocoa-palms bespeak the homes of human beings, of whose existence, however, there is little else to remind one; but our eyes are straining rather in the opposite direction of Java.

## JAVA.

Java, until lately, was less known for real natural beauties and undeveloped wealth, than for the policy of convenience, which put us in temporary possession of its government during our Napoleonic wars, and its name embroidered on the standards of a few of our regiments, keeps alive the memory of these events.

Anjer, although not the principal town of the island, is from its situation, perhaps, better known to seafaring Englishmen, than the capital, being on the coast, and convenient for ships passing through the Straits of Sunda.

In the face of one of those heavy squalls, so frequent in these latitudes, we steamed into the open roadstead of Anjer, where we found four other vessels straining their cables in the heavy sea that was running, but owing to the wildness of the day and the heavy surf, there were no small boats about; presently, however, on our approach, a frail canoe formed of the trunk of a tree, freighted with bananas and paddled by two Javanese, made its way to us, and was shortly followed by a larger well-managed boat, on board of which was the quasi agent of the Dutch harbour master. The background of lofty hills was partially obscured by heavy clouds and driving showers, while the little settlement itself cowered timidly to the beach with its red tiled houses, small fort, and conspicuous patriarchal tree, from the summit of which waved the tricolour of Holland. A large grove of cocoa-nut palms stretches away in one direction, and in the other a dense forest or jungle is apparently in full possession of its allodial rights.

As the waves were running high, and the pelting shower gave no signs of cessation, no one seemed disposed, even for the sake of our ready-written letters, to submit to such a ducking; so the task of posting these missives to friends, and which would be taken on by the next steamer to Singapore, devolved on myself. I had some difficulty in getting into the boat, however, as at one moment she was sunk ten or fifteen feet in a trough of the sea, and the next was cresting a wave that nearly reached our gangway. At last, watching my opportunity, I caught the hand of the harbour master's servant and jumped on board his boat.

This servant (or Captain, as he was called), was a slight man with a small moustache and blue black hair. An ill-rolled cheroot was never out of his mouth, while under his arm he carried an account book, and in his hand some official documents and a pencil. His costume was rich in colour although poor in material. Indeed, it was only in an æsthetic point of view that he could have been admired, and then merely as an accessory, to relieve the all-pervading greens of the landscape. His costume consisted of a blue and white striped banyan, over which was a loose buff muslin jacket with a deep orange arabesque pattern, loose payjamas of a greenish colour, with alternate broad and narrow stripes of blue. Thrown negligently across his right shoulder and round his waist was a bright crimson scarf crossed with lines of yellow, and bordered with stripes of dark blue. His *tout ensemble* was completed by a carelessly folded white muslin turban of voluminous proportions, sprigged with a brown seaweed pattern.

As we tore through the waves, under a press of canvas, this fellow remained imperturbably silent; but when the boatmen took to their oars (which latter by the way have scarcely any fluke, and are little better than leaping-poles), and raised their wild song, as we neared the threatening surf, he discharged volley upon volley of the grossest abuse, strange to say, in Hindostanee, although his auditors were Malays. Whether or no they understood what he said I cannot vouch; I trust, however, that they did not.

It was raining heavily all the while, and as the surf was breaking furiously on the shore I felt serious doubts about our affecting a landing, but I soon observed a well-constructed breakwater on either side of a long and narrow sluice. At the critical moment our oars were suspended, a huge curling wave bowled us up the sluice in long undulations, and deposited us safely about two hundred yards inland, underneath the overspreading branches of the large tree so conspicuous from the roadstead.

Following the official of the voluminous turban, I sprang ashore in front of the small custom-house, where the chief Dutch functionary was seated in the verandah, surrounded by a group of picturesque natives, each holding in his hand his remarkable hat, which I mistook for a very gaudy target.

The hard-featured old Batavian received me courteously, and buttoning up his white cotton jacket authoritatively—not suspiciously—took me under cover of his large umbrella to his own house. Here I posted my letters, for this officer performs all the functions of the Government and executive, and had some difficulty in exchanging my Mexican dollars without loss.

My new acquaintance spoke of a recent English traveller in Java, as having given his pen to one of the two parties in the island, from which in return he received much valuable information that otherwise was not within his reach.

Presently the harbour-master, &c., rang a tiny French hand-bell, on which a boy brought in a veletah, on an iron rod fixed to a pedestal like a gaff-boom, a box of cheroots, and sundry bottles of Scheidam, &c. The lad was then ordered to gather me a bunch of the best flowers in the garden, while the lady of the house made her appearance, and presented me with two beautiful large lemons. She spoke English perfectly well, and was slightly coloured. Her

husband alluded to the affairs of China, and noticed the joke in
"Punch" about the Elgin Marbles, on which the lady, to show her
acquaintance with contemporaneous history, remarked, in her sweet
artless way, "It is very strange, is it not, what they say, that this
very same Lord Elgin's father once went to China long ago to get
marble too?"

I had not the heart to destroy the pleasant coincidence, perhaps
the only (quasi) political fact, which had ever made an impression
on her tender domestic mind.

In this old gentleman's drawing-room, there was a very fine
portrait painted in oils on oak. It arrested my attention the moment
that I entered; and observing the effect it produced, he informed
me that it was the likeness of one of his sturdy ancestors, by the
hand of no less an artist than the great Sir Anthony himself, and,
in truth, its merits justified the assertion. The artist had invested
the lineaments of the old Batavian worthy's countenance with a
grim vitality, and had happily individualised its every peculiarity,
from the angular high forehead to the small, firm, and avaricious
mouth, as none but a master could. This able, but somewhat
illiberal face, was set in a broad-plaited white cambric ruff, which
seemed almost to bear the impress of the laundress's skill. Such
was the portrait of "Roelef Warmolts, of Gröningen," and I trust
that I may never owe such a man a farthing, much as I may
respect him.

The walks in the harbour-master's garden were laid down with
fragments of coral instead of gravel. It is a pity that the variety
known as the Astraea, and indeed the rock corals generally, have
not been adopted by the architect in the pavements of conservatories
and bath-rooms, where not only their beauty in transverse slabs, but
their porous nature would make them very desirable.

Amongst several unfamiliar plants, I noticed one which emitted
at night, as I afterwards discovered from its leaves only, a delightful fragrance like that of common garden sage.*

A number of natives offered me Java sparrows, and a beautiful
variety of small blue-headed parrot, at comparatively trifling prices;
but then the trouble and risk of taking them a long voyage to
England are, under ordinary circumstances, sufficient to deter a
casual visitor from trying the experiment.

### MAURITIUS.

Each break in a long voyage seems to renovate both the mental
and the physical nature, not so much by any actual novelty—for,
indeed, there is little new under the sun to an old voyager in the
outward aspect of things—but rather by the reappearance of those
outward objects which are generally associated with our earliest
recollections or impressions. After living for weeks within the
narrow limits of shipboard, and in contemplation of the serener

* It bears a striking resemblance to the "Bryophyllum Calcinum."

beauties of sea and sky, with their solemn associations, what a relief to gaze again on quiet villages nestling amongst trees, on verdant pastures, or on leafy uplands, mingling their green tints with the neutral violets of the far distance! It is then that the ruddy wanderer of the deep seems intuitively to recognise his own " complimentary colour."

Several small islands, for the most part barren, intercept the approach to Port Louis, in Mauritius, and dangerous reefs are encountered at a league's distance from the shore.

The former, in general configuration, somewhat resemble those that lie scattered about the Straits of Sunda, but on a nearer approach the absence of umbrageous vegetation forms a marked distinction. Here a large rocky islet, hoary and streaked with guano, is known as " Le Colombier ;" near it is a long spit of land, with patches of green, speckled with white houses, which terminates in a bold headland crowned by a light-house. Still nearer the coast is the " Gunner's Quoin," which sloping from the sea at a sharp angle terminates suddenly in a precipice, whose perpendicular face of strangely and apparently closely stratified rock, rises to a height of (I should suppose) fully 600 feet. Sea-birds are ever soaring about its lofty summit, or gyrating on snowy wings about the black and gloomy recess that marks the entrance to a large cavern.

The first impressions of the island of Mauritius are very pleasing. Highly cultivated fields in all shades of green undulate in rich crops from the yellow surf-beaten beach, near the scene of Virginia's apocryphal shipwreck, to the accumulating spurs that unite in a lofty range of mountains, whose grotesque peaks rise to the height of nearly three thousand feet, and are swept by eddying mists. The numerous white chimneys of sugar-boiling houses, the neat cottages of the peasantry, and the larger residences of the upper classes, even at the distance from which we saw them, conveyed the impression of a thriving colony, and a charming natural combination of the useful and the romantic.

The opportune arrival of a pilot on board hastened our entry into the harbour of Port Louis, which is land-locked, and protected by two small forts, one on either side of the narrow entrance.

The clouds that had rested in the early morning on the background of mountains at whose base the town is situated, now cleared away gradually, first disclosing the peak called the Pousse, then the Cap of Liberty, and in a higher range, the Peter Botte, towering in basaltic majesty into the blue empyrean, like the spire of some wonderful cathedral. Yet this celebrated mountain in some respects disappointed the most of us. Its form was not exactly that of the Impracticable Straight-Jacket, as represented to our boyish admiration in ancient Penny Magazines, but had certainly all the fulness of rocky skirts more conformable to modern fashion, and the peculiar shape, from our first point of view of its rocky head, being strictly perpendicular on one side, presents a *coup d'œil* far more like the flowing contours of a modern belle than that of any straight-laced old Batavian.

From the aforesaid woodcut, many an unreflecting lad has grown old in the faith that the wondrous ascent was made in the face of that fearful angle subtending the abyss, but alas! it is not so, a bight in the rock where it is simply vertical, enabled the first, as it has since enabled several other enterprising visitors, to accomplish what would otherwise seem to be an impossibility.

On the right of the harbour on entering, a long row of light and tall Madagascar pines* (as they are here called) and low white walls, mark the graveyard, and place of public execution; and stretch away from Fort William, or as it was named formerly by the French, Fort Blanc, to the town, which latter is connected with the opposite fort by a narrow causeway about a mile in length. In the basin thus formed the shipping is closely moored, stem and stern.

Port Louis, as might be supposed, in its general features is a close approximation to many of the towns of the West Indies, where the French and other European colonists still give a tone to the locality. The houses, too, are built much in the same style, with verandahs and jalousies, and a surrounding garden or shrubbery, where during our visit the superb Flamboyant,† being then in bloom, ruled with undisputed sway the empire of flowers, and seemed to absorb in his lofty crimson masses even the aspiring glories of the brilliant Poincianas. This tree is perhaps the most intensely flaming, as indeed its name imports, of any I remember having seen, and, if I am not mistaken, might even dispute for precedence with the Amherstia, of recent notoriety. Popularity, even in the botanical world, depends at first on accident as much as on desert, and many plants of the most eminent beauty are still born to blush unseen, until rescued from undeserved obscurity by some casual observer who does not forget its claims because it seems to be common in its own locality.

Opposite the landing-place there is a fine statue of M. de la Bourdonnais, who governed the island during its occupation by the French from the year 1744 to 17—; and further on, about the centre of the town, there is a pretty grove of ornamental trees enclosing an elegant fountain.

There is an excellent market, but provisions are on the whole dear, a fault traceable here, no doubt, as in some of the West Indian islands, to mismanagement. What fish I tasted was of an inferior description. I believe that many kinds are poisonous, and I was shown some excellent coloured drawings of a few remarkable varieties, and amongst them the dull grey mud-fish, a wound from whose sharp dorsal spines is said to be fatal.

French bijouterie is conspicuous in the shop windows, but there seemed to be no indigenous arts. Seed bracelets and tortoise-shell combs are made for sale, but clumsily; and the latter are far more

* Casuarinas.                           † A species of Acacia.

expensive than in England. The small stained rush caps, and red and yellow matting, come from Madagascar. Excellent light claret is to be had at ten shillings a dozen, but fruits on the other hand are correspondingly dear. The mangosteen has been successfully cultivated, and bananas, pine apples, cocoa nuts, and mangoes, are plentiful, and just coming into season, while we were in harbour. Tomatoes, potatoes, carrots, brenjals, &c., &c., are to be had in abundance. Animal food is remarkably expensive, and apparently this is the result of unavoidable causes.*

This colony is one of those interesting ethnological crucibles, in which it seems to be our especial mission to fuse and amalgamate the various races of mankind, and that too with no inconsiderable success. The population consists of English, French, Chinese, Indians, and Africans, and all their intermediate varieties. The concomitant diversity of peculiar manners, and sumptuary tastes, are as interesting as they are often amusing, from the tortuous embellishment of intractable wool, to the pale brow and delicate features, shaded by dark flowing braids, where large-petalled flowers seem to sleep, of the not unworthy successors of Virginia herself, as they lean over a balcony, or show their frilled or lace-worked Bloomers at garden-gates. A proportion of Artillery, Engineers, and two regiments of the line, constitute the strength of the garrison, one of the latter being generally broken up into detachments to occupy various small outposts.

Amongst the amusements of the island, I heard of fishing, as well as deer-stalking. Shell collecting is also carried on to a great extent, and there are several valuable collections in the island, which it is to be hoped will at some future period find their way into the public museums of the mother-country. It is to be regretted that such collections by remaining in private hands come in the ordinary course of events to be broken up or lost.

The Mission to Madagascar,† which was lately sent to congratulate the new sovereign of that imperfectly known island, on his accession to the throne, had just returned, and was one of the chief topics of interest at the period of our visit. The published report, although rather meagre, throws out some indistinct sug-

* No pasturage apparently in the island.
† " Papers relative to the Congratulation Mission of (sic) Radama, Queen of Madagascar, laid before Council on the 29th November, 1861."
Although the Mission was avowedly non-commercial, we showed a very laudable desire to make the royal palate acquainted with some of our most popular comestibles, for in the list of presents forwarded by the Governor of Mauritius, we find 14 cases of tongues and sausages, 20 cases of preserved European fruits, 50 hams and 20 Cheddar cheeses, besides such other luxuries as a pair of gold epaulettes, a thermometer, and a revolver " complete "
In this curious document there occurs some names which would sound almost familiar to the translators of Pali inscriptions, and the collectors of Bactrian coins. Thus " Radama" writing by his secretary " Rahaniraka," from his capital " Antanarivo" adverts to the death of his mother " Ranavalomanjaka."

gestions relative to the future commercial intercourse between the two islands.

The object of the visit is stated to have been purely of a friendly nature, and entirely unconnected with commerce or politics, but of course such professions should be taken at what they are worth. It was no doubt a politic step on the part of the Governor, to secure the friendship of his strange neighbour—a man, be it remarked, who had in early life visited England, and who appears to be far in advance of his subjects.

The purely French inhabitants of Mauritius are accused by the English of being unsocial and exclusive, while the mixed population of the lower orders consider them as hard taskmasters. How far the latter may be true I cannot say; but as regards the former it seems not unlikely that there may be faults on both sides, and that the French might with equal justice retort that Englishmen in receipt of large salaries abroad, have an overweening desire of saving money to spend it on sociality at home, and that in consequence of the levity and indiscretion of a few of our youthful spirits they have resolved on keeping aloof. Moreover, with their morbid sensitiveness and great national pride, Frenchmen can never be well affected under English rule.

The tombs of Paul and Virginia, about six miles from Port Louis, and near the Botanical Garden, are considered amongst the lions of the island, and thither flock the majority of visitors to pay an unconscious tribute to genius; for it is a remarkable fact, that of all my acquaintance who performed the pilgrimage with such eager enthusiasm, one only had ever read the story, or knew what it was about, beyond the bare names and the fact of a shipwreck— a tale "signifying nothing."

These tombs were felt to be one of the requirements of the age and in consequence they were erected, and no doubt are very pretty objects, which, if they serve to keep alive the sentiment embodied in a tale of perennial freshness, will in a certain degree have done their duty well, but to mortuary distinction they have no claim so far as concerns the lovers of St. Pierre.

It was not without a feeling of regret that we bid adieu so soon to ancient Peter Botte and his group of grotesque offspring, that rear their gnome heads about the paternal knee. We had heard of genuine deer forests where there were *bonâ fide* trees, of pleasant waterfalls, and shady walks bordered by lilies, and the pink-eyed tropical periwinkle (*vinca rosea*), and of tamarind, and other delicate trees, plaiting their branches overhead. Of rural retirements, where the juicy sugar-cane rustles in the sea-breeze, and the homely sounds of well-kept poultry-yards have a cheery music of their own. There was also something to be seen in the French phase of the colony, and perhaps even amongst a few of us a lingering ambition to belong to the select band of those, who had surmounted the difficulties of standing on the head of the local genius, "Peter Botte!"

Still as we passed ever-varying profiles of mountains, and the rich woodlands that skirt the western shores, our glasses were focussed to pierce those leafy coverts, or climb the rocks as gradually they faded into azure——   *   *   *

Another day, and we were passing the island of Bourbon, in a heavy swell, and under a troubled sky.

## THE FRENCH CAMPAIGN IN COCHIN CHINA.

By the treaty negotiated between the French Bishop of Adran and Djallong, the dethroned monarch of Cochin China, in 1787, the latter ceded to the French the district of Tourane in return for military assistance which the former were to give him in recovering his throne. This assistance was not, however, given him, at least not directly, or to any appreciable extent; the only services he received being from French adventurers sent to him from the West Indies. It does not appear to us at all clear that a cession of territory made on conditions which were never fulfilled can be binding on the person who ceded it, or that a just claim can be based on such a document. Be this as it may, the ambition of France is gratified by the conquest of a province likely to be of more value to her than Algeria, and which is of great extent, comprising all Lower Cochin China lying between Cape St. Jacques and the river Saigon to the east, the river Cambodge to the west, and the province of Laos to the north. Before the termination of the war in China the French Government resolved that a portion of the forces engaged in that expedition should be sent to strike an effective blow in Cochin China. Vice-Admiral Charner was the officer to whom the command of this expedition was entrusted. Dividing the naval force under his orders into two parts, he left one under the command of Rear-Admiral Protet to look after French interests in China, with injunctions to send first one ship and then another at short intervals to Japan, with the view of impressing on the Japanese the power of France.

The necessary arrangements having been made with Baron Gros and General Montauban, the embarkation of the troops destined for Cochin China commenced. This operation was performed under circumstances of the greatest possible discomfort. The winter had set in, the thermometer marked from 10° to 12° below zero, the rigging and every part of the vessels was covered with hoar frost, and the chopping sea breaking against the sides of the boats sent the spray flying over the men and wetted them to the skin. The crews of the gunboats that had been stationed for two years previously in the high temperature of Cochin China were great sufferers. These gunboats had rendered most important services during the Chinese campaign. Not only were they of great assistance in the reduction of the forts of the Peiho, but they were exceedingly useful in the conveyance of troops and supplies up the river, and saved the sailors an immense amount of labour in bringing off the troops to the ships. This duty having been satisfactorily performed, their guns and ammunition were taken out, their coals removed to their bows, their sides fresh caulked, and they were towed by the ships to Saigon, through a rough sea twelve hundred leagues, with the loss of only two during the voyage.

The powers conferred on Admiral Charner, says M. Pallu writing in the *Revue des Deux Mondes*, were greater than any that had been delegated to any officer since the first empire. Besides the power of appointing and promoting officers, he was vested with authority to make peace or war with the Annamite empire. The total number of vessels under his orders amounted to seventy, fifty-six steam vessels, and fourteen sailing vessels, with seven others hired from the Peninsular and Oriental Company to serve as transports. The condition of a portion of the fleet, however, was very bad, which is not to be wondered at, seeing that some of the vessels of which it was composed had been cruizing in those seas between four and five years. The total number of men engaged in this expedition was a little over 4,000, and included chasseurs à pied, chasseurs d'Afrique, artillery, engineers, commissariat, besides 800 marines, and so perfectly organized and provided with necessaries as to form a complete little army, capable of marching through a hostile country without having to rely on any other resources than its own. Moreover, to spare the troops the necessity of exerting themselves, except in actual fighting, under a climate so hot and pestilential as that of Cochin China, 600 coolies were taken from China.

As Spain had some time before united with France in operating against the Annamites, Admiral Charner communicated with the Spanish commander, and sent a requisition to the Governor-General of the Philippines for an addition of cavalry and infantry to the Spanish contingent of 230 men already established at Saigon, but for some reason or other, though Manilla could have easily furnished the cavalry, the reinforcement was never sent.

The expedition reached Cochin China on the 7th February, and anchored in the Donnai before Saigon. This is one of five noble rivers which traverse Lower Cochin China, and flows into the sea by one of the largest estuaries in the world. The banks of these rivers are low, and well covered with vegetation, among which grow numerous mangoes. They are connected with each other by canals, some of them entirely the work of men's hands, others only partially so. The vegetation on the banks of these canals is passably rich, but has none of the magnificence of the tropics. All that is seen beside the mangoes already mentioned, are dwarf palms, large shrubs bearing a white flower, and others of every tint of green, but of no kind of use; at some distance from the banks, however, grow cocoa and palm trees, displaying their graceful proportions above a thick mass of aloes and prickly cactus, which none but a native could penetrate. The whole of this part of the country, like all rice lands, is, in fact, little better than a mud flat; but beyond this are forests from which drugs are obtained which command a very high price in China. The staple produce of the country is rice, and there is no doubt that this was the principal reason of the desire of the French Government to get possession of it, inasmuch as any quantity of rice finds a ready market in China, and French ships will then have a commodity which they can exchange for the silk and tea they are now forced to pay for in silver. There can be no question either of the seriousness of the intention of France to establish a permanent station there, and the Government is of opinion that Frenchmen may be induced to emigrate thither and colonize the country, and that it offers a great many advantages to colonists which are wanting in Algeria. Possession has already been guaranteed in a few instances where they have squatted on the ground, and allotments have been made for public buildings, for a station for the *Messageries Impériales*, which is becoming a powerful rival to the Peninsular and Oriental Company, and for other purposes.

Saigon is a straggling kind of place; the houses, or to speak more correctly the wooden huts covered in with palm leaves, are scattered here and there without regard to symmetry. Since the French have had possession of it, the Corps of Engineers, with the assistance of a few hired labourers, have drained the land about it for a considerable distance, and laid out broad streets, which only lack houses to make it a handsome town. Its position made it to the Annamites what Portsmouth is to us, but their London was at Mytho; a commercial depôt difficult of access to European vessels, but easily approached by the flat-bottomed boats of the country, and by junks.

Saigon was defended by a kind of citadel, built on the highest ground, the principal contents of which in 1861 were two long mounds of rice, still burning, though it was two years since it was set on fire. The fortifications, such as they were, were designed by Colonel Ollivier, who was one of the twenty Frenchmen taken there in 1791 by the Bishop of Adran, the sole relics of a fleet of twenty vessels and seven regiments detained on their way from France to Cochin China by the English Governor of Pondicherry. Forty years later the place was taken by the Cambogians, after a two years siege, and rased to the ground. It was afterwards rebuilt by the Annamites, and stored with large quantities of provisions and ammunition, and was made so strong as to resist all the attacks of Camboge and Siam, though it was less successful in resisting the attack made on it by Admiral Genouilly in 1859, who destroyed and then abandoned it. The natives retired to an immense cemetery about four miles distant, and entrenched themselves there so strongly that a French force sent against them was repulsed with loss.

At the end of 1859, or beginning of 1860, Rear-Admiral Page resumed possession of Saigon, laid out the defences, ordered the erection of a hospital, barracks, and magazines, and opened the port to trade, with such beneficial results that within four months seventy vessels and about a hundred junks shipped from thence sixty thousand tons of rice, which was sold at Hong Kong and Singapore at an enormous profit. For some reason or other the Chinese located in the town did not approve of these proceedings on the part of the French. Having possession of the immense warehouses in which the rice was stored, they induced the Annamites to cut off the communication with the latter by means of a double sap and trench. The foreigners, who were only a handful of men in comparison with the Annamites, instantly seized and began to fortify a couple of pagodas. Before they could complete the works, a force at least two thousand strong attacked them. At the same time the native artillery poured a constant fire into them from their guns, without any regard to the fact that their own troops were mixed up with the French and Spanish troops defending them. The struggle was terminated by the arrival of reinforcements to the French, when the Annamites retired; but only to carry out additional entrenchments, which effectually cut off the foreigners from the roads leading to Mytho, Hue, and Cambodge, while it left perfectly open the access to the Chinese part of Saigon. The manner in which these defences were constructed proved that the natives are exceedingly skilful in availing themselves of the means at their command.

The state of affairs we have just described was that which existed in 1861 at the date of the arrival of the French expedition. Admiral Charner, in concert with the Spanish commander, and the principal French officers, at once proceeded to survey the position of the enemy, and to plan the best method of attacking them. The result was a determination to make the attack according to the following plan. The gunboats were to ascend the Donnai, sweeping away in their course the obstructions placed there by the enemy, destroy the forts, and take up a position commanding the upper part of the river. Armed with a powerful artillery, including some rifled cannon landed from the ships, the pagodas, supported by the men-of-war, moored in a semicircle before Saigon, were to keep the enemy in check on the front and right flank. Emerging from this line, and following a course beyond the reach of the enemy's fire, the expeditionary army was to march round the Annamite camp, and attack it in the rear; thus closing it in on all sides, and leaving the defenders no alternative between a successful defence or an unconditional surrender. The preparations for carrying this plan into execution were not made in a day, and the greatest watchfulness had to be observed at night in order that no sudden onslaught might be made on the town under cover of the darkness by the enemy, who were estimated to be at least thirty thousand strong, and agile as so many North American Indians. The French troops showed no unwillingness to attack, but the recollection of the previous attack and repulse, and the close vicinity of the enemy's lines, which extended a distance of nearly thirty miles, made them more serious than they usually are under such circumstances, or than they have been since in that country; the defeat of the Annamites and the destruction of their camp having changed the feeling with which they then regarded them into contempt. The share taken by the sailors in the preliminary preparations was an arduous one. Not only had they to bend at the oars from morning till night under a burning sun in landing troops, guns, and ammunition, but they furnished also a detachment of 900, who were to be employed in the subsequent operations. These were armed with boarding cutlasses and revolvers, and were to act as a kind of pioneers, and a number of others were employed to work the guns landed from the ships.

It was four o'clock in the morning, and still dark when the bugle sounded to summon the men to their standards. They had already drunk their coffee and their ration of brandy, and their haversacks had been packed the night before, each man being supplied with biscuits for eight days, and two rations of cooked meat. Notwithstanding the darkness, they had fallen into their places at five o'clock, and half an hour later were on the march. Escorted by a troop of Chasseurs d'Afrique, the Admiral led the advance. Next came the Spanish infantry, then two companies of riflemen, the artillery, including three rifled 4-pounders, four rifled 12-pounders, and some howitzers; the sailors with their cutlasses and revolvers, who were to attack the fortifications; the marines, and lastly, the military train and ambulance. The coolies and baggage animals followed a different route, so as not to impede the movement of the column. It was now pretty nearly broad daylight, and the temperature was not yet so high as to make marching a difficult labour. Some of the forts had already opened fire on the enemy's lines, rather to occupy their attention than with the expectation of doing them any substantial injury, and the deep sonorous booming of these rifled 30-pounders was readily distinguished from the weaker and more ringing sound of the small iron guns of the Annamites, who were now in full movement, though the air was filled with the sounds emitted by their gongs summoning them to their posts, which was only overpowered when one of the guns thundered from the fort, and sent a ball ploughing through the hurrying mass of soldiers. At the entrance to the plain in front of the enemy's line, the French artillery made a dash forward, unlimbered, and directly afterwards the clear ringing sound which issued from their batteries showed that they had commenced practice. This allowed the soldiers forming the column to take breath a little after they had debouched upon the plain, though the firing was not supposed to have much effect beyond inducing the Annamites to waste their ammunition in fruitless replies.    The distance between the opposing lines was now diminished by one half, the new position taken up by the artillery being within five hundred yards of the enemy, whose balls poured in thick and fast among the French and their Spanish allies.   The troops were now divided into two columns of assault ; the left formed of sailors under the command of one of their captains, and led by a captain of engineers ; the right composed of two companies of riflemen, the corps of marines, and the Spanish infantry.   The fire of the Annamites was well-sustained, accurate, and directed with great skill and judgment.   In a few minutes several artillerymen and horses were struck, and whenever the Admiral and his staff took up a stationary position, a concentrated fire was opened upon it instantly.   The short interval which separated the French batteries from the enemy's camp, neutralised the superior accuracy of the rifled guns ; and after the firing had continued a considerable time there was not the faintest sign of any relaxation in the replies of the native cannon.   The losses of the allies were growing serious, when the Admiral, taking the direct command of the troops, gave the signal for the assault.   Under the protection of a smart fire of grape the troops advanced at a steady pace in the face of a well sustained fire of musketry.   A cry of " Vive l'Empereur" was heard above the sound of the guns, and the next instant the troops were cutting their way through the obstacles raised by the enemy, and advancing cautiously among the innumerable pitfalls till they had crossed the ditch and mounted the ramparts.   The Annamites remained at their post till this moment, when firing a parting volley point blank at the assailants, they retreated, but in such good order, that to the Frenchmen who entered the works in time to see them, they looked like labourers who had just finished their work, and were going quietly home.   In a few moments they had joined the main body of their troops, and the French were left in undisturbed possession of the works.   Though the Annamites stood well to their guns, in spite of serious losses, they did not attempt to sustain a hand to hand conflict.

The fight ended, the wounded were transported to the fort, the troops returned for the knapsacks they had thrown off before making the assault, and in a short time they were in quiet occupation of the low wooden sheds vacated by their opponents.   This was about nine o'clock, and they had been on foot since four o'clock, and a few hours rest was absolutely necessary before they continued their march, in consequence of the danger of fatiguing men under a blazing sun in the marshy districts.   About three o'clock the same afternoon, the bugle again sounded the call. Leaving a company of marines and a howitzer in the fort, the troops were marched along a moss-covered plain towards a point which would cut off the enemy's retreat.   It is possible the Annamites may by this time have become aware of, or at all events suspected the intention of the French commander, for suddenly a troop of elephants issued from their camp with colours flying, as if it were their purpose to dispute the further advance of their antagonists. But the sortie was speedily checked by a few discharges of grape from the French guns, most likely from the impossibility of getting elephants to advance against the fire of artillery, and the natives re-entered their camp. After a march of two hours, the allies reached the point desired, which had been the site of a village. Admiral Charner took up his quarters in one of the abandoned huts, and the men had already begun to make preparations for camping for the night, when suddenly so hot a fire opened upon them from among the shrubs and underwood which lay between them and the enemy's lines, one of the balls knocking the roof to pieces beneath which the head-quarters were established, that they were obliged to retreat till the skirmishers and artillery had driven the enemy from their shelter, which was not accomplished without considerable difficulty. At last the worn-out men were allowed to rest themselves in peace, most of them being content to make their evening meal of biscuit washed down with water; after which they stretched themselves on the ground and slept till they had got pretty well into the small hours, when they were roused by the command to assemble, and at five o'clock the artillerymen were again in the saddle.

The army was divided into two parts of unequal strength, the main assault being devolved on the left, and the right, supported by three howitzers, being led against the camp by an enfilade movement intended to lighten the task of the column of assault; those who headed the attack on the previous day now forming the reserve.

Amidst the obscurity which surrounded it the advancing column looked almost like a company of phantoms. The moss-covered ground rendered the footsteps and the rolling of the wheels of the artillery inaudible at the leisurely pace at which they marched. There was nothing of the excitement of war here except the danger. No music, nor flashing colours, no idea that the eyes of the world were upon them; and the only sound which broke the silence was the rush of the balls from the heavy guns of Ki-hoa which swept over their heads.

The exterior defences of the camp were of a primitive character, but it is doubtful whether with the same means at their disposal any European troops could have constructed better. Numerous deep and artfully concealed pitfalls with spikes at the bottom extended nearly two hundred yards in advance of the earthworks, the spaces between the rows being filled with palisades and stakes. Beyond these were two broad ditches, each containing liquid mud to the depth of about three feet, the opposite sides being raised to a height of fifteen feet, and bristling with pointed bamboo stakes, with which were interwoven branches of shrubs covered with sharp thorns.

These defences, formidable enough in themselves, were defended by
swarms of Annamites, who kept up an incessant fire of musketry
upon their assailants, who were obliged to advance slowly in consequence of the pitfalls.  When these had been traversed, those
who escaped falling into them made an impetuous attack on the
remaining obstacles.  The fight was long and obstinate ; and when
at last the Annamites retired, it was only within their forts and
another line of earthworks.  The attacking force was now in as bad,
or worse, position than before.  The guns of the forts had been laid
with skill, so as to cross their fire, and the whole of the open space
in front of this internal line of fortifications was capable of being
swept by the fire of musketry.  It is not improbable that if the
Annamites-had had only the outer line of works, and had concentrated their whole exertions to its defence, the little army of Frenchmen would have been so cut up that they could not have persisted
in their attack against such odds ; but having once penetrated this
outer line the latter were encouraged to make a more furious attack
on the inner line of defences.  The fire from the forts opened
the instant after the natives had retired within their protection,
and a perfect shower of musket balls hailed among the allied
forces.  Officers and men were dropping in every direction, and
still there was no sign of any slackening in the vigour of the
resistance offered by the besieged.  The main attack was urged
unsuccessfully for three-quarters of an hour under a burning sun.
Nearly the whole staff and escort surrounding Admiral Charner
were wounded, the men were getting exhausted, and no human cry
was now heard except the occasional shriek or imprecation of a
wounded man.  Even the trumpet was silenced for a time from the
trumpeter being stunned by a ball striking him on the forehead.
At this juncture the reserve was ordered up, and every man that
could be made available ; the baggage waggons and even the artillery being left almost unprotected.  With a sudden access
of energy inspired by discipline, tradition, and the feeling that
salvation depended on immediate success, a rush was made against
the entrances to the forts and defences, which were cut down with
axes, wielded as frequently by the officers as by their men.  The
assault was now successful.  The Europeans forced their way into
the interior, and a scene of carnage ensued not difficult to imagine
when it is remembered that the allies had suffered severe losses, and
were so near being discomfited.  The forts were at once occupied by
the victors, and also the huts from which the enemy had been
driven out.  Ammunition, stores, and provisions were brought
from the depôts ; and at the same time intelligence was brought of
the complete success of the flotilla in its encounters with the forts
in forcing a passage up the river.

  It was found when the muster roll was called over that one-thir-
teenth of the allied army had been placed *hors de combat* in this
affair.  How many the enemy lost is not known, inasmuch as they

had facilities for carrying off their killed and wounded as they fell to a distant part of the camp. When account had been taken, it was found that the Annamites had abandoned nearly a hundred and fifty pieces of ordinance of different calibres; above two thousand flint muskets of French manufacture, all in good condition, more than four thousand pounds of well made gunpowder, a considerable quantity of copper money, and numerous plans and maps.

From the absence of cavalry, for the Chasseurs d'Afrique did not amount to a score in all, the enemy could not be pursued as they fled, and, therefore, their retreat was not changed into a rout; and instead of being cut up or captured, they made their escape from the camp by two gulleys known only to themselves, which traversed a district so soft and muddy and of such extent, that a large army might have been engulphed in it.

The next step taken by the French commander was an advance to Tongkeau, a place of some importance as being an arsenal of the Annamites. This was captured after a brisk cannonade with little loss; and the stores of guns, ammunition, and provisions which fell into the hands of the allies was considerable. After a short halt the advance was continued, but it would have been better to have encamped for the night where they were, for the sun was so powerful, and the air so filled with heated impalpable dust that the men suffered greatly, some dying, and others losing their senses from the effect of sunstroke. The ultimate result of these continual advances into the interior was the dissolution of the Annamite army. Driven from point to point, the vassals who held their farms by a military tenure threw off their uniform and returned to the cultivation of their land, while the regular troops, or what remained of them, dispersed and made their escape to other districts. Twelve months later, peace was signed between France and the empire of Aunam, favourable, of course, to the former; but it is doubtful if such terms would have been yielded if the Emperor had not had to contend against a very serious insurrection. Subsequently, the French have had to enter the field again to put down a rising among the population in the territory ceded to them.

With the differences of opinion which have since arisen in France as to whether it would not have been better to have kept the troops at home and saved the expenses of the expedition we have nothing to do; but the operations of France in such a distant part of the world shows that this invasion, taken in conjunction with the resumption of possession of New Caledonia on the coast of Australia, and the expedition to Mexico, forms part of a vast scheme on the part of the Emperor Napoleon to aggrandise his empire. The campaign was not one of very great importance, but our sympathies with France are strong enough to cause us to regard with interest the struggle of so small a force of Europeans against an entire empire of Asiatics.

## REMINISCENCES OF A CADET.

" Temper justice with mercy" ought to be one of the leading principles of those who are placed in authority over youth.  Discipline, stern unbending discipline, will not suffice; allowance must be made for the ebullitions, the follies, and, alas! we must add the budding vices of the incipient—man.  Admitting the truth of " Just as the twig is bent the tree's inclined," we must still remember that in bending we must avoid breaking; an experienced and patient gardener may succeed in judiciously training the rising plant, while a hasty man may too often "nip the flower in its bud."  What a distressing spectacle would it prove to some of the educational authorities could they see the termination of the earthly career of some of their erring pupils; who, though guilty of misdemeanours, or perhaps youthful vices, had only just wandered from the paths of rectitude, morality, and religion; and by clemency, advice, and not over severe treatment might have been reclaimed from their approaches to crime, and have lived to become ornaments to society; whereas, by harsh and unfeeling punishment, many of these headstrong, or misguided youths became callous to consequences, and stubbornly pursued their evil habits, or, with even a maddened feeling of indignation, rushed headlong into a course of life at the mere thought of which a few months previously they would have shuddered.  Records are kept and published of the career of many of our distinguished countrymen in their scholastic and collegiate progress from boyhood to manhood; and to the press too we are indebted for interesting accounts of the customs and regulations established at the various institutions; but the *black letter books* have not appeared, the feelings of the outcasts and of their relations have been spared ; and, in some instances, the absence of this very publicity has added to the self-satisfied feelings of an over-strict and ill-judging disciplinarian, who, to carry out his own views, has unhesitatingly and unjustifiably condemned a youth who merited not so harsh a sentence as that awarded for his erring conduct.

Since the following tragic career of one of our associates at a military educational establishment, many years have passed, but the sad termination of it is still fresh in our memory, and induces us to give publicity to it, not only as a warning to youths, but also as a caution to those in authority, lest they should at any time unwisely and heartlessly forget "to temper justice with mercy."  At the termination of one of the vacations, a cadet received from his father a liberal supply of pocket money for his petty expenses, and for his journey to ——.  Similarly to too many pilgrims in the course of life, he wandered from the straight path, and, instead of returning direct to his post, he became so fascinated with the allurements of pleasure and freedom that he remained in the metropolis until all his funds were flittered away; and then, with a heavy heart, made his appearance at his place of military instruction. Anticipating severe notice of his absence, most unjustifiably, and most imprudently he had prepared a false medical certificate, which he produced to the inspector of studies on being called upon to account for his delayed return. The manner and tone of this officer were rather peculiar, and, having looked at the certificate, he said, in his usual drawling tone, "Why, Mr. ——, I really think this is a forgery." Uttered as it was, the appeal was irresistibly ludicrous, and quite disconcerted the intended steady demeanour of the absentee, who, without a moment's thought, replied, "Why, of course it is." This drew forth, "Then, Mr. ——, you are placed in arrest, and I shall report the circumstance to the Governor." This having been done, the delinquent was sent to the black hole for some days, and then ordered *to be degraded*. To the inexperienced in these matters we must make known that degradation of a cadet implied separation from his comrades at meals, studies, and at night; moreover, when the cadets marched past at the garrison parade on Sunday morning, the degraded embryo soldier was dressed in his daily undress costume, and marched in the rear of the division, while the other cadets were attired in their full-dress suit; thus pointing out to all the soldiers the delinquency of the outcast. Aware of the intention of thus exposing him on public parade, the indignant and proud youth determined not to submit to so harsh an ordeal, and his decision was well known not only to the body of cadets, but also to the officers of the garrison, all of whom felt for his distressing position, and in their hearts applauded him for upholding the rank of a cadet, which would have been indelibly disgraced by his appearing on parade in the conspicuous manner intended by the Governor. The eventful Sunday came, the parade was formed in front of the Cadet barracks, the body of the military students, and poor —— in the rear dressed in the costume previously described; but, on the word "March" being given, *one cadet* obeyed not the order, the degraded one moved not, and, on being desired to follow his late associates, he replied to the officer—"No, sir, I will never disgrace the cadets by appearing thus on the garrison parade, the punishment is degrading to the Company, the soldiers would see a cadet thus humiliated who before long might be an officer over them. I will never march to that parade: I have submitted to every other portion of my punishment without a murmur, but I will not disgrace the Company: send me again to the black hole, or do anything else you please with me, but do not expect that you can induce me to attend the garrison parade to-day." All the officers and cadets sympathised with the determined recusant, and approved of his feelings of pride and self-devotion. Not so the stern Governor, who (indignant that his orders had been disobeyed, and not duly appreciating the sensitive feelings which caused the doomed cadet to refuse compliance with his harsh mandate) lost no time in

reporting the case to the highest authority, and the direful result
was the dismissal of poor —— from the Cadet Company. Alas!
for him; he was a favourite with his comrades, his character had not
been tarnished until the perpetration of the recorded improper conduct, and now he was cast upon the world destitute and penniless—
for his refusal to obey the Governor's orders having been made
known to his father, he, too, forgot "to err is human, to forgive
divine;" he too, a father and a clergyman, closed the gates of
mercy, and heartlessly perpetrated a deed that Christians well might
blush at—"But if ye forgive not men their trespasses, neither will
your Father forgive your trespasses."

All the erring ones have, we believe, quitted this world of trial,
and we may therefore terminate the recital of the mournful event
without distressing their feelings. On receiving his dismissal, and
being made cognizant of the total blight to his hopes of ever obtaining a commission in the army, another death-blow was in store
for him, a letter from his father was received conveying his most
severe censure, banishing him from his home, and casting him off
for ever. The grieving associates of poor ——, having learnt this
cruel treatment, collected together all the money they could for the
unlucky cast-away, and, all shaking him by the hand, parted from
him with regret. Months elapsed, and nothing further was heard
of him, until, accidentally, on a Sunday afternoon a cadet, on leave
of absence, was struck by the resemblance of a private in the Guards
to his late associate; and, on looking steadily at him, the soldier
came towards him, and said, "I see you have recognised me, and I
had better, therefore, not attempt to conceal my present position,
which I now make known, with a request that, in mentioning it to
the other cadets, you will beg them never to notice me should they
meet me in London. When I quitted you all, entirely deserted by
my relations, I endeavoured to obtain some employment as a clerk,
but not succeeding in this, and the subscription you kindly gave me
having been quite exhausted, to avoid starving I enlisted as a soldier,
and thought it advisable to make my colonel aware of my former
course of life. He was much pleased with my military drawings,
and said he would communicate what I had told him to the other
officers, and promote me to non-commissioned officer as soon as
he could."

Thus terminated the history of the discarded cadet's enlistment;
and several years elapsed without any further account of him. Accidentally, however, we became acquainted with an officer of the
same name, who related that, a short time after the battle of
Waterloo, an officer of the Guards called upon him, and stated that
a serjeant in his regiment was in a dying state, and that as it was
known in the corps that the serjeant was by birth a gentleman, it
was thought that perhaps the officer might be connected with him,
and that he would therefore like to accompany him to the dying
non-commissioned officer. They proceeded without delay to the

hospital, but arrived, alas! too late to have any conversation with our early associate, whose constitution gave way under the hardships he had endured in the campaign, and who thus unfriended, and almost unknown, quitted the world, in which for several years his life must indeed have been a life of sorrow and disappointment; all his troubles and sufferings having been caused by one act of youthful folly and reprehensible conduct.

In scanning the deeds of our fellow-man, let us not judge too harshly; there is no doubt that severe blame, censure, and punishment ought to have awaited the erring cadet; but let stern moralists take a lesson from the injury, destructive of all that life holds dear, inflicted on a mere youth; let his melancholy fate prove a lesson to future disciplinarians, let them not imitate the unfeeling judge, let them "temper justice with mercy," and thus prove themselves a blessing instead of a curse to those over whom they are placed in authority.

> " The quality of mercy is not strained,
> It droppeth as the gentle rain from heaven
> Upon the place beneath; it is twice bless'd,
> It blesseth him that gives, and him that takes:
> 'Tis mightiest in the mightiest; it becomes
> The throned monarch better than his crown:
> His sceptre shows the force of temporal power,
> The attribute to awe and majesty,
> Wherein doth sit the dread and fear of kings;
> But mercy is above his scepter'd sway,
> It is enthroned in the hearts of kings,
> It is an attribute to God himself,
> An earthly power doth then show likest God's
> When mercy seasons justice."

In our reminiscences of the sad termination of the career of some of our old associates, we will now instance the life of one who as a youth was quiet, well-disposed, and apparently had every prospect of rising in his profession, and becoming a comfort and blessing to his parents, of whom he was the only son and heir to a landed estate. Though not possessing good abilities as a scholar, still he was not deficient in mental qualifications; the latter portion of his life, however, made it but too apparent that his strength of mind, and appreciation of right and wrong were not such as to keep him in the path of religion, morality, and honourable conduct. Shortly after obtaining his commission, he formed an attachment to an unprincipled and degraded woman, who obtained so much power over him that he made her his wife, though for some time he did not acknowledge his marriage to his brother officers. This disreputable connection reached the ears of his father, who forthwith went to his misguided son in the hope to reclaim him from his abandoned course of life. After a most distressing interview with him and his disreputable wife, the unhappy parent at length succeeded in inducing them to consent to a separation from each other for ever; the woman, in consequence, to receive one hundred pounds a year for life, and the son's conduct to be forgiven, and a liberal pecuniary allowance continued to him on condition that he never again cohabited with his vicious wife. To ensure breaking this abominable connection, the young officer was removed to another station, and the woman went her way, separated, as it was expected, for ever from the victim she had entrapped. Bad as matters had been thus far, there was still hope and prospect that the future life of the young soldier might be gentlemanly and moral, and make amends in some measure for his entrance into the paths of vice and degradation; but, alas! the tares had been too firmly rooted to be separated from the wheat, the good seed sown was completely choked up, the weeds of evil obtained their full growth, and furnished baneful and destructive food, instead of the wholesome and nutritious nourishment that the soil by judicious culture would have produced. The converse of "Drink deep, or taste not the Pierian spring" is, in too many cases, applicable to the poisonous cup of Circe, whose votaries, having once indulged in a draught of her attractive, though destructive beverage, "banish reason from her throne," and, without a pang or a murmur, drink deep and—perish. This too truly was the result in the case of the officer whose course of life became worse and worse: the promises made to his anxious parent were unheeded and broken; the woman rejoined her degraded husband, whose pecuniary allowance from his justly-irritated father was in consequence immediately stopped; the disapprobation and censure of brother officers were expressed; debts increased, which were not paid; and eventually the commission, that had been disgraced, was resigned, and the vicious couple were thrown upon the world without friends and without any means of subsistence. After some time, intelligence was received that they had been fortunate enough to support themselves in a very humble way by teaching the children of poor parents in a day-school; but this pause in the downward career of the man (who wilfully sacrificed for a worthless woman all that would have made life a blessing to himself and his parents) was, we believe, of short duration. The descending wheel of fortune, once in motion, pursued its course, and the next report that reached us was that the miserable man had been seen ascending a long ladder, as a bricklayer's labourer, with a hod of mortar on his shoulder. We heard no more of him; but, as he was neither strong in body nor of a good constitution, his life must have been brief, enduring such hardships, to which there could be no termination, for his broken-hearted father had disinherited him, and all friendship and sympathy were alienated between the outcast and the companions of his youth. In the recital of the misfortunes that attended the misconduct of the first cadet, who, by less harsh treatment than he experienced, would in all probability have done credit to his profession, we attached blame to the too severe authorities; but, in this latter reminiscence, to "temper justice with mercy" had not

been forgotten; mercy had been fully shown, every endeavour had
been made to reclaim the votary of vice, the prodigal son had been
intreated to return, the fatted calf would have been killed, bright
and happy would have been his welcome; but he sealed his own
doom in this world: and, degraded and discarded from the position
he ought to have occupied in life, he terminated his days an outcast
from enlightened and high-principled society; furnishing another
beacon to deter men from risking shipwreck on the rocks and quick-
sands of self-gratification, immorality, and vice.

> " What lost a world, and made a hero fly?
> The timid tear in Cleopatra's eye.
> Yet be the soft Triumvir's fault forgiven,
> By this—how many lose not earth but heaven;
> Consign their souls to man's eternal foe,
> And seal their own, to spare some wanton's woe?"

The two previous reminiscences have been of a sombre and distressing character, but it must not be imagined that, in our thoughts
of past times, we always look at the gloomy side of life, and remember not the light scenes of pleasure and conviviality. What
amusing, aye! and edifying books of anecdotes might be published
if men, on their entrance into professional life, would but more often
devote an idle half hour now and then to dot down the quaint
sayings and humourous doings of their friends and associates. A
few volumes of anecdotes may certainly be found in large libraries,
but what a starvation diet may they be considered when we remember the myriads of men who have, each in their day, enjoyed
the merry joke, and been themselves often present in scenes the relation of which would be found very interesting, whether the transactions had reference to deeds of daring, escapes from danger, ebullitions of wit, practical jokes, in short any acts commendable for
their good intentions, and consequent good results, or for the effects
they may have had in raising drooping spirits, and proving that in
this world " all is (not) barren."

Returning again to our Reminiscences, we will give an instance
of stretching the point of honour to its extreme bounds. Youthful
spirit will have its fling, and at a fair, in the vicinity of the barracks,
a party of excited and mischievously-disposed cadets were one
evening determined to sweep away everything that opposed them in
their promenade between the booths. For a short time they carried
all before them, but at length they were encountered by a body of
civilian pleasure seekers, who were determined to hold their ground
against the embryo soldiers. The opponents met face to face, "then
came the tug of war;" flesh and blood would not give way, but the
stalls of gingerbread, dolls, toys, and the usual heterogenous collection of rubbish at these fairs were soon upset, and trampled on the
ground amidst the scolding of women and the abuse, followed by
the pugnacious assaults of the male possessors of the insulted property. Heavy and hearty fell the blows on both sides, hats were

smashed, garments, the pride of tailors and their dandy wearers' were rent and destroyed; faces and figures were severely punished, but still the fight went on, each party obstinately disputing every inch of ground. At length a strong body of constables made their appearance, and endeavoured to secure some of the most active in the fray, but the cadet combatants closed their ranks, and thus prevented the capture of any individual. Not such was the good fortune of an inoffensive cadet, who was on the outskirts of the skirmish, and had not taken any share in the encounter, but was merely a quiet spectator of the misconduct of his comrades: he, poor youth, was pounced upon by the police, and of course easily captured.

> " Thus when two dogs are fighting in the streets,
> With one of these two dogs t'other dog meets;
> With angry teeth he bites him to the bone,
> And *this* dog suffers for what *t'other* dog has done."

Rejoiced at having secured one of the cadets, they triumphantly carried their victim to the cage, locked him up, and returned to the fair just as the fight had terminated.

As the cadets were moving homewards, they learnt the fate of their unoffending associate, and lost no time in proceeding in a body to the cage, in which they found him incarcerated. This was unendurable; so, without a moment's hesitation, they procured the means of bursting open the well-locked door, which soon yielded to their united strength; and, having thus succeeded, they told the released prisoner to return with them to the barracks. To their great surprise and indignation he refused to do so, influenced by his own peculiar views and feelings of the point of honour. In vain did his friends endeavour to persuade him to accompany them, he would not quit his cell, refusing all entreaties, saying "The same power that put him in should take him out." With open door there he remained all the night; and, as a climax to his misfortunes, he was the following morning fined by the magistrates for being in the fray, had to bear his portion of the expenses for damage to booths, &c.; and, furthermore, he lost the good opinion of his youthful comrades by making known the names of the cadets " who had fought the good fight, and gained the victory;" and who, but for his high fangled notions of honour, would have had their spree at the fair without any of the unpleasant consequences which followed their uproarious and mischievous conduct.

---

# A TRIP TO VANCOUVER ISLAND, AND BRITISH COLUMBIA.

## CHAPTER IX.

### The Passage Home.

Who the Major is, and what the Major does, I have not the slightest idea, but he will be eternally associated in my mind with

San Francisco shipping. Directly you arrive in port you see the Major, who is a man of immense importance, looks as if he had swallowed a poker, pounces upon the mail, pumps the captain with questions, and winds up by saying, "Gentlemen! have you got any newspapers?" Whether the Major has any connexion with the departure of steamers, and whether he was on board or not, I did not know. Every saloon, every cabin, every nook and corner, was a dense conglomeration of juvenile newsvendors, who persuaded or forced you to buy a paper, of nurses and babies in caps and out of caps, of busy porters, frantic stewards, passengers and passenger's baggage. A jolly-looking gentleman in black which is very respectable, and with very big collars, which added considerably to that respectability, and who looked like something between a bishop, a dean, and an archdeacon, was bowing, shaking hands, chatting and laughing, or rather roaring with everybody. "Celebrated preacher that," said some communicative gentleman; "runs away from his parish every year, and is as jolly, I guess, as a sand-boy;" and then, as if one had any desire to controvert such a statement, added, "an uncommon smart preacher." And there was the girl-mother tossing her baby up and down to keep it quiet, and chatting about the general who had sent her a telegraphic dispatch, most precious of all military dispatches, to the pleasant-looking Scotch stewardess, who, with the experience of twenty-five different passages from Liverpool to New York, had left the Atlantic, and was now chirping to the baby, just as if she hadn't to work very hard to get a living, understood babies, and was herself a mother. There, too, was a pale-faced old gentleman, who had just kissed some little lads who was going away and crying badly; and a peddling chemist had espied him, and with a preparatory cough, said: "Wright's pills, Wright's inimitable pills, Sir!" "But are they genuine?" asked the pale-faced gentleman. "To be sure, Sir, of course, good for everything," answered the Chemist, pocketing a dollar, "and take a copy of 'Snoggins Illustrated Advertiser,' free gratis, to read with them. Won't make you bilious, and you'll find it vastly improving. Just examine it." Then, turning to me, the Chemist says, "Seidlitz powders! seidlitz powders, Sir! a pleasant beverage for the tropics."

"By your leave, madam! Gangway! gangway!" and there sets in a stream of modern Atlasses, breathless and deploringly bent under the weight of mail bags, sacks of all sizes, duly addressed and ticketed. Then your ears are stunned by a hand-bell which is carried about and rung in a desperate manner, until even a lazy gentleman, who is airing his feet on the arms of a chair, and spitting at intervals into a wooden tray half full of saliva, becomes excited, and endeavours to force his way into some extraordinary place, where the door is locked, and there is evidently no admittance. Thus, after a moment's peace, the hand-bell begins again, worse than ever, the passengers' friends clear away, and we begin to feel quite deserted. The crowd which throngs the shore waves "good-bye" to everybody, and we are off, creeping very slowly from the wharf. " When shall we be regularly under weigh, captain ?" says the lazy gentleman. "Impossible to say," answers the captain, bustling off; "there is half the crew on shore yet, because they've cut their wages." "Smart man that, captain!" ejaculates the lazy gentleman. "That's so," chimes in a seedy-looking individual with a long beard, "and a good phrenologist,—knows something about it, too, into the bargain."

There was a lady among the passengers of lofty stature, a grave, saturnine expression of countenance and a benignly pitying smile, who answered exactly to my conception of the Delphian Pythoness. Whichever way you looked you caught this lady's eye, and you were at once conscious that she was endeavouring to interpret your mouth, read your eyes, and make observations upon your temperament. Occasionally there were responses from this oracle which were sufficiently mysterious. The British aristocracy were intrinsically bad, and would terminate in some violent way during the present century. The badness of selection in the creation of peers of the realm was something incredible. They didn't make George Combe a duke. "The Whole Duty of Man" was the most original and finest work in the English language. When I learned that the Pythoness was a female M.D., a water-cure doctor, a spiritual medium, and a lecturer on Woman's Rights and Woman's Wrongs, and, further, that she had been particularly warned by spiritual manifestations not to travel by the Golden Gate steamer, my curiosity was considerably increased. We were chatting about Spiritualism one day when an English gentleman asserted that it was anything but what it ought to be, and added, that the first question we ought to ask respecting it was, " of what use is it ?" " Decidedly not," said the Pythoness; " the first question which we ought to ask respecting Spiritualism and all other things is this :—Is it true ?" Although no Spiritualist, I thought that the lady had the best of the argument. I was exceedingly sorry when I was told that I had lost what the passengers call the first " hen" lecture, but I was more fortunate as regards the second. It was a novel sight to see ladies sitting in groups, some with babies in their arms, around the female lecturer, who looked particularly prim, and to whom a look of extra genius was afforded by the addition of spectacles. The lecture was on Woman, her position in the world, and her duties ; and I was surprised to find so little that any one could quarrel with in the doctrine propounded. We were told, of course, that woman's reasoning was inductive, man's deductive ; the one derived from natural instinct, the other from facts. Woman's genius was aspiration ; it had to do with the unseen. Man's ambition, to rise in the outer world. Great Britain was instanced as an example of ambition—America of aspiration. The character both of man and of woman was affected by great crises. A great crisis had stamped its character in the physiognomy of the American. A story was told to illustrate the necessity of intelligence in a mother to ensure talent in a child. In a remark-ably stupid family, known to the lecturer, one child was a genius, and she learned eventually that the mother had during pregnancy discovered some pretty book and taught herself to read. It was not woman's mission to take part in politics, and labour for hire was not her proper work. A masculine or strong-minded woman—a character cordially disliked by men—was one whose sympathies were deadened by study. A strong-minded was not merely an intelligent woman. No man objected to intelligence in woman; he did not want a fool for his wife. Some wonder was expressed that Mr. Buckle had not referred to woman's work in the " Progress of Civi-lization, but the admission was amply atoned for by a lecture delivered by this historian at the Royal Institution. The lecturer, who spoke fluently for more than an hour, concluded her lecture with the words, " Well, I guess I've talked enough."

The steamer which preceded us was the Golden Gate which met with an appalling disaster. When several miles from the shore she took fire, and upwards of two hundred passengers, men, women, and children, were either burned, drowned, or torn to pieces by the paddle-wheels. It was a melancholy sight to see the hull of this splendid steamer stranded among the heavy breakers on a shelving shore. We touched at Mazanilla, a deadly-lively village of thatched cottages, to take in cotton and to land some ninety odd tons of quicksilver, an article for which there is a considerable demand in mining countries. Here we took up two dreamy-looking passengers, man and wife; the former an American, the latter English, a native of Yorkshire. The lady, approaching to *embonpoint*, wore her hair à *la* Rosa Bonheur, and was suffering from a fortnight at Maximilian, a wretched fiery place, all dust, sandflies, and mosquitoes. Anima-tion had to be restored with copious draughts of champagne. It was not long before I discovered that those singular passengers were spiritual mediums. A friend of their's, who although not an orthodox spiritualist himself, was a waverer, and who had been par-ticularly warned, it seems, not to travel by the Golden Gate, but laughed at the warning, was among the missing passengers. The extraordinary couple held a communication with the spirit of the missing gentleman, but the spirit was obstinate and would not re-spond, and they accordingly concluded that the missing gentleman was alive. I need hardly say that the industrious search after the missing passenger, which must have been made at a considerable expense, proved of no avail.

On Saturday, August 30th, we reached Acapulco, where we tar-ried a few hours to take in coal. A French frigate had arrived on or about the 24th ult., and had scared nearly every one away. The United States sloop, Lancaster (Commodore Huff), had taken up a position between the French frigate and the shore, and when the frigate moved she changed her position also. The French frigate was not allowed to land a boat. An old fort had been abandoned and served as an hospital, while two new forts out of gun range from the harbour, had been constructed on the heights. They could be readily taken in rear by mountain howitzers. Acapulco is a decayed Mexican town. Very lean pigs with very long snouts, wander dejectedly about the streets in search of stray cabbage stalks. Lazarus covered with sores, lay looking up reproachfully at the "botica legal," well stored with drugs. Here and there were dark Spanish beauties, dressed in white, long black hair hanging naturally down their neck. The bed-rooms looked clean, white and chalky, and some of the bedsteads were of brass, nearly as big as the great bed of Ware, covered with very neat Damask counterpanes. Hammocks, generally well filled, were suspended in every verandah. An American hotel is a poor place, but my companion, an Italian priest, conjured me to turn in and take breakfast. Girls entered at the open doors with shell flowers and necklaces, one of which the priest purchased for a rosary; without were fruit stalls, and there girls sat working, chatting or smoking, not paper cigarettes, but good honest cigars. The brigadier seemed rather more mercantile than military. Sailor-looking soldiers in white trousers fastened by a black silk belt, and straw hats, were pacing up and down, before his office. We found the climate intensely hot and moist. I suggested to an American naval officer that it was a dull, disagreeable station; but he replied in the negative, "We don't dislike it much, for we can buy plenty of capital fowls here." I was glad to discover for the first time in my life that there lived a man in the world so easily satisfied. A gun warned us to betake ourselves to the steamer, and none probably regretted our departure more than a shoal of juvenile, swarthy divers, whose mouths were all well filled with silver. Here we lost sight of the pair of spiritual mediums, who awaited the mail steamer returning to San Francisco.

I was fated throughout my journey to become acquainted with men whose business had been, or was, connected with investments. Some had merry faces, but money was expressed in most, and sternness, anxiety, and rapacity, had taken away all that was high and noble, and left all that was odious and contemptible. With all these gentlemen money was the theme of conversation; and they had a happy idea that money was the great reformer, the end of life, the outward and visible sign of respectability, the foundation of religion. It was sad to see the men with one foot in the grave so convinced that trade and all its littlenesses was the sole business of man's existence, to observe the energy with which he reiterated, striking his clenched fist at intervals upon his chair: "What gives you clothes, what gives you friends, what makes you independent, what enables you to travel?—Money." To one of these gentlemen I had lent Mr. Trollope's "North America," and the first question he asked upon returning it was, "Will that book sell in England?" He entered at length into the way in which books and newspapers are got up in Great Britain ; and I believe that he was perfectly right in asserting, that if less attention was paid to outward show and to the material of which our paper is composed, the cost of production would be considerably lessened, and the circulation and profits of the undertaking materially increased.   He then assured me that an International Copyright Act was in course of passing at Washington, when he stopped it.   It was simply envy that prompted the desire on the part of English authors, but did they never consider that if there was such an Act it would enhance the price of their books, they would not have half the readers which they have at the present moment in the United States, and their gains would be inconsiderable?   It is impossible to convince an American, who sees nothing objectionable in smartness, that there is anything unjust in the matter.   I asked one young capitalist who was going to college, and who told me that he had been in the money-lending line of business, if he had ever lost money.   He replied, " A man who lends money must lose occasionally, however sharp he is," and he mentioned the name of a well-known capitalist in San Francisco, who advanced a large sum on hams in bond without securing himself by inspecting them, and who found to his cost that not one ham was worth a single cent.   " I will give you an instance," he said, " of Western smartness.   I went one day with a friend to a town where we had both got town lots.   I was in the hotel when the landlord, who was game to trade about anything and everything, said, ' That's a nice gold watch of your's : let's trade! How many land lots will you take for it ?'   ' I did not want to lose my watch,' said the speaker, and I left the hotel and went to a neighbouring shop.   Presently my friend came in, and said, ' I have struck a bargain.   Change watches, old fellow,—mine is much the best, and he will never discover it.'   My friend in his desire to deceive the landlord of the hotel forgot that he was selling himself, considerably to my advantage.   He found it out, and came to me in a few days, when I gave him some small gold key to split the difference."   A French capitalist who has risen to wealth in San Francisco was pointed out to me.   The secret of his success is, that he has the facility of borrowing money in France at four, and can lend it in California at thirty-six per cent. per annum.   I could name an English military officer, who went to San Francisco with some three thousand pounds sterling, and who was simply a victim in the hands of those whom he accommodated.   Only a Scotchman can hope to cope successfully with a Yankee money-lender.

It was dusk when we arrived at Panama, and rode out of the boat upon the backs of the Spanish boatmen.   Being accompanied by an English merchant from Valparaiso or its neighbourhood, who did the talking, I got my baggage transported to the Aspinwall Hotel on far more favourable terms than many of the other passengers.   There must be something German about my face, for a German who spoke English perfectly, addressed me on entering the

hotel in German, and on one occasion I was similarly interrogated
in Sardinia.  I chatted frequently with this gentleman afterwards,
and he told me that Panama was the most "awfully miserable place"
he was ever in.  It was the rainy season, and Panama was certainly
hot and muggy.  I thought that the streets might have been cleaner,
for they were the common sewer in which every species of filth
breathed forth pestiferous vapours.  The high and crazy houses in
the neighbourhood of the hotel were chiefly low beershops and
brothels.  Every house has its green parrot, which betrays the
character of the neighbourhood—shrieking, cursing, swearing, and
indulging in obscene language from morning to night.  There is
next to no trade, and activity lies dead.  The lower classes fall asleep
over their cigars.  The private soldiers are very dirty and billeted
about everywhere; the officers are rather picturesque.  An American
omnibus rattles perpetually about the town in a promiscuous manner,
not starting from anywhere exactly nor arriving at any place in particular, and driving into desperation nervous passengers for Southampton, who purpose to travel by a train which is itself highly
irregular, and starts when the passengers grow irritable, or the British
Consul imagines that it would be advisable to accommodate a Naval
Agent.  Panama fever is a disorder of a malignant type.  You run
a chance of catching it upon making the shortest stay; and if it
does not carry you off it hangs about you for the natural term of
your existence.  I fortified myself daily with doses of sulphate of
quinine, an invaluable medicine, which restores confidence in the
most gloomy regions.  I must confess that I did not thank my
neighbour for telling me a sad story about a gentleman with two
little children, who was merely passing through some weeks previously, and who lost both his children in two days.  There is a
wretched newspaper here with a small circulation, edited by two
Irish gentlemen, whose taste in regard to climate I consider exceedingly depraved.  The paper is bad, the ink is bad, and the journal
itself seems very much at the mercy of the Spanish printers' devils,
who make havoc of Anglo-Saxon.  At night you are frequently
treated to serenades, the vocalists singing in parts.

The charge made at the Aspinwall Hotel for board and lodging
is three dollars a-day.  Here you can get rain-water baths alive with
interesting natural species.  As the fowls were so forgetful of their duty
as not to lay eggs, I had not an opportunity of testing the powers
of the cook in respect to omelette or pudding.  The claret is 6s.,
and is procured, I fancy, from some crazy den round the corner,
where it is sold at eighteen pence a bottle.  There is nothing good
about the hotel but beefsteaks, not the legitimate tough English
steak with the due proportion of bone and gristle, but a viand
manufactured from the choicest cut.  Some Spanish nobleman
attached to the hotel, interests himself about your luggage, forwards
it to the station, and charges you handsomely for the privilege.  The
Aspinwall Hotel is the exchange where the foreign merchants or

traders—chiefly American, German, and French—most do congregate, discuss politics, and imbibe "long" and "short" drinks. In this delightful locality we saw the sunny face of Mrs. Seacole, of Crimean renown, gadding about with naval officers, on leave from the frigate Orlando. The railway company is generous, putting naval officers on the free-list.

There is a railway from Panama to Aspinwall, which is composed of violent curves running through pestiferous marsh and tangled forest. Every iron sleeper is said to have cost the life of an Irish navvy. There is only one class of cars here as throughout America, with seats placed crosswise, invented previous to the introduction of crinoline. The locomotive engine is not covered up like ours but is very naked, is fed with wood, and is accompanied by an agonized shriek and a hollow consumptive cough. The ragged-looking guard, who wears no uniform of any kind, peeps first into one carriage and then into another, and smokes industriously. They are not regardless of weight on this line, charging you five cents. for every lb. over fifty. It came on to rain when we were jolting along upon this railway so that we had to close the wooden shutters, which left us in darkness, and still the water spirted in, which was not pleasant. Nobody got out at the stations and nobody got in, and nobody did anything but some dusky natives, who exchanged the fruit of the country for small coin. The check system by which the safety of your luggage is secured is good, and worthy of adoption on our English railways; boxes and portmanteaus, with a family likeness, being apt to go astray, especially when the address is illegible.

I regretted not saying good bye to several passengers bound to New York. It is a mistake to suppose that you cannot enjoy yourself—better often to my mind—upon an American than upon an English steamer. American women are pretty—but they are more than this, for they are intelligent and winning in their manners. Their forwardness and pertness is combined with such artless coquettishness, that it becomes rather a virtue than a vice. The men are straightforward and honest, and there is nothing of the Dundreary school about them. Probably if the men did not "liquor up" so much before breakfast, and the women did not put their knives into their mouths so often, I should like them better; but then we must make allowance for a people who so closely resemble ourselves in conquering everything but prejudice. That new ways are often improvements is obvious to every one but the English mechanic. The helmsman who is placed at a wheel-house forward, where there are no passengers to intercept his view, and he can catch the lowest words from the captain in the most windy weather, is certainly in the proper position. Then the arrangements at the table are excellent. No Government people give themselves high and mighty airs, and protest that the best places must be reserved for them at the captain's table. The day after you go on board you are summoned to the purser's office, and receive a ticket bearing a similar number, and a similar number appears in your plate until you have learned your place, and there you sit at all your meals from the beginning to the end of the voyage.

Unless the weather is very good or highly unsatisfactory, and the passengers are very pleasant or extremely disagreeable, there is very little to record respecting the West India Mail Line. On some of these steamers the Jamaica "nigger" is musical, and the notes of a violin facilitate the weighing of a anchor. I am under the impression that even the sails are set to jigs and are taken in to dirges.

## LIEUT.-GENERAL THE EARL OF CARDIGAN AND LIEUT.-COLONEL CALTHORPE.

Some of the commanding-officers of our Cavalry regiments have been of late creating an unenviable notoriety for themselves, and doing their best to bring into disrepute that noble branch of their profession. Not many months since there was the case of Colonel Bentinck, of the 4th Dragoon Guards; now we have Colonel Crawley, of the Enniskillen Dragoons, who is to be brought to a court-martial, and at the same time Colonel Calthorpe, who at present commands the 5th Dragoon Guards, appears before the public.

It is true there is no complaint against the latter officer with respect to the mismanagement of the regiment under his command, but, in common with the other officers, he has been guilty of an act calculated to undermine the discipline of the army, and destroy the good and honourable feeling that ought to exist between all ranks in the service. In the case of the first officer mentioned, he applied the screw so sharply with the view of compelling a captain in his regiment to leave it, that a court-martial was the result, which ended in the discomfiture of the Colonel. In the next, the Lieut.-Colonel, it is stated, required his Paymaster to sign a false return, and on his refusal used the provocative power to such an extent that caused the Paymaster to write a letter addressed to him, his commanding-officer, couched in insubordinate language, for which he was brought to a court-martial, and sentenced to be cashiered. Opinions differ materially as to the terms made use of in this letter, but it forms no part of the present subject further than to shew the strange anomaly between the cases of the Paymaster of the Enniskillen Dragoons, and Lieut.-Colonel Calthorpe, commanding the 5th Dragoon Guards. The first addresses a letter to his superior officer, for which he is tried by a court-martial and cashiered; the second writes a series of letters to his friends in England while he is on foreign service, foully calumniating a general-officer, which letters he afterwards publishes—consequently addresses to the whole world.    This is said not to be a military offence, while the writing a single letter to a single individual is so construed.    The Earl of Cardigan, who ought to be as good a judge as any man in the Service of what constitutes a military offence, evidently considered that Colonel Calthorpe had committed a very grave one, or he never would have applied for a court-martial to be held upon that officer. His Lordship was informed that his remedy was to bring an action for the publication of a libel—a remedy that is not, and never has been, consonant with the feelings of an officer and a gentleman.    Had Lord Cardigan applied for a court-martial, and preferred charges against Colonel Calthorpe for *unofficer-like* and *ungentleman-like* conduct, that application could not have been refused without setting at naught the Articles of War.    This refusal to some extent marred Lord Cardigan's cause by shutting the doors of the Court of Queen's Bench upon him in the steps he ultimately adopted.

Now this rule of the Court, as explained by the Lord-Chief-Justice, was perfectly well known to Colonel Calthorpe's legal advisers, therefore Mr. Serjeant Shee could very well afford to make a fine splash about his client's (the Colonel's) disdain to mount a horse of the breed of "The Statute of Limitations;" he knew the Colonel would be carried quite safely by a different charger; in short, that the rule for a criminal information neither would nor could be made absolute.    There was no other necessity for a long set speech from the learned Serjeant, than that leading counsel are always expected to make long speeches.

The relative rank and position of the Earl of Cardigan and Colonel Calthorpe at the time these letters were written should be well considered by all who desire to arrive at just conclusions.    His Lordship had served for thirty years in the Cavalry, and had just attained his rank as a general; Colonel Calthorpe was a Lieutenant in the 8th Hussars of some four years standing, one of the regiments forming a part of Lord Cardigan's brigade, but with which Lieutenant-Calthorpe was not present in the charge he takes upon himself to describe, although he was a looker-on.    He had the good fortune to be on Lord Raglan's staff.

Had Lieutenant Calthorpe followed the noble example of the late Duke of Richmond, then Earl of March, who previous to the battle of Waterloo, quitted the staff of the Duke of Wellington to join in the battle with his own glorious regiment, the 52nd, the public would have been more disposed to place reliance upon his statements.    At all events he could have said that he described scenes in which he had taken part.    But this does not seem to have struck him; he takes his stand upon the reports of officers who probably never saw Lord Cardigan during the whole affair after he placed himself at the head of his troops until it was all over.

Colonel Calthorpe cannot produce a single witness from the 13th or 17th, whose four weak squadrons formed the first line, to confirm his statements respecting the conduct of the General he had the opportunity of following, if he had thought fit so to do. The tables may be fairly turned upon him, and the question asked—"why were you not with your regiment so that you might say, you yourself saw what you have written?" It is not intended to impute want of personal courage to Colonel Calthorpe, but other staff officers have been, and were, on that day, too eager to remain inactive. The bearer of the order to Lord Lucan, the late Captain Nolan, might, if he had so chosen, have returned instantly to his General who dispatched him, without a question being asked as to his courage, but he preferred to see the order executed, and share the danger, and he was the first of the memorable six hundred who was killed.

One of Colonel Calthorpe's principal witnesses of what took place, a Lieutenant Clutterbuck of his own regiment, says that Lord Cardigan never was in the engagement at all. That the Lieutenant who was probably in a cavalry charge for the first time in his life on that day, should have lost his head, and not have known what occurred, is not wonderful; but that Lieutenant Calthorpe who did not join in the charge should have lost his, which he must have done when he produced his brother subaltern's statement, is surprising, for it could have no other effect than that of holding up his friend to ridicule. However, when men are bent upon vituperation, they seldom know when and where to stop, and no dependance can be placed upon them when they have been compelled to confess they have made statements for truth, which are at variance with facts. Such is the position in which Colonel Calthorpe has placed himself. He first asserted that Lord Cardigan without entering the battery, turned, and galloped to the rear past the squadrons of the 4th Light Dragoons and the 8th Hussars, before those squadrons got up to the Russian guns, and when this was proved to be false, excused himself by saying that, he relied upon information supplied to him by officers actually engaged in the charge. He admitted that he could speak to nothing of his own knowledge, for he was too distant from the scene of carnage, and that the advancing squadrons were hidden by the smoke from the Russian batteries. So upon hearsay evidence he gives publicity to a notorious falsehood, which he partly acknowledges, by stating that he heard Lord Cardigan tell Lord Raglan that on coming up to the battery, a gun was fired close to him which caused his horse to swerve. There is some difference between a horse swerving, and turning short round, and had the latter been the case, the chances are that Lord Cardigan would have been ridden over by his immediate followers, at all events it could not have passed unnoticed. But what does his aide-de-camp, Lieutenant (now Lieutenant-Colonel) Maxse say? Lord Cardigan was under the impression that he was wounded before they fell upon the Russian battery, but it was not until after they had passed through the guns that he was hit, and as it is not customary for an aide-de-camp to ride in front of his General, that fact alone would render conclusive the question of Lord Cardigan's presence at the moment when Colonel Calthorpe's informants pre-tend he was absent.

The different commentators on Lord Cardigan's conduct, especially Colonel Calthorpe as a cavalry officer, ought to know that the officer who leads a charge cannot by possibility direct the operation of the reserves, or supporting bodies of troops; that duty is always assigned to another, and on that day it was undertaken by Lord Cardigan's chief, the Earl of Lucan. How it was performed has been placed upon record by the late Lord Raglan. When Lord Cardigan received the order to charge, his brigade was mr-shalled by Lord Lucan, and Lord Cardigan had no choice but to obey and lead it into action. The second and third lines were not, as some writers seemed to have imagined, formed, or ordered to act as reserves, nor were they in any way independent or separately commanded, they followed the first line at the same pace; in short the charge may be said to have been made in double open column, and the rear of the column would naturally be closing up when the speed of the head would be checked by coming in contact with the enemy. Hence if Lord Cardigan had turned to go to the rear on reaching the guns, he would have had to have forced his way through six ranks of cavalry, which is scarcely consistent with the story of his being seen galloping to the rear on one of the flanks.

The remarks said to have been made by the Russian General Liprandi, are most probably the invention of some fertile brain; a Russian General would have had something else to do than watch an officer belonging to his enemy riding to the rear at that conjuncture, besides it is well known that the Russian Artillery was playing upon friend and foe alike, and Colonel Calthorpe informs us what is the effect of the smoke from the fire of artillery on the field of battle. If, however, the story is true, it goes to confirm the fact of Lord Cardigan having advanced to some distance beyond the guns, else he could not have been nearly made prisoner, and that at all events he could not have been among the first to get out of the mess.

The affidavit of Lord Lucan is said to be the one which tells most against Lord Cardigan. With all due deference to those who hold that opinion it ought not to carry any weight whatever. It is in direct contradiction to his official report; either that document, therefore, or the affidavit his lordship has sworn must be incorrect.

Supposing that Lord Cardigan had been the first to get out of the fray, and gallop to the rear, he must have been seen by those men who had their horses killed, and were themselves uninjured, and by wounded men also who were struggling to the rear; he

would likewise, as a natural consequence, have gone straight to
Lord Lucan, who was with Sir J. Scarlett's brigade, to report the
disaster; but no witnesses such as might be found amongst those
officers or men have been forthcoming, and yet they were the only
ones who could tell positively what was passing in the rear.   The
witnesses who are called, are men whose sole attention at that
moment must have been directed to their front.   No doubt the
officers and men who have given their testimony in favour of Colonel
Calthorpe's statements fancied they saw Lord Cardigan going to the
rear because he was not seen by them in their front, than which
nothing can be more easily accounted for.   In such a *melée*, and
amidst the din, the clash of arms, the shouts, the roaring of cannon,
the crack of rifles, and the smoke, it is not wonderful the leader
should be invisible—in this instance particularly so—for he was
far in front, isolated from his men, beset by Cossacks; and but for
the timely aid of a man of the 13th Dragoons would possibly have
been overpowered.   Besides this—and the author speaks advisedly,
for he has taken part in more than one cavalry charge—on most
occasions when the charging squadrons come in contact with their
enemy, not only the leader himself, but the commanders of regiments and squadrons are constantly lost sight of by their men; it
is the natural result of the disorder and confusion which always
follow upon the coming to blows; each man must then look to
himself, and if he gets no orders, must judge from the action of
others near him whether orders have been issued somewhere or
other to retreat, and re-form on the reserves, or to continue fighting.
The charge of Lord Cardigan's brigade at Balaklava was precisely
one of these cases; the first and second lines lost fully half their
numbers, and were scattered and confused.   The third line coming
close upon their heels, it appears, separated, one regiment inclining
to the right the other to the left, which fact at once destroys the
notion of any further command having been held by Lord George
Paget beyond that of his own regiment. These two corps were
speedily hemmed in by the Russian cavalry, and in common with the
other three which had preceded them by about a minute, or at most
two, were overwhelmed by superior numbers in front, flanks, and
rear.   Under such circumstances, how could Lord Cardigan have
been seen by those men riding to the rear?   It is most probable
that no order whatever was given to retreat, for it is clear that Lord
Cardigan was in front and separated from his men, and he had
staff officer with him to convey an order.   More likely one
and all being convinced of the inutility of contending against such
masses, and with other artillery, (for there was plenty more in addition to the captured battery playing upon them, besides hordes of
riflemen firing upon them regardless of their own men) came to the
conclusion simultaneously that they must cut their way out as best
they could.   The story of the 4th Light Dragoons retiring in good
order, and finding Lord Cardigan in the rear ready to receive them,

is simply the reverse of fact; for it happened to be what was left of that very regiment was the first remnant of his brigade that Lord Cardigan found re-formed when he got to the rear, and he was received by the men with cheers.

The sneering remark upon "the excellence of his Lordship's horsemanship" is a puerile attempt at wit, and intended in a very nasty manner to offer a graver insult, as much as to say, if his horse had not run away with him he must have run away himself.   One of our contemporaries has truly observed that strange language is used now-a-days; and this was certainly an insult that neither Colonel Calthorpe nor any man breathing would have dared to make to such a man as Lord Cardigan a few years back, when he would have been called before a different tribunal.   The idea of accusing Lord Cardigan of cowardice is supremely ridiculous, and might be treated with silent contempt, but for its being published in a book which may be read by many of the present day who, residing at a distance, are ignorant of Lord Cardigan's well-known qualities, and by posterity, who may take for granted what is written without taking the trouble to inquire.   To those who know him personally, by reputation, or by sight, it would seem much the same thing as making the same accusation against our own lion-hearted Richard. One has only to look at the man to see the personification of courage.

A very plain question may be asked.   Is it possible that a man with a single grain of cowardice in his composition could have led his squadrons as straight and true as ever he did at a review, for a mile and a quarter through a murderous fire, his men and horses dropping every instant, up to the muzzles of the enemy's guns, capturing them, and cutting down the gunners who continued to serve them to the last moment?   The attacking Artillery with Cavalry is the same to them as is the forlorn hope to Infantry, and is seldom ordered except in extreme cases.   Our allies the French have laid it down as a rule that to attack a battery with Cavalry it should be done by a few, and in *loose* order, which is no doubt the true principle.   They have had great experience, and probably the heavy losses sustained by some of their columns on such occasions in the wars of the first Empire, gave rise to the ordinance as laid down in their last regulations for Cavalry movements.

Such a mode of attack does not seem to have been contemplated by Lord Lucan; possibly he might have been unacquainted with the French Book of Instructions, or did not approve them; but Lord Cardigan, whatever the formation, had a right to look to his chief for support, for he himself has informed us that he had repeatedly told Lord Cardigan he might rely upon him for support whenever he was engaged with the enemy in front.   On this occasion, Lord Lucan appears to have forgotten his assurances.   It has been said that Lord Cardigan, when his first line was nearly demolished, should have gone to the second and third lines and directed their movements, so he would, as a matter of course, had those two lines been warned to act as supports, but he knew this was not the case; and even if he could have got back instantly to give any orders, he would have found all his regiments engaged in a hand to hand fight, and in such disorder that it would have been impossible to make any regular movement.

He is a bold man who can venture to say who was first out of such a crash; who was first in most could see, and it was never disputed until Colonel Calthorpe, in the first edition of his book, said Lord Cardigan never passed the battery at all; he did not go quite so far as his friend Lieutenant Clutterbuck in his hallucinations, but he published what was notoriously incorrect, and was subsequently compelled to acknowledge it—a very undignified position for an officer and gentleman to be placed in.

The slur cast upon Lord Cardigan about living on board his yacht is most unworthy of the authors. His health had broken down, and it was said he was afflicted with a painful disorder besides, added to this he was then approaching his sixtieth year, and at that time of life few men preserve a robust constitution. They may have all the spirit and energy of earlier days, but it is out of the nature of things that they can endure the same amount of fatigue and exposure which they could formerly do with impunity. The only wonder is that he lasted so long; for many, younger in years and of high rank, had been compelled to give in before him. He may be haughty in his manner, but not to those who really know him. He has always entertained a sense of duty in his military capacity, although it may be admitted he has occasionally allowed that feeling to overrule his sober judgment. He is not a Liberal in politics, but, nevertheless, a more liberal-minded man does not exist. The great error he fell into after his return was that of saying too much in his after dinner speeches; his representations in some trivial points varied, and as a marked man, of course, they were taken advantage of, and made more of than they really deserved; but he was elated with his success, and the reception he met with was enough to turn any man's head, whose conduct hitherto had been the reverse of popular, but to accuse him of cowardice is preposterous.

No two men told precisely the same tale as to what did happen, but it does not follow that all were misrepresentations; it was not possible for any one to say to a certainty what was passing excepting close to him. It is not surprising, therefore, that there should be some apparent discrepancies in Lord Cardigan's explanations, for he could see no better than any other, and of necessity must have depended upon the reports made to him. Thus what would apply to one regiment might not to another, and what was intended possibly to describe the action of one part of his brigade was wholly inapplicable to another, but being taken all together was assumed to be contradictory. He was not singular, for many others fell into the same error, and by mixing up what they saw with what they heard from others caused their accounts to vary each time of telling, without the most distant intention of misleading or misrepresenting, but rather to be more explanatory.

Had Colonel Calthorpe confined himself to giving as accurate an account as he could of the war, without taking upon himself to condemn the conduct of a general-officer in the army who had never been found fault with by his chief (Lord Raglan), his book would have had value, as it is natural to suppose that in his position as aide-de-camp to the Commander-in-Chief, he would have been acquainted with many circumstances not generally known, particularly as to motives for different orders and movements. The fact, however, of his having been forced to withdraw some of his statements naturally throws a doubt on his representations in general, and makes it questionable whether he derived any information from the highest authority. None of the evidence produced by Colonel Calthorpe can weigh in the scale against that brought forward by Lord Cardigan, for at the time they fancied they saw Lord Cardigan going to the rear, it was incontrovertibly proved by competent witnesses that his Lordship was personally engaged in defending himself from the attacks of the Cossacks.

Colonel Calthorpe would seem to have written his book more with a view to disparage his superior officer, than to give such an account of events as might have been expected from an officer in his position. The publication is an unfortunate event for himself, and the animadversions upon, and misrepresentations of the conduct of a general-officer under whose immediate command he would have been but for his relationship to Lord Raglan, is setting a very bad example to the officers under his own command, and to young officers in general.

Although the rule for a criminal information was discharged, Lord Cardigan may rest satisfied that his reputation has not suffered. The public Press is almost universally in his favour. Amongst professional men Colonel Calthorpe is generally condemned, and his Lordship's shortcomings as a general, on which the Lord-Chief-Justice dwelt, he had no opportunity of showing, having no discretionary power left to him. Even supposing he had not been cut off from his men by being so far in front himself, the confusion and disorder were so great, that one order only could have been given with any chance of being obeyed, which was to retire as quickly as possible, and that, officers and men alike seem to have acted upon of their own accord. The 8th Hussars claim to have retired in good order; they may have done so, but certainly not until after they had got out of the ruck.

There could be no question about generalship in the part allotted to Lord Cardigan, he had only to carry out his instructions, and that he did to the admiration of all who saw him lead fearlessly

into the jaws of death, but not without remonstrance, and pointing
out the impossibility of doing any good. The generalship rested with
the officer who held the chief command of the Cavalry. Lord Cardigan
received the order to charge, but no supports, or reserves, or artillery,
were placed at his disposition. Lord Lucan had the handling of them,
and whatever generalship was displayed, must be placed to his
Lordship's credit.

---

## GREENWICH CHARACTERS.

"You will find mine a very tedious story, I fear, if I go on at
this rate, detailing every little incident."

"Not in the least, Morgan," said I, "you will be tired first."

"Well, to say the truth, I am very nearly tired already, and yet
it is a pleasure to me to live over again some of the bright scenes of
my existence. Bright they were just at this time, but they were
soon overclouded again. I was serving in one of the fastest
schooners in the West Indies, and with one of the smartest commanders that ever trod a deck. The fine schooner which I mentioned the other day was purchased in part with the Commander's
money, and manned with fifty as fine seamen as any man would
wish to look upon ; but unluckily, in one sense, we were no longer a
tender. The Fox had been commissioned by Lieutenant F—, although
only temporarily, and she was too fine a vessel for an officer of no
interest to be allowed to retain. In a short time we made many
captures, and destroyed one of the largest privateers on the station,
and our Commander's reward was—what do you think ? "

"Promotion of course."

"Not a bit of it. We arrived at Port Royal after a successful
cruize, and our Commander returned on board, after having reported
himself to the Admiral, mad as any Bedlamite.

"Had he not been habitually sober, even to water drinking, I
should have thought he had been drinking to excess. Mr. Cheeseman, the Master's mate, had gone on shore to the Dockyard, and
left me in charge of the schooner ; the Doctor also was on shore.

"The Commander looked at me, as I thought, angrily—then
burst out laughing—and was literally beside himself. ' Mr. Jones,'
said he, when more composed ' you have behaved well since you
have been under my command.

"He was sitting at his desk, and the cabin was strewed with
papers.

"' Yes,' he continued, ' you have done your duty, and here is
your certificate.' It was a bill of exchange for I forget how many
dollars.

"' What is this for, Sir ?' I asked, looking at the slip of paper.

"' That is your certificate, as I am going home.'

"'Certificate—going home,' said I, bewildered.

"'Yes, Sir; don't you believe me?'

"'Yes; no, Sir. I hope not,' I stammered out; 'but I will, if you will allow me, go with you to the end of the world and share your fortunes.'

"'Nonsense boy,' he replied, bitterly; 'go with a ruined man! I am superseded.'

"'What's that, Sir?'

"'Why, what a blockhead you must be—superseded means, in my case, robbed, deprived of my ship; but I will—'

"'Sir,' said I, 'you are distressed. You have been very good to me, and have taught me my duty. I want no better certificate than your good opinion—not a dollar of your's will I touch. I can, I have worked for my bread, and will do so again, without being indebted to any one.'

"Alas! it was too true. A young Lieutenant had been appointed from England to take command of the Fox, and all our gallant Commander's labour and expense had been thrown away— he had been deprived of his fine command! Never shall I forget the effect of the news upon all hands. The attempt, however, to make the fortune of the new Commander was most unfortunate. The goose that laid the golden eggs had been killed. Mr. Cheeseman left her, and I never heard what became of him, and half the crew deserted in the course of a few days. I applied to be discharged, but the Commander would scarcely listen to me, so I ran with the crew of the Captain's gig. In the dead of the night we reached a hovel well known to run-away sailors, from whence we were conveyed across the country to Kingston, and shipped on board the Janet Brown, West-Indiaman, bound to Bristol, laden with sugar and rum, for which run the rascally crimp received fifty dollars upon each of us, handing us over about ten."

"I suppose," said I, interrupting my old friend, "you are now telling me what happened to you without knowing many of the details."

"Exactly. All I remember distinctly is reaching the Crimp's house, and being plied with rum, to the use of which I was unaccustomed, and my finding myself, with two of my shipmates, in the fore part of an old lumbering vessel deeply laden. Whether I was sent in a sugar hogshead or not, I cannot tell; but there I was, and stowed away until the convoy sailed.

"Oh! the misery of that voyage. Work, work, kicks and cuffs, pumping and reefing topsails, and short-handed in the bargain, only eight men besides myself to do everything in a five-hundred-ton ship. It was enough to break down the proudest and strongest spirit, and I fell sick—so sick that there seemed no life in me. The master was half his time drunk and quarrelsome, and the mate very little better; but they were both, on the whole, tolerably civil to me, and sent me food from the cabin. As to navigation, we were guided by the convoy, at least I never remember seeing any one take an observation.

"On nearing the Channel a tremendous gale from the eastward dispersed the convoy, and left us, no one knew where. I was still very weak, but the love of dear life prompted me to make some exertion. Finding the Master tolerably sober—for his helpless condition had sobered him—I volunteered to ascertain the position of the ship if he would lend me his quadrant and books, a proposition to which he at once assented. The dead-reckoning had been very badly kept, and my only chance was to get the latitude by observation. Availing myself of a break in the heavy clouds, I got a meridian altitude, and found we were then in the latitude of Scilly. We got soundings, but as they did not correspond with those at the entrance of the British Channel, I concluded we were to westward of the Land's End, and in St. George's Channel. Under this impression I advised the Master to make sail on the starboard-tack, close hauled. For a week previously we had been lying-to under close-reefed maintopsail and storm-staysails, drifting bodily to leeward. The wind rising, had got more round to the southward and we laid up northeast, and I hoped we should soon get sight of Lundy island. The old brute was rolling like a porpoise. All night it blew strong, and, ere the morning dawned—it was in the month of March—it was blowing a gale from the westward. We still kept her north-east, as I did not wish to be caught on a lee-shore in a deep-laden West-Indiaman. By the dead reckoning, I found we were in the latitude of Lundy, and, that being the case, the Master and Mate relieved of any further responsibility, satisfied in their own knowledge, and kept her away east, considering, I imagine, that they were actually in the Bristol Channel.

"At noon next day I again managed to get a glimpse of the sun, and, to my dismay, found we were in 52 deg. 20 min. north. It was then blowing a heavy gale, and we were staggering and rolling with four hands at the wheel, but not making more than five or six knots. When I told the Master that we were already to the northward of St. David's Head, he would not believe me. He thought the quadrant must be incorrect, or that I had not had a good sight, and continued to stand on.

"Night was closing in when a man on the forecastle shouted out breakers a-head. The helm was put hard a-starboard, in the hope of wearing; but, before the old brute would pay any attention to it, she was in the midst of the roaring waves, and tearing herself to pieces on the oyster rocks off Aberystwith. Of all the sensations in the world there is nothing which equals that of a ship striking. Well might Falconer say of such a moment:

'Then shrieked the timid and stood still the brave.'

We had no women on board to shriek, but man looked upon his fellow-man as if to say—'It is all up with us.' We could discern the outline of high land, but it appeared very distant, and the haze and rapidly-increasing darkness prevented our getting a sight of anything likely to be within reach.

The long-boat was lumbered with hawsers and rubbish. We set to work to clear it; but, before we could accomplish that, and get the tackles hooked on to hoist her out, the ship gave a tremendous lift, broke in two amidships, and saved us the trouble of hoisting the boat out. I had just time to catch hold of her as she floated on the top of an enormous wave, clear of the wreck. There were five or six of us, but we had gained little by being in the boat, for the plug was out, and she leaked at every seam, and before we could do anything to remedy the defects another monster sea struck her, and she turned bottom upwards. I had a narrow escape of being extinguished under her, as some of my shipmates were, and clung to her still as my ark of refuge, Who can describe the struggle for life under such circumstances?

"All that long night I held on like grim death to the boat, now clinging to the keel, then washed off and with difficulty regaining my position. At length she struck against the point of a rock, or piece of floating wreck, and again turned over. I succeeded in getting hold of the gunwale, and, after a time, got inside. Although full of water, the boat was some protection against the force of the sea. I was alone. The lifeless bodies of my shipmates had been washed out, and I was left to fight the battle by myself.

" It seemed to me the sun was never going to rise again, it was so very long; but, when nearly exhausted, a grey streak appeared on the horizon, and hope, which had been almost dead, revived. By slow degrees the light increased, and at length I could discern to leeward a line of coast, along which I was slowly drifting with the tide; but the bright line of foam convinced me that it would be impossible to effect a landing there in a water-logged boat. It would have been folly to have attempted to clear the boat of water, so I was content to sit with my head just above water, not always that, and bide my time. The distance was too great to warrant any attempt at swimming, in fact I was too much exhausted to make the slightest exertion ; and what with weakness, hunger, and the helplessness of reaching the shore, my condition was most deplorable. The rising sun somewhat reassured me. The waves seemed to beat with less violence on my water-logged boat, and, noticing a broken plank floating near me, I managed to haul it into the boat, and placing it on the gunwales, made a seat of it which left only my legs in the water. I had, however, great difficulty in retaining my seat, as my weight seemed to immerse the boat more deeply, and at one time my frail support was nearly swept from under me.

" How long I floated in this precarious way without seeing any one I can hardly tell, but I think it must have been noon when I noticed a sail, that of a fishing-boat, standing out from under the land. This gave me hope of rescue, but the hope sank again as I observed that, after apparently catching hold of something, she stood in for the shore with it in tow. It was a cask of rum, probably, which had floated out of the broken-up West Indiaman. Very soon, however, as the weather moderated, I observed a small fleet of boats coming out, tempted no doubt by the hope of picking up wreck. Weak as I was, I succeeded, after many futile attempts, in standing upon my plank, and having taken off my jacket, held it out as a signal. But it seemed that no one cared to search for the living, and, had my boat drifted far from the wreck and casks which had floated up, my prospects would have been bad indeed. But the search for wrecked property induced one boat to approach within a short distance of myself, and I was seen. I do not think I could have held out another half hour, for when the fishermen came alongside they were obliged to haul me on board, and all sense deserted me.

" When I regained consciousness I found myself in a fisherman's hut, lying upon a decent bed, and attended by a buxom dame. She spoke in Welch to those about her, and her words were those of pity and kindness. She appeared to think my life not worth much, and I was so low that I found it difficult to murmur my thanks, which, however, I did after a time in my mother tongue. . The effect was good. I was a countryman—a Briton. After partaking of some warm buttermilk I went off to sleep again, and did not awake until the following morning. The kindness and hospitality of the poor fisherman's wife and her neigbhours restored me to life and partial strength ; so much so that I expressed a wish to set out for my home at the other extremity of the bay. I had only thanks to offer in return for the services rendered me, but they were received as sufficient. I succeeded in getting a cast across the bay, and I was supplied moreover with shoes and a decent suit of clothes, which had been washed ashore in a seaman's chest, and one fine morning in April I landed at Point Linney, and started off for my father's house, from which I had been absent upwards of four years.

" The country over which I passed was interspersed with small farms, and I found at each a welcome and refreshment. My journey had already occupied three days, and on the fourth I drew near to my father's house. The site of the old moss-covered walls brought to my mind the scenes of my boyhood, which, alas ! were not over blissful, and I was doubtful as to what sort of a reception I should meet with, now that I had returned.

" There was a small cottage not far from the Fron, as it was called, in which a farm labourer had lived when I was at home, and of whom and his wife I was very fond. Evan Evans was a hard-working, sober man, and his wife who at one time lived as servant in our house, was very partial to me. I presented myself at the door, and craved a drink of water. Poor Annie brought me some butter-milk. Thanking her, I looked hard at her, and asked her if she remembered me.

"The poor woman screamed, 'Yes, yes, you are Morgan Jones—my poor lad; here come in and rest yourself—her is not dead.' 'Here, Evan,' she called out, 'here's Morgan, the Squire's son, come back alive!'

"Evan, who had been chopping wood, came forward and greeted me cordially. Their honest welcome was warm, and it cheered my sad heart, and I remained an hour talking to them, and inquiring after my old friends and playmates. The accounts I received of my home were the reverse of pleasing or satisfactory. My father had not acquired popularity, my eldest brother was much disliked, and only my sister Lucy was spoken of kindly.

"It was believed that I was dead. Mason, my schoolfellow and companion, had written to his friends to say that he left me dying from the wounds I had received in the privateer, and no one but Lucy expressed any concern.

"After washing my face, and refreshing myself, I marched boldly up to the house. The door was opened by a stranger, and as my attire seemed to mark me as a beggar, none of whom were ever relieved at the Fron, it was as hastily slammed in my face before I had time to speak. I repeated the summons, however, and the door was re-opened—this time by an old servant, the butler, armed with a stick to drive me away. After taking a brief survey of me, however, the man uttered my name, and, leaving the door open, ran with all speed to inform his mistress.

"Without waiting to be invited, I walked into my father's house, and into a well-known room. Lucy was there, and immediately recognised me, and in an instant her arms were round my neck—the only joy, alas, of that day. Mrs. Jones, now a stately dowager, strutted in and opened fire upon me. She was surprised, so she said, at my daring to show my face again at the Fron, that my father would have me put in prison as soon as he returned; but Lucy sat by my side, and did all that a girl of sixteen could do to show me that by one at least I was beloved. The sufferings and fatigue I had undergone had broken my spirit. I heard all that the unfeeling woman had to say with unconcern, and for a time without reply. At length, when she ceased, I said 'I want nothing of you but house-room and food for a few weeks, to enable me to regain my strength, and then I will be off and you shall see me no more.'

"My father now came in, and at first evinced some show of sympathy, but it was soon dissipated. He was completely in the hands of his wife, and when he found how unwelcome I was to her, his coldness returned; but finding me poor, half naked, almost shoeless and weakened from sickness and suffering he consented to my remaining a short time under his roof. A room was provided for me, very slenderly furnished, and upon the plea that my clothes were not fit to appear in, I was not allowed to take my meals at his table. What a position was mine. I wished that the waves had been less merciful to me; and but for dear Lucy I should have left the house the night I entered it.

"Lucy was a privileged person. Being the only daughter, she had acquired a sort of independence and power over her parents, and she insisted upon taking her meals with me in my room, as I was forbidden to appear at the family table. Only one brother, the youngest, remained at home; the eldest, William, was at college, and the second at school. The one at home was very sickly, and had no recollection of me. He was a cold, unloveable boy, and I took no trouble to make him friendly.

"After the lapse of a week, I had recovered my strength, a good deal, and having been supplied with a suit of clothes, I was enabled to go out for a ramble in the country with my sister. But this pleasure was of very short duration. Lucy was the idol of her home, but devotedly attached to me, and the latter fact was enough to place her in the black books of her mother, who forbade her accompanying me in my rambles.

"Wandering about by myself was slow work; and my only place to hear what was going on in the world was the little cottage of Evan Evans, and not much, generally speaking, could I learn there. I was, however, interested in anything which related to my old acquaintances.

"A few days after Lucy had been forbidden to go out with me, I strolled over to Evan's. He had just returned from the town, and to my surprise had a budget of news for me.

"'Master John, what do you think I heard to-day? Why, I was told that a constable was coming over to the Fron to take you away to prison.'

"'Prison!' said I, in astonishment, 'what for?'

"'Why, that old hag Peggy, that was at Owen Hall when it was burnt, has been up before the Justice to say that she wants you taken up to be tried for burning down the master's house, and she claims the reward. The old wretch swore that you and your schoolfellow, that ran away with you, set fire to the house. She said so a long while ago, and a reward of £50 was offered to any one that would take you.'

"'And how did you hear that?'

"'Why, I was sitting smoking my pipe at the Horns, when the constable came in and told me about it, knowing that I lived on your father's property; and he said that the Justice had told him that he was to have a warrant, and that he should be over here as to-morrow.'

"'Then,' said I, 'they may take me, but I know no more about it than you do.' Still I did not understand anything about the law, and felt rather uneasy. Just as I left the cottage, I met my father on horseback going towards home.

"'I want you, young man,' for that was his usual affectionate mode of addressing me.

" ' Very well,' I replied, curtly.

" ' Do you know,' said he, 'that you are very likely to be hung.'

" ' It would not grieve you much if I was,' I answered grumpily, but he did not, or seemed not to hear me.

" ' Yes; to be hung at the gallows: very fine prospect for the family of Morgan Jones.'

" ' What for ?' I asked.

" ' Only on a charge of arson—burning a house down—a hanging matter.'

" ' But I did not do it,' I replied doggedly.

" ' Oh, there are witnesses to swear you did.'

" ' And you believe them?"

" ' Of course. They have made affidavits to that effect, and to-morrow there will be a warrant over here for your apprehension.'

" ' But, Sir,' I repeated, 'I am not guilty; I was nearly burnt to death with Slingsby Mason, and had we not been able to get out of the window we should have been burnt as sure as fate.'

" ' Serve you right, too, for your rebellious conduct to the master.'

" ' Thank you,' said I, 'for your fatherly feeling.'

" ' Don't be insolent,' he said, raising his whip, 'or I'll chastise you.'

" ' You had better not try it,' said I; for my Welch blood was rising, and I dare say I looked defiance.

" ' You are a disgrace to my name and family,' and the old man made a cut at me with his whip. I caught hold of the whip, tore it from his hand, and threw it over the wall of a garden.

" I know not to what further extremities we might have proceeded, had not Lucy, like an angel of light, interposed. She saw that we were angry, and knew what a passionate man our father was. A short truce was mutually agreed to; but, before opening the gate, his enmity returned, and my father forbade me again entering his house. Had he invited me, however, to go in, it would have been the same thing; for, after such expressions of feeling, I never could again have lived under the same roof with him.

" I sat down on a bank. I could not shed a tear. My heart seemed breaking. I fell into a kind of stupor, from which I was aroused by Lucy. She had stolen from the house in search of me. She wished me to return with her, and said she would make my peace with father, but I felt that to be impossible. The scene I shall never forget, but I cannot describe it.

" I got up and returned to the cottage of poor Evan, determined to rest there that night, and leave early next morning for Liverpool, of which port I had heard much. The distance I knew to be great, but I could take my time about it, and beg my way. Before I was up, however, Lucy was by the side of my straw bed.

" ' Jack,' said she, 'if you will go, you must not go without money. Here,' she said, 'is my purse, it contains my quarter's allowance for clothes, but I can do without anything new for the next three months. I wept like a child. Her tenderness was too much for my proud heart to withstand. No amount of severity could have overcome me, but her love subdued me entirely. I refused the money, but she told me that my taking it was the only comfort she could enjoy in my absence. The purse contained five guineas, and, as I knew that she would not be allowed to want for anything, I consented to accept it, determining to repay it with interest when in a position to do so. Alas! I never saw her more. She was too good for this world."

Poor Morgan was so overcome with the recital of this scene that it was a long time before he could resume his story.

"After that parting, I took leave of Evan Evans and his wife, neither of whom would accept anything in return for their hospitality; and, in light marching order, but with a heavy heart, I walked a distance of four miles to a cross road, where I expected to meet the stage coach for Llangollen.

"It would have taken me a long time to have walked the distance, for my journey by stage occupied two days and nights, and when I had reached Liverpool I had expended more than half my money in coach hire.

"I thought at one time of surrendering to take my trial. It seemed cowardly to run away; but I acted wisely, for had I waited to be apprehended, the probability is I should have been condemned and executed, as arson was a capital offence, and I have no doubt that my father, instigated by my step-mother, had suborned the witnesses. It seems an awful thought but subsequent events convinced me that it was so. Had I been taken, and thrown into prison, I should have been entirely at the mercy of my persecutors, as I could not have retained any one to plead for me; but this was never so plain to me until I heard the death-bed confession of Peggy. Then the truth flashed across my mind, and I saw that I was providentially directed in getting away as I did.

"I made my way to Liverpool, as I told you, and found myself in that great town with two guineas and a few shillings in my pocket. I made my way to the docks, and walked on board the first ship that seemed ready for sea. Her name was the Ibis, a fine ship of about seven hundred tons. The first mate, a smart young man, was on board, and in reply to my question, if he wanted any hands, he answered in the affirmative.

"'We want,' said he, 'a second mate; but you look young. Where have you served?' The question was a difficult one to answer.

"'I have been five years at sea chiefly as an officer.'

"'I see,' said he, 'you are a roving blade—a privateersman, I can tell that by the cut of you.'

"'I have been a privateersman, a merchant-seaman, and a man-of-war officer.'

"'The Captain will be here presently, and, if he thinks you fit, we can ship you at once, as we are off to-morrow for Bengal; and shall run the passage as soon as we get clear of the Channel.'

"The Captain at once closed with the chief-mate's suggestion, and I was duly ensconced in my new position with five pounds a month and everything found at the cuddy table.

"During the voyage out and home nothing very remarkable occurred, and we made quick passages both ways; but, on nearing Scilly, a man-of-war hove in sight—a small frigate outward-bound. She chased and brought us to, and a young Lieutenant, Mr. Williams, whom you may remember, boarded us to muster our crew and press all they could find worth taking. The curses of the crew were heaped bountifully upon the head of the British officer, who, however, was only doing his duty. The practice was most inhuman, but in the then state of the country it was necessary.

"'And what may you be, Sir?' asked the Lieutenant addressing myself.

"'Second Mate.'

"'Then I shall press you, unless you will save me the unpleasant duty and volunteer.'

"'I will volunteer,' said I, 'upon one condition, namely, that you will not trouble these other poor fellows. I don't think you could take them legally, as we have only our smallest established number of men on board, and the poor fellows are looking forward to seeing their friends.'

"'My orders were to muster, and not to press unless there was a surplus number of men.'

"'We lost three on the passage home, and are short-handed already. There is only one above the number that you must leave to navigate the ship, and I will volunteer to be that one.'

"My shipmates heard what I said, and, I believe, would rather have drawn lots than that I should leave them; but I was perfectly careless what became of me. The Captain and chief-mate hoped I would not leave them; but I had said it; and I had my traps put in the boat, and received payment of the wages due to me; then bidding adieu to my shipmates in the Ibis, receiving a lusty parting cheer, we pulled away for the H——."

"And became my shipmate."

"Yes, your shipmate; but you do not, perhaps, remember what happened on my joining. Captain S— was on deck, and seeing a smart young fellow, well dressed, come up the side, he seemed pleased. The Lieutenant reported me as a volunteer.

"'Worth three pressed men,' said the Captain, who happened to be in a good humour.

"I bowed to the compliment.

"'Where have you served?'

"'I have just been a voyage to Bengal as second mate of that ship the Ibis, and here is my certificate,' which was an unusually good one.

" ' Would you like a rating as Master's Mate ?'

" I replied, I should be much obliged ; but I could do my duty in any part of the ship.

" ' We shall see that,' said the Captain, turning on his heel. ' Here, Mr. Simpson,' calling the mate of the watch, ' go down into my clerk's office with Mr. —— what's your name ?'

" ' John Morgan,' I replied, for I dropped the Jones.

" ' And tell him to rate Mr. Morgan, master's mate.' "

---

## THE POLISH REVOLUTION WITH SPECIAL REFERENCE TO THE RELIGIOUS QUESTION.

There is no doubt that religious interests play a great part in the complications of the Polish question, and that the Poles have taken up arms not only for the independence of their country, but also with the view of liberating their altars from the intolerable yoke of the Orthodox Greek Church. The ill-treatment of the Roman Catholics in Poland is a standing grievance with the Church of Rome; and as far back as the 22nd July, 1840, Pope Gregory XVI. addressed a very explicit allocution to the Sacred College in the Secret Consistory on the odious persecution then suffered by the Roman Catholic Church in Poland.

The suppression of convents, the forced conversions, and the flogging of nuns, were then fresh in the memory of every one ; and when the Emperor Nicholas visited Rome in the year 1845, his reception by the Holy Father at the Vatican was such as to cause the Autocrat of all the Russias and Chief of the Greek Church to hasten his departure from the dominions of the Spiritual Chief of the Roman Catholic world.

The following extracts from the most important treaties between Poland and Russia may serve to throw some light upon the religious element of the Polish question, and the facts which we record will expose the enormous persecutions to which the Roman Catholic populations of Poland have been subjected for very nearly a century.

It is to be remembered that the first pretext fixed upon by Russia and Prussia for interfering in the affairs of Poland, was for the protection of the dissenters. Poland at that time had eighteen millions of inhabitants, of whom twelve millions were Roman Catholics, four million dissenters (i.e., Protestants)), and the remaining two millions Jews and Mussulmans. The Roman Catholic religion was the religion of the State, the Dissenters having the free exercise of their creed, being, however, excluded from civil and political rights.

In order to appreciate the hollowness of this pretext for interference, it is necessary to bear in mind the different laws regarding Dissenters in use at that period throughout Europe ; the Empress Catherine, however, got her pretentions supported by an alliance

with the Northern Powers, Great Britain, Prussia, Denmark, and
Sweden; and it is worthy of especial notice that in none of those
countries the Roman Catholics enjoyed privileges similar to those
enjoyed by the Protestants in Poland.    Treaties were quoted by
Russia in support of this plea for intervention in the internal affairs
of Poland.   That of Moscow between Russia and Poland in 1686,
that of Velan between Prussia and Poland, 1657, and finally that
between Sweden and Poland, 1660.

Now all these treaties stipulated for the free exercise of the dis-
senting faith, which was *de facto* granted; but none of them guaranteed an equality of civil and political rights to the Protestants, as
was now demanded.

As it is not our purpose to trace the course of Russian intrigues
in Poland prior to its partition, nor to doubt the right Poland had
to continue united, we simply allude to these circumstances with the
view of exposing the shallow ground upon which Russia based her
complaints respecting the persecution of her co-religionists in Poland
in the time of the Republic, and founded the plea for intervention
in the internal affairs of that country.   The treaties of the partition
of Poland are in themselves a sufficient ground to condemn the
conduct of the Russian Czar's towards the Roman Catholics of
Poland, and they cannot surely be renounced by those who framed
them.

The fifth article of the first treaty of partition between Poland
and Russia, dated 18th September, 1773, is conceived as follows:

The Roman Catholics *utriusque ritus* will enjoy, in the provinces
ceded by the present treaty, all their properties and possessions; and
as regards religion, the *statu quo* will be observed, that is to say:
they will continue to enjoy the free exercise and discipline of their
creed, together with the possession of all and every church, and all
ecclesiastical properties which they held at the time they passed
under the domination of her Imperial Majesty in the month of
September, 1772; and her Imperial Majesty and her successors will
never avail themselves of their sovereign rights to the prejudice of the
*statu quo* of the Roman Catholic religion in the abovenamed countries.   The 8th Article of the first partition between Prussia
and Poland, bearing the same date, is conceived in precisely the
same terms.   The 5th Article of the treaty with Austria is also
identical, save that Austria being herself a Roman Catholic State,
the stipulations are made on behalf of the Protestants and non-
united Greeks.

As soon as the partition was effected, immense properties passed
from the hands of the United Ruthenians to those of the Greco-
Russians, by whom they were ceded to the Crown.   The Bishop of
Posen on the 21st of February, 1774, endeavoured to interfere, and
remitted a Note to Count Stackelberg, the Russian Minister in
Poland, and renewed his complaints on the 8th of March; and in
1775 a separate agreement was entered into between Russia and

Poland, with the view of remedying the evils complained of; but, as has been the case with all these stipulations, we find the Russians ever ready to promise everything and assume every engagement, and violating both the one and the other. The protests of the Polish Church continued and were supported by the Papal Nuncio, but in vain.

At the second partition of Poland the 8th Article of the Russian treaty of the 3rd of August, 1793, and the 5th Article of the Russian treaty of the 25th of September, are as explicit about the rights conceded to the Roman Catholics who passed away from under the Polish dominion. One of the most flagrant violations of the promised *statu quo* was, the obligation imposed upon the Ruthenians of choosing between the Latin Church and the Schism, which resulted in the suppression of the whole united Ruthenian Church.

In 1779, a ukase was published, establishing that on the death of a priest in a commune or parish of the United Church, the commune would have to name as successor any priest whom they chose to select, of whatever creed he might be; but the true electors were schismatic magistrates named by Russia. This ukase was clearly framed with the view of deceiving Catholic Europe and the Court of Rome.

The see of Polock having been vacant four years, that diocese lost eight parishes with 100,000 members of the church, who were all forced to embrace the schism. All this time Catherine II. was making the most fulsome protestations to the Pope regarding her Catholic subjects; an extract from one of her despatches to Count Stackelberg has, however, the following passage: "The Pope cannot ignore that the greater part of my subjects professing the Catholic faith belonged formally to our orthodox religion, and that they only await the opportunity to return to the bosom of the church which they had only left with regret and to escape from persecution."

Whenever Russia is accused of persecuting the Roman Catholics, this passage is quoted in extenuation. At a council held at Petersburg to devise the best means of recalling the members of the united to the orthodox church, Catherine resolved to establish a seminary of Schismatic Missionaries. After the publication of a sanguinary manifesto against the Catholics, priests were sent escorted by soldiers to make conversions, and they resorted to the most violent measures for this purpose. The governors of the provinces were ordered to adopt any means they liked to force the Ruthenians to embrace the orthodox faith; and the knout, floggings, confiscations, and the most horrible mutilations were resorted to for this purpose.

In a Circular dated May 25th, 1795, the schismatic Archbishop of Mohilew boasted of having made a million of conversions in one year; and the Bishop of Leopol, in Podolia, having endeavoured *to encourage his clergy* in their faith, was ordered to desist from opposing the intentions of the Empress.   The Pope and the Emperor Leopold II. in vain interposed.

A few days after the final partition of Poland, Catherine II. suppressed all the dioceses of the Ruthenian United Church with the exception of Polok (those of Leopol and Przemyst having passed under the Austrian dominion), confiscating a part of their property and distributing the rest among her followers.   The Basilian monasteries were nearly all destroyed, their churches given over to schismatic priests, and the priests who would not change their faith either reduced to penury or exiled.   A great number fled to Gallicia.   Barely two out of five thousand parishes of the four dioceses, Kiew, Wladimir, Luck, and Karnience, remained Catholic.

The nine dioceses of Poland contained in 1771 twelve millions of Catholics; and there were thirteen thousand large and seven thousand small parishes, and about two hundred and fifty-one Basilian monasteries and convents.   In 1814 there only remained in Russia one million three hundred and ninety thousand members of the united church, ninety-one convents, and one thousand three hundred and eighty-eight parishes, adding for Gallicia (census of 1826) two thousand two hundred and ninety-six parishes, 2,136,666 followers, and fourteen Basilian convents, giving a total of 3,534,144 Catholics, 3,684 parishes, and 115 Basilian convents.   Thus, in eight years the United Church had lost eight millions followers, 9,316 parishes, and 145 convents.   The constitutional charter of the kingdom of Poland, granted at Warsaw on the 15th and 27th of November, 1815, says : " § II. Art. II.   The Roman Catholic religion, which is professed by the majority of the inhabitants of Poland, will be the object of especial care to the Government."

Art. XIII. The funds actually possessed by the Roman Catholic clergy and the clergy of the united Greek Church, and that which we may accord to them by a special decree, are declared inalienable and common to the general ecclesiastical hierarchy, as soon as the government shall have distributed to the said clergy the national domains which form their dowry.   This was but putting into execution the engagements entered into at the Congress of Vienna, and the obligation imposed on the three Powers who were parties to the partition, of conserving the Polish nationality; and, what is more, of protecting the national church.

To pass to more recent times, in 1832, the Emperor Nicholas published several ukases of the most sweeping character.   The Catholic churches were turned into Greek Cathedrals, the Catholic prayer-books in the churches replaced by those of the Greek Church; and Greek bishoprics were established wherever Roman Catholic ones had existed, and it was sufficient ground for such a step, to receive the simple information that such and such a curacy had in former times belonged to the dominant religion.   In the diocese of Karnienice, there remained not a single Roman Catholic church, and in some of the towns the priests were obliged to pre-

serve the holy sacrament hidden at their homes. In 1838, a terrible ukase of the Empress Catherine's was revived; to punish as a
rebel every Catholic, whether priest or layman, of whatever degree,
whensoever, by either word or deed, he should be found opposing
the dominant religion. In virtue of this law, every person refusing
to embrace the schism could be imprisoned. Nevertheless, some
villages had for two years to be occupied by Russian troops before
they could be made to embrace the schism.

The government replied in the same words as the Empress Catherine to those who complained, that in declaring individuals and
families orthodox, their consciences were not violated, as it was
simply bringing them back to the faith of their fathers, whose
religion they had left through ignorance. In 1834, a law was
established in the kingdom of Poland, obliging the priests to bless
mixed marriages, and establishing the right of women, whose hus-
bands were exiled in Siberia, to re-marry. By an ukase, published
in 1839, it was made known that every Catholic condemned to the
knout, the mines, the galleys, or to prison, for murder, robbery, or
any other crime, would receive a free pardon on embracing the
schismatic faith. The direction of all the educational establishments in the kingdom of Poland was confided to Greco-Russians by
the Emperor Nicholas. The Catholics had to demand the permission of the government for the establishment of private institutions. The catechisms were modified by official agents. The
priests were furnished with ready made sermons, and the subjects
on which the two churches differed interdicted. The Pope endeavoured to interest all the Roman Catholic powers in favour of
Poland, and in consequence of steps taken by Gregory XVI, a
Concordat was signed at Rome on the 3rd of August, 1847, precisely at the same time at which the Emperor Nicholas published
the criminal code of Poland, and according to which the slightest
offence against the Russian form of worship entailed Siberia or the
knout. The Concordat was never observed.

On the present Emperor ascending the throne, great hopes were
entertained that the persecution of the Roman Catholics would
cease, and one of his first acts having been to publish the Concordat of 1847, which had remained secret, the Roman Catholics
of Poland were elated. The Concordat was, however, no more
attended to than in the days of the late Emperor Nicholas, and
under the rule of his son, Alexander II, the most odious persecutions have been continued, and whole populations forced to
renounce their religion, and embrace that of their usurpers.

From the above observations, and from the facts quoted, it will
be seen that the religious side of the Polish question forms a not
inconsiderable element in the grievances of that unfortunate country. If we are rightly informed, his Holiness Pius IX has addressed a letter to the Emperor of Russia on this subject, which
was presented to Prince Gortschakoff a few days after the Notes of

the three Powers, through the intermedium of the Austrian chargé-d'affaires; the Holy Father, as it is known, not having an official representative at the Court of Russia. In this letter, the Pope says that considering the terrible spectacle now offered by Poland, he should be wanting in his most sacred duties if, as father of the Great Christian Community, he did not raise his voice in favour of his children, plunged into the deepest misery, and a prey to all the evils consequent upon war. That the duty to do so was the more binding upon him, as the evils which have now befallen that unfortunate people, are to be attributed solely to the Russian Government itself, which has never kept the promises contracted by treaties, therefore he follows the example of his venerable predecessor, Gregory XVI, who, in the secret consistory of the 22nd July, 1840, addressed to the Sacred College, a very explicit allocution on the odious persecution then suffered by the church in Poland, and he now reminds the Czar of the Concordat of 1847, the prescriptions of which have never been fulfilled. His Holiness concludes by appealing to the sentiments of humanity, of justice, and of clemency of the Emperor Alexander, and urges him to restore at length to the Catholics of Poland, freedom of religion, and of their faith, as the only means likely to put a term to actual troubles, to stop the effusion of blood, and to effect the reconciliation between the Poles and the Russian Government.

In former numbers of this Magazine, we have sketched the progress of the Polish Revolution, the course of the negociations entered into by the three Great Powers, and the expression of public opinion in all countries in favour of the unfortunate people who are struggling for every right which man holds dear: To this is now added the powerful sympathy of the Roman Church and Catholics throughout the world, and the Russian Government must indeed be stubborn, if it lends an unwilling ear to the last appeal of the Great Powers, in the face of this all-powerful expression of both the civilised sense of Europe, and strong religious feeling. The Russian reply to the first three Notes on the affairs of Poland was, as is now generally known, most unsatisfactory, and now three Notes have been despatched to St. Petersburg, identical in substance. These Notes are framed on the grounds of European peace and humanity. France, which was the first to take the initiative in the diplomatic action in favour of the Polish cause, now speaks out more plainly. The armies of the French Emperor have been victorious in distant Mexico. Puebla, the principal stronghold, has fallen; and this circumstance is most opportune to strengthen the representations of the French Emperor. The semi-official press of the French Empire now denounces the Russian Government in Poland in no measured terms, charging it with the extermination of those whom it can never conciliate; and hinting in plain terms, that if diplomacy is powerless it has behind it the argument of bayonets.

In the meanwhile the revolution in Poland, although it cannot be said to be victorious, gains daily in extension, assuming a character which renders the action of the Russian troops more difficult than ever, as the whole of the country which before the year 1772 was an independent Power is now in a state of insurrection, spreading even to parts which are, strictly speaking, Russian. It would not be unreasonable to suppose that such a state of things would influence the Russian Government to give way and accord concessions; the very extent of the disaffection and the revived national spirit, however, oppose obstacles to concession. In the face of this state of things, and considering the attitude assumed by the great Powers, and France in particular, the Polish question bids fair to lead to a general European war, in which the Emperor of the French may find the opportunity of carrying out the enterprise of restoring independence to Poland, as he has already done with regard to Italy. Of the popularity of such an enterprise after the general expression of the public opinion of Europe, and the religious interest which is interwoven with it, it would be needless further to dilate.

## MILITARY STUDIES.—No. III.

### CAVALRY.

It is amusing enough that at the termination of every campaign a great controversy is seen to arise on the subject of the Cavalry. This arm has certainly for a long period not had the good fortune to decide, single-handed, any action of consequence, as it used to do in the olden time; and it is, therefore, at once taken for granted that it has become wholly superfluous, if not an impediment or an expensive nuisance that should be forthwith abolished.

But it appears wholly illogical and inconsistent to put forward, as the oponents of Cavalry do, the otherwise incontestable doctrine, that the Infantry is the main stay of all modern armies, and in the same breath fall foul of the Cavalry for not deciding every battle that is fought. Let us look for instance to the campaign of 1859 in Italy, and the relative strength of the two arms. In the French army the Cavalry amounted, at the beginning of the campaign, to about one-twelfth of the Infantry, in the Sardinian to less than one-tenth, and in the Austrian to little more than one-thirtieth, in the end, perhaps, to one-twenty-fifth. We ask, is it reasonable to expect that such small fractions of the total strength of the respective armies, acting in a country so little suited to the movements of Cavalry as to the plains of Lomellina and Lombardy undoubtedly are, should do more than act a subordinate part?

But in truth the Cavalry performed in 1859 services of very great importance, and, particularly as regards the French, such as were wholly incommersurate with its numerical strength as shall presently be shown. That it might have done more, in despite of Minié carbines and rifled guns, it is impossible to deny; nay, the events of the campaign have proved, beyond a doubt, that the real practical value of all the modern improvements in fire-arms is by no means so wonderful as the "ignobile vulgus" supposes, and certainly insufficient to diminish sensibly that of the bayonet and sabre.

If the French generals know how to make the best use of their Cavalry, such as it is, it is equally certain that the Austrians have a better material, which they do not well know how to use, and this old maxim has been fully justified by the events of 1859. There is an anecdote of Napoleon I exclaiming, at a review of Austrian Cavalry at Schönbrunn in 1809, " Le français n'est pas homme à cheval," and adding, that if he had always had such troops as those before him at his disposal, he could have conquered the whole world. Under these circumstances, then, it is strange that the anti-Cavalry movement should have originated in France, whilst in Austria that arm, although somewhat reduced from purely financial motives, seems to have lost nothing of its credit.

The proximate cause of the outcry against the Cavalry in the former country, was simply the fact that the documents laid before the Cavalry Committee in 1860 proved beyond a doubt that the 10,600 sabres with which the French Cavalry entered the field, had dwindled down to 3,000 on the 24th June; that is to say, in the short period of some ten weeks, almost exclusively in conse- quence of sore backs and other similar injuries inflicted on the horses by their own riders; for at Magenta, only one Cavalry brigade belonging to the 2nd Corps d'Armée, and two or three squadrons of the Light Cavalry of the Guard came into action. This is certainly a fearful tale to tell; but it proves in reality nothing against the Cavalry as an arm, and simply that the above mentioned dictum of Napoleon I still holds good.

It is evident that a variety of questions are opened by this *exposé*, and we shall endeavour to examine them, and, if possible, answer each in its turn; but first of all let us take a rapid glance at the services performed by the Cavalry on both sides during the several actions of this short campaign.

To begin with Montebello, 20th May, we find the Sardinian Cavalry brigade De Sonnaz, although taken by surprise, struggling successfully to retard the advance of the Austrian Infantry brigade Schafgolsche at the farm Genestrello, and thereby affording General Forey time to bring up his troops from Voghena. De Sonnaz Cavalry no doubt suffered very heavy losses in repeatedly attacking the Austrian Infantry, and one or two battalions of the regiment Archduke Charles successfully imitated the exploit of our Infantry at Maida, and charged the Cavalry in line with the bayonet. But De Sonnaz gained his point in a great degree, and his repeated

arges prove that the fire of Minié rifles is wholly incapable of
nihilating Cavalry as certain people pretend.

At Magenta, on the 4th of June, the Cavalry brigade Gaudin,
ght squadrons of Chasseurs à cheval,) supported it would seem
one or two Italian squadrons, mainly prevented an Infantry
igade of Clam's Corps d'Armée from penetrating into the interval
tween the French divisions De Lamotterouge, which had advanced
Cuggioni and Casate, and De l'Espinasse, which marched direct
Magenta by Buscate and Meseco. The junction of these two
visions enabled McMahon to decide the fate of the battle by
nking the whole of the Austrian position.

Again, when the Infantry brigade Gablentz, of the Austrian 7th
rps, had driven back a column of the Grenadiers and Zouaves of
Guard on Ponte Nuovo di Magenta, taken a gun, succeeding in
occupying the buildimgs on the left bank of the canal, and was
out to storm those on the right bank still occupied by the French,
further progress was arrested for a moment by General Cas-
gnolles charging at the head of a squadron of Chasseurs à cheval of
Guard; but this moment was sufficient to enable the Grena-
rs and Zouaves, that had been driven across the bridge in double
ick, to rally and take a position that kept Gablentz at bay until
rt of Vinoy's division coming up just in the nick of time
abled the French to resume the offensive, and secure the passage
the canal.

The remainder of the French Cavalry remained on the right bank
the Tessin during the action, the roads being so thronged with
antry columns, artillery and baggage, that it was impossible to
ing it forward. Part of the Sardinian Cavalry crossed the river
Turbigo, and was employed in reconnoitering to the north-west,
ere Urban's division showed itself.

The Austrians had a considerable Cavalry force, 36 to 38 squad-
is in the immediate vicinity of the field of battle. The 1st
rps, Clam-Gallais, had two squadrons of the 12th regiment of
ussars, which were scattered in all directions in small parties;
2nd Corps, Prince Edward Liechtenstein, had four ditto of the
th regiment of Hulans, which were attached by squadrons to the
ir brigades of the corps, and, of course, could do nothing beyond
ffectual skirmishing with McMahon's Cavalry brigade. The
valry division of Count Mensdorff, or rather that part of it that
s on the ground, was posted early in the morning on the high
id to the east of Magenta, near Corbetta, with instructions to
ver the road to Milan; it was never brought into action nor was
commandant in a position to undertake anything on his own
ponsibility. Towards the end of the battle, it covered the retreat
the beaten troops of Clam's corps, all that remained for it to do.
account for the reasons why this division was not employed to
pport the movement, attempted for a moment by Clam, for the
rpose of isolating the two divisions De Lamotterouge and De

l'Espinasse of McMahon's corps, would be to give a general history
of the battle, for which this is not the place.

What became of the four squadrons of the 1st regiment of Hussars attached to the 7th Austrian Corps is hard to say; they were
detached by squadrons to the Infantry brigades, and as a matter of
consequence, could do but little.

The only portion of the Austrian Cavalry that did anything
worth speaking of, or indeed capable of being ascertained, was the
10th regiment of Hussars attached to the 3rd Corps, Prince Edmund Schwarzenberg, which arrived on the field at about five
o'clock in the evening. The entire regiment, then eight squadrons
strong, with some 11 to 1200 horses, was attached to this corps,
then consisting of four Infantry brigades; the other Corps d'Armée,
some of which had five brigades, had only one-half or one-quarter
the number of squadrons. This was all the result of circumstances
bearing so directly on certain questions concerning the Cavalry, that
it is necessary to detail them at some length.

Colonel Baron Edelsheim, then commandant of the 10th Hussars,
is a man of undoubted ability and knowledge of the details of
Cavalry service; we suspect, however, nothing worse than this. He
had been pushed on with great rapidity in consequence of his services, ability and connexions, and obtained his rank and the command of a regiment, after an unusually short period of service.
At the great Cavalry manœuvres at Parnsdorf, in 1857, Colonel
Edelsheim first brought forward his new system of *moving Cavalry;*
we know no better term to employ, for it was not a new system of
tactics; its chief features being, to make bold riders, instead of
school riders, to emancipate the Cavalry from the monotony of
eternally filing past at a short canter, the favourite criterion applied
in Austria, to prove that this arm can be moved across the most
difficult country, when occasion requires, and to show further that
the best way of preventing sore backs, &c., on the march, is by
substituting an alternation of trot and walk for the old established
respectable snail's pace.

The reader will perceive that these are very important results.
If the number of sore backs can be reduced to a minimum, the
efficiency of a given body of Cavalry will be nearly doubled, and
such catastrophies as happened to the French regiments in 1859
avoided, and if further, the very means employed to attain this end,
brings this arm more rapidly to the scene of action, and moreover,
the difficulties of the ground cease to form an impediment to its
movements, then its value may be supposed to be quadrupled in
comparison with what it had hitherto been.

But the being able to bring cavalry intact and with greater
rapidity than hitherto to the scene of combat, however important
and valuable in itself, is unfortunately insufficient to restore to that
arm the preponderance it once possessed, because the defensive
power of the Infantry is tripled or quadrupled by those very diffi-

culties of the ground that Edelsheim's system teaches us to surmount, in other words being able to cross a difficult country in
tolerably good order, does not mean being able to encounter
therein with advantage an enemy, whose means of defence are
*eo ipso* raised to a higher power.  This fact seems not to have been
duly recognised before the campaign, and even now its importance
is underrated, although Edelsheim himself has furnished us with the
most positive proofs of its accuracy.

This officer was sent to Italy with his regiment some months
before hostilities commenced, and put it regularly in training so as
to be able to surmount even the difficulties of the Italian country.
When the Austrians took the field, the 10th Hussars was attached
to Prince Schwarzenberg's Corps d'Armée, and Edelsheim had interest enough at head-quarters to manage to have the whole regiment
left together, so that even where three or four squadrons were attached to the infantry brigades he always had five or four at his
own disposal; and Schwarzenberg, himself a cavalry officer, gave
him *carte blanche*.

It was half-past five o'clock on the evening of the 4th of June,
1859, when Niel came up with a portion of his corps to the aid of
Canrobert, who had been struggling to gain ground on the plateau
between the Naviglio Grande and the Tessin.  The brigade Hartung
of the Austrian 3rd Corps d'Armée had repeatedly, six to seven
times, stormed and carried the western half of the small village of
Pontevecchio di Magenta on this canal, and been as repeatedly
driven out of it by reinforcements of fresh troops that continually
arrived.  Another brigade, Dürfeld, had long and gallantly struggled
to turn the French right towards the river, and been repulsed in
the same manner.  Niel's arrival with part of Vinoy's division,
two battalions of the 85th and one of the 73rd at length enabled
the brigade Picard of Canrobert's corps to hold its ground firmly
in this part of the village; and when the brigade Jannin of the
latter corps came up at six o'clock, the French felt themselves strong
enough to assume the offensive and attempted to debouch from the
village, while Hartung and Dürfeld were compelled to retreat.

At this moment Edelsheim arrived on the immediate scene of
action with five squadrons that had hitherto been held in reserve at
Carpenzago.  His line of advance was parallel with the road leading from this village to Pontevecchio, and formed, consequently, a
very acute angle with the front of Hartung's brigade.  Edelsheim
could not, however, advance on the road itself, which is very narrow
and was moreover crowded with obstacles; he, therefore, formed his
force into two columns on the fields to the right and left, and indicating generally the direction in which the charge was to be made,
for the rows of trees and festoons of vines rendered it quite impossible to see a hundred yards in advance, put both columns into a
canter.  Never, perhaps, did Cavalry attempt such a task as this,
the ground being not only intersected with festoons of vines, sus-

pended five to six feet above the surface, which the men at the head
of the column had to cut through with their sabres, but also with
deep ditches used for the purpose of irrigation and drainage.
Away, however, went the two columns over hedge and ditch in true
steeple chase style, a glorious sight to see; one of them deviated
too much to the left and missed the village, the other encountered
the French Infantry just in the act of debouching from Pontevecchio in the direction of Carpenzago, drove it *pêle mêle* before it,
and never stopped till it reached the canal bridge.  This had been
broken down by the Austrians some time previously, and these gallant Hussars were, therefore, compelled to turn their horses' heads
and ride back through the streets, from every house of which, now
lined with Infantry, a deadly volley was poured into the retreating
column.   The loss was, of course, enormous.   One major, three to
four captains, several subalterns, and a great number of rank and
file were left dead or wounded in the streets of this fatal village;
but the attack meditated by the French was paralysed, and they did
not venture to renew it, whilst on the other hand, Hartung's and
Dürfeld's brigades gained time to rally and take up a new position,
which they held till the close of the action.   As may be supposed,
from the difficult nature of the ground and the pace that was ridden,
many parties straggled off to the right and left of both columns,
and one of these fell in with Canrobert and his Staff as the Marshal
was giving directions to the fresh troops just arrived.   Canrobert
had a narrow escape of being taken prisoner; the officers of his
staff, several of whom were wounded and others fairly rode down,
amongst these Colonel Bellecourt, were obliged to draw their sabres
and defend themselves; but General Renault, who saw the *melée*
from the other side of the canal lined its bank with Infantry, whose
fire compelled the Hussars to retreat.

   At Melegnano, the next action in this campaign, the Cavalry on
both sides had but little to do.   A French squadron imitated Edelsheim's example in so far, that it attempted to force the entrance
of the town from the high road, but getting into a heavy cross fire
of the Austrian Infantry posted in the houses and gardens on the
right and left, combined with that of a battery in the front, it was
glad to withdraw after a few minutes.

   In order to understand perfectly the part played by the Cavalry
at Solferino, it is necessary to present the reader with a general view
of, at least, that part of the action that was fought on the plain,
which we do the more readily, because it affords the opportunity of
stripping off some of that load of meretricious ornament with
which the true facts of the case have been hitherto disguised.

   There can be no objection to the French, who fought most gallantly and achieved a most decisive and brilliant victory, making as
much political and military capital as possible out of it; this is
human nature, and every one does the same, more or less.   But it
is scarcely polite or even politic to do it in a way that implies that

all the rest of the world are born asses or sleeping babes. For instance, to represent the victory of Magenta to be the result of sublime strategical combinations, and extol that of Solferino as an instance of the Emperor's proficiency in the *haute tactique*, is a very strong insinuation.   With the former battle and the movements that preceded it we have for the moment nothing to do, but it must be evident to even the most moderately competent judge of such matters, that the victory of Solferino is mainly to be attributed to the clever and well judged strategical disposition for the movements of the French army issued on the 23rd of June—that is, the day before the battle, having been so judiciously and energetically carried out by the French generals.

There was scarcely an occasion or even an opportunity for changing the direction of the march of one single battalion; what remained for Napoleon to do he did promptly and cleverly; and this was to bring up his reserve, the Infantry of the Guard, to the decisive point, and prevent the Corps d'Armée of his right wing (4th and 3rd) from being separated during their concentric march from the 2nd or central one, on which the whole army pivoted up to two o'clock, p.m.; and this he effected by throwing the whole of his reserve Cavalry, combined with Artillery, into the gap, which brings us precisely to our point.

McMahon, whose corps had bivouacked at Castiglione, marched from thence at three o'clock, a.m., the whole corps in one column on the high road leading to Guidizzolo.   He had orders to turn off to the left towards Cavriano before reaching the former town, but he halted the head of his column soon after five o'clock, a.m., near the Monte Medolano, a small eminence on the right of the road halfway between Castiglione and Guidizzolo.   Nearly two English miles to his right Niel, who had orders to march on Guidizzolo, was engaged at Medule with the Austrian 9th Corps, and about a mile and a half mile to his left, between La Grole and Solferino, Baraguay d'Hilliers with the 5th Corps; he stood, therefore, nearly in the centre of a three-and-a-half mile wide gap in the French line of battle.   The key of the Austrian position was on the heights of Solferino, and this could only be carried by his co-operation.   But if he moved his corps to the left towards San Cassiano for that purpose, the two mile gap between him and Niel would have been widened to a three or four mile one; and towards that already existing the Austrians soon after ten o'clock directed their 3rd Corps, supported by Mensdorff's Cavalry on its right wing.   It was, therefore, the first consideration to stop up this hole, which was done at first by Niel's throwing into it the two Cavalry reserve divisions, Devaux and Partonneaux, with their batteries, and then flanking the front of these with the thirty guns of his Artillery reserve.   General Auger, on the other hand, formed the twenty-four guns of the Artillery reserve of McMahon's corps into one battery in front of the latter, and to the left of the two Cavalry divisions; and finally Napoleon ordered up the Cavalry of the Guard, which was hastening up from Castenedolo, to prolong the line formed by Devaux and Partonneaux towards the right of McMahon's corps, which was thus at length enabled to assume the offensive after having been compelled to remain perfectly inactive for several hours.

But long before McMahon was thus enabled to co-operate with Baraguay d'Hilliers and the Infantry of the Guard in their attack on Solferino and Caosiana, the Austrians had made repeated attempts to penetrate into the interval occupied by the two Cavalry divisions, and thus separate the right wing of the French army from its centre and left; and it was here and for this purpose that Mensdorff's Cavalry was employed. Thus it came to pass that, contrary to all tactical rules, the reserve Cavalry of both armies* came to be employed nearly in the centre without having a line of Infantry in front or rear.† On the part of the French, however, the deficiency was supplied by the judicious employment of the fire of about eighty guns concentrated nearly on one point, to which the Austrians, who had a much more numerous artillery, opposed nothing, but the fire of a few isolated batteries, chiefly light 6-pounders.

It is necessary to remark here that the disposition for the march of the Austrian army issued on the 22nd and renewed on the 23rd of June, threw the three Corps d'Armée of their left wing, 3rd, 9th, 11th, into an eccentric direction as regarded the ground on which the battle was actually fought, that is to say, towards Medole. Unfortunately, too, for the Austrians, Niel's attack on the last-named village, early in the morning, naturally drew them off in the same false direction, and rendered it impossible to remedy the error by throwing these three corps into the space between the hilly country, and the high road from Castiglione to Goito, the only means of bringing the attack on Solferino to a stand still ‡ Moreover, McMahon, with the most consummate judgment, abstained for several hours from making any movement that might have tended to draw the attention of the Austrian leaders to this vulnerable and important point of the allied line of battle.

And thus it came to pass, that the 3rd Corps d'Armée, Prince Schwarzenberg, flanked on the right by Mensdorff's Cavalry, attempted soon after 10 o'clock A.M., to penetrate into the opening between Niel and McMahon, on the right of the latter. There

---

* The services of the reserve Cavalry division Zedwitz were lost in consequence of Major-General Baron Laningen having withdrawn his brigade at the commencement of the action in the most unaccountable manner.

† This was partly a consequence of the peculiarities of the ground, the heath of Medole lying in this direction, partly of the battle of Solferino having been altogether improvised on both sides.

‡ If the rencontre of the two armies had not taken place, or if the Austrians had commenced their movement at the same moment as the French, that is at three o'clock, a.m., this eccentricity in the march direction of these three corps would have ceased to exist.

were no troops available to throw into the equally fatal hiatus on McMahon's left, between him and the 1st Corps, with the exception of Colonel Edelsheim, with his four squadrons of Hussars.

Having now placed before the reader a general view of the situation, and of the circumstances under which the Cavalry on both sides were employed on this memorable day, we proceed to the details, and commence with Edelsheim, whose action has become the object of much discussion, excited a very peculiar interest, and let us add, been very much overrated in a tactical point of view.

Like all apostles of new systems, Edelsheim thought only of his own hobby, charging across the most difficult piece of country he could pick out; perhaps, too, the prospect of gaining the much-coveted Order of Maria Theresa may have occurred to him, but we are inclined to doubt that he had any very clear idea of the general tactical situation. Every one, too, seems to have been doing, at the moment, what best pleased himself, for the Emperor Francis Joseph was still at Valleggio, or just about to leave it, in perfect ignorance of all that had happened up to the moment.

However this may be, away went Edelsheim across country, his four squadrons in line, with a wide interval between each pair.* His starting point was Val di Termini, half-way house between Guidizzolo and Caosiana, from whence he moved nearly in a straight line towards Castiglione. At first, he fell in only with small detachments of the 7th regiment of Chasseurs à cheval, placed here in observation by McMahon, and these were soon compelled to fall back on their supports.

We must here remark, that McMahon in his report, deceived no doubt by the great difference in the strength of the French and Austrian squadrons, and seeing two lines of considerable length, with a large interval between them, represents this charge or series of charges to have been made by two regiments; and this has given rise to the very erroneous idea, that it was Mensdorff's Cavalry that acted here, whereas this general never came into contact with McMahon's left wing having had to do, as we shall presently see, with Devaux and Partonneaux, who were on the right of the French 2nd Corps d'Armée. It is also necessary to observe that blame has been attached to Mensdorff for not having followed Edelsheim, who cursorily informed him of what he was about to undertake, at a moment that the two columns came nearly in contact during their first advance, but this is perfectly absurd, as we shall presently prove to the reader's satisfaction.

Edelsheim progressed steadily in his onward course, and was met with equal gallantry by the French chasseurs, then ensued a series of charges and countercharges, in which the latter had decidedly the worst of it, and lost a great number of men and many horses.

* Two squadrons form in the Austrian cavalry a division without intervals, under the command of a field-officer, just as with us, two troops a squadron under the command of a captain.

McMahon had, meanwhile, deployed his Corps across the road, front towards Guidizzolo, one brigade of the 1st division to the right, the whole of the 2nd division to the left, and the 2nd brigade of the 1st division being placed in reserve at Barcaccio; he had also withdrawn two squadrons of the 4th Chasseurs à cheval from his right wing, on finding that the presence of the two Cavalry divisions enabled him to do so with safety. When Edelsheim arrived at Barcaccio the reserve Infantry brigade posted there endeavoured to bar his passage by throwing out a swarm of tirailleurs, but these were speedily driven in on their respective battalions, by a successful charge of his left squadron, whilst the other three kept on straight ahead, and encountered the above-mentioned two squadrons of the 4th Chasseurs, which had just arrived, and effected their junction with those of the 7th regiment. These six squadrons united, charged Edelsheim's three, but were in their turn broken, not, however, before they had made one or two determined countercharges, during which, part of the Hussars were driven in under the fire of squares formed by the 11th battalion of Chasseurs, and the 72nd of the Line, and suffered severely. According to McMahon's report, several prisoners, including an officer, and some 30 horses were captured. By this time, it was nearly 12 o'clock, and Edelsheim had reached Le Grole, a village taken by Forey's troops two hours previously. It is stated that he now sent patrols to the rear to look for Mensdorff's division, which he seems to have fancied should have followed him, but in truth he must have begun to see that his expedition was a tactical " nonsense," for the heights on his right were already occupied by Baraguay d'Hilliers' corps; and his patrols, who, of course, saw nothing of Mensdorff, brought him the news that McMahon was closing up his line of retreat with squares of Infantry, the prelude to his movement on San Cassiano. Nothing daunted by this, Edelsheim rallied his squadrons, and sent one under Captain Baron Lederer ahead as avant-garde, and followed with the remaining three in line, with double or treble intervals. Lederer soon after encountered the head of the column of the Cavalry of the Guard, which was advancing on the high road from Castiglione towards McMahon's right wing, and, although himself menaced in the flank and rear by a squadron of Chasseurs, he did not hesitate a moment in charging the avant-garde, which he drove back on the head of the column; the Chasseurs in his rear were, meanwhile, driven off by one of the squadrons that followed in his wake.

In consequence, the progress of the Cavalry of the Guard was retarded for some time, but General Morris ordered it to deploy, and Edelsheim, seeing that he had no chance of resisting so large a body, was compelled to think of retreating, the more so because a French battalion posted behind some stone walls at the point of intersection of the cross road, leading from Le Grole to Carpenedolo, with the main road on which McMahon had advanced, galled him with its fire, although his brave Hussars jumped the walls and dashed into the midst of the infantry. But his horses and men were, by this time, quite done up, and he retreated by Casa Morino, in the rear of McMahon's corps, where he again encountered French Infantry, but finally made his way unmolested to the brigade of General Rösgen which formed the right wing of Schwarzenberg's corps, and was posted at the cross-road leading from Medole to San Cassiano.

Thus ended Edelsheim's exploit, which proved beyond a doubt that Cavalry may be moved, in small bodies at least, over the most difficult country, and perform the most valuable services despite of rifled guns, both big and small, indeed from the former it has nothing to fear at close quarters. But really important results can be attained, only when this arm is used at the proper moment, and in the right direction, neither of which was here the case; however we must not anticipate, and can only repeat what was aptly said of our own Balaclava charge, "c'est magnifique, mais ce n'est pas la guerre." The only other parallel that occurs to us, is Colonel Baron Meiendorff's charge at the battle of Grochow, on the 25th February, 1831, with four squadrons of the Russian cuirassier regiment, Prince Albert.

Edelsheim's squadron lost in this affair 8 officers, 125 rank and file and 126 horses, or as nearly as possible one-fourth of their actual strength at the time. It is by no means true, as has been asserted, that all these were killed and wounded in the melée, and only one man by a shell; for the French made several prisoners and captured only thirty horses. A great number of the men and three-fourths of the horses were killed or wounded by the fire of the infantry and artillery, although perhaps the majority of the rank and file may have been sabred. The only real result of the affair was, that a second practical proof was afforded of the possibility of carrying out Edelsheim's system of moving cavalry, and that he himself gained the Order he coveted—tactical results it had none, nor could it under the circumstances have had, even if Mensdorff's division had followed, indeed these gallant troops, so recklessly sacrificed, could have been much better employed at a later period of the battle and in a different direction, as shall be presently shown.

Mensdorff had left his bivouac at Tezze nearly an English mile and a half to the rear of Valdi Termini, from whence Edelsheim had started, between six and seven o'clock A.M., and the direction of his march brought the two columns into contact soon after eight o'clock, when the casual communication alluded to, took place. A certain degree of blame has been thrown on Mensdorff for not following Edelsheim with his division (3 regiments, 20 squadrons, about 2000 sabres.) It is therefore but fair to enquire into the circumstances of the case which were as follows.

Mensdorff's division formed the Cavalry reserve of the right wing of the Austrian army under Schlick.   The disposition for the march previously issued instructed this general officer, to cover the ground between Camarino, on the high road, and Caosiana, on the edge of the hilly country, during the advance of the army, and to cover Schlick's left and secure his communications with Wimpffen. Zedivitz who was attached to the wing commanded by Wimpffen had received precisely similar orders for his division in the open country near Medole, of course *mutatis mutandis*, and this would naturally have brought the two divisions into contact in the open country, that lay between the two wings of the Austrian force, but they were perefectly independent of each other.   Mensdorff had therefore a perfectly well defined and specific task to perform, and at the time when Edelsheim communicated with him, his instructions had not been altered nor indeed was it then possible to say whether the combats going on at the moment at Medole and Le Grole were mere avant-garde affairs, or the prelude to a general action.

Under these circumstances it would have been perfectly unjustifiable and wholly contrary to the spirit and letter of his instructions, and indeed to common sense, to engage the whole of the reserve cavalry in an expedition, whose consequences it was wholly impossible to foresee in the slightest degree, and this too, at the very commencement of an affair, the nature of which was not yet clearly defined, and moreover leave a space of two or three English miles in the centre of the Austrian army wholly uncovered. We, of course, do not mean to say that the reserve Cavalry of an army should never be engaged at the commencement of an action, although it is in most instances better to avoid doing so, nor that the commandant should hold himself so bound by instructions as never to deviate from them or follow his own inspiration; on the contrary, we consider his doing so occasionally to be the real test of fitness for the command of Cavalry, but he must then be quite sure that he knows what he is doing, and not ride tilts at windmills.

Edelsheim was in a very different position, but he was attached to an Infantry Corps d'Armée belonging to the left wing of the army, Wimpffen's, and had received the permission of his immediate chief, Prince Schwarzenberg, to try a *coup* wherever he saw a chance of success, and it seems to us not a little strange to censure a general officer commanding a division for not following the lead of a Colonel commanding four squadrons in every wild-goose chase it might please the latter to undertake, whether this harmonised with his instructions or was perfectly opposed to them.

It is, however, a very different question to ask, whether as things turned out it would have been better if Mensdorff had directed his movements against the interval between McMahon and Baraguay d'Hilliers, or, as he actually did, against that between the former and Niel.   Now we have already shown that McMahon was compelled to inaction, and could not move to support Baraguay d'Hilliers' attack on the heights of Solferino until Niel's corps had formed a junction with his; there was therefore nothing for the Austrian cavalry to prevent in this direction, and further that Niel had thrown the two cavalry divisions Devaux and Partonnaux with their batteries in addition to the whole of his own reserve artillery into this interval, for the purpose of securing the junction of the 4th and 2nd Corps d'Armée so soon as Canrobert's arrival with the 3rd should have enabled him to incline to his left, and finally, that the Emperor Napoleon had moved the Cavalry of the Guard on the same point for the same purpose.

Is it necessary to draw the deduction, that the longer this junction could be deferred, so much the longer would McMahon's action remain paralysed and so much the later would he be enabled to co-operate with Baraguay d'Hilliers and the Infantry of the Guard at the decisive points San Cassiano and Solferino; this was precisely what occurred, for McMahon could not commence his movement for many hours. There was, therefore, something for the Austrian Cavalry to prevent in this direction.

Mensdorff arrived on the ground about nine o'clock or a little later, he placed the two Dragoon regiments (twelve squadrons) of the brigade Prince William of Holstein in the first line and the regiment of Hulans, Count Civillart (eight squadrons) of the brigade Zichy in rear of his right en échelon, the second regiment of the latter brigade had not as yet joined the army; his artillery consisted of one light six-pounder battery of the absurd construction that the Austrians are pleased to call "cavalry batteries." Directly opposed to him were the two Cavalry divisions Devaux and Partonneaux* with their guns in front, flanked on their right by the cross fire of the 36 guns of Niel's reserve artillery, whilst 24 guns of McMahon's reserve, under General Auger, were opposed to his right; that is to say between 70 and 80 guns in all.

It would, however, be a gross misrepresentation to pretend that Niel's junction with McMahon was delayed for so many hours solely by the action of Mensdorff's Cavalry. Canrobert arrived late, and with only a portion of his corps, to Niel's assistance, and the latter could not in any case have continued his movement of conveyance towards McMahon till the former joined him. Again the Austrian 9th corps supported by portions of the 11th, offered a direct and very obstinate resistance to his progress, and finally the 3rd corps under Schwarzenberg endeavoured to turn the left wing of his Infantry and cut off his communication with McMahon, whilst Mensdorff's Cavalry endeavoured to bring Devaux and Partonneaux to action with the same intention and also cover the right wing of Schwarzenberg's corps, and keep open its communication with Schlick's force.

* Each of these consisted nominally of 16 squadrons, consequently 32 in all, but these were very weak in consequence of the enormous number of disabled horses already alluded to.

But Schwarzenberg and Mensdorff's efforts to penetrate into the interval between Niel and McMahon were frustrated by the French artillery posted here, although the greater part of the 11th corps (3 brigades) was by degrees employed to support the former. Mensdorff, who had meanwhile received orders from the Emperor Francis Joseph to support Wimpffen's wing of the army in its advance, drew off his squadrons when the fire of the French guns compelled him to do so, advanced again in line of columns of divisions at intervals, or in échelons from his right wing, and endeavoured unceasingly to entice the French Cavalry out of its favourable position on the edge of the heath of Medole, where it was impregnable under the protection of its artillery, but in vain; neither of the French generals ventured once during the whole action to encounter Mensdorff, and in so doing, they acted with perfect judgment; for a successful charge on their part would have been comparatively useless to the French, whereas if beaten and driven off the ground, the artillery must have also been withdrawn or sacrificed, and thus the way opened to Schwarzenberg to break through the French centre and separate the right wing from the left. At a later period, however, they renounced their inactivity and charged repeatedly with great bravery and considerable effect the Infantry brigades of the Austrian 3rd and 9th corps at Canuova and Boite, as we shall presently see.

Mensdorff's battery had soon five of its eight guns dismounted, and was compelled to retreat; another badly horsed reserve battery was brought forward, and had three of its guns dismounted in a few minutes. Its commandant wished to push on with the remaining five to case-shot range of the French guns, his only chance, but Mensdorff would not permit this. Five or six batteries of genuine horse artillery might have been able to do the trick even with the old fashioned smooth-bored guns, but with one maimed battery it would have been absurd.

While Mensdorff was thus fruitlessly endeavouring to bring the French reserve Cavalry to action, McMahon threw forward some Infantry from his right wing, covered by two squadrons of the 4th Chasseurs, to turn the right wing of the Austrian Cavalry. Mensdorff immediately detached four squadrons of Hulans to oppose this force; notwithstanding the hedgerows, ditches, and walls, with which the country is intersected, the Hulans charged successfully, and drove the French back in this direction; but pursuing too hotly, they got under the fire of the squares of the first brigade of Delamotterouge's division, and lost a number of men and horses. Subsequently, between twelve and one o'clock, the head of a Cavalry column appeared on Mensdorff's right, it was the first échelon of the Cavalry of the Guard that had just arrived, and been ordered by McMahon to deploy between his right and the left of Devaux and Partonneaux, so soon as he should have commenced his movements on San Cassiano, which happened soon after. Mensdorff sent two squadrons of the 5th Dragoons to oppose this column, but no charge ensued, for the French Cavalry was withdrawn; but the Dragoons got under the fire of the Infantry of the 2nd Corps, and were compelled to retreat.

The French accounts of the action of their Cavalry against Mensdorff are altogether incorrect; we do not mean to say that there is intentional misrepresentation, for it is quite evident that they confounded Edelsheim with Mensdorff throughout. Thus the charge of the six squadrons of Chasseurs was made against Edelsheim's four squadrons formed in two divisions, and not against two regiments of Mensdorff; the *attaque en muraille* of the brigade Cassaignolles, Chasseurs and Guides de la Garde, was directed not against a brigade of Mensdorff, but against one or two squadrons of the 10th Hussars attached to Infantry brigades of the 3rd Austrian Corps. The partial charges of the Austrian regiments which the French authors mention as having been directed against the right wing of McMahon's Corps towards the end of the action, and chiefly repulsed by échelons of the Cavalry of the Guard, were, in fact, isolated charges of the very same single squadrons attached to the Infantry brigades during the last gallant effort made to retake Canuova; in fact, Mensdorff's Cavalry never once came in contact with anything but skirmishers, or isolated *attaques en fourrageurs*, which were repulsed with considerable loss to the French of killed, wounded, and prisoners.

Our object being, not to give an account of the battle, but merely to point out certain details connected with the action of the Cavalry, we must here leave Mensdorff, with the remark, that he lost about 500 horses, or one-fourth of his total strength, and this wholly by the fire of the French Artillery and Infantry.

Although the French reserve Cavalry certainly never came into serious contact with the Austrian, and even seems to have avoided doing so, for the reasons already stated; it nevertheless played a most active and successful part in the operations of the right wing of the French army, and mainly contributed by its distinguished gallantry, as Niel expressly declares in his report, to the defeat of the Austrian Corps d'Armée under Wimpffen in their attempts to retake Canuova and Boite, so much so indeed that it seems perfectly incomprehensible how, in the face of such facts, an outcry against the Cavalry should have arisen in France; had it taken place in Austria it would have been more intelligible.

An article in the Seventh Number of the Austrian " Militärische Zeitschrift" for 1860, giving an account of the two attacks on Canuova led by Prince Charles Windischgrätz, and in the last of which that gallant officer was killed, furnishes a striking proof of this assertion.

The half brigade led by Windischgrätz consisted of the 1st Field and the Grenadier battalions of the regiment Khevenhüller, the former with six, the latter with four companies; it advanced on the left of the road leading to Canuova from Guidizzolo, the remainder of the brigade under General Greschke advancing on the right. The 1st battalion was formed in three partial columns of divisions (two companies each) at distance, the Grenadier battalions following in reserve, a swarm of skirmishers in the front and on the flanks.

During the advance, a heavy fire was opened on this column by the French Infantry posted in Canuova, which made it wave for a moment, but the officers seconded the example given by their colonel so gallantly that the onward movement was resumed after a few minutes. The major commanding the 1st battalion lined the ditches and hedgerows with skirmishers, and was about leading his three divisional columns against the front and flanks of the building, when all of a sudden a squadron of French Hussars made a vehement charge on his left flank, threw the whole battalion into disorder, and compelled Windischgrätz to withdraw his troops, the French pursuing them with skirmishers rendered it impossible to re-form the columns, which were driven back to the stone bridge at Guidizzolo, behind which they were at length rallied.

The second attack was attempted at half past three o'clock, p.m., the same two battalions advancing this time in column of battalions at quarter distance, supported on the right by the brigade Ballin of the 3rd Corps, the brigade Wetzlan following in reserve. Everything went on prosperously till Windischgrätz came within eighty yards of the farm-house, when his men again hesitated for a moment, but went ahead again and reached the hedgerows surrounding the main building, where they were again brought to a stand still by a charge of French Lancers on their left flank, but the battalions formed squares and the skirmishers clumps, and beat off the Cavalry, which had charged without sufficient energy. But this had given the French Infantry time to prepare a counter attack; and just as Windischgrätz's two columns reached the farm-building, and some few men had even penetrated into the court-yard, they were taken on both flanks with the bayonet, Windischgrätz killed, and away went the whole back to Guidizzolo hotly pursued by swarms of Cavalry, that rendered all attempts at rallying perfectly vain.

The Austrian accounts of the affair say that the brigade Ballin offered no support to this attack, which was undertaken without the aid of Artillery, and not flanked by Cavalry as it should have been. The loss of the two battalions was 19 officers, including the colonel, and 626 rank and file, killed and wounded, and the colours of one battalion, consequently, as nearly as possible, one-eighth of the total strength.

We could cite a number of similar instances in which the French Cavalry charged the Austrian Infantry both in squares and when advancing in columns of attack, at Boite and Rebecco, and the Austrian Cavalry made also repeated charges in the same manner. In many instances, single French Cavalry officers even penetrated into the Austrian squares, but were all either killed or taken prisoners; the squares, however, were never broken as far as we can ascertain.

The consideration of what may be fairly deduced from the above facts, we must refer to a future article, but every impartial reader will have already arrived at the conclusion that the services of the Cavalry were by no means so unimportant or insignificant, during the war of 1859 in Italy, as has been represented by its enemies, and that not only what is technically termed divisional Cavalry, but also the Cavalry reserves have still, each of them, its own sphere of action.

## EDITOR'S PORTFOLIO;

### OR,

# NAVAL AND MILITARY REGISTER.

It is surely a fit subject for congratulation in a professional Journal to be able to record that the great geographical problem of ages has, at length, been solved by the patient endurance and hardihood of British officers.  Of course, we allude to the discovery of the real source of the Nile, by Captains Speke and Grant, who have recently returned to England, and who were most justly honoured with an ovation by the Royal Geographical Society on the 22nd of last month.

After some very complimentary remarks from the Chairman, Sir Roderick Impey Murchison, Captain Speke gave, by request, an outline of the labours of himself and his gallant associate, which will no doubt be printed in a more convenient form than the newspaper report. As to the great discovery made, it is now established by the indisputable means of actual inspection and astronomical observation, that the Victoria Nyanza (Nyanza means, indifferently, lake, pond, and river) is the great reservoir of the Nile. The river issues from the lake, flowing over rocks of igneous character, to which Captain Speke has given the name of the Ripon Falls, in honour of the noble lord who was the President of the Royal Geographical Society when this successful expedition was set on foot.

The Chairman of the meeting presented to Captain Speke a gold medal sent by the King of Italy, and intimated that a similar one was on its way for Captain Grant.  He also stated that Her Majesty had expressed her lively interest in the result of the expedition, and he believed that she also would show her satisfaction in the like substantial form.   This announcement gave great satisfaction to the crowded meeting, and we trust that we shall very soon have the pleasure of recording that it has been carried into effect.

Of the personal adventures of the explorers, and the hardships that they experienced, Captain Speke said nothing in his most interesting address, but we may form some idea of what they must have been, when we find him stating that of 185 natives, whom he engaged at Zanzibar to accompany him, only 18 adhered to him throughout the journey.   He accounts for this mistrust by saying that the Arabs, whom alone they have hitherto seen, have so cheated them, that they have now no confidence in anybody. To remedy this, he proposes that some of them should be brought to Europe and educated, and then being sent back as Consuls on the coast, they would gradually lay the foundation of that belief in the good intentions of the white man towards them, without which they can never be brought into profitable connexion with Europe.   This seems a practical suggestion, and well deserves serious consideration.

----

The principal events in connection with the Polish Revolution during the last few weeks, have been the continued expression of public opinion, not so much in favour of the Polish cause as against the action of the Russian Government.   The religious element, which forms an important egredient in the just complaints of the Polish people, has been most significantly brought before the world by the letter addressed by the Pope to Alexander II. The three Great Powers, England, France and Austria, have addressed fresh and identical notes to the Russian Cabinet, and the attitude of France since the late victories in Mexico, has become more menacing.   Thus we see the Polish Question raised to the most prominent position, and threatening to involve the Powers of Europe in a general war, unless the Russian Government, giving ear to the general expression of public opinion and the combined action of the Great Powers, should consent to carry out the provisions of the treaties which were passed for the safeguard of the national rights of Poland, and for the preservation of the peace of Europe.

Puebla has fallen, and a heavy load of anxiety has thereby been taken off the mind of the Emperor of the French. The war was not popular. The unexpected, determined defence, made by the Mexicans, and the ravages committed by sickness, were becoming serious sources of concern, not only to the French Government, but to France generally. Moreover, it was a heavy drain upon the French finances. With the fall of Puebla, the war will probably terminate. Whether Mexico will surrender is doubtful. The French army can now return with honour and victory, and the indefatigable mind of Napoleon III can turn to the consideration of other questions—for instance, Poland, or mediation in America. In another portion of the Magazine, we publish a narrative of the Mexican question, and the last official details respecting the Capture of Puebla.

———

The latest news from America contains one satisfactory item, and that is, the removal of the renowned Wilkes from the command of the "flying squadron," which has *not* captured the Alabama or any other of the "English pirates." Whether his successor will have better luck, or more enterprise, remains to be seen, but it is pretty certain, that he cannot do more to bring another war on the hands of the Federals than the great Antarctic discoverer has already done; and as to finishing the present pretty little quarrel, he cannot well do less.

The rest of the news, though it comes exclusively through the Federals, is entirely of a negative character. Vicksburg, which was going to "fall in a few hours" some two months ago, is probably not taken yet, for the last "rumour from Murfreesborough" to the effect that it had fallen, is most likely only a delicate way of breaking the news that the siege has been raised. At least, such is a fair conclusion from the scores of "great Union victories" that have turned out to be defeats. Further south, the Federals have succeeded no better; an attack by Banks on Port Hudson having confessedly failed, but there they had the consolation of knowing that one of their negro regiments was nearly annihilated, a matter that would reconcile most Yankees to the defeat. Misled by a rather improbable tale that General Lee had taken himself off, the "injudicious" Hooker ventured to pass some of his troops over the Rappahannock, where they soon discovered their mistake; and though, of course, they performed "prodigies of valour," they returned much faster than they came.  Meanwhile, a strong peace party is springing up in the North, and if the talk at public meetings in New York is worth anything, State rights are to be the ground of a pretty general disclaimer of the authority of the Government at Washington.  If this is not "the beginning of the end," perhaps the appearance of M'Clellan, before whom several regiments, returning heart-sick from the war, lately "passed in review," may be.  But we shall see what we shall see, for the Yankees are not to be judged by ordinary rules.

Although there is no actual war on the continent, except in Poland, to which we have elsewhere alluded, still "fears of change" apparently perplex more monarchs than one.  It remains to be seen how the Emperor Napoleon will treat his "Opposition;" but we know that the King of Prussia has taken steps with his Parliament, which, according to our English ideas, must have very serious consequences.  The Emperor of Austria is playing at Constitutional Government, and so is Victor Emmanuel, but it does not appear that either of these royal performers gives much satisfaction to his audience.  Greece, at last, has got a King, and the Greeks in London have indulged in a *Te Deum* on the occasion, everything being *couleur de rose* with them just at present.  We can only, like the good Vicar of Wakefield, hope "they may be all the better for it this day six months."

One of the three great military scandals by which the nation has recently been disturbed, has just been cleared up, and an opinion authoritatively pronounced thereon, that we are sure will commend itself to the right feeling alike of the profession of arms and the public.  Of course, we allude to the Calthorpe and Cardigan controversy, upon which some remarks will be found in another page, as well as a summary of the legal judgment.  The case of Colonel Dickson against the Earls of Combermere and Wilton and General Peel, and the Mhow court-martial and its melancholy results, being still *sub judice*, we do not at present touch upon them, though we put on record in our pages the memorandum of H.R.H. the Commander-in-Chief on the latter subject; but when the time comes that the legal proceedings are closed, we shall state our views with the same fairness and decision as we have done in regard to the brilliant though ill-advised Balaclava charge.

Any of our London readers who have a half hour to spare, may turn it to account by looking in at the Gallery of Illustration, 14, Regent Street, where Mr. Armytage's fine picture of "The Vision of St. John" is to be seen. It is an illustration of the 4th, 5th, 6th and 8th chapters of the Book of Revelations, and treats its sublime theme in a truly noble manner.

———

In the Court of Queen's Bench, on Wednesday, the 10th of June, the Court gave judgment in the case of the Earl of Cardigan *versus* Lieutenant-Colonel Hon. Somerset Calthorpe, which arose out of imputations cast upon the Earl in a work written several years ago by Colonel Calthorpe, entitled "Letters from a Staff Officer in the Crimea." The noble Earl had obtained a rule calling upon the writer to show cause why a criminal information should not issue against him for libel. Mr. Sergeant Shee, on behalf of Colonel Calthorpe, urged as reason for discharging the rule, first, that the statements in the "Letters from Head Quarters" were based upon information obtained at the time; secondly, that since the publication of the book Lord Cardigan had done all he could against Colonel Calthorpe, and was therefore disentitled to the special interference for which he asked; and thirdly, that Colonel Calthorpe had a right to express his views in reference to the war in the Crimea and the conduct of officers there, which were now matters of history. Several affidavits were read to the effect that the Earl was not in the battery which was charged at Balaklava at the time when he was wanted. It was further stated that Colonel Calthorpe destroyed the unbound copies of one edition of his book, and that he had done his best to make peace with Lord Cardigan. On the other side, Mr. Garth said— that this was a slander by an officer of comparatively low rank, and but of few years' standing, against a general officer of thirty or forty years' service; and its retractation, if it could be called such, was made in the most unhandsome, the most uncandid, the most unbecoming, and the most ungenerous style, for its effect was only to change the charge which he had been brought before the court to answer. His Lordship justly felt indignant at the libel, and it was not to be surprised that he applied at first to the Horse Guards for a court-martial, believing that to be the proper tribunal to afford him that redress which was denied him by Lieutenant-Colonel Calthorpe. Attempts were then made by mutual friends, which only led to further provocations. The admission that had now been made might have been done in a more generous spirit. The Lord Chief Justice said—I can entertain no doubt that the passage in the work upon which this application has been made for a criminal information contains a most serious libel on the Earl of Cardigan. I think it is impossible to read the passage without coming to the conclusion that that which it is intended to convey is an imputation on the Earl of Cardigan of his having been wanting in his duty at a time when he was in command of the detachment of cavalry ordered to take the Russian battery, and of having been wanting in his duty throughout of personal courage. It is true that in the first edition of the work the absence of Earl Cardigan (whose presence as a general officer was necessary) was ascribed to an accident. It was said that his horse, alarmed by the discharge of a gun close to his head, swerved, and carried him in spite of himself off the field ; which was clearly intended to convey that the Earl of Cardigan never reached the battery with the detachment under his command, owing to an accident. The Earl of Cardigan, feeling that he had reason to complain of this statement, as well as others contained in the work, made it the subject of complaint and remonstrance, and in the second edition a notice was prefixed to the work, which in the third edition was incorporated in the shape of a note into the body of the work. The failure of Lord Cardigan's reaching the battery with his men was withdrawn, and in the shape of a compliment, ostensibly on the face of it, but which in my judgment, conveys the bitterest sarcasm disguised under a compliment. The imputation was that it was not owing to the fault of his horse, but to his own fault, that he did not reach the scene of danger and conflict into which the others entered and passed. That conveys, and was intended to convey, an imputation that the Earl of Cardigan was wanting in personal courage in the discharge of his military duty. To say that a soldier ordered to attack an enemy—much more a general officer, whose duty it was to lead others into action —stopped short midway in the path that led to danger and perhaps death, whilst others went on, without any obstacle to prevent his accompanying them—must convey to the minds of all, whether military men or civilians, imputations of personal cowardice, disgrace, and dishonour. It is therefore impossible not to feel that this is a matter of the most libellous character. Heaven forbid that the time should ever come when the honour, courage, and reputation of our soldiers and sailors engaged in the service of our country should be deemed to be that which the law will not protect when unjustly and unjustifiably assailed. Looking to the position of the parties and also its importance to the services to which the objectionable passages refer, it is a matter to be properly made the subject of a criminal information unless some special cause be shown to the contrary. His Lordship then, at considerable length, entered into the details of the circumstances of the case, and observed that the Court did not regret the time the case had consumed, as it had given Lord Cardigan an opportunity of justifying his conduct, and he regretted that Lieutenant-Colonel Calthorpe had not made a more gracious retractation. The fact disclosed by the defendant in his affidavit and also Mr. Murray's, that the un-

published copies of the last edition on which alone a rule could
have been granted were destroyed, entirely cut away the ground
for this rule, and had that circumstance been known when the
rule was moved for, it would not have been granted. It had,
however, been clearly shown that that fact was unknown at the
time to Earl Cardigan or his solicitor. Under that circumstance
the rule must be discharged, but without costs." The rule was
discharged accordingly.

*The Case of Sergeant-Major Lilley*

The following is an authentic copy of the Memorandum of his
Royal Highness the Commander-in-chief on this case:—

"Horse Guards, S.W., Dec. 18, 1862.
"Memorandum.

"His Royal Highness the Field-Marshal Commanding-in-chief
having perused the proceedings of the general court-martial on
Paymaster Smales, of the 6th Inniskilling Dragoons, and having
had under his consideration not only these proceedings, but also
many facts bearing on them, has seldom found himself in a more
painful position, or one in which it appears more difficult to deal
out even-handed justice to all parties who have become mixed up
with these unfortunate events, and at the same time to do justice
to the service.

"Not only is the reputation of one of the most highly distinguished regiments in Her Majesty's cavalry service implicated by
them, but they have taken such a course that his Royal Highness
is most unwillingly forced into the position of differing to a great
degree from the views which appear to be taken by officers of
high rank, great reputation, and usually of excellent judgment,
to differ with whom he feels it to be not only painful to himself,
but in some degree embarrassing to the service.

"His Royal Highness has, however, but one course to pursue,
and that is, after mature consideration, and a patient hearing of
the opinions of those who, from their rank and position, are most
likely to give unbiased advice, to act upon his own sense of justice
to all parties, and with due regard to the interests of the service
over which he is called to preside.

"In the mind of his Royal Highness there can be no doubt
that the Court have come to a proper verdict as regards the insubordinate tone of the letter written by Paymaster Smales to his
commanding officer; and it would have been quite sufficient for
the purposes of discipline, and have saved a great mass of evidence
and extraneous matter, had the charges been directed solely
against the tone and spirit of that letter, and the letter itself been
laid before the Court as the only evidence required; in which
opinion his Royal Highness finds himself fortified by that of
the Judge Advocate-General of Her Majesty's Forces herewith
annexed.

"With regard, therefore, to Paymaster Smales—without entering into the minute points which the prosecutor has brought evidence, with more or less success, to rebut,—there can be no doubt, upon the broad principles of discipline, that that officer was guilty of most insubordinate conduct in writing such letter, and his removal from the army is an act of justice to the service.

"Unfortunately, however, in bringing down on his own head a just retribution for his contumacy in writing an insubordinate letter, this trial of Paymaster Smales has exposed a state of things in the Inniskilling Dragoons which his Royal Highness will endeavour to take an impartial view of.

"There is no doubt that the Inniskilling Dragoons under Colonel White and his successor, Colonel Shute—two distinguished officers, in whom his Royal Highness has great confidence,—before their embarcation for India, were all that could be desired as to *esprit de corps*, unanimity, and good feeling among the officers, and as to drill and discipline among the men.

"On their embarcation for India some changes took place among the officers, and the regiment had not been long in India when some unfavourable reports of the behaviour of one or two individuals when off duty, or at the mess, called down his Royal Highness's severe displeasure, the more so that it formed so strong a contrast to the previously acquired reputation of the corps.

"Still, with such exception, the regiment remained in the highest state of discipline, as elicited from all the confidential reports that have reached his Royal Highness from the Commander-in-chief and inspecting general officers in Bombay, till Colonel Shute was succeeded by Lieutenant-Colonel Crawley from another corps.

"In permitting Lieutenant-Colonel Crawley to succeed Colonel Shute, his Royal Highness believed he placed—and he did, in fact, place—at the head of the Inniskillings an officer of experience in the lower ranks of the service, of considerable talent, knowledge, and zeal; but, unfortunately, as has been proved, an officer not gifted with the special talent which unites with the firmness of command the tact which inspires confidence and creates goodwill.

"From the first Lieutenant-Colonel Crawley appears to have taken an unfavourable view of some points in the regiment, and to have expressed himself in no measured terms as to the changes he contemplated, which His Royal Highness cannot but think was uncalled for and unnecessary, and which was sure, to create an unfavourable feeling on the part of the regiment.

"The conduct of Lieutenant-Colonel Crawley subsequent to the court-martial, if the address he made to his regiment, both officers and men, be correctly reported, was, to say the least of it, exceedingly reprehensible and injudicious.

"There are other points in Lieutenant-Colonel Crawley's

conduct of which his Royal Highness cannot speak in too strong terms.

"His Royal Highness alludes to the confinement, under arrest, of certain non-commissioned officers during the trial, under a charge of conspiracy, which was never attempted to be proved against them, and for which there seems not to have been a shadow of foundation.

"His Royal Highness has also reason to believe that had the Commander-in-chief in India been better acquainted with some of the facts of Sergeant-Major Lilley's case he would have taken a different view of it from that which his remarks prove him to have done, and would not have attributed the death of that unfortunate non-commissioned officer to excess.

"Under these circumstances nothing but the high opinion expressed of Lieutenant-Colonel Crawley by the general officers in immediate command has induced his Royal Highness to continue him at the head of the regiment, and he does so only upon trial, and under the hope that for the future he will be able to carry on discipline without outraging the feelings of the gentlemen under his command.

"With reference to Major Swindley, his Royal Highness considers his conduct to have been most reprehensible, and he finds it difficult to make any excuse for it.

"'The tone and manner in which his evidence was given were highly unbecoming, and if his Royal Highness had not been obliged to make the remarks he has done on Lieutenant-Colonel Crawley he would at once remove Major Swindley from the Regiment; but, as he has given Lieutenant-Colonel Crawley the benefit of the character he has received from the general officers under whom he is serving, his Royal Highness will also give Major Swindley the advantage of the reports he has previously heard in his favour.

"His Royal. Highness now warns both Lieutenant-Colonel Crawley and Major Swindley that unless they hereafter conduct themselves in their relative positions in a manner to set an example of discipline to the regiment generally he will feel it his duty to remove one or both of them from the important stations they occupy.

"His Royal Highness feels it to be his duty also not to pass unnoticed the conduct of Captain Weir and Surgeon Turnbull.

"Nothing can excuse a subordinate officer for showing, by manner or act, disapprobation of his commanding officer before the younger members of a corps, who should look up to the captains and officers of station and experience as examples of discipline and obedience.

"In conclusion, his Royal Highness trusts that the future conduct of the officers of the Inniskillings will be such as to eradicate the evil spirit which momentarily appears to have crept into the corps, and to have tarnished a reputation which was second to none in the cavalry for all that constitutes a well ordered and most efficient regiment.

"J. YORKE SCARLETT, A.G."

# CRITICAL NOTICES.

ADVENTURES AND RESEARCHES AMONG THE ANDAMAN ISLANDERS. By Frederic J. Mouat, M.D., F.R.C.S., Surgeon-Major Her Majesty's Indian Army, &c.

The Andaman archipelago, in the Bay of Bengal, lies in the track of commerce, but being surrounded by coral reefs and inhabited by a race of apparently untameable savages, called Mincopies, who have the character of being cannibals, it is only of late years that it has been voluntarily visited. The first expedition of the kind that we know of, was that under Captain Blair and Colonel Colebrooke, who in the year 1789 surveyed the Andamans by direction of the East India Company, and the last, in the year 1857-8, is the subject of the present volume. The objects of both expeditions were much the same, namely, to find suitable sites for harbours of refuge and a penal settlement. These were found, and a settlement established, under Captain Blair, in the year 1789; but after struggling with many difficulties, it was abandoned in 1796, in consequence of the extreme unhealthiness of the position. The project was revived in 1855; but before proceeding further, it will be well to quote from Dr. Mouat some account of the scene of his labours.

"The Andaman Archipelago, is situated in the Bay of Bengal, near the meridian of 93 deg. E., and between the 10th and 15th parallels of North latitude. The largest and most important of the islands is that termed the Great Andaman, the configuration of which is remarkable in one respect, namely that, consisting of three great tracts of land, divided from each other by narrow passages, it forms apparently one island. About twenty miles to the southward is situated a second island, which, being considerably smaller than the other, is termed the Little Andaman. The surrounding waters are studded in many directions with numerous small islets, many of them exceedingly pretty and picturesque in appearance, rising as they do like beautiful oases in the wild waste of ocean that lashes their rocky shores. All of them are clothed with the richest tropical vegetation, which, from the level of the lowest swamp to the summit of the highest hill, grows in that un-restrained profusion in which Nature indulges in such climates. The entire group is surrounded in every direction by a natural fortress of coral reefs, which, extending for many miles, guards the approach to the islands, and in stormy weather, or in dark nights, renders it a matter of no little difficulty, and attended with considerable danger, to attempt to land upon them.

"Of the Great Andaman it may be observed that its western section is about forty-four miles in length, while its breadth may be computed at about an average of fourteen miles. In this part of the island is the magnificent harbour called Port Cornwallis, which, being locked in by land, affords a secure refuge for ships. The surface of this spacious natural harbour is diversified by several small islands, in one of which, in the year 1791, a place of refuge for such mariners as had the mis-fortune to be shipwrecked on that dreaded coast, and a burial settle-ment for those who sank under their hardship, were founded. They were discovered, however, to be in several respects unsuited for the purpose intended, and in the course of a few years were ultimately abandoned. The principal reasons for taking such a step, after a good deal of trouble and expense, were the extreme unhealthiness of the locality that had been selected, and the great additional expenditure that was requisite in order to supply those temporarily settled there with the various necessaries of life.

"The Saddle Mountain is situated to the south of Port Cornwallis, at the distance of a few miles. It rises to a considerable height, and forms the highest point to be seen in the whole group, its elevation being about 2,400 feet. On a favourable day, when the atmosphere is clear and cloudless, it is visible to the practised eye of the mariner at a distance of twenty leagues from the land.

"The middle division, known as the Middle Andaman, is separated from the northern portion of the island by a narrow strait. It is somewhat larger than the latter, extending in length to fifty miles, and being fifteen miles in width. The narrow strait is quite innavigable, and on examining it we found that, at a distance of six miles from its eastern outlet, it became a mere mud marsh at low water. At its north-western extremity, on the other hand, it was ascertained that it opened into a fine broad expanse, forming an excellent and capacious harbour, with secure anchorage for ships, at the extremety of which is Interview Island, one of the largest detached islets of the whole group. The South Andaman is forty-three miles in length, and its average breadth about the same as that of the Middle division. On its eastern side there are two commodious harbours, to which the names of Port Meadows and Port Blair have been given. There are also two harbours on its western coast, distinguished as Port Mouat and Port Campbell. The strait by which the Southern Andaman is separated from the Middle is navigable throughout its whole extent; and near its western extremity is an extremely fine harbour, which has only recently been discovered by Major Haughton, the second superintendent of Port Blair. On the southern side of the South Andaman, from which it is separated by Macpherson's Straits, another small island is situated. It is known by the name of Rutland Island, and it is nearly ten miles long, by four broad. The northern extremity of this island rises to a considerable height."

The author of the work before us was, in 1857, Inspector-General of Prisons in Bengal, and this is the account that he gives of the origin of his mission.

"The continually recurring outrages committed by the natives of the Andaman Islands on such shipwrecked mariners as had been thrown by the tempests on their inhospitable shores, were at length carried to such a formidable extent that the Government of India was imperatively called on to interfere. In the year 1855, therefore, when this matter became so urgent that it could no longer be neglected, the measure proposed as a remedy for the evil were taken into consideration without any further delay. The object in view was not only to make the islands safe asylums for those who had the misfortune to be wrecked on their coasts, but also to ultilize them in such a way as would prove ultimately beneficial to the inhabitants themselves, supposing their suspicious fears overcome, and their confidence gained. Two plans were accordingly proposed. One was the formation of a harbour of refuge on a suitable part of the coast, the expediency of which was generally admitted. The second was the establishment of a penal settlement on the principal island, in the most advantageous locality that could be selected. The advisability of carrying this proposal into effect was under discussion in the Indian Council at the time when the late dreadful mutiny broke out in 1857. Startling the world by its sudden, savage, and unprovoked nature, its immediate effect was to lay all such useful measures and plans in abeyance for the time; and it was not until the neck of this treacherous rebellion was completely broken that the subject was again submitted to the Councils of Government, in circumstances that rendered a speedy decision necessary. A settlement was now required to which those misguided agents of the late mutiny, whose crime, however great, was not attended with circumstances of such unpardonable atrocity as rendered imperative the forfeiture of their lives, might be transported. There were many whose hands had not been actually imbued in blood, yet who, from the share they had openly taken in the revolt, could not with safety be included in any measure of amnesty, however comprehensive, until either the last traces of disaffection had entirely disappeared, or the natives of India were thoroughly convinced that any further attempt at rebellion against the authority of England must infallibly be put down. It was believed that the transportation of these mutineers to the Andaman Islands would be an adequate punishment for the crime of which they had been guilty. There was something poetical in the retributive justice that thus rendered the crimes of an ancient race the means of reclaiming a fair and fertile tract of land from the neglect, the barbarity, and the atrocities of a more primitive, but scarcely less cruel and vindictive race, whose origin is yet involved in such a dark cloud of mystery. To the combination of these causes is due the visit which I paid to the Andaman Islands in 1857.

"The object of the expedition which I was called upon thus suddenly to join was to explore the coasts of these islands of the Indian sea, to examine how far they were adapted for the establishment of a convict station, and to select a suitable site for such a settlement. It was my good fortune, in this enterprise, to be associated with able, intelligent, and agreeable associates, and I could therefore undertake it with the confident hope of bringing it to a successful issue. My colleagues were Dr. George Playfair, of the Royal Army, and Lieutenant J. A. Heathcote, of the Indian Navy; and I am sure I can be guilty of no indiscretion in affirming that no army or navy in the world could have produced men better fitted by their talents for the tasks especially assigned to them. Their scientific ability was undoubted, and their practical skill had been more than once put to the test, and with the most successful results. Nor was their personal character less worthy of all the approbation that can be bestowed upon it. I have never met with men more noble-hearted, more self-sacrificing, or of more kindly disposition; and I need hardly say that my satisfaction in being associated with two such officers was almost—I should rather say entirely—unalloyed. I knew that no enterprise was too arduous for them, and that the prospect of danger would rather increase than impair their energy and devotion.

"My last evening in Calcutta was spent in the society of the Governor-General and his kind-hearted and accomplished lady. Alas! it is only a few years since, and they are now both no more! To my certain knowledge they are both mourned throughout our Eastern empire with a depth and intensity of sorrow, with feelings of such deep personal regret as are seldom felt for those who have occupied a station so exalted, their authority, although only derived and representative, exceeding that of many European kings and rulers "

The commissioners embarked in the Semiramis for Moulmein, and after a short stay at that port were transferred to the war-steamer Pluto, a vessel of light draught, and so better suited for experimental navigation among coral reefs and shallows. They were accompanied by a French photographer, a body of Burmese convicts to act as pioneers, a party of Europeans to serve as an armed guard, and a native crew of so heterogeneous a character, that the description is worth quoting.

"The ship's company had, by some good fortune, a fair proportion of musical amateurs, and from these was formed a band of serenaders, whose strains at occasional intervals relieved the tedium of the slowly-passing hours. The musicians were all natives of Goa, a peculiar composite race, who supply India with the more humble professors of the arts of cookery and music. Ethnological inquirers have been baffled in their attempts to determine, with anything like certainty, the origin of this very remarkable class of fiddlers and cooks; but judging by the result of previous investigations, the problem is apparently one that would baffle the ingenuity and learning of a Darwin. They are genuine hybrids of the true sable hue, looking as if they had been covered with a coat of tar wash. In many cases, the dark lustre of their skins could be appropriately compared only to the polished blackness of a life-guardsman's boot.

"This model crew likewise boasted the possession of a superior piper, whose renown was in all their mouths. Very probably, in other circumstances, we might have been disposed to dispense with the strains with which, with a liberality we were scarcely sufficiently grateful for, he was at all seasons ready to entertain us. We thought it right to encourage his musical abilities, particularly for one reason. The Andamanese would no doubt be able to appreciate the melody he produced from his favourite instrument, and we anticipated wonders from the war-dance with which we intended to gratify the natives on the celebration of our *fête* of fraternization with that interesting race of cannibals. But poor Sandy, like so many of his countrymen, even in these days of rampant teetotalism, was a thirsty soul. He dearly loved a drop of something stronger than either water or tea, and unfortunately he was inclined to be unreasonable in the frequency with which he repeated the doses that he considered necessary for his constitution—absolutely necessary in so trying a climate, and especially when engaged in an expedition in which all might find it requisite to be able to screw their courage up to the sticking point. We were not sorry that ere long we were deprived of the ear-piercing strains of our enthusiastic piper, although we regretted the cause that condemned him to silence. It was found necessary, after repeated warnings had been of no avail in restraining him in the gratification of his favourite appetite, to deprive him of his liberty, with the hope that the stocks would have some moral influence upon a character which was thrice armed at all points against every description of rational argument—at least, on this particular question. His vagaries became so extravagant, and his conduct so obstreperous, that we were compelled to resign ourselves to the loss of his assistance in the exercise of that civilizing and softening influence in which music has always been represented as playing no inconsiderable part. It was destined that the rude manners were not to be softened, nor the savage soul soothed to rest, by any strains that the bagpipe could produce.

"Our crew consisted of a strangely mingled collection of human beings. Anyone devoted to the study of ethnology would have had ample means for adding to his store of knowledge in that science, by observing the peculiarities of the various nationalities of whom there were specimens on the deck of the *Pluto*. Limited as was the number of our European crew, among them might be found the self-dependent Anglo-Saxons, active and fiery Celts, fair Norsemen, stout Findlanders, swarthy Italians, and Maltese distinguished by their bronzed faces and their guttural speech. In addition to these, we could boast of one Frenchman and a Hamburgher, with a Portuguese or two as swarthy and as guttural in speech as the Maltese. These constituted the European complement, forming, it must be allowed, with two natives of North and South America, a pretty varied representation of the white

branch of the Arian family of the human race.  As regarded the dark,
or rather the black portion of our crew, Africa supplied us with stokers
and pokers, well seasoned for their hot and laborious occupation by
the burning sun of their native plains and deserts.  China was laid
under contribution to supply us with carpenters.  We had sailors of
various castes from the Malayan peninsula, the ports of Hindostan, and
the Malabar coast.  Our cooks hailed from Burmah, from which we
had also a party of convicts, to whom were to be assigned some of the
laborious tasks that we might find necessary on reaching our destination.  Last of all, Bengal supplied us with our personal attendants.
There was considerable truth in a remark by one of my companions,
that if the earth were overwhelmed by a deluge during our absence,
or if the whole race of mankind were swallowed up by any earthquake
—we alone being left to show that such a creature as man had once
trod the surface of the globe—an ethnological inquirer, endowed with
the skill and knowledge of a Cuvier or an Owen, would not find it
difficult, with this comprehensive representation of the original stock,
to form a pretty accurate conception of the principal tribes, nations, and
tongues existing npon the face of the earth at the period of this supposed calamity."

On the 11th December, 1857, in the evening, Chatham Island, in
Port Cornwallis, was reached, and on the following day a landing was
made in the vicinity of the spot where the old settlement had been
established.

" Here we discovered some of the first native huts that had yet come
under our observation; and miserable apologies for human dwellings
they were, being merely small open sheds, the roofs of which were
formed of dried leaves of the wild palm, supported on four small central
posts.  The earthern floor was covered nearly a foot deep with the
shells of oysters, muscles, and other molluscæ, which were also scattered about in profusion on the open space by which these primitive
habitations were surrounded.

" Our course led us along the sandy beach.  It was pleasant to remain
within the influence of the inspiring sea-breeze, which, in comparison
with the sultry atmosphere of the valleys of the interior, or the me-
phitic exhalations from the deadly marsh already described, seemed to
be laden with the very essence of health and strength.  The sparkling
silvery sea-sand, which had rarely been trod by any civilised race of
men, was crisp and firm beneath our feet.  As we wended our way
along, enjoying our work in a way that made it seem like play, our
attention was attracted by a small group of cocoa-nut palm trees, evidently planted by the old settlers, for none were found elsewhere in the
vicinity of this great harbour.

" The hill, on the summit of which was built the settlement that owed
its foundation to the enterprising and interpid Blair, was now before
us.  We were anxious to ascend to the slope on which we might still
find its remains, but the eminence was so thickly covered with the
luxuriant vegetation of the island, that the task appeared to be one attended with no inconsiderable difficulty.  Our Burmese convicts, however—a patient, quiet, uncomplaining lot, to whom all the more laborious tasks were assigned—were set to work; and though it was not
executed without considerable difficulty, we had the pleasure of seeing
a path cut out by which we could easily ascend  As we made our way
up the hill, we soon came upon the vestiges of which we were in scarch,
even the most familiar objects of which excited our lively interest, as
testifying to the former presence of those who were once engaged on a
mission of the same nature as that which had brought us to this solitary
island.  Broken bricks, tiles, and stone that had been used in building,
were lying about in every direction, all so thickly covered with the

vegetation that had grown during the intervening years, that they appeared imbedded in the soil, and it was not until we had stumbled over
them in our onward progress, as we frequently did, that in some cases
we became aware of their presence, we were able to ascertain what
they were. Although the elevation was by no means considerable,
not more, I believe, than one hundred and fifty feet, yet from the
numerous trifling difficulties that constantly impeded us in our ascent,
and from the necessity under which we were of clearing our way before
us, the day was far advanced before we had completed our upward progress, and when we at length stood upon the summit of the hill
the sun was fast declining below the horizon.

"The scene upon which we looked from the summit was one well calculated to fix the gaze of all who delight in new varieties of natural
scenery. All around the hill, as far as the eye could see, extended
what literally appeared to be an ocean of vegetation, gently swaying
and undulating before the light breeze of the evening. The rich crimson of the tropical sunset contrasted with the endless shades of silvan
green that distinguished the spontaneous vegetable growth of successive
years. The remarkable profusion of trees and plants, the closeness
with which the various parasites were laced and interlaced together,
may be gathered from the fact that not only our light Burmese followers,
but also several of our more robust English, or, at any rate, European
nautical companions, walked, without the assistance of their hands, as
in climbing, almost to the top of several of the loftiest trees, the path
that they took being over the twining trunks of the creepers, unex-
ampled for their prodigious size. To the very verge of the horizon
this astonishing exuberance of vegetation extended. All that we heard
was the gentle rustling of innumerable leaves, slightly moved by the
gentle breeze of evening; all that we saw was this ocean of green, in
which not even an opening the size of a man's hand could be discovered
after the longest, closest, and most searching observation."

A brief investigation showed that the unhealthiness of the old settlement had arisen from the vicinity of a salt marsh, which might easily
be drained, and when that was done it was considered that the original
site was the most eligible that could be found for the required purposes.
The whole archipelago, however, was visited, but no place was discovered that could be fairly put in competition with it. The purpose of
the expedition being thus answered, Dr. Mouat returned to Calcutta
without delay and made his report, which was favourably received and
acted on; the Mutiny having just then furnished an abundant supply of
very proper candidates for the new penal settlement. Whilst in the
Andamans, Dr. Mouat and his party tried most perseveringly to conciliate the natives, but without success. Nothing could induce them to
hold any communication with their visitors; and at last things came to
the usual result—two or three skirmishes, in which the little people
showed desperate bravery, and inflicted some very severe wounds,
though their arms were nothing better than spears and arrows tipped
with fish bones or crooked nails; but of course they had the worst of it,
and their dead bodies enabled the Doctor and his scientific confederates
to make more minute investigations as to their osteology and dental
characters than would otherwise have been possible. In one of the
skirmishes a young native was made prisoner, and being carried to
Calcutta became the lion of the day. The sailors on board, who had
named him Jack, took a great liking to him; and Dr. Mouat, from close
observation of his demeanour, is inclined to give his countrymen credit
for more intelligence and good feeling than is usually ascribed to them.

" On learning that we had brought back a living representative of life
in the Andamans, in the person of our friend Jack, Lord and Lady
Canning at once expressed their anxious desire to see him. He was

accordingly invested with a becoming suit of clothes, and taken to
Government House, where he was treated with the utmost kindness by
their Excellencies, which perhaps induced him, on a subsequent occasion, to attempt to salute her ladyship in the native manner, namely,
by blowing in the hand with a cooing murmur; but, however kindly
disposed, her ladyship preferred to reject the offered civility. Most
of the time Jack spent in their presence he was greatly absorbed in self-
admiration. Observing his figure at full length in the large pier-glasses
with which the apartment was adorned, he stationed himself before one,
and, regarding his own image with undisguised satisfaction, he continued grinning at himself with a leer expressive of the utmost self-ad-
miration, constantly repeating, with a strange chuckle, as if speaking
to himself in the glass—"Jack! Jack!" and then bursting out, in vio-
lation of all good manners, into an irrepressible fit of laughter, in which
we found it difficult to prevent ourself joining. After he had sufficiently
admired himself, and Lord and Lady Canning had repeated to me the
gratification which they felt at having had an opportunity of seeing
poor Jack, they expressed their determination not to forget him, but,
if he should remain in Calcutta, to keep a watchful eye on him during
his future career. The interview was then considered at an end; and
having been removed from their presence, he was taken back to my
house, where quarters had been provided for him."

Civilized life, however, did not do for poor Jack; he fell ill, and at
last he was sent back to the Andamans, loaded with presents of all kinds
by Lord Canning, in the hope that, if restored to health, he might be
able to teach his countrymen, for he was naturally quick in his percep-
tions, and had become very observant during the latter portion of his
sojourn in Calcutta. The parting of this new Omai and his civilized
friends was painful to both.

"As he had been captured at South Reef Island, we had made arrangements for putting him ashore there, as the place where he would
stand the best chance of being immediately recognized by former friends
and relatives. He was at first conveyed ashore in the clothes he usually
wore at Calcutta, but the reflection immediately occurred to those in
whose charge he was, that in that condition it might not be possible for
any of the natives to recognize him. He was therefore stripped, with
his own consent, and left naked on the shore, a condition to which he
had been accustomed all his life, except during the short period of his
sojourn at Calcutta, and from which, therefore, it was probable he
would suffer no injury. None of his fellow-countrymen appeared to
claim him while any of the men belonging to the *Pluto*, by which he
had been carried back, remained with him on the island. It was therefore resolved to bid him farewell, leaving his clothes by his side, and
with the hope that when they had left, he would be claimed by his
kindred, or that he himself would be able to find them out. He took
an affectionate leave of all who had accompanied him, appearing very
dejected and low. The crew of the boat were very unwilling to leave
him behind, and were it not that they believed it was for the benefit of
his health, they would not have done it, so lonely and sad did the poor
fellow appear. After taking a last farewell, they rowed out to the ship,
gradually losing sight of him, still standing silent and melancholy in
the same place; and, as soon as they had got on board, they steamed
away from the Reef Island on their return to Calcutta. After this sad
parting nothing was ever seen or heard of our captive again. Alas,
poor Jack!"

The latter part of Dr. Mouat's book is devoted to as minute an account
of the Mincopies, their manners and customs, as his materials and
observations have enabled him to compile. As we have said, he regards
them as not quite so black as they have been painted.

Those who wish to pursue this subject further can consult Professor Owen's remarks on the Mincopies, founded on a skeleton sent to him by the author, and printed in his book, as is also an Appendix on the Zoology of the Andamans by Mr. Blyth, the Curator of the Calcutta Museum. In parting with Dr. Mouat we must not omit to mention that his book is furnished with a coloured chart of the Andaman archipelago, and several spirited engravings, of which, whilst some exhibit the Mincopies in all their unmitigated ugliness, others display their canoes, weapons, and implements, and these, strange to say, are marked by an amount of skilful and even elegant finish that would not be expected. Taken altogether, the book is an extremely interesting one, and such as could only be produced by a wise and benevolent man.

FIFTY YEARS BIOGRAPHICAL REMINISCENCES. By Lord William Pitt Lennox. 2 vols.

We have received this work at too late a period of the month to allow of our doing more than bestowing a mere glance at it. That glance, however, has shown us that it is full of life and interest, and abounds in amusing anecdote. We shall endeavour to do justice to it next month, but in the meantime, if our readers take our advice, they will pass many a pleasant hour over its diversified pages.

RESPECTABLE SINNERS. By Mrs. Brotherton, Author of "Arthur Brandon." 3 vols.

"Marry in haste, and repent at leisure," might be the motto of this clever novel. Pretty little Louisa Danbaye offends her father, the Colonel, by a runaway match with Captain Ashton, and in a short time is left a widow, with an infant daughter. After a while she contracts a second marriage with Mr. Grinston Hartley, a "respectable sinner" of the first order, who has broken the heart of his first wife, but finds his second quite able to hold her own against him. In course of time his only son falls in love with Helen Ashton, and another runaway match is the consequence. The young man is a weak, dissipated fellow, and makes his wife very wretched; but in the end he succeeds to the estates of which his father had tried to deprive him, and, as luckily, his morals improve with his circumstances, Helen is rendered happy at last. Beside the mother and daughter, who are the joint heroines of the story, and very charming ones too, we have a complete portrait gallery, evidently from life, of the class that gives name to the book. Among these "respectable sinners" appear the vindictive old Colonel Danbaye, and his still more detestable sister, Mrs. Nettlefold, who is a very pattern of pharisaic malignity, and devotes herself to the amiable task of preventing her brother ever being reconciled to his daughter. On the other side are some true-hearted people, as Montagu Ashton, who is a real friend to his widowed sister-in-law; Robert Hartley, the ill-used young brother of the magnate of Hartley Hall; and, though last not least, Tatt, the devoted nurse and humble friend of Mrs. Ashton in all her troubles. These and a few other characters are skilfully played off against one another, and the result is as agreeable a book as we have for a long time met with.

CHURCH AND CHAPEL. By the Author of "High Church," &c. 3 vols.

There is not so much controversy in this book as might be expected from its title, although the author claims the right, and exercises it too, of bringing in reflections, in which all may not concur, on various occasions. The story is of the wooing and winning of Amy Saville, a young lady who exhibits a rather undue amount of feminine fickleness, and so forms a good contrast to the two puritanical "strong-minded women," Susan Bayford and Dorcas Glade. Among the men, "Church" has for its representative a Puseyite rector, the Rev. Frederic Alland, and "Chapel" is equally well supported by the humble but stout-hearted minister of Vale Street Chapel, James Bayford; whilst meek Mr. Chark, an Evangelical vicar and Amy's guardian, labours hard to bring them to an agreement. But unluckily, Robert Bayford, who has returned from India a millionaire, and Mr. Alland, both have an affection for Amy, and worse still, she is by no means insensible to the merits of either; how the matter will end is cleverly kept in suspense until the very last, and we will not, by an imprudent revelation, deprive the reader of the pleasure of learning for himself how it is settled. Amy of course is "married and settled in life," but what name she thereby takes in lieu of Saville it is not our business to tell.

MAN; OR, THE OLD AND NEW PHILOSOPHY: Being Notes and Facts for the Curious, with Especial Reference to Recent Writers on the subject of the Origin of Man. By the Rev. B. W. Savile, M.A., Author of "Revelation and Science."

This is a very amusing *exposé* of the outrageous nonsense which is now attempted to be palmed on the world under the names of "advanced thought," "free handling," "enlightened Biblical criticism," &c. Professor Huxley, and Bishop Colenso, and the whole tribe of "Essayists and Reviewers," are "tossed and gored," as sturdy old Samuel Johnson used to say, and Man is traced from his origin to his end, in a way that will find more readers than a serious refutation of the absurdities of the new school would command. Not the least amusing part of the work is the last chapter, which gathers together a choice collection of epitaphs, of which take this specimen, "on a gallant soldier, who lies buried at Bristol."

> "I went and listed in the Tenth Hussars,
> And gallop'd with them to the bloody wars;
> 'Die for your Sovereign—for your Country die!'
> To earn such glory, feeling rather shy,
> Snug I slipped home. But Death soon sent me off,
> After a struggle with the whooping cough."

MISTRESS AND MAID. By the Author of "John Halifax, Gentleman," &c.

Having recently noticed this work, on its first appearance, we have now only to express our gratification at seeing it added to Messrs. Hurst and Blackett's cheap and excellent Standard Library.

THE REAL AND THE IDEAL. Poems by Arthur Llewellyn.

We have here a number of poems of fair promise, and hope some day again to meet the author when he has attained a more thorough mastery of the lyre. Probably we ought to say of the harp, as Wales, her mountains, and streams, her castles, her warriors, and her bards, are the frequent subject of his theme, and excite in him a glowing enthusiasm worthy of the native of such a land of glorious scenery and proud historic memories. One poem especially, entitled "Cambria," is well deserving of a permanent place in our literature.

# MILITARY OBITUARY.

General Sir John Hanbury, K.C.B., K.C.H., colonel of the 99th Regiment of Foot, expired on June 7th, at his house in Charles Street, Berkeley Square, after a protracted illness, in the 81st year of his age. This venerable officer entered the army in 1799, and had in his early career seen much active service. The late general served in the Egyptian campaign of 1801, as lieutenant in the 58th, including the actions of the 8th, 13th, and 21st of March, and has received the gold medal from the Grand Seignoir. He was the aide-de-camp to Major-General Warde in the campaign of 1808-9, and was present at Sir John Moore's retreat, and at the Battle of Corunna. He served with the 1st Guards at Walcheren, in 1809, and subsequently in the Peninsular campaign, including the retreat from Burgos, passage of the Bidassoa, and Adour, battles of Nivelle and Nive, investment of Bayonne, and repulse of the sortie. Sir John received the war medal with four clasps for Egypt, Corunna, Nivelle and Nive. Shortly after the late King William the Fourth's accession to the throne, he was, in consideration of his military services, made a Knight Commander of the Hanoverian Order of the Guelphs. He was appointed Colonel of the 99th Regiment, Oct. 6, 1851. His commissions bore date as follow :—Ensign, July 20, 1799; Lieut., Sept. 26, 1799; Capt., June 3, 1802; Lieut-Col., Dec. 20, 1812; Col., July 25, 1821; Major-Gen., July 22, 1830; Lieut-Gen., Nov. 23, 1841; and Gen., June 20, 1854.

Lieutenant-Colonel Flamank, formerly of the 51st Light Infantry, died on the 29th May, at Newbridge, hill, near Bath, aged 75. He served in the Peninsula with the 51st, from Jan., 1811, to the end of that war in 1814, including the battle of Fuentes d'Onor, second siege of Badajoz, covering the sieges of Ciudad Rodrigo and third siege of Badajoz, affair in front of Moresco, battle of Salmanca, retreat from Burgos, battles of Vittoria and the Pyrenees (30th and 31st July), passage of the Bidassoa, battles of Neville and St. Pé, and battle of Orthes. Served also the campaign of 1815, including the battle of Waterloo and capture of Cambray.

Major George Seymour Crole, late of the 23th Foot, died on the 13th June at Chatham, aged 63. •

Major W. S. Prenderleath, late of the 81st Regiment, died suddenly on the 5th June, at Ramsgate, aged 88.

Deputy-Inspector-General William Barry, M.D., on half-pay, died, 2nd June, at Bath, aged 80. He entered the service April, 1808, became Deputy-Inspector-General Nov. 1825, and was placed on half-pay, June, 1828. He served in the Peninsula from August, 1811, and again from August, 1813, to the end of that war in 1814, and has the war medal with four clasps for Busaco, Nivelle, Orthes, and Toulouse. Also the campaign of 1815, including the battle of Waterloo (medal).

Captain W. S. Moorsom, formerly of the 52nd Foot, died 3rd June, at Great George Street, Westminster.
The deceased, who was in his 58th year, was the youngest son of the late Admiral Sir Robert Moorsom. He entered the Royal Military College at Sandhurst in 1819, and quickly rose to the first position among the cadets of that establishment. He joined the 79th Regiment in Ireland in 1823; and while following the ordinary duties of the garrison in Dublin, found time to make a trigonometrical survey of the whole of that city and surrounding district, extending over an area of about 150 square miles. This survey was the one used in the Quarter-master-General's Office at the Horse Guards, until the Ordnance survey of Ireland superseded it. This work brought Mr. Moorsom under the notice of the Adjutant-General, Sir H. Torrens, who offered him a lieutenancy by purchase in the 7th Fusiliers. In this distinguished regiment Lieutenant Moorsom served as adjutant under the command

of Lord Frederick Fitzclarence, until his promotion to an unattached company. Shortly afterwards Captain Moorsom was brought on full pay in the 52nd Light Infantry, when stationed in Nova Scotia. In 1828 Captain Moorsom became known to the public by his work, ' Letters from Nova Scotia.' At the same time his industry in exploring the province, and particularly his survey of the harbour and environs of Halifax, which still remains as the best plan for reference in the Quartermaster-General's office at the Horse Guards, led to his being appointed by Major-General Sir P. Maitland to be Acting Quartermaster-General of the division upon the retirement of Lieutenant-Colonel Beresford. His industry again showed itself by the office being soon supplied with routes and copious notes of capability of supply and maintenance of troops over every part of the provinces of Nova Scotia and New Brunswick. Domestic circumstances now led to Captain Moorsom's return to England, and finding that promotion to an unattached majority by purchase was denied him, notwithstanding he had been selected to fill a post involving the duties of a lieutenant-colonel, he quitted the Army, and soon afterwards, under the advice and with the assistance of the late Mr. Robert Stephenson, entered upon the profession of a civil engineer. In this profession Captain Moorsom is known by many important public works, which it would be out of place to refer to here. We may just allude, however, to his first great work, the Birmingham and Gloucester Railway, because in this undertaking he first achieved the previously unattempted task of carrying a train up a steep incline of no less than 1 in 37. The work was not considered practicable by Brunel, Locke, and the other engineers of the time. Captain Moorsom accomplished it by taking the railway over the Lickey, though he had to get his engines made in America, the English engine-makers at that time refusing to make such engines as were required for the purpose. His last great engineering work was his survey, made for the Government, of a line of railway between Colombo and Candy, in Ceylon, particularly referred to in the "Transactions of the Royal Engineers" of 1859. In 1860 Captain Moorsom, though suffering from illness, edited, by the desire of the officers of his late regiment, the "Historical Record of the 52nd Light Infantry"—a record which, in numerous reviews, has been held to be a perfect example of what such a work ought to be. The death in action, at Lucknow, in 1858, of his eldest son, William Robert, Quartermaster-General on the Staff of Sir H. Havelock, and subsequently of Sir James Outram, and other domestic afflictions, had produced a marked effect on Captain Moorsom's general health, and seemed to lay the seeds of a disease which eventually proved fatal on the 3rd inst. Captain Moorsom leaves three sons in the Army, one of whom, Captain C. Moorsom, 30th Regiment, was severely wounded at the final assault of Sebastopol.

———

Captain James Barton, of the 65th Regiment, died on the 12th of Feb., on board the Ida Zeigler on his passage from New Zealand. He entered the service in June, 1845, and served at Taranaki during the Maori war of 1860-61.

———

Captain Charles D. Bevan, Royal Artillery, died on the 8th June, at Twickenham, aged 27. He entered the service in February 1855; was promoted to 2nd Lieut., Dec., 1854, and to his late rank of 2nd Capt. in March, 1862. He served at the siege and fall of Sebastopol in 1855 (medal and clasp, and Turkish medal).

———

Captain James Hannay, late of the 8th Foot; died on the 4th June, suddenly, at Ballylough, county Antrim.

Captain J. A. Lane, of the 50th Regiment, died on the 5th May, at Colombo. He entered the service in February, 1849.

Captain the Hon. H. J. Liddell, formerly of the 15th Regiment, died on the 4th June, at Ravensworth Castle, aged 38.

Captain T. A. Macreight, of the 17th Regiment, died on the 14th of May, after a few days' illness, at Quebec, Canada, aged 28. He entered the service in April, 1854, and served at the siege of Sebastopol from June, 1855, and at the assault on the Redan on the 8th Sept.; also at the bombardment and surrender of Kinburn (medal and clasp, and Turkish medal).

Captain Arthur Watson Palmer, late of the 5th Foot, died on the 5th June, at Carlton Park, Northamptonshire, aged 37.

Captain E. A. Stotherd, of the 60th Rifles was drowned on the 27th of April, from the wreck of the Anglo-Saxon near the Cape Race, Newfoundland, aged 30. He entered the service in Feb. 1851. He served with 93rd Highlanders the Eastern campaign of 1854 and to the 14th July, 1855, including the battles of Alma and Balaklava, siege of Sebastopol, and expedition to Kertch (medal with three clasps, and Turkish medal).

William Stothert, Esq., formerly Captain in the Coldstreams died at Edinburgh on April 23. The deceased officer served during the Peninsular war, and was wounded and taken prisoner at Fuentes d'Onoro. In a recent controversy between a French author and General Napier, as to the truth of a relation with reference to the above battle, Captain Stothert was able entirely to corroborate the General's history, having been a subaltern engaged on the spot, and in the operation in question. The present Empress of the French is a blood relation of the family: her Majesty's brother bearing the names of Robert Stothert Kirkpatrick.

Captain W. Wynne, of the Coldstream Guards, died on the 22nd May in London, aged 32. He entered the service in Feb. 1856.

Lieutenant Denzil Ede, on half-pay, Royal Marines, and a justice of the peace for the county of Essex, died at Billericay on the 17th June, aged 83. He entered the service June, 1798; became Lieutenant, August, 1804, and was placed on half-pay, January, 1816.

Lieutenant Jesse Hilder, late 15th Regiment, died at Milton-next-Gravesend, on the 11th June, aged 81.

Lieutenant Charles James Holbrook, 95th Regiment, died on the 13th April, from a fall from his horse. He entered the service May, 1855; and became Lieut., Nov., 1857. He served in 1858 at the siege and capture of Awah and Kotah, battle of Kota ka Serai, general action resulting in the capture of Gwalior, siege and capture of Pouree (medal and clasp).

Captain Richard Hart, on half-pay of the 6th Foot, died latterly, at Hythe, Kent, aged 81. He entered the service, March 27, 1805, became Lieut. April 1805, Capt. March, 1825, and retired on half-pay in May, 1825. He served with the 78th at the capture of Java, in 1811, for which he received the war medal with one clasp.

Lieutenant Charles James Dundas Napier, Royal Marine Light Infantry, died at Bridgend, Glamorgan, on the 8th June, aged 30. He entered the service as 2nd Lieut. in June, 1853, was promoted to his late rank of 1st Lieut. in July, 1854. He served in the Eastern campaign of 1854, with the R.M. Brigade, including the battle of Balaklava; attached to the Light Division in the trenches, and at the battle of Inkerman, with the combined forces before Sebastopol during the siege in 1855, and with the expedition to Kertch, and occupation of Yenikale (medal and three clasps, Sardinian medal, 5th class of Medjidie and Turkish medal). Served on the China expedition of 1857-59, including blockade of the Canton river, the landing before and capture of the city. Also campaign of 1860, as aide-de-camp to Sir Robert Napier, including the action of Sinho, the taking of Tonghoo, storm and capture of the North Taku Forts, and subsequent operation (medal and three clasps).

## NAVAL OBITUARY.

Captain Henry Benjamin Wyatt, 1855, on the Retired H I K. List died at Ryde, Isle of Wight, on the 11th of June, aged 77. He entered the Navy, 1803, as Midshipman of the Unicorn, and served in her boats at the capture of the French privateer Tape-à-Bord, in 1805. Served on shore with the Army at the storming of Monte Video, and assault upon Buenos Ayres, 1807; and took an active part at the attack on the French fleet in Aix Roads, 1809. He was made a Lieutenant on the 3rd July, 1809; and served in Walcheren expedition as Lieutenant of the Magnet. He afterwards joined the Ruby, and saw much service against the Danish gunboats in the Baltic and Belts; and was made Commander, 18th Sept., 1815, and had not been employed subsequently.

Captain Edward Hooper Senhouse, 1860, on the Retired H.I.K. List died at Worthing, Barbadoes, on the 22nd May from paralysis aged 76. He entered the Navy, in 1800, and, after serving in the West Indies, was made a Lieutenant, May 23, 1807. He commanded a gunboat at the siege of Flushing, and was actively employed till the close of the war. He was made a Commander in 1843; and in 1860 was retired with the rank of Captain.

Commander William Hoghton, on the P Retired List died at Northcote, near Melbourne, on the 27th March, aged 73.

Paymaster-in-Chief Edward Thorne, 1862, died at Southsea on the 5th inst. This officer served as Clerk of the Eclair, and was severely wounded in the boats at an attack upon a French convoy protected by two gunboats at Languilla in 1812; and again served as a volunteer at the same place and at Port d'Auzo in 1813. He was not made a Purser, however, until 17th of Aug., 1829; and was retired as Paymaster-in-Chief in Jan., 1862.

Surgeon James Niven, M.D., serving on board the Pembroke, at Harwich, died on the 10th June, after a short illness, aged 43.

Paymaster Robert Scott, 1806, on the Retired List, died at Devonport on the 5th June, aged 80. This officer served as Midshipman of the Audacious in the action off Algesiras, in 1808; and was Purser of the Cornwallis, and his services were officially mentioned at the capture of Amboyna. He served in the same ship at the reduction of the islands of France and Java in 1810.

# STATIONS OF THE ROYAL NAVY IN COMMISSION.

### (*Corrected to 27th June*)

### *With the Dates of Commission of the officers in Command.*

Aboukir, 86, sc. Commodore P. Cracroft, C.B., 1854, Jamaica

Acorn, Hosp. Ship, Mast.-Com. H. Hutchings, 1861, Shanghae

Active, 20, Training Ship, for Naval Reserve, Com. T. Heard, 1860, Sunderland

Adder, st. ves., Second Master W. Blakey (acting) Chatham

Adventure, 2, sc. troop ship, Com. T. B. Lethbridge, 1857, particular service

Ajax, 60, sc. Cap. M. de Courcy, 1862, Coast Guard Kingstown.

Alacrity, 4, sc. Com. J. K. E. Baird, 1857, Mediterranean (ordered home)

Alecto, st. ves., 5, Com. W. H. Blake, 1860, S.E. Coast of America.

Alert, 17, sc., Com. H. Majendie, 1854, Channel Squadron

Algerine, 1, sc. gunboat, Lieut.-Com. A. B. Blane, 1856, China.

Antelope, 3, st. ves., Lieut.-Com. C. O. D. Allingham, 1856, Coast of Africa

Archer, 13, sc. Capt. J. Bythesea, V.C. (1861) Coast of Africa

Ardent, 5, steam vessel, Capt. J. E. Parish, 1857, S.E. Coast of America. (Ordered home.)

Argus, 6, steam ves. Com. L. J. Moore, 1860, China

Ariadne, 26, sc. Capt. E. W. Vansittart, 1856, North America and West Indies

Ariel, 9, sc. Com. W. C. Chapman, 1855, Cape of Good Hope

Asia, 84, Rear Admiral George Elliot, Capt. H. Broadhead, 1855, Portsmouth

Bacchante, 51, sc. Capt. D. McL. Mackenzie, 1859, Pacific

Barracouta, 6, st. ves. Com. G. J. Malcolm, 1859, North America and West Indies

Barrosa, 21, sc, Captain W. M. Dowell, 1858, East Indies and China

Beagle, 4, sc. Com E. Hay, 1858, East Indies, ordered home.

Black Prince, 40, sc, Capt. J. F. B. Wainwright, (1853) Channel Squadron

Blenheim, 60, sc. Capt. Lord F. H. Kerr, 1852, Coast Guard, Milford

Bloodhound, 3, st., ves. Lieut.-Com. J. E. Stokes, 1858, Coast of Africa

Boscawen, 20, Com. H. Campion, 1855, Southampton Training Ship

Bouncer, 2, sc. gunboat, ———— China

Brilliant, 16, Com. Grey Skipwith, 1848, Naval Reserve Drill Ship, Dundee

Brisk, 16, sc. Capt J. P. Luce, 1858, West Coast of Africa

Britannia, 6, Cadet Training Ship, Captain R. A. Powell, C.B., 1855, Portland

Buzzard, st. ves., 6, Com. T. H. M. Martin, 1859, North America and West Indies

Cambridge, gunnery Ship, Capt. C. J. F. Ewart, C.B., 1855, Devonport

Cameleon, 17, sc. Com. E. Hardinge, 1856, Pacific

Canopus, Naval Barrack, Capt. C. H. May, (1859) Devonport

Caradoc, sc., 2, Lieut.-Com. E. H Wilkinson, 1856, Mediterranean

Castor, 22, Com. J. Palmer, 1855, Naval Reserve Drill Ship. Shields

Centaur, 6 steam ves. Com. J. Z. Creasy (acting) 1862. China, ordered home

Challenger, 22, sc. J. J. Kennedy, C.B., 1856, North America and W. Indies

Chanticleer, 17, sc. Com. C Stirling, 1856, Mediterranean

Charybdis, 21, sc. Capt. R. W. Turnour, 1857, Pacific

Clio, 22, sc. Captain T. Miller, 1855, Pacific. (Ordered home.)

Cockatrice, 2, sc. Lieut. Com. R. M. Gibson (1855), Mediterranean

Colossus, 80, sc. Captain E. S. Sotheby, C.B., 1855, Coast Guard, Portland Roads

Columbine, 4, sc., Com. T. Le H. Ward, 1861 Channel Squadron

Coquette, 4, sc., Commander J. H. I. Alexander, 1860, East Indies and China

Cormorant, 4, sc. Com. C. M. Buckle (1860) East Indies and China

Cornwallis, 60, sc. Capt. J. N. Strange, 1854, Coast Guard, Hull

Cossack, 20, sc., Capt. W. R. Rolland, 1857, Mediterranean

Cumberland, 24, Capt. W. K. Hall, C.B., 1858, Sheerness

Curacoa, 26, Commodore Sir W. Wiseman, Bart., Australia

Curlew, 9, sc. Com. J. S. Hudson, 1861, S. E. Coast of America

Cygnet, 5, sc. Com. H. P. De Kantzow (1863) North America and West Indies

Dædalus, 16, Com. W. H. Fenwick, 1856, Naval Reserve Drill ship, Bristol

Dart, 5, sc. Com. F. W. Richards, (1860) Coast of Africa

Dasher, 3, st. ves., Com. P. De Sausmarez, 1854 Channel Islands

Dauntless, 31, sc. Capt. J. B. Dickson, 1854, Coast Guard, Southampton

Dee, 2, st. Store Ship, Mas.-Com. G. Raymond, 1858, Woolwich

Defence, 18, sc. Capt. A. Phillimore, 1856, Channel Squadron

Desperate, 7, sc. Com. A. T. Thrupp, 1858, North America and West Indies

Devastation, 6, screw, Com J. W. Pike, 1860, Pacific

Doterel, 2, sc. gunboat, Lieut. Com. W. F. Johnson, 1853, South America

Dromedary, sc. store-ship, Mast.-Com. A. Brown, (1854), particular service

Duke of Wellington, 131, Capt. J. Seccombe, 1859, Portsmouth

Eagle, 50, Commander J. W. Whyte, 1855, Naval Reserve Drill Ship, Liverpool

Eclipse, 4, sc., Com. R. C. Mayne, 1861, Australia

Edgar, 71, sc. Rr. Adml. S. C. Dacres, C.B., Capt. G. T. P. Horby, 1852, Channel Squadron

Edinburgh, 60, sc. Captain C. F. Schomberg, 1851 Coast Guard, Queen's Ferry, N.B.

Egmont, receiving ship, Capt. F. A. B. Craufurd, 1856, Rio de Janeiro

Emerald, 35, sc. Captain A. Cumming, 1854, Channel Squadron

Enchantress, 1, st. Admiralty Yacht, Mas.-Com. J. E. Petley, 1844, Portsmouth

Encounter, 14, sc. Captain R. Dew, CB., 1858, East Indies and China, (ordered home)

Esk, 21, Capt. J. F. C. Hamilton, 1858, Australia

Espoir, 5, sc. Com. S. Douglas, 1858, C. of Africa

Euryalus, 35, sc. Vice Adml A. L. Kuper, C.B., Captain J. J. S. Josling, 1861, China

Excellent, gunnery ship, Capt. A. C. Key, C.B., 1860, Portsmouth

Fairy, sc. yacht, tender to Victoria and Albert Portsmouth, Mast.-Com. D. N. Welch, 18

Firefly, 5, st. ves. Com. A. L. Mansell, 1855, Mediterranean

Fisgard, 42, Commodore Sir. F. W. E. Nicolson, Bart C.B Woolwich

Flamer, sc. gunboat, Lieut. Com G. S. Bosanquet, 1855, China

Formidable, 26, Vice-Adml. Sir G. R. Lambert, K· B·, Capt. J. Fulford, Sheerness

Forte, 39, sc. Rear Admiral R. L. Warren, Capt. A. Mellersh, 1856, S E. Coast of America

Forward, 2, sc Lieut Com. the Hon. H. D. Lascelles, 1855, Pacific

Fox, sc. store-ship, Mast.-Com. J. C. Pullen, (1844) particular service

Foxhound, 4. sc. Com W. H. 'Anderson, 1859, Mediterranean

Galatea, 26, sc. Cap. R. Maguire, 1855, North America, and West Indies

Geyser, 5. st. ves. Com. M R. Pechell, (1856), Channel Squadron

Gorgon, 6, st. ves. Com. J. C Wilson, 1861, Cape of Good Hope. ordered home

Grappler, 2, sc. Lieut. Com. E. H. Verney, 1858, Pacific

Grasshopper, sc gunboat, Lt. Com. F. W. Bennett, 1854, East Indies and China

Greyhound, 17, sc. Com. H D Hickley, 1858, North America and West Indies

Griffon, 5, sc. Com. J. L. Perry, 1858, Coast of Africa

Hardy, 3, sc. gunbt, Lieut. Com. A. G. Bogle, 1855, East Indies and China

Harrier, 17, sc. Com. F. W. Sullivan, 1859, Australia

Hastings, 60, sc. Rear-Admiral Sir L. T. Jones, K.C.B., Capt. C. F. A. Shadwell, C.B., 1853, Queenstown

Havock, 2. sc. gunbt, Lieut. Com. G. Poole, 1858 East Indies and China

Hawke, 60. sc. Capt. E. Codd, 1851, Coast Guard Queenstown

Hecate, 6, st. vessel, Capt. G. H. Richards, 1854, passage home,

Hesper, 4, sc. store ship, Mast. Com. A. F. Boxer, 1854, East Indies and China

Hibernia, rec. ship, Rear Adm. H. J. Austin, C.B., Com. R. B. Harvey, 1859, Malta

Himalaya, 6, sc. troop ship, Captain E. Lacy, (1862), Devonport.

Hogue, 60, sc. Captain A. Farquhar, 1849, Coast Guard. Greenock

Hornet, 17, sc. Com. J. Dayman, 1858, East Indies

Icarus, 11, sc. Com. N Salmon, V.C. 1858, Mediterranean

Hydra, 6, st. ves , Lieut. G. R Wilkinson, 1854, Woolwich

Immortalité, 51, sc. Capt. G. Hancock, 1855, North America and West Indies

Implacable, 24, Com. S. B. Dolling, 1856, Training Ship, Devonport

Impregnable, 78, Capt. F. S. Tremlett (1863) Training Ship, Devonport

Indus, Rear Admiral T M. C. Symonds. C.B., Capt. W. Edmonstone, C.B., 1853, Devonport

Industry, 2, sc. store ship, Mast. Com. E. C. T. Youel, 1850, particular service

Insolent, 2, sc. gunbt. Lieut. Com G. Parsons, 1864, East Indies and China

Investigator, 2, st. ves. Lieut. Com. P. R. Sharpe, 1854, Coast of Africa

Jackal, 4, st. vessel, Lieut. Com. E. F. Lodder 1854, Coast of Scotland

Jaseur, 5, sc Com. W. J. H. Grubbe (1861) Coast of Africa

Jason, 21, sc. Capt. E. P B. Von Donop, 1855, North America, W Indies

Landrail, 5, sc. Com. W. Arthur, 1861, N America and West Indies

Leander, 39, sc. Commodore T. Harvey, Pacific

Lizard, 3, st. ves. Lieut.-Com. H J. Challis, 1854, Sheerness

Lee, 5, sc. Com. C. E. Foot (act.) 1860, Coast of Africa

Leopard, 18. st. vessel, Capt. C. T. Leckie, 1858, East Indies and China

Leven, 1, screw gun vessel, Lt. Com. H. P. Knevitt (1855) East Indies and China

Liffey, 39, sc Captain G. Parker, 1854, Mediterranean

Lily 4, sc., Com. H. Harvey, 1857, North America and West Indies

Liverpool, 35, sc., Capt. R. Lambert, 1855, Channel Squadron.

Mæander, 10, Cap. F. L Barnard, 1855, Ascension

Magicienne, 16, st. ves. Capt. W. Armytage, 1860, Mediterranean

Majestic, 80, sc. Capt. E. A. Inglefield, 1853, Coast guard, Rock Ferry, Liverpool

Malacca, 17, st. ves. Cap. G. J. Napier, (1856), Mediterranean

Manilla, sc. Mast. Com. H. W. Burnett, 1856, East Indies and China

Marlborough, 121, sc. Vice Adml. R. Smart, K H., Captain C. Fellowes, 1858, Mediterranean

Medea, 6, st ves Com. D'Arcy S. Preston, (1860) North America and West Indies

Medina, 4, st. ves. Capt. T. A. B. Spratt, C.B. 1855, Mediterranean

Medusa, 2, st. ves . Mas.-Com. J. Loane, 1846, particular service

Meeanee, 60, Captain G. Wodehouse, 1854, Mediterranean.

Megæra, 6, sc. Com. E. Madden, (1858)

Miranda, 15, sc Capt. R. Jenkins, 1857, Australia

Mulle sc. Com. C. H. Simpson 1860, Coast of At. 5æ

Mutine, 17, sc. Com. W. Graham, 1858, Pacific.

Naiad, 6, store ship, Mas. Com. G. Reid, 1850, Callao

Narcissus, 39 sc. Rear Adm. Sir B. W. Walker, Bart , K C.B , Capt. J. G. Bickford, (1860) Cape of Good Hope

Nereus, 6, store depot. Mast. Com. C. R. P. Forbes, 1848, Valparaiso

Nile, 78, sc. Vice-Adml. Sir A. Milne, K.C.B.. Capt. E. K. Barnard, 1859, North America and West Indies

Nimble, 5, sc. Com. J. D'Arcy, 1854, North America and West Indies

Odin, 16, steam vessel, Commodore Lord J. Hay, C.B. 1854, East Indies, ordered home

Orestes, 21, sc. Capt. A. H. Gardner, 1856, Cape of Good Hope

Orontes, 3, sc., troop ship, Capt. H. W. Hire, 1862, Portsmouth

Orlando, 46, sc. Capt. G G. Randolph, 1854 Mediterranean

Osborne, st vessel, Mas Com. G. H. K. Bower, 1842, Portsmouth

Osprey, sc , 4, Com. A. J. Innes 1861, East Indies and China

Pandora, 5, sc. Com. W. F. Ruxton, 1861, Coast of Africa

Pantaloon, 11, sc. Com. F. Purvis, (1860), East Indies.

Pearl, 21, sc. Capt J. Borlase, C.B 1855, East Indies and China

Pelican, 17, sc. Com. P. Brock, 1859, Mediterranean.

Pembroke, 60, Commodore A. P. Ryder, 1848, C B., Capt. J. O. Johnson, 1856, Coast Guard Harwich

Perseus, 17, sc , Com. A. J. Kingston, 1860, China

Peterel, 11, sc. Com G. W Watson, 1858, North America and West Indies

Phaeton, 39, sc Capt E. Tatham, 1854, North America and West Indies

Philomel, 5, sc. Com. L. Wildman, (1858) Coast of Africa

Phœbe, 35, sc., Captain T D. A. Fortescue, 1857, Mediterranean.

Pigmy, 5, st. v. Master Com. W. W. Vine, 1861 Portsmouth.

Pioneer, 6, sc. Com. F. C. B. Robinson (acting), Australia, ordered home

Plover, 5, sc. Com. the Hon. A. L. Corry, 1859, North America and West Indies

President, 50, Com W. Mould, 1855, Naval Reserve Drill Ship, London.

Princess Charlotte, 12, Captain M. S. Nolloth, 1854, Hong Kong

Prserin, 2, Capt. E. Ommanney, 1846, Lieut. Com. Hon. J. B. Vivian, 1856, Gibraltar.

Psyche, 2, st. vessel, Lieut.-Com. R. Sterne 1854, Mediterranean

Pylades, 21, sc. Capt. A. W. A. Hood, North America and West Indies

Queen, 74, sc. Captain C. F. Hillyar, 1852, Mediterranean

Racchorse, 4, sc. Com. C. R. F. Boxer, 1860, China

Raccoon, 22, sc. Capt. Count Gleichen, (1859), particular service

Ranger, 5, Com. H. R. Wratislaw, 1858, West Coast of Africa

Rapid, 11, sc. Com. C. T. Jago (1860) C. of Africa

Rattler, 17, sc. Com. E. H. Howard, 1857, East Indies and China

Rattlesnake, 21, sc. Commodore A. P. E Wilmot, C.B., Coast of Africa

Renard, 4, sc. Com. C. J. Rowley, 1861, Sheerness

Resistance, 18, sc. Capt. W. C. Chamberlain, 1856, Channel Squadron,

Revenge, 73, sc. Rr.-Ad. H. R. Yelverton, C.B., Capt. Hon. F. A. Foley, 1860, Mediterranean

Rifleman, 8, sur.-ves. Mast. Commander J. W. Reed, 1857, China Seas

Rinaldo, 17, sc. Com. J. A B. Dunlop, 1860, 1858, North America and West Indies

Ringdova, 4, sc. Com. R. A. O. Brown, 1857, East Indies and China

Rosario, 11, sc. Com. H. D. Grant, 1859, North America and West Indies

Royal Adelaide, 26, Vice-Adml. Sir H. Stewart, K.C.B. Capt. C. Vesey, 1860, Devonport

Royal Oak, 34, sc. Capt. F. A. Campbell, 1854, Channel Squadron

Russell, 60, sc. Capt. S. Grenfell, (1860) Coast Guard Falmouth

Satellite, 21, sa. Capt. S. S. L. Crofton, 1856, S. E. Coast of America

Saturn, Captain W. Loring, C.B., 1846, Pembroke

Scout, 21, sc. Capt. J. Corbett, 1857, East Indies and China, ordered home

Seringapatam, Receiving Ship, Capt. J. H. Cockburn, 1856, Cape of Good Hope

Severn, 35, sc. Commodore F. B. Montrésor, East Indies

Shannon, 35, sc. Capt. O. J. Jones, (1855) N. America and West Indies

Sheldrake, 2, sc. gunboat, Lieut.-Com. John Nott, 1854, S. E. Coast of America

Shearwater, 11, sa. Com. R. G. Douglas, 1860, Pacific.

Slaney, 1, sc. gunboat, Lieut.-Com. W. F. Lee, 1855, East Indies and China

Sparrow, 5, sc. Com. Hon. E. G. L. Cochrane, 1860, C. of Africa.

Sphinx, 6, st. ves. Com. T. M. Jones, 1859, East Indies and China, passage home

Spider, 3, sc. gunboat, Lieut. Com. E. A. T. Stubbs, 1854, South America

St. George, 86, sc. Capt. the Hon. F. Egerton, 1854, Mediterranean

Staunch, 1, sc., Lieut.-Com. J. S. Keats 1860, China

St. Vincent, 26, Com. M. Lowther, 1859, Portsmouth

Steady, 5, sc. Com. Fred Harvey, 1861, North America and West Indies

Stromboli, 6, sc. Com. A. R. Heury, 1857, S.E Coast of America

Styx, 6, sc. Com. the Hon. W. J. Ward, 1856, North America and West Indies

Supply, 2 sa. store ship. Mast. Com. C. Bawden, 1849, particular service

Surprise, 4, sc. Com. W. H. Whyte, 1856, Mediterranean

Sutlej, 35, sc., Rear-Adml. J. Kingcome, Captain M. Connolly, 1858, Pacific

Swallow, 9, sur. ves. Mast. Com. E. Wilds, 1855, East Indies

Tartar, 20, sc. Capt. J. M. Hayes, 1855, Pacific

Terror, 16, Capt. F. H. H. Glasse, C B. 1844, Bermuda

Topaze, 39, sc. Commodore the Hon. J. W. S. Spencer, (1854) Pacific

Torch, 5, sc. Com. F. H. Smith, 1858, Coast of Africa

Trafalgar, 70, sc. Capt. T. H. Mason, 1849, Mediterranean.

Tribune, 23, sc. Capt. Viscount Gilford, 1852 Pacific

Trident, 6, st. Com. C. J. Balfour, 1859, Gibraltar

Trincomalee, 16, Com. E. Field, (1859) Naval Reserve drill Ship, Hartlepool

Triton, sc., 3, Lieut.-Com. E. V. Kerby, 1854, S.E. Coast of America

Valorous, 16, st. ves., Capt. C. C. Forsyth, 1857, Cape of Good Hope

Vesuvius, 6, sc. Capt. R. V. Hamilton, 1862, North America and West Indies

Victoria and Albert, steam yacht, Capt. H.S.H. Prince Leiningen, (1860,) Portsmouth

Victory, 12, Vice Adml. Sir Michael Seymour, G C B. Captain Francis Scott, C.B., (1849) Portsmouth

Vigilant, 4, sc., Com. W. R. Hobson, 1859, East Indies and China

Vindictive, store ship. Mas.-Com. W. F. Lew 1857, Fernando Po

Virago, 6, st ves. Com. W. G. H. Johnstone, 185 particular service

Vivid, 2, st. v. Mast Com. H. W. Allen, 1842, particular service.

Vulcan, 6, sc. troop ship, Capt. A. C. Strode, 1863 East Indies and China, ordered home

Wanderer, 4, sc. Com. M. C. Seymour, 1859 Mediterranean

Warrior, 40, sc. Capt. the Hon. A. A. Cochrane, C.B. 1854, Channel Squadron Portsmouth

Weazel, 2, sc. gunboat, Lieut. Com. H. G. Hale, 1855, East Indies and China

Wellesley, 72, Captain Superintendent E. G. Fanshawe, 1845, Chatham

Weser, 6, st. v. Com. A. H. J. Johnstone, 1859, Mediterranean

Winchester, 12, Drill Ship for Naval Reserve, Com. C. J. Balfour. 1846, Aberdeen

Wrangler, 4, sc. Com. H. H. Beamish, 1858, Coast of Africa

Wye, 2, sc. store-ship. Mast. Com. V. G. Roberts, 1844, Sheerness

Zebra, 17, sc., Com. A. H. Hoskins, 1858, Coast of Africa

## STATIONS OF THE BRITISH ARMY.

### (*Corrected up to 26th June, 1863, inclusive.*)

[Where two places are mentioned, the last-named is that at which the Depot is stationed.]

1st Life Guards—Regent's Park
2nd do.—Hyde Park
Royal Horse Guards—Aldershot
1st Dragoon Guards—Madras, Canterbury
2nd do.—Bengal, Canterbury
3rd do.—Bombay, Canterbury
4th do.—Curragh
5th do.—Curragh
6th do.—Aldershot
7th do.—Bengal, Canterbury
1st Dragoons—Birmingham
2nd do.—Birmingham
3rd Hussars—Piershill
4th do.—Newbridge
5th Lancers—Aldershot
6th Dragoons—Bombay, Maidstone
7th Hussars—Bengal, Maidstone
8th do.—Bengal, Canterbury
9th Lancers—Brighton
10th Hussars—Newbridge
11th Hussars—Dublin
12th Lancers—Aldershot
13th Hussars—Aldershot
14th do.—Manchester
15th Hussars—Dublin
16th Lancers—York
17th do.—Madras, Maidstone
18th Hussars—Aldershot
19th do.—Bengal, Maidstone
20th do.—Bengal, Canterbury
21st do.—Bengal, Canterbury
Military Train (1st bat.)—Woolwich
Do (2nd bat.)—Aldershot
Do. (3rd bat.)—Canada
Do. (4th bat.)—Woolwich
Do. (5th bat.)—Aldershot
Do. (6th bat.)—Curragh
Grenadier Guards (1st bat.)—Canada
Do (2nd bat.)—Wellington Barracks
Do. (3rd bat.)—St. George's Barracks
Coldstream Guards (1st bat.)—Portman Street
Do. (2nd bat.)—Windsor
Scots Fus. Guards (1st bat.)—Aldershot
Fus. (2nd bat.)—Canada
1st Foot (1st.)—Madras, Colchester
Do. (2nd bat.)—Aldershot, Colchester
2nd do. (1st bat.)—Plymouth, Walmer
Do. (2nd bat.)—Corfu, Walmer
3rd do. (1st bat.)—Aldershot, Limerick
Do. (2nd bat.)—Gibraltar, Limerick
4th do. (1st bat.)—Bombay, Chatham
Do. (2nd bat.)—Corfu, Chatham
5th do (1st bat.)—Shorncliffe, Colchester
Do. (2nd bat.)—Cape of Gd. Hope, Colchester
6th do. (1st bat.)—Aldershot, Colchester
Do. (2nd bat.)—Corfu, Colchester
7th do. (1st bat.)—Bengal, Walmer
Do. (2nd bat.)—Gibraltar, Walmer
8th do. (1st bat.)—Sheffield, Templemore
Do. (2nd bat.)—Gibraltar, Templemore
9th do. (1st bat.)—Cephalonia, Limerick
Do. (2nd bat.)—Corfu, Limerick
10th do. (1st bat.)—Dublin, Preston
Do. (2nd bat.)—Cape of Gd. Hope, Preston
11th do. (1st bat.)—Curragh, Fermoy
Do. (2nd bat.) C. of Good Hope, Fermoy
12th do. (1st bat.)—N. S. Wales, Chatham
Do. (2nd bat.)—Curragh, Chatham
13th do. (1st bat.)—Bengal, Fermoy
Do. (2nd bat.)—Mauritius, Fermoy
14th do. (1st bat.)—Jamaica, Fermoy.
Do. (2nd bat.)—New Zealand, Fermoy
15th do. (1st bat.)—N. Brunswick, Pembroke
15th do. (2nd bat.)—Malta, Pembroke

16th do. (1st bat.)—Canada, Templemore
Do. (2nd bat.)—Nova Scotia, Templemore
17th do. (1st bat.)—Canada, Limerick
Do. (2nd bat.) Nova Scotia, Limerick
18th do. (1st bat.)—Madras, Buttevant.
Do. (2nd bat.)—New Zealand, Buttevant
19th do. (1st bat.)—Bengal, Chatham
Do. (2nd bat.)—Dublin, Chatham
20th do. (1st bat.)—Bengal, Chatham
Do. (2nd bat.)—Portsmouth, Chatham
21st do. (1st bat.)—Barbadoes, Birr
Do. (2nd bat.)—Curragh, Birr
22nd do. (1st bat.)—Malta, Parkhurst
Do. (2nd bat.)—Malta, Parkhurst
23rd do. (1st bat.)—Bengal, Walmer
Do. (2nd bat.)—Malta, Walmer
24th do. (1st bat.)—Aldershot, Cork
Do. (2nd bat.)—Mauritius, Cork
25th do. (1st bat.)—Malta, Athlone
Do. (2nd bat.)—Edinburgh, Athlone
26th do.—Gosport, Belfast
27th do.—Bengal, Cork
28th do.—Bombay, Fermoy
29th do.—Curragh, Preston
30th do.—Canada, Parkhurst
31st do.—China, Chatham
32nd do.—Curragh, Preston
33rd do.—Bombay, Fermoy
34th do.—Bengal, Colchester
35th do.—Bengal, Chatham
36th do.—Dublin, Athlone
37th do.—Aldershot, Pembroke
38th do.—Bengal, Colchester
39th do.—Bermuda, Templemore
40th do.—New Zealand, Birr
41st do.—Glasgow, Preston
42nd do.—Bengal, Sterling
43rd do.—Bengal, Chatham.
44th do.—Bombay, Colchester
45th do.—Curragh, Parkhurst
46th do.—Bengal, Buttevant
47th do.—Canada, Athlone
48th do.—Bengal, Cork
49th do.—Manchester, Belfast
50th do.—Ceylon, Parkhurst
51st do.—Bengal, Chatham
52nd do.—Bengal, Chatham
53rd do.—Portsmouth, Birr
54th do.—Bengal, Colchester
55th do.—Portsmouth, Preston
56th do.—Bombay, Colchester
57th do.—New Zealand, Cork
58th do—Dublin, Birr
59th do.—Aldershot, Preston
60th do. (1st bat.)—Tower, Winchester
Do. (2nd bat.)—Aldershot, Winchester
Do. (3rd bat.)—Madras, Winchester
Do. (4th bat.)—Canada, Winchester
61st do.—Jersey, Pembroke
62nd do.—Canada, Belfast
63rd do.—Canada, Belfast
64th do.—Aldershot, Colchester
65th do.—New Zealand, Birr
66th do.—Madras, Colchester
67th do.—China, Athlone
68th do.—Madras, Fermoy
69th do—Madras, Fermoy
70th do.—New Zealand, Colchester
71st do.—Bengal, Stirling
72nd do.—Bombay, Aberdeen
73rd do.—Aldershot, Colchester
74th do.—Madras, Perth
75th do.—Plymouth, Chatham
76th Foot—Aldershot, Belfast
77th Foot—Bengal, Chatham

78th do.—Dover, Aberdeen
79th do.—Bengal, Stirling
80th do.—ditto, Buttevant
81st do.—Bengal, Chatham
82nd do.—Bengal, Colchester
83rd do.—Shorncliff, Chatham
84th do.—Shorncliff, Pembroke
85th do.—Dover, Pembroke
86th do.—Curragh, Templemore
87th do.—Aldershot, Buttevant
88th do.—Bengal, Colchester
89th do.—Bengal, Fermoy
90th do.—Bengal, Colchester
91st do.—Madras, Chatham
92nd do.—Gosport, Stirling
93rd do.—Bengal, Aberdeen
94th do.—ditto, Chatham
95th do.—Bombay, Fermoy
96th do.—Cape, Belfast
97th do.—Bengal, Colchester
98th do.—Bengal, Colchester
99th do.—China, Cork
100th Foot—Gibraltar; Parkhurst
101st do.—Bengal, Chatham

102nd do.—Madras, Chatham
103rd do.—Bombay, Colchester
104th do.—Bengal, Parkhurst
105th do.—Madras, Pembroke
106th do.—Bombay, Birr
107th do.—Bengal, Fermoy
108th do.—Madras, Fermoy
109th do.—Bombay, Cork
Rifle Brigade (1st bat.)—Canada, Winchester.
Do. (2nd bat.)—Bengal, Winchester
Do. (3rd bat.)—Bengal, Winchester
Do. (4th bat.)—Malta Winchester
1st West India Regiment—Nassau
2nd do.—Bahamas
3rd do.—West Coast of Africa
4th do—Jamaica, for Africa
5th do.—Jamaica
Ceylon Rifle Regiment—Ceylon
Cape Mounted Rifles—Cape of Good Hope
Royal Canadian Rifle Regiment—Canada
St. Helena Regiment—St. Helena
Royal Newfoundland Comps.—Newfoundland
Gold Coast Artillery Corps—Cape Coast Castle
Royal Malta Fencible Artillery—Malta

---

## DEPOT BATTALIONS.

1st Depot Battalion—Chatham
2nd do.—Chatham
3rd do.—Chatham
4th do.—Colchester
5th do.—Parkhurst
6th do.—Walmer
7th do.—Winchester
8th do.—Pembroke
9th do.—Colchester
10th do.—Colchester
11th do.—Preston
12th do.—Athlone
13th do.—Birr

14th Depot Battalion—Belfast
15th do.—Buttevant
16th do.—Templemore
17th do.—Limerick
18th do.—Fermoy
19th do.—Fermoy
20th do.—Cork
22nd do.—Stirling
33rd do.—Aberdeen
Cavalry Depot—Maidstone
    do.—Canterbury

---

## ARTILLERY AND ENGINEERS.

1st Hrs. Brig.—Woolwich
2nd Hrs. Brig.—Meerut
3rd Hrs Brig.—Bangalore
4th Hrs. Brig.—Kirkee
5th Hrs. Brig.—Umballah
1st Brig—Gibraltar
2nd Brig.—Dover
3rd Brig.—Malta and Corfu
4th Brig.—Aldershott
5th Brig.—Plymouth
6th Brig.—Portsmouth
7th Brig.—Montreal
8th Brig.—Dublin
9th Brig—Shorncliffe
10th Brig.—Canada
11th Brig.—Bengal
12th Brig.—Mauritius
13th Brig—Woolwich
14th Brig—Bengal
15th Brig.—Halifax N.S.
16th Brig—Delhi
17th Brig.—Madras
18th Brig.—Kirkee
19th Brig.—Peshawur
20th Brig.—Kamptee
21st Brig.—Mhow
22nd Brig—Jullundur
23rd Brig.—Secunderabad
24th Brig—Mean Meer
25th Brig.—Agra
    *Royal Engineers.*
A Troop Royal Engineer Train, Aldershott
    1st Compy—Devonport
    2nd Compy—Kensington
    3rd Compy—Gibraltar
    4th Compy—Halifax, N.S.

5th Compy.—Bermuda
6th Compy.—New Zealand
7th Compy.—Chatham
8th Compy.—China
9th Compy.—Woolwich
10th Compy.—Aldershott
11th Compy.—Mauritius
12th Compy.—Cape
13th Compy—Dublin (survey)
14th Compy.—Dublin (survey)
15th Compy.—Canada
16th Compy.—Southton (survey)
17th Compy.—Curragh
18th Compy.—Canada
19th Compy.—Glasgow (survey)
20th Compy.—Chatham.
21st Compy—Mauritius.
22nd Compy.—Chatham
23rd Compy.—Shorncliffe
24th Compy.—Aldershott
25th Compy.—Cape
26th Compy.—Chatham
27th Compy.—Gibraltar
28th Compy.—Malta
29th Compy.—Corfu
30th Compy.—Corfu
31st Compy.—Malta
32nd Compy.—St. Helena
33rd Compy.—Gibraltar
34th Compy.—Bermuda
35th Compy.—Chatham
36th Compy.—Chatham
37th Compy.—Chatham
38th Compy.—Chatham
39th Compy.—Chatham
40th Compy.—Chatham

# PROMOTIONS AND APPOINTMENTS.

## NAVY.

### PROMOTIONS.

WAR OFFICE, JUNE 16.

The Queen has been graciously pleased to give orders for the appointment of Rear-Adm. the Hon. Edward Alfred John Harris, Her Majesty's Minister Plenipotentiary to the Swiss Confederation, and Horatio Nelson Lay, Esq., employed with the special mission of the Earl of Elgin to China, in the years 1857 and 1858, to be Ordinary Members of the Civil Division of the Third Class, or Companions of the Most Hon. Order of the Bath.

To be Captain—Com. David Miller.

To be Retired Master, with rank of Captain—John E. Ellis.

Engineer—James Orchard of the Tyrian.

First-Class Assistant-Engineers —Evan L. Williams, Peter Eckford, and Peter Murray, of the Asia; James Wilson, of the Echo; Joseph Wyllie, of the Valorous; William Frazer, of the Indus; William Pearson, of the Emerald; Thomas Scott (B), of the Cumberland; Joseph T. Robinson, of the Scout; James M'Gough, of the Surprise; Frederick Pointon, of the Orestes: James Crawford, of the Mutine; Richard Wyllie, of the Bustard; Angus Leitch, of the Kestrel; William Barclay, of the Medea.

### APPOINTMENTS.

Captains—W. J. S. Pullen to the Terror, additional, for surveying service; Hon. G. D. Keane to the Cumberland, for service at the Naval Barracks at Sheerness; E. W. Turnour to the Charybdis, vice Keane.

Commanders—John A. Shears to the Aboukir; Henry L. Cox, John Henderson, and Frederick W. Sidney to the Miranda, for surveying duties; Arthur W. Gillett to the Marlborough.

Lieutenants—G. G. Duff and W. E. Mitchell to the Esk; W. D. D. Selby to the Cumberland; W. J. Botelor to the Orlando; H. F. Cleveland to the Resistance; Stratford Tuke and John A. F. Luttrell to the Excellent.

Masters—Daniel M'D. Jago to the Saturn; John Molloy to the President; Haben B. Hunt to the Phaeton; John Palmer to the Barossa; Percy V. James to the Rattler; John A. Collinson to the Jackal; J. P. C. Clements to the Prince Consort; John T. H. Norris to the Hawke; George Raymond to the Dee; Henry S Ley to the Sans Pareil.

Chaplains and Naval Instructors —Rev. Thomas E. G. Bunbury to the Esk; Rev. E. R. Colby, M.A., to the Cossack.

Surgeons—John Caldwell to the Osprey; Thomas J. Breen and George Moore, M.D., additional, to the President, for the Naval Reserve; John Ward to the Trincomalee; George F. M'Donough, M.D., to the Active; G. P. Cooke to the Dee.

Paymasters—Edward Jas. Bennett to the Trincomalee; R. F. E. Morison to the Active; Edmund A. Rowe, additional, to the President; William B. Hutchinson to the Eclipse; Frederick T. Robins to the Esk.

Sub-Lieutenants—Hugo Lewis Pearson, Henry James Fairlie, and Hon. Edward Stanley Dawson, to the Victoria and Albert; G. W. Osmond and Pearson C. Johnstone to the Edgar.

Assistant-Surgeons—Dld. MacIver, M.D., Josh Whitaker, M.D., and John Fraser, additional (acting), to the Royal Adelaide; Alfred William Whitley and William D. Woodsworth, additional (acting).

to the Victory; W. D. Longfield to the Styx; Francis H. Moore to the Victory for the Royal Marines; Matthew Coates to Haslar Hospital; John Barnett (acting) to the Vivid.

Second Masters—James G. Liddell, Silas H. Liddell, George White, Selwyn S. Sugden, Clement Hertzell, Charles S C. Watkins, and James C. Thomas to the Euryalus, as supernumeraries; E. H. C. Smith, Herbert D. Walker, John F. Barns, and William C. Spain to the Victory, as supernumeraries; E. B. D'Arcy and H. J, R. J. Pearch to the Dee.

Master's Assistants—W. H. Brickdale to the Cossack; Theodore G. Fenn, Richard R. B. Hopley, and Edwin H. Richards to the Eask; Richard S. Stewart and Thomas H. James to the Cossack; Robert T. Hodges to the Lizard; James S. Barrett to the Narcissus, as supernumerary; G. K. Moore and Richard Godden to the Dee.

Assistant-Paymasters — W. H. Haswell (in charge) to the Dee; Edward M. Roe (in charge) to the Firefly; Joseph G. W. Hoare to the Victoria and Albert; Robert F. W. Soady to the Magicienne; F. W. S. Ponsonby to the Aboukir.

Midshipmen—Lord W. de la P. Beresford to the Defence; C. E. Bell, C. E. Wood, G. S. Parker, E. H. Oldham, and J. H. T. Chowne to the Esk; Arthur C. B. Bromley, Alexander De C. Crawford, John H. Bainbridge, Edward B. Boyle, Vesey Knox, and Bernal W. Fielding to the Cossack; E. M. S. Claremont to the Revenge; Chas. Lindsay to the Esk.

Naval Cadets (nominated)—Chas. R. Arbuthnott, Henry Vashon Baker, Frank J. Grasse, Frederick G. Ree, Charles C. Stuart, James C R. Scott, George Huntingford, Robert H. Hutchings, Charles G. W. Aylen, Henry C. A. Morshead, Nugent B. M. de Geytt, Ferdinand Beauclerk, William Harvey, Chas. W. Hicks; Arthur Henry Stone and Henry W. Savill; Maurice S. R. Bayley, Frederick Brind, Hon. Robert Walter Craven, William C. H. Gill, Walter H. B. Graham,

Richard N. Grealey, Arthur F. T. James, Henry D. Mackenzie, Arthur W. E. Prothero, Thomas B. J. Ross, Edward Walker, Dixon S. B. Mackenzie, Harry H. Glaybrook, Charles H. Cochran, Andrew W. Rogers, C. E. Grissell to the Esk, J. G. M. Field, and E. H. Gamble.

Clerks—Alfred G. Roberts to the Virginia; Edmund H. Key to the Racoon; E. E. Richmond to the Fisgard, as supernumerary; Arundel Smith to the Royal Adelaide.

Assistant-Clerks—Charles F. W. Edwards to the Edgar; H. S. Dobson to the Royal Adelaide, as supernumerary; George H. Bradley (additional) to the Curaçoa; W. L. Fenoock to the Warrior; H. W. Paul (additional) to the Indus; A. G. Hill and W. F. Banbury (additional) to the Edgar; W. H. Fox (additional) to the Majestic; R. Osborn and C. K. O'Mahoney (additional) to the Fisgard; C. Reid and E. G. Whitmore to the Royal Adelaide, as supernumeraries; Charles Walker to the Black Prince.

Chief Engineers—R. Sampson to the Prince Consort; Benjamin Barber to the Salamander; William Pitt to the Sans Pareil.

Engineers—William Hardie to the Asia, as supernumerary; F. W. Sutton (B) to the Indus, as supernumerary; Edward Fowell (acting) to the Orlando; Edwin Daniels to the Salamis.

First-Class Assistant-Engineers —Edward Judge to the Cockatrice; Richard W. Trubshaw (acting) to the Louisa.

Assistant - Engineers — William Reid to the Dasher; James Croll to the Racoon; H. J. Iles to the Cumberland, as supernumerary; F. C. Ford to the Indus for hospital treatment; J. Gray to the Fisgard, as supernumerary; John West to the Columbine; T. R. Butters to the Sprightly; H. D. Garwood and Frederick Moore to the Enchantress; H. G. Hall to the Prince Consort; Thomas Catchpole to the Charger; Thomas Scott (B) to the Cumberland, as supernumerary; James Legate to the Tender; Peter Samson to the Sans

Pareil; C. F. H. Burt and James Parry to the Indus, as supernumeraries.

Second-Class Assistant-Engineers—David B. Keiller to the Curaçoa; Robert Sutherland to the Miranda; Frederick Smiley to the Cockatrice.

## ROYAL MARINES.
ADMIRALTY, JUNE 1.

Maj.-Gen. Fortescue Graham, C.B., to be col. of the Plymouth Division, under Order in Council of the 20th March, vice Wearing, deceased.

Royal Marine Light Infantry—First Lieut. Wingrove Laugharne Tinmouth to be capt., vice Gritton, retired on full-pay; Sec. Lieut. William Henry Wells to be first lieut, vice Tinmouth.

## COAST-GUARD.

Inspecting-Commanders—S. P. Brett to Penzance, vice C. J. Austen, superseded at his own request; Thomas H. B. Fellowes to Penzance, vice Austen, resigned.

Chief Officer (Second Class)—William Pollard to Tarbert.

## ROYAL NAVAL RESERVE.

To be Lieutenants—John Trelfall Bragg and Richard Gully.

To be Sub-Lieutenants—Michael Sydney and Alexander Oughton.

## ARMY.

WAR OFFICE, PALL MALL, May 22.

1st Regt. of Dragoon Guards—Lieut. John Buchan Hepburn, from the 5th Dragoon Guards, to be lieut., vice Quin, who exchanges.

4th Dragoon Guards—Lieut. Augustus Gladwyn Churchill Inge, to be capt., by purchase, vice Thomas Clarke Gillespie, who retires; Cornet George Hall Ringrose, to be lieut., by purchase, vice Inge; Philip Edward Poppe, gent., to be cor., by purchase, vice Wm. John Brooke, promoted.

5th Dragoon Guards — Lieut. Thomas Albert Quin, from the 1st Dragoon Guards, to be lieut., vice Hepburn, who exchanges.

7th Dragoon Guards—Ens. Geo. Tomkyns Morris, from the 38th Foot, to be cor., vice Joseph Thos. Cammelleri, promoted.

5th Lancers—Assist.-Surg. Robert Sutherland from the 24th Foot, to be assist.-surg.

12th Lancers—The services of Paymaster Randal H. Roberts have been dispensed with.

9th Regt. of Foot—Lieut. John Haycroft Bolton to be capt., by purchase, vice William Augustus Elmhirst, who retires, Ens. Wm. Hawkins Hathway to be lieut., by purchase, vice Bolton; Thomas John Buchanan, gent., to be ens., by purchase, vice Hathway.

10th Foot—Ens. George Wm. Carter to be lieut., without purchase, vice Hargood Thomas Snooke, deceased; Ens. Christopher Campbell Oldfield to be lieut., by purchase, vice George William Carter, whose promotion, by purchase, on the 31 March, 1863, has been cancelled; George Daniel Hall Brookes, gent., to be ens., without purchase, vice Oldfield; Staff Assist.-Surg. Baynes Reed to be assist.-surg., vice John Clarke, M.D., promoted on the Staff.

18th Foot—Maj. James Harwood Rocke, from a Depot Battalion, to be maj., vice Swinburne, who exchanges.

21st Foot—Cecil Bowes Robinson, gent., to be ens., by purchase, vice Forbes George Vernon, whose appointment has been cancelled.

22nd Foot—Chas. Leslie Sykes, gent., to be ens., by purchase, vice Joseph King Barnes, who retires.

24th Foot—Staff Assist.-Surg. Campbell Millis Douglas, M.D., to be assist.-surg., vice Robert Sutherland, appointed to the 5th Lancers.

31st Foot—Staff-Surg. Duncan Robertson Rennie to be surg, vice David Field Rennie, M.D., appointed to the Staff.

38th Foot—James Alexander, gent., to be ens., by purchase, vice George Tomkyns Morris, transferred to the 7th Dragoon Guards.

39th Foot—H. French Cotton, gent., to be ens. by purchase, vice Francis Shortt Arnott, who retires.

41st Foot—Ens. Henry Webb Byng to be lieut., by purchase, vice Edgar Younghusband, who retires; Edward Eden Hughes, gent., to be ens.. by purchase, vice Byng.

43rd Foot—Ens. Wm. M'Neile Cairns, from the 96th Foot, to be ens., vice Wellington James Denton, who retires; John Bingley Garland, gent., to be ens., by purchase, vice Charles Yates Peyton, who retires.

44th Foot—Lieut. George Evatt Acklom to be capt, without purchase, vice Arthur de Montmorency Fleming, deceased—1st April; Ens. William John Edward Graham Sutherland to be lieut., without purchase, vice Acklom—1st April; Ens. Lloyd Fenton, from the 15th Foot, to be ens., vice Sutherland.

57th Foot—Lieut. Edward Gould Hasted to be capt., by purchase, vice Edward Gorton, who retires; Ens. Arthur Cecil Manners to be lieut., by purchase, vice Hasted; James Richard Knox Tredennick, gent., to be ens., by purchase, vice Manners.

61st Foot—Ens. Francis John Wakeman Pigott Long to be lieut., by purchase, vice Charles John Griffiths, who retires; James Thos. Gilfoyle, gent., to be ens., by purchase, vice Long.

73rd Foot—Ens. James Fergusson to be lieut., by purchase, vice James Fraser, who retires; Geo. Edward Earle, gent., to be ens., by purchase, vice Fergusson.

77th Foot—Lieut. Thos. Howard M'Dougall Murray, from the Gold Coast Artillery Corps, to be lieut., vice William Minieter, promoted to an Unattached Company, without purchase.

83rd Foot—Ens. Charles Lucius Smith to be lieut., by purchase, vice Edwyn Thomas, who retires; Sir Keith George Jackson, bart., to be ens., by purchase, vice Smith.

94th Foot—Lieut. Sydenham Malthus to be capt., without purchase, vice Francis Hamilton Elliot, deceased—30th March.

96th Foot—Frederick William Lambert Cassidy, gent., to be ens., by purchase, vice Cairns, transferred to the 43rd Foot.

2nd West India Regt.—Ensign Edmund Ashton Boss to be lieut., without purchase, vice Andrew Truelove Edge, deceased—3rd May; Ens. Archibald Hamilton Duthie to be lieut. by purchase, vice Thomas Peach, who retires; John Barclay Jackson, gent., to be ens., without purchase, vice Boss; Beaufort Henry Vidal, gent., to be ens., by purchase, vice Duthie.

DEPOT BATTALION.

Maj. the Hon. William Leopold Talbot, from half-pay, unattached, to be maj., vice Dawson Cornelius Greene, who retires upon temporary half-pay; Maj. John Swinburne, from 18th Foot, to be maj., vice Rocke, who exchanges.

COMMISSARIAT DEPARTMENT.

Deputy Assist.-Com.-Gen. Joseph Marsh to be assist.-com.-gen., vice Hector John Macaulay, placed upon retired pay—1st May; Deputy Assist.-Com.-Gen. Geo. Home Telfer, from half-pay, to be deputy assist.-com.-gen. vice Marsh—1st May.

MEDICAL DEPARTMENT.

Surg. David Field Rennie, M.D., from 31st Foot, to be staff surg.; Assist-Surg. John Clark, M.D., from 10th Foot, to be staff surg, vice Duncan Robertson Rennie, appointed to the 31st Foot.

CHAPLAIN'S DEPARTMENT.

The Rev. William Anderson, Chaplain of the Fourth Class, has been permitted to resign his Commission; the Rev. Matthew R. Scott. M.A., Chaplain of the second class, to be chap. of the first class —10th April; the Rev. J. Browne Wilson to be chap. of the fourth class, vice the Rev. William Anderson, resigned — 18th Sept. 1860.

UNATTACHED.

Capt. and Brev.-Col. Thomas E. Lacy, half-pay unattached, Maj. and Superintendent of Studies, Royal Military College, Sandhurst, to be maj., without purchase; Ens. Peter Gill, on the Unattached Indian Establishment, to have the rank of Lieut. on the Indian Establishment.

BREVET.

The Commission as Brevet-Maj. of Sec. Capt. John Bonham, Royal (late Bengal) Artillery to be antedated to 2nd Oct., 1861.

Capt. David Mac Farlan, Royal (late Bengal) Artillery, to be maj. in the Army—9th Feb.

Capt. Astell Thomas Welsh, 8th Foot, to be maj. in the Army.

Paymaster William Dowler, 98th Foot, to have the hon. rank of Capt.—26th March—

Paymaster George Montgomerie Davidson, 22nd Foot, to have the hon. rank of Capt.—1st April.

The undermentioned officers having completed five years' Qualifying Service in the rank of Lieut.-Col., under the provisions of the Royal Warrant of 14th Oct., 1858, to be cols.—Lieut.-Col. H. Meade Hamilton, 12th Foot—12th April; Lieut.-Col. the Hon. Frederick Augustus Thesiger 95th Foot —30th April.

The following promotions to take place in Her Majesty's Indian Military Forces, consequent on the deaths of Lieut.-Gen. James Perry

Madras Infantry, on the 17th March; Maj.-Gen. David Forbes, Bombay Infantry, on the 2nd April; Lieut.-Gen. Duncan Gordon Scott, Bengal Infantry, on the 5th of April; Lieut.-Gen. Thomas Fiddes, Bengal Infantry, on the 13th April; and Lieut.-Gen. Wm. Henry Hewitt, Bengal Infantry, on the 16th April.

To be Lieutenant-Generals.

Maj.-Gen. James Parsons, C.B., Bengal Infantry—18th March; Maj.-Gen. George Warren, Bengal Infantry—6th April; Maj.-Gen. Henry Fisher Salter, C.B., Bengal Cavalry—14th April; Maj.-Gen. Thomas Matthew Taylor, Bengal Cavalry—17th April.

To be Major-Generals.

Col. Sir Chas. Shepperd Stuart, K.C.B., Bombay Infantry—18th March; Col. Thos. Henry Shuldham, Bengal Infantry—3rd April; Col. John Butler, Bengal Infantry —6th April; Col. William Barclay Goodfellow, Bombay Engineers— 14 April; Col. William Marcus Coghlan, Bombay Artillery—17th April.

The undermentioned Officers of Her Majesty's Indian Military Forces, who have retired upon full-pay to have a step of hon. rank as follows:—Lieut.-Col. Grant Allan, Madras Infantry, to be col.; Maj. Henry William Rawlins, Madras Staff Corps, to be lieut.-col.; Maj. Robert Cowpar, Bombay Staff Corps, to be lieut.-col.; Captain Blackett Revell, Madras Infantry, to be maj.; Capt. Henry Michell, Bengal Infantry, to be Major; Deputy Inspector-General of Hospitals Henry Gibbon Graham, to have the hon. rank of Inspector-Gen. of Hospitals; Surg.-Maj. Henry Goodall, to have the hon. rank of Deputy Inspector-Gen. of Hospitals.

---

## THE MILITIA GAZETTE.

War Office, Pall Mall, May 19.

Artillery Regt. of Royal Lancashire Militia—J. Clifton Brown, Major in the 1st Regt. of Lancashire Artillery Volunteers, to be first-lieut., vice George Wood, resigned.

1st Regt. of the Duke of Lancaster's Own Militia—Her Majesty has been graciously pleased to accept the resignation of the Commissions held by Lieuts. John Wood Younghusband and Francis John Shortis.

6th Regt. of Royal Lancashire Militia—Her Majesty has been graciously pleased to accept the resignation of the Commission held by Assist.-Surg. Frederick Foulkes.

Memorandum—The Queen has been graciously pleased to accept the resignation of Commission held by the following Officers:—

4th or Royal South Middlesex Regt. of Militia—Lieut. Chas. Rodney Huxley.

Memorandum—The Queen has been graciously pleased to accept the resignation of the Commissions held by the following Officers:—

5th or Royal Elthorne Light Infantry Regt. of Middlesex Militia—Capt. Wm. Thos. Llewellyn Lloyd; Lieut. Charles Randall.

1st Devon Yeomanry Cavalry— Lieut. William Basnes to be capt., vice Walcot, resigned.

Shropshire Regt. of Militia— Capt. Sir George Samuel Brooke Pechell, Bart., to be sec. maj.

Leicestershire Regt. of Militia— William Beauclerk Powell, gent., to be lieut.

2nd Regt. of Surrey Militia— William Richard Barnes, Esq., late Maj. Turkish Contingent, to be lieut., vice Molineux, promoted; Frederick Pontifex, Esq, to be lieut., vice Elyard, promoted.

King's Own Light Infantry Regt. of Militia—William Hall Graham, gent, to be lieut, vice Robertson, resigned.

Queen's Own Light Infantry Regt. of Tower Hamlets Militia— Sir James Lawrence, Cottor, Bart, to be capt.

---

War Office, Pall Mall, May 22.

Royal East Kent Regiment of Mounted Rifles Yeomanry Cavalry —The Right Hon. Sackville George, Baron Conyers (late Royal Horse Guards Blue), to be lieut., vice Loftus Pemberton, promoted.

Memoranda—Her Majesty has been graciously please to accept the resignation of the Commissions held by the following officers :—

2nd West York Militia—Lieut.-Col. Joshua Samuel Crompton, with leave to retain his rank and wear the uniform of the corps in consideration of his long service.

6th West York Militia—Capt. William Alcock; Lieut. William Deans West.

[The following appointment is substituted in the *Gazette* of the 15th inst.]

1st or Western Regt. of Norfolk Militia—Lieut. George Longueville Bedingfeld to be capt., vice Stirling, deceased.

5th Regt. of Royal Lancashire Militia—Her Majesty has been graciously pleased to accept the resignation of the Commission held by Capt. Edward Petre.

Memoranda — Royal London Militia—Her Majesty's Commissioners of Lieutenancy have been pleased to accept the resignation of the Commmission held by Capt. Augustus Henry Garland in the above Regt.

———

THE VOLUNTEER GAZETTE.
WAR OFFICE, PALL MALL, May 19.

The Hon. Artillery Company of London—Lieut. George Ritherdon to be capt.; Serg. John Hornby to be ens.; Serg. Charles Edward Webb to be ens.

1st Lancaster Rifle Volunteer Corps—Thomas Taylor, gent., to be ens.

2nd Manchester or 28th Lancashire Rifle Volunteer Corps—Francis Beaufort Wyndham Quin, gent., to be lieut.

Memorandum — Her Majesty's acceptance of the resignation of the Commissions held by Sec. Lieut. Thomas Dawson, in the 21st Lancashire Artillery Volunteer Corps (inserted in the *Gazette* of 8th of May inst.), has been cancelled.

26th Middlesex Rifle Volunteer Corps—Ens. John Leggat Irish to be lieut., vice Jones, promoted.

48th Middlesex Rifle Volunteer Corps—Daniel Henry Ashford to be lieut.

26th Cheshire Rifle Volunteers —Francis Hampson, gent., to be super.-lieut.

Prince Albert's Own Leicestershire Regt. of Volunteer Cavalry—Charles Thomas Freer, Esq., to be maj., vice Haynes, resigned; Geo. Henry Nevill, Esq., to be capt., vice Freer, promoted; Edward William Craddock Middleton, gent., to be cor., vice Douglass, promoted.

Memorandum—Prince Albert's Own Leicestershire Regt. of Volunteer Cavalry—The Queen has been pleased to accept of the resignation of the Commission held by Major Haymes in the above Regt.

Memorandum—6th Company of Leicestershire Rifle Volunteers—The Queen has been pleased to accept of the resignation of the Commission held by Lieutenant Eddowes in the above Corps.

12th Gloucestershire Rifle Volunteer Corps—John Irving, gent., to be lieut., vice Onslow, promoted.

1st Lanarkshire Artillery Volunteer Corps—Thomas Rowan, gent., to be first lieut., vice David Storer, resigned; John Matheson, gent., to be sec. lieut., vice Thomas Taylor Hay, resigned.

2nd Lanarkshire Engineer Volunteer Corps — James Morris Gale, gent., to be first lieut., vice Thomas Currie Gregory, resigned.

1st Lanarkshire Rifle Volunteer Corps—Ens. John Harvey to be lieut., vice Robert Readman, resigned; Henry Stewart, gent., to be ens., vice John Harvey, promoted.

3rd Lanarkshire Rifle Volunteer Corps—James Struthers, gent., to be lieut., vice John Granger, resigned; Ens. Daniel Fleming to be lieut., vice Henry Herbert Carr, resigned; George Lindsay, gent., to be lieut., vice James Landels Selkirk, resigned; Alexander Easton, gent., to be ens., vice Ernest Clausen, resigned; James Sloane McCaul, gent., to be ens., vice Daniel Fleming, promoted.

4th Lanarkshire Rifle Volunteer Corps—John Tennant, Esq., to be hon.-col.; Lieut. William Simpson to be capt., vice George Anderson, promoted; Ens. James Dalgiel Johnston to be lieut., vice William Simpson, promoted.

25th Lanarkshire Rifle Volunteer Corps — Ens. Samson George Goodall Copestake to be lieut., vice Thomas Barclay, promoted; Geo. McIntosh Neilson, gent., to be ens., vice William McWhirter Wilson, resigned.

Memorandum—Her Majesty has been graciously pleased to accept the resignation by the following gentlemen of their Commissions:

1st Lanarkshire Artillery Volunteer Corps—Sec. Lieut. Thos. Osborne.

25th Lanarkshire Rifle Volunteer Corps—Capt. J. McIntyre; Ens. James Clark Bunten.

1st Herefordshire Rifle Volunteer Corps—James Thomas Owen Fowler to be super.-lieut., on condition of his acting as Quartermaster, to the 1st Administrative Battalion of Herefordshire Rifle Volunteers.

2nd Tower Hamlets Rifle Volunteer Corps—Charles Morris, gent., to be ens.

Memorandum—Her Majesty has been graciously pleased to accept the resignation of the Commission held by Ens. J. Simpson.

Memorandum—1st Administrative Battalion of Aberdeenshire Rifle Volunteers—Adjt. Charles Gilborne to serve with the rank of capt., from the 7th of Jan., 1863.

Memorandum—1st Lincolnshire Rifle Volunteers—Her Majesty has been graciously pleased to accept the resignation of the commission held by Hon. Assist.-Surg. Wm. Pauli.

Memorandum—2nd Pembrokeshire Rifle Volunteer Corps—Her Majesty has been graciously pleased to accept the resignations of the Commissions held by Lieut. Allen Long and Ens. James McLean.

Memorandum—3rd Forfarshire Artillery Volunteer Corps—Her Majesty has been graciously pleased to accept the resignation of the Commission held by Sec. Lieut. John Charles Bell in the above Corps.

Memorandum—11th Forfarshire Rifle Volunteer Corps—Her Majesty has been graciously pleased to accept the resignation of the Commission held by Lieut. David Carnegie in the above Corps.

War Office, Pall Mall, May 22.

1st Administrative Battalion of Fife Rifle Volunteers—Lieut.-Col. Robert Anstruther to be maj.

8th Fife Artillery Volunteer Corps—Sec. Lieut. Andrew Wilkie to be first lieut.; James Anderson, jun., gent., to be sec. lieut.

11th Fife Artillery Volunteer Corps — John Benjamin Lord, gent., to be capt.; James Hepburn, gent., to be first lieut.; Alexander Darney, gent., to be sec. lieut.; The Rev. Matthew Bowie to be hon.-chap.; John Stoddart, M.D., to be hon. assist.-surg.

Memorandum—Her Majesty has been graciously pleased to accept the resignation of the Commission held by Capt. Robert Dalgleish Pryde in the 1st Fifeshire Artillery Volunteer Corps.

1st Administrative Battalion of the Isle of Wight Rifle Volunteers—John Farmery Ollard, Esq., M.R.C.S., to be assist.-surg.

2nd Hampshire Rifle Volunteer Corps—Ens. Henry Abraham to be lieut., vice Coles, promoted.

5th Hampshire Rifle Volunteer Corps—The Rev. John George Francis Knapp to be hon. chap., vice McGhie, resigued.

1st Warwickshire Rifle Volunteer Corps—Thomas Middlemore, gent., to be ens., vice Sargant, resigned; John Charles Edward Stroud, gent., to be ens., vice Ledsam, resigned; Assist.-Surg. Geo. Yates to be surg., vice Hill, resigned.

Oxford University Rifle Volunteer Corps — Horatio Charles Maurice, esq., to be ens., vice Wickman, promoted.

1st Administrative Brigade of Sussex Artillery Volunteers—

Thomas Hayter Johnston to be maj.

1st West Riding of Yorkshire Artillery Volunteer Corps—First Lieut. Walter Holdforth to be capt.; First Lieut. Frederick Horatio Barr to be capt.; Sec. Lieut. William Thomas Jackson to be first lieut.

37th West Riding of Yorkshire Rifle Volunteer Corps—Herbert Hodgetts Taylor, gent., to be ens., vice Potter, promoted.

Memoranda—Her Majesty has been graciously pleased to accept the resignation of the Commissions held by the following Officers:—

1st West Riding of Yorkshire Artillery Volunteer Corps—Capt. Richard Dyneley Dyneley.

2nd West Riding of Yorkshire Artillery Volunteer Corps—Capt. Charles Smythe Johnson.

25th West Riding of Yorkshire Rifle Volunteer Corps — Lieut. Henry Granville Baker.

26th West Riding of Yorkshire Rifle Volunteer Corps—Capt. J. Thomas Coates.

Memoranda—4th London Rifle Volunteer Corps—Her Majesty has been pleased to accept the resignation of the Commission held by the following officers: — Lieut. John Brockhouse in the above Corps.

East York Artillery Volunteers —4th Corps (Hull)—Capt. George Christopher Roberts and Captain Herbert Archibald Gibson Mends.

East York Rifle Volunteers— 1st Administrative Battalion—6th Company (Beverley) — Captain Harold Barkworth.

1st Corps (Hull)—Hon. Assist.-Surg. Thomas Stephenson Usher.

1st Forfarshire Rifle Volunteer Corps—Capt. John Jack, jun.

1st Cambridgeshire Rifle Volunteer Corps — Capt. William Prest.

3rd Cambridgeshire Rifle Volunteer Corps — Surg. Henry James Haviland.

---

THE ARMY GAZETTE.

*₊* Where not otherwise specified, the following Commissions bear the current date.

WAR OFFICE, PALL MALL, May 29·

2nd Regiment of Life Guards— Lieut. and Capt. Robert Thomas Lowndes Norton, from the Grenadier Guards, to be capt., paying the difference, vice Ed. Stratton Fitzhardinge Berkeley, who retires.

6th Dragoons—H. Allen Gosset, late Lieutenant 22nd Foot, to be paymaster, vice Thomas Smales, cashiered by sentence of a General Court-Martial.

9th Lancers—Cor. William H. Lawrence to be lieut., by purchase, vice John Geo. Buchan Hepburn, who retires.

Royal Artillery—Lieut.-Colonel Bladen West Black to be col., vice Charles John Cooke, retired upon full-pay, 6th Jan.; Capt. Charles Alexander Purvis, to be lieut.-col., vice Black, 6th Jan.; Second Capt. Henry William Lumsden to be capt., vice Purvis, 6th Jan.; Lieut. Benjamin Lumsden Gordon to be second capt., vice Lumsden, 6th Jan.; Lieut. Joseph George Marshall to be second capt., vice Brev.-Maj. Lancelot Francis C Thomas, removed to the Supernumerary List, 3rd March; Second Capt. Benjamin Lumsden Gordon to be adjt., vice Lumsden, promoted, 6th Jan.; Gent.-Cadet Francis Blake Knox to be lieut., vice Gordon, promoted, 1st April; Gent.-Cadet George Black to be lieut., vice Marshall, promoted, 1st April; Acting Vet.-Surg. Daniel Maclean to be vet.-surg , vice John Surtees Stockley, placed on half-pay, 8th Aug., 1862

Grenadier Guards—Ensign and Lieut. Robert Charles de Grey Vyner to be lieut. and capt., by purchase, vice Norton, transferred to the 2nd Life Guards; John Arthur Thomas Garratt, gent., to be ens. and lieut.. by purchase, vice Vyner; Lieut. and Capt. Alfred Walter Thynne to be adjt., vice Earle, promoted.

6th Regiment of Foot—Lieut. Dawson Kelly Evans to be capt.; by purchase, vice Easton John Cox, who retires; Ens. Alfred Teevan to be lieut., by purchase, vice Evans.

7th Foot—Maj. Thomas Tryon

to be lieut.-col., by purchase, vice Brev.-Col. Richard William Aldworth, who retires; Capt. Lord Richard Howe Browne to be maj., by purchase, vice Tryon; Lieut. Francis Burton Cole to be capt., by purchase, vice Lord Richard Howe Browne; Lieut. Cornelius George O'Brien to be capt., by purchase, vice James Kennedy McAdam, who retires; Ens. Rd. Spencer Hall to be lieut., by purchase, vice Cole; Eus. Henry Ferdinand Oakes to be lieut., vice O'Brien; Pierce Crosbie, gent., to be ens., by purchase, vice Oakes.

8th Foot—Capt. Fraser Newall, from the 109th Foot, to be capt., vice Brev.-Maj. Welsh, who exchanges; Francis Moore, gent., to be ens., by purchase, vice Charles Thomas Frederick Blair, who retires.

16th Foot—Ens. Leonard Ball Anderson Poynter to be lieut., by purchase, vice Charles Presaly Pen er, who retires upon temporary half-pay; Jas. Ramsay Akers, gent., to be ens. by purchase, vice Poynter.

17th oot—Ens. Arthur Vesey Nugent Fto be lieut., by purchase, vice Francis Wood, who retires; Herbert Charles Marryat, gent., to be ens., by purchase, vice Nugent.

24th Foot—Lieut. Charles Jas. Bromhead to be adjt., vice Lieut. John Cusack, promoted to an unattached company without purchase.

36th Foot—Lieut. Charles Dere James to be capt., vice Joseph Osmund Walter Scott; who retires; Ens. Edward Staples Bond to be lieut., by purchase, vice James; Arthur Montagu Neave, gent., to be ens., by purchase, vice Bond.

43rd Foot—Capt. Henry Alex. Atchison, from half-pay unattached, to be capt., repaying the difference, vice Capt. and Brev.-Maj. Thomas Hugh Cockburn, promoted to an unattached majority, without purchase; Lieut. Arthur R. Close to be capt., by purchase, vice Atchison, who retires; Eus. St. Vincent Alexander Hammick to be lieut., by purchase, vice Close; Robert

Barclay Allardice, gent., to be ens., by purchase, vice Hammick.

48th Foot—Ens. Walter Benson Hattyn to be lieut., by purchase, vice George Nugent R. Goddard, who retires; Alexander William Fair, gent., to be ens., by purchase, vice Hatton.

60th Foot—Ens. Edward Digby O'Rorke to be lieut., by purchase, vice Richard Albert Massey, who retires; Gerald Henry Talbot, gent., to be ens., by purchase, vice O'Rorke.

93rd Foot—Quartermaster John Joiner to be Paymaster, vice Blake, transferred to the 4th Hussars.

96th Foot—Albert John Molyneux Treeby, gent., to be ens., by purchase, vice Edward Shilson, who retires.

109th Foot—Capt. and Brev.-Maj. Astell Thomas Welsh, from the 8th Foot, to be capt., vice Newall, who exchanges.

### DEPOT BATTALION.

Capt. George Robert Stewart Black, 60th Foot, to be instructor of musketry, vice Capt. Thomas Biggs, 60th Foot, who has completed the regular period of service in that appointment—5th May.

### UNATTACHED.

Capt. and Brev.-Maj. Thomas Hugh Cockburn, from the 43rd Foot, to be Maj., without purchase. Lieut. Richard Bunn, from the 37th Foot, to be capt., without purchase.

### MEDICAL DEPARTMENT.

The second Christian name of Staff-Assist.-Surg. Curtis is *Lindsey*, and not *Lindesey*, as stated in the *Gazette* of the 7th April.

### BREVET.

Col. Charles John Cooke, on the retired full-pay list of the Royal Artillery, to be maj.-gen., the rank being honorary only—6th Jan.

Capt. Henry Alexander Atchison, 43rd Foot, to be Maj.—9th Nov., 1846.

Capt. and Brev.-Maj. Henry Alexander Atchison, 43rd Foot, to be Lieut.-Col—20th June, 1854.

Capt. John William Henry Chafyn Grove Morris, Royal Marine Artillery, to be maj.

Paymaster Henry Barrett Bromley, 10th Foot, to have the honorary rank of capt.—22nd Feb.

## THE MILITIA GAZETTE.

WAR OFFICE, PALL MALL, May 26.

Royal Bucks (King's Own) Regiment of Militia—Alfred de Rothschild, gent., to be lieut., vice Crewe, resigned.

Leicestershire Regiment of Militia—Jas. Palliser Gostobadie, Esq., late Capt. 70th Foot, to be capt., vice E. A. Paget, resigned.

2nd Regiment (Light Infantry) of West York Militia—Maj. Henry Van Straubenzee to be lieut.-col., vice Crompton, resigned.

2nd or Edmonton Royal Rifle Regiment of Middlesex Militia—Herbert Ashton Blount to be lieut., vice Bridger, promoted.

Memorandum—Her Majesty has been graciously pleased to accept the resignation of the commission held by Lieut. James Scott Ogle in the West Kent Regiment of Yeomanry Cavalry.

West Kent Regiment of Yeomanry Cavalry—Cornet James Frederick Edmeades to be lieut., vice Ogle, resigned; Nevile Lubbock, gent., to be cor., vice Edmeades, promoted; Adam Rae Martin, gent., to be surg., vice Smith, resigned.

WAR OFFICE, PALL MALL, May 29.

Hertfordshire Militia—Capt. H. Grimston Hale to be adjt., from the 21st Feb., 1863.

Dorset Regiment of Militia—Arthur B. Leach, Esq., to be lieut., vice Bower, promoted.

West Essex Yeomanry Cavalry—Lieut Thomas Duff Cater to be capt.; Cor. George Edward Pritchett to be lieut., vice Cater, promoted; Joseph Frederick Jessopp, gent., to be cor., vice Pritchett, promoted.

Memorandum—Her Majesty has been pleased to accept the resignation of the commissions held by Capt. Robert Swann and Lieuts. William Gordon and Bertram Aynsley James Mitford in the Essex Rifles Regiment of Militia.

2nd Regiment of Royal Surrey

Militia—Thomas Beckworth, gent., to be lieut.

Memorandum—Her Majesty has been graciously pleased to accept the resignation of the commission held by Capt. Nicholas Kendall in the Cornwall Rangers Militia.

Cornwall Rangers Militia—Capt. James Rennell Rodd to be maj., vice Johns, resigned.

[The following appointment is substituted for that which appeared in the *Gazette* of the 26th instant.]

2nd or Edmonton Royal Rifle Regiment of Middlesex Militia—Herbert Aston Blount to be lieut., vice Bridger, promoted.

Memorandum—Her Majesty has been graciously pleased to accept the resignation of the commission held by Capt. G. H. Rose Briscoe in the Royal Denbigh Militia; and Lieut. James Dunlop in the Edinburgh County Militia.

## THE VOLUNTEER GAZETTE.

WAR OFFICE, PALL MALL, May 26.

2nd Administrative Battalion of Northumberland Rifle Volunteers—Frederick Fox, late Lieut. 20th Foot, to be adj.

4th West Riding of Yorkshire Artillery Volunteer Corps—George Ferriers, gent., to be adj. from 11th March, 1863.

6th Company of Leicestershire Rifle Volunteers — Isaac Blount Dobell, gent., to be lieut. vice Eddowes, resigned.

5th Administrative Battalion of West Riding of Yorkshire Rifle Volunteers — Thomas Pearson Crosland, Esq., to be maj.

1st West Riding of Yorkshire Rifle Volunteers — Super. Lieut. John Forth Munby to be lieut.

2nd Administrative Battalion of Aberdeenshire Rifle Volunteers—Sir William Coote Seton, Bart. to be lieut.-col.

5th Aberdeenshire Artillery Volunteer Corps—Sec. Lieut. John Mellis to be first lieut. vice Wallis, resigned.

Memorandum—Her Majesty has been graciously pleased to accept the resignations of the Commissions held by Capt. Sir William Coote Seton, Bart. in the 2nd

Aberdeenshire Rifle Volunteer Corps, and by First Lieut. George Wallace in the 5th Aerdeenshire Artillery Volunteer Corps.

1st Administrative Battalion of Hertfordshire Rifle Volunteers— The Hon. Hugh Henry Hare to be capt.

3rd London Rifle Volunteer Corps—William Webb Venn the younger to be ens.

4th London Rifle Volunteer Corps—George Packer to be ens.

West Middlesex Rifle Volunteer Corps—Ens. Cyrus Daniell to be lieut. vice Price, removed.

London Irish Rifle Volunteer Corps — Lieut. James William Dusack to be capt.

Memorandum—The Queen has been graciously pleased to accept the resignation of the Commission held by Assist.-Surg. William Riddell Brunton in the 1st Surrey (or South London) Rifle Volunteer Battalion.

2nd Surrey Artillery Volunteer Corps—William North Rees, gent. to be sec. lieut.; John Veasey Franklin, gent. to be sec. lieut.

1st Surrey (or South London) Rifle Volunteer Battalion—Charles Browne, gent. to be assist.-surg. vice Brunton, resigned.

1st Company of Ayrshire Artillery Volunteers — John Smart Crawford to be super.-lieut This appointment is sanctioned on condition Mr. Crawford acting as quartermaster to the 1st Administrative Brigade of Ayrshire Artillery Volunteers.

Memorandum — Her Majesty has been graciously pleased to accept the resignation of the Commission held by Capt. Tyndal Bright in the 1st Lancashire Rifle Volunteer Corps.

———

WAR OFFICE, PALL MALL, May 29.

1st Flintshire Engineer Volunteer Corps—Thomas Leacroft Cottingham, gent. to be lieut.; Dashwood Parry, gent. to be sec. lieut.

4th Cinque Ports Artillery Volunteer Corps—The Rev. Barrington Stafford Wright, M.A. to be hon. chap.

12th Cheshire Rifle Volunteer Corps—George Oswald Luckman, gent. to be ens. vice Griffin, resigned.

25th Cheshire Rifle Volunteer Corps—William Arthur Harrison, gent. to be ens. vice Ledward, promoted.

26th Cheshire Rifle Volunteer Corps — George William Mould, gent. to be hon. assist.-surg.

1st Lancashire Artillery Volunteer Corps—Henry Hulme gent. to be hon. assist.-surg.

4th Lancashire Artillery Volunteer Corps—First Lieut. James Poole to be capt.; Walter Duckworth, gent. to be sec. lieut.

19th Lancashire Artillery Volunteer Corps—Maj. John Isaac Mawson to be lieut.-col.; Henry Houldsworth Grierson, Esq. to be capt.; Sec. Lieut. James Mawson to be first lieut.; Thomas Brown, gent. to be sec. lieut.

67th Lancashire Rifle Volunteer Corps—Lieut. John Nightingale Key Grover to be capt.; Ens. Peter Rasbotham the younger to be lieut.; William Innes Beechley gent. to be ens.

14th Kent Artillery Volunteer Corps—Hon. Assist.-Surg. Harry Browne to be surg. vice Harding, deceased; George Daniel Harding, gent. to be hon. assist.-surg. vice Browne, promoted.

12th Kent Rifle Volunteers— William Craycroft Fooks, Esq. to be capt. vice Fleet, resigned.

Memorandum—Her Majesty has been graciously pleased to accept the resignation of the Commission held by Lieut. Charles Edward Rashleigh in the 12th Kent Rifle Volunteer Corps.

East York Artillery Volunteers 4th Corps (Hull)—First Lieut. Charles James Todd to be capt.; First Lieut. Charles Heaven to be capt.; First Lieut. Richard George Smith to be capt.; Sec. Lieut. Thomas Richardson Humphrey to be first lieut.

Memorandum—Her Majesty has been graciously pleased to accept the resignation of the Commission held by Cor. Francis Day in the 1st Huntingdonshire Light Horse Volunteer Corps.

1st Huntingdonshire Light Horse Volunteer Corps—Charles Isham Strong to be cor.

Victoria Rifle Volunteer Corps —The Rev. William Bentinck Hawkins to be hon. chap. vice Bolton, deceased.

36th Middlesex Rifle Volunteer Corps—Alfred Constantine Cross to be ens.; Frederic Waterloo Jennings to be ens.

Memoranda — The Queen has been graciously pleased to accept the resignation of the Commission held by the following officers, viz.:—

St. George's Rifle Volunteer Corps—Honorary Chap. the Rev. William Bentinck Hawkins.

14th Middlesex Rifle Volunteer Corps—Lieut. Benjamin Greene-Lake.

London Irish Rifle Volunteer Corps—Ens. Maurice Cavanagh.

39th Middlesex Rifle Volunteer Corps—Lieut. James Frederick Corben.

42nd Middlesex Rifle Volunteer Corps—Ens. Rupert Flindt.

7th Administrative Battalion of Middlesex Rifle Volunteers—Capt. and Adj. Charles Foveaux Kirby.

Memorandum—Her Majesty has been graciously pleased to accept the resignation of the Commission held by Capt. Penry Lloyd in the 1st Brecknockshire Rifle Volunteer Corps.

---

THE ARMY GAZETTE.

WAR OFFICE, PALL MALL, June 2.

*₊* Where not otherwise specified, the following Commissions bear the current date.

GARRISON.

The Rev. Joseph Yates Dod, M.A., to be chap. to the Tower of London, vice the Rev. Henry Melvill, who resigns—1st April.

COMMISSARIAT DEPARTMENT.

Assist.-Com.-Gen. Alfred Salwey to be dep.-com.-gen. vice Edwards, placed upon Retired Pay—1st June.

Assist.-Com.-Gen. Thomas Forsyth Moore, from half-pay, to be assist.-Com.-Gen. vice Salwey, 1st June.

Act. Dept. - Assist. - Com.-Gen.

John Igglesden Troupe, from Ens. 5th Foot, to be dept.-assist.-com.-gen. 1st April.

CHAPLAIN'S DEPARTMENT.

The Rev. T. H. Cole, M.A. to be chap. to the Fourth Class, 8th November, 1862.

---

ADMIRALTY, May 28.

Corps of Royal Marines—Lieut.-Col. George Brydges Rodney to be assist.-adj.-gen. of the Corps, vice Col. Travers, resigned.

May 29.

Corps of Royal Marines—Maj.-Gen. John Alexander Philips to be lieut.-gen. vice Wearing, deceased; Col.-Com. Thomas Holloway, C.B. to be maj.-gen. vice Philips; Col. and Sec. Com. John Hawkins Gascoigne, C B. to be col.-com. vice Holloway; Lieut. - Col. Joseph Oates Travers, C.B. to be col. and sec. com. vice Gascoigne; Capt. Charles William Adair to be lieut.-col. vice Travers; First Lieut. Fitzmaurice Creighton to be capt. vice Adair; Sec. Lieut. Nassau William Irwin Hampden Stephens to be first lieut. vice Creighton.

---

INDIA OFFICE, June 5.

Her Majesty has been pleased to approve of the undermentioned promotions and alterations of rank amongst the Officers of Her Majesty's Indian Military Forces.

---

BENGAL ARMY.

Medical Officers — Assist.-Surg. Frederick Freeman Allen to be surg. vice Crozier, deceased.

---

MADRAS ARMY.

General List of Cavalry Officers— Cor. Thomas Deane to be lieut.— 4th March.

Army Rank — The undermentioned officers having completed fifteen years' service, to be capt. by brevet:—Lieut. William Mellish Parratt—25th February.

Medical Officers — Assist.-Surg. William Judson Von Someren to be surg. vice Linton, retired, 1st March.

Alterations of Rank—Surg. William Aitken to take rank from 25th February, vice Pattison, deceased.

## BOMBAY ARMY.

*General List of Infantry Officers*
—Ens. Edward Robert Reay to be
lieut. vice Packe, 30th Native Infantry, removed from the Army—
13th February.

*Medical Officers*—Surg. William
Thom to be surg.-maj. 8th April.

## THE MILITIA GAZETTE.

WAR OFFICE, PALL MALL, June 2.

King's Own Light Infantry Regiment of Militia—Henry Turner,
gent. to be lieut. vice Wilkinson,
promoted.

Royal North Gloucestershire
Regiment of Militia — Gerald
Henry Baird Young, gent. to be
lieut. (super.)

Memorandum—Forfar and Kincardine Militia—Her Majesty has
been graciously pleased to accept
the resignation of the Commission
held by Capt. Alexander Moncrieff
in the above Regiment.

----

WAR OFFICE. PALL MALL, June 5.

West Essex Yeomanry Cavalry
—Cor. Frederick Edenborough to
be lieut.; Sir Charles Henry Leslie, Bart. to be cor. vice Edenborough, promoted.

Argyll and Bute Artillery Militia—John Pirie, M.D. to be surg.
vice Campbell, deceased.

1st (Rifle) Regiment of West
York Militia—Lieut. Henry Cox
Wilkin to be capt. vice Hercy, re-
signed.

2nd Regiment (Light Infantry)
of West York Militia—Richard
Sterne Carroll, Esq. to be maj. vice
Straubenzee, promoted.

[The following Appointment is
substituted for that which appeared in the *Gazette* of the 1st
ultimo].

1st West Regiment of Yorkshire
Yeomanry Cavalry — Lawrence
Kiernan, gent. to be assist.-surg.
vice Cooke, resigned.

[The following Appointment is
substituted for that which appeared in the *Gazette* of the 29th
ultimo].

Dorset Regiment of Militia—
Arthur B. Leech, Esq. to be lieut.
vice Bower, promoted.

----

## THE VOLUNTEER GAZETTE.

WAR OFFICE, PALL MALL, June 2.

2nd London Rifle Volunteer
Corps—Lieut. Frederick William
Jones, of Her Majesty's Indian
Army, to be adj. from the 24th
March, 1863.

Memorandum—6th Tower Ham-
lets Rifle Volunteer Corps—Her
Majesty has been graciously pleased
to accept the resignation of the
Commission held by Capt. Valentine Hicks Labrow.

2nd London Rifle Volunteer
Brigade—Cholmeley Austin Leigh,
Esq. to be capt.

East York Rifle Volunteers—
1st Corps (Hull)—Henry Gibson,
Esq. to be surg.

1st Norfolk Rifle Volunteer
Corps—Nathaniel Henry Caley to
be ens.

19th Lancashire Artillery Volunteer Corps—Charles Sacie, Esq.
to be capt.

Memorandum—Her Majesty has
been graciously pleased to accept
the resignation of the Commissions held by the following Officers: viz.: Capt. Joseph Corbett
Lowe and First Lieut. Hugh Mey-
ler Bright in the 4th Lancashire
Artillery Volunteer Corps; and
Lieut, Richard Long Cooke, in the
1st Manchester or 6th Lancashire
Rifle Volunteer Corps.

3rd Renfrewshire Rifle Volunteer Corps—Ens. Robert Graham
to be lieut. vice Mackean, resigned; John Fullerton to be ens.
vice Graham, promoted.

4th Durham Rifle Volunteer
Corps — Lieut. William Culley
Stobart to be capt.; Ens. James
Thompson to be lieut.; Henry
Forster to be ens.

4th Derbyshire Rifle Volunteer
Corps—Francis Nicholas Smith,
Esq. to be capt., vice Curzon, resigned; Ens. James Shewin
Clarke to be lieut. vice Boden, resigned; Robert Harvey, gent. to
be ens. vice Clarke, promoted.

Memorandum—Her Majesty has
been graciously pleased to accept
the resignations of Captain Nathaniel Charles Curzon and Lieut.
Walter Boden in the 4th Derbyshire Rifle Volunteer Corps.

1st Sussex Artillery Volunteer Corps—First Lieut. Samuel Hannington to be capt.; Sec. Lieut. Philip Hannington to be first lieut.; Sec. Lieut. Edward Martin to be first lieut.; Sec. Lieut. George Grantham to be first lieut.; Thomas Dunnill to be first lieut.; Henry Catt to be super. first lieut.; Jack Thomas Whalford to be sec. lieut.

Memorandum—The Queen has been graciously pleased to accept the resignation of the Commission held by Ens. John Green in the 1st Surrey or (South London) Rifle Volunteer Battalion.

Memorandum—The Queen has been graciously pleased to accept the resignation of the Commission held by Lieut. Robert Payne in the 4th Surrey Rifle Volunteer Corps.

4th Surrey Rifle Volunteer Corps—William Cuthbert Quilter, gent. to be ens.

2nd Surrey Artillery Volunteer Corps—Edwin Payne, gent. to be surg.; William Ponsby Johns Llewellyn, gent. to be hon. assist.-surg.

Memorandum—6th Argyllshire Rifle Volunteers—Her Majesty has been graciously pleased to accept the resignation of the Commission held by Capt. Richard Roper Kelly in this Corps.

---

War Office, Pall Mall, June 5.

2nd Durham Artillery Volunteer Corps—James Crawford, gent., to be adjt., from the 18th March.

13th Worcestershire Rifle Volunteer Corps—Ens. Henry Stafford Gustard to be lieut.

1st Warwickshire Rifle Volunteer Corps—John St. Swithun Wilders, gent., to be assist.-surg., vice Yates, promoted.

6th Berwickshire Rifle Volunteer Corps—Alexander Mitchell to be capt.; James Smail to be lieut.; and Charles Wilson, junr., to be Ens.

6th Durham Rifle Volunteer Corps—The Rev. Thomas Henry Chester to be hon. chap.

1st Cambridgeshire Rifle Volunteers—Lieut. Albert Decimus Claydon to be capt., vice Prest, re-signed; Ens. John Fuller to be lieut, vice Claydon, promoted; Joseph Garratt to be Ens., vice Beales, resigned; Edward Harry Adcock to be ens, vice Fuller, promoted.

Memorandum—Her Majesty has been pleased to accept the resignation of the commission held by Lieut. William Henry Haslehurst in the 2nd Essex Rifle Volunteer Corps, also of the commission held by Surg. Philip Humbly Banks in the 5th Essex Rifle Volunteer Corps.

4th Lancashire Artillery Volunteer Corps—First Lieut. Henry Duckworth to be capt.; James G. Robinson, gent., to be first lieut.

Memorandum—Her Majesty has been graciously pleased to accept the resignation of the commissions held by the following officers, viz:

Capt. Charles Birley and Hon. Chap. the Rev. William Law Hussey, in the 10th Lancashire Artillery Volunteer Corps.

Ens. Percy Wollaston, in the 42nd Lancashire Rifle Volunteer Corps; and,

Capt. Peter Hopwood Moore, in the 48th Lancashire Rifle Volunteer Corps.

23rd Norfolk Rifle Volunteer Corps—Lieut. Thomas Lancelot Reed to be capt.; Ens. William Thorpe Brackenbury to be lieut.; the Rev. Edward Charles King to be hon. chap.

4th West Riding of Yorkshire Artillery Volunteer Corps—Henry Bomhead, Esq., to be capt; Fredk. Chalmer, gent., to be sec. lieut.

Memorandum—13th Somersetshire Rifle Volunteer Corps—The Lord Lieutenant has, with the approval of the Queen, appointed that Capt. James Whalley Dawe Thomas Wickham shall bear the designation of capt.-commandt. in this corps from the 1st of June.

Memorandum—26th Somersetshire Rifle Volunteer Corps—The Lord Lieutenant has, with the approval of the Queen, appointed that Capt. Henry Bridges shall bear the designation of capt.-commandt. in this corps from the 2nd June.

Memorandum—17th Aberdeen-shire Rifle Volunteer Corps—Her Majesty has been graciously pleased to accept the resignation of the commission held by Ens. James Milne in the above corps.

Memorandum—Her Majesty has been graciously pleased to accept the resignation of the commission held by Ens. Wentworth Clay in the 11th Herefordshire Rifle Volunteers.

## THE ARMY GAZETTE.

*₀* Where not otherwise specified, the following commissions bear the current date.

WAR OFFICE, PALL MALL, JUNE 12.

Royal Regiment of Artillery—Lieut.-Gen. Alexander Maclachlan to be col.-commandt., vice Lieut.-Gen. Richard Jones, deceased—19th May.

2nd Regiment of Life Guards—Lieut. George Augustus Curzon to be capt., by purchase, vice Hamilton Sandford Pakenham, who retires; Lieut. Augustus Fredk. Arthur Lord Sandys, from 96th Foot, to be lieut., paying the difference, vice Curzon; Cecil Alfd. Hughes, gent., to be cor. and sub-lieut., by purchase, vice Frederick French Townshend, promoted; Alexander Cockburn, gent., to be cor. and lieut., by purchase, vice Sir Samuel Hercules Hayes, Bart., promoted; Clarence Peter Trevelyan Kendall, gent., to be cor. and sub-lieut., by purchase, vice Nassau Clark, promoted.

Royal Horse Guards—George Charles, Marquis of Blandford, to be cor., by purchase, vice Arthur Hamilton Scrope, who has retired.

1st Dragoon Guards—Captain Henry Alexander to be maj., by purchase, vice Thomas Nisbet, who retires; Lieut. Leonard Wilson Atkinson, to be capt., by purchase, vice Alexander; Cornet Edward Hoare Reeves to be lieut, by purchase, vice Atkinson.

10th Hussars—Cornet Combré Brabazon Ponsonby to be lieut., by purchase, vice William Morgan Maunder, who retires; Cor. John Charles Stephen Fremantle to be lieut., by purchase, vice Wilfred Brougham, who retires; Edward Spencer Watson, gent., to be cor., vice Ponsonby; the Hon. Henry George Louis Crichton to be cor., by purchase, vice Fremantle.

Royal Regiment of Artillery—Capt. Andrew Aytoun to be lieut.-col., vice Henry Lee Gibbard, deceased—18th May; Sec. Capt. and Brev. Maj. William Howley Goodenough to be capt, vice Richard Paget Campbell Jones, cashiered by sentence of a General Court Martial—22nd Feb.; Sec. Capt. and Brev. Maj. Richard Pittman to be capt., vice Aytoun—18th May; Lieut. John Robert Dyce to be sec. capt., vice Brev. Maj. Goodenough—1st April; Lieut. James Cecil Grove Price to be sec. capt., vice Frederick Ely Smalpage, deceased—3rd April; Lieut. Arthur Carey to be sec. capt., vice Brev. Maj. Pittman—18th May.

The promotions of the undermentioned officers to be antedated as follows:—Captain Herbert Mark Garrett Purvis to 12th Feb.; Sec. Capt. Turner Van Straubenzee to 12th Feb.; Sec. Capt. Henry Webster Shakerley to 22nd Feb.

Military Train—Lieut. Edmund Weston, from half-pay, late Osmanli Horse Artillery, to be lieut., vice Isaac Cummin, who retires upon temporary half-pay; Ens. Thomas Gerard Lockyer to be lieut, by purchase, vice Weston, who retires; Franklin Ludovic Berthon, gent., to be ens., by purchase, vice Lockyer; Lieut. James Milne to be adjt., vice Lieut. Cummin.

Coldstream Guards—Ens. and Lieut. Henry Robert Brand to be lieut. and capt., without purchase, vice William Wynne, deceased—23rd May; the Hon. John Robert William Vesey, to be ens. and lieut., by purchase, vice Brand—12th June.

Scots Fusilier Guards—Ensign and Lieut. the Hon. Henry Thomas Fraser to be lieut. and capt., by purchase, vice Richard Augustus Cooper, who retires; Lord Charles John Innes-Ker to be ens. and lieut., by purchase, vice the Hon. Henry Thomas Fraser.

1st Regiment of Foot—The promotion of Capt. John James Heywood to be antedated to the 29th July, 1862, such antedate not to carry back pay.

2nd Foot—Lieut. Heber Reeve Tucker to be capt., by purchase, vice William Charles Coghlan, who retires; Ens. Reginald Thoresby Gwyn to be lieut, by purchase, vice Tucker; John Campbell, gent., to be ens., vice Gwyn; Neill Roger, gent., to be ens., by purchase, in succession to Lieut. A. Baird, appointed paymaster; Ens. George Herbert Woodard to be adjt., vice Lieut. and Adjt. Alexander Baird, appointed paymaster.

20th Foot—Lieut.-Col. Henry Ralph Browne, from half-pay, late particular service, to be lieut.-col., vice Lieut.-Col. and Brev.-Col. W. Pollexfen Radcliffe, who retires upon temporary half-pay.

21st Foot—Maj. Frederick Cockayne Elton, from a depot battalion, to be maj., vice Maj. and Brev.-Lieut.-Col. George Neeld Boldero, who exchanges.

23rd Foot—Ens. George Pepper Lowry, from the 100th Foot, to be ens., vice William Phineas Bury, who retires.

24th Foot—Lieut. Charles Fredk. Lloyd to be capt., by purchase, vice David Gibson, who retires; Ens. Albert Frank Adams to be lieut., by purchase, vice Lloyd.

27th Foot—Lieut. Wm. Stuckhouse Church Pinwill to be capt., by purchase, vice Henry Mitford, who retires; Ens. Robert Bruce Robertson Glasgow to be lieut., by purchase, vice Pinwill; Henry Burch Pye Phillips, gent., to be ens., by purchase, vice Glasgow; Lieut. Robert Bruce Robertson Glasgow to be adjt., vice Lieut. Walter H. Twemlow, promoted.

45th Foot—Lieut. Adam Perry to be capt, by purchase, vice Arthur William Knox Gore, who retires; Ens. Augustine Hugh Lefroy to be lieut., by purchase, vice Perry; Nevill H. Reeve, gent., to be ens., by purchase, vice Lefroy.

49th Foot—Ens. Philip Julius Honeywood A. Barne to be lieut., by purchase, vice Ernest Christian Wilford, seconded on appointment as lieut. intructor of musketry on the establishment of the schools of musketry.

52nd Foot—Henry Coker Adams, gent., to be ens., by purchase, vice Edward Stewart Ker, who retires.

56th Foot—The promotion of Serjt.-Maj. Joseph Whittaker to be quartermaster, to bear date the 30th Jan, 1863, and not 10th Oct., 1862, as previously stated.

58th Foot—Capt. Henry Carver Treacher, from the 90th Foot, to be capt., vice Perryn, who exchanges; Lieut. Henry John Wynyard to be capt., by purchase, vice Capt. and Brev.-Maj. Wm. Temple Parratt, who retires; Ens. Joseph Barrington Deacon to be lieut., by purchase, vice Wynyard; Oliver Beauchamp St. John, gent., to be ens., by purchase, vice Deacon.

60th Foot—Lieut. James Arthur Morrah to be capt., without purchase, vice Ed. Augustus Stotherd, deceased, 28th April; Ens. John Miller to be lieut., by purchase, vice John East Hunter Peyton, who retires; Ens. Courtenay Forbes Terry to be lieut., by purchase, vice James Kiero Watson, seconded on appointment as lieut. instructor of musketry, on the establishment of the schools of musketry; Fredk. Chas. Blenkinsopp Coulson, gent., to be ens., by purchase, vice Miller; Henry Donald Browne, gent., to be ens., by purchase, vice Terry.

67th Foot—Lieut. Robert Ed. Colborne Jarvis, from the 87th Foot, to be lieut., vice Stevenson, who exchanges.

74th Foot—Ens. John Francis Darvall to be lieut., by purchase, vice John Thomas Evans, who retires; Evelyn John Hamilton, gent., to be ens., by purchase, vice Darvall.

79th Foot—Lieut. Arthur Walker, to be seconded on appointment as lieut. instructor of musketry on the establishment of the schools of musketry.

83rd Foot—Quartermaster Thos. Copeland, from half-pay late Land Transport Corps, to be quartermaster, vice Patrick Hayes, who retires upon half-pay.

86th Foot.—Noel Hovenden Bryan Vardon, Esq., late capt. 13th Foot, to be paymaster, vice paymaster, with the honorary rank of maj., Charles Fade Heatly, transferred to the 18th Foot.

87th Foot—Lieut. Thos. Rennie Stevenson, from the 67th Foot, to be lieut., vice Jarvis, who exchanges.

90th Foot—Capt. George Ed. Perryn, from the 58th Foot, to be capt., vice Treacher, who exchanges.

93rd Foot—Col.-Serj. Harry McLeod to be quartermaster, vice Joiner, appointed paymaster.

96th Foot—Ens. Henry Kimberly Gould to be lieut., by purchase, vice Lord Sandys, transferred to the 2nd Life Guards; Robert William Blackwood, gent., to be ens., by purchase, vice Henry Kimberly Gould.

99th Foot—Ens. George Ivau Thompson to be lieut., by purchase, vice Charles Coates, promoted; Robert Patch, gent., to be ens., by purchase, vice Thompson.

100th Foot—Augustus William Whitworth, gent., to be ens., by purchase, vice Lowry, transferred to the 23rd Foot.

108th Foot—Capt. Arthur James Shuldham to be maj., vice Conolly Dysart, who retires; Lieut. Leslie Creery to be capt., vice Shuldham; Ens. Charles James Dyke to be lieut., vice Creery.

Rifle Brigade—Ens. Walter Caradoc Smith to be lieut., by purchase, vice William Steward Travers, who retires; Ens. the Hon. Thomas Charles Scott to be lieut., by purchase, vice John Francis Mair Winterscale, who retires; Robert Dundas, gent., to be ens., by purchase, vice Smith; Lionel Richard Stopford, gent., to be ens., by purchase, vice the Hon. Thomas Charles Scott; the Hon. Jeffery Charles Amherst to be ens., by purchase, vice the Hon. Thomas John Wynn, who retires.

DEPOT BATTALIONS.

Maj. and Brev.-Lieut.-Col. Geo. Neeld Boldero, from the 21st Foot, to be maj., vice Elton, who exchanges; Capt. Francis George King, of the 21st Foot, to be instructor of musketry, vice Capt. Frederick Stansfield Herries, of the 65th Foot, who has filled the appointment the regulated period —1st June.

MEDICAL DEPARTMENT.

Staff-Surg. Maj. James Stewart, who retires upon half-pay, to have the honorary rank of deputy inspector-general of hospitals; Staff Assist.-Surg. John Coote Ovens to be staff-surg., vice Staff-Surg. Maj. James Stewart, who retires upon half-pay; the promotion of Surg.-Maj. James Gordon Inglis, M.D., C.B., to the rank of deputy inspector-general of hospitals, to bear date 1st May, and not 5th May, as stated in the *Gazette* of the latter date.

BREVET.

Lieut.-Col. and Brev.-Col. George Maxwell, retired full-pay 66th Foot, to have the honorary rank of maj.-gen.; Lieut.-Col. Jas. Peter Robertson, C.B., of the Military Train, having completed five years' qualifying service in the rank of lieut.-col., under the provisions of the Royal Warrant, of 14th Oct., 1858, to be col.—18th May; Paymaster Robert Savery Rouse, 3rd Hussars, to have the honorary rank of capt. —16th April; Quartermaster Patrick Hayes, half-pay late 83rd Foot, to have the honorary rank of capt.

The following promotion to take place consequent on the death of Lieut.-Gen. Richard Jones, Royal Artillery:—Maj.-Gen. Henry Wm. Gordon, Royal Artillery, to be lieut.-gen., 19th May; Maj.-Gen. Sir William Fenwick Williams, Bart, K.C.B., from Supernumerary List, to be maj.-gen., vice Gordon, 19th May.

THE MILITIA GAZETTE.

WAR OFFICE, PALL MALL, JUNE 9.

Norfolk Artillery Regiment of Militia—First Lieut. Ed Henry Gervase Stracey to be capt., vice Harbord, removed.

Northumberland Regiment of Militia Light Infantry—Lieut. W. Pears to be capt., vice Potts, promoted; Lieut. George Pringle

Hughes to be capt., vice John Adamson, resigned

Isle of Wight Artillery Militia—John Young, gent., to be first lieut., vice Brigstocke, resigned.

Memorandum—Her Majesty has been graciously pleased to accept the resignation by Assist.-Surg. John Holt of his commission in the 1st Royal Lanarkshire Militia.

76th, Highland Light Infantry or Inverness, Banff, Elgin, and Nairnshire Regiment of Militia—John F. Baillie to be capt., vice Cameron, resigned.

Queen's Own Light Infantry Regiment of Tower Hamlets Militia—Lieut. Robert Kirkwood to be capt., vice Lawrence, resigned.

Memorandum—Cornwall Rangers Militia—Her Majesty has signified her pleasure that Lieut. Joseph Lyle be removed from the strength of the regiment.

———

WAR OFFICE, PALL MALL, JUNE 12.

Bedfordshire Regiment of Militia—Lieut. Alfred Herbert Lucas to be capt., vice Morhan, resigned.

Queen's Own Regiment of Oxfordshire Yeomanry Cavalry—Cor. Holford Cotton Risley to be lieut., vice Elwes, deceased; the Hon. Gerald Normanby Dillon to be cor., vice Risley, promoted.

Memorandum—90th or Stirlingshire, &c., Regiment of N.B. Militia (Highland Borderers)—Her Majesty has been graciously pleased to accept the resignation of the commission held by Lieut. George Scott.

Memorandum—Her Majesty has been graciously pleased to accept the resignation of the commission held by First Lieut. Thomas Mackinlay, in the Fife Artillery Militia.

———

THE VOLUNTEER GAZETTE.

WAR OFFICE, PALL MALL, JUNE 9.

2nd Essex Rifle Volunteers—Ens. Webster Glynes to be lieut.; John Henry Mitchell to be ens.

5th Essex Rifle Volunteers—Assist.-Surg. Chas. Gibson Taylor to be surg.

Dumbartonshire Rifle Volunteer Corps, 9th Company—Andrew Wyllie, gent., to be lieut., vice James Wyllie, resigned.

20th North Riding of Yorkshire Rifle Volunteer Corps—The Rev. Francis Henry Morgan to be hon. chap.

Memorandum—Her Majesty has been graciously pleased to accept the resignation of the commissions held by Lieut. Henry Gardener Patrick in the 6th Company, and Lieut. John Graham in the 10th Company of Ayrshire Rifle Volunteers.

6th Company Ayrshire Rifle Volunteers—Ens. James Anderson Faulds to be lieut, vice Patrick, resigned.

10th Company Ayrshire Rifle Volunteers—Ens. John Grant Gordon to be lieut., vice Graham, resigned.

4th Lancashire Artillery Volunteer Corps—Sec. Lieut. Danson Cunningham to be first lieut.

1st Lanarkshire Artillery Volunteer Corps—John Kidston, gent., to be sec. lieut., vice Osborne, resigned.

1st Lanarkshire Rifle Volunteer Corps—Ens. David Mitchell to be lieut, vice Alexander Brown, resigned.

4th Lanarkshire Rifle Volunteer Corps—Hugh Rae, gent., to be ens., vice McGregor, resigned.

5th Lanarkshire Rifle Volunteer Corps—William Stirling, Esq., to be hon. col.

25th Lanarkshire Rifle Volunteer Corps—Jas. Cumming Swan, gent., to be ens., vice Bunten, resigned.

55th Lanarkshire Rifle Volunteer Corps—Edward Gilroy, Esq., to be capt., vice Bertram, resigned.

1st Lanarkshire Artillery Volunteer Corps—First Lieut. John Wilson Robinson to be capt, vice Archibald Campbell Holms, resigned; Archibald Gray, gent., to be first lieut., vice Robinson, promoted.

Memorandum—Her Majesty has been graciously pleased to accept the resignation of the following gentlemen of their commissions, viz.:—

1st Lanarkshire Artilllery Volunteer Corps—Assist.-Surg. Bruce Barclay.

1st Lanarkshire Rifle Volunteer Corps—Lieut. David Arnott Reid.

5th Lanarkshire Rifle Volunteer Corps—Surg. James Drummond.

96th Lanarkshire Rifle Volunteer Corps—Ens. John Bowman Graham.

97th Lanarkshire Rifle Volunteer Corps—Surg. Hugh Rae

5th Company of Banffshire Artillery Volunteers at Cullen—John Peterkin to be sec. lieut., vice Sim, resigned.

9th Tower Hamlets Rifle Volunteer Corps—Charles Downes Manning. Esq., to be capt.-commandt.; Lieut. John Back Fisher to be capt.; Ens. Samuel Joseph Ball to be lieut.; Edwin Hooke, gent., to be lieut.; Samuel Henry Croxton, gent., to be ens

Memorandum—Her Majesty has been graciously pleased to accept the resignation of the commission held by Capt. Thomas Chandler.

Memorandum—1st Administrative Battalion of Hertfordshire Rifle Volunteers—Adjt. the Hon. Hugh Henry Hare to serve with the rank of capt., from the 21st May, 1863.

Memorandum—Prince Albert's Own Leicestershire Regiment of Volunteer Cavalry—Her Majesty has been pleased to permit Maj. Arthur Haymes, late of the above Regiment, to retain his rank and wear his uniform.

Memorandum—Her Majesty has been graciously pleased to accept the resignation of the commissions held by Lieut. Jas. Douglas Clephane Wickham in the Oxford University Rifle Volunteer Corps.

Memorandum—Her Majesty has been graciously pleased to accept the resignation of the commissions held by Lieut. George Alexander Augustus Coates in the 2nd Monmouthshire Rifle Volunteer Corps.

WAR OFFICE, PALL MALL, JUNE 12.

1st Flintshire Rifle Volunteer Corps—Lieut. Chas. Butler Clough to be supernumerary lieut.; Ens. William Fitz Ev Jones to be lieut.

4th Flintshire Rifle Volunteer

Corps—John Hancock Wolstenholme, gent., to be supernumerary lieut.

Memorandum—Her Majesty has been graciously pleased to accept the resignation of the commission held by Capt. Henry Talbot Moore in the 14th Kent Rifle Volunteer Corps.

14th Kent Rifle Volunteer Corps—Lieut. William Bartram to be capt., vice Moore, resigned; Ens. William Carr to be lieut., vice Bartram, promoted; William Ireland Blackburn Maze, gent., to be ens., vice Carr, promoted.

1st Warwickshire Rifle Volunteer Corps—Ens. Falkland Samuel Thornton to be lieut., vice Turner, resigned.

19th Lancashire Artillery Volunteer Corps—Hon. Assist.-Surg. Jonathan Wilson to be assist.-surg.

Memorandum—Her Majesty has been graciously pleased to accept the resignation of the commissions held by the following officers, viz: Capt. David Fernie in the 12th Lancashire Artillery Volunteer Corps; and Lieut. Robert Hall in the 10th Lancashire Rifle Volunteer Corps.

11th Gloucestershire Rifle Volunteer Corps—Ens. Wm. Cornock to be lieut., vice Bloxsome, resigned.

1st Surrey Light Horse Volunteer Corps—Cor. Henry Walker to be lieut.; Joseph Daw, gent., to be cor.

19th Surrey (or Lambeth) Rifle Volunteer Battalion — Valentine Hicks Labrow, Esq., to be maj.

Memorandum—The Queen has been graciously pleased to accept the resignation of the commissions held by Lieut. Robert Barclay and Ens. Charles Arthur Barclay in the 14th Company of Surrey Rifle Volunteers.

Memorandum—Her Majesty has been graciously pleased to accept the resignation of the commission held by Ens. Alexander Brebner in the 2nd Aberdeenshire Rifle Volunteer Corps.

## THE MILITIA GAZETTE.

WAR OFFICE, PALL MALL, June 16.

1st or Royal East Middlesex Regiment of Militia—Godson Godson to be lieut. (super.)

Memoranda — The Queen has been graciously pleased to accept the resignation of the Commissions held by the following Officers, viz :—

2nd or Edmonton Royal Rifle Regiment of Middlesex Militia— Surg. Nicholas McCann.

5th or Royal Elthorne Light Infantry Regiment of Middlesex Militia—Capt. Dean John Hoare.

Worcestershire Regiment of Militia—Wilmer Mackett Willet, gent. to be lieut. vice Lieut. Rainforth, appointed to the 24th Regiment.

Edinburgh County Militia— Benjamin Wilson, gent. to be lieut. vice Dunlop, resigned.

Cornwall Rangers Militia — Lieut. Owen Henry Morshead to be capt. vice the Earl of Mount Edgcumbe, resigned.

Artillery Battalion of the Royal Sussex Militia — William John Tonge, gent. to be first lieut. vice Fraser, resigned.

Norfolk Artillery Regiment of Militia—First Lieut. John Stanley Mott to be capt. vice Brereton, resigned.

Memorandum—Her Majesty has been graciously pleased to accept the resignation of the Commission held by Capt. Robert Alured Denne in the Kent Artillery Regiment of Militia.

Kent Artillery Regiment of Militia—Wilfred Simpson, gent. to be super. first lieut. vice Bailey, promoted.

WAR OFFICE, PALL MALL, June 19.

2nd or Edmonton Royal Regiment of Middlesex Militia—Chas. Thomas Carter to be surg. vice McCann, resigned.

Royal Sherwood Forester's or Nottinghamshire Regiment of Militia — Ernest Boteler Lloyd, gent. to be lieut.

North Durham Regiment of Militia—Percival Forster, gent. to be lieut. vice Eames, promoted.

Memorandum—Her Majesty has been graciously pleased to accept the resignation of the Commissions held by Maj. Alexander Cockburn and Capt. Thomas William Usherwood Robinson in this regiment.

Durham Artillery Regiment of Militia — Her Majesty has been graciously pleased to accept the resignation of the Commission held by Capt. Charles Spencer Malley in this Regiment.

5th Regiment of Royal Lancashire Militia—Lieut. John Witham Sutcliffe Witham to be capt. vice John Joseph Middleton, promoted; Lieut. Harry Creeke to be capt. vice Edward Petre, resigned; Lieut. John Grimshaw to be capt. vice Daniel Brereton, resigned.

6th Regiment of Royal Lancashire Militia—Lieut. John Clarke Swanton to be capt. vice Moore, resigned.

5th Regiment of Royal Lancashire Militia—Lieut. Francis Edward Hassard to be removed from the strength of the Regiment.

[The following Appointments are substituted for those which appeared in the Gazette of the 15th ultimo].

Sherwood Rangers Yeomanry Cavalry — Cor. Charles Tylden Wright to be lieut. vice the Earl of Lincoln, resigned; Francis Foljambe Anderson, Esq. to be cor. vice Wright, promoted.

## THE VOLUNTEER GAZETTE.

WAR OFFICE, PALL MALL, June 16.

St. George's Rifle Volunteer Corps—The Rev. Henry Howarth, B.D. to be hon. chap. vice Hawkins, resigned.

26th Middlesex Rifle Volunteer Corps—John Owens, jun. to be lieut.

London Irish Rifle Volunteer Corps — Assist-Surg. Reginald West, M.D. to be surg. vice Duncan, resigned.

37th Middlesex Rifle Volunteer Corps—Lieut. Joseph Day to be capt. vice Ware, resigned.

46th Middlesex Rifle Volunteer Corps—Henry William Bagster to be ens.

Memoranda — The Queen has been graciously pleased to accept the resignation of the Commissions held by the following officers, viz:

Victoria Rifle Volunteer Corps —Ens. John Parnell.

St. George's Rifle Volunteer Corps—Capt. Campbell Munro.

Queen's (Westminster) Rifle Volunteer Corps — Lieut. William Roe.

36th Middlesex Rifle Volunteer Corps—Lieut. Octavius Adolphus Field; Lieut. Robert John Child.

37th Middlesex Rifle Volunteer Corps — Capt. Charles Tayler Ware.

44th Middlesex Rifle Volunteer Corps—Capt. James Paine.

Memorandum—Her Majesty has been graciously pleased to accept the resignation of the Commission held by Capt. George Wauchope in the 1st Midlothian Coast Artillery Volunteer Corps.

Memorandum—Her Majesty has been graciously pleased to accept the resignation of the Commission held by Ens John Milne in the 1st Midlothian Rifle Volunteer Corps.

1st Midlothian Coast Artillery Volunteer Corps—Sec. Lieut. John Reid to be capt.; Matthew Montgomerie Bell to be sec. lieut.; David Younger to be sec. lieut.

1st Midlothian Rifle Volunteer Corps—William James ·Brodie to be lieut.; James Henry Bennett to be lieut.; Thomas Cameron to be ens.; Peter Bell to be ens.

4th Lancashire Rifle Volunteer Corps—William Murray, gent. to be ens.

46th Lancashire Rifle Volunteer Corps—Lieut. Jonathan Waddington to be capt.

Memorandum—2nd North Riding of Yorkshire Artillery Volunteer Corps—Her Majesty has been graciously pleased to accept the resignation of the Commission held by Sec. Lieut. Thomas Stephenson in the above Corps.

Memorandum—1st North Riding of Yorkshire Rifle Volunteer Corps—Her Majesty has been graciously pleased to accept the resignation of the Commission held

by Ens. Thomas Robinson Etty in the above Corps.

Memorandum—19th North Riding of Yorkshire Rifle Volunteer Corps—Her Majesty has been graciously pleased to accept the resignation of the Commission held by Lieut. Henry Rutson in the above Corps.

3rd North Riding of Yorkshire Artillery Volunteer Corps—Sec. Lieut. William Barry to be first lieut.; George Taylor, gent., to be sec. lieut.

2nd North Riding of Yorkshire Artillery Volunteer Corps—Thos. Bagnall, gent., to be sec. lieut.

1st Derbyshire Rifle Volunteer Corps—Lieut. William Turpie to be capt., vice Newton, resigned; Robert Turner, gent., to be lieut., vice Turpie, promoted.

15th Derbyshire Rifle Volunteer Corps—Lieut. Thomas Bateman to be capt., vice Wilmot, resigned; Ens. William Thomas Edward Cox to be lieut, vice Bateman, promoted; Thomas Cartlich, gent., to be ens., vice Cox, promoted.

Memorandum—Her Majesty has been graciously pleased to accept the resignations of Capt. Henry Wilmot in the 15th Derbyshire Rifle Volunteer Corps, and Ens. Robert Turner in the 5th Derbyshire Rifle Volunteer Corps.

7th Isle of Wight Rifle Volunteers—Lieut. John Randall Mann to be capt., vice Graham, resigned.

Memorandum—Her Majesty has been graciously pleased to accept the resignation of Capt. William Stewart Graham in the above corps.

Memorandum—1st Administrative Battalion of Lincolnshire Rifle Volunteers—Her Majesty has been graciously pleased to accept the resignation of the commission held by Lieut.-Col. the Earl of Yarborough.

Memorandum—3rd Lincolnshire Rifle Volunteers—Her Majesty has been graciously pleased to accept the resignation of the commission held by Capt. Parker.

Memorandum — 13th Lincolnshire Rifle Volunteers—Her Majesty has been graciously pleased to accept the resignation of the commission held by Capt. Hilliam.

13th Lincolnshire Rifle Volunteers—Lieut. Francis Thos. Selby to be capt., vice Hilliam, resigned; Ens. Ashley Maples to be lieut., vice Selby, promoted; Joseph Henry Bugg, gent., to be ens., vice Maples, promoted.

2nd Monmouthshire Rifle Volunteer Corps—Lieut. Edwin Richards to be capt.; Ens. Tudor Lamprey Skinner to be lieut.

1st Hampshire Engineer Volunteer Corps—First Lieut. Henry Philip Buchan to be capt.

Memorandum—12th Hampshire Rifle Volunteer Corps—Her Majesty has been graciously pleased to accept the resignation of the commission held by Capt. Sir Wm. Wellesley Knighton.

1st Kincardineshire Artillery Volunteer Corps—Hercules Scott to be capt.; Sec. Lieut. James Crockatt to be first lieut.; James Taylor Thorn, M.D., to be hon. assist.-surg.

Memorandum—Her Majesty has been graciously pleased to accept the resignation of the commission held by Capt. Alfred Farrell in the 3rd Kincardineshire Rifle Volunteer Corps.

Memorandum—1st Administrative Brigade of Argyllshire Artillery Volunteers—Her Majesty has been graciously pleased to accept the resignation of the commission held by Adjt. George Hewson in the above brigade.

---

WAR OFFICE, PALL MALL, JUNE 19.

1st Middlesex Engineer Volunteer Corps—Roger Pocklington to be sec. lieut., vice Simkins, resigned. .

4th Middlesex Rifle Volunteer Corps—Benjamin Alfred Corben to be lieut.

St. George's Rifle Volunteer Corps—Lieut. Henry Browne to be capt., vice Munroe, resigned; Ens. Francis Otter Hodgkinson to be lieut., vice Browne, promoted.

46th Middlesex Rifle Volunteer Corps—John Grenville Syms to be ens,

5th Cumberland Rifle Volunteers

—Michael Rimington to be ens., vice Arnison, promoted.

Memorandum—Her Majesty has been graciously pleased to accept the resignation of the commission held by Lieut. Henry Hodgetts and Ens. John Towerson in the 9th Cumberland Rifle Volunteer Corps.

East York Rifle Volunteers, 1st Corps (Hull) — Edward Stokes Roberts, Esq., M.R.C.S., L.S.A. England, to be assist.-surg., vice Walton, resigned.

6th Corps (Beverley) — Lieut. Richard Hodgson to be capt., vice Barkworth, resigned; Ens. Henry William Bainton to be lieut., vice Hodgson, promoted; Thos. Fredk. Champney, Esq, to be ens., vice Bainton, promoted.

Robin Hood Rifle Volunteer Corps—The Most Noble William Amelius Aubrey de Vere, Duke of St. Albans, to be hon. col.

Newark or 3rd Nottinghamshire Rifle Volunteer Corps—Ens. Wm. Edward Tallents to be lieut., vice Betts, deceased; Joseph Gilstrap Branston, gent., to be ens., vice Tallents, promoted; the Rev. John Garrett Bussell, M.A., to be Hon. Chaplain, vice Ellison, resigned.

4th Forfarshire Artillery Volunteer Corps—First Lieut. Alexander Rae to be capt., vice Shaw, resigned.

11th Forfarshire Rifle Volunteer Corps—Ens. William Davidson to be lieut., vice Carnegie, resigned; David Carnegie, gent., to be ens., vice Davidson, promoted.

Memorandum—Her Majesty has been graciously pleased to accept the resignation of the commission held by Hon. Assist.-Surg. Robert Charles McWatt in the 1st Berwickshire Rifle Volunteer Corps.

1st Administrative Battalion of Berwickshire Rifle Volunteers—Robert Charles McWatt to be surg.

Memorandum--Her Majesty has been graciously pleased to accept the resignation of the commissions held by Sec. Lieut. George Thomas Jolley in the 10th Kent Artillery Volunteer Corps; Sec. Lieut. H. Morgan in the 13th Kent Artillery

Volunteer Corps; Capt. John Robin Harris in the 13th Kent Rifle Volunteer Corps; Capt. Wm. Chas. Butter and Ens. Peter Brown in the 26th Kent Rifle Volunteer Corps.

13th Kent Artillery Volunteer Corps—John Francis Lacy, gent , to be first lieut., vice Pennell, promoted.

13th Kent Rifle Volunteer Corps —Lieut. William Bristow to be capt., vice Harris, resigned; Ens.

Thomas William Marchant to be lieut., vice Bristow, promoted.

Memorandum—Her Majesty has been graciously pleased to accept the resignation of the commission held by Hon. Chap. the Rev. Edward Pigot in the 1st Westmorland Rifle Volunteer Corps, and of the commission held by Ens. Frank Maude Taylor Jones in the 5th Westmorland Rifle Volunteer Corps.

# COLBURN'S
# UNITED SERVICE MAGAZINE

AND

## NAVAL AND MILITARY JOURNAL.

### No. CCCCXVII.—AUGUST, 1863.

## CONTENTS.

### TO CORRESPONDENTS.

The letter of " Manchester" has been forwarded to the writer of the Papers to which he refers, and we hope to be able to reply to our correspondent in our next. Lines on the Battle of Inkermann are declined with thanks. Captain Acklom's "Steam-ship Ventilator" in our next. The article entitled "The Broad Arrow" is under consideration.

### LONDON:

# HURST AND BLACKETT, PUBLISHERS,
### SUCCESSORS TO HENRY COLBURN,
## 13, GREAT MARLBOROUGH STREET.

SOLD ALSO BY BELL AND BRADFUTE, EDINBURGH ; M'GLASHAN AND GILL,

DUBLIN ; AND ALL BOOKSELLERS.

# MILITARY STUDIES.—No. IV.

## CAVALRY.

The preceding portion of this Paper contains facts which seem to justify the conclusion that there is, to say the least, still room for the employment both of divisional cavalry and cavalry reserves. Two questions present themselves here in the first instance; what is the proper kind of cavalry—light, heavy or intermediate to be employed for each, and how should they be organised? With the former we have for the moment nothing to do and apply ourselves therefore to the examination of the latter.

This involves, however, the consideration of a principle that is put forward in almost every tactical work, and has become a sort of shibboleth amongst military men, although its precise value and real meaning seem not to be very generally understood; we mean the doctrine of the combined action of the three arms.

Few general principles will admit of being pushed to their utmost limits or even taken literally, in *ré militari*, and this is precisely what has been done in the most absurd manner with regard to this theory, for the result of its application has too frequently been to mix up cavalry, artillery and infantry in the general organization, without paying the slightest regard to their several peculiarities. Now a combined organization of the three arms far from promoting the combination of this action is a serious impediment to it, because the latter, in consequence of the very great difference in the nature of infantry, cavalry and artillery and their modes of combat can rarely be simultaneous; moreover, the necessity and opportunity for this combination of action never present themselves at all points indiscriminately with the same intensity, whilst the mixed organization, if pushed beyond certain limits, seriously impedes the employment of both cavalry and artillery in the way most fitted to enable them to produce decisive results, that is to say, united in comparatively large bodies. The uniform combination of the three arms in the organization of an army presupposes what never takes place in fact, namely a perfect uniformity in the character of the ground on which the troops are to be employed, and is moreover wholly at variance with strategical and tactical science which teach us, that there are certain decisive points in every line of battle.

What are the limits beyond which, for purely tactical reasons, the mixed organization should not be pushed? the sketch we have given of the action of the Cavalry in the campaign of 1859 in Italy, affords the best answer we can give to this question. The French did not parcel out their batteries and attach them singly to their infantry brigades, the two batteries belonging to each division were kept together in the hands of the general officers commanding these bodies, the reserve artillery of each Corps d'Armée was moreover, as has been shown, in the hands of a

General belonging to that arm; with fewer guns, of a better description it is true, than the Austrian, they performed the most important services, because they were kept together and used *en masse*. The French Cavalry was kept in hand on precisely similar principles; the whole of that arm was under the immediate superintendence and command of Cavalry generals on the field of battle, subject only to the control of the commandant of the Corps d'Armée, it was of inferior quality as is proved by the fact of its having dwindled almost to nothing before it really came into action, but its being kept together, far from preventing the combination of its action with that of the other two arms, favoured this in an extraordinary degree, because it could be and was directed at the proper moment, to the proper point.

The great mass of the Austrian Cavalry was, on the contrary, parcelled out into single squadrons attached to the infantry brigades, it must have suffered severely from the enemies fire, and still we find no trace of its having rendered any service of importance. Edelsheim alone, who had at Magenta five, and at Solferino four squadrons at his disposal, was enabled to do anything worth talking of. In the first named battle he was employed at the right moment and in the right place, in the last named he was permitted to sacrifice his men at the most inopportune moment and in a perfectly false direction.

It is perfectly clear from all this, that the French understand the combined action of the three arms in a very different way from what the Austrians and Germans in general, including the Prussians, do, and, we need scarcely add, in a much more rational manner. Although their Generals deserve this title, to wit an officer capable of undertaking the general command of all arms; in a higher degree than those of most European armies, we still find them employing a greater number of special Cavalry and Artillery Generals than any other nation and this with the best success.

It is a commonly received opinion that the great majority of Cavalry and Artillery Generals have but little acquaintance with general tactics—whether this be founded in fact or not, we cannot pretend to decide, but it might be very fairly retorted that the great majority of Infantry Generals know nothing whatever of Cavalry and Artillery, and usually employ both in the most absurd manner possible. But even supposing this to be an extreme view of the matter on both sides, which it probably is, the general officer commanding a brigade of several battalions has his hands so full of other and more important work, that it is quite impossible for him to devote his attention to the small body of Cavalry usually attached to an Infantry brigade without at the same time neglecting his proper business, and in armies on a large scale, that is such as are organized into Corps d'Armée, the same holds good of the General commanding a division. The French system of keeping their Cavalry and Artillery united in larger bodies and employing

general officers belonging to these arms to command them, is
founded on the principle of the division of labour and a just appreciation of the advantages arising from the employment of special-
lities; and to this much of the success of the French arms in the
field may be fairly attributed.

There are, however, other reasons for avoiding as much as possible, the dismemberment of Cavalry regiments. Detached squadrons
are deprived for the time being of all the resources and benefits of
regimental organization, and when permanently detached they must,
and experience proves they do, melt away with rapidity. It may
be objected that the French Cavalry although kept united in regiments, brigades and divisions during the campaign of 1859 melted
away with much greater rapidity than the Austrians which was
chiefly parcelled out by single squadrons, but it is very clear that
this is to be fairly attributed to other causes; and we have no doubt
that if the Austrian system had been adopted in the French army,
the latter would have arrived on the battle field of Solferino without
a single squadron fit for duty, moreover we don't know what the
Austrians really lost in this way. So much for the question of
mixed organization, and having disposed of it we proceed to consider another portion of our subject.

Nothing can, in our apprehension, be more ill-judged or useless
than to appeal to the feats of the Cavalry in the Seven Years' War,
or at any other distant period of military history, for the purpose
of proving that this arm is still capable of doing great things—we
hold this style of argument to be a great and positive injury to this
arm. All the circumstance of the past and present differ so materially, that is quite absurd to assert that what has been, must
always be possible. The question we really have to solve is:
what are the mutual relations of the three arms now, and what
can be done by one or the other under the present circumstances?

Looking back to former periods of military history we find, to
begin with, the proportion of Cavalry to Infantry not only to be
absolutely greater in the times to which reference is usually made
than at present, in Frederick's army it was about one-fifth, but its
relative strength to have been increased by its being kept together
and employed more judiciously. No wonder then that the Cavalry
played a different and much more important part then than now,
and without underrating the influence exercised by the subsequent
improvements of fire-arms of all descriptions, and the obstacles
presented to the movement of troops by the extension of cultivation,
both of which by the way are enormously exaggerated, we may
safely conclude that the Cavalry has lost much of its importance both
from being absolutely and relatively less numerous, and injudiciously
organized and mixed up with other troops.

There are certain hot-headed partisans of our arm* who affect
to believe that the old pre-eminence of the Cavalry might be once

* The writer of this article is a cavalry officer of nearly thirty years standing.

more attained by a numerical increase of it; and thus far we agree
with them, that an army of genuine Cavalry combined with a
certain quantity of really efficient horse artillery would in the end
carry all before it.  But they lose sight of the fact, that the old
armies, into which the Cavalry entered in so large a proportion,
were in themselves numerically infinitely inferior to the overgrown
hosts of modern times, and seldom exceeded the strength of a
Corps d'Armée of the present day.  There is no civilized country
in the world possessing riders, horses and money sufficient to realize
the idea of such an army of Cavalry, the Infantry is much cheaper
and more easily organized and kept, and will therefore always form
the great bulk of our forces, consequently the Cavalry must be
content to remain what it has now become—an auxiliary.  But the
time is coming, there are already symptoms of its approach in
various quarters, when old Europe will be reduced to huge armies of
Infantry Militia, unsupported by a Cavalry deserving the name,
and then the mounted nations will again ride forth from the north
and east, and new Attilas arise,—the old game will be played
over again and the Cavalry remain for a time in the ascendant; for
it can always throw the Infantry on the defensive, and in this lies
its real force if we were only wise enough to see and acknowledge
it.

What has been related of the deeds of the Cavalry on the plains
of Lombardy during the summer of 1859 in the first portion of
this Paper should suffice to open our eyes on this subject.  Numerous instances occurred in which small bodies of Cavalry, launched
at the proper moment and in the proper direction, not only brought
strong Infantry columns to a standstill, but wholly defeated their
enterprises.  Nor is there anything wonderful in this.  The main
tactical difference between Cavalry and Infantry is, that the former
possesses no power of defence and still less offence when stationary,
but when put into motion its offensive power is very great and may,
in this condition, be applied to defensive purposes; whereas, the
defensive power of Infantry is at its maximum, and, as regards
Cavalry, nearly insuperable so long as it remains stationary; its
offensive power is also increased by its being put in motion, but it
loses in this state all its defensive pre-eminence, and regains this to
its full extent only on resuming its stationary condition which is in
most cases equivalent to an interruption of its offensive movement,
even supposing the line or column not to have been wholly broken
and routed, a chance that always lies on the cards.

The common sense deduction to be drawn from this is; that the
Cavalry, having but slight chances of success against Infantry
when stationary, the defensive power of the latter being then at a
maximum, should as a general rule direct its efforts against that
arm when in motion, that is to say when this same defensive power
is at a minimum; and notwithstanding this, all the controversies on
the Cavalry question that have taken place for the last forty or fifty

years show plainly that Cavalry officers always dream about taking the bull by the horns, and that those of the Infantry but too easily demonstrate that this can rarely succeed. The proper arm to employ against Infantry in position, and supposing the moment for using the bayonet not yet to have arrived, is very evidently masses of artillery, and this latter arm can also continue its efforts against the former when this has been put in motion. But when the Infantry columns or lines approach within a certain distance, the artillery must either limber up and retreat, or lose its guns, and this is the moment for the action of the divisional Cavalry, which should then be directed against the flanks of the Infantry as was so clearly done by the French during the defence of the farm-house Casa Nuova against Windishgrätz.

From charges of Cavalry conducted with energy on this principle the following results and advantages may be fairly expected. If the surprise be complete, which will depend on the ground, and the enemies Infantry be not of the highest order, its total rout will probably follow, our own Infantry will be saved a murderous conflict with the bayonet, and the projected attack will be defeated. In the less favourable case, and supposing the enemy to have time and steadiness enough to form squares, he is nevertheless brought to a standstill, and time is gained for our Infantry to organize a counter-attack, the only safe system of defence, for artillery to reopen its fire, having shifted its position if advisable and what is equally valuable, for fresh troops to arrive.

We must, however, view the question from both sides; and what first presents itself, is the probability that the attacking column of Infantry will be covered on the wings with Cavalry, for the very purpose of protecting it from such interruptions of its progress, or total defeat, as above alluded to. Granted, and we have a negative confirmation in the Austrian account of the failure of Windishgrätz's last attack on Casa Nuova, where it was said that this was mainly attributable to the want of Cavalry on the wings. What follows? simply, that one portion of the divisional Cavalry, on the side of the defence, must be opposed to the enemy's covering Cavalry, and the other to his Infantry column, during its advance. The final result is : first then, here we have the combined action about which so much fuss is made; secondly, it is clear that this work cannot be done by single squadrons attached to Infantry brigades; finally the proof is afforded that the Infantry is by no means so independent of the Cavalry, and the latter far from being so useless as some people would have us believe.

It would be easy to cite from history facts, some few positive, by far the greater number negative, in support of the above views, but the limits of this article prohibit our doing more than refer the reader to Siborne's History of the Waterloo campaign; a work from which those who are desirous of studying tactical questions of this nature, will learn infinitely more than through the distorted medium of theoretical treatises; there one finds, in the descriptions of the battles of Quatre-Bras, Ligny and Waterloo, but especially in the account of the affair of Gemappes, most instructive instances of the good and bad employment of Cavalry, the latter being, to say the truth, predominant.

In the course of this article, we have more than once expressed our opinion, that Edelsheim's feat at Solferino, however brilliant and gallant, and even valuable, as a proof of what may be done with Cavalry, was still merel   a tactical *nonsens*, and that his Hussars might have performedyreally important services at a later period of the day.   McMahon covered his movement on San Cassiano and Caoseana, which contributed so essentially to the victory achieved by the French, on the one flank by the Cavalry of the Guard, on the other by the few squadrons of Chasseurs at his disposal.   It was while this movement was being effected, and not before it had commenced that the Austrian Cavalry should have been employed to prevent it.   Edelsheim drove the Chasseurs off the field, but his efforts against the stationary French Infantry were unavailing, its defensive power being in that condition at a maximum, and the same would have been the case, even if Mensdorff had followed him.   But when the 2nd Corps had commenced its movement and thereby lost half its defensive power, there was no longer any Austrian Cavalry at hand capable of attempting to arrest its progress.   Edelsheim's squadrons were done up, Mensdorff engaged in another direction, and the remainder of the arm scattered about by single squadrons over the field.

It is not so totally useless as many persons suppose to fight lost battles over again on paper, and endeavour to ascertain what might have been the consequence if matters had been managed differently; because few things are more instructive than a clear insight into the faults or omissions committed on both sides.   This may serve as our excuse for calling the reader's attention for a moment to what happened at Medole, in consequence of General Laniugen having withdrawn his Cavalry brigade at the very commencement of the action, and General Vopaterny, who commanded the other brigade of Zedwitz division, having followed too strictly the letter of his instructions, to cover the extreme left of the Austrian Army.

If the Austrian 9th Corps d'Armée, Schaffgolsche, could have maintained its ground against Niel and those portions of Canrobert's corps that came to his assistance, not only would the former have been prevented from forming his junction with McMahon, but the Austrian 3rd and 11th Corps, Schwarzenberg and Veigl, been enabled to convert the eccentric movement in which they were unfortunately involved into a concentric one that would probably have changed the whole face of affairs.   But Schaffgolsche's Infantry was completely decimated and worn out by the never ceasing bayonet charges of Niel's troops, and gradually lost ground before them. If Zedwitz's Cavalry had been present and employed in the way indicated above, the Austrian Infantry would have been spared many of these murderous conflicts, and time gained to bring the reserve Artillery into action, for Niel's Cavalry and reserve Artillery were all employed on his left wing and could scarcely have been withdrawn from thence.

The mode of employing Cavalry against Infantry, here recommended, is, although of late seldom employed, because generally neglected in favour of the very questionable system of launching this arm against squares of Infantry, in truth nothing new. It was that adopted during the most brilliant period in the history of the Cavalry of the Seven Years' War, for instance at Hohenfriedberg, Freiberg, Zorndorf, &c. Frederick the Great says, the true moment for the Cavalry to attack the Infantry is, when the latter has begun to whirl round its colours, in consequence of the fire of the Artillery. Now if we consider that the tactics and arms of the Infantry at that period were very different from what they now are, and moreover that the great improvements effected in the Artillery render it wholly impossible for the Cavalry to post itself cooly in front of the enemy's Infantry and wait for the propitious moment, it is evident that the altered circumstances demand a modification of the original principle, of not attacking unbroken Infantry, which can be best attained in the way we advocate. For Infantry columns in motion, if unexpectedly attacked, are, next to those that have been shattered by Artillery, in the most vulnerable condition we can expect to find them; a combination of both circumstances would of course form the climax.

We shall now endeavour to lay before the reader the link that connects the action of the reserve with that of the divisional Cavalry, to which latter we have hitherto chiefly devoted our attention. We have supposed a column of Infantry to be engaged in an important offensive movement; the enemy launches a portion of his divisional Cavalry against it to arrest its progress, but its wings being covered by Cavalry to protect it against attacks of this nature, the remainder of the divisional squadrons must be employed to meet this. Then results a combination of combats of Cavalry against Infantry, and Cavalry against Cavalry, in which the reserve Cavalry is finally involved. Leaving out of the question, for the moment, the part the Artillery may be called upon to play in actions of this nature, it is evident that the advantage is likely to remain with the party possessing the best or most numerous Cavalry, and knowing how to employ it in the most efficient manner.

There is another point to be taken into consideration. We have shown how McMahon secured the junction of the two divisions of his Corps at Magenta by throwing all his Cavalry into the interval; and how Niel's junction with McMahon and the combined action of the three French Corps d'Armée against the key of the Austrian position at Solferino was secured by Niel and Napoleon throwing the whole of the reserve Cavalry of the French army, covered by masses of Artillery, into the interval between the 4th and 2nd Corps.*

Finally the reserve Cavalry may be employed for the purpose of covering the wing of an army in position, or when advancing to attack one.

The sphere of action and the importance of the reserve Cavalry result very clearly from the above. In olden times, both before and since the invention of Artillery and portable fire-arms, the fate of a battle was frequently decided immediately and directly by the Cavalry of one army driving that of the other off the field at the very commencement of the action; this happened more than once in the Seven Years' War. Leaving the most ample margin for the effect of the improvements of fire arms, big and little, the mutual dependence of the three arms on each other is still sufficiently great to enable the Cavalry even now to bring about similar results immediately and indirectly; the pursuit of the beaten enemy or the task of covering the retreat, to which many would confine the sphere of its action, remain, therefore, as they have always done, subordinate and secondary to the primary object of gaining the battle.

Enough has been said here to show, that the command of the Cavalry of an army is one of the difficult and important duties that can be confided to a general officer; the opportunities for employing this arm successfully occur unexpectedly and suddenly, and are equally evanescent, they may present themselves at the very commencement of a battle, in the midst of it, at its termination, or not at all; it requires the greatest judgment, intelligence, and steadiness, and military knowledge of the highest order, to enable the commandant of the Cavalry to determine the proper moment for daring the utmost, and the greatest fortitude and self-denial to enable him to withstand the frequently occurring temptations to commit acts of foolish gallantry, or Don Quixotism. It is impossible to lay down one simple positive rule for any part of the conduct of the chief of the Cavalry of a large army, and this is one of the reasons why this arm performs so little in proportion to its cost. The hour and the place present themselves frequently, but the man is seldom to be found.

Whilst candour, however, compels us to acknowledge that it is impossible to lay down positive rules on this subject, it is easy enough, and may, perhaps, be useful, to point out faults and misconceptions that have been committed and entertained at various periods up to the present day. Amongst the former, the most prominent and injurious to this arm is, perhaps, the mania for organizing monster Cavalry Corps d'Armée to be worked in one mass

---

* In the number of the 'Spectateur Militaire' for October, 1852, there is an article entitled, " Le Camp de Chalons et la Cavalerie," giving an account of manœuvres of this nature, which show that the French have turned their attention to this point, and are fully alive to its great importance.

by the agency of a system of tactics much more fitted to the Infantry than the Cavalry, that has raged at intervals since the peace of 1815, and came to a climax under the Emperors Nicholas of Russia and Francis Joseph of Austria. Some peculiarity in the personal character of these two sovereigns was, more probably, than any just appreciation of the tactical questions, the inciting motive.

This mania seems to have arisen in the first instance in a spirit of purely servile imitation of Napoleon I, without taking the trouble to inquire to what extent such bodies had answered the purpose for which they were intended, or carefully weighing the positive and well known evils inherent to them against their presumed advantages, or even taking into serious account the detail of their organization.

The latter point is of such importance that it seems desirable to follow it through the several stages of its developement.

In 1805 there is no trace to be found of the application of the principles of the corps organization to the Cavalry in the French army. We find simply a Cavalry reserve under Murat's command, consisting of two divisions of Cuirassiers, four divisions of mounted Dragoons, varying in strength from 2,200 to 3,200 sabres and one division of dismounted Dragoons, 5,800 men,* altogether 112 squadrons and 2,200 men; and in the course of this campaign, this Cavalry was employed by divisions, and no attempt made to unite permanently the action of larger bodies.

In 1807, we find a Cavalry reserve again under Murat's command consisting of three Cuirassiers and five Dragoon divisions altogether 14,990 men 13,269 horses. The divisions varied in strength from 1500 to 2,200 horses, the principle of employing the Cavalry by divisions is still adhered to, and these latter bodies are weaker than before.

In 1809, after Eckmühl and Ratisbonne, the reserve Cavalry under Bessières consisted of one division, twenty-four squadrons, Carabiniers and Cuirassiers, 3,500 horses; two ditto Cuirassiers, sixteen squadrons each, 1800 and 1500 horses; one ditto Chasseurs and Hussars, ten squadrons, 1550 horses; one ditto ditto, fourteen squadrons, 1430 horses, and two light brigades, altogether 97 squadrons, with about 12,000 sabres—the same principles as above being still adhered to.

1812 shows, for the first time, the reserve Cavalry organized into Corps d'Armée much more as a consequence of the gigantic proportions of the Army destined for the invasion of Russia than for tactical reasons. The first and second Cavalry Corps consisted each of one light and two Cuirassier divisions with 12,000 horses; the third had one light, one Cuirassier, and one dragoon division, 10,000 horses; the fourth, one light and one dragoon division, 8,000 horses; the whole under the command of Murat. The divi-

* These were subsequently mounted on horses procured by requisition in Germany, or taken from the Austrians.

visional system, as it then existed and still continues to exist in the
French Army, remained however applicable to these Corps d'Armée,
no attempt being made to handle them *en bloc*.

In 1813, we find the first Cavalry corps with two light and two
heavy divisions, 78 squadrons, 16,000 horses; the second, third and
fifth ditto, with one light and two heavy divisions each, 52, 27
and 46 squadrons respectively, and an average of 10,000 horses
each.  The number of squadrons raised in the division from six to
twenty-two in consequence of the great variety of regimental
organizations and the number of allied troops acting with the
French.

1814 shows merely the *débris* that had been saved from the
Campaign of the preceding year.

In 1815 the Cavalry corps were composed as follows : 1st. two light
divisions, eighteen squadrons, 2,500 sabres; 2nd. two Dragoon
divisions, twenty-four squadrons, 2,500 sabres, one division
Cuirassiers and Dragoons another; Cuirassiers and Carabiniers,
twenty-four squadrons, 3,300 sabres; 4th. two divisions Cuirassiers,
twenty-one squadrons, 3,300 sabres.  Looking at the above dates,
one sees that the successful campaigns and those during which
Napoleon's Cavalry performed important services, were by no
means coincident with the massive organization of that arm, but let
us turn our attention for a moment to the imitators of Napoleon's
Cavalry Corps d'Armée.

It would be incorrect to include amongst these the Prussians,
and much nearer the truth to represent the former as having been
invented for the purpose of copying Frederick's mode of employing
his Cavalry during the Seven Years' War.  The modern Prussian
Cavalry Generals fancy, no doubt, that this system is a continuation
of that adopted by Seydlitz, Ziethen Belling, &c., but on looking
into it more closely, one discovers so many traces of the Infantry
tactics of the nineteenth century, especially of the theory of the
combined action of the three arms, that this may be fairly
doubted.

According to the Prussian organization as determined by the
regulations of 1823, a Cavalry Corps d'Armée should consist of
four regiments of Cuirassiers, four ditto Hulans, the latter being in
Prussia heavy cavalry, two ditto Dragoons, light, and two ditto
Hussars, altogether twelve regiments, forty-eight squadrons, on the
war footing, upwards of 8,000 sabres, or for each of the three divisions about 2,700.  The normal formation places the Cuirassier
division in the first, the Hulan ditto in the second line, and a light
brigade, Dragoons or Hussars, on each wing somewhat rear of the
latter—one of these light brigades being eventually employed as
avant garde, the other for the purpose of acting on the enemy's
flank as occasion might require.  It seems, however, to be the
opinion of the best Prussian Cavalry officers, that eight regiments
or thirty-two squadrons is the maximum that should be employed

as one body, and we find on looking to the manœuvres of 1843 that
the corps employed on that occasion consisted of ten regiments and
forty squadrons, there having been only two instead of four regiments of Hulans.*

The dimensions and internal organization of such a corps as this
are very reasonable, and would permit of the Cavalry being handled
in an efficient manner; perhaps the greatest objection to be made
is to the large number of guns, five batteries attached, although
the Austrian critic of the manœuvres of 1843, supposed to be the
present Field-marshal Hess, was of opinion that the combination of
action of the Artillery was too little dwelt on.

The Emperor Nicholas' three corps of reserve Cavalry consisted:
the first and second each of one division of Cuirassiers, twenty-four
squadrons, 4,368 sabres and one ditto Hulans of the same strength,
consequently for each corps fifty-eight squadrons with 8,736 sabres;
the third or Dragoon corps consisted of eight regiments, eighty
squadrons of heavy Dragoons in two divisions of the enormous
strength of 7,160 sabres each, or 14,320 for the whole corps.
Two batteries, sixteen guns, were attached to each of these enormous
Cuirassier divisions, and three ditto (twenty-four guns) to each of
the Hulan or Dragoon ditto.

A number of normal formations were devised for these divisions,
the chief characteristic being, either multiplication of lines of
double squadrons (regimental divisions) deployed, or in lines of
columns at deployment distance, sometimes supported by a brigade
mass, close column at quarter distance, or one whole division in
the first named formation, the other in the reserve ditto, mass or
column at quarter distance. The Artillery is almost always disposed in single batteries on the wings of the first line, but is sometimes united into one large battery before its centre.

It is evident on looking at these formations with their multiplied
supports and covering detachments, all at stated intervals and
distances, and especially at the disposition of the Artillery, that the
author had constantly in view the stiff precision of parade
manœuvres; that if any thought of actual combat crossed his vision,
it was that of a cannonade covered by masses of Cuirassiers and
Hulans, and that there is not a vestige of real Cavalry tactics in
the whole affair, indeed the Dragoon corps was nothing but mounted
Infantry and treated altogether as such.

We have shown in a former Paper how defective the organization
of the Austrian Infantry brigades was up to 1860, that of the
Cavalry brigades and Corps d'Armée was perhaps still worse. A
corps consisted of two divisions, four brigades, and each of the
latter of two heavy regiments, Curassiers or Dragoons, with a light
regiment attached, as also a battery of eight guns. The strength
of a heavy regiment was at the time six squadrons of 162 sabres

* A detailed account of these very interesting manœuvres is to be found in the
first volume of the " Aust. Milit. Zeitschrift for 1844, Old Series."

(mounted) consequently in all 972 ditto; that of a light regiment, eight squadrons with 192 sabres (mounted) or 1,536 ditto, and the brigade had therefore twenty squadrons with 3,580 sabres, a division forty ditto with 7,160 ditto, and the whole Corps d'Armée eighty ditto with 14,320 ditto.

Some of Napoleon's Corps d'Armée were no doubt even stronger than this, for instance in 1813, the first corps with seventy-eight squadrons and 16,000 horses, but this was organized differently, and had four divisions with an average strength of 4,000 horses, consequently little more than an Austrian brigade. The staffs of the Austrian Cavalry Corps, divisions and brigades were moreover organized in precisely the same defective manner as those of the Infantry, and to crown all, the Cavalry regulations were assimilated as much as possible to those of the latter arm.

On comparing these Austrian formations* with the Prussian and French, we find the same names applied to bodies of double the effective strength conducted by staffs containing less than one half the corresponding number of officers, and, as a general consequence, a system of tactics wholly unsuited to the Cavalry.

So called great manœuvres were perpetrated in 1851, 52, 53 and 57, the attempt being made at first to work a whole corps *en masse*, then a division, and finally a brigade; each set of manœuvres proving the inefficiency of the system adopted and engendering new Cavalry regulations, four of which appeared in the space of five years.

The enormous sums these great Cavalry manœuvres must have cost, although onerous enough in the then state of the Austrian finances, was not the worst part of the evil, the attempt to move such unwieldly bodies symmetrically and in unison, naturally led to the substitution of formal drill and parade for genuine manœuvoring, and encumbered the regulation with complicated difficult and wholly useless formations and movements.

But to those who take an interest in Cavalry tactics, the plans of these Austrian manœuvres which have been published at Vienna from time to time afford valuable instruction; they prove in the most convincing manner that the attempt to unite very large bodies of Cavalry in permanent organizations and apply to these the rules of formal tactics, leads directly to results, wholly at variance with the principles on which the efficiency of the arm really depend. We find, for instance, one single charge to be the usual result of manœuvres that lasted four or five hours, or even longer. Now it is universally admitted both by the opponents and admirers of the Cavalry, that its best, if not only, chance of success mainly depends on surprise, and consequently on rapidity of evolution, and this can never be attained by such unwieldly formations as the Austrian Cavalry corps we have here described.

* It is right to mention that there were also cavalry brigades, consisting of 2 light regiments, 16 squadrons, 3072 sabres; but these were destined to act independantly, the regular formation of the brigades of the reserve cavalry was a detached force.

It would seem, however, that these manœuvres have not been altogether devoid of positive and valuable practical results, for although the object proposed has certainly not been attained, the efforts made in its pursuit have not only had the effect of gradually eliminating from the Austrian Cavalry regulations a vast number of antiquated and useless formations and movements, but what is still more important, they have engendered new principles of formal tactics, whose value will be easily appreciated by Cavalry officers. The most striking of these is, that all formation and the transitions from one to the other, can be effected without halting, a vast progress as compared with what has hitherto obtained and still exists in the regulations of other armies. It results from this, that all formations may be effected towards the front, more properly speaking in the direction of the march, whether in advance or retreat, and it is no longer necessary to lead troops or squadrons to the rear for the purpose of enabling them subsequently to move to the front. This facility and rapidity of evolution has been attained by adopting the principle of invasion as a general rule, the tactical unity at the head of a column or on the right of a line being always No. 1 for tactical purposes, although of course it retains its proper number for those that are administrative, &c. The temporary number applied to the other unities depends on their place for the moment, and varies in almost every formation.

The organization, too, of the Austrian Cavalry has been changed, and as appears to us in the right direction; the heavy cavalry regiments have been reduced to four, the light ones to six squadrons each, and the number of horses equalized throughout, namely 136 for each squadron, exclusive of officers' chargers. A heavy regiment will therefore bring into the field about 540 sabres, and a brigade consisting of two, 1,080 ditto; a light regiment about 800 sabres, or a brigade of two, 1600 ditto. We cannot, however, state exactly what the new brigade organization is to be, and whether, as in the Infantry, the division has been abandoned or not, the Corps d'Armée seem to have been altogether abolished. The permanent organization of overgrown Corps d'Armée is very evidently equally ill-adapted to secure a rapidly combined action of large masses of Cavalry on the field of battle as the system of attaching single squadrons to infantry brigades, the combined action of the three arms. It is probable that one and the same system of organization, namely in divisions of sixteen to twenty-four squadrons, or 2,400 to 3,600 horses, would answer the purposes of the divisional and reserve Cavalry equally well, and therefore being generally applicable, render all higher combinations unnecessary. The organization in separate divisions cannot be an obstacle to the concentration of masses of Cavalry on the field of battle, Frederick the Great never concentrated his squadrons till the moment they were wanted; the divisional organization, however, presupposes good Cavalry generals and a good staff, and when these are wanting the organization Corps d'Armée will scarcely remedy the defect.

We do not mean to say that such formations as the Prussian Cavalry corps might not be successfully handled by clever generals aided by efficient staffs, but there are other than merely tactical considerations that render it expedient to avoid the permanent concentration of a great number of squadrons. The columns of march of such bodies are monstrous nuisances and impediments to the whole army, and to the Cavalry itself, their length, the heat, the clouds of dust, the obstruction of main roads are bad enough; the worst is, that here the sore backs and other injuries that render horses unserviceable, are produced with the greatest rapidity and certainty.

It will be found that the proportion of sore backs almost at zero in the case of single orderlies, increases rapidly as we ascend the scale of patrol squadrons, regiments, brigades, &c., and the reason is obvious. The individual management of each rider decreases in proportion as the number of riders increases. In the case of large columns the heat and dust fatigue the rider, and a regular and steady pace is rendered impossible by the vain attempts made to keep distance; moreover, the control of the squadron officers and the possibility of preventing mischief by re-saddling, when necessary, are reduced to a minimum. The injuries to the horse's backs occur almost always during the latter third of the day's march, when the rider is tired and has grown stiff, and this is the reason why the plan of trotting down the *étapes* is found useful, but this is only then practicable when the Cavalry marches in a great number of small columns.

It is also sometimes a matter of great difficulty to find bivouacs suited to large bodies of Cavalry, and the difficulties of foraging are increased tenfold thereby.

On the 27th of August, 1805, Napoleon I. gave orders for the troops at Boulogne to disembark and march on the Rhine. The Cavalry division of the 2nd Corps d'Armée (infantry) was concentrated at Mayence on the 25th September, that of the third ditto at Speyer on the 28th, of the 4th ditto at Pirmasens on the 25th, of the 5th ditto at Waesth on the 26th, and the divisions of the reserve Cavalry reached Permasens, Schlettsladt, Molsheim and Oberstein between the 16th and 20th of September. All these troops marched through France in small bodies, sometimes by separate squadrons, and reached the Rhine in the best possible condition.

In 1812, after the corps organization had been introduced, the French Cavalry marched by divisions from the moment it crossed the Rhine, although the whole country between that river and the Niemen was either under French authority or in close alliance with France. Thus two heavy Cavalry divisions of the 2nd Cavalry corps marched united from Cologne and Bonn to Weimar, and thence with the remainder of the corps and its Artillery *en masse* to the Niemen. The 1st Cavalry corps was concentrated on the Elbe and pursued its march in one column to the Russian frontier. The losses sustained in consequence, and before a shot was fired, were enormous.

A question that has been much agitated is, whether Artillery should, under all circumstances, or only occasionally, be combined with Cavalry? The advocates of the great Cavalry corps, a certain number of Artillery officers, amongst others Monhaupt, and, it would also seem the majority of the Austrian authorities, Radetzky, Hess &c., not only insist on the necessity of combining the two arms, under all circumstances, but go the length of laying it down as a rule; "that the action of the Cavalry can only succeed when it has been prepared beforehand by Artillery." It has always been a matter of astonishment to us to find these same persons putting forward, in the same breath, the other doctrine, "that the success of the Cavalry mainly depends on the enemy being taken by surprise." these two dogmata cannot be made to harmonize with each other, it is evidently because one or the other is false, and if we attempt to combine them, the monstrous absurdity is engendered, "that the successful action of the Cavalry depends on the enemy being prepared to be surprised."

But a careful and impartial examination of all the normal formations of the Cavalry Corps d'Armée, and of the plans so called great Cavalry manœuvres, prove that these people had always in view combats of great masses of Artillery covered by Cavalry which latter was intended to go in and finish at the end of the cannonade, much in the way in which the Cavalry divisions Devaux and Partonneaux and the Cavalry of the Guard were employed at Solferino. But such an employment of the Cavalry can only be exceptional, especially since the introduction of rifled artillery, and can never be put forward as a general rule.

If we analyze this question, we find it to consist of a number of separate elements that admit of multiplied combinations, and therefore exclude the idea of any one general solution. Taking the divisional Cavalry, in the first instance, we may conclude that it is absurd to attach guns to it permanently; because the Artillery of a Corps d'Armée is best employed *en masse,* as we have already shown, to combine these two arms is to weaken one without strengthening the other other.

Let us next take the case of Cavalry acting against Infantry, and we find, that the latter arm having always Artillery attached, the small number of guns usually attached to the divisional cavalry will be in the most favourable case, perhaps equal, more usually much inferior in number, and therefore in all cases too weak to do anything more than enter into a combat with the enemy's artillery, the Cavalry can gain nothing by this but the loss of men and horses. But some one will say, increase the proportions of guns

attached to the Cavalry—this would be to convert the latter into
an escort or covering party for the former; a strange proposition in
the mouth of those who assert, that rifled guns can destroy Cavalry
at the distance of an English mile or further.

We now come to Cavalry against Cavalry, that is to say to the
work of the reserves.   There are two cases possible, first that both
parties are nearly equal in strength, or secondly, that they are
unequal.   If my enemy be about equal in number, or if somewhat   superior,   my   Cavalry   better   than   his,   I   shall   pitch
into him at once without waiting till he is prepared to be surprised.   This is what the thorough-bred Cavalry General will say,
and we hold that he is right.   If, however, the superiority of
number or quality be very great on the one side, then the weaker
party may certainly advantageously combine Artillery with his
squadrons, or with a portion of them, thus keeping the remainder
available for a favourable opportunity; and if he be sheltered by
a great number of guns, then one can hardly get at him otherwise
than by bringing up guns enough to silence his.   We have already
shown that Mensdorff could do nothing at Solferino against the
French Cavalry because he had no guns to bring up.

But this very instance proves beyond a doubt that the question
at issue is, how is the Artillery best employed—*en masse*, or scattered by single batteries over the whole line of battle?  there can
be no doubt as to the answer, and, therefore, as the Artillery always
loses by being scattered about piecemeal by single batteries, and a
combination of Artillery with Cavalry is indispensable to the latter,
only in the one single case when it is too weak to stand on its own
legs, it follows that the combination of the two arms should only
be temporary and exceptional, and not permanent and regular.

The doctrines of the united action of the three arms must there·
fore be understood only in the sense of their being employed harmoniously, each at the proper moment, and in the right direction,
to the furtherance of the general design or plan of the Commander-
in-Chief, and as this can never be the same in any two actions, and
is impossible to foresee or determine, except in the most general
manner; the attempt to secure this combined action by a combination of organization, to the extent to which it is pushed by the
German school, can only defeat its own object, for each arm loses
thereby more or less of its own independence, and consequently
moral strength, and none more certainly than the Cavalry.

What is called the decline of this arm is therefore the necessary
consequence of a variety of circumstances, many of which are perfectly fortuitous, although others have no doubt a real and deeply
founded existence.   The armies of the present day are so numerous
that they must consist almost exclusively of Infantry, and this alone
condemns the Cavalry to a secondary *rôle*.   Fire-arms in general,
and Artillery in especial, have made enormous progress within a
few years, this too is unfavourable to the Cavalry.   But in the same

proportion as our armies have grown numerically stronger, they have become in many respects intrinsically inferior to what they were.   The enormous drain on human capital on the one hand, and the progress of civilization on the other, have exercised an unfavourable influence on the physical qualities of the soldier.   Whatever may be said to the contrary, it is certain that the three arms have lost much of their former self-dependence, the basis of their strength.   The Infantry considers itself sacrificed unless supported by Artillery and covered by Cavalry, and the latter is readily sacrificed to the more numerous, and if the reader will, more important arm.   The field artillery commenced its career as a secondary and merely auxiliary arm, it has worked itself up to the rank of a principal one, and would now, like the Infantry, convert the Cavalry into its handmaid.   This is not as it should be, let each stand on its own legs, and all three will fare the better.

But there are other reasons for the decline of the Cavalry, inherent in its own nature, any man with straight limbs, a sound chest and good feet can be made into a good Artillerist or Infantry soldier, genuine good Cavalry can only be made out of men that are accustomed to horses from their childhood, in one shape or the other, and really love these animals; otherwise we have more sore backs than sound ones in a short time.   But this subject shall form the conclusion of our paper in a future number.

## COST OF HER MAJESTY'S SHIPS.

It will be remembered how much stress was laid by the Commissioners entrusted with the inquiry into the control and management of Her Majesty's Naval Yards, on the importance and necessity of having accurate and detailed accounts of the expenditure incurred in those establishments, and how warmly the subject was at the time taken up by Parliament.   The Report made by Sir Henry Willoughby and his brother commissioners dwelt, in fact, much more on the system adopted in keeping accounts, than on that which prevailed in managing the officers and men employed in the yards; and as there was no real fault to be found with the mode in which that part of the business of the Navy was conducted, the Commissioners were obliged to assume that there must be *something* wrong, and that this *something* was connected with the statements of the receipt and expenditure of the stores.

"The system of accounts is elaborate and minute," they stated, "but as far as we can judge, its results are not to be relied upon for any particular purpose;" and after explaining at great length the mode in which the accounts were made out, and bringing prominently under notice the plan adopted in ascertaining the value of the articles supplied for various purposes, they wound up with the following suggestions.   First, that the Accountant-General should frame a new system of accounts on the principle of double entry; 2nd. That the accounts should be made up in the dock-yards each month; 3rd. That an annual account should be laid before Parliament, giving a detailed statement showing how the money voted for the dock-yards has been expended on ships and services; 4th. That the forms of accounts should be carefully revised; 5th. That the Accountant-General should consult with the officers and decide upon an uniform system of classification of heads of services at the different yards; 6th. That the storekeepers should be cashiers, and should pay the wages at the yards; and 7th. That the practice of issuing stores without vouchers should be checked by the Superintendents of the dock-yards.

When this Report was printed, it was at once pronounced to be an able, but not an impartially prepared document, and although the larger number of persons were rather inclined to take the same view of dock-yard affairs as the Royal Commissioners, and to conclude that there was some radical defect in the plan on which these establishments were conducted, those who were practically acquainted with the real merits of the case were not surprised to find that the Accountant-General of the Navy, who was described by the Commissioners as "an officer well fitted by his great expierence and acknowledged ability to remodel the department," shortly afterwards reported that, although the returns were not so satisfactory in their results as might be desired, they were sound on the whole, as a basis for a great account to show the expense of each establishment, and that the public need be under no fear that one shilling of the public money is applied to any other purpose than that for which it is voted by Parliament.   But unfortunately the great mass of readers are too ready to receive implicitly any statement which tends to throw discredit on the Government departments, or anything which seems to confirm their pre-conceived notions as to the superiority of private over public establishments; so much so, that they frequently quote as true, and repeat as correct, assertions which have been shown to be false and unfounded.   This was the case with the author of the pamphlet entitled "The Three Panics," which appeared about twelve months after Sir Henry Willoughby presented his Report on the Dock-Yards, as well as with the author of the work on "Taxation, its Levy and Expenditure," published last winter.   They both allude to the incorrectness of the dock-yard accounts, and the statements relating to the cost of Her Majesty's ships prepared therefrom; but they make no allusion whatever to the speeches of responsible ministers, or to the official reports presented to Parliament correcting the mistakes to which we have adverted.

It should always be borne in mind when considering the question of accounts of such magnitude as those kept at the various naval yards necessarily are, that improvements can only be effected

by degrees, or as may from time to time be found to be requisite.
Up to 1830, for one hundred years, there had been little change
in the manner of keeping the public accounts; but from that time
they began to improve, and they have gone on improving ever
since; so that any impartial person who looks into them now, and
who looked into them in former days, will say that, with all their
imperfections, they are much better than they have been before.
The attention of Sir James Graham was given to this subject when
he was at the Admiralty in 1852, and arrangements were made by
his successor, Sir Charles Wood, for ensuring much greater correctness in the accounts, as well as for establishing a proper check
on the expenditure.   These measures have been followed up by
the numerous "First Lords" who have since presided at the
Whitehall Board; and the public are now furnished every year,
soon after Parliament meets, with detailed accounts of the receipt
and expenditure of all monies voted for Naval Services, and of the
expenses incurred on Her Majesty's ships building, converting,
repairing, and fitting.

When the Duke of Somerset was under examination before the
Select Committee of the House of Commons on the Board of
Admiralty, he stated that if it were known exactly what information respecting the cost of building, converting, or repairing ships
were wanted, it could easily be given; and that as it was a great
undertaking to alter the accounts in all the dock-yards, it was very
desirable before they were established on any system, to see that
that system will be such as will give Parliament the information it
wishes to have.   Also, that when they are so established, there
would be no difficulty in keeping them according to the system.
And when his Grace was asked whether he was of opinion that
under the existing system of Admiralty management, it would be
easy to adopt such checks and revisions as would obviate all risk
of inaccuracy for the future, he replied, "That can be done; but
I don't think it very easy.   I think that establishing a system of
double entry in the dock-yards for all the various accounts that
have to be brought together is not a very easy matter.   I think
that when you go into the value not only of the stores brought in,
but of stores manufactured in the yards, of stores returned from
ships, and also from the variety of articles and of value of the
different stores, that there is considerable difficulty in having a
very accurate account."

The old saying, that "where there is a will there is a way," has
proved true with regard to these dock-yard returns.   Directly the
members of the Board were convinced that an alteration in the
plans of keeping them was necessary, and that they required to
be put on an improved footing, they called upon the Accountant-
General to prepare a system of books by double entry for the
dock-yards.   This plan, after being duly considered by the other
principal officers at Somerset House, whose duties were very much

involved in the question, was then adopted, and from the returns which have been recently laid on the table of the House of Commons, we are enabled to form a correct opinion as to whether the Admiralty have carried out the views expressed in both Houses of Parliament on the subject.

The report made by Sir Richard Bromley shortly before be left the Admiralty to become a Commissioner of Greenwich Hospital, shows that in leaving this matter to be dealt with by the Duke of Somerset and his colleagues, the country acted most wisely, and that the executives had the power as well as the will to place this much vexed question of the cost of constructing men-of-war on a satisfactory footing. Every item contained in the Return is based upon orders for materials drawn from store, and for labour applied, signed for by the respective shipwright and factory officers in charge of each particular work; the whole has been checked and audited, and may therefore be relied upon. It is however susceptible of great improvement, and we have no doubt that, under the superintendence of Mr. Stansfeld, who is well versed in mercantile business, we shall see it approach year by year much nearer perfection than it is at present.

Until March, 1860, there was no means of ascertaining correctly the cost of any particular ship, except from the Doomsday Book which was kept in the office of the Controller of the Navy, and which was not of course open to public inspection. At that date, the first of the Returns showing the expenses incurred on Her Majesty's ships, prepared at the instance of Lord Clarence Paget, was presented to Parliament by her Majesty's command. It was an abstract account, accompanied by detailed statements, showing the expenses incurred under the heads of, 1. Ships and vessels building; 2. Ships commenced as sailing vessels, and converted to screws; 3. Ships launched as sailing ships, and subsequently converted; 4. Fitting and maintaining steam ships in commission and in ordinary; 5. Repairing and maintaining sailing ships in commission and in ordinary; 6. Fitting and maintaining hulks, yard craft, boats, &c.; and was signed by the Controller of the Navy. The Return which was printed in February, 1861, was made up on very nearly the same plan; as also was the one presented in the year following; except that ships built in the dock-yards were distinguished from those built by contract and purchased. To each of these papers a memorandum was appended, to the effect that the aggregate expenses incurred under the various heads may in any one year greatly exceed or fall short of the aggregate amount of money voted; in other words, that those sums ought not to balance unless the value of materials in store at the commencement and at the end of the year happened to be the same; and this can never be ascertained without the laborious and costly process of taking and valuing stock.

Since the Accountant-General has had charge of these returns, the difficulty alluded to by the Controller of the Navy appears to have been overcome; and we have now the advantage of seeing the two sides of the account placed in juxta-position. On one hand there is given a statement of the charges incurred under the various heads, and on the other a list of the sums expended at the dock-yards and at the Admiralty. To enable a correct idea to be formed of the business-like manner in which this account is now rendered, and of the vast sums which are included therein, it may be well to give an abridged abstract of it, as follows:

Charges incurred for

| | |
|---|---|
| Ships building in Her Majesty's dock-yards . | £613,829 |
| Ships built by contract, or purchased . . . | 932,323 |
| Ships commenced as wooden vessels converted into iron-cased ships . . . . . | 368,292 |
| Ships launched or commenced as sailing ships converted into screws . . . . . | 118,530 |
| Steam ships fitting out, refitting, repairs, &c., in commission and in reserve . . . | 1,186,442 |
| Sailing ships, fitting out, refitting, repairs, &c., in commission and in reserve . . . | 71,538 |
| Fitting and maintaining hulks, breaking up old ships, building and repairing yard craft, coal depots, &c. . . . . . . . | 82,759 |
| Stores supplied, &c., for other Government departments, private individuals, and foreign Governments, and for making machinery for permanent yard plant . . . . . . | 102,466 |
| | £3,476,179 |
| Deducted for stores, &c., returned from sailing ships, and for breaking up of old vessels . | 41,318 |
| | £3,434,861 |
| Expenditure at Her Majesty's dock-yards . . | £1,894,540 |
| Payments for machinery made by contractors . | 727,794 |
| Payments for vessels purchased or built, and repaired at private yards . . . . . | 770,706 |
| Payment for stores purchased by captains, consuls, &c. . . . . . . . . | 11,637 |
| Expenditure for wages of Metropolitan police, &c. | 30,184 |
| | £3,434,861 |

From this statement it will be seen that the sum paid to the contractors and others for the purchase of vessels and machinery, is nearly equal to that expended at the dock-yards, a proportion with which even the Cobdens, and Brights, and Lindsays, and all the other members who are constantly advocating the employment

of private establishments, may be satisfied, but one which we hope
may not be maintained in future years. The theory that greater
reliance should be placed on the yards belonging to private firms
for building the ships of the Royal Navy, and that the dock-yards
should be used principally for repairing and refitting those vessels,
may be very good in the sight of those who are interested in this
diversion of the money voted by Parliament from its legitimate
channel, but in practice it will be found that in time of peace it
is more expensive, and during the pressure of war it will fail us
altogether.    Even if it could be shown that in an economical point
of view it would be better for the Crown to employ private individuals in preference to its own officers and servants in constructing
the fleet, the mere pecuniary advantage would be greatly out-
balanced by the risk which must in that case be incurred of the
country being placed at the mercy of those whom it could not
control.    The voluntary system may be a very good one, but in
our opinion the establishment system is a much better one.
    This question has, however, received a practical answer within the
last twelvemonths.    When it was determined that the example of
the Emperor of the French should be followed, and that some of
the most powerful ships of the Navy should be built of iron, the
Admiralty entrusted the construction of those ships to private
firms and public companies, and the result has been that " in no
one instance have the contractors kept to their agreements, either
as to time or cost," not only, " has one contractor, or one iron
ship builder, failed in his agreement, but all have done so."    When
to these facts are added the difficulties which, necessarily surround
the question, such as, " the general slovenliness of the work performed, rendering the presence of an inspector necessary on the
premises of the contractor, the great temptations that beset
contractors to use inferior and cheaper materials, the probability of
strikes of workmen, strikes of colliers, disputes in trades," we
think it must be admitted that, however desirous the government
may be to allow the country to benefit by the advantages which
may possibly be derived from occasionally employing private
firms, it would be most impolitic for them to reduce the power
which it now possesses of building, repairing, and re-fitting ships
of all classes. Moreover, it appears that, of the vessels built by contract and launched in 1861, two were returned to the contractors
" not being fit for the service."
    The sums expended on this part of the Navy are no doubt
large, they may indeed be termed enormous ; the results should be
enormous also.    Let us see then what return the country has
received for the three and a half millions expended during the
financial year ended on the 31st of March, 1862.    The following
ships are stated to have been launched from Her Majesty's Dock-
yards, and by contractors, viz. :—

## From Her Majesty's Dock-yards.

| Name | Number of Guns | Tonnage | Horse Power | Total sum expended |
|---|---|---|---|---|
| Africa | 4 | 669 | 150 | £22,135 |
| Aurora | 51 | 2,558 | 400 | 90,775 |
| Defiance | 89 | 3,475 | 800 | 140,036 |
| Glasgow | 51 | 3,037 | 600 | 105,654 |
| Investigator | 2 | 149 | 34 | 6,023 |
| Perseus | 17 | 955 | 200 | 33,265 |
| Rattler | 17 | 952 | 200 | 34,756 |
| Rattlesnake | 21 | 1,705 | 400 | 64,552 |
| Royalist | 11 | 669 | 156 | 25,846 |
| Shearwater | 4 | 669 | 150 | 21,475 |

## From Private Yards.

| Name | Number of Guns | Tonnage | Horse Power | Total sum expended |
|---|---|---|---|---|
| Defence | 16 | 3,720 | 600 | 209,075 |
| Dromedary | 2 | 654 | 100 | 11,562 |
| Resistance | 16 | 3,710 | 600 | 213,047 |

The wooden ships Caledonia, Ocean, Prince Consort, and Royal Oak, were each advanced considerably towards conversion into iron-cased vessels, and the following ships launched as sailing ships were converted into screw steam vessels, viz. :—

| Name | Number of Guns | Tonnage | Horse Power | Total sum expended |
|---|---|---|---|---|
| Arethusa | 51 | 3,141 | 500 | £85,965 |
| Albion | 86 | 3,117 | 400 | 57,450 |
| Bombay | 81 | 2,782 | 400 | 74,556 |
| Collingwood | 80 | 2,611 | 400 | 52,359 |
| Octavia | 51 | 3,161 | 500 | 68,687 |
| Prince Regent | 86 | 2,762 | 500 | 56,816 |

While the ships thus enumerated have been added to the Fleet, 431 steam ships and vessels have been fitted out, refitted, repaired, and maintained in commission and reserve, 64 steam vessels permanently employed as troop, store, and surveying vessels, tenders, yachts &c., have also been fitted out, repaired, and refitted, as also have 200 sailing ships,—and 76 hulks have been fitted and maintained.

For the first time an attempt has been made to institute a comparison of the rate per ton for ships built of wood in Her Majesty's dock-yards, and by contract, from which it appears that the charge on the former varies from £22 19s 3d to £27 18s 2d per ton, and on the latter from £21 19s to £23 15s per ton ; but this statement must not be taken as a fair test of the relative cost of the vessels launched from the public and private establishments ; by a note appended to the return it appears that "owing to the different state of advancement of ships at the period of launching, it is liable to lead to erroneous opinions being formed as to the ultimate cost of the ships, some of them having considerable sums expended upon them for fittings while on the stocks, while on others they are comparatively trifling, the value also of the timber materials increases in proportion to the increase in scantling, which materially affects the rate per ton for large ships." The latter remark is most important in this case, as none of the vessels built in private yards (of wood) exceed 300 tons, while those constructed in the naval yards range from 149 to 2,558 tons, in fact one only of the latter is even approximately of so small a tonnage as the former. In order to institute an exact comparison of the cost of ships built in different places, the capital account of the cost of a ship should not be closed until she is fitted for sea and has left the port in commission, for the money expended for fitting and preparing for the reserve and commission is, in many cases, very large, as will be seen by the following table—

| Ship | Description of charge | | Charge during the year 1861-62. |
|---|---|---|---|
| Albion, fitting, repairing &c. in reserve | | | £9,566 |
| Arethusa | „ | „ | 10,860 |
| Barrosa | | | 13,086 |
| Bombay | | „ | 15,204 |
| Chanticleer | „ | „ | 14,245 |
| Defence | „ | in reserve and in commission | 28,495 |
| Devastation | „ | „ | 15,966 |
| Duncan | „ | in reserve | 16,175 |
| Euryalus, fitting, repairing, &c., in reserve and in commission | | „ | £21,617 |
| Galatea | „ | in reserve | 21,453 |
| Glasgow | „ | „ | 10,158 |
| Marlborough | „ | in commission | 30,939 |
| Orestes | „ | in reserve and in commission | 12,457 |
| Orpheus | „ | „ | 15,958 |
| Phœbe | | „ | 21,347 |
| Resistance | „ | in reserve | 10,690 |
| Sutlej | | „ | 12,031 |
| Tribune | „ | in reserve and in commission | 40,148 |
| Warrior | „ | „ | 67,855 |

Amongst the various items of expenditure of which the Parliamentary return under consideration is composed, there are none which we notice with so much pleasure as those for training ships by boys, and drill ships for the Royal Naval Reserve. By the use of the training ships we feel confident that hundreds of thousands of pounds will ultimately be saved to the country. They are the nurseries from which the supply of trained seamen will be obtained for the fleet; and the education given to the boys, as well as the good habits formed by them while on board those ships, will be the means of improving the service in a manner which can now hardly be estimated. The advantages of having a Reserve of some of the finest seamen in the world, ready to man a fleet of line of battle ships immediately their services are required, have been so fully discussed during the last few years, and are now so generally admitted and appreciated, that we need not enlarge on that gratifying subject. We cannot, however, allow the subject to pass without expressing a hope that this magnificent force may be speedily raised to the number authorized by Parliament, and that some more of the sailing ships remaining in reserve may be appropriated for this purpose; unless it should be found that they are better suited for being placed in commission as troop ships, a purpose for which it would be far preferable to use them, rather than to hire merchant vessels at a much heavier cost to the country.

We cannot conclude our remarks on this subject of Dock-Yard Expenditure, and the cost of Her Majesty's Ships, without noticing the elaborate Return last week laid by Mr. Stansfeld on the table of the House of Commons, containing a copy of the balance sheets showing the cost of manufacturing articles in the workshops of the several dock-yards and steam factories for the year 1861-62; a well prepared Blue-book which we confidently commend to the attention of Sir Hugh Willoughby, Mr. Dalglish, and others, who have hitherto been under the impression that the value of the numerous articles manufactured in the Government establishments has not been correctly ascertained. An examination of this Blue-book will perhaps induce them to change their opinion on this subject.

## MILITARY SCIENCE; ANCIENT, AND MODERN.

In our notice of "Professional Papers of the Corps of Royal Engineers," February, 1863, we expressed our intention of extending our observations on some portions of the subjects to similar transactions of other nations; and we now therefore purpose entering into a comparative survey of the ancient and modern engines of war, and their relative powers for offence, and defence; this practical branch of military science being well worthy attention, and probably such as will be considered interesting not only to those officers who study the theory of their profession, but also to our general readers, many of whom are perhaps unwilling to devote much time to the acquirement of any knowledge excepting that which is practical, and bearing immediately, as it were, on events the results of which may be of vital importance to themselves when engaged in military operations in the face of an enemy. A zealous and good soldier will admit the correctness of the following judicious opinion of the Chevalier Folard, "La guerre est un métier pour les ignorans, et une science pour les habiles gens."

The ancient engines of war, or artillery, may be divided into three classes; 1st, those used for projectiles; 2nd, those for approach and demolition of walls, &c.; 3rd, a miscellaneous class, applicable to various offensive operations.

First Class. The Ballista hurled stones of enormous weight and size. Athenæus relates that a ballista threw a stone of three talents weight, about 330 lbs. Stones weighing 1 cwt. were projected by the Romans at the siege of Jerusalem; and bodies of 1200 lbs. were thrown against the Roman fleet at Syracuse.

The Catapulta threw either stones or darts. Montflaucon had a catapulta, only five inches in length, which projected its dart 400 feet, and Folard possessed a model, only a foot in each dimension, which threw a dart with such force as to cause it to penetrate, and remain in freestone at the distance of 1,300 feet. At the siege of Marseilles, beams of wood twelve feet long, and pointed with iron, were propelled from the top of the walls. The invention of the catapulta caused as great a sensation in ancient times, and led to similiar exertions to overcome its destructive effects, as in the present days are exemplified in the manufacture of gigantic ordnance, and corresponding iron plates to resist the ponderous projectiles of the guns of Armstrong, Whitworth, Blakeley, and others. When the catapulta was first introduced into Sicily, Archimedes exclaimed, " By the gods, the valour of man is now useless;" and good grounds had he for thus expressing his astonishment at witnessing the effect produced by this destructive engine, which hurled stones of such immense weight and bulk, that the angles of square towers were demolished, merlons knocked to pieces, and the most powerful defences of masonry were destroyed and levelled with the ground.

The Scorpion and the Arcobalista were smaller engines, for discharging arrows and darts.

Second Class. There were two descriptions of Battering Rams; the one suspended, which vibrated similarly to a pendulum; the other moveable on rollers.

These were denominated the Swinging and Rolling Rams, and when either of these were worked under a cover or shed, they were denominated Tortoise rams. The swinging ram resembled in form and magnitude the mast of a ship, and it was suspended horizontally at its centre of gravity by chains or cords from a wooden frame. The rolling ram was, in its general construction, similar to the foregoing, except that instead of receiving a pendulous motion, it was a motion of simple alternation or impulsion, produced by the strength of men applied to cords passing over pulleys. Appian declares that at the siege of Carthage he saw two rams so colossal, that one hundred men were employed in working each; and Vitruvius affirms that the beam was often from one hundred to one hundred and twenty feet in length; and Justus Lipsius describes some as one hundred and eighty feet long, and two feet four inches in diameter, with an iron head weighing at least a ton and a half. Such a ram as that described by Lipsius would weigh more than

45,000 lbs.; and the momentum of this, supposing its velocity to be about two yards per second, would be nearly quadruple the momentum of a 40 lb. ball, moving with a velocity of 1,600 feet per second.

The moveable towers employed by the ancients in their sieges, were often of astonishing magnitude. Their height was sometimes forty or fifty feet, to bases of thirty feet square, to be above the walls and stone towers of a besieged city. Vitruvius states that the weight of one of the (helepoles) towers brought against Rhodes was 260,000lb., and that to man and work it 34,000 soldiers were required.

Crows, and Cranes. These were defensive machines used in sieges and engagements at sea. It has been stated that when Marcellus had advanced his galleys close under the walls of Syracuse, Archimedes directed against them enormous machines, which being projected forward, there were let down from them large beams, from which were suspended long ropes, terminating with grappling hooks, which laying hold of the vessels, and rapidly elevating them by the employment of counter weights, upset and sank them to the bottom of the sea; or after raising them by their prows, and setting them as it were on their sterns, plunged them into the water. Other vessels were swung round towards the shore by the application of cranes, and after being whirled through the air were dashed to pieces on the rocks beneath.

The Telleno was a machine for raising a few soldiers higher than the top of the enemy's walls, to discern the movements within, and for aiding the escalading parties.

Having completed the foregoing brief description of ancient artillery, we will give a few more instances of their employment at sieges, and the means taken to avert the destructive effects that would otherwise have resulted from the use of them in the attack of a place.

At the siege of Yotapata, Vespasian placed around the city one hundred and sixty engines for throwing darts and stones; some threw lances, and stones of the weight of 113lb. 10oz. (a talent) together with fire, and a vast number of arrows. At the siege of Jerusalem, Titus employed three hundred catapultæ of diverse magnitudes, and forty ballistæ.

When the Consul Censorinus marched against Carthage, and obliged the inhabitants to give up their arms, they surrendered to him two thousand machines constructed for throwing darts and stones; and afterwards when Scipio made himself master of the same city, there were no less than one hundred and twenty-one catapultæ of the large size, two hundred and eighty-one of the smaller, twenty-three of the large ballistæ, fifty-two of the smaller kind, and innumerable scorpions, arms, missiles, and weapons. When Marcellus laid siege to Syracuse, Archimedes exerted the powers of his mind in the invention of warlike machines. Marcellus had brought with him a stupendous engine, mounted on eight galleys, which Archimedes destroyed by discharging at it single stones of enormous weight while it was at a considerable distance from the walls. Athenæus, speaking of King Hiero's ship, which was built after a model contrived by Archimedes, relates,

"That in this ship they erected a platform, from whence with their engines they threw stones of three talents weight, and at the same time a spear or javelin of twelve cubits in length, (twenty-one four-fifths feet) to the distance of a furlong." Æneus Scipio in a sea fight, found out a way of throwing vessels full of pitch and pine wood at the enemy's fleet, which were as dangerous in their fall because of their weight, as they were hurtful on the score of the burning matter they contained.

Red-hot balls. It was the custom of the ancients to defend themselves with red-hot iron, as is testified by Diodorus Siculus, who saith that "The Tyrians threw great bodies of red-hot iron from ballistæ to burn the besiegers' works."

Ancient Sieges. When the Ancients besieged a place of strength, they surrounded and attacked it on all quarters at once; this the Romans termed *corona cingere*. The corona was single, double, or triple; if three-fold, as was generally the case, the first, or innermost circle was composed of the heavy armed foot, who always began the assault; the middle circle consisted of the *velites*, or light-armed, who with their slings, darts, and arrows, drove the defenders from their parapets, that the heavy-armed might urge the assault with less opposition; the third and outmost body was composed of the cavalry. The army, thus prepared, commenced the attack, the advance carrying scaling ladders, and hurdles to fill up the ditch. This effected, the heavy-armed men formed themselves into the *testudo*, or military shell, by means of their bucklers, forming a slope, from which the stones or darts thrown by the defenders slid off without effecting any injury to the assailants. Sometimes also in storming, a kind of crane was employed termed a tolleno; which was constructed by fixing a mast upright in the ground; across this was placed a beam that moved on an axis; and to one end of the beam a basket was attached, in which soldiers were hoisted up to the top of the walls, to force the defenders from their works, and to facilitate the attack of the troops below. The lines of circumvallation, and countervallation generally consisted of a double ditch and rampart, fortified with towers, or redoubts, breastworks, and palisades.

The Testudo, the Musculus, the Vinea, and the Pluteus were covered machines made of strong planks, under which the pioneers advanced securely to the walls and undermined them, &c. The pluteus moved on wheels, the rest were usually laid on rollers, and were moved forward with levers. The Aggeres were mounds of earth, stone, timber, &c., upon which were placed the battering engines and ambulatory towers. Some of these mounds were raised to a great height; that erected by the Romans against Massada, in Judea, was three hundred feet high, upon which was laid a stone platform to support a wooden tower forty feet high, all coated over with iron. The mound constructed by Cæsar at Avaricum was three hundred and thirty feet broad, and eighty feet high.

Further to corroborate the mechanical knowledge, the military science, and the undaunted perseverance exemplified by the Ancients in besieging a place, we will briefly describe the siege of Tyre, a city strongly fortified both by nature and art; but the capture of which was effected by Alexander at the expiration of seven months, after desperate struggles on both sides; for we learn that, in this obstinately contested siege, no less than eight thousand Tyrians were slain. In order that the battering engines might be able to produce the desired effect against the walls of Tyre, a mole was first formed from the continent to the city; the depth of the sea being three fathoms, and the workmen being galled from the walls by the missiles of the besieged, as well as attacked with vigour by well manned galleys. To oppose these assaults two wooden towers were erected at the extremity of the mole, on which were placed the engines, covered with raw hides and leather, to resist the ignited darts and fireships of the enemy. To frustrate and defeat these scientific operations, the Tyrians prepared a large hulk, filling it with pitch, sulphur, branches of trees, and other combustibles; slinging also to the yards of the two masts cauldrons containing ingredients to add to the conflagration. A favourable wind contributed to the success of the fire-hulk, which was towed to the mole by two galleys; and the combustibles having been thoroughly ignited, the skillful and persevering labours of the Macedonians were set at nought by the conflagation of the towers, &c. Alexander lost no time in constructing another mole, on which were erected the formidable battering engines; and reinforcements arrived to revive the courage of his troops, raising the strength of the naval armament to two hundred vessels. Thus outnumbered, but still undaunted, the bold Tyrians retired to their posts, assailing the hulks and galleys of their enemy with fiery darts, immense stones, and other missiles; and covered vessels were also employed in carrying men to cut the cables of the besiegers' hulks. A squadron was then ordered to drive back the Tyrian vessels, but this availed not, for expert divers plunged into the sea, and cut the cables of the Macedonian vessels. Chains having been substituted for ropes, and the ponderous stones removed, the dreaded battering engines were brought up to the walls of the doomed city. During two days did the resolute and valiant besieged oppose the desperate assaults of the besiegers. Hand to hand, from towers equal in height to the walls, did the equally gallant foemen struggle desperately for the mastery. The bravest of the assailants at some parts reached the battlements by means of spontoons and scaling ladders; at other parts grappling irons, books, burning sand, &c., were successfully employed by the Tyrians in the repulse and destruction of the besiegers. In the attack and defence, courage, perseverance, and militar science were equally conspicuous. Ingenious contrivances and methods of assault were met by equally subtle and adroit modes of resistance. The shock of the battering engines was deadened by raw hides and bags of wool; and breaches when effected, were resolutely defended. The vigour of the enemy at length gave way to the indomitable perseverance of Alexander. On the third day, simultaneously, did the whole of the engines desperately assail the walls, while the fleet attacked the harbours. A wide breach having been made, the hulks with the engines retired, and others with scaling ladders and troops advanced to the assault. Desperate was the struggle, but at last the discomfited Tyrians were forced to yield to the irresistible prowess of the victors, and to submit to the capture of the city. In this obstinately contested siege, which lasted seven months, eight thousand Tyrians were slain, and thirty thousand reduced to servitude.

In our retrospect of ancient warfare, and the *modus operandi*, we will now refer to the pictorial and interesting work, entitled *"Veteres de re militari scriptores,"* (CICDCLXX) by Vegetius, and other Roman writers. The old saying of "there's nothing new under the sun" appears to be verified, with reference to the science of war; for we find in this old publication an invaluable record of military operations, and also a minute description of the various engines used in the attack and defence of cities, the construction of bridges, mode of encamping, and even the employment of paddle wheels for propelling vessels. From the perusal of this publication, it appears quite evident that the boasted military science of the present day amounts to but little; for, in the power of destruction, in the ingenuity, and in the high mathematical knowledge manifested in the construction of some of the engines, proudly may the Ancients contrast their evidences of mental ability even with the gigantic and scientific ordnance, and implements of warfare of the present times.

Confining our attention, chiefly to the military machinery, and projectiles of the Ancients, we will now pass in review the detailed accounts of their construction, and application to the purposes intended; noticing, however, matter having reference to field operations.

Encamping: By Polybius the best mode of forming a camp is laid down, the *fossæ et valli* are described, *Pedites, Equites, Forum, Prætorium*, &c., have each their places assigned to them, all confusion thereby avoided, and the health and comfort of every soldier attended to.

Contrast this with some of the modern operations in the field, look at the Peninsular War, Crimean Campaign, warfare in India, China, Cape of Good Hope, and New Zealand; after all our ex-

perience, may we not hang our heads, and blush for shame when we
reflect how many thousands of our countrymen have perished for
want of wholesome food, the absence of proper attention to their
bodily comforts and health; the blind, or wilful ignorance of those
who sent armies into the field without any regard to their organization, and to the provision of clothing, and food for their sustenance.

Commencing with the Tyrones (recruits) the instruction in the
mode of using their various arms is clearly described, the progressive steps in the completion of a perfect Roman soldier is minutely
detailed, and, reading these, we are not surprised at the result—a
result which entitled Rome, justly, to style herself "the mistress of
the world." Compare our dry and uninteresting "regulations and
orders for the army," "field exercise, and evolutions of infantry"
with these instructions, and we shall understand why the monotony,
the machine like-life of a private soldier in the British Army is
distasteful, and wearisome to all but an automaton. A profitable
lesson might indeed be learnt, if the writers, or compilers of our
military publications would study Vegetius, and the other Roman
authors in the work under notice, and, we will prompt a step in the
right direction, by advising that at the examination of Candidates
for commissions in the Army, passages from Vegetius should be
taken instead of selections from the obsolete and uninstructive
classical authors Ovid and Horace, many portions of which exemplify
the depravity of the human heart, and by raising the evil passions
of youth induce them to enter into vice and profligacy at a more
early age than they otherwise probably would do, if they were
not led astray by the exciteable descriptions of feelings and
actions not only immoral, but some of them having reference to
vices that ought not to have been brought before the youthful
mind;

"Nil dictu fœdum visuque, hæc limina tangat,
        Intra quæ puer est," being totally unheeded;
for contamination, to a certain extent, must be the consequence;
and when a previously artless, innocent boy evinces precocious and
immoral feelings, possibly he is dismissed from the school by the
very man who ought himself to be held responsible for all the evil
that has followed his own want of judgment, and just appreciation
of right and wrong.

Returning to Vegetius' lucid exposition of the art of war, we
would fain extract largely from "Regulæ bellorum generales," but
our limits forbid this, and we therefore only introduce a few of the
rules, as specimens of the style of writing, and of the profitable
instruction to be derived from Chapter XXVI.

Occasio in bello amplius solet juvare, quàm virtus.

Amplius juvat virtus, quàm multitudo.

Amplius prodest locus sœpe quàm virtus.

Qui frumentum, necessariumque commeatum non prœparat,
vincitur sine ferro.

Magna dispositio est, hostem fame magis urguere, quam ferro.

Passing over directions relative to the attack and defence of cities, the construction of the works, and the employment of the various engines of war, we next come to the fourth book of Sextus Julius Frontinus, which, though replete with most interesting directions and anecdotes (relative to operations in the field) is not eligible for our present article, which would be extended to too great a length were we to introduce extracts from Frontinus' work. Far preferable would it be for classical students, who are preparing for commissions in the army, to acquire the knowledge of the Latin language by perusing these anecdotes instead of being crammed from the publications of authors, whose feelings, and descriptions of life are now obsolete, and in many respects repugnant to good taste and virtuous principles. In the compilation of the valuable works of Vegetius, and the other ancient writers, all subjects of warfare are well entered into, and their principles explained, commencing with the use of weapons and engines, the formation and movement of troops, sieges, construction of bridges, castrametation, &c.; in short, every branch of the science of war in the olden times is well explained, and we can only regret that "Veteres de re militari scriptores," has never been translated into English, for the benefit of those who are unwilling, or unable to search for knowledge at the fountain head, in the language of ancient civilization.

Additional value will be given to the Latin publication, when we mention that well executed woodcuts illustrate the description of the application of the weapons, engines, &c., from which much benefit will be derived in considering the results to be expected from the employment of them. Commencing with Funditor (the Slinger) a fine old Roman soldier is depicted, with one stone poised in his sling, and another to succeed it in his left hand. Slingers were practised in throwing stones at marks distant six hundred feet, which were scarcely ever missed. We must not pass over unnoticed the war chariots of the Romans, which are represented drawn by four, or two horses abreast, they being defended with armour, and having across their backs a slight wooden frame, in each of the ends of which three sharp pointed spearheads were fixed. To the wheels of the chariot, scythe blades were attached, and the vehicle, thus armed, and filled with bowmen and spearmen was driven furiously into the ranks of the enemy. The services of the ponderous and sagacious elephant were also made available for battle by the Romans, who erected towers on their backs, and very interesting is the representation of the elephant of war with an armed guide on his neck, and on his back a tower containing eight combatants with their javelins and shields. The invention of gunpowder, and its application to successively improved fire-arms, and guns, soon terminated the employment of war chariots and elephants; and we therefore need not enter further into the Roman mode of breaking through the enemy's line of battle.

*Variarum scalarum figuræ* represent several very ingenious scaling ladders, from which, even in our more enlightened days of military science, our engineers might advantageously copy. One of these ladders appears to have been constructed on the same principle as those at present in our service, consisting of portions which were raised above each other and fastened together. *Inter alias,* light ladders were formed from single poles, on which small blocks of wood were nailed to form steps. The rope ladders were also cleverly made, and, being aware of the difficulty often experienced in campaigns of procuring ladders for storming a fortress, we clearly perceive that the Moderns in this instance have retrograded, instead of evincing any superiority over the Romans. During the Peninsular War, the Duke of Wellington used to ascertain if there were any long ladders in the churches of the cities en route, or in those captured, and, whether from friend or foe, similar was the fate of the long ladders, which, on the army quitting the towns, were no longer to be found in the churches, but in the British siege trains. On one occasion when ladders were wanted for an immediate storm, and the Engineer officer in command stated the impossibility of making them in time, the Duke exclaimed, " have you no baggage waggons, take their sides (which were framed like ladders) and alter them for the purpose." The direction was attended to, and good ladders thus extemporised. The Testudo, and the Masculus were also proofs of the inventive genius of the Ancients ; who, by means of these machines, were enabled to approach in safety the walls of an enemy's city, and, by employing a powerful screw or an oscillating ram within the machine, the walls were demolished.

Aries, the ram, of which there were several kinds, which though simple in their form were tremendously powerful in the effects they produced on masonry, supposed previously to be impenetrable to the blows of any engine that could be invented. Having previously described the two classes of the ram, which were in general use, and most destructive in the attack of enclosed cities, we need not allude further to the pictorial, and detailed accounts of what may be termed the heavy ordnance of the Romans. Boast as we may of our knowledge of the science of projectiles, and plume ourselves, as we do, more and more from day to day on the successive improvements in the construction of gigantic ordnance, and in the formation of iron plates to resist the penetration of projectiles of enormous weight and extraordinary velocity, still we must admire the mechanical skill, and the strong evidence of practical mathematics exhibited by the military engineers of the Ancients. Let any zealous and thoughtful soldier cast his eyes on the representation of the Roman implements and machines of war; let him observe the towers armed with men on the roofs, containing also in the lower story the insidious and destructive ram; these towers, in some instances, being made high enough to overtop the

walls of the besieged city, and provided with a bridge to lower from
a window, smaller towers being constructed in a framework that
by means of a powerful screw they could be raised to a limited
height; all Turres ambulatoriœ being on wheels, and moved by
men to their destined place of assault.  Let the military student
consider the sagacity and mechanical skill displayed in taking advantage of the power of the lever, by means of which cases containing about eight men, fully armed, were raised above the walls and
lowered on the defenders of the beleaguered city, at the same time
that the battering ram was doing its work, and, by repeated blows,
effecting a breach in the masonry surrounding the city.  From
the foregoing exemplifications, let each unprejudiced soldier admit
that more inventive genius was manifested by the Ancients than is
generally imagined; making it clear that though the Moderns may be
termed apt scholars, still the Romans well deserved to be called our
masters in the art of war.

In the construction of military bridges, a few hints may be pro-
fitably taken from Vegetius' work, in which are representations of
every species of extemporaneous bridge, formed from inflated skins
of animals, air-tight boxes, and cylinders, as well as various boats,
&c.; one of the bridges being constructed by laying down planks
on air tight compartments, these cases being most ingeniously
fastened together, and forming a well-shaped boat.  Moreover, to
elucidate the method of exhausting the air in the several compartments, there are drawings of the description of bellows employed
for the purpose.  Let not the inventors of the pontoons, at present
in the service (as well as of those which have been tested and discarded) plume themselves on the inventive genius they imagine
they have displayed; in the indian rubber coats in compartments
which we remember seeing tried many years ago, in the various
descriptions of pontoons, we do not perceive any march of intellect
to boast of, indeed we may almost venture to add our doubts,
whether, notwithstanding the experience in late wars, and the costly
and cumbersome appendage of the present pontoon train, a British
army would as readily effect the passage of rivers as the Ancients
did by using such materials as could be procured on the spot, and
by turning them to profit by mechanical and scientific ingenuity.
How often is a military operation thwarted for want of a little
common sense in subordinates; if the usual means for effecting what
is desired are not at hand, the work is stopped; but, if an officer is
" worth his salt," he should not allow any impediment to frustrate
the execution of the duty imposed upon him.

During the Peninsular war, a field battery of Artillery was constantly in the rear of the division, the commanding officer stating
that, in consequence of the bad roads, the horses were unable to
keep pace with the troops.  Contrariwise to this, another officer's
guns were always ready for their work, simply, because he had the
good sense to call in the aid of bullocks from the commissariat

department when the roads were very heavy. Again, the same officer, when in Canada, was asked for his advice and co-operation in rapidly constructing a temporary magazine for gunpowder, there not being sufficient time for the engineer department to erect one of a permanent nature that might be considered proof against fire and the weather. The true soldier of the Peninsular campaign shrunk not from the arduous undertaking, and merely asked for an order for timber, and for hides of bullocks. His requisitions were complied with, the bullocks slaughtered, carpenters were set to work, the magazine, erected and well covered with layers of skins within the stipulated time, was reported proof and serviceable by the commanding officers of engineers and artillery; the large supply of powder for the war in America was removed from the vessel, in which it had been brought from England, and the ship quitted Quebec before the ice formed in the St. Lawrence, (thus saving a heavy charge for demurrage) this being a second instance of the application of rapid thought, and the employment of appliances at hand for effecting the purpose required, by a sensible and ready-minded soldier.

Reverting to the invaluable writings of the old Romans, unwillingly do we quit the descriptions of the ingenious modes of constructing bridges for the transport of an army across rivers, for modern soldiers might, indeed, derive much profit by copying their predecessors in the game of war; but, as our notice of the works of Vegetius and other Roman authors has already been rather extensive, we must bring the interesting subject to a conclusion by making known the scarcely credible fact that even the application of paddle wheels was in existence in the time of the Romans. Witness "Liburnœ rotatœ figura," in which is depicted a Roman galley with the metal beak of a bird to act as a ram, and also *mirabile dictu*, three pair of paddle wheels, each pair being turned by two oxen, harnessed to bars affixed to three short masts on the upper deck of the vessel of war. The prow of another galley, "Prora rostrata" appears doubly armed for impulsive strokes, for, below a metal boar's head, three sword blades are firmly affixed, "et non raro perforata navigia mergebantur."

Surprising as was the representation of the well armed galley, the drawing of "Navale propugnaculum cum turri," out-herods Herod, for this large galley was armed at the prow with a projecting metal head of a boar, with three sharp-pointed metal blades below it, and was rowed by twenty-four men, over whom a platform was strongly supported; and, on this flooring, two towers were erected with twelve men on their tops, armed with javelins, bows and arrows, and large stones, the space between the towers being occupied by about sixteen men, armed for hand to hand combats. Verily the old Romans were right good soldiers, and it is not surprising that with their knowledge of the details of military science, their fortitude, their discipline, and their indomitable courage, they acquired for their nation, the rightful appellation of "the mistress of the world." Having reached this proud pinnacle, their destiny was fulfilled, and the fall of the Roman empire was such that we can hardly credit that such warriors ever existed on the classic ground now trod by the degenerate Italian race.

> " Oh, Rome, whose steps of power were necks of kings!
> Europe—the earth—beneath her eagle's wings—
> How like a thing divine she ruled the world !
> Her finger lifted, thrones to dust were hurl'd;
> High o'er her site the goddess Victory flew.
> Mars waved his sword, and Fame her trumpet blew.
> What is she now ?   A widow with how'd head,
> Her empire vanished, and her heroes dead ;
> Weeping she sits, a mute and dying thing,
> Beneath the yew, and years no solace bring.
> What is she now ?   A dream of wonder past,
> A tombless skeleton, dark, lone, and vast,
> Whose heart of fire hath long, long ceased to burn,
> Whose ribs of marble e'en to dust return.
> Her shade alone, the ghost of ancient power,
> Wanders in gloom o'er shrine and crumbling tower,
> Points with its shadowy hand to Cæsar's hall,
> Sighs beneath arches tottering to their fall,
> And glides down stately Tiber's rushing waves,
> That seem to wail through all their hoary caves."

We cannot close our survey of " *Veteres de re militari scriptores,*" without introducing one more instance of the Ancients having clearly proved that in the art of war the Moderns will have considerable difficulty in surpassing them; often, perhaps, profitting by their science and experience, without having the generosity to acknowledge from whence they derived the information they palmed upon the world as their own. In " Figura Testudinis" we have depicted a large iron shield composed of rectangular bucklers, closely held together in the form of a sloping roof by Roman soldiers, who thus covered from the impetus of large stones, &c., hurled upon them, were able to approach close to the walls of a besieged city. Thus did the Ancients, and we Moderns do but imitate them, having recourse to iron plates to resist the shock of the projectiles of the present ordnance, instead of the ponderous stones and darts showered from the bulwarks of ancient cities. Interesting and instructive as it may be to trace the progress of military science from age to age, we are unwilling to risk being considered prolix in our expositions and comparisons. Having opened the subject to zealous and meditative soldiers, we leave them to follow in our wake; and (beneficially for themselves and country) may they avail themselves of the knowledge exhibited by the long invincible Romans in the art of war.

" My task is done—my song hath ceased—my theme
Has died into an echo; it is fit
The spell should break of this protracted dream.
The torch shall be extinguished which hath lit
My midnight lamp—and what is writ, is writ.
Would it were worthier.  But I am not now
That which I have been—and my visions flit
Less palpably before me—and the glow
Which in my spirit dwelt is fluttering, faint, and low."

---

## THE SENTIMENT OF WAR.

### By. W. W. Knollys.

The feeling which leads soldiers to hazard their lives in the most
dangerous enterprises, for the sake of apparently intangible results,
may be termed the sentiment of war.  Philosophers and civilians
may be puzzled to account for it, nevertheless it affords one of the
most powerful levers by which a general can move his troops.
Napoleon placed the moral far above the physical in war, and the
history of his campaigns proved most conclusively how correct was
his opinion.  Abstractedly, the "gros bataillons," if composed of
men possessing natural courage, strength, and skill in arms, to an
equal degree with their opponents, being also as well handled, and
occupying as good a position, cannot fail to be victorious.  Practically, we know that many other considerations are involved.  The
consciousness of a good cause, pride of race or birth, the memory of
past achievements, a feeling of hatred or revenge, with last, not
least, a feeling of emulation or enterprise, each of these may over-
throw every arithmetical calculation, every prognostic of the tacti-
tian.  There are many instances of the truth of this remark.  Leonidas and his three hundred Spartans at Thermopylæ.  The resistless
onset of Rupert's cavaliers during the civil war, when proud of
ancient lineage, and confident in the holiness of their cause, they
struck their way through a mass of tapsters and clowns, superior in
numbers, and each of them probably their superiors in physical
strength.  The subsequent success of Cromwell's Ironsides against
these very same Royalists, whose chivalry was, by the sagacious
general, skillfully met by fanaticism.  The triumph of the 42nd
Highlanders at Alexandria, when animated by the soul-stirring
words of Sir Ralph Abercrombie, "Highlanders, remember your
fathers," they overcame, in a series of single combats, the impetuous
onset of the French cavalry, who had broken their ranks.  The
above may be cited as amongst the most striking examples of what
we have asserted.
More powerful perhaps than any other motive, is however the

desire of personal distinction, the fear of personal disgrace.   This feeling not only produces individual acts of courage, in themselves tending largely to success, but also causes a spirit of emulation in the doer's comrades, which brings about esprit-de-corps.   What one man has done, his companions feel it disgraceful not at least to attempt.   A regiment also appropriates to itself what one of their body has effected; and if it can number among its annals many glorious achievements, the conduct of that regiment in action may ever be depended on with certainty.   The necessity is felt of sustaining the existing reputation, and knowing that much is expected, it is eager to prevent public disappointment.   This wholesome feeling extends beyond the ranks of the corps themselves, and other regiments become anxious to acquire an equal success.   "Highlanders, remember Egypt," from the lips of Sir John Moore, who had commanded them in the gloriouspcampaign in that country, animated the 42nd at Corunna with a courage which nothing could resist; while it may be easily credited that the consciousness that they had still a name to make, was not without its influence on the 95th at Alma.   In the history of Napoleon's wars, there is one instance, if not more, of a regiment wiping out past disgrace by the most devoted courage, and eagerly seeking to retrieve the right to carry the eagle of which it had been deprived.   A bit of silk of the intrinsic value say, ten pounds, a silver coin worth a few shillings, a cross made of gun metal, or a simple kettledrum, at once becomes the dearest object of a soldier's devotion or desire, when recognised as a symbol of honour, or valour, and the standard, the medal, the drum, and the Victoria Cross are defended and won at the expense of torrents of blood.   These are not in themselves sufficient to induce men to risk life, wounds, and captivity, were they not regarded as permanent substantial proofs of courage and victory. In all ages, and most countries, has this been acknowledged, though the philosophy of the thing has been probably comprehended by but few.   We find that among the ancient Greeks the loss of a shield was the greatest disgrace that a warrior could suffer.   This impression proceeded from the idea that to retire from a battle without a shield, was a tacit acknowledgment of want of prowess or resolution.   The Romans considered the death of the enemy's leader as a signal triumph, and awarded the title of "spolia opina" to the trophies torn from his corpse.   With them also, the first over the battlements of an assaulted town received, as the proud token of his valour, the mural crown, a wreath which presented in any other way, would have been regarded but as a bundle of worthless twigs.

Among the nations of the East, the loss of their leader in battle is the greatest disgrace that can happen.   There is palpable reason in this feeling, which is founded on something more than mere sentiment; for deprived of their officers, the best troops soon become a rabble.   Among these races, the loss of a kettle-drum is also viewed as discreditable, and every effort is made to capture and defend it.  A chivalrous feeling, however, protects the kettle-drummer, who is rarely molested himself.  Again, on examination, we find a basis for this motive.  The music of the kettle-drum speaks of unbroken ranks ; as long as its sound strikes the ear, the troops know that they are not yet defeated ; while its music exercises that animating influence on the hearers which noise has always produced on men engaged in strife.  The Highland bagpipe is no less stimulating to the Gael ; and here in addition to the influences above mentioned, its spirit stirring tones bring back to the kilted warriors the thoughts of home, of their heather crowned braes, and the grey-haired sires in Scotland, eager to hear of their sons' glorious deeds of arms, and whom the tidings of disgrace would bow to the earth with shame.  Oh, there is something which quickens the blood, and expels fear as by a charm, in the shrill notes of the great war pipe, with all its memories of former victories.  At Lucknow, the gallant Pipe Major, McKay, of the Sutherland Highlanders, who pushed up the breech by his comrades, amidst a storm of whistling bullets, bursting shells, and rushing round shot, never ceased to animate the stormers with their national war music, had no small share in the success, and may claim no slight portion of the glory of that glorious day.  In the account of the Thirty Years' War, we read of the disgrace suffered by a cavalry regiment which had lost its kettle-drum ; while our own military history presents numerous instances of desperate devotion exhibited in defence of that square piece of silk, which when placed at the end of a pole, blessed by a clergyman, and presented by a lady, becomes at once the embodiment of the regimental honour, and the record on which is inscribed the names of the various victories in which the corps has borne a part.  In the mercer's shop it was but a simple piece of silk, liable to be bought for a few shillings by any passer by, and made into a lady's dress.  As a standard it immediately assumes a sacred character, and the true soldier would die sooner than see the revered emblem in the hands of a foe.  Guarded like an idol, with obeisance rendered to it, resembling that paid to the Host, there is something almost fanatical in the soldier's love for the rag which serves as his rallying point in battle.  The different sorts of standards on record are various, and in some cases most whimsical.  The Janissaries at the commencement of a mutiny, always, as the first step, elevated their cooking kettles on long poles, and employed them as their military ensigns.  The standards of the Turks were horse tails, either one, two, or three, according to the rank of the Pacha who commanded.  The Dutch insurgents in 1490, painted the likeness of a loaf and a cheese on their banners.  Many other instances of whimsical fancy might be related if the reader cared to know them.

The French, from the time of the sacred Oriflamme downwards, have ever regarded the colours with the utmost reverence.  In the disastrous retreat from Moscow, when every influence which restrains man, every tie which binds him to his fellow, every thought save that of self-preservation, was utterly swept away in the general demoralization—even then, when the actual present was everything, and the future unthought of, the strongest element in a soldier's faith did not altogether disappear. The 3rd corps—Marshal Ney's—which at the beginning of the campaign had numbered 40,400 men, and had since received numerous reinforcements, was reduced after the passage of the Beresina, to about one hundred men able to bear arms. Then, and not till then, was the order given to abandon the eagles. They were to be broken up and buried. The Colonel of the 4th Regiment, though it seemed doubtful whether he and the few exhausted skeletons he commanded, would ever reach France alive, could not make up his mind to a sacrifice, the severity of which none but a military man can appreciate. He ordered the staff to be burnt, and the eagle to be carried in the knapsack of one of the eagle-bearers, by whose side he himself constantly marched. The writer of this article has seen a snuff-box made out of a preserved fragment of the staff in question. The general commanding the Westphalian regiments exhibited a similar jealousy of the military honour of his men. He caused the silk of the colours to be torn off and distributed among the field-officers, and the staves to be burnt. Just previous to the occurrence of these episodes, the 3rd corps, then scarcely existing but in name, halted to take a few moments repose at the close of three days and two nights almost incessant marching. They could scarcely have been blamed if, at such a moment, they had thought only of their individual comfort. Not so, faithful to their well-earned glory, these military bigots still cherished the emblems of their former fame, and while some of the exhausted, starving, frozen soldiers snatched a hasty slumber, the others mounted guard over the eagles.

The inhabitants of the British Islands have ever exhibited the most dogged courage in the defence of the colours. We read of the 12th Regiment, that when in the war of succession, they were, with the rest of the garrison of Barcelona, compelled to surrender to the forces of Philip V, they destroyed their colours sooner than permit them to become the trophies of the enemy. At the battle of Dettingen, a fierce cavalry combat took place, in which Cornet Richardson, carrying the standard of the 7th Dragoon Guards, was surrounded by the enemy's mail-clad gens-d'armes. Alone in the midst of a surging sea of threatening horsemen, bent brows, flashing swords, and imprecations met him on every side; still he remained undaunted. "Give up the standard," sternly and confidently shouted the nearest Frenchmen. What could the young cornet do? one hand holding the bridle, and the other the colours, he was perfectly helpless. To give up his charge was a thing not to be thought of, but yet how defend it? His resolution was indeed severely tested. Blows were showered on him in such numbers, that his escape from being instantly slain can only be attributed to the fact that the strikers, in their eagerness, got in each others way. The standard pole was hacked in pieces, the cornet received thirty wounds, yet was the standard still held with bull-dog tenacity.  At length, reinforcements coming up, the brave cornet covered with blood and glory, succeeded in carrying the colours into his own ranks.  It is satisfactory to learn that his numerous wounds did not after all prove fatal.

The case of Captain Souter exhibits another signal instance of devotion.  During the dreadful retreat from Cabul in 1839, the 44th Regiment, to which that officer belonged, was, as is well known, almost literally annihilated.  Among the few survivors was Captain Souter.  When the last remnant of the ill-fated force melted away before the combined power of intense cold, and the murderous onslaught of the Affghans, he tore the silk from the regimental colour, and wrapped it round his waist.  He was soon after taken prisoner, and lived to recount at the termination of hostilities, how, even when instant death was staring him in the face, he had still been mindful of the honour of his corps.  The history of the battle of Waterloo displayed two brilliant examples of the strength of that feeling which we have designated as the sentiment of war.  Some of the Polish Lancers succeeded in reaching the 79th Highlanders, at that time drawn up in line, and one of them made a dash at the colours.  He inflicted a painful wound in the eye on one of the young ensigns who bore them, and succeeded in seizing the flag.  The gallant boy, though suffering the most dreadful agony, had resolution enough, even while in the act of falling, to retain his grasp of the precious charge.  Ere another instant had passed, the adventurous horseman was killed, and the wished for prize remained in the hands of him who had shown himself so well fitted to be its guardian.

In another regiment, we cannot remember which, the ensign, a mere boy, who bore one of the colours was shot.  The enemy were advancing in overwhelming force, the regiment was being gradually pushed back, and the colour that had waved above their heads in many a dearly bought victory, seemed destined to become the prize of the foe, in whose discomfited faces it had so often proudly flaunted.  At this instant a gallant serjeant rushed to the front, determined to avert the threatened calamity.  The attempt appeared certain death, but he had only one thought, the honour of his regiment.  Reaching the spot where the colour lay dabbled in mud and the blood of its bearer, he seized it with a nervous grasp, and strove to tear it from the dead man's hands.  He found it impossible to do so.  In the moment of death, the ensign's fingers had tightened round it like a vice.  The flag could not be moved. His own comrades were retiring, the French advancing, nay were almost upon him.  Without a moment's hesitation, the serjeant, by a vigorous effort, cast the corpse and the standard together, across his shoulders, and thus nobly freighted, rejoined his own ranks, friends and foes both uniting to greet the exploit with hearty cheers.   When the Scots Fusileer Guards at Alma, staggered by a storm of shot, thrown into confusion by the retreat of the remnants of the Light Division through their ranks, and misled by an order not intended for them, retired for a short distance, the colours were for a few minutes in great danger, Lieutenants Lindsay and Thistlethwayte who bore them, undismayed by the havoc around, and comprehending no command save that to advance, stood firm, though only supported by the four sergeants who formed their escort.   The Russians, encouraged by the temporary withdrawal of the regiment, came pouring out of the battery, and a crowd of them attacked the colours.   Lindsay and Thistlethwayte bravely resisted with their revolvers, and were well seconded by the centre serjeants. A fierce though brief combat ensued.   Several of the small party had fallen, and the colours seemed lost, when Captain and Adjutant Drummond, whose horse had been killed under him, hurried up to the rescue.   Using his revolver with deadly effect, he somewhat checked the Russian onset.   The regiment now charged up the hill, the Russians fled, and the colours were saved.   In this battle the Queen's colour was struck by twenty-three shots.   The present war in America shows how desperately men will risk certain death for the sake of that object of adoration, which the imagination alone has rendered sacred.   At Alexandria a Secession banner had been erected by one Jackson the landlord of an hotel, on the roof of his house, in full view of the indignant inhabitants of Washington.   Orders were repeatedly sent to bid Jackson take down the obnoxious emblem.   He haughtily refused to strike the flag, swearing to defend it with his heart's blood.   Colonel Elsworth, a young officer of the Federal Army, burned to avenge this insult, and swore to the President that he would bring the trophy and lay it at his feet.   Early one morning the Federal troops attacked Alexandria, and Colonel Elsworth, accompanied by a few of his men entered the hotel, and hastily mounting the stairs seized the standard.   Jackson was in bed at the time, but hearing what had occurred, quickly dressing himself, hurried up-stairs.   On the landing-place he met Colonel Elsworth attended by his men, and carrying with him in triumph the captured flag.   That officer did not long enjoy his triumph, Jackson true to the oath he had taken, and reckless of consequences, at once shot him through the heart.   Neither had Jackson much time allowed him for exultation.   The soldiers infuriated at the death of their commander, and heedless of the presence of his slayer's wife and children, pierced the luckless man with a score of bayonet wounds.   Here was a genuine instance of the power of mere sentiment, two lives staked and lost for the sake of what had neither intrinsic value, nor exercised influence over armed men, nor any large mass of people, but was a mere manifestation of individual opinion.   Sometimes the force of custom causes the preservation of the symbol after a separation has taken place between it and the sentiment it typified. During the Indian mutiny, when military honour had been cast on one side, and loyalty become a stigma, the Sepoys with superstitious reverence still retained the colours which their English rulers had entrusted to them. In the same manner, these same mutineers used to make their bands play "God save the Queen," at the very period when they were striving their utmost to destroy the Queen's rule. The numerous acts of gallantry recognized by the grant of that little simple bronze cross, which is the proudest reward of British valour, afford many interesting themes for the pen of a military historian. The hearts of his readers will swell with pride when they learn—how Probyn at the head of his wild horsemen rivalled the chivalry of the ancient crusaders; how Butler swam the Goomtee at Lucknow, in spite of the shot of the enemy, and fierce alligators, to communicate with Outram; how Home and Salkeld advanced to almost certain death in order to blow in the Kashmirgate; and how the civilian Mangles, though wounded himself, yet carried for miles a soldier who had been shot in the leg.

What influence the thought of the Victoria Cross had in causing these brave deeds to be performed, can only be known to the individuals themselves; but a consideration of attendant circumstances induces us to think that in many cases, the idea of reward did not present itself till after it had been earned. With Englishmen the sense of duty is so powerful, that often the most heroic deeds are performed with a total unconsciousness that any particular merit attaches to them. This national characteristic received an impulse and development from the Duke of Wellington, likely to endure for ages. An example of the feeling is, that it is one of the traditions of Her Majesty's Brigade of Guards that no officer is allowed to volunteer for a storming party, but the first on the roster is taken for that, as for any other duty. Among all nations, the hot-brained, and the impetuous are to be found, therefore in the English Army and Navy, are many who eagerly thrust themselves into any service of danger. As a rule, however, we English, particularly the natives of England proper, are not much addicted to volunteering. What is required to be done, whether the service be dangerous, desperate, or safe, is done, and that is enough. It is either in somebody's province, or else the person nearest performs it, and there is an end of the matter. Notwithstanding, when volunteers are called for by the general in command, there is never any lack of men. On the contrary, the difficulty generally lies in selection, for whole bodies often step forward as one man, ready to cut each other's throats for the sake of incurring ten chances of death, to one of life. With such soldiers and sailors, no artificial incitements in the shape of prizes are required, and the history of the Peninsular War presents as many instances of

daring courage, as does that of the campaigns which have taken
place since the institution of an order of valour. Because, however, British soldiers do not need the stimulus of reward to urge
them on to heroism, there is no reason why such heroism should
not be rewarded.

To withhold the meed of valour, because that valour has not
directly sprung from the hope of obtaining it, would be base indeed.
Moreover, the Victoria Cross is one of those of things which tends
to make the service popular with men before entering the army,
however little the same individuals may be influenced by the hope
of obtaining it after they have become soldiers.  It is a reward,
and a recognition, not a bribe, and is a means of rescuing from
oblivion, deeds which act as useful examples to after ages, and are
amongst the precious ornaments of the military history of the
country.  With regard to decorations, our neighbours are different
from ourselves.  The numerous political convulsions they have
undergone, the constant change of rulers and forms of Government,
have done much to destroy that feeling of patriotism, that sense of
duty, that looking to public approval, and to the pride of the home
circle, which with us has effected so much.  When the public conscience becomes seared, the obligations due to the country are forgotten, and might takes the place of right.  The soldier so often
employed against the liberties of his fellow-countrymen, feels that
he is no longer one of them, that he is a being apart, that he is a
soldier, not a citizen.  The service becomes his home, the applause
of his native place sinks into insignificance when compared with
the approval of his comrades and his general, and ceasing to be a
Frenchman, he merges into that nation within a nation, the French
Army.  Such being the case, nothing save promotion, glory, and
the expression of it, in the shape of crosses and medals, possesses
any influence over him.  This insatiable thirst must perforce be fed
by him who wields that dangerous weapon, a body of unprincipled
armed men.  To retain his authority, he is compelled to supply
the deficiency of the sense of duty, by personal attachment to himself.  He must shew that he is the best purveyor to their desires.
Now promotion alone does not suffice.  All cannot be promoted,
and the soreness of those passed over must be soothed by other
means.  Vanity is the balm employed, and the history of the wars
of France, from the time of the first revolution, shows how successful has been the prescription.  Unfortunately, peculiar conditions
are required, even the self-conceit of a Frenchman would despise
the reward which had no pretext to be considered as earned.  We
have known one exception : seeing a French officer at Varna who
wore the Cross of the Legion of Honour, the writer said with reference to it "Monsieur has doubtless served in Algeria," "No Monsieur," he replied, "I gained it *par ancienneté de service.*"  This is,
however, but an isolated instance, and does not affect the truth of
our assertion.  A continual state of war is necessary for the proper

management of the French army, and that, to do them justice, the rulers of France during the last three quarters of a century have ever been careful to procure.

Another cause of the greater value and importance of conventional modes of reward in the armies of France, than in those of England, may be found in the national characteristics.  Essentially vain and frivolous, a Frenchman is devoted to personal adornment, and often regards the Cross of the Legion of Honour as being desirable as a mere ornament, without reference to what it typifies. The French soldier also fights better as one of a mass than as an individual.  He is doubtless most gallant, but is subject more than any one else to the contagion alike of panic and enthusiasm.  Consequently, individual acts of heroism under depressing or discouraging circumstances require to be elicited by the stimulus of immediate reward.  The distinction between an English and a French soldier, may be summed up as follows : the one fights from a sense of duty, the other from a love of glory.  Under the influence of the latter, the French army has displayed numberless instances of brilliant courage.  Among the most striking of these may be mentioned the following anecdote extracted from Napier's Peninsular War.  "The bridge of Tordesillas over the Duero had been destroyed by the English, and the regiment of Brunswicks Oels sent to prevent its being repaired by the enemy, or a passage effected.  A tower behind the ruins was occupied by a detachment, while the remainder of the Brunswickers took post in a pine wood at some distance. The French arrived and seemed for sometime at a loss, but very soon sixty French officers and non-commissioned officers, headed by Captain Guingret, a daring man, formed a small raft to hold their arms and clothes, and then plunged into the water, holding their swords with their teeth, and swimming and pushing their raft before them. Under protection of a cannonade, they thus crossed this great river, though it was in full and strong water and the weather very cold, and having reached the other side, naked as they were, stormed the tower.  The Brunswick regiment then abandoned its position, and these gallant soldiers remained masters of the bridge.  In conclusion, we will remark that however inadequately the utilitarian may consider the gift of a metal cross, or silver medal compensates for extraordinary risks of death and mutilation, however childish the "sentiment of war" may appear to the philosopher, yet there is no doubt that, under great trials, the soldier has need of every adventitious incentive which can be afforded by an excited mind to a trembling body.  To ignore this fact, is to be ignorant of human nature, to neglect the teachings of history, and to treat men as mere machines.

The "vanity of war" is also very useful, scarcely less so in truth than the "sentiment of war," and indeed the two are often scarcely to be distinguished from each other.  It is astonishing what the trifles are, by which the pride of a regiment is created, and esprit de corps maintained. Green or blue patches of cloth on the cuffs or collars, or as they are called facings, the distinctive marks of a light company man, the piece of black ribbon representing the disused pigtail hanging down the back of the coat of the officers of the Welsh Fusiliers, all possess influences of no slight extent. We know one recent instance, when on the order being given to break up the light company of a distinguished Highland regiment, those of the men who composed it, and were entitled to their discharge, same in crowds and desired their names to be put down for permission to quit the service. Be it remembered these were the very élite of the corps, and had served with it through several campaigns. They liked their profession, but their vanity had been hurt. In the same way, the pride of the Rifle Brigade is so great that the most offensive expression that can be made of to an awkward rifleman is to call him "a red soldier." The privileges of the Guards, one of these, so the story goes, was supposed some years ago, to consist in stepping off with the right instead of the left foot, increase the martial bearing and feeling of this gallant corps to an extent which is palpably apparent. In other corps, even nicknames are treasured up with the warmest affection. The "die-hards" the "dirty half hundred" and "the lambs," for the information of civilians the 57th, the 50th, and the 2nd Regiments, are as proud of these terms as if they were titles of honour given by the Sovereign. There is scarcely an old regiment in the service, which has not got some tradition, some memory attached to it. These are sometimes ludicrous. In reference to the great antiquity of the 1st Royal Regiment of Foot, or, as they proudly term themselves, the Royal Regiment, it has been jokingly asserted that they took their origin from the Roman soldiers forming the garrison of Jerusalem at the time of our Saviour's crucifixion. They have in consequence been nicknamed Pontius Pilate's Guards. In connection with this subject an amusing story is told of the late Duke of Kent. His Royal Highness was Colonel of the Regiment, and exceedingly proud of its fame and reputation. General — aware of this feeling on the part of his Royal friend, determined to "take a rise out of him." "Your Royal Highness' Regiment," said the General, "never misconducted itself but upon one occasion." "When was that? when was that?" said the Duke very gruffly, and with considerable irritation. "When they went to sleep on guard at the Sepulchre," replied the bantering General. With reference to the titles of regiments, an anecdote is related which it may not be out of place to insert here, as it shows what sensitiveness and consequently envy is sometimes felt on this subject. Several regiments were on one occasion being drilled together in brigade. All the corps present with the exception of one had some distinctive title in addition to their numerical and county designation, such we will say as "Royal Welsh Fusiliers." "The Prince of Wales' Light Infantry, &c. The Colonels proud of the names of their regiments invariably prefaced the word of command with the titles belonging to them. For example, "The Royal Welsh Fusiliers, shoulder arms," "the Prince of Wales' Light Infantry, " fix bayonets," and so on. The commanding officer of the one regiment which possessed no distinction became irritated at this, as he considered it, perpetual swagger, and determined to administer a cutting rebuke. His corps was a Nottinghamshire Regiment, so the next time he had to give a word of command, he shouted out at the top of his voice, "Stocking weavers, shoulder arms." The amusement of his listeners may be imagined.

It has been justly remarked that life is made up of trifles, this is particularly the case with the soldier. Whoever neglects to base his conduct on this principle, wilfully divests himself of much power, and in the day of trial finds too late that the study of human nature is to a general but little inferior in utility, to a knowledge of his profession.

## PROPOSED SUBSTITUTES FOR DEPOT BATTALIONS.

As stated in the last number of the "United Service Magazine," I propose in this Paper to sketch and consider shortly some of the plans which have been suggested as Substitutes for the Depot Battalion System, with a view to ascertain whether they offer any means of escape from the sacrifices which the continuance of that system entails on us.

I have already noticed the most important of the objects which the depot or reserve organization of the army is intended to secure. Let us not forget these as we proceed, for they afford the surest test by which the eligibility of all schemes that may be proposed for adoption can be tried.

I need scarcely do more than allude to the four company depot organization which we abandoned some years ago, as a possible substitute for the present system. Although not altogether without advantages, it is liable to such objections as render a return to it inexpedient. It is not necessary to mention more than one of these objections. The four company organization entails a minute division of our depot forces in battalions of too low a numerical strength to be convenient in peace, or serviceable in war. It encumbers us with a number of establishments under separate responsibilities, which is out of all proportion to the aggregate strength of the men employed. Such an arrangement besides adding greatly to the labour of departments, and enhancing the difficulty of supervision, complicates the details of the depot service, and impares the efficiency for any service of a large and important branch of our army. The depot service of the army instead of being conducted as at present by twenty-three Commanders of Battalions, would, if the system were fully carried out, pass into the hands of about one hundred and forty commanding officers, each of whose relations with the departments, the military divisions, and the central authority, would be nearly as troublesome as those of a battalion under the present more compact organization. A little consideration will show this objection to be so fatal, that I need not dwell on it, or contemplate further the possibility of this organization being seriously proposed for re-adoption.

A project has lately been promulgated which attracts a good deal of attention, and deserves careful consideration. It advocates doing away with depots, and forming each regiment into three battalions, of which two, taking it in turn, should be always abroad; the third acting as a reserve at home. This general outline of a scheme appears to promise the solution of at least some of our difficulties. Let us fill in some of the details, and put them to the test we have already proposed.

The training of recruits, the command of home service men, the instruction of young officers, and the custody of attestations and records for the entire regiment, would devolve upon the commander of the home or reserve battalion. The battalions abroad would thus be composed entirely of trained soldiers fit for any description of service. The Reserve Battalion would not, however, like the Depot Battalion, consist exclusively, or even principally, of recruits and men unfit for the fatigues of general service, but would contain only such a proportion of these men as the casualties of the two battalions abroad might render necessary. In other respects its composition would be that of an ordinary regiment on home service. The system of discipline and instruction would be an essentially regimental one, and therefore free from many of the objections urged against Depot Battalions.

The recruit's training would be conducted by instructors of his own regiment, and his duties when dismissed from drill would be performed with officers who might be expected to feel an interest in his proficiency, and of whom the majority would be men of some experience. The young officers and recruits being those of three battalions only instead of six as at present, the objection to their being employed on duty together would to that extent be diminished. The recruits would moreover be exposed to less risk from intercourse with home service men, as the latter, being drawn from three battalions only, would be half as numerous as at present, and as the disadvantages of such intercourse would be corrected by a greater leavening of general service men, and by the frequent changes of station which the necessity of taking part in garrison and camp duty would entail on the battalion.

In case of actual or threatened war, however, on our own soil, the Reserve Battalion, like the Depot Battalion, would necessarily cease to act as a training school. On being called into the field it would either be hampered with a number of untrained men in its ranks, or it would have to be relieved of its training staff, young officers and recruits altogether. In either case we should find ourselves without our accustomed means of disciplining, arming, and clothing reinforcements, except at some hastily formed depot. The formation of such depots during the excitement and general disturbance which would be the consequence of threatened invasion, would be attended with great difficulty, and it is to be feared could not be accomplished in time to be of much use during the emergency.

As a corps for actual employment in defensive operations in the field, the Reserve Battalion is not open to the same objections as those justly urged in that respect against Depot Battalions. It would simply form a battalion of one of our existing regiments, with an old name and high reputation to sustain, and would be composed of officers and men who have devoted the best part of their lives to service in its ranks.

As a school for young officers, the reserve battalion when not employed in the field, would have much to recommend it. The young officer on joining, would find himself amongst the officers of his own regiment, who are known to be the safest companions he can have under such circumstances. His instruction and duty would be superintended by those who are most likely to feel real interest in his progress.

As far then as our test goes, the proposed organization appears to be one that would suit us under ordinary circumstances; but which, if war threatened us on our own soil, would cease to provide for the training of recruits and young officers, and for the care of attestations and records. There are, however, other points connected with the proposed scheme which although not touched by the test we have been applying, must be studied.

It is a prominent feature of the scheme that it would substitute a regimental for the present general system of foreign relief, and that it would fix absolutely the relative numbers of battalions to be employed at all times on home and foreign duty. During peace this would perhaps present no difficulties, except such as might be met by regulating the strength of battalions according to the wants of particular localities, but during foreign war it might be otherwise. We cannot count upon being always able during foreign war to retain so large a force as one third of our battalions on home service. That some such proportion ought to be always available for home defence may be granted, but practically we know that when the emergency abroad arises, we shall probably give way to it as we have so often done before, and lean for the time on our naval, our militia, and our volunteer forces. The possibility that some temporary modification of the plan might become necessary during emergencies abroad, must therefore be contemplated. That this modification would probably consist in establishing depots of some kind or other to fulfil for a time the functions of the reserve battalions temporarily employed abroad, is, I think, evident. The only practical alternative would be to add fourth battalions to the regiments engaged, and this we know is a measure we should avoid as long as possible. The temporary establishment of a certain number of depots to take the places of Reserve Battalions sent abroad during emergencies such as we have alluded to, would not, however, affect the general character of the plan. Such a necessity would be only one of the many inconveniences consequent on a state of foreign war, which, like any other augmentation, we should get rid of on the restoration of peace. It would not, like the hasty formation of depots during threatened invasion, interrupt the working of any part of our system, or be productive of more than temporary inconvenience.

Next, we find that under existing circumstances it would be impracticable to apply the proposed scheme to the whole of our army. To a partial extent we might carry it out by converting the four depot companies of each of our twenty-five double battalion regiments into third or reserve battalions of six or eight companies. The total increase of strength consequent on this conversion would be in the former case fifty, in the latter, one hundred companies. Or we might convert the two battalions of our first twenty-five regiments, consisting at present of twelve companies each, (including depots), into three battalions of eight, nine, or ten companies each. The first number would entail no increase of total strength, simply a re-distribution of companies; the second an increase of seventy-five, the third an increase of one hundred and fifty companies. To meet any increase, a corresponding reduction would of course have to be made elsewhere. The proposed scheme might likewise be extended to the 60th Rifles, and the Rifle Brigade, each of which consist at present of four battalions of twelve companies. The reduction of each to three battalions of twelve companies, would give us a total reduction of thirty-six companies towards balancing any increase of strength caused by the conversion of the first twenty-five regiments. As all our regiments are now composed of riflemen, and as many of them actually occupy higher places in the musketry classification return than the 60th and Rifle Brigade, this measure would not in any way operate injuriously on the service.

Any more general extension of the proposed scheme could only take place simultaneously with a considerable increase of strength, or by the conversion of a number of existing regiments into second and third battalions. I need not say that these conditions are out of our reach. Even if all the arguments in favour of the scheme then were to be granted, it would still remain a question for grave consideration whether it would be expedient to introduce a change which cannot at present be more than partially carried out.

On the whole, however, it appears to me that while we cannot express unqualified approbation of the proposed scheme, it offers many advantages, and even its partial adoption would free us from much of what we complain of at present. Moreover, the system is one which may be very gradually introduced, and its operation tested by experiment before we commit ourselves to its general adoption.

Another plan which has long been a subject of discussion amongst military men, has never, as far as I know, been advanced in public. It proposes to abolish regimental depots altogether; to drill and discipline recruits and young officers in special training establishments; to embody soldiers unfit for any but home duty in garrison battalions; to send invalids to an invalid depot; to establish a central depot for soldiers belonging to regiments abroad, who although neither recruits, home service men, nor invalids, happen to be temporarily within the United Kingdom; and to keep the records and attestations of the entire army in a central office. Let us consider the details of this proposal.

Recruits after attestation would be sent to large establishments especially and exclusively devoted to purposes of instruction, where they would be clothed and thoroughly disciplined before being passed on to their regiments. Each training establishment might have a staff of officers and non-commissioned officers specially selected from the whole army as being the men best fitted for the distinct and peculiar duties of instruction. In order to facilitate by means of example the acquirement by recruits of habits of discipline and a knowledge of military duty, as well as to assist in the training of young officers, a certain number of old soldiers might when no emergency required their presence with their regiments, be attached to each training establishment. By making this temporary duty the reward of good conduct and high soldierly qualities, and attaching to it a small rate of extra pay, a benefit might be conferred on deserving men, and safe guides would be provided for the recruits. The exact proportion of old soldiers required to leaven a mass of recruits, is a matter of detail upon which we need not now enter. Such establishments, besides affording the best possible training for recruits, would enable regiments to take the field unencumbered by untrained men; whilst under almost any emergency of war that could arise, they would themselves remain undisturbed and free to proceed with the clothing, arming, and disciplining of new levies.

It is next proposed that the power should be vested in Her Majesty, to be used only in cases of great emergency at home, of causing recruits of Regiments abroad who happen to be at the training establishments to be drafted when fit for the ranks to regiments on home service; their restoration to the regiments they enlisted for when the emergency shall have ceased being provided for. One is here tempted to consider whether enlistment for general service would not constitute an improvement on our present system; but as it is not an essential element of the scheme under consideration, we may defer doing so to some other opportunity.

The next part of the scheme to be considered is that which deals

with the difficult question regarding the instruction of officers.
Not only is the necessity of home training for the young officers of
regiments on foreign service recognized in this scheme, but it forms
a part of it that a system of preparatory training should be generally adopted throughout the army.  While suggesting the means
of securing this object, an effort is made to show that the evils complained of in depot battalions may at the same time be avoided.
In order to explain this part of the plan fully, I must beg the
indulgence of my readers whilst I venture to go a little more into
detail than has hitherto been necessary.

It is suggested that certain of the proposed training establishments for recruits should have attached to them schools for the
professional training of officers.  This professional training, it is
suggested, might be given immediately before appointment to commissions, or immediately after, the details of the scheme being equally
applicable to either course.  The system of discipline to be pursued would, however, necessarily differ in the two cases.  In the
former some such system as is now in force at the Royal Military
Colleges might be adopted, in the latter such close supervision and
control would neither be practicable nor expedient.  When it is remembered that the staff officers of the training establishments would
be men specially selected for their posts, and their success in the
performance of their duties judged of by results, either of these
courses might, it is urged, be accepted as offering satisfactory means
of supervision, and as much freedom from the risk of bad example
as it is possible to secure.

It is further suggested that the young officer's course at the training school should be one of instruction exclusively, and that when
considered qualified to perform duty on his own responsibility, he
should be at once sent to his regiment.  On an average, three or
four months' instruction would be found sufficient to qualify for the
performance of duty.  The object contemplated in thus restricting
the course is to guard against the possibility of any part of the
actual duty of the recruit establishment being entrusted to the young
officers ; it being an essential condition of this scheme that such
duty should be performed by the selected staff-officers, and by them
only.  The young officer would  go through the whole of the
recruit course of instruction in drill and musketry with the recruits,
armed and dressed as a private.  He would then be dismissed from
recruit drill, and his connection with the recruit branch of the
establishment would finally terminate.  He would next enter on a
second course of instruction, in which he would be attached exclusively to the old soldiers serving with the establishment.  In this
he would practice the duties of non-commissioned officer, and officer
in company and battalion drill, after which his course of drill would
come to an end.

Simultaneously with the instruction in drill and musketry, daily
lectures and examinations in such professional subjects as are re-

quired to qualify for the proper discharge of regimental duty, might
take place under competent instructors. Every court-martial held
in the establishment might be attended by the young officers for
instruction, minutes of the proceedings being made out by each for
the inspection of the officer-instructor afterwards. The young
officers might likewise in turn accompany the staff orderly officers
during their daily duty to receive practical instruction on every
point connected therewith, but without authority or responsibility
regarding the duty on their own part.

The young officer would thus, it is believed, be more thoroughly
grounded in the details of his work than he is or can be at present.
He would in a great measure be safe from the risks he must run
amongst chance companions and without proper supervision at a
Depot Battalion, whilst the recruit training would not suffer in any
way from his inexperience.

To provide for the useful employment of men temporarily or permanently incapacitated for foreign service, whether belonging to
regiments at home or regiments abroad, it is proposed that garrison
battalions should be organized, to be officered in the usual manner
and employed on home service exclusively. By requiring that
every man proposed for transfer to a garrison battalion should first
pass through the invalid or central depot, from which he might
be forwarded as intended, or be returned to his regiment, or
discharged as the case might require, and by periodical medical
examinations of battalions, in order that men considered fit for
service with their regiments might be restored thereto, all risk of
abuse would be obviated. It is believed that this organization
would render the services of the large class of man it deals with
more useful for purposes of home defence than any other that can be
devised. The whole of the officers and a large majority of the men
would have a permanent interest in the reputation of their battalions,
whilst the men temporarily attached for the recovery of health would
be placed under conditions of discipline identical with those existing
in their own regiments. The demoralizing influences of constant
intercourse with recruits and of stationary quarters which operate
so injuriously under the present system would be altogether
avoided.

For the disposal of soldiers who have become confirmed invalids
and are unfit even for home service, it is suggested that no better
plan can be devised than that which we pursue at present of sending
them to an invalid depot as a preparatory step to their final
discharge.

The next suggestion is, that one central depot for the army
abroad should be established at home for the purpose of fulfilling
certain requirements of our foreign service. Such an establishment
would be charged with the discipline of soldiers belonging to
regiments abroad, who although neither recruits, home-service men,
nor invalids, happen to be temporarily within the United Kingdom.

This class includes soldiers awaiting discharge; soldiers re-enlisted, transferred, returning from furlough, proceeding on or returning from recruiting service, apprehended deserters, and others arriving from or proceeding to their regiments abroad. Another important function of the central depot would be that of carrying into effect the final discharge of soldiers, other than invalids, sent from abroad for that purpose.

The last part of the plan I need allude to is that which provides for the care of the attestations and records of regiments. It is proposed that a central office in London or elsewhere should be established for the custody of these documents, the information necessary for filling up the entries in them being transmitted, as at present, periodically from the various regiments. The office, it is suggested, might be divided into two departments, one for the attestations, the other for the records. The roll books of regiments would then contain as at present a duplicate of each soldier's record which would accompany him throughout his service.

Let us recapitulate the advantages which this scheme offers. A perfect system of training recruits either in peace or war, the means during emergencies of employing all recruits fit for the ranks with regiments on the home establishment, a satisfactory system of training young officers, an efficient organization for home defence of home-service men, and provision for the due care of attestations and records. Further, it has been shown that these advantages may be obtained without impairing the constant efficiency of regiments for immediate service, and without interrupting any of the details connected with our home and foreign service.

Here then is a substitute for Depot Battalions which appears likely to attain all the ends contemplated in such institutions without one of the drawbacks to which they are liable, and to which it is difficult to find any objection stronger than that it contains novel proposals which require time for digestion.

We have now at some length studied two of the plans which have been proposed. The discussion, I hope, has been sufficient to shew that no unsurmountable difficulty lies in the way of finding a satisfactory substitute for the Depot Battalion system, and that it rests with the Government to cause such investigation to be made by means of a military commission or, otherwise, as shall satisfy the country that in their hands the important public interest involved has not been neglected.                    B.

# GREENWICH CHARACTERS.

## XII.

### JOHN IRELAND.

Dropping one morning into the office of my friend—as I was proud to call him—the Adjutant, my business being a gossip, I found him engaged in settling a dispute between a pensioner and a shopkeeper who claimed a small debt. I took a seat near the window, for I was much more interested with the examination of the newly admitted men, who had attended at the office to be registered, than with the roundabout story about a pound of candles. The study of physiognomy had always had charms for me, and here I had ample opportunities for its exercise. There was the marine, with head erect, and features carved out of wood, marked with the sort of determined unflinching spirit which had probably led him to be a target for an enemy, or to be the recipient of three dozen at the gangway with as much apparent unconcern as if all the time standing sentry at the cabin door. The monosyllabic reply, 'Brown, John.'—'Sixty-nine.'—'Troubridge.'—'Marine.'—'Widower.'— &c., &c. Not a word nor a sentence needlessly spoken. Then came a cautious Scot, a ship-carpenter, with stooping gait, red nose, hand in pocket—Archibald Maclachlan, of Dundee. In reply to the question, 'Were you ever wounded in the service?' the hand was withdrawn from the pocket to demonstrate the fact that he had lost two fingers. These and others passed in review before me; and, although amused, I thought how difficult it would be to extract from such materials two interesting facts.

But who have we next? A short, broad-shouldered, round-faced and full-chested veteran, limping along aided by a short walking-stick. My friend the Adjutant, having adjusted the dispute between the pensioner and the chandler, now joined me. The new comer had a remarkable expression of countenance. He had a round, healthy-looking face, and having been just shaved, his massive chin was of a fine dark blue. His eyes were of the same colour; but it took time to determine that fact, as they were deeply sunken, and shaded by large black projecting eye-brows.

"What is your name?" asked the clerk.

"John Ireland."

"How old are you?"

"Eighty-one."

"Bet you that's a purser's name," said my friend, in an under tone.  "I'll find that out when he has answered all the questions."

So, just as the old man was going away, my friend called him back.

"How many other names have you had besides the present one?"

The old man scratched his head, and with a knowing turn of his quid—for his distorted cheek showed that he relished the delicious moisture of the Virginian weed—said, "Can't remember exactly. More nor one," he added after a time.

"I said so," to me *sotto voce*. "Now how long have you been John Ireland?"

"Why—let's see. Ever since I rinned, that is—left the ould Eggymemnon, in 1806."

"Now then we shall have it," said my friend, writing down, "and who commanded the Eggymemnon?"

"Sir E. Berry, to be sure he did, and didn't I sarve with him at Trafalgar and off Saint Domingy?"

"Well, but what made you 'rin' after serving with such a gallant officer as some thought him?"

"A good many reasons for why? I had an old 'oman at home as I hadn't set eyes on for seven year, and here was the ship ordered out to South Ameriker with another Captain; and was it likely I was going to be bundled off again like that? No. So I tuk French leave; and from John England I got to be John Ireland in my next ship."

"But England is not your name neither," said my catechising friend.

"Well no, not exactly. England was my mother's maiden name."

"And you 'rinned' before you took up that?"

"Well, what if I did?" replied the old man, testily.

"Oh, nothing at all," said my good-humoured friend, laughing, "only it strikes me as if you had been a good many years in the service, or at sea, that is, before you joined the 'Eggymemnon.'"

"Perhaps I had; but the Admiralty would not take away the 'R' if I asked for it, although there's a main lot of prize-money ahind that 'R,' I can tell you; and it's no manner of use my asking it, or saying any word about it."

"I only asked out of curiosity. How much good servitude have you got?"

"Only about ten years and six months, out of thirty-five. If I could have got all my time and pension, I would have stayed down at Whitehaven and ended my days there; but when I made application for a pension, I was told I might come into the House."

The 'next man' was now called in, and John Ireland *alias* England, *alias* Simpson, as I afterwards found out, hobbled out, for he was rather lame.

"What ward are you in?" asked the Lieutenant, as the old man moved away.

"Clarence." Did I not note down that fact?

Quite promiscuously, as a man would say, I toiled up the dirty stone staircase—dirty from the constant traffic of some five hundred men up and down at least three or four times a day—and on reaching the Clarence inquired of the boatswain if the new man, naming Ireland, was in.

"Tuk him over to the 'fermary day before yesterday. He had a fall and hurted his leg; and I made 'en go to the Doctor whether he would or no; and the Doctor swore at 'en in a good-natured way, and said as how the man was too old to go up four pair of stairs."

"And so he is in the Infirmary?"

"Yes, he's in the surgery side, Old Dicky's got him, and he won't let him go till he is all right."

"Is the poor man much hurt?"

"Only sprained his ankle, I think."

Further inquiries satisfied me that the old man was tolerably steady in his habits, and that the accident he had met with was not occasioned by imbibing too much. The following day I asked at the Infirmary for John Ireland.

"Kitty, show this gentleman up to No. 10, second floor, said the boatswain of the Infirmary.

A lively character was Kitty White; a little woman, whose accent soon satisfied me that she was from the Emerald Isle.

"Ah! what, you here, Mr. —— ?" said a well-known voice, seconded by a thump on the floor, which made me aware that my friend the Adjutant was by. "What are you about with Kitty? She is an old friend of mine."

"Now, Mr. R——," said the nurse, "sure and it's kind of you to call the likes of me frind."

"None of your blarney, Kitty; have you got another watch to sell?"

"Watch is it now, your honour, you're always up to your jokes; what about watches?"

"Why, the one you sold to Johnny G——?"

"Ah now, Mr. R——, and you're hard upon Kitty. Well," said she, laughing, "if he did buy it and found it daer at the price it was his bad luck sure.

"'Do you want a watch, Mr. G——?' says I.

"'What for?' ses he.

"'Cause I'll sell you one chape,' ses I.

"'How much?' ses he.

"'Quartern o' whuskey,' ses I.

"'But I must see it first,' ses he.

"'No, no, Mr. G——, you must take it upon my recommenda-tion, and you, gentlemen,' says I to the young doctors standing round, 'will say that's fair, considering the lowness of the price.'

"'Buy it, Johnny,' says one, 'I know,' he whispered, 'it's a bargain; only Kitty got it by the sly from one-of the men that died suddenly.'

"'How much will you take?' ses he.

"'Well, a quartern of whuskey, that's the best, and costs nine-pence.'

"'Well,' ses he, 'then you shall have it, and here's the money;' and now let's see the watch.'

"'Oh, thank your honour,' says I, after I had got the money, and made a low curtshey, 'if you'll look in about twelve o'clock to-night you shall have it, for it's *the middle watch.*'

"Lor, you never heard such a screech as the young doctors give, they laughed ready to split; and all but Johnny laughed, and he turned blue."

"So you want to see old John Ireland. I want to see him too; for the Doctor says he is too old to be warded at the top of the building, and I want to ask him where he would like to go when he comes out. Here comes the Doctor going his rounds, I will introduce you to him. A friend of mine, Doctor."

"Must be a good fellow to be a friend of yours; let me shake your hand, Sir."

A fine specimen of the rough old school of medicine was Dr. D——. A spacious open countenance, strong features, and full of life, always happy to oblige, and ready at any moment to amputate a limb, or send his probe deeply into a wound. Liked much, but feared more. He was kind to the sick; but a mortal foe to a skulker; and having had much to do with men of the latter class during his service afloat, he was naturally suspicious still.

Dr. D—— was of tall stature when he stood erect; but at the present time he was suffering from weakness in the loins, occasioned by a fit of the gout, and walked with his body much bent. He, however, threw himself back on speaking to me, and with one hand on the small of his back under his coat tails, and the other holding a small stick, he asked me if I needed any of that, pointing to a large tin tray. I thanked him most cordially, while a cold shiver ran over me as I glanced at the array of knives and other surgical instruments which an attendant was carrying in the rear. Two other medical officers were in attendance, going the rounds.

We entered one of the cabins, a cube of about eighteen feet, lighted by one window, and at each corner was a bed, containing a patient, covered with a horse rug. At the bed's head was a dingy striped linen curtain; and there was nothing prepossessing in the general appearance of the room, nothing cheerful—all was gloom; the walls were painted of a dull drab, the floor, tolerably well scrubbed, was destitute of carpet, hand-stools without backs there were to sit upon, but everything was very gloomy and dispiriting; and many of the old men preferred death outside rather than enter the Infirmary to be cured. The prejudice against the Hospital was so strong, that my friend the Adjutant, in order to remove it as far as he could by example, being ill, entered the Infirmary as a patient himself, and remained a considerable time under surgical treatment. The nurses were women, neither young nor particular, and the surgeons of the old school were not famed for the mildness of their treatment. Dr. D—— was most skilful and ready with the knife, and he expected his patients to submit without wincing to operations which are now seldom performed without chloroform.

"This is No 10," said Kitty White; but on entering we found that No. 3 patient was out on the leads. The place indicated by 'the leads' was the passage leading from one side of the quadrangle to the other; but as it served as a cover to the passage beneath it was leaded.

The old man whom we were in search of, was found seated on a stool with a pair of crutches beside him. The injury to his ankle was not very serious, and there was no doubt entertained of his speedy recovery, his habit of body being evidently good.

"Now do not try to get up, my old friend," said my companion to the old man, who was endeavouring to rise from his seat. "You must not try the Clarence again, I will put you in a ground-floor ward when you come out; but you must not be in a hurry."

"But I am in a hurry," said the old man, pettishly, "I don't want to stop in here."

"Why what's wrong?"

"Why everything's wrong. I can't get out, nor get a drop of grog, and there's no one to buy me pig-tail, and precious little money to buy it."

"Have patience, my old man."

"And for the matter of the pig-tail," said I, chiming in, "here's a fathom or so to go on with."

The old fellow's eyes glistened, and almost before thanking me for the unexpected treat, he had notched off with his knife about fourteen inches of it. After discharging his old quid, he rolled the new length of weed up in a ball, and placing it in his cheek looked perfectly at his ease. "Ah, ha!" said I, inwardly, "I have got the length of your foot, pig-tail will do it I see."

Watching my opportunity, I caught my old hero a few days afterwards, seated on a bench by the side of the new helpless; and quite by accident, of course, I had a length of pig-tail in my pocket.

"Talking of pig-tail," said I, "when did you dock off your tail?"

"About 1800, I was sick of the 'tie for tie.' The tail was more trouble than enough. I had plenty to do without sarving a messmate's tail, and if you wouldn't do that for your messmate he wouldn't do it for you."

"Tie for tie and no favours," said I.

"Yes, that was it, so I took it into my head to cut mine off one day, and I stowed it away in my bag intending to sell it."

"Sell it, who would buy it?"

"The barbers to be sure. Why, my tail was as thick as your wrist at the upper end, and a yard in length, and all long black hair; but when I took it to sell, I had kept it too long, and it was quite rotten and good for nothing."

"What did you say your name was before you changed it to England?"

The old fellow eyed me with a knowing leer, as much as to say " what business is that of yours;" but just then I felt in my pocket for the pig-tail. He smelt it.

" What was that you axed, Sir ?"

" Oh, nothing, only to know your name before you changed it to England."

" To Ireland you mean," said he, " my name is Ireland now, and it was England."

" Yes, I know; but what was it before that ?"

" Now I see your drift, you want to get your chain pumps to work upon me; but I don't mind you. I wasn't going to tell the Leftenant; though, for the matter of that, he's as good a man as ever stepped on one or two legs, and never harmed nobody in his life, so they tells me here: and I believes them, for he's got the true cut of a sailor; but then you see he's an officer here, and maybe he wouldn't like to hear what I have got to say."

" You might trust him as well as you could me," said I.

" Why, you see," said the old man, in a cautious whisper, " I was near hand being hung as a delegate, and perhaps I should have been sarved right if I had; and afore that I was one of a boat's crew that runaway from a ship in a sinking state."

" Not much harm in that," said I.

" I don't know that; I thinks, and always did, that we acted like cowards; and mayhap if we hadn't rinned away the ship would have been kept afloat till such times as a friendly sail hove in sight."

" I have read something about that," I answered, " but the ship was sinking, and the captain could not do any good by stopping to go down in her; and the boat had not got a sail or compass."

" That's all a pack of lies; I have had that yarn read over to me, and what I says, I means, it's all a pack of lies; and if so be as I had been axed to speak out at the Court-Martial I could have told them better."

" And have been hung for your trouble."

" Yes, very like. Hanging was no hard matter then; and the man who wanted to keep clear of the yard-arm or the gangway was always forced to clap a stopper on his jaw."

" But tell me what you recollect of that affair."

" You see, after the battle with Count de Grasse, there was nine sail-of-the-line that had been in the action and had been knocked about a good bit, that sailed from Bluefields in July, I think, for England, and a large convoy. The Admiral's flag was then in the Ramillies."

" Oh, the fatal Ramillies, as the song says."

" Yes, fatal enough; but not so bad as some other ships, and the Admiral had shifted his flag to the Ville de Paris before that. Part of the convoy was for New York, and the rest for England. When off the banks of Newfoundland, a gale came on, and threw us on our beam-ends. We cut away the mizen and mainmasts, and the foremast and bowsprit went of their own will. The rudder was also washed away. It was a mercy we did not founder there and then; but she righted, and we got nearly all the guns overboard. The ship rolled and laboured as you may suppose; but instead of trying to get up jury-masts to steady her, we tried a sea anchor."

"What's that?"

"I'll tell you. We slung the stream anchor to a boom and some gun-carriages, and got it over the bows, with a large hawser bent on to it, hoping that it would bring the ship head to wind, but it had no effect; whereas, if so be we had got up our spare spars, and set anything upon the ship to steady her, she would have been more under command, and not have strained as she did. Owing to the heavy working of the ship, and the water shipped as she rolled her lower deck ports under, we soon had seven or eight feet of water in the hold, and our pumps got choked with coal-dust that washed out of the after-hold into the pump-well. There we laid rolling about like a porpoise for five blessed days and nights, sometimes blowing hard, and at other times scarcely a breeze; but no jury-masts, although we did begin to think about it, and got up sheers forward to raise a foremast by. We got a fothered sail under the bottom, but that had no effect; and as the pumps were choked and the leathers worn out, we turned to and bailed, and at one time got her nearly free of water; but it came on to blow again, and having no sail of any sort to steady her, the ship rolled about frightfully, and the leaks increased and gained upon us. We could get very little water to drink, however, but plenty of rum, and that did more mischief than enough.

"As there seemed no chance of saving the ship, the large boats were got over the side and provisions put in them. The Captain first had his eye on the yawl, a fine roomy boat, but she got stove alongside, and then the pinnace took his fancy. I belonged to that boat, and was in her alongside to keep the crew from jumping in. So we got the boat all ready for a start, and then the Captain he persuades the officers that he could mayhap find out the leak by going round the ship outside. The ship was in a fair way of foundering as we all knew, but while there's life there's hope you know; and so long as a ship floats, there is no telling what may turn up to save the lives of the crew, and, Sir, it's my opinion, though I am only a poor man, that the Captain ought always to be the last man to leave a sinking ship."

"No doubt you are right," said I, "and many captains before and since that event have stood at their post, and have calmly met their death rather than attempt to save themselves while those under their command were in peril; but it seems, from what I have read, that the ship was actually sinking, and that the Captain caught at the boat as a drowning man would catch at a plank."

"That's all good what you say, but the ship was in sight hours after we had stole away from her.  We ran away from the ship like a thief in the night, and bitter was the cursing and swearing at us as we made sail upon the boat."

"Made sail, avast there! what's that you say? why, you had no sail on board, only an old blanket."

"That is all gammon," rejoined the old man, "we had a sail and a mast too, and a compass to steer by, and as much grub as the boat would carry, all put in by the Captain's orders.  I remember well the carpenter of the ship looking over the side and threatening us that if ever the ship got into port what he would do to us.  What happened to the poor fellows after we left them no one can tell; but I expect they got at the rum again, and—but it's no use talking.  I know this, that if I'd been captain, and had had a hundred lives, I would have given them all up before I would have left my ship as our captain did.

"We calculated that we had about from two hundred and fifty to three hundred leagues to run before we got to the Western Islands, and we had the Master in the boat to navigate us.  What we should have done without him, I don't know; but we kept the boat's head the right way, and made Fayal in thirteen days."

"Not bad sailing under a blanket," said I.

"Blanket! why, it was a lug sail, or how should we have made sixty miles a day, taking one day with another, and sometimes with a foul wind?"

"I am only speaking by the book, you know; and the book says you had no compass or quadrant."

"How should we have made that passage without a compass? You are a fine sailor to think such things.  We had contrary winds, and yet we made the island of Fayal as straight as a line; but we were almost famished with hunger and thirst, and our limbs were cramped with the wet and want of exercise.  My tongue was as hard as a board.  Old Thompson, the quartermaster, died of drinking salt water, and another day would have killed one or two more of us.  I was the man that first saw the land.  It was thick weather, but I got a sight of the high land above the fog; and when I reported it I thought the crew would have gone mad.  They jumped, and screeched as loud as they could; and the Master, when he had satisfied himself that it was all right as I said, altered the course for it, and soon all hands could see it as well as myself, though I daresay it was forty miles off.

"We fell in with a fishing-boat, and they piloted us into the harbour at midnight, and thankful we all felt, leastways, I know I did; but I was so weak I could not walk, and had to be carried up the town to the British Consul's house.  The officers were better off.  The good people only gave me a tea-spoonful of soup at a time, and I could hardly swallow that; and it took a week before I could eat any meat, my gums were so sore, and teeth so loose. My joints are stiff now at times."

"The narrative made out that you had no compass, yet the writer of it states that a reckoning was kept.  I never could understand how a reckoning could be kept while the boat was steering without a compass, and with only an old blanket for a sail."

" Don't you believe it.  You understand if the Captain had not made up a fine yarn, he must have been turned out of the Service, and there was no one to contradict his yarn.  In course he wasn't tried by cooks.

"I suppose not," said I, "for at the court-martial he was called 'a cool and resolute officer,' and the court told him that his conduct 'reflected the highest credit on him,' and so forth."

"I know all that ; I was at the court-martial, in course, as one of the prisoners, and saw the sword given back to the Captain, and heard all that was said to him ; and then I went on the lower deck of the flag-ship, and heard what some others had to say ; but as I was asked no questions at the court, why I could not say anything.  But never mind, I'm a Collegeman, and the Captain died a great man ; but I hope that when my time comes I may be able to say that I never turned my back on messmate or shipmate in time of trouble."  A plentiful discharge of tobacco juice accompanied this outpouring of pent-up feeling.

" We was called cowards," he continued, "and hooted by the poor fellows we left behind, and I felt half inclined to jump overboard and go back to the ship and share their lot sooner than run away from them, but I was under command and it was my duty to obey orders.  One young midshipman jumped overboard after us and was taken in, and in all we had four officers, one of them a surgeon's mate, and only lost one out of the twelve.

" Ah," added the old man with a sort of sigh, " I've seen many more troubles besides that, and plenty of them; but I did not like being called a coward, and I knowed it was true.  I was nearly burnt to death after that."

" Aye, aye how was that ?"

" Oh, that was in the Hindostan store ship.  I jounded her at the short peace.  Mr. Weir, a master, had command of her then, but when we took fire we had a master and commander; he was a Guernsey man named Captain Le Gros."

" And when did that happen ?"

" We were bound out to Malta with stores and provisions for the fleet, and in storing the hold, the dock-yard people put in paint, and turpentine, and rope, and all sorts of stores all mixed up together.  The Hindostan had been an East Indiaman, teak built, and very strong.  If she had not been I should not have been here now to tell you the story.  Besides stores we had a great many passengers, women and children besides, shipwrights going to Malta to serve in a dock-yard there.  I think I was in the luck of it, just before I jounded the Hindostan I had been cast away in the Pallas frigate, and that was the third time I had been wrecked ; but now again I was near upon being roasted alive."

" We encountered some heavy weather before we got to Gibraltar; and just as we had passed through the Straits we got a fresh gale after us, and the old ship rolled like a water-butt.  No doubt the stores got adrift with the rolling, and some of the turpentine jars broke, and what do you call it ?"

" Spontaneous combustion, I suppose."

" Yes, something of that sort took place, and the smoke began to come out of the hold through the hatches, enough to choke old Nick himself.  I was boatswain's mate at the time, and was sent down with the master and a party of hands to put the fire out.  The master was for unshipping the hatches, and pouring water into the hold; but, says I, Sir, if you do that we'll all be burnt up, as sure as death.  Keep the hatches down, and cover them up with wet swabs and blankets and hammocks.  The lower deck ports had all been well closed in before to keep out the sea.

" ' You are right, my man,' said the captain, who had come down to see what we were doing; ' keep all fast and cover the hatches as England recommends.'

" By this time the lower deck was a mass of thick smoke, and all hands were on the main and upper decks, for she was a fifty gun two decked ship you must know; the poor women and children were crying and expecting every minute to see the flames burst up the hatchways, or that the fire would reach the magazine, and blow us sky-high.  Meantime the Captain had put the ship right before the wind, running in for the Spanish coast, with studding-sails set on both sides.

" When nearly every soul had been driven off the lower deck by the smoke, I volunteered to go down in search of the purser's steward, who had been left below.  I had a rope fastened to me, and I got down on the deck, and crept along on all-fours, as the smoke was not so thick there.  I came across the steward lying on the deck senseless.  He had a bag of money in his hand.  I bent a hauling line on to his leg, and they pulled him up the hatchway, but too late to save his life.  I then worked my way to the master's cabin, and brought up a black canvas bag.  After me no one ventured below.  We kept pumping water down, and flooded the lower deck which helped to keep the fire from breaking through.

" Everything was done as regular as possible, just as if nothing whatever was the matter.  We hoisted out all the boats, and towed them astern with a boat keeper in each; and every man had orders not to allow anyone to get into the boats on any account.

" The fire was discovered at daybreak in the morning, and it was noon before we got sight of the land.  The wind seemed lighter than it was, but the ship was going six knots; although such was the anxiety to get ashore, that she seemed hardly to move.  The smoke got thicker every minute, and poured up in such volumes as to deaden the force of the wind.

The boats would not have held one half of the ship's company and passengers, so we all knew that if the flames burst out, the chief part of us would perish. Every turn of the half-hour glass we thought would be the last for us; but notwithstanding that, all hands were quiet and obedient. The Captain and officers walked the deck quite composed, and the poor women and children had been all assembled aft on the quarter-deck and poop. The land appeared to run away from us, and the breeze gradually dropped, until we could not have been going more than three or four knots. As we got closer in, we saw some Spanish launches; but they all gave us a wide berth, as it seemed to them the ship was in flames.

"It was near sunset before we touched the ground. We were in the Bay of Roses and it was a bay of roses to us. As we grounded gently forward, the motion seemed to give the fire more power, for a thick cloud of smoke burst up which seemed to say our destruction was at hand. Some of the blue jackets I am sorry to say made a rush off to get at the boats, and one man jumped overboard from the poop, and caught hold of the gunwale of the pinnace. Bob Collinson, coxswain of the boat, up stretcher and hit the man over the knuckles until he let go and fell astern, and was drowned."

"Sharp practice," I remarked.

"Yes, but not a bit too sharp, for if Bob hadn't done that, a hundred fellows would soon have followed, and the boats would have been swamped in quarter less no time, but seeing how the coxswain served the first who tried it, the rest kept quiet, and so we lost one man instead of a hundred."

"As soon as the ship was hard and fast aground, the boats were ordered up alongside one by one, and the women and children handed down into them. The Spanish launches took the passengers from our boats, and landed them, and after the passengers the ship's company went, and after them, the officers, and last of all the captain. In consequence of the good order, every one was saved but the purser's steward who went down after the money, and the man who jumped off the poop."

"I stuck by the Captain, and was in the last boat that left the ship, and I don't think we had shoved off more than five minutes when the flames burst out of the lower deck ports and in five minutes more the ship was one bright flame. The magazine was reached soon afterwards, and up went the old Hindostan skyhigh, sending fiery splinters right and left. We all reached the shore that night, thanking Providence for our miraculous deliverance, we were famishing with hunger and thirst, for few of us had tasted food the whole of that day. The water in the scuttle butt was exhausted, and we could not get a drop from below. Our Captain deserved the thanks of all hands, for nothing but his coolness kept the people quiet."

"You deserved thanks, too," said I.

" Perhaps I did, I have always had the luck of it. If they had lifted one of the hatches, the ship would soon have been on fire fore and aft and the loss of life would have been terrible, and had I not been of the party the hatches would have been taken off."

" I suppose," said I, " the Captain got posted."

" Not a bit of it. I don't think he was ever employed afterwards, and he was never rewarded for his noble behaviour."

" What a contrast, how very curious," I said to myself, after wishing good bye to old Ireland. One Captain deserts his ship and crew, and is rewarded by another ship, and afterwards by one of the most desirable positions an officer of his rank could have enjoyed, while another by his cool determination saved hundreds of lives, was never afterwards employed and died a Commander! for I found upon searching that Captain Le Gros died about six years afterwards in the rank which he held when he lost the Hindostan.

## ARTILLERY—HORSE AND FOOT.

Two articles which have recently appeared on the subject of Artillery, do the writers infinite credit. Yet it is hoped that a few remarks from an old officer may not be taken so as to give offence, or be unacceptable in general.

The first article treats of Horse Artillery and Cavalry as to combined movements and general effect if acting together, which of course they ought to do, yet occasions may occur when they may be separated and act independently of each other. Another thing to be considered is, the increased range of Artillery, which may be brought to bear upon a body of Cavalry at a much greater distance than formerly; this shews how much more necessary it is for Cavalry to have Artillery attached to them, which is able to keep pace with their movements, and always be at hand to cover their advance, to repel the attack of the enemy should they make one, or if their own Cavalry should be obliged to retire, and so adapt their movements as to be of mutual advantage to each other.

If Cavalry are opposed to Cavalry alone, one side or other must advance to meet its enemy, and countries where Cavalry are most useful and likely to come into contact, are mostly level or tolerably open, there must have been a bad look-out kept, if the Artillery did not get due notice of their proceedings, and as they can reach them now from so much greater distance than they could formerly, the attacking party could be seen and fired at so much further, that they might be greatly injured before they would come to actual blows with their own branch of the service. That in fact, if Cavalry is well supported by Artillery, we may look upon the days of Cavalry fighting solely with Cavalry, as among things that have been.

We quite agree in the opinion that the Horse Artillery and
Cavalry must know how they can best support and protect each
other; and that this point is not sufficiently taken into consideration by either party, and that the commanding officers do not sufficiently understand or appreciate the benefits that may arise by duly
consulting each other. An officer commanding a Brigade of Cavalry
does not always know, how, where and when, the Artillery may be
best employed, as he may not have sufficient knowledge of that
branch of the service, and he may not like always to take the
opinion of a junior, but gives an order to the Artillery officer to
act at once, without duly considering, how it is to be carried into
effect, and when the latter comes to act upon it, he may find difficulty or impossibility to carry out what may be required.

As regards what is said of escort duties of Cavalry to Artillery,
it is certainly right that Artillery, when in action, especially when it
may be at some little distance from the main body, should be
properly supported, as all Artillerymen must know the old maxim, that
the last discharges when the enemy are nearest the muzzles of the
guns are the most effective and cover him with glory; but if the
Artillery find or know that they are not properly supported, they
might be apt to "limber up" when they ought to give the last discharge, under the conviction that their guns would be taken and
perhaps turned upon their own side, and that it would be better
to carry them away than allow of such a contingency, whereas if
they knew that they had a squadron or two to support them, they
would fight to the last.

This was exemplified at Talavera, by Captain Cleeves of the
German Legion Artillery, he saw the celebrated Polish Lancers
about to charge his guns, he had just time to load with grape and
canister in addition to the round shot already in. He gave the
word to fire when the Lancers were about 50 yards off. Of
course he emptied many saddles, but did not prevent the charge, as
those who remained, from the impetus with which they were
moving, charged through his guns and got back again, spearing
everything they could reach, right or left. After they retired,
Cleeves could only man two guns, to give them a shot, and had
only horses, left unhurt, sufficient for two guns and one ammunition
waggon, however the Polish Lancers never appeared before the
British Army, before or since, this was their only action in the
Peninsula.*

Had Cleeves' brigade been supported by a squadron of Cavalry,
his loss would not have been so severe, as the Lancers might have
been met upon the last discharge of the guns and would not have
succeeded in passing through as they did. The battery was a
brigade of foot Artillery and was attached to Infantry only.

This is a case in point of having all Artillery properly supported
in the field, whether horse or foot. But it is to be feared that the

* The writer had this account from Captain Cleeves himself.

plan suggested in the able article alluded to, would meet with some
objections before it could be carried out, nothing can be · better
than the suggestion itself, nevertheless it is to be feared that if
any particular corps of Cavalry was to be picked out, and the
Colonel told that his regiment was to be particularly attached by
troops or squadrons to serve as escort to the Artillery, that he would
grumble not a little.   He would consider it derogatory to Cavalry to
do so, that from the regiment being detached it would lose its high
state of discipline, for which he could not be responsible, and many
other causes would be assigned why his corps should not be told
off for such a duty; never thinking at the same time, that he might
have many opportunities on the Special Escort duty of earning
distinction which might not happen in the regular way.

Another objection might occur which would be unpleasant unless
especially attended to in the commencement, that is that the rank
of the officers might clash; for it would often happen that the
Cavalry officer would be senior to the Artillery one, and would consider all the movements of the battery to be under his control, and
give orders accordingly, whereas the reverse ought to be the case,
and it would generally speaking be a very difficult matter to find a
Colonel of Cavalry willing to give up this prerogative.   Certainly
this Special Escort duty should not be given to any particular
regiment for any length of time, and all the corps in each brigade
should take it in turn.   If only one battery is attached to a corps
of Cavalry, a squadron of any regiment might perform the escort
duty for a certain period, then be relieved at the end of a month or
week by another, and so on till the whole regiment had gone
through the duty, after which another would take it up in turn.
This would be of the greatest benefit as it would give so much
instruction to the service, and give the officers and men of the
Cavalry some idea of the Artillery service, of which at present very
few have any knowledge, as the safety of the Artillery is a matter of
the greatest consequence to an army.

The writer of this is old enough to remember the first formation
of the Field Artillery, the *Car Brigade* as it was then called, under
the direction of Brigade-Major Spearman, before he (the writer)
was a cadet.   There were six guns (six-pounders) and six cars, the
gunners were mounted, three upon the gun limber, and six back to
back upon the car, which had only two wheels, and a most delightful tendency to upset if taken out of the barrack-field to the common,
which in those days had not been levelled; as it was considered
this tendency would not be found advantageous on service, the car
was condemned, though we did see some of them in Canada in
1814, and the present ammunition waggon was brought into use
just before the commencement of the Peninsula War, or rather,
they were taken from the model of those used there by the Horse
Artillery which has not been materially altered since.   The Foot
Brigades, as batteries were called in those days, were in a very bad

state. The drivers were a corps by themselves and had the sole management of the horses; for officers were not regularly, even at Woolwich, told off to field guns. About twice a week a brigade was ordered out for exercise, and officers appointed from the regular roster for the day. Each officer sent his saddle and bridle to the stable, and a horse was prepared for him which was not accustomed to be ridden, and there often used to be serious conflicts before the horse and his rider could come to a mutual understanding, so as to be able to go through the drill. It would sometimes happen that a Captain was appointed to command a brigade, who had been for years in the West Indies, or some other foreign station where field-guns were unknown; of course as he had never seen a brigade he could not command one, so he generally appointed one of the subalterns as his adjutant, who used to prompt him in the words of command. This was pretty much the state previous to the Peninsular War, at its commencement the horses were still under the Driver-officers and those of the regiment did not trouble themselves much about them, and as there was only one Driver-officer to do everything, looking after his men, horses and harness gave him so much to do, that often he did nothing. Such a state of affairs could not last, as everything went to the bad and nobody responsible. However, in a little time subalterns of the company attached, were told off to divisions and made responsible for everything belonging to it, in a short time a spirit of emulation sprung up among them as to who would turn his division* out in the best manner, and from this was formed the field-battery of the present day.

The writer of the pleasant sketch of "Some of the Artilleries of Europe," gives many interesting observations upon the different systems in several countries, but though there may be some faults in our own, there are no Foreign Artillery taking them in general that surpass ours. At the great review at Paris after the Battle of Waterloo, the British Artillery had the credit of being the most efficient and serviceable corps on the ground.

Certain it is that no country comes up to ours in horse appointments, or the knowledge of harness, and how a horse can be put to work to the greatest advantage; look at the manner in which they are attached to gentlemen's carriages, there is not an inch of leather to spare, or one wanted, the horses are close up to their work, that one ignorant of the business would imagine that if the horse moved he must be caught by some part or other of the carriage when it is put into motion, yet it is found he is not, but steps off with the greatest freedom. There is nothing astonishes a foreigner more than our English carriages, carts and horses of every description. The gun carriages are on the same principle, not an inch of draught is wasted. The French have copied our field artillery in many respects. They used to drive with single poles between the wheel horses and long traces—now they are better. A few years ago in

* A division consisted of two guns and their ammunition waggons.

Spain I saw a battery of Spanish Horse Artillery, which was thought by them to be, a *ne plus ultra*. The fore wheels were lower than the hind ones, they had not any limber boxes, and a pole from the front axle passed between the two horses and was attached to a bar which passed from the pad of the off-horse, to the front of the saddle of the driver, like the bars of the curricles, which were so much in vogue some forty years ago for gentlemen's open carriages. On full dress occasions the horses, draught as well as riding, had shabraques hanging down over the saddles nearly to the ground. They moved very well on smooth ground, but the horses were too light and vicious and would jib if they found any stiff pulling. The Americans used sometimes to drive " four-in-hand," the driver seated on the limber boxes.

As the last writer alluded to, speaks a good deal of the movements and equipment of Artillery, we have been induced to make some remarks and feel happy in bearing testimony to the justice of his.

The power of moving Artillery so as to be able to get it into certain positions at certain times is of the greatest consequence, for sometimes the fate of a battle or campaign may depend upon it.

In the Foot Artillery on the ordinary line of march, the gunners should always march by the side of their respective guns or carriages, and on no occasion be permitted to ride, the horses have enough to do to get the guns along with their proper load without carrying either the men or their knapsacks, yet a small part of the kitt might be placed upon the carriages and a light one be carried by the men, containing only a change of linen, a pair of trousers and a pair socks and shoes; this is quite enough for the gunner to carry, as it often happens on service that he may be required to repair a piece of road, pull down a bank or wall, or take an occasional pull at a drag rope, so that he should not be overloaded, for he is not only liable to have some heavy work to do on the march, but is sure of something when it is over; greasing wheels, cleaning things, looking over everything that may have occurred on the march, so as to have all in order for next day. He should not be encumbered with the care of a carbine, it is only in his way when employed in his own legitimate duty of working the guns in action, and is likely to become broken or lost, all his arms ought to be a short double-edged sword about twenty inches long, with a solid handle, rather broader towards the point, or shaped like the old Roman sword—this will enable him to cut down brushwood, or a hedge, so as to allow the gun to get through, it would answer all the purpose of a bill-hook, and be a formidable weapon at the same time. There were no carbines or fire-arms used by the Artillery during the Peninsula War, yet still a few would do no harm, each mounted man might carry a revolver and they could be given over to the Sergeant of the Guard, who would be responsible when they were returned to the men who had carried them. Certainly the present nondescript weapon in shape of a crooked sword, carried by both gunners and drivers, is the most absurd thing ever put into a soldier's hand.

As to Artillery, when wanted to move to the front quickly, some means ought to be adopted for carrying the men, as it is not always convenient or proper to bring the ammunition waggon into action, the men who are thus carried for show at Woolwich, would not be up with the guns, or if they did run for a short distance they would be blown when they arrived, as a man cannot run very far when encumbered even with a very light kitt.

Let us suppose the guns were required to advance at a trot for about a mile, what would be the best way of conveying the men? We should think that if the gun was divested of all extra weight of such things as are often carried extra, that three men might ride on the limber; seats with springs might be made for two more on the axle-tree on each side of the gun, and by having a pad upon the centre off horses, if there were six to the gun, one man might ride on that, and he and the centre driver on the near horse might dismount to work the gun, thus giving seven men. Numbers two and three from the axles, would be ready for the sponge and loading, one, four and five, would unlimber, while six and seven would be ready to bring up ammunition—thus the gun would be speedily brought into action.

As so many changes have taken place since the old Board of Ordnance was done away with; whether for better or worse, remains to be seen, some more may still be made. We have often thought that the corps should be divided into three distinct parts. 1st. The Horse Artillery; 2nd. Field Artillery; 3rd. Garrison and Siege Artillery. The first to remain as they are, the second would be nearly on the same establishment as the first, but attached to Infantry, as the other to Cavalry. The third to be posted in garrisons and only to take field as a siege force to work the heavy guns for that purpose, or guns of position. When men have served a certain number of years in the Horse or Field-artillery, they should be drafted into the garrison corps from which they would not be so likely to be moved; and though they might not be so active as they were, they would do very well for garrison work, and the old soldier would be able to end his days or the full period of his service in an easy and comfortable way.

The promotion of the corps might go in the usual manner and exchanges be effected from one department to another as heretofore.

The instruction of the men would be more simple, for in the first instance they would have only one species of ordnance to become acquainted with, namely, the light guns, or field-work, and the other duties might easily be acquired when quartered in garrison.

The concentration of a force of Artillery is of the greatest con-

sequence at the present day, and the necessity of keeping guns in
the most complete state, so that they can be moved in the shortest
time is very essential ; and if due care is not taken of the condition
of the horses as well as keeping everything connected with field
guns in the most perfect and complete order, the General in
command of an army may find himself grievously disappointed in
the time of need.  So that in order to prevent this, no pains ought
to be spared to render everything effective ; the great changes that
have taken place recently have caused an almost complete revision of
this branch of the service necessary, especially in the field, for though
the Artillery have the advantage of a longer range than formerly,
at the same time the Infantry have a similar one, for their range is
also much greater, and the effect of their fire more certain ; for they
can pick off the Artillerymen from a distance where they may have
taken shelter, and a few men well posted will have more effect upon
the Artillery, than a large body had formerly.  This shews the necessity of having them properly protected under every circumstance
whether by Cavalry, or Infantry, or both ; for if a large body of
Artillery should be brought together in one place, then the sharpshooters of the enemy would be attracted, and in order to keep
them in check it would be necessary to push our own light troops
at least 1,000 yards in front, so as to keep the enemy at a proper
distance to allow guns to be worked to enable them to fire with
effect upon some point, probably, between two or three miles off,
a thing that a few years ago would have been deemed impossible.  This
is quite a new phase in warlike movements and one that ought to
be particularly considered, for in that distance though a body of
men, an encampment, or a fortress may be perceived, there is no
knowing what vallies and undulating country may intervene, or
what number of troops may be moving or concealed in the intermediate space, or what movements may be making to the right or
left, and the first intelligence a General may have is, that a fire
from Artillery is opened upon his flank from a battery two or three
miles off.  This we may say is a new epoch in strategy, and our
Generals should consider in time of peace and at their leisure,
what steps they would take, if they were sent upon active service,
for it will not do to wait till such an event occurs—they must be
prepared to meet things at once.

The time is now approaching for field days and reviews at the
different camps of instruction, and things must be managed on the
extensive scale ; the enemy must be supposed to be in position three
miles off, and an attack made by the Artillery.  In order therefore
to have sham fights at that distance, it will not do suppose that
there is an enemy, when there are no troops to represent one, but
one half of the troops, say at Aldershot, should be sent to that
distance, no plan previously made out by either party, the distant
one should try to get home in spite of the opposition he might
meet with, and by taking some circuitous route circumvent the

plans of the other party, and take up another position so that the party who were left within the camp might find him where they least expected; some such work as this would give our Generals something to think of, instead of acting upon plans concocted beforehand in London.

As each General would have to act for himself and upon his own judgment, it would give the staff something to do to get information for their respective generals as to the moves of the opposing parties. These long distances would give opportunity for sending scouting parties out to gain information, and would lead to many skirmishes and give opportunities of practising "*La petite guerre*," as it would cause captains and young officers to be constantly on the alert to prevent surprise and capture, and give Cavalry officers instruction in one of the most important parts of their duty, that of patrolling in front of the enemy.

In the course of these movements experiments may be tried of the best way of moving or carrying the gunners of the field-batteries so as to cause the least fatigue to the men or horses, that both may be effective when the gun is brought into action.

The movements of Artillery on service are generally along the roads and they seldom have to cross country for any distance, or with great speed, a good opportunity will offer at the field-days and reviews for trying experiments upon this and many other points to which allusion has been made in this article, and hope that what has been suggested may lead to something, which if not quite the thing, may be the means of producing something useful, by setting others to think on the subject.                                    C. S.

---

## SHOEBURYNESS AND ITS EXPERIMENTS, OR SHIPS
### *versus* FORTS, *and vice versa.*

The House of Commons having long since voted a round sum of money for the purpose of putting Portsmouth and the anchorage at Spithead in a state to be defended by a comparatively small force of Volunteers or Militia, against the attack of an invading enemy, in case of such a contingency at any future time occurring, one would have supposed that the principle being once admitted by a majority of the representatives of the people, the minority would have desisted from further factious opposition, and have allowed the annual instalments to be voted *sub silentio,* as the necessity for their application recurred periodically. Such a reasonable course of proceeding, however, would be at variance with the tactics of party, (that curse of representative government), and we have consequently seen that although many of the land defences of Portsmouth have been entirely finished, and the remainder are in an advanced stage towards completion, Sir Morton Peto, Sir Frederic Smith, and Mr.

Bright, the *tria juncta in uno* of the minority, with their supporters,
have left no stone unturned, and no art untried to stop the good
work in its progress, and leave the forts unfinished, as a memorial
to future generations of the changeable nature of the popular
chamelion called a House of Commons.   Fortunately, however,
their absurd and miserably factious attempts have failed for the
moment; to be again revived, no doubt, next session, or at every
recurring vote for the annual instalment; and we shall probably
have the pain of witnessing the periodical party fight as we have
done this year and last.

On the recent occasion, it was more particularly the forts on the
Horse Sand, No Man's Land, and Stourbridge at Spithead, that
were chosen as the "cheval de bataille," and certainly if we must
have had a Jonas to throw overboard as a sacrifice to the infernal
gods, in order to save the ship from the fury of the elements, we
should have preferred to leave those three isolated sea-batteries in
abeyance until all the rest were completed.   But by so doing the
unity of the whole scheme would be impaired; and it would have
been necessary to have floating batteries in the very place of these
fixed ones, and that being the case, we do not see what would have
been gained by the sacrifice.   The forts at Cronstadt were quite
effective in keeping our wooden walls and steamers at a distance
from St. Petersburgh, and our ships could not lie against the stone
forts at Sebastopol; and as it has been now satisfactorily demon-
strated by all the costly experiments at Shoeburyness, that guns can
at any time be produced to throw shot and shell that will penetrate
any armour that any ship can carry and float, we consider that the
question is left precisely where it was before the invention of
armour-plated ships, and rifled cannon, and that the relative
strength of ships and forts is in no way changed with respect to
each other.   On the contrary, it must be now rather admitted by
every unprejudiced person who is capable of appreciating the subject,
that iron-plated forts with rifled cannon, shooting with increased
facility and accuracy to a longer range than formerly, will be much
more formidable, even to the armour-plated ships that can cross
the ocean, or the channel in anything but a dead calm, than the old
stone casemated batteries used to be with respect to ordinary men-
of-war.   At Copenhagen in 1801 and 1807, and at Algiers in
1816, as well as on some other occasions, we did certainly see fleets
able to silence, for a time, the fire of land batteries; but then there
were circumstances of a peculiar kind in favour of the ships, which
might not again occur, and even those particular cases were
purely accidental.   If the Copenhagen batteries had been better
distributed, for instance, and had fired red hot shot and shells, and
if there had been a few heavier guns well placed at distant intervals,
so as to enfilade the line of attack from points where the ships could
not bring a concentrated fire to bear upon them, it is probable the
English fleet might have had the worst of the encounter, and the

bombardment of the town of Copenhagen, with the previous loss of the Danish fleet itself, had great influence in causing the surrender of that place.    At Algiers in 1816, the English fleet might not have been so successful as it was, if the defenders had not allowed the ships to anchor quickly before they fired a shot, and as it was, many of the ships were very badly handled, and with a more resolute defence, and under other circumstances, the place might have held out.

The question is not whether forts can take the place of ships, but whether ships can be used instead of forts for the protection of a particular roadstead, and we consider that the answer is self-evident. In the first place, floating-batteries to be effectual, must be at least as costly as fixed ones, and they cannot be so durable.    In the second place, they cannot be so steady, except in a dead calm, and in proportion to the number of guns, an iron-plated ship or "floating battery" will be even more costly than a fixed iron fort on a sandbank.    In the third place, a fixed fort can be mounted with artillery of such weight and power, worked by machinery, as no ship or floating battery could bear, and a few such guns will be more effective for sinking an enemy's ship than a whole broadside of even eight or ten inch guns such as can be used on board ship. Then again, the fixed batteries can be entirely open at the back, so that the smoke may escape at once, and the guns on the upper platform can be so placed that though they can see the enemy, the latter will hardly be able to perceive the gun by which he is hit, except by the momentary flash and puff of smoke from which the shot issues.    One effective shot from such a battery may smash in the side of a ship and sink her; but a great many broadsides from a ship will not sensibly damage a well constructed sea-battery. The cost of the three forts in question at Spithead, though considerable, is nothing in comparison to three times as many iron-plated ships that would have to be anchored in their place, and iron-plated ships are better kept disposable for attack, than if made to do duty as mere citadels or hulks.

As for ships *versus* ships, they will be just where they were. Two powerful fleets meeting at sea may be imagined as equally matched as regards the number of vessels, their size, and the weight of metal they carry respectively, and whether both sides are coated with impenetrable armour or not, the equality remains the same, as far as their intrinsic worth is in question.    It is just the old story over again : the richest nation or the longest purse will in the end prevail, provided always that the ships are equally well handled, and therein lies the rub.    The more ships a nation sends to sea, the more will become a prey to the waves or the enemy, if they are not well manned and commanded; and in a naval war that nation will prevail in the end, which is able to man efficiently the greatest number of ships.*    This being the case, we are of opinion that

* At the close of the year 1862, there belonged to the ports of the United

England can maintain her superiority at sea, if she wills to do so. Let other nations build fleets, and use them as long as they remain at peace with England. If they treat us unjustly, or attempt to bully us, as the Northern States of America are now trying to do, it may become a question whether war is not preferable to pretended peace. John Bull is long suffering, and it takes a good deal to "ryle" him, but if his back is once up, he may become an ugly customer; and we fancy somehow that in case of need we could turn out a good number of fast iron-clads that would match those of any other nation, Yankee or not.

As for continued experiments of improved guns against iron targets at Shoeburyness, it seems a useless waste of money to carry them any further. If a manufacturer imagines he has attained to such perfection that he can construct a ship's side that is impervious to the heaviest shot, while at the same time it shall be lighter than the hitherto accepted model, there can be no harm in allowing and giving him every facility of testing his invention, on the condition that he puts it in place at his own expense. The Government will always be able to keep a piece of artillery or two of the first magnitude for practice or for experimenting on samples of such plates as they may wish to prove before adopting them; but it is surely unnecessary to go on manufacturing 'Warrior targets' at a vast outlay, merely for the sake of demolishing them at the first encounter. By all means let Mr. Whitworth, or anybody else, offer the newest improvement in artillery for adoption, and let the Government adopt the very best model for each class of ship, and for sea batteries that they can procure, but having once got a good gun that will pierce through any armour that a ship can carry and float, we do not consider it advisable to be always changing and altering the pattern for the sake of some fancied improvement which may after all be only an alteration. For ship guns, there is clearly a limit fixed to their weight, by the class of vessels for which they are intended, and the rolling and pitching in a gale of wind, to which even the largest ships are exposed as well as the smallest. Even the Great Eastern in a gale of wind, is no more than a shuttlecock in the hand of the mighty ocean, and if the largest ship has one very powerful piece of artillery fixed in midships for particular occasions, it is probably as much as she can bear, in addition to her broadside of eight or ten inch guns, of which there must be few compared with the former armament of our three-deckers. What we gain in size and weight of metal, we necessarily lose in the number of guns with which a ship can be armed. But there is no reason why a sea battery on shore should not have as many guns of the very largest calibre that can be managed by machinery, as the

Kingdom 28,440 vessels, of 4,934,400 tons, usually navigated by 228,139 men and boys—an increase of 402 vessels, 127,574 tons, and 3,315 men and boys over the former year. The vessels belonging to the British plantations were 10,967, of 1,107,696 tons, manned by 75,934 persons.

extent of the front will admit.*   Within certain limits, necessarily fixed by circumstances of situation, the more the guns are distributed the better.   Two heavy guns which can concentrate their fire on a ship will be much more effective if they are far apart from each other than in juxta-position.   The ship will be hit by both of them, and cannot so well reply to both at once; and the same argument holds good for two separate batteries of two, three, or more guns each.   Two earthen batteries bearing on a channel by which ships must pass, will be much more effective than one in which all the guns of the two were crowded together.   It must, however, always be borne in mind that the batteries in question must be secure from a coup-de-main or surprise, and each fort or battery must have an efficient and properly instructed officer to command them.   The efficiency of a battery against ships will depend on the accuracy multiplied by the rapidity of its fire; quick firing without hitting the mark is worse than none, but at the same time it is not necessary to be slow and dilatory to ensure accuracy. Both at once are indispensable; and to attain either, practice under good instruction is indispensable.

We consider it superfluous to insist further on this matter, and refer the reader to our June No., (pp. 159 to 168), for the substratum on which the present remarks are based, as well as to former ones, (see Jan., Feb., and March last).   We are glad to observe that our Volunteer Artillery Corps are wide awake to this important subject, and the Government now allow ammunition and projectiles very liberally both to the Militia and Volunteer Artillery for gunnery practice with shot and shells.   In case of necessity, there is no doubt that all our coast batteries can be efficiently manned and commanded by the Militia and Volunteers, leaving the regular troops disposable for active operations in the field.   Of the importance of intrenched camps such as Portsmouth affords, it is impossible to speak too highly; and when our dockyards and arsenals are safe from insult, there is little fear but that we shall be able to give a good account of any possible invader before he got to London.                                                                        H.

---

## THE POLISH QUESTION.

The Polish question has arrived at a culminating point. We are now in possession of the identical notes of England, France, and Austria to the Government of the Emperor of Russia,—if not identical in words, at all events in substance,—and the reply of Prince Gortschakoff to the same.   The object of these notes of the

---

* It is self-evident that batteries are more advantageous when in only one, or at the utmost two tiers of guns.   It is only when built in the sea, as those at Spithead must be, that they should be made in three or four tiers, to save the enormous outlay of more extended foundations under water.

Western Powers was to induce the Czar by amicable advice to adopt such conciliatory measures towards Poland as would lead to a suspension of hostilities, put an end to the inhuman slaughter which is carried on in that unfortunate country, and, pending an armistice, to initiate diplomatic negotiations with a view to effect a solution of a question which threatens to disturb the general peace of Europe, and to give to Poland such constitutional rights as would satisfy the Poles without infringing too much upon the prerogatives and dignity of the Czar. To any careful observer of the political events of the day, the difficulty of the task taken upon themselves by the Great Powers, under the plea of "humanity," is at once patent. Any concessions of Alexander II would naturally be regarded by the revolted Poles as a triumph, unless such concessions were on so magnanimous a scale that the Powers who are now exerting their "good offices" with the Russian Government, should insist upon their being adopted under the alternative to the Poles of abandoning them to their fate if not accepted by them.

Prince Gortschakoff's tardy reply is not satisfactory, and it now remains to be seen whether the "minimum" contained in the identical notes will not be made an "ultimatum," backed with the bayonets of France; or whether the Poles will be once again abandoned to the ruthless sway of the Russian Commanders, discouraged and disheartened by hopes engendered by false promises. That the revolution, unaided, must necessarily succumb before the overwhelming strength of the Russian armies, no reasonable man can doubt. It would be premature to conjecture how the Emperor of the French will act. The popular feeling in Paris runs high in favour of an armed intervention, but England, as well as Austria, are averse to hostilities. Great questions are often decided by circumstances not in the control of the rulers of nations, and, to say the least, the political horizon at the present moment is pregnant with storm.

Before we enter into a narrative of the events which have taken place on the actual scene of warfare during the last month, let us carefully examine the diplomatic side of the question. Europe has on more than one occasion been indebted to the efforts of diplomacy for the preservation of peace, and the pen has often achieved greater victories than the sword. The Governments of England, France, and Austria, whilst making the solution of the Polish difficulty the common object of their united efforts, seem resolved not to deviate from the path of moderation and conciliation until every diplomatic argument shall have been exhausted to induce Russia to give ear to the legitimate wishes of Poland. This delicacy in not wishing to ruffle the susceptibilities of the Czar, by only asking from him what is just, equitable, and possible, would seemingly imply a more energetic line of action should the Emperor Alexander II refuse to listen to the friendly remonstrances made in the name of the general interests of Europe. A conference has been proposed to meet at

Brussels, but Prince Gortschakoff's reply is of a nature to leave the whole question in abeyance. The Court of St. Petersburg accepts in *principle* the programme laid down by the three Cabinets of Paris, London, and Vienna as the point of departure for ulterior negotiations tending to restore to Poland the conditions of a solid and durable peace—that is to say, Russia reserves to herself the right of pointing out the changes which, without altering the preliminary bases, should be made in the common programme, in a spirit of conciliation calculated to favour the work of pacification. The Russian Note, however, endeavours to insinuate that the development of the programme might be obtained in the ordinary diplomatic way, keeping in view the previous understanding which might appear to be established upon one part or the other. Russia does not, therefore, precisely decline the conference, to which she had previously already assented; she merely represents it as superfluous. While sincerely coinciding in the desire of the three Courts for the speedy cessation of bloodshed in Poland, the Emperor Alexander, says Prince Gortschakoff, would be unable to enter upon the initiative course suggested by the Western Powers without compromising the dignity of his Crown. Nevertheless, disposed to give ear solely to the voice of clemency and of magnanimity with respect to his erring subjects, the Czar promises, conformably with the first stipulation of the preliminary bases, to promulgate immediately a full and complete amnesty in favour of the Poles. Prince Gortschakoff thinks that the Poles would find so extensive an act of clemency a sufficient pledge for laying down their arms and producing the immediate suppression of all hostility. Written, as ever, with rare skill, the reply of Russia is couched in the most courteous and friendly terms. To judge of the real impression, however, the reply will have produced upon the three Courts, it will be requisite to wait until they have had time to exchange their reciprocal estimates.

Earl Russell in his despatch of the 17th June, to Lord Napier, the British Ambassador at St. Petersburg, thus states the views of the English Government:

"Foreign-Office, June 17, 1863.

" My Lord,—Her Majesty's Government have considered with the deepest attention the despatch of Prince Gortzchakoff of the 26th of April, which was placed in my hands by Baron Brunnow on the 2nd of May. Her Majesty's Government are not desirous, any more than Prince Gortschakoff, of continuing a barren discussion. I will therefore pass over all the controversy regarding my previous despatch. I will not endeavour in the present communication to fix the precise meaning of the article regarding Poland in the Treaty of Vienna, nor will I argue, as Prince Gortschakoff seems to expect I should do, that there is only one form under which good government can be established. Still less will I call in question the benevolent intentions of the enlightened Emperor who has already in a short time effected such marvellous changes in the legal condition of his Russian subjects. Her Majesty's Government are willing with the Emperor of Russia to seek a practical solution of a difficult and most important problem. Baron Brunnow, in presenting to me Prince Gortschakoff's despatch, said, 'The Imperial Cabinet is ready to enter upon an exchange of ideas upon the ground and within the limits of the Treaties of 1815.' Her Majesty's Government are thus invited by the Government of Russia to an exchange of ideas upon the basis of the Treaty of 1815, with a view to the pacification and permanent tranquillity of Poland. Before making any definite proposals, it is essential to point out that there are two leading principles upon which, as it appears to Her Majesty's Government, any future Government of Poland ought to rest. The first of these is the establishment of confidence in the Government on the part of the governed. The original views of the Emperor Alexander I. are stated by Lord Castlereagh, who had heard from the Emperor's own lips, in a long conversation, the plan he contemplated. The plan of the Emperor is thus described by Lord Castlereagh :—'To retain the whole of the Duchy of Warsaw, with the exception of the small portion to the westward of Kalisch, which he meant to assign to Prussia, erecting the remainder, together with the Polish provinces formerly dismembered, into a kingdom under the domain of Russia, with a national Administration congenial to the sentiments of the people.' The whole force of this plan consists in the latter words. Whether power is retained in the hands of one, as in the old monarchy of France, or divided among a select body of the aristocracy, as in the Republic of Venice, or distributed among a Sovereign, a House of Peers, and a Representative Assembly, as in England—its virtue and strength must consist in its being a 'national Administration congenial to the sentiments of the people.' The Emperor Alexander II, speaking of the institutions he has given, says, ' As to the future, it necessarily depends on the confidence with which these institutions will be received on the part of the kingdom.' Such an Administration as Alexander I. intended, such confidence as Alexander II looked for, unhappily do not exist in Poland. The next principle of order and stability must be found in the supremacy of law over arbitrary will. Where such supremacy exists, the subject or citizen may enjoy his property or exercise his industry in peace, and the security he feels as an individual will be felt in its turn by the Government under which he lives. Partial tumults, secret conspiracies, and the interference of cosmopolite strangers, will not shake the firm edifice of such a Government. This element of stability is likewise wanting in Poland. The religious liberty guaranteed by the solemn declarations of the Empress Catherine, the political freedom granted by the deliberate Charter of the Emperor Alexander I., have alike been abrogated by succeeding Governments, and have been only partially revived by the present Emperor. It is no easy task to restore the confidence which has been lost, and to regain the peace which is now everywhere broken.   Her Majesty's Government would deem themselves guilty of great presumption if they were to express an assurance that vague declarations of good intentions, or even the enactment of some wise laws, would make such an impression on the minds of the Polish people as to obtain peace and restore obedience.   In present circumstances it appears to Her Majesty's Government that nothing less than the following outline of measures should be adopted as the bases of pacification :—

" 1.  Complete and general amnesty.

" 2.  National representation, with powers similar to those which are fixed by the charter of the 15-27th November, 1815.

" Poles to be named to public offices in such a manner as to form a distinct national Administration, having the confidence of the country.

" 4.  Full and entire liberty of conscience ;  repeal of the restrictions imposed on Catholic worship.

" 5.  The Polish language recognized in the kingdom as the official language, and used as such in the administration of the law and in education.

" 6  The establishment of a regular and legal system of recruiting.

" These six points might serve as the indications of measures to be adopted, after calm and full deliberation.   But it is difficult, nay, almost impossible, to create the requisite confidence and calm while the passions of men are becoming daily more excited, their hatreds more deadly, their determination to succeed or perish more fixed and immovable.   Your lordship has sent me an extract from the *St. Petersburg Gazette* of the 7th (19th) of May.   I could send your lordship, in return, extracts from London newspapers, giving accounts of atrocities equally horrible, committed by men acting on behalf of Russian authority.   It is not for Her Majesty's Government to discriminate between the real facts and the exaggerations of hostile parties.   Many of the allegations of each are probably unfounded, but some must in all probability be true.   How, then, are we to hope to conduct to any good end a negotiation carried on between parties thus exasperated?   In an ordinary war, the successes of fleets and armies, who fight with courage, but without hatred, may be balanced in a negotiation carried on in the midst of hostilities.   An island more or less to be transferred, a boundary more or less to be extended, might express the value of the last victory or conquest.   But where the object is to attain civil peace, and to induce men to live under those against whom they have fought with rancour and desperation, the case is different.   The first thing to be done, therefore, in the opinion of Her Majesty's Government, is to establish a suspension of hostilities.   This might be done in the name of humanity by a proclamation of the Emperor of Russia, without any derogation of his dignity.   The Poles, &

course, would not be entitled to the benefit of such an act, unless they themselves refrained from hostilities of every kind during the suspension. Tranquillity thus for the moment restored, the next thing is to consult the Powers who signed the Treaty of Vienna. Prussia, Spain, Sweden, and Portugal must be asked to give their opinion as to the best mode of giving effect to a treaty to which they were contracting parties. What Her Majesty's Government propose, therefore, consists in these three propositions :—

"1st. The adoption of the six points enumerated as bases of negotiation.

"2nd. A provisional suspension of arms, to be proclaimed by the Emperor of Russia.

"3rd. A conference of the eight Powers who signed the Treaty of Vienna.

"Your Excellency will read and give a copy of this despatch to Prince Gortschakoff.

"I am, &c.,<br>"RUSSELL."

The despatch of M. Drouyn de L'Huys, the French Minister of Foreign Affairs, dated 17th June, is identical in tenor with that of Lord Russell. In conclusion, the French Minister makes the following observations :

"Poland presents at this moment a melancholy spectacle. As the struggle is prolonged, mutual animosity and resentment render it more and more sanguinary. It is assuredly the wish of the Court of Russia to see these hostilities terminated, which carry desolation and mourning into the ancient provinces as well as into the kingdom of Poland. The continuation of these calamities during the negotiations cannot but irritate a discussion which, to be useful, should be calm. There is, then, room to anticipate a provisional pacification founded upon the maintenance of the military *status quo*, which it would be the duty of the Emperor of Russia to proclaim, and which the Poles should, on their side, observe on their own responsibility. As to the form which the negotiations ought to assume, the Russian Government has itself foreshadowed its views in its communications to the three Cabinets. It has fully recognised in its despatch to Baron Budberg the right of the Powers formerly called to regulate the political system of Europe to occupy themselves with the complications which may disturb it. It has been more explicit still in addressing Baron Brunnow. 'His Majesty,' said Prince Gortschakoff to the Ambassador of Russia at London, 'admits that the particular position of the kingdom, and the troubles which agitate it, may affect the tranquillity of the neighbouring States, between which were concluded, on the 3rd May, 1815, separate treaties intended to regulate the fate of the duchy of Warsaw, and which interest the Powers who signed the general compromise of the 9th of June, in which were inserted the principal stipulations of these separate treaties. Thus the Cabinet of St.

Petersbur has beforehand, and spontaneously, given us to understand that it will accept the assistance of the eight Powers who
participated in the general act of the Congress of Vienna.   Wishing
to reply to terms the conciliatory character of which it appreciates,
the Government of His Majesty is ready, so far as it is concerned,
to take part in these deliberations, and to be represented in the
conference which it will be convenient to assemble; and if, as we
hope, Russia adheres to the basis proposed for her acceptance by
the three Cabinets, we shall be happy should the resolution to which
the Emperor Alexander shall arrive be in harmony with the great
interests which considerations at once legitimate and powerful have
induced us to recommend to his enlightened solicitude; for this
question, withdrawn from the decision of force, which might cut it
once more without solving it, would henceforth enter on the path of
friendly discussion—the only way to prepare a solution vainly sought
up to the present day, and which would be worthy alike of the
enlightenment of the epoch and of the generous sentiments by which
all the Cabinets are animated."

The despatch of Count Rechberg, the Austrian Minister of Foreign
Affairs, to Count Thun, the Austrian Chargé d'Affaires at St.
Petersburg, is dated the 18th of June.   After repeating the six
points as given above in Lord Russell's despatch, the Austrian
Minister concludes as follows:

"To Judge from a passage of Prince Gortschakoff's despatch to
Baron Brunnow, the Cabinet of St. Petersburg seems to admit the
interest which all the Powers who signed the General Act of the
Congress of Vienna have in participating in deliberations concerning
the country designated in that Act as the Duchy of Warsaw.

"We should have no objection, for our part, to such a form of
negotiations, and we should be ready to accept preliminary negotiations or Conferences between the Eight Powers signing the General
Act of the Congress of Vienna if Russia recognized the expediency
of such Conferences, in order to discuss the development and application of the programme which we have drawn up above.

"When we addressed to you, M. le Comte, our despatch of the
11th of April we were distressed at the effect of a sanguinary conflict, the consequence of which was felt on Austrian territory, and
which thus became a source of calamity to the subjects of the
Emperor, our august master.

"We feel great sorrow at the prolongation of such conflicts.
Guided no less by considerations of humanity, than by the special
interests of Austria, we sincerely trust that the wisdom of the
Russian Government and the conciliatory efforts of the Powers who
offer their concurrence will succeed in arresting a deplorable effusion
of blood.   We have pleasure in believing that the generous sentiments of the Emperor Alexander will powerfully aid in the attainment of this result, which, if it could be obtained, would greatly
facilitate the task of the Cabinets at the Conferences.

"We shall be happy if the resolution which the Court of Russia will take, be in harmony with the great interests which powerful motives have induced us to recommend to its enlightened solicitude.

"In bringing such an intricate question as that which now occupies us into friendly discussion, a solution will be prepared which will be pacific, and at the same time one worthy of the sentiments which inspire the Cabinets."

So stands the diplomatic point of the question.

We must now turn to the popular feeling to the *vox populi vox Dei* of Europe. Let us begin with England, which is by no means desirous of war, but where generous sentiments and the love of liberty pervade the masses, where tyranny is detested, but where prudence stands wisely at the helm. In the House of Commons, on the 21st July, Mr. Horsman moved the following resolution:

"That the arrangements made with regard to Poland by the Treaty of Vienna have failed to secure the good government of Poland or the peace of Europe, and any further attempt to replace Poland under the conditions of that treaty must cause calamities to Poland, and embarrassment and danger to Europe."

In a very able speech Mr. Horsman reviewed the whole Polish question. Poland had been "diplomatized to death." What was it proposed to do now? Nothing more than to settle the Polish difficulty by "reviving the exploded hypocrisy of 1815." As a practical settlement of the question the six points would be laughed at by the Emperor of the French. But England made two additions —an armistice and a conference of the Powers. To everything proposed by England, Russia had given an unqualified rejection. This reduced the question to the narrowest compass. The Poles were fighting for independence; the Cabinet were the instigators and advisers of the Poles; did they mean to give them their nationality? Did they mean to apply to the Poles the principles they had applied to Italy? How could we, without violating the laws of justice and morality, without committing a fresh crime, deliver up the Poles once more into the hands of their oppressor? Poland for the Poles. Let us repair the wrongs of Poland by welcoming her into the brotherhood of nations. Then, could the restoration of Poland be accomplished without recourse to war? It depended upon whether Austria would give up Galicia. We had, however, raised the flame, and must meet the exigency wisely. The Polish question was the special property of Lord Palmerston. It was to him he looked to correct the feeble utterances and to repudiate the ignoble sentiments of others in high places.

The reply of the Ministers indicates that the Government has no intention of going to war to help the Poles. Mr. Gladstone denied that the Poles had been encouraged by hopes of aid from without, and the present was not the moment when a developement of the future policy of England would be expedient. Mr. Hennessy on the other hand maintained that Russia had forfeited, by her gross and barbarous outrages upon the people of Poland, all right to the kingdom. The House was justified in asking what were the intentions of the Government. Lord Palmerston said it appeared to him that the speech of Mr. Horsman was not consistent with itself or with his motion. He had told the House that there was no alternative between our remaining passive or insisting upon the establishment of Poland in its ancient state. If all the Powers of Europe were prepared to go to war to force Russia to relinquish her possession, this might be done; but it was clear that it could not be accomplished by persuasion. The only ground that could justify our remonstrance with Russia was the Treaty of Vienna; if that was abandoned, we should deliver the Poles, bound hand and foot, to Russia. He hoped, therefore, the House would not agree to the motion, or would press the Government to declare the course they should pursue. It would be their duty to communicate with the Governments of Austria and France.

The debate, which was, in many respects an important one, as testifying the strong feeling in favour of Poland which pervades the great community of England, terminated by Mr. Horsman withdrawing his resolution; and every sensible Pole must now see that they must not expect any material aid from the English Government.

The effect of this debate upon Austria and France has still to be seen. Popular feeling, as we have already stated, runs high in France in favour of armed intervention. The following may serve as a specimen. It is a petition got up in the Paris workshops to the Emperor.

"Sire,—With the crimes committed against humanity there are no longer political parties in France; there is but one nation, ever ready to strengthen the community of interests among peoples. Russia murders Poland. She murders the citizens whom our fathers baptized as their brothers in arms, and who showed themselves deserving of that glorious title in our reverses as in our triumphs. Russia murders old men and children. She murders mothers, wives, and young virgins. All at the hour of death think of their country, and turn their suppliant eyes towards France. And these orgies of blood Mouravieff seasons with barbarous atrocities which make our civilization shudder with horror. At the story of such deeds our mothers weep, our wives weep, our sisters and our children weep. For our own part, we feel our French blood boil in our veins. Sire, you hold in your hands the sword of France; employ that sword in cutting what diplomacy is powerless to resolve. Sire, unfurl the national flag, and proclaim at once to the world that a holy cause precedes it, and that a great people follow it. Sire, save, let us save Poland! And in this hope we are, Sire, &c.

In the cafés at Paris a proximate war with Russia is the common topic of conversation, and the termination of the Mexican campaign strengthens the popular opinion that sooner or later France will throw her sword into the balance as she did in Italy. Russia entertains the same idea, and is making every possible preparation both by land and by sea to be prepared for such an eventuality.

To turn to the actual events of the war during the last month, we find that the Poles, though nothing daunted, have had the worst of it. Gliszanski and Horodinski have fallen at Radziwilow; and the expedition into Volhynia has proved a failure. The following account of this disastrous affair is taken from a correspondent.

" Galician-Volhynian Frontier, July 2.

" The combined expedition from Galicia to Volhynia, after being organized, disorganized, and re-organized on various plans, was declared ready for the frontier last week, and on Sunday the points of rendezvous were made known, and orders issued to assemble the same evening. Three thousand names had been inscribed, and arms for that number of men concealed in the wood near the border, but so many seizures were made by the Austrian soldiers and police that, at the last moment, it was found impossible to arm more than 2,000. Then came the news that Minniewski, who was to command the left wing, and who had had more than the usual difficulties to contend with in getting his force together, would not be ready to cross with the main body; and, ultimately, when the centre, under General Wysocki, and the right wing, under Colonel Horodinski, had succeeded in reaching the forests which extend from Galicia far away into Volhynia, it appeared that between them they could only muster from 1,100 to 1,200 men. With this very small army, in two divisions, it was resolved to attack Radziwilow, the nearest Russian town to the Austrian frontier town of Brody; and it was hoped that if it were taken Minniewski would be able to enter the place next day with 500 new troops. To wait for Minniewski was impossible, as there was reason to believe that the Austrians were already on the track of Wysocki and Horodinski; indeed, the rear-guard of the latter had scarcely crossed when the approach of Austrian troops was announced, and some of the Polish gentlemen of the neighbourhood who had undertaken to see the detachment to the frontier would, but for the darkness and storminess of the night, in all probability have been made prisoners.

" The plan agreed upon was that Wysocki and Horodinski should both make for Radziwilow—the former from the immediate neighbourhood, the latter from a point about six English miles to the south. If Horodinski was attacked first Wysocki was to march to his assistance. Otherwise it was the intention of Wysocki to remain on the defensive in the woods before Radziwilow until Horodinski announced his approach.

" This plan for various reasons could not be carried out. Wysocki, pursued by the Austrians, had to take a difficult and circuitous road to the border, or he would have been stopped before he had fairly started, and when he had at last got over, his men had marched nearly 30 miles and had eaten nothing for 24 hours. Worse than that, it was 7 in the morning, and there were no signs of Horodinski, who had promised to advance towards Radziwilow at daybreak, and expected either to arrive at 3 o'clock, or, in the event of being attacked by superior forces, to receive aid from Wysocki within an hour, at the utmost, from the commencement of the battle.

" However, at about 8 o'clock some 500 Russians had collected outside Radziwilow, and were gradually improving their position, when Wysocki, though still ignorant as to the position of Horodinski, found it necessary to attack them. The opposing forces were nearly equal, but the Russians, it is to be presumed, had had a few hours' sleep, and something to eat the day before, and had not worn themselves out by a march of 30 miles. There was plenty of cover on both sides, the Poles firing for the most part from a forest, while the Russians aimed coolly and quietly enough from a field of rich, ripe corn, which if it could not protect at least sufficed to conceal them. Between the wood and the wheat there were a few houses and huts, chiefly inhabited by Jews. Here a number of Russian sharpshooters established themselves, and for some time kept up a murderous fire, from which the Poles could only save themselves by burning the miniature village. When the Russians came out they were charged and driven into the corn by a company of sythemen. This was the only instance of anything like hand-to-hand fighting throughout the battle. No cavalry were engaged, there were no bayonet charges, nor was a single volley fired. The Russians, like the Poles, fought in open order from beginning to end, and did not once give them the opportunity which they have so often profited by in other engagements of firing upon dense masses. The Polish infantry were too enfeebled by hunger and fatigue to be allowed to charge, though several companies were very anxious to be led forward; as for the cavalry, the horses were so tired that many of them could scarcely move. On the other hand, the Russians, when the Polish General called back the foremost lines of the skirmishers into the forest, showed no disposition to follow them, and the battle ended as it began — with the Poles half-covered in the wood, and the Russians entirely concealed in the corn-fields. The only persons who found themselves in a totally new position were the unhappy Jews and other neutral inhabitants of the little village so unfortunately situated between the two bodies of combatants.

" While Wysocki was wondering where Horodinski could be, and why he did not come to his assistance, that gallant officer had actually entered Radziwilow at 1 o'clock, and his detachment (consisting of from 400 to 500 men) was not beaten back until 5, when all that was left of it retired to the frontier and entered Galicia without being pursued. If Wysocki had been able to keep his

appointment, Radziwilow might and doubtless would have fallen
into the hands of the Poles.  As it was, Horodinski's corps was so
fearfully cut up and so completely beaten, that Wysocki, when
he came up at seven, could see no signs of his having been anywhere near the appointed place of meeting.    He did not even
know that the right wing had passed the frontier, until the news
was given him by an English gentleman who had gone as an amateur to visit Radziwilow under the impression that it was already
in the hands of Wysocki, and who, finding that a battle was going
on, and perceiving that 'some one had blundered,' went into the
thick of the fire and told the General that he had seen Horodinski
cross over into Volhynia the night before.

"Wysocki thought that if he went on fighting Horodinski must
soon be near enough to hear the firing; but Horodinski was dead.
He had fallen in a desperate hand-to-hand struggle in the middle
of the market-place at Radziwilow at the head of his troops, urging
and calling them on to the very last.   It is feared that Major Synkiewicz, who commanded the infantry, shared his fate.   My infor-
mant saw him fall from his horse just as the Russians were pressing around him, and if, as is said, all the best and most daring
of the officers were killed, Synkiewicz is certainly not among the
living.   But it must be hoped that there has been some exaggeration on this head, for no detachment with so many excellent
officers as that of Horodinski possessed had appeared in Poland
since the beginning of the insurrection.

"Ultimately Wysocki, after holding a council of war, decided on
Wednesday evening to repass the frontier, and he is now, with by
far the greater part of his men, in Galicia.   I do not think the
entire number of killed and wounded in Wysocki's corps can have
amounted to anything like a hundred, and very few indeed fell into
the hands of the Austrians.   The arms they left in a place of
safety.

"Wysocki having been too late for Horodinski, and not having
waited long enough for Minniewski, it is thought, nevertheless, that
Minniewski will enter Volhynia to-day, and try for the third time
whether a few companies of Poles can drive the Russians out of
Radziwilow.   The three detachments together, attacking the town
in three different places, could doubtless have taken it yesterday
morning; but now that the Russians are prepared, I see no reason
for supposing that Minniewski will succeed where Horodinski
failed, and Wysocki was scarcely able to make a serious attempt.

"Wysocki's loss in officers was very great, and of the aides-de-
camp, who were much exposed, scarcely one escaped being hit.
Garczinski and Domogalski, the chiefs of this service, were
wounded, the former mortally, the latter very seriously, and in
three places.   Another staff officer, Captain Glisszinski, after being
actively employed throughout the day in placing and keeping the
tirailleurs in position, and in filling up the gaps along what appeared

to be a very long line, considering the small number of men engaged, fell just at the end of the action, which lasted from 8 until 12, and again from about a quarter-past 12 until 2.

"In spite of the report spread a few days ago that Colonel Jordan had been killed while leading the centre of the last detachment which left Western Galicia for the Kingdom of Poland (1,100 strong, in three separate bodies), it appears now, to the great joy of his numerous friends, that he is alive, and not very seriously wounded. About 200 of the entire force are said to have penetrated into the kingdom. The rest were either killed, wounded, and made prisoners, or driven back into Galicia. Among the dead are several young men belonging to the principal families in Poland."

Our space will not admit us to give a detailed account of the various engagements which have taken place in many points. In every engagement the same heroic and determined courage is displayed by the patriots, who have, however, generally been compelled to retire before superior numbers. General Mouravieff has established martial law in the governments of Wilna, Kowno, Gardno, Mink, Witepsk and Mohilew. From Cracow, under date of the 27th June, we learn that the Russians have fallen back upon Suwalki, that the insurrection in Podlachia continues undiminished, that the insurgents have occupied three places in the government of Augustowa, that the Polish leader Andrusskiewicz has occupied Lomza, Stycan, and Grajewo, in the government of Augustowa. We also learn that a sanguinary engagement occurred at Serolk on the 22nd June.

Executions continue to take place by order of the Russian Government. Macewicz, Ancypa, and Korsak were shot at Mohilew upon the 18th, and Zietinski was executed at Kiew. Czarnecki, Micewicz, and Bokiewicz have been hung at Siedlce and Piotrkow. Two sanguinary conflicts have occurred at Krolowymost and Luelniki, in Lithuania.

The *Czas* says : "The denial given by the Russian Government to the statement that General Mouravieff had issued an order of great severity against women wearing mourning is false. The fact is that General Mouravieff has condemned women who wear mourning to a fine of 25 to 100 roubles; but if they cannot pay they are flogged with rods. This order has provoked disturbance among the population of Wilna, in the suppression of which the troops have killed forty persons."

A murderous encounter occurred in Podolia on the 23rd June, and on the same day an engagement took place at Orany, in Lithuania, terminating in favour of the Russians.

Archbishop Felinski has been banished to Jaroslaw.

## THE IONIAN ISLANDS.

The winter of 1862-1863 being most probably the last in which the British Flag will have flown in the Ionian Islands, it may also be termed the last season of Corfu. But few English, whether naval, military, or civilian residents, or of that happier community who pay it flying visits, free to leave when they like, will feel otherwise than sorry at parting with the Ionian Islands. To the soldier they have ever been and are the pleasantest of foreign stations; their short distance from England—one can get to Corfu from London in five days and a half, without great exertion, and for less than £20— the excellent sport to be had on the opposite coasts of Albania and the Morea, the numerous places of interest within easy reach to be visited, very pleasant society, all combine to make Corfu a specially favourite quarter. Few would, however, choose Corfu as it now is for a home. The English are in anything but a comfortable or proper position under the present form of government. To the man, sensible of the dignity attached to the word Englishman, constant vexations and annoyance arise. As protectors we are snubbed, restricted, and imposed upon in many ways. The passport system in Austria is mild compared to that in force in the Ionian Islands. The sporting but needy sub, who unable to bear the expense of a yacht, hires a ditch boat to cross to Albania for a day with the woodcock, has in addition to the hire of the boat, a series of Dogana, Sanita, and Polizia fees; yet he goes and returns from that rugged bit of " contumacious" Turkey without having seen a soul, save a hill-shepherd or two. Not even can one take a boat to sail or pull down the Benizza, a village on the island, some six miles off, and in full view of the citadel, without the said customs, health office and police stamps on his permit. But perhaps one of the most glaring impositions on the Protectorate, is the compelling it to pay an import duty upon the supplies sent by the British Government for the use of the protecting troops. Further, the very oil purchased by the Royal Navy for consumption on the ships in port, has an export duty charged upon it. In round numbers, some £200,000 are spent annually by the English in the islands, and in that sum is included an average for the private expenditure of officers and temporary winter residents. Yet we are constantly having it cast in our teeth that the Islands contribute towards the maintenance of the Protectorate. It is true that after much haggling, the annual sum of £35,000 was determined on as a fixed contribution, but so irregular has its payment been, that at the present moment, (to say nothing of occasional tips of £10,000 from the British Government) the Islands are some £80,000 in our debt.

Can anyone imagine the change in affairs when these Islands become an integral part of Greece? Will she, already eight millions in debt, and raising fresh loans, spend anything on the Islands? So far from it, the Unionists will see it just the other way. Hungry Athenians will fill their public offices, grinding taxes will be their share in the Administration. But they wish to be annexed, and so—they must pay for it. Within three years, if the Greeks hold the Islands so long, they will be the resort of the pirate and the fillibuster, and Corfu—spite of its ignorant, dishonest municipality—charming Corfu, will have sunk to the level of a Levantine town. From its position it might be made as healthy as any in the world, now it is a sink of filth and wretchedness; the commonest sanitary rules disregarded, and the word decency not understood in it. One scarcely knows which to resent most, the dishonesty of the municipality, the lethargy of the Government, or the superstition of both. Refuse and garbage crowd the streets and choke the drains; pestilential smells, and consequent fevers are rife, during the past spring scarlatina has decimated the children, and instead of clearing and ventilating, flushing sewers, &c., the church is appealed to, and out comes St. Spiro, and parades through the town with an escort a mile long of plumed and helmeted musicians, gentry carrying banners, and the *oi polloi* bearing candles, our Protestant Royal Artillery firing salutes, and our Lord High Commissioner with his staff, all uncovered, doing reverence to the wretched mummery. The Ionians and English do not get on together. There are but few of the former in society, and yet they are well educated, high bred people, mostly speaking English, French, and Italian, and of course Greek, though the two last tongues are a villainous patois as spoken by them. The reason of this want of *entente cordiale* is difficult to make out. The Ionian nobility—and Counts are in profusion—is a very proud one, and it does not like the too readily expressed, "What can you expect from a Greek?" or, "He is only a dirt Greek."

The society is chiefly military, and very agreeable. As there is but little intercourse between the garrison and the natives, so also is there but little between the British civilians and the military. There appears to be an assumption of status amongst the former, they are all Knights, K.C.M.G., and Knights' wives think much of themselves, and this will not go down with even a junior ensign if of any breeding. Let a big-wig arrive in Corfu, and never mind his or her antecedents, quickly shoots my lady's pasteboard on the new comer, shortly to be followed by a request for the honour of the Duchess of ——s, or Lord ——'s company. It is pleasant enough for the stranger, for where ladies compete to have their card baskets well filled with names of notabilities, the latter are not likely to suffer for want of attention. Unhappily, Corfu has no lady at the head of its domestic or fashionable world. Whilst the late and sincerely regretted Sir John Inglis commanded, his wife, the very personification of the well-bred, courteous, kind-hearted Englishwoman, kept people together, and prevented the miserable airs and jealousies of parvenues. It must be owned the English st

Corfu do not tend to raise the British character in the eyes of those they dwell amongst. The palace scandal, the ill-nature amongst married women, the *effronté* manner in which certain young ladies throw themselves into the arms of the gallant red coats, give to the Ionians an unfavourable opinion of our state of society. Again, it is a lamentable thing to watch "young Corfu," as represented by the unemployed cadets of the old families there, politics *à l'outrance* with cigarettes and cups of coffee ad libitum, constitute the existence of "Young Corfu." Gambling, too, is carried on to a fearful extent, but though forbidden by the laws, its existence is officially ignored, for it would be awkward to make a swoop at a hell, and find nine-tenths of the gamblers were amongst the highest employés under Government. Not long since a young man robbed the Monte di Pieta, in which he held an appointment, to meet some gambling debts; ill-luck stuck to him, and he could not replace the loan. It was discovered, but he contrived to escape arrest; why? he was the nephew of a senator, and his arrest would have caused difficulties.

Corfu boasts an opera-house, and each winter a troupe goes from Italy to occupy it. But few people patronize it, the stench in and about the house render it unbearable. The singing and acting, moreover, are only tenth-rate. The Ionians chiefly keep it up. The English have no club in Corfu, an unusual thing in a garrison town abroad, and it is a want very much felt; but there is a very excellent garrison library and reading-room in a wing of the Palace, to which strangers are admitted for a time as honorary members, and afterwards on payment of a trifling subscription, and in this institution it must be mentioned that strangers meet with very great courtesy. If, however, there be no regular club, Corfu has its rendezvous, Taylors' shop, and the One-Gun Battery, the latter so called, *lucus a non lucendo*, for neither gun nor battery is or ever was there. It is a high bluff, about three miles from the citadel, at the entrance to Lake Calichiopulo, on the road to which the *beau monde* rides, drives, walks, and meets its friends. Seated on the low wall around, on the road to the "One-Gun," are to be seen on fine afternoons, smoking subs, and the demi-monde of Corfu, and right well got up too is that demi-monde, vieing with the professional Phrynes in the sailor's straw hat and brass be-buttoned paletôt. The Ionians are said to study the Follet very carefully, the English on the contrary affect—and certain young ladies very successfully—the pretty horsebreaker line.

The past shooting season was a very poor one, indeed, the sport has year by year been going off, and no wonder; not a day passes from October to March, but that parties cross over to Albania, and between the officers of the garrison and the navy, and the "travelling gents," wild boar, deer, jackals, &c., have a hot time of

it, whilst the small covers are so incessantly worked that cock
will not lie in them.

There were no less than twenty-seven English yachts in and
about the Ionian Islands last winter, and the officers at Corfu
complain, with some reason, of the strangers, or "T. G's," as
they are called in the Ionian Islands—"Travelling Gents"—whose
time is their own, and who have the means of locomotion, hanging
about Corfu and harrying those near places, which the former, with
their short forty-eight hours' leave, can only reach.

The Ionians have an idea that when the English, with the money
spending garrison, have left the islands, the price of everything
will be so much reduced, that numbers of English families will
come and reside there for economy's sake, as well as on account
of the climate and other inducements. But that is not probable,
for Corfu then, will not have the attractions it has now. The
English hotel and shopkeepers talk of seeking a new field—the
Protectorate gone, they will find no customers. It is with infinite
regret the garrison looks back on the last winter as being possibly
the last that it will be seen with under British colours. There are
those who, being compelled to reside there, do not consider it
the paradise the migratory folks do. The heat in summer is
insupportable, from May to October there is an utter stagnation
of life; young children suffer sadly, and happy are those who
can leave Corfu and travel northwards. Laybach is a favourite
resort for families. The natives, however, delight in the heat;
but during the cold season there is hardly a day that one cares
to wear gloves, or aught but a light coat. Yet throughout the
winter months, the Ionian will be seen shuffling along in cloak
or capote, and comforter well wrapped round his face.

The Esplanade affords a curious scene by night in summer
time, it is turned into one huge bed; the poorer classes give up
their lodgings, stow all their goods into one room, and live *al
fresco*.

The Lord High Commissioner gives dances during the winter.
The Palace rooms are very fine, good floors, tolerable music, but
the suppers—well, in charity one can only say they must be
intended for the low salaried Government employés, who thus
get a heavy meal out of their chief. Still it seems that something
more *recherché* than bad Marsala and Corfu beer might be afforded
by our representative. A more affable, courteous person than Sir
Henry Storks does not exist, yet he has failed to please every one,
civil and military.

# EDITOR'S PORTFOLIO;

## OR,

# NAVAL AND MILITARY REGISTER.

The capture of Puebla has been followed by the surrender of the Mexican capital. The news was thus briefly telegraphed by M. De Montholon, the French Consul-General at New York to his government.

"New York, 1st July;

"A telegram from San Francisco announces the surrender of Mexico.

"MONTHOLON."

The French campaign in Mexico may therefore be said to be drawing to a close, or better to express it, the military phasis is past, and the diplomatic phasis is on the eve of commencing. The city of Mexico does not imply the surrender of the country. From the details which have as yet been received, and which are up to the 6th June, we learn that it was only after lengthy discussion that Juarez and his Cabinet decided to evacuate the city of Mexico, believing that the most effectual resistance to the French could be made outside the walls. On the 31st of May, the Government moved to San Louis de Potosi taking all the moveable fire-arms and ammunition with them. They also took 2,000,000 dollars from the Treasury. The Mexican troops estimated at 20,000 men, withdrew to Cuernevoca Plaza and to intermediate points round the city for the purpose of carrying on guerilla warfare. On the 1st of June a meeting was held in the city of Mexico by the principal leaders of the so-called Church party, and a Commission was sent to General Forey to offer their allegiance to the Emperor Napoleon. On June 5th, General Bazaine, who it will be remembered had advanced on Mexico immediately after the capture of Puebla, entered Mexico and offered protection to the Church party against the excited population; the whole French army was expected to occupy the capital on the 8th of June. The official reports of the losses sustained by the French since the commencement of the campaign, and the sums of money spent in this war have not been published. They will form a curious volume, nor have we received any fuller details of what has occurred since General Forey took possession of Puebla.

Acccording to a correspondence in the *Panama Star*, General Comonfort was held responsible for the defeat of the Mexican troops at Cerro de San Lorenzo, ten days before the capture of Puebla. This defeat was considered to have decided the fall of Puebla, and General Comonfort is held responsible for it by having disobeyed the orders of the President in sending the convoy of provisions and arms destined for the garrison of Puebla by a different route to that indicated to him. For this reason General Comonfort was replaced by General Juan de la Garza. The *Panama Star* also quotes a private letter from Acapulco, dated the 30th of May, which states that the Mexicans lost in the battle at Cerro de San Lorenzo above 1,000 men, killed, wounded and missing, and 800 prisoners, besides 200 waggon-loads of provisions and munitions of war destined for the garrison, eighty pieces of artillery, and the medical ambulance. The Mexicans fought with the greatest obstinacy, but were compelled to give way before the numerical superiority of the French.

The question which naturally rises, is: "What does France intend to do now that she is in possession of the capital and that the campaign may be said to be terminated?" we have various *data* to go upon. The second article of the Convention of the 31st October last between France, Great Britain, and Spain prohibits " any acquisition of territory, or any particular advantage or interference in the internal affairs of Mexico, or the exercise of any influence of a nature to attack the right of the Mexican nation to freely choose and constitute the form of its government." The right of conquest may, however, materially alter the views of the French Government in this matter. If we refer to the views expressed by the French Minister of Foreign Affairs in his *Exposé de la situation de l'Empire*, at the commencement of the year, we find M. Drouyn de l'Huys thus expressing himself: "the Mexican question has entered into a military phasis, the solution of which we must wait for. The government, therefore, must confine itself to express its confidence that the expedition will soon terminate gloriously for our flag, and that the moment is not far distant when the success of our arms will assure to the interests which led us to Mexico those durable guarantees of which they have so long stood in need."

The above words were penned before the capture of Puebla and evacuation of Mexico. Let it be hoped that the brilliant success which has crowned the French expedition will shortly lead to the establishment in Mexico of a regular and firm government unswayed by foreign influence, and under which all legitimate interests will find sure guarantees for their protection.

The tone of the French press, including the Government organs, is decidedly in favour of immediate negotiations to put an end to a distant war; the *Pays*, however, announces that M. Hubert Delisle proceeds to Mexico charged with the administrative organisation of that country. What this means it is impossible to say. Meanwhile the French Emperor, with that tact which endears him to the army, has instituted an order of Mexico, and honours and rewards will be at once showered upon the officers and men who have taken part in the campaign. General (now Marshal) Forey will, it is said, return to France, and the chief command of the French troops in Mexico will be entrusted to General Bazaine.

---

Most men, whether they have ventured their lives in "the imminent deadly breach" or not, will allow that ten years appears a long time for questions of Prize of War to hang over, yet from the speech of Colonel North in the House of Commons on the 14th of last month, that would appear to be about the average. The gallant Colonel spoke but too truly of "the universal dissatisfaction at present pervading the Army, both officers and men, who had taken part in those glorious campaigns, which resulted, owing to the gracious consideration of the Sovereign, in their right to receive prize money. What they complained of was, not only the small amount received, but the immense length of time which elapsed between the time of the capture and the period when the money was distributed to the captors. He had endeavoured to make himself master of the details, but considerable mystery appeared to exist on the subject. He naturally applied in the first instance to Chelsea Hospital for information, but the answer he received was, that that establishment was only the depository of unclaimed or forfeited shares after distribution was made. Without wearying the House by a reference to very distant campaigns, and confining himself only to campaigns with which they were all conversant, and almost all of which had occurred in India, he would be able to show that most unreasonable delays had occurred in the distribution of Prize Money. He had moved for a return of Army Prize Money granted, stating the name and date of capture, and the date when the distribution in India was authorized in

general orders.  The first on the list was the Isle of France, and
the date of the capture was 1810, while the first award for prize
money took place on the 2nd of February, 1819.  But, not to go
so far back, he would refer to the Burmese war in the years 1824,
1825, and 1826; and he found that the order for the first payment of prize money was dated December 19, 1836, or ten years
after the war was closed.  In July, 1839, the capture of Ghuznee
took place, but no prize money was distributed until March 17,
1848, or nine years after the event.  Then came the case of
Khelat, in November, 1839, and six years elapsed before the prize
money was paid.  With regard to Pegu, the contest terminated
in 1853, but the prize money was not paid until March, 1863,
after a delay of ten years, and he understood that the prize money
to each private soldier only amounted to about a couple of rupees.
No one, then, could be surprised that the soldiers were disgusted
at the treatment they experienced in this matter."

The Colonel's motion was for "An address to the Crown for
the issue of a Royal Commission to inquire into the realization of
Army Prize property, and its mode of distribution, and into the
cause of the extraordinary delays which had, in most cases, occurred
in its distribution to the captors, with a view to a remedy for the
same."

Lord Palmerston readily agreed to the grant of the Commission,
but he took exception to the term "extraordinary delays," maintaining that they were in reality "ordinary" ones, though he hoped
they would be so no longer.  He trusted that the proposed investigation would tend to a great abridgment of the delays which
now take place, and he promised that in the composition of the
Commission the Government would take care that it shall contain
within itself those elements of information and authority which
will render its recommendations satisfactory to the Army and
Navy, as well as to the country.

We heartily hope that it may be so, and that the booty of any
future war may come promptly into the hands that have won it,
and not be bought up for a mere song by greedy speculators, as is
too often the case at the present day.  We are not forgetful of the
real difficulties connected with the subject of prize distribution,
but we do think ten years rather too long a time to wait for their
solution, and we are glad to find Lord Palmerston admits that this
is his opinion also.  ———

Though the news comes from Federal sources, and no doubt is made the very most of, it appears certain that Dame Fortune has for the nonce changed sides, and allowed the Confederates to suffer severely. A really desperate battle of three days' duration, seems to have been little to the advantage of either party; but Meade, the newest Federal General, is a pupil of West Point, and if he could not absolutely defeat Lee, has so held him in check, that the Confederates have retired into Virginia, and Washington, like Richmond, has not as yet changed masters. On the Mississippi the fortune of war has been decidedly against the Confederates. Vicksburg seems to have surrendered from exhaustion of supplies; our latest arrivals tell the same tale of Port Hudson, and the Federal partisans in this country exult over these matters as a certain proof of the utter exhaustion of the South. It may be so, though we hope not, as already on the strength of these successes we have the foul mouthed New York papers blustering about calling England and France to account for various high crimes and misdemeanours against the Union. They seem rather too hasty in this, as the long expected enforcement of the conscription has given New York into the power of the mob for a couple of days, and there are unmistakeable symptoms that something of the kind impends in other places. A Government thus threatened with at least as great a failure of its "food for powder" as its adversaries, can hardly be very formidable to the nations of Europe, and we are not much disturbed at the idea of the vengeance to be dealt out to us when the "Union is restored."

––––––––

The case of the outrage on the officers of the 'Forte' at Rio de Janeiro has at length been decided on by the King of the Belgians, and the conclusion at which His Majesty has arrived is, that no insult to the British Navy as such was perpetrated, though the individuals in question were badly used. To endeavour to prevent the recurrence of such scenes, the Admiralty have issued directions which only require to be carried out judiciously to have a good effect. My Lords order the Naval uniform to be worn on all occasions of officers going on shore; but of course they must have left a large discretion to the Commander-in-chief on each station. No one can believe that it is desired to make uniform imperative in such places as Malta or Corfu, though we think that officers for their own sake should wear it more frequently than they now do;

but it is the dictate of the most ordinary prudence not to give the ignorant officials of a half savage population the excuse which plain clothing affords them. These people generally have a wholesome awe of the British uniform, and happy are they when any incautious wight who is entitled to wear it affords them the opportunity of paying off old scores by appearing among them without it. A quarrel is pretty sure to be picked with him, and whatever injury he suffers, his chances of redress are very slight indeed. Naval officers should consider this, and not play into unfriendly hands by violating a regulation which has their honour and safety primarily in view, although, like every thing else, it is capable of being made a "grievance" if not regarded in its proper light.

The Polish question has reached a culminating point. We publish in another portion of the Magazine a careful analysis of the diplomatic correspondence which has passed between the Governments of England, France, Austria and Russia, with a view to put an end to the horrible and sanguinary deeds which are being daily perpetrated in Poland. The Russian reply to the identical notes of the three Powers can scarcely be looked upon as satisfactory. It leaves the whole question in *status quo*. The Emperor Alexander declines the armistice proposed by Lord Russell, but notifies his willingness to grant an amnesty if the Poles will lay down their arms. It is not likely they will do this without concessions and guarantees. The expedition into Volhynia has proved disastrous to the National cause, and the recent debates in the House of Commons show that there is no intention on the part of the English Government to go to war for the liberation of Poland. The Poles now look beseechingly towards France as their last resource, and once again the fate of Europe may be said to depend upon the will of the mysterious ruler who sits on the throne of France.

By general consent the Guards' Ball to the Prince and Princess of Wales has been pronounced the most satisfactory of all the entertainments offered to their Royal Highnesses. The Picture galleries of the Exhibition Building were almost magically transformed into ball and supper rooms, &c., in which some 2000 of the *élite* of society assembled, and the entertainment in all its features was worthy alike of the givers and receivers. To add to the splendour of the scene many of the nobility lent services of plate, and, most remarkable of all, the famous Waterloo shield, the triumph of Flaxman's art, left Apsley House for the first time, being sent by the Duke of Wellington. Military trophies, flags, figures in armour, appeared on every side, but after all, none could be so satisfactory to the Guards as the noble Shield on which the glories of the Great War are depicted, and accordingly it occupied the place of honour, and attracted more attention than perhaps anything else.

Like the Brighton Easter Monday Review, the Wimbledon Meeting seems firmly established as a national institution. The one that has just closed was a decided improvement on that of last year, and the scores made by the various competitors were really astonishing, so as to prove to demonstration that our Volunteers can hold their own against all comers. We used in former years to be told that the Swiss, the Tyrolese, and the Backwoodsmen had a mastery of the rifle that was altogether unapproachable by ourselves; this is now shown to be a mere popular delusion; but it would be a more serious error than this, if we were to believe that the production of a good number of first-rate marksmen is the most important result of these meetings. To fire between two boards at a target placed at a known distance, and with danger to nobody except the unlucky markers to disturb the nerves, bears not the most distant resemblance to the incidents of the field of battle, and it by no means follows that the crack shot may prove a steady soldier; it is drill, and that well kept up, which alone can make the Volunteers a force to be depended on as an auxiliary to the Army. This well attended to, and the interior economy of each corps assimilated as far as possible to that of the regular troops, the Volunteer movement will prosper as well as its warmest friends can wish, but not without.

In addition to the flattering testimonials already presented to Captain Brown, the late Registrar-General of Seamen, by the Royal Naval Reserve of Sunderland, Seaham, and Hartlepool—a handsome Service of Silver Plate has just been forwarded to that gallant officer, purchased by the Shilling Contributions of the Force belonging to the other ports of the United Kingdom; every one, who had the opportunity, being desirous of adding his mite, as a token of respect to this popular and meritorious officer, who appears by his strenuous and unceasing efforts to benefit this class, to have won the affections of the Merchant Seamen of the United Kingdom, and to have contributed in no small degree to establish that feeling, which now so happily prevails amongst them.

The testimonial was accompanied by the following flattering address, handsomely embossed on vellum, to which Captain Brown returned a suitable reply, requesting the Committee to make it known to the Volunteers of the Naval Reserve, who have contributed to the testimonial.

### TO CAPTAIN BROWN, R.N., C.B.

Sir. — We, the Seamen of the Royal Naval Reserve, hearing that you had recently retired from the cares of office, after long and arduous service, desire to express to you' our warm gratitude for the great benefits, which we, in common with our brethren throughout the United Kingdom, owe to your friendship, and unwearied exertions in our behalf.

It is because we deeply feel this, that we now intrude for a brief space on your retirement, to ask you to carry with you this our warm acknowledgments of your services in our cause, and, more especially of that crowning service, which has linked us, the Seamen of the Merchant Marine, with our brethren of the Royal Navy, in the common defence of our Queen and country. In obtaining for us this privilege, you have gratified our national patriotic pride, by raising for the protection of our beloved Queen and country, a body of men, who, in time of need, will be found, " Ready, aye Ready."

Along with this sincere expression of our feelings, we beg you to accept the accompanying Testimonial, which may serve to perpetuate in your family, more effectually than mere words, the sentiments of gratitude, of those British Merchant Seamen, who owe to you, amongst other benefits, that of being members of the Royal Naval Reserve. That you may long enjoy, in honoured retirement, the fruits of a public career, began at Trafalgar, and worthily closed in organizing a new National Bulwark, is our earnest prayer.

Presented on behalf of the Royal Naval Reserve by the Committee.

# CRITICAL NOTICES.

FIFTY YEARS' BIOGRAPHICAL REMINISCENCES. By Lord William Pitt
Lennox. 2 vols.

Lord William Lennox is the son of the fourth Duke of Richmond,
who, whilst plain Colonel Lennox, fought a duel with the Duke of
York; he is the godson of William Pitt, the cousin of Charles James
Fox, and the nephew of the Duchess of Devonshire and the four other
lovely daughters of "the beautiful Duchess of Gordon." Thus by birth
connected with the very *élite* of society, he has been in succession
a Westminster boy, an officer of the Blues, an aide-de-camp to Wellington, and an M.P. in both the unreformed and the reformed Houses.
In a less public capacity, he has been an amateur actor from childhood,
and was a frequenter of the Green-Room in the days of Kean; he has
lived the life of a man about town, and has tried every kind of excitement, from driving a stage-coach to yachting, pugilism, and a footrace
at midnight in Hill Street, Berkeley Square, where he won the bet, but
lost his shoes; and he has made war on the *feræ naturæ* in both Europe
and America, killing his grouse and his foxes in company with royalty,
and his elk under the superintendence of a chief of the Red Indians
in the Hudson's Bay country. Such varied experiences, beside those
gained as a "friend" in several duels, recorded by a man who has been
the editor of the "Sporting Review" and a successful novel writer,
make a book which no one who has begun is likely to leave half read,
but which is still of so discursive a character that, open it where we
may, we are sure of meeting something that will interest and amuse
independently of all the rest.

Lord William is far from professing to give anything like a complete
outline of the history of the first half of the present century, but there
are few of its celebrities who do not figure in his pages. The Duke of
Wellington and Dr. Cary, the master of Westminster School, Lady
Blessington and Lady Morgan, Count d'Orsay and Romeo Coates,
Colonel Berkeley, Pea-Green Hayne, the "Golden Ball," Malibran, the
Duchess of St. Albans, the Bourbons, William IV., the Barrymores,
pugilists, yachting men, sportsmen of every grade, many of the
dramatic stars, Stephenson the banker, &c., &c., are to be met with
wherever we open the book, and having said this we have but to
give a few specimens of the way in which men and things are depicted
by its author.

Let us first take a picture which Old Westminsters will agree is true
to the letter:

"The life of a Westminster boy, by the way, is not all *couleur de rose*;
indeed, while he remains a fag, it presents a totally different complexion
—at least it did in my time. The young gentleman was then obliged
to rise at six in summer, and seven in winter. He commenced the
labours of the day by fetching water from the pump in Dean's Yard,
and then applied himself to light his master's fire—usually with an
insufficient allowance of wood. He next boiled his water, and prepared
his breakfast. Later in the day he had to fag for him at cricket or
fives, or run messages, and do his little marketings for sausages, rolls,
muffins, tarts, and fruits, with the risk, if caught out of bounds, of
having a flogging, to encourage the others, as a Frenchman said of
the execution of Admiral Byng. He had also to prepare tea and supper,
to brush boots and clothes, and clean cord breeches, and top-boots,
gridiron, frying-pan, and all other cooking utensils, the property of his
master. As a recompense for these multifarious duties the fag sometimes obtained ten shillings or a guinea at Christmas—more frequently

the reversion of an old tea-pot. Such suit and service I performed for the Honourable Mr. Erskine, afterwards Earl of Mar. The nature and extent of my reversionary interests I cannot remember, but I doubt whether they were more munificent than those which fell to the other juvenile victims of the system—a system, however, which was carried out in my time far more harshly than I believe it is now.

"One day when I was to fight a boy 'after four,' Erskine sent for me.

"'If you don't lick him,' said he, 'I'll lick you!'

"I fought till I was blind, and was vanquished. When on the sick-list in the housekeeper's room, Erskine came in.

"'You fought well,' said he, 'I shan't fag you for a week; here's half-a-guinea for you.'

"Tyrant as I had considered him, and not without cause, his kindness won me, and I slaved on for him as long as I remained in the lower school, without a murmur."

The Westminster lad passed his Christmas holidays in Ireland, where his father was then Lord Lieutenant (he died Governor-General of Canada), and there attracted the notice of the Irish Secretary whose aide-de-camp he afterwards became. At the age of fourteen he was gazetted to the Blues, was, probably in consequence, "not so steady as he had been," and received a hint from good Dr. Cary that he had better finish his education elsewhere; therefore he was removed to the care of a reverend gentleman in Berkshire, who was bringing forward some youths for the profession of arms, and here he was able to exercise his talents for theatricals, field sports, driving, &c., to his heart's content. At length he received a summons to wait on the Duke of Wellington, passed muster along with the present Lord Downes, and in an hour or two was on his way to the Continent, the trio travelling in the same carriage. He afterwards accompanied the Duke to Paris, and next to Vienna, but an accident prevented his sharing in the battle of Waterloo, though he witnessed a part of it as a non-combatant. After a while he returned to England, varied the routine of duty in the Blues by appearing as a page at the coronation of George IV., took decidedly to theatricals, which offended the Iron Duke, went to Canada with his father, the Duke of Richmond, and at length sold out of the Army, a peculiar custom in the Blues of not allowing exchanges, seeming to leave him no hope of advancement. He of course now mixed even more freely than before with every grade of society, and his active mind found employment for a while in Parliament; but it is more as the shrewd yet kindly sketcher of the remarkable men and women of the first quarter of this century that he claims attention. We will, with his assistance, glance at one phase of fashionable society about the year 1806:

"Among the clubs the most fashionable went by the name of the 'Pic-nics.' They assembled for a supper, to which all were forced to contribute by lot. A bag containing tickets inscribed with the names of certain edibles and drinkables, was passed round, and each took a chance in this strange lottery. Individuals of both sexes belonged to it, and had to forward within a given time whatever they had drawn—a haunch of venison or a Welsh-rabbit, ortolans or oysters, pigeon-pie or lobster-salad—in short, anything the maître d'hôtel chose to put down in the proper bill of fare for the occasion. A good deal of amusement was occasioned by the difficulty of procuring, or of sending the required comestible—but wherever the supper was to come off, there the delicacy must appear. The young ladies however youthful, and the elderly gentlemen however aged, frequently had to use extraordinary exertions to fulfil their obligations.

"The idea is said to have originated with the Lady Albina Buckinghamshire—a belle esprit of that day; but it had long been in familiar

usage in good society in France. Colonel Greville, well-known in the
fashionable circles, assisted her ladyship in naturalizing it in this
country; and the first meetings of the club were held at Le Texier's
public rooms in Leicester Square. They were also given at the Pan-
theon in Oxford Street.

"Such reunions were not solely devoted to the material pleasures
of eating and drinking—amateur concerts and amateur plays were
occasionally got up by the members; but the club did not prosper. It
elicited lampoons innumerable, and the squibs of the wits, or would-be-
wits, were shortly accompanied by ludicrous attacks from the carica-
turists. The honorary secretary, Colonel Greville, became embarrassed
in his pecuniary circumstances. His handsome person was withdrawn
to a distant part of the globe, where he had obtained an appointment,
and the ladies, whom his winning manners had drawn together,
abandoned the Pic-nics; shortly afterwards the club was dissolved."

\*       \*       \*       \*       \*       \*

"Concerts and operas increased in fashion, and the aspirants for *ton*
were not always satisfied with patronizing the artist—some of them
sought proficiency in the art. The Royal Family were conspicuous for
this amateurship. The Duke of Cumberland gave his leisure to the
violin; whilst the Prince of Wales, and the Duke of Gloucester practised
quite as zealously on the violoncello. The Prince, too, possessed an
excellent voice, which had been cultivated by Latour, the Court music-
master, and his Royal Highness organized a private orchestra in Carlton
House, to which he lent his assistance. The Duke of Queensberry, the
Marquis of Buckingham, Lord Boyle, Lord Hampden, and many other
leading personages in society, were in the habit of entertaining their
company with concerts, for which the greatest attraction in the musical
world, vocal and instrumental, was sure to be engaged. The com-
positions most in favour were those of Handel and Mozart, Cimarosa
and Glück, Paesiello, Sacchini, Sarti, Winter, and Haydn.

"Several ladies of rank not only played well on the pianoforte, an
improvement on the harpsichord, but wrote many pleasing melodies—
the beautiful Georgina, Duchess of Devonshire, for instance, set to
music Sheridan's melancholy lyric, 'I have a silent sorrow here.' A
sentimental effusion equally in favour with the fair of May Fair was,
'The Banks of Allan Water,' written by Monk Lewis. The Prince of
Wales obtained the reputation of having been the author of 'The Lass
of Richmond Hill,' which was said to have been inspired by Mrs. Fitz-
herbert, then a resident in that picturesque neighbourhood; but, independently of the absurdity of calling a woman of thirty a lass, must be
added this singular combination of negatives. The scene of the ballad
was not Richmond Hill, Surrey, but Richmond Hill, Yorkshire. The
heroine of the ballad was not a fashionable widow, but a damsel in her
teens—a Miss I'Anson; and the author was not an heir-apparent who
had crowns to resign, but a briefless Irish barrister, whose half-crowns
only, and those perhaps not without some reluctance, could have been
parted with to gain the desired object. He was Bernard McNally,
known in Ireland as the advocate of the Irish rebels—known in England
as the author of the libretto of a comic opera called 'Robin Hood,' and
of various fugitive pieces of poetry."

Among the celebrities whom Lord William met with was Sydney
Owenson, whose acquaintance he made long before she attained the
"full-blown dignity" of Lady Morgan. If the old dame were alive now,
we fancy she would be "exceedingly indignant indeed," even more than
she was when Colburn advertised her works at half-price, at the picture
given, part of which reads thus:

"While my family were stationed at Dublin, its members became
more or less acquainted with all the noble and intellectual, gentle and

simple of the Irish metropolis and neighbourhood, who desired to be presented to the Viceroy. Among these were Lady Moira, Catherine Countess of Charleville, with the Marquis and Marchioness of Abercorn —the former a superlatively fine gentleman of the olden time, who, in his exceedingly studied get up, looked so superior an article of humanity, as was only fit to be seen under a glass shade. His lady was quite as elegant and refined in her costume—indeed, aspired to set the fashion at the Irish Court in manners as well as dress.

"In their suite they had secured a young woman who had obtained no small degree of celebrity as a writer of fiction. She was one of the two daughters of a person named Owenson, who had been a farmer, a wine merchant, and an actor—but was much more widely known on the boards of one of the Dublin theatres, than as a trader or agriculturist. Like scores of similar adventurers of the same class and country, he had always been better acquainted with Fortune's eldest daughter than herself—nevertheless, being an amusing fellow, he was frequently found in good society. Though he could not afford to give his children a regular education, they contrived to acquire as much of it as fitted them to play a respectable part on the great stage of life. Indeed, one got on so far in reading and writing, that when she ought to have been at school, she took a situation as governess; and when she should have been qualifying for so onerous a post, she was writing a novel.

"Imaginative literature was at a very low ebb in the sister island— 'The Sorrows of Werter,' and the 'Poems of Ossian,' were the chief sources of sentiment and taste; and Sydney Owenson, having fallen in love with a clerk, wrote the result of her experience and her reading, in a tale called 'St. Clair, or First Love,' which was published in Dublin in 1802. The moderate success which attended this production emboldened her to try another venture, and she produced 'The Novice of St. Dominic,' which had the distinction of being brought out by a London publisher, Sir Richard Phillip's, to whom it was taken by the authoress in person, in 1805. This had a much more extended success. It has been affirmed that Mr. Pitt was delighted with it, and re-perused its pages when suffering from the illness that proved fatal. Dr. Johnson, we know, was equally enraptured with Miss Burney's early attempt at fiction. The literary merit of both works, notwithstanding, has long ceased to be appreciated.

"It was Miss Owenson's third venture, 'The Wild Irish Girl,' that established her fame as an Irish novelist. The extent of her imaginative power may be understood from the fact, that in the story she represents the rollicking Dublin actor and bankrupt tradesman, her father, as the 'Prince of Innismore,' herself as Glorvina the Princess; a man of the name of Everard, and his scape grace son, with whom she had been carrying on an amorous correspondence, as an English nobleman, Lord M., and his heir.

"Never before or since had such homely materials been so transformed. They took the shape of a melo-dramatic romance, written in a series of letters—a favourite mode of romance writing in the last century, the best example of which exists in Smollett's 'Humphrey Clinker.' The work had a success equal to the best of Maturin's equally flighty productions, and the reputation it brought, gave Miss Owenson easy access to the best Irish society. Ladies of rank were glad to patronize the popular authoress—as she became a lionne in their circle, and was so completely identified with her own heroine, that everyone called her Glorvina. Whether her father was similarly elevated, is not affirmed.

"Lord and Lady Abercorn took Miss Owenson into their establishment 'to amuse them;' and it is but justice to say, that she entertained them and their friends amazingly. She was always ready to make herself generally entertaining, if not generally useful, to the throngs of gay Irishmen and Irishwomen who filled the fashionable drawing-rooms of her patrons. She played tunes on the harp, sang Irish songs, and danced Irish jigs, with equal vivacity. Her small figure, dark complexion, round head of curly hair, and laughing eyes, being displayed to the best advantage, but with a theatrical manner that could only have been tolerated in 'A Wild Irish Girl' and a 'genius.'

"The ladies were more amused than edified by her exhibitions—in truth, some of them thought her a quiz, and ridiculed her displays. The gentlemen professed immense admiration, particularly those with whom she flirted, which was said to include everyone who required, or was thought to require, a wife. It so happened that the more desirable of her numerous admirers looked at the enticing bait, but did not seem to care to be hooked. Stories were in circulation respecting a poor subaltern who had drowned himself, and a small poet who had pined away for the peerless Glorvina, which may possibly account for the reticence of her fashionable adorers.

"I remember well the fun my brothers and I found as spectators of the young lady's performances. To us schoolboys they afforded a rich treat. Nothing we had seen of Irish life we found half so amusing.

"Lady Abercorn at last became afraid that her lovely *protégée* might get herself into a scrape, if she did not make some effort to have her respectably off her hands. So, after long consultations with her husband, and subsequent conferences with my father, it was determined to marry her to Lord Abercorn's family doctor, who, forming a part of his lordship's establishment, was at hand for the much-desired purpose.

"The young lady's friends, however, were well aware that she was ambitious—that in her heart she had cultivated the hope of realizing the aristocratic pretensions of her 'Wild Irish Girl.' The Marquis and Marchioness therefore made earnest suit to the Lord Lieutenant, that he would assist them to elevate the amusing Glorvina. This petition he could not very well deny, as he just before, in his Vice-regal capacity, had done the same service for her sister, by knighting a certain Dr. Clarke, whom that young lady had married. It was therefore resolved that Dr. Morgan should straightway be made Sir Charles, and that he should be the husband of Sydney Owenson. This programme was fulfilled, and in the month of January, of the year 1812, she became Lady Morgan; after having been seriously abjured by her considerate friends to give up flirting, and mind her ps and qs—for her reluctance to abandon her ambitious aspirations was evident to them all."

The following picture of the Barrymores is one that we trust cannot be paralleled at the present day:

"A great patron of the turf was Lord Barrymore, about one of the wildest spirits then to be met with among the most reckless of the votaries of pleasure found in the metropolis, or anywhere else. Ireland contributed a large per centage of the sowers of wild oats, who made London their field of operations. His lordship, moreover, belonged to a family possessed of a celebrity for such cultivation—indeed, in the last generation, thus employing both sexes.

"By the death of the sixth Earl, his progeny were consigned to a long and not undistinguished minority, the last years of which were spent in London society, where each succeeded in establishing for him, or herself, a 'local habitation and a name;' but for particular reasons it was connected with distinct districts within the liberties of the city. One of this hopeful lot had been incarcerated, probably among the debtors—and was, in consequence, known as 'Newgate;' the next was lame to some extent, and was christened 'Cripplegate;' their sister, who was notorious for a too free use of the vulgar tongue, was ungallantly called 'Billingsgate.' There was another brother, said to have been educated for the Church, whose discourse so abounded in reference to a place not to be mentioned to ears polite, that he received the equally characteristic appellation of 'Hellgate.'

"The elder, Richard, succeeded to the earldom, and by the time he had arrived at years of discretion, had become a most indiscreet member of the Peerage. It is impossible to do justice to his extravagance, his freaks, and his follies. Rich as modern society may be thought to be in the follies of fashion, they would shrink into commonplace vagaries compared with the excesses of his career. He began early—when a boy at Eton he is said to have gone to the Spring Meeting at Newmarket, where he betted a thousand on Rockingham. The horse won. He received his wager in pounds, when he demanded guineas—his lordship being already too knowing to be done out of fifty pounds.

"He subsequently made a bet with the Duke of Bedford for £5,000, on the result of an election—which he also won, and doubtless took equal care of the odd shillings. His speculations in this way were, however, far too numerous for me to chronicle.

"His lordship was so great a patron of the Prize-Ring, that he occasionally got up fights near a little country house of his at Wargrave, near Reading. He frequently entertained pugilists at his table, and betted largely on them. One Tom Cooper he took into his service. This man not only wore his livery and waited on his guests at table, but attended his master in his most hazardous escapades, for the purpose of interposing in his behalf should Lord Barrymore get himself into a scrape. On one occasion, when a frolic was designed to come off at Vauxhall, Cooper was sent disguised as a clergyman. His vulgar cockney tongue betrayed him—he was identified, and the temporary representative of the Church militant was violently expelled the Gardens.

"Lord Barrymore's end was sudden and unexpected. As a captain in a militia regiment, his lordship was marching with his company, guarding some French prisoners on the road between Folkestone and Dover, when a musket, in the hands of one of his men, accidentally went off, killing the commander.

"His younger brother, Henry ('Cripplegate'), succeeded to the title—Augustus ('Hellgate') having previously 'shuffled off this mortal coil;' and it is only justice to say, that the eighth earl was acknowledged to be a fit successor to the seventh. Fortunately he proved the last of such Mohicans; but his career extended to the year 1824. The name of Barrymore continued to appear in the public papers for some time afterwards, though the earldom was extinct—a female constantly coming before the magistrates to answer for most unladylike misdemeanors, who took the title of Lady Barrymore—one of a very large number of the sex who had quite as good a claim to it. She was a 'Billingsgate,' indeed, but not the original one, who, having married a French nobleman, had become Countess Melfort."

One of Lord William's acquaintances was Ball Hughes (the "Golden Ball" of some forty years ago), who died at Paris very recently. Hughes' impulsive nature more than once brought himself and his friend into odd scrapes, one of which may interest the good people of Croydon even at the present day.

"Ball Hughes, albeit the kindest-hearted creature that ever lived, was a spoiled child of fortune; for having become his own master at an early period of life, he ever acted on the inclination of the moment. I remember dining with him upon a sultry summer's evening. The day had been intensely hot, and my companion began to sigh for country air; it was about eight o'clock.

"'Shall we,' he asked, 'run down to Brighton to-night?—I fancy a dip in the sea, and we can return in time for dinner to-morrow.'

"I consented. His travelling chariot and four was ordered round, and, having directed his postilions to call at my lodgings for my *sac de nuit*, we proceeded on our journey.

"Scarcely had we passed the suburban villas dotted about in the neighbourhood of Brixton, than Ball Hughes exclaimed,

"'It's awfully hot!—what say you to putting the postilions inside, and our taking their places? I'll get on one of the leaders, and you shall ride a wheeler; anything is better than this stewy carriage.'

"My companion hailed the postilions; the trusty valet descended from the rumble behind, we were soon on our saddles, the 'boys' got inside, and away we started.

"The fashionable costume of the day was tight leather pantaloons and hessian boots, and in this dress my companion happened to be, while I was equipped in a loose pair of nankeen trousers, silk stockings, and shoes. Of course my trousers would not keep in their place, and I soon began to experience the discomfort of my post; my knees were chafed, and every now and then I ran the risk of having my leg broken by the sudden jerking of the pole; then the leaders would not keep a direct course—occasionally they bolted to the left, then to the right, then their traces became loosened, and then the pole began to stir them up, after the fashion of the man who used to look after the lions at Exeter 'Change.

"At length we came in sight of Croydon, and, exerting our best endeavours, brought the carriage well up to the door of the inn.

"'First and second turn out,' cried the ostler.

"'Here she is,' exclaimed a voice in the crowd. The bells rang—the landlord, landlady, waiter, barmaid, boots, rushed out—the idlers in the street and in the yard came forward.

"'Hurrah! hurrah!' shouted the assembled crowd.

"In the meantime curious people were peeping into the carriage, the blinds of which had been pulled down by its temporary occupants.

"'That's she, and there's her chamberlain. Brayvo, Wood! Don't you see his gold-laced cap?'

"While this was going on, no one seemed to pay much attention to the riders of the horses, and as we were rather ashamed of our posts, we quietly dismounted, leaving the ostler to stand by the leaders' heads.

"'Will your majesty please to alight,' said the landlord, as he opened the carriage door.

"What the answer was we knew not, but to the great surprise of Boniface, the two postilions, who, from their gold-laced caps and jackets, had been taken for royalty, jumped out, and nearly knocked over the landlord and his waiters.

"'Why, what's up?' asked a fellow in the crowd.

"Ball Hughes and myself, walking unnoticed through the crowd, gained the bar, where we explained the cause of our appearing in the characters we did, and were then informed that a rumour had got abroad that Queen Caroline was expected on her way to Brighton, to take possession of the Pavilion, and that, seeing a well-appointed carriage and four drive up, with blinds down, and a glimpse of gold lace inside, had strengthened the report; and many of the loyal inhabitants of Croydon had turned out to get a glimpse of one whom, if they could not respect, they could, at least, sympathise with, on account of the ill-usage she had received.

"Fresh horses were soon produced, and, after a journey, during which no other event occurred, we reached the York Hotel, at Brighton, about half-past three o'clock in the morning. After a few hours in bed, a dip in the sea, a prawn breakfast, a stroll on the Steine, we started back for London, and reached Brook Street in time for dinner and the play."

Want of space precludes our giving an idea of the wit, if not wisdom, of the Rev. Mr. Cannon (Hook's "Dean of Patcham"), the jokes of Hook himself, the fancies of Edmund Kean, or the vagaries of others not so well known to fame, with which the book literally overflows; but we cannot resist the temptation to quote, as a wind up, the account of a practical joke with which the 'country quarters' of Flanders in 1816, were enlivened. We must premise that amateur theatricals had been got up by our author and others, and some professionals occasionally came over from from England to assist; one of these, Joe Kelly, whose singing made him a great favourite, was the victim.

"A practical joke was played one night upon poor Joe Kelly, which caused a great laugh at his expense. He had been dining with some convivial friends in the guard-room, and, to the surprise of all, showed the greatest anxiety to get away at ten o'clock, pleading an engagement to escort some ladies to a suburban masquerade. The rest of the party, who had anticipated a musical treat, among them myself, were loud in our wailings; but Kelly was inflexible. The ladies, dressed *en costume*, had called for him, and had sent in a pilgrim's garb, in which their chaperon was to disguise himself—not the only *disguise*, for the wine had passed freely, and all were more or less under the influence of the jolly god.

"Kelly was now called upon to sing the 'Irish Dragoon,' but he resolutely refused, and rose to attend his fair friends, who were impatient to get to the masquerade.

"The officer of the guard ordered the sergeant to allow the carriage to pass inside the gates, and the pilgrim got in.

"'Drive to the *Temple de Flore*,' shouted Kelly, '*Faubourg St. Louis.*'

"The coachman drove on, and, arriving at the outer gate of the fortress, found it locked.

"I must here explain that the guard-room, which had been the scene of festivity, was the inner gate near the town.

"'What's to be done?' exclaimed the disappointed masqueraders. Kelly alighted; spoke to the sergeant, found the keys had been sent to the commandant's office, and, greatly crest-fallen, ordered the coachman to return. They had not got many yards, during which the ladies were loud in their lamentations, when they came to a sudden stop—the drawbridge was up, and there was no possibility of proceeding farther. A sentry was on the opposite side, and the guard-room where the poor victim of the hoax had dined, was within hail. In vain did Kelly call for the officer on duty—a deaf ear was turned to his entreaties.

"Nothing then was to be done but to bivouac for the night in the glass-coach; and upon the gates being opened in the morning, a few of my boon companions of the preceding evening and myself amused ourselves by strolling within the fortifications to see the coach pass, which it shortly did, containing our hero, dressed in a coarse camlet cloak, ornamented with scallop shells, two ladies in the costume of Swiss peasants, and one in the sober garb of a nun of St. Olave's, all looking jaded, and thoroughly ashamed of their day-light appearance.

"Kelly vowed vengeance against the perpetrator of this practical joke, who, fortunately, was never discovered."

---

WAR PICTURES FROM THE SOUTH, by B. Estvàn, Colonel of Cavalry in the Confederate Army.

A series of graphic descriptions of the battles which occurred in the Civil War in America, with Sketches of the leading Generals, and various other matters of historical and political interest cannot fail to have considerable attraction for the great reading public at a moment when the battle-ground still remains the same; especially when the account comes from an eye-witness of events. The Narrative, under the heading of ' War Pictures,' commences with the secession of South Carolina, and terminates with the celebrated seven days battle before Richmond which ended in the defeat of McClellan. The fact of Colonel Estván having served with the Confederate army might lead astray to the belief that a partial account in favouring the Confederates would be the result. Far from it. Colonel Estván's sympathies are more · North than South. This he distinctly states, not only in the Preface, but in various other portions of the book, though at the same time he pretends to give due justice to both parties.

The fight at Bull-Run, the battle of Manassas, where the lamented Jackson earned the immortal cognomen of ' Stonewall' are given in great detail. The death of Zollikofer, of General Sydney Johnston, the capture of Fort Donnelson, the adventures of the Guerilla chieftain Morgan, are truly ' War Pictures' and fully justify the title. The Confederates, however, will scarcely be pleased with some chapters in the book.

The work which consists of two handsome volumes is enriched by portraits of President Davis, Stonewall Jackson, McClellan, and other Generals both Federals and Confederates, and with Maps of the Battle of Manassas, and the Seven Days fight.

We make a few extracts. The Secession of the Southern States:

" I had only been a few days in the camp when the news arrived that the Convention at Montgomery had elected Jefferson Davis as President, and Alexander H. Stephens as Vice-President of the Confederacy. I took a hasty farewell of General Bragg and of the chief of the staff; ordered Sam to pack up my things, and on that same evening started on my way back to Montgomery.

" In a very short time the circumstances of the South had undergone a great change. After the secession of South Carolina, that of other Southern States soon followed. Early in January, 1816, Mississippi, Alabama, and Florida seceded from the Union, and at the end of the same month Georgia and Louisiana did the same. Texas seceded in February. So that in less than three months after the election of President Lincoln all the cotton States had separated from the Union, taking, moreover, at the same time, the precaution to seize all State property, with the exception of the forts in Charleston Bay and Fort Pickens in Florida, which were held by the troops of the United States, who did not show the least inclination to give them up at the first bidding.

" At the end of January the Legislature of the State of Virginia proposed a Peace-Congress, to avert, if possible, the calamity of a civil war. This Congress actually met on the 9th of February at Washington, for the purpose of taking counsel to devise friendly and conciliatory measures calculated to quench the smouldering sparks of revolution, and Mr. Tyler, a former President of the United States, was elected to preside; but after a few days' sitting the Congress broke up, as it was found impracticable to come to any understanding. The seceding States thereupon organised a government of their own, and thus laid the foundation of the future Confederacy.

" The delegates of the six seceding States met at Montgomery, and there, on 8th of February, a constitution for the Confederate States was framed and adopted. The Congress then proceeded to the election of a President, and Vice-President, and after some discussion, Jefferson Davis was, as already stated, elected President, and Alexander H. Stephens, of Georgia, Vice-President of the Confederacy."

The ceremony of the installation of Abraham Lincoln as President of the United States is thus described :

"The hour for his installation at last struck, and General Scott, commander-in-chief of the United States army, received instructions to take all possible precautions to put down any attempt at an outbreak, as it was currently reported that a demonstration had been resolved upon by the many thousand Southerners who had assembled on the occasion. The old General displayed the greatest activity on this occasion. He occupied the Capitol with regular troops; he ordered the bye-roads which lead into Pennsylvania Street, the main avenue leading from the President's house to the Capitol, to be closed; while the flat roofs of the houses were occupied by riflemen, and large bodies of infantry and cavalry were stationed at various points, ready at a given signal to act in concert. Cavalry was ordered to form the advanced and rear-guards of the Presidential procession, and to serve also as an escort. The marine brigade in the port was likewise ordered to be ready in case of any emergency.

"A portentous cloud thus hung over the Capitol of the Union. Had a single unlucky shot been fired, the city of Washington was doomed; for General Scott was not the man to shrink at trifles, and would certainly have cleared the streets with grape had any mad attempt been made to oppose the installation of the President. When favourable reports from different quarters came in on all sides, the old General, addressing his officers, said: 'Thank Heaven that I was not compelled to have recourse to force, for in that case it would have been a very sad business.'

"Merry peals of bells and the roar of cannon announced the ceremony of the installation. Thousands of people had arrived from all parts to see the old rail-splitter of Kentucky installed in one of the highest of earthly dignities, and I too formed one of the curious spectators. The procession which left the White House was headed by a number of volunteers, detachments of military, and various deputations; then came a plain carriage, wherein sat the ex-President Buchanan, and, on his right, his successor, Abraham Lincoln. The President elect appeared pale and care-worn from the fatigue and excitement he had undergone, and he cast a weary and cold glance at the moving mass of human beings at each side of the procession. Was he endeavouring to discover his Brutus among them?

"Buchanan sat at his side with a beaming face; it was quite clear he was delighted at being relieved from the duties of his responsible position. The representatives of foreign States followed the simple carriage of the President in magnificent equipages, attended by the whole personnel of their respective embassies and consulates in their official costumes.

"President Lincoln made his inaugural speech—a serious and dignified oration—from the east portico of the Capitol. He swore solemnly with upraised hand that he would observe and defend the rights and laws of the United States, and that he would govern in such wise that he should be able one day to render a good account of his acts before his Supreme Judge. He declared that there was no necessity for the shedding of blood, or to have recourse to force, at least not unless—and he placed great emphasis upon that word—the insurgent people should drive the Government to it. He further declared that he should make use of the power entrusted to him by the majority of the people to maintain with a firm hand, under all circumstances, every town and citadel which belonged to the Government."

The account of the battle of Manassas is too long for an extract, but the following passage will be read with great interest:

"Johnston was now in a state of despair; all seemed to be lost, and the exertions of the whole day fruitless. Like a wounded boar, he rushed about endeavouring to collect the last remnants of his defeated

corps; and the tide of fortune was fast setting in against the cause of
the Confederacy, when, as an expiring effort, Hampton's legion was
now brought up to support Jackson. ' You cover the retreat,' shouted
Jackson : 'we are beaten, and must fall back. Then,' added he resolutely, 'I will again show the enemy our bayonets.' In a very short
time he had formed his troops into order; and General Bee exultingly
exclaimed : 'Here stands Jackson like a 'stone-wall,' and here let us
conquer or die !'

"The exclamation was received with enthusiasm along the whole line.
'Stone-wall! stone-wall!' shouted the men; and their courage was
renewed as if by magic. Here it was that Jackson earned the imperish-
able term of *Stonewall* as a prefix to his name."

According to Colonel Estvàn, it was the timely arrival of Kirby
Smith which alone saved the Confederates from a defeat at Manassas.
The battle was nearly lost :

" Johnston and Jackson rode like madmen through the ranks of the
disheartened soldiers, but their zeal was of no avail. The confusion
increased, and masses of Beauregard's routed division came hurrying
back, adding to the general bewilderment. All discipline was at an
end; the enemy's bullets already began to shower in upon us, and the
shout of 'Run!' was raised. And now at this moment appeared in
sight, at no great distance too, advancing columns of the anxiously-ex-
pected corps of Kirby Smith.

"Like an electric shock, the words ran from mouth to mouth through
the ranks, 'Kirby is coming!' and a thousand voices thundered forth,
'Kirby is advancing with 30,000 men!' Each eye now flashed with
enthusiasm, and each breast heaved with renewed courage.

"It was now an easy task for the officers to restore order amongst
their men. The new comers are greeted with shouts of 'Welcome!'
The help that was needed to save the army had come at last. Kirby
Smith advanced at once to attack, and every one felt that his opportune
arrival had operated a miraculous change in the state of affairs. The
loud cheer that rang along our broken lines now startled the elated
advancing enemy.

"Like a thunderbolt, Kirby Smith fell upon the foe; our men fought
desperately; and in a moment the Federal troops, who had felt certain
of victory, were everywhere driven back. Scarcely had they commenced
retiring, when it became impossible to restrain our troops. A giant
Texan, throwing away his rifle, took out his Bowie knife. With one
blow he split the skull of a wounded man who had fallen to the ground;
and this became the signal for a general butchery. Like wild beasts,
the incensed soldiery fell upon their victims, hewing, stabbing, and
slashing like madmen."

The report that Kirby Smith had fallen (p. 167) was false, that brave
officer is still doing good service for the Confederate cause. A 'War
Picture' after the battle :

"The picture of human misery displayed in these ill-provided asylums
was a heartrending one. A young Federal officer especially engrossed
my sympathy. Pale as death, he lay with eyes shut and closed lips,
whilst tears rolled down his cheeks. 'Courage, comrade,' I said,
cheeringly; "the day will come when you will calmly remember this
battle as one of the things of the past.' Gradually opening his eyes,
and holding out his hand, he pressed mine, and exclaimed, in a trembling voice, 'Do not give me false hopes, sir: it is all up with me.'
In vain did I endeavour to cheer his flagging spirit. 'I do not grieve
that I shall die,' he quietly observed; 'for with these stumps' (and
he lifted the coverlit, to show me that both his feet had been smashed
by a round shot,) 'I cannot live long; but I weep for my poor dis-
tracted country. But had I a second life at my command, I would

willingly sacrifice it for the cause of the Union.' Deeply moved, I stood by the couch of this gallant youth, who with his dying breath still spoke in the same patriotic strain. His eyes had again closed,; a faint smile passed over his face, like the young dawn of another world. Suddenly he rose nervously in the bed, while his whole frame quivered; and, after exclaiming in distinct tones ' Mother!—father!' he fell back His features became rigid—his spirit had fled.

"Here, amongst enemies, he breathed out his young life, far away from his beloved relations, and none of them will probably ever learn where and how he died. There was nothing to give us any clue to his identity, with the exception of a small locket with the portrait of a fair young girl, which he wore round his neck. I put it upon the dead man's breast, and took care to have it buried with him in the small grave that had been dug to receive his body, under the shade of a large cherry-tree. How many must have died in a similar manner, far from their friends, without one word of consolation, without one friendly look to cheer their last moments!"

The Battle in Tennessee, in which General Zollikofer was killed, is a graphic picture. The Confederates, under Crittenden and Zollikofer, commenced a march at midnight to take the Federals by surprise:

"Zollikofer's Brigade being the first ready to start, commenced its midnight march; the other troops followed in silence; and the cavalry formed the van and rear-guards. The march was a most fatiguing one; the ground being so saturated by snow and rain that it was difficult to get along, especially as we had to carry our arms and provisions with us. Added to this, the night was so dark that we could scarcely see a hand's length before us; and the men were therefore obliged to keep together in the closest order. Morning was beginning to dawn, the rain still continued to fall in torrents, and yet it seemed as if our weary march would never come to an end.

"Suddenly the solemn sound of bells was faintly audible in the distance; some church or chapel was evidently not far off, and its bells were inviting the pious to prayer: it was Sunday morning. The effect this produced upon our men was peculiar and striking. In the distance, peaceful chimes betokened piety and brotherly love, while on the spot we occupied hostile columns were advancing in the dark, bent upon destruction; proceeding, not to pray, like good Christians, but to slay and maim their fellow-men.

"Suddenly a shot was fired—then a second. A general halt was now made, and orderlies galoped about like gaunt shadows in the mist. In a few minutes a heavy roll of musketry followed. Like wildfire the news spread that the enemy had discovered the approach of our advanced guard, and had fired upon them. The heavy sound of cannon soon added its deep base to the musketry. 'Chapman's battery, forward!' shouted the commanding officer, and our men pressed up close to the roadside to allow the battery and ammunition cars to pass: the lighted matches of the gunners looking like so many fire-flies in the misty gloom that surrounded us.

"As soon as the battery had passed, the spirits of our men revived. Orders were issued with decision, and were promptly obeyed. General Zollikofer alone seemed not to share in the general confidence displayed by the troops. Silent and sad he sat on his horse at the mouth of the pass, casting an anxious look on the animated troops as they marched forward. Nothing seemed capable of rousing him. Like a statue he remained on one spot: indeed, had it not been that his black charger sent forth incessant volumes of steaming breath from his nostrils, both the rider and his steed might have been supposed to be cast in iron. Usually so cheerful, why was the brave general now so melancholy and sad—was his mind depressed by any mournful presentiment? Suddenly he put spurs to his horse, and in a few minutes both were out of sight.

"In a very short time the Confederate troops were hotly engaged. The intention of their leaders had been, as we have seen, to make an unexpected attack upon the enemy, and the very reverse had happened; they had been anticipated. The whole air now resounded with the roar of cannon, the roll of musketry, and the cheers of the contending combatants. Zollikofer, as was always his custom, headed the first attacking columns in person. Despite the snow, the rain, and the fog, which spread like a pall over the surrounding country, the spirits of our men were excellent. The different columns advanced cheerily to the respective positions allotted to them. As soon as it was sufficiently light to allow friend and foe to be distinguishable, General Zollikofer, placing himself at the head of the 15th and 17th Mississippi regiments, addressed them in a few appropriate words and led them against the enemy. The first man to fall was the standard-bearer, who, grasping his flag, sunk mortally wounded. This somewhat disconcerted our advancing columns, when two or three men rushed forward to seize the flag, which was again raised on high. Our troops now boldly advanced against the enemy's well protected position, and were received by a murderous fire, which spread death and devastation in their ranks. The officers showed the most determined bravery, leading on their men sword in hand. General Zollikofer was aware that he must persevere in this attack without flinching, so as to allow the other troops sufficient time to take up their positions. The two Mississippi regiments fought with courage which excited universal admiration, although their loss was most severe: more than half their number fell dead or wounded on the ground, and it was impossible to remove the latter in the heat of the fight. The enemy were well aware that, if once driven out of their strong position, there was but little hope left for them, as owing to the state of the ground it would have been impossible for them to manoeuvre with any chance of success.

"Crittenden having ordered up Carroll's brigade to support Zollikofer, these sun-burnts sons of the West rushed furiously upon the enemy, Zollikofer in person leading them on. His black charger was now seen suddenly to leap a barrier, and at the same moment the general fell backwards, horse and man rolling over together, both of them struck dead.

"A cry of anguish and revenge ran along the ranks. 'Zollikofer is shot! Zollikofer is killed!' Then using the butt-ends of their muskets, which were of little use as fire-arms, owing to the wet, the infuriated soldiery rushed upon the foe felling them, to the ground right and left. The battle now became a regular mêlée: the Federals, overcome by the furious onslaught of the Confederates, gave way: their batteries were left unprotected, and as the artillerymen did not flinch, they were bayoneted at their guns. Both attack and defence were most obstinate and the fierceness of the struggle showed that kindred blood ran in the veins of the contending foes.

"The officer in command of the Federal batteries was cut down in front of one of his own guns, and a regular massacre ensued, which was only put a stop to by the arrival of the Confederate Colonel Morgan."

A night sortie from Fort Donnelson, and the successful flight of the Ex-Federal Minister of War is another graphic 'War Picture.' The sketch of John Morgan, the guerilla chieftain is a picture in itself:

"Of vulgar extraction and of no education, but gifted with extraordinary courage and self-possession, John Morgan had formed a body of men of his own stamp, who preferred fighting, and the hardships of a roving life, to any peaceable occupation. His band roamed about the country with such audacity as to become a perfect dread to the enemy. Scarcely a day passed without some daring act being recorded of John Morgan and his horsemen. Although he and his band belonged properly speaking, to General Hardee's division, and his duty was to watch the enemy's movements, he much preferred doing a little business on his own account.

"One day he proposed to his men to make a raid upon the little town of Gallatin, twenty miles north of Nashville, then occupied by the enemy. The very idea of such an expedition created a joyful excitement amongst his desperate followers, and like lightning they fell upon the town and took possession of it. Whilst his men were robbing and plundering to their hearts' content, Captain Morgan proceeded to the office of the telegraph, in the expectation of finding important despatches there. The official on duty had not the slightest idea of what was going on in the town, and when Captain Morgan asked him with great politeness what news he had received, the agent taking him for an officer of the United States army, replied, 'Nothing particular; but inquiries are being made continually respecting that rebel bandit, Morgan. But if he should ever come across my path I have pills enough to satisfy him!' pulling out his revolver as he said this and flourishing it in the air before he thrust it back into his belt. As soon as he had finished, the strange officer thundered forth, 'You are speaking to Captain Morgan; I am Morgan, you miserable wretch.' The poor official sank on his knees, and with the fear of death full upon him sued for mercy. 'I will not hurt you,' retorted Morgan, 'but send off this despatch at once to Prentiss.*

"'Mr. Prentiss,—As I learn at this telegraph office that you intend to proceed to Nashville, perhaps you will allow me to escort you there at the head of my band.

"'JOHN MORGAN.'

"It is easy to conceive what a fright Mr. Prentiss must have been in, when the authenticity of this despatch was proved a few days afterwards.

"After sending off this friendly invitation, Morgan hastened to the railway station to see the train come in. In a few minutes it came up, upon which Captain Morgan ordered one of his men, with pistol in hand, to take charge of the engine driver, whilst he examined the carriages, and proceeded to take five officers prisoners. He then had all the carriages set fire to, and other inflammable matter, stopped up the vents, and sent it back on fire in full speed, towards Nashville. The engine, however, exploded after going a few hundred yards. After this exploit Morgan and his men, with their prisoners, remounted their horses and gained the camp in safety, where they were enthusiastically welcomed by their comrades.

"On another occasion he surprised a picket of six Federal soldiers, and made them prisoners. He was quite alone. On coming across them he went straight up to the corporal in command, and, passing himself off as a Federal officer, expressed his indignation at their slovenly appearance, and ordered them to lay down their muskets, and regard themselves as under arrest. The order was obeyed; but when the men saw that he was taking them in a contrary direction, they observed that they were going the wrong road. 'Not so,' he retorted; 'I am Captain Morgan, and know best what road you have to take.' These little adventures, amongst many of a similar nature, made his name well known, and acquired for him a wide-spread popularity."

The battle of Shiloh, in which Sidney Johnston fell, is described in great detail. Our space will not admit us to give any further extracts.

* Editor of a paper at Louisville, and a mortal enemy of Morgan.

It was at the Battle of Seven Pines that Joe Johnson was so severely wounded as to be compelled for a time to seek rest. We behold him again now with the gallant Lee among the most active officers in the Confederate army.

The investment of Richmond by McClellan, and the Seven days battle form a distinct chapter in the work.

The concluding observations of Colonel Estvàn, though many may differ from them, are well deserving attention, they are as follows:

"If the question be raised, how it has happened that the success which the Federal Government reasonably look forward to obtain, in the struggle for the maintenance of the Union, turned chiefly in favour of the South, the only safe conclusion we can come to is, that it must be ascribed to a want of unity amongst the Federal generals.

"If that Government had only possessed a few such men as Sterling Price of Missouri, the Leonidas of the Confederate army; if the leading members of that Government could have been content to sacrifice their own ambition and vanity to a patriotic regard for the real interests of their cause, affairs might have taken a very different turn. The honour awarded by the nation to its sons is not based on the rank or titles they may hold, but is a consequence of the acts which they perform. All the distinction which mere vanity strives to obtain are utterly barren; it is only the memory of disinterested, undaunted patriots that endures in the hearts of their countrymen. What the Washington Government had to contend against, was both a want of unity and a general craving for personal notoriety.

"Such was the nature of the cancer that ought to have been cut out before it was so deeply rooted as to become incurable. Why did Fortune, it may be asked, smile so often upon the arms of the Confederates? Because, we reply, with few exceptions, their generals acted harmoniously together, and were well supported by their Government and press; whilst the Federal Government, on the contrary, had to contend with three distinct political parties, each of which endeavoured to impede the action of the other, and this practical source of disunion caused the troops, as well as the people, occasionally to lose confidence in their leaders, political and military, and necessarily rendered the task of the latter much more difficult than it would otherwise have been. In fact, it is beyond question that the Federal Government, with its inexhaustible resources, with its powerful fleet and army, might long since have annihilated the Seceding party in the Southern States, whom they regarded in the light of rebels, if its generals had but energetically concentrated their operations.

"The United States Government should only have had two points in view in directing their offensive operations: the first and cardinal point being Richmond, which ought to have been taken at any cost, for if once in their power, the death-blow to the Confederacy would have been given. Whatever people may say about moving the seat of Government further south, it matters not; with the fall of Richmond, the Confederacy would have succumbed likewise, for Richmond was not only the abiding-place of the most rabid Southern fire-eaters, but of the thousand overawed partisans of the Union, who would have plucked up courage to judge and act for themselves, had the pressure upon them been removed. The Confederate Government—which it must be remembered, had not been really acknowledged, for President Davis was elected merely by a small body of partisans—would then have fallen to the ground.

"The Confederate Government is perfectly well aware of this, and this is why they exert every nerve to make a stand at Richmond. All the resources indispensable to carry on the war are concentrated in and around that city. Virginia is a rich and productive State, quite capable of providing for the wants of a large army: iron and coal-mines, rich pastures, corn-land, and all kinds of cattle, are to be found plentifully within it. Richmond, besides being the seat of the Confederate Government, is rich in arsenals, arm-founderies, manufactories of different kinds, and great baking establishments for the army. If driven from Richmond, the Confederate Government might possibly make a stand for a fortnight in North Carolina, but would then be compelled to decamp hastily to the other side of the Mississippi.

"When General M'Clellan took post before Richmond, he was perfectly well aware of the momentous task he had before him. Knowing the enemy's strength, he never treated them with contempt; but he well knew the vast importance of unity and self-confidence. It was not his fault that he was beaten before Richmond; his failure must be attributed to the blindness of his Government, who looked upon the foe as one easily to be vanquished. When M'Clellan had placed round the throat of that foe an iron collar, which he intended to draw tighter, and had obtained a footing so close to Richmond that he could send his cannon-balls into the very centre of the city, the Government at Washington ought to have concentrated all its thoughts and energies to the one great object, of sending M'Clellan as many troops as would enable him to assume and maintain the offensive.

"The second point which the Union Government should have kept in view is the command of the Mississippi. The Federal Government ought, at any price, to have taken possession of that great road of communication, no matter what amount of troops it would have been necessary to employ for that purpose. If it could have obtained the possession of this great watercourse, it would at once have cut off a portion of the Confederate States from all communication with those places on which they depended for supplies, and compelled them, through sheer necessity, to return to the Union. With various stations for her ships on the Mississippi, and an army of 200,000 men in the field, the United States could hold its own against all comers. The Government at Washington should not have attached so much importance to its flanks; for on the one side they were protected by their powerful fleet, on the other by a brave and numerous people ready to step forward in the defence of their Government as soon as they were satisfied that the latter was in earnest. If it had collected together all the troops scattered over the different parts of its vast territories; if it had put at their head a leader provided with the means of conducting the large army we have designated—a leader who had gained the love of his soldiers—there can be no question that he could have achieved the greatest results. One decisive blow—one great victory—would have sufficed to induce the soldiers to follow him willingly unto death wherever he chose to lead them; and that, too, without the allurement of bounty, or of any promised reward, but simply for the honour of fighting for the national cause.

"The various acts of cruelty that have been occasionally perpetrated during this war may be accounted for by the fact of the armies being composed of heterogeneous elements. There was no true soldier-like spirit, no clear conception of the laws of military honour amongst these great masses, such as are to be met with in the armies of more civilized nations. The troops comprised a singular mixture of semi-savages, civilized men, patriots, and hot-headed partisans, with some few chivalrous adventurers.

"This lamentable war would long since have terminated if the Union Government had actively and resolutely bestowed at the commencement of the contest serious attention on its more important issues, and have then readily made those sacrifices which it is now driven to. The whole affair was treated with too much levity; indeed, it appeared

almost as if a wish prevailed amongst many to provoke the war. Over-
confidence in their resources, national vanity, party spirit and private
interests, all served to kindle the spark which has grown up into a
mighty conflagration, that has let loose the hell-hounds of war to ravage
this unfortunate land. When will a controlling hand be stretched forth
to restore peace between the fratricidal opponents? when will the mild
angel of peace descend with the olive-branch to restore tranquillity and
order in the dwellings of man, and to implant love within hearts that
are now filled with deadly hatred and revenge?

" Who can tell?

" Ere long, let us hope and pray, for who does not sincerely desire
it? But it needs the combined efforts of strong will, powerful intellect,
and untiring energy, as well as of undaunted courage, to recover and
reunite the loosened elements of former content, prosperity, and
liberty. Anticipating, as I fervently do, so desirable a consummation,
I trust that thousands will join me in heartily wishing that the American
Republic, once the pride of the world, may arise strong and powerful
from this disastrous struggle; that the blood which has been shed in
torrents during this war may serve to fertilize the soil of liberty, and
that a new Union may arise, greater, stronger, and more free than its
predecessor."

A MILITARY VIEW OF RECENT CAMPAIGNS IN VIRGINIA AND MARYLAND.
By Captain C. C. Chesney, R.E., Professor of Military History,
Sandhurst College. With Maps.

Our professional readers will do well to make themselves masters of
this pocket volume, for the preparation of which Captain Chesney has
consulted the very numerous periodicals of France, England, Germany,
and America, where the narratives of eye-witnesses of the contests of
the Civil War have appeared. The Captain has toned down the "extravagance of writing" by which so many of the published accounts are
disfigured, and he has been enabled to correct their errors, and supply
their deficiencies, by means of private communications that he has
received from numerous other parties, who have either themselves been
spectators of portions of the war, or have had relatives actively engaged
in it. By careful comparison of the conflicting accounts, he is enabled
to lay before the reader a record of the Virginia and Maryland campaigns, which is a marvel of clearness and completeness when its
sources are considered. The work, in what we may term its finished state,
only extends to the year 1862; but there is a postscript on Chancellors-
ville, which Captain Chesney has not had time to work out as thoroughly
as he could wish, and in which he fears that some minor inaccuracies
may be found, for which he bespeaks consideration. We cannot believe
that there will be much to alter, but even if there should be, the second
edition, which this most useful work will assuredly shortly reach, will
no doubt see everything rectified; and we hope that we may have at a
future day the advantage of so able a guide in tracing the course of the
contest to what we conceive its inevitable conclusion, the independence
of the South.

We should mention that Captain Chesney has supplied some small
sketch maps, which will enable any one to follow the leading operations
step by step. In them, all features of the country not actually needful
have been omitted, and the result of a few minutes' study of them
is a much clearer idea of the scene of operations than can be readily
attained by any other means.

THE FIRST YEAR OF THE WAR IN AMERICA. By Edward A. Pollard,
Editor of the " Richmond Examiner."

We own to no further acquaintance with the " Richmond Examiner" than the extracts which appear in our English newspapers give us, but in this book we have its editor coming forward in his own name, and showing that his print must be a formidable rival to the notorious "New York Herald." Of course, he professes himself an ardent champion of the South; but he is at least as ardent a hater of Mr. Jeff. Davis, who is fiercely denounced as an "autocrat," "tyrant," &c., &c.; and the Southern Government, which people in Europe generally think highly of, it seems, is far inferior to the Cabinet of Washington. "Drunken patriots, cowards in epaulettes, crippled toadies, and men living on the charity of Jefferson Davis" have ventured to question some of Mr. Pollard's statements, and very reasonably we think, but still his coarse publication has reached a second edition, which brings down the narrative to September, 1862. To attempt to analyze the book would be useless. Mr. Jefferson Davis is the author's pet aversion, but scarcely any one else is mentioned in much better terms; indeed, so indiscriminate a reviler we hardly ever met with; and though perhaps there may be some facts not known to the English reader that would be discovered on a very attentive perusal, still they are so hidden under the mask of the very worst style of American newspaper writing, that we cannot recommend any one to look for them.

---

RECOLLECTIONS AND ANECDOTES: Being a Second Series of Reminiscences of the Camp, the Court, and the Clubs. By Captain R. H. Gronow, formerly of the Grenadier Guards, and M.P. for Stafford.

We spoke favourably some little time ago of the first series of the gallant Captain's Recollections, and are glad to have another instalment of his Reminiscences, which are quite as agreeable as ever. The second series is more confined to members of the fashionable, literary, or artistic world that the former was; but there are some anecdotes about Waterloo, and Wellington, and the Allies in France, which are worth preservation. Towards the end, Captain Gronow appears in a new character, and gives us some reminiscences of his own parliamentary career, in which Lord Althorpe, Daniel O'Connell, and other celebrities of St. Stephen's are introduced.

---

TEN YEARS OF THE SCHLESWIG-HOLSTEIN QUESTION. An Abstract and Commentary by Otto Wenkstern.

Mr. Wenkstern is a practised writer, and puts a very plausible appearance on the question of Germany against Denmark. His case is, that though Denmark is weaker than Germany, she is stronger than the Duchies, and that Germany is therefore bound to protect the latter. It is not, he says, Germany that wishes to overawe Denmark, but Denmark that not only wishes, but actually does oppress Schleswig and Holstein. This has all along been the statement of the German party, and a careful selection is made by Mr. Wenkstern from the interminable state papers that have passed on the subject. Still, they are "selected" papers, and no doubt the Danes could produce plenty that would tell a different tale; but they do not use the press so freely as their German rivals. Instead, they stand calmly on what they have ever maintained as their "right," and seem hardly likely to be driven from it by either the long-winded dispatches or the slow action of the German Confederacy.

# MILITARY OBITUARY.

General Sir James L. Caldwell, G.C.B., Royal (Madras) Engineers. This gallant and distinguished officer died at an advanced age at his residence, Beachlands, Ryde, Isle of Wight, on the 28th of June. He entered the service of the late Hon. East India Company in the year 1788, and was employed at the attack and capture of the minor Hill Forts of Woohadroog, Ootradroog, Bhynumghur, Ramjurry, and others. At the attack of Tippoo Sahib's camp at Bangalore, under the command of General Floyd. In 1792, at the assault of the Pettah or Lower Fort of Bangalore, under Lord Cornwallis, where the Colonel Morehouse, the Commandant of Artillery, and many officers and men were killed. At the siege of Bangalore, where he was wounded in the trenches. At the assault of the breach of Bangalore under General Meadows ; entered the breach with storming party, and was near the Killydar (the Commander of the Fortress) when he was killed defending the top of the breach ; many thousands of the enemy fell at this assault. At the siege and capture of the strong hill fortress of Savendroog, under the command of Lord Cornwallis ; mounted breach with storming party directed by General Meadow. At the surprise and capture of the Pettah of Nundedroog. At the siege and capture of the fortress of Nundedroog ; mounted breach with storming party. At the battle of Caragaut with Tippoo Sultaun's army under Lord Cornwallis. In 1799 at the first siege of Seringapatam under Lord Cornwallis ; slightly wounded in the trenches. At the attack of Tippoo's camp and line of redoubts under Lord Cornwallis previous to the siege.  At the battle of Malwelly under General Harris. At the second siege and capture of Seringapatam, 1799 ; commanded the brigade of Engineers accompanying the storming party ; had charge of the scaling ladders ; twice wounded during siege ; shot at the top of breach in rear of forlorn hope, and rolled into the ditch shortly before the Sultaun Tippoo Sahib was killed ; received pension for wound, and medal ; the only officer of Engineers wounded during the siege. Appointed in 1810 senior Engineer and Surveyor on the expedition against the Isle of France, under the command of General Abercrombie ; thanked in the public despatch, and favourably mentioned in General Orders ; General Abercrombie observes, "To Major Caldwell, of the Madras Engineers, and who accompanied me from India, I am indebted for the most able and assiduous exertions. Since his arrival in these islands, he was indefatigable in procuring the necessary information in respect to the defence of this colony, and through his measures, I was put in possession of an accurate plan of the town some time previous to the disembarkation of the army ; and I trust your Lordship will permit me to recommend to your Lordship's protection this valuable and experienced officer." Was on board Her Majesty's frigate Ceylon, when attacked off, and in sight of, St. Denis, Isle of Bourbon, by the French frigate Venus, of very superior force ; both vessels dismasted, and after a night's hard fighting struck to the Victor, a third ship ; recaptured next morning by Commodore Rowley. Appointed to the charge of the Engineer's Department in Centre Division of the Madras Army in March 1811. Appointed to superintend the repair of the fortress of Seringapatam in 1812, and as Special Surveyor of Fortresses in 1813. Appointed a Commissioner in 1816 for the restoration of the French Settlements on the coasts of Coromandel and Malabar. Appointed to act as Chief Engineer of the Madras Army in the same year. In 1815 he was nominated a Companion of the Order of the Bath ; in 1837 was made a Knight Commander, and in 1848 a Grand Cross of the Order. His commissions bore date as follows—

Ensign, 27th July, 1789; Lieutenant, 2nd December, 1792; Captain, 12th August, 1802; Major, 1st January, 1806; Lieutenant-Colonel, 26th September, 1819; Colonel, 27th May, 1825; Major-General, 10th January, 1837; Lieutenant-General, 9th of November, 1846; and General, 20th June, 1854.

---

General Sir Thomas Erskine Napier, K.C.B., Colonel of the 71st Foot, died 5th July, at Polton House, Lasswade. He was the younger brother of the late Admiral Sir Charles Napier, was born in 1790, entered the service July, 1805; became Lieutenant., May, 1806; Captain, October, 1808; Major, December, 1813; Lieutenant-Colonel, June, 1817; Colonel, January, 1837; Major-General, November, 1846; Lieutenant-General, June, 1854; and General, September, 1861. He served with the 52nd Regiment at the siege of Copenhagen and battle of Kioge in 1807. Aide-de-camp to Sir John Hope on the expedition to Sweden in 1808; and subsequently to Sir John Moore's campaign in Spain, including the retreat to and battle of Corunna. In Sicily with the regiment until the autumn of 1810. Served afterwards in the Peninsula on the staff, including the defence of Cadiz, oattle of the Fuentes d'Onor, second siege of Badajoz, battles of Salamanca, Vittoria, Nivelle, and the Nive—including the various engagements near the Mayor's house, slightly wounded on the 10th December, and severely on the 11th—lost left arm. He received the war medal with seven clasps.

---

Major-General Thomas Kelly, K.C., died on the 27th of June, at Lansdowne Square, Rosherville, at the age of 87. He entered the army nearly 70 years ago, and was early engaged with his regiment, the 26th Light Dragoons, in the operations carried on towards the close of the last century in the West India Islands, and was actively employed against the Caribs and the French till he was ordered to Portugal. On the voyage the transport was attacked by a Spanish gunboat, which was beaten off, and in the conflict he much distinguished himself. He proceeded to Egypt with the force under Sir R. Abercrombie, and participated in the engagements which crowned the expedition with success; and he was present at the siege of Aboukir, and in the operations under Sir Eyre Coote, near Alexandria. He was also engaged in the action of the 21st of March, and was wounded in a night attack on the 25th of August, when he captured the whole of the enemy's pickets with a far inferior force. For these services he received the gold medal from the Grand Seignor, and he also had the silver war medal with one clasp. But he was one of those who suffered from the great disadvantage of being sent away to the West Indies on foreign service on the outbreak of the great European war—the Peninsula and Waterloo—so that he had no opportunity of sharing in the glories and in the promotions which fell to the lot of his more fortunate comrades, and his career from 1810, when he became a captain, was so slow that it was 20 years before he attained the rank of major. He was appointed Commandant of Tilbury Fort, where he discharged the duties, which were more onerous than might be supposed, with zeal and ability for 46 years, and only retired in consequence of age and infirmity a short time ago, with the rank of major-general.

---

Colonel E. W. Crofton, Royal Artillery, died at Malta on the 26th June. He entered the Service in 1831. He served in Spain during the Christino and Carlist war in 1837 and 1838, and was taken prisoner by the Carlists. He had received the order of St. Fernando, 1st class. He was nominated to the 3rd class of the Medjidie for services as a Brigadier-General with the Osmanli Cavalry. As Brigadier-General he commanded the Royal Artillery throughout the campaign of 1860 in China.

and was present at the action of Simho, taking of Tangku, capture of the Taku Forts, action of Tangehow on the 18th and 21st of September, and surrender of Pekin. He was twice mentioned in despatches, was made a Companion of the Bath, and received the medal and two clasps. He was in command of the Royal Artillery at Malta at the time of his death.

Lieutenant-Colonel James M'Grigor was drowned at Aden on the 28th of June. This officer belonged to the Bombay Native Infantry, and served in one of its regiments throughout the campaign of Scinde, under Sir Charles Napier, on which occasion he was favourably noticed by his great commander. His other services were also meritorious. During the Indian Mutiny his conduct was such that the Secretary of State for War attributed the suppression of an outbreak in the Bombay Presidency to the prompt and vigorous measures of Major M'Grigor. A plot had been formed by the men of one of the regiments at Bombay to murder the officers, and, in concert with other Sepoys, to pillage and massacre all the Christian Residents in Bombay. Major M'Grigor, however, possessed the confidence of the soldiers, one of whom divulged the particulars of the plot, and named the hour, viz., midnight, which was fixed for its execution. Accordingly he galloped off for reinforcements, summoned the regiment for parade a quarter of an hour before midnight, and obliged the intended mutineers to lay down their arms. The late Colonel M'Grigor was not more remarkable for courage and presence of mind than for generosity and kindness of heart. His life was unselfish and his death premature. He was son of the late Colonel M'Grigor, who commanded Her Majesty's 70th Regiment, and nephew of the late Sir James M'Grigor, who was for thirty-eight years Director-General of the Army Medical Department.

Lieutenant-Colonel John Ouchterlony, of the Royal Engineers, died 29th April, at Ootacamund, India, aged fifty. He entered the service, June, 1832; became Lieutenant, March, 1842; Captain, June, 1847; Major, October, 1860; and Lieutenant-Colonel, February, 1861.

Lieutenant-Colonel Richard Palmer Sharp, late of the 72nd Foot, died near Dublin on July 4. He served with the 26th Regiment in the first China expedition (medal). Commanded the 72nd in the Crimea from the arrival of the regiment on the 13th of June to the 31st July, 1855, including the expedition to Kertch, and siege of Sebastopol (medal and clasp, and Turkish medal).

Major the Honourable Henry Littleton Powys-Keck, formerly of the 60th Foot, died the 10th of July at Stoughton Grange, near Leicester, aged 51.

Doctor T. C. Gaulter, Surgeon-Major, late Surgeon at the Royal Hospital at Chelsea, died, June 25. He entered the Service in March, 1827, and served in India, Cape of Good Hope, &c. He was one of the most intelligent, benevolent, and kind medical officers that the Army ever had on its staff, and is a great loss to the service.

Captain John Cassidy, formerly of the 68th Foot, died on June 30, at Upper Norwood, aged thirty-six. He served the Eastern campaign of 1854-55, including the battles of Alma and Inkerman, siege and fall of Sebastopol, (medal and three clasps, and Turkish medal).

Captain A. S. Craig, late 3rd West India Regiment, died at Jamaica on the 11th of May, aged thirty-nine. He served as Lieutenant in the

62nd Regiment in the Sutlej campaign in 1845, and was present at the battle of Ferozeshah (medal), where he was severely wounded by a cannon ball, causing amputation of the right arm.

Captain Herbert H. Moseley, 42nd Royal Highlanders, died on the 19th of May, at Calcutta, aged twenty-seven. He entered the service in June, 1853. He served the campaign of 1857-58 against the mutineers in India, including the actions at Kudygunge and Shumsabad, siege and fall of Lucknow, and assault of the Martinière and Bank's Bungalow (medal and clasp).

Lieutenant Frederick William Ramsbottom, of the Rifle Brigade, died on June 25, at Winchester. He entered the service in July, 1855, and became Lieutenant, May, 1858. He served with the 2nd Battalion during the Indian Mutiny, including the actions at Cawnpore, and relief of Lucknow; subsequently with Ross's camel corps from November, 1858 (medal and clasp).

# NAVAL OBITUARY.

Admiral the Hon. Sir George Elliot, K.C.B., on the Reserved Pension list, died on June 24, after a somewhat lengthened illness, at his town residence, aged 79. The gallant deceased entered the Navy on the 4th June, 1794, as a volunteer on board the St. George, afterwards serving in different ships until 1800, when he obtained his Lieutenant's commission. In the St. George he witnessed, while at a distance, the action off Copenhagen. Attaining the rank of Commander in 1802, he was appointed to the Termagant. In 1808, while in command of the Modeste, he captured a French corvette of 18 guns after a running action of one hour, and in the summer of 1805 commanded the Aurora, in the action of three hours duration with some Spanish gunboats, near Tarifa, three of which he captured. At the reduction of Java, in 1811, he superintended the landing of the troops; and in June, 1813, joined in an attack on the pirates of Sambas, in Borneo. He was next appointed to the Victory, in 1827, guardship in Portsmouth harbour, the command of which he retained for three years; and in January, 1837, was nominated Commander-in-Chief at the Cape of Good Hope. Being transferred in 1840 to the chief command in the East Indies, he sailed for China, where, in the capacity of joint plenipotentiary, he superintended the earlier operations of the war from July to November of the same year. He was then invalided home. From December, 1834, to April, 1835, he filled the office of Secretary to the Admiralty, and from the latter date, until his appointment to the chief command at the Cape, that of a lord of the same Board. Sir George married in 1810, and has had issue five daughters and five sons, one of whom, the eldest, George, is now serving as Rear-Admiral Superintendant of Portsmouth Dockyard, and the second, Gilbert George, in the Army.

Admiral William Wolrige, 1862, on the Retired C list, died at Nutwell, Devon, on the 19th June, aged 77. This officer entered the Navy in February, 1793, in the Jason, and was present, in company with the Mars, at the capture of the French 74 gunship Hercule, 1798, and after assisting at the capture of the French frigate Seine in the same year, was wrecked off Brest, and made prisoner. Having been exchanged, he joined the Revolutionnaire in 1799. In April, 1805, he joined the Viper as Sub-Lieutenant; and was promoted, to the rank of Lieutenant, March 23, 1807, and appointed to the

Volage. In the latter ship he assisted at the capture of the French 16 gun brig Requin, co-operated at the defence of Sicily, and distinguished himself as first Lieutenant in the action off Lissa, 1811; for his services on which occasion was made Commander. After serving for a time in the Stag as acting Captain, and successively in command of the Bermuda, Albacore, and Wasp, he obtained post rank, his commission bearing date December 7, 1818. Never having been employed subsequently, he accepted the retirement in 1846.

Captain George Pierce, 1852, on the Reserved F.G. list, died at Holloway on the 24th of June, aged 71. This officer joined the Navy in 1803, and served continuously in the Baltic, North Sea, and West Indies, in the flag ships of Lord Gardner, Admirals Sir E. Thornborough, Sir James Saumarez, Lord Gambier, Sir A. Cochrane, and Sir F. Laforey, until made a Lieutenant, 21st March, 1812. He was present in the Walcheren expedition, where he commanded a gunboat. As a Lieutenant he served in the Mulgrave, in the Mediterranean, and saw much boat service; and afterwards in the Comus on the coast of Africa, where he was engaged in the suppression of the slave trade. In 1816 he joined the Beelzebub, was present at the bombardment of Algiers, and was for a long time afterwards employed in flag ships in the Medway, and after being made a Commander, 5th September, 1833, became an Inspecting-Commander of Coastguard. For many years Captain Pierce was well known and esteemed as the Secretary of the Sailors' Home, Well Street, and as principal shipping master of the Port of London.

Commander John Bingham, 1853, on the Retired O list, died at Exeter on the 25th June, aged 78. He entered the Navy, 1798, as Volunteer of the 1st class of the Minerva, from which he moved to the Minotaur, and was present at the siege of Genoa, and expedition to Egypt, 1801. He served successively and without intermission in the Amphion, Victory, and Agincourt as Midshipman, and, having been made a Lieutenant in 1806, and appointed to the Endymion, was present at the passage of the Dardanelles. He was captured in September, 1807, while reconnoitring off Cephalonia, and remained a prisoner at Verdun till the peace in 1815.

Commander Thomas H. Downes (1856), on the Reserved M N List, died on the 2nd of July at Gosport.

Commander Henry Rich, 1859, on the O Retired List, died in Down Street, Piccadilly, on the 26th of June, aged 74. He entered the Navy, 1801, and served as Midshipman of the Diligence in Lord Nelson's attack on the Boulogne flotilla. He joined the Defiance in 1804, and took part in that ship in Calder's action, and at Trafalgar, 1805. He continued serving till the peace in 1815, and was actively employed in the meanwhile at the defence of Cadiz and Tarifa.

Lieutenant Samuel Sparshott Shore, 1842, on the Reserved List, died on the 11th of July, at Southgate, aged 48.

Surgeon John Clark, 1808, retired on a commuted allowance, died at Weldon, Northamptonshire, on the 1st of July, in his 78th year. He had been upwards of forty-eight years surgeon at the above place, and one of the few survivors of the battle of Trafalgar, at which he was present as Assistant-Surgeon.

# STATIONS OF THE ROYAL NAVY IN COMMISSION.

*(Corrected to 27th. July)*

*With the Dates of Commission of the officers in Command.*

Aboukir, 86, sc, Commodore P. Cracroft, C.B., 1854, Jamaica

Acorn, Hosp. Ship, Mast.-Com. H. Hutchings, 1861, Shanghae

Active, 20, Training Ship, for Naval Reserve, Com. E. Field, 1859, Sunderland

Adder, st. ves., Second Master W. Blakey (acting) Chatham

Adventure, 2, sc. troop ship, Com. T. B. Lethbridge, 1857, particular service

Ajax, 60, sc Cap. M. de Courcy, 1852, Coast Guard Kingstown.

Alacrity, 4, sc. Com. J. K. E. Baird, 1857, Sheerness

Alecto, 5, st. ves., Com. W. H. Blake, 1860, S.E. Coast of America

Alert, 17, sc, Com. H. C. Majendie, 1864, Channel Squadron

Algerine, 1, sc. gunboat, Lieut.-Com. A. R. Blane, 1856, China

Antelope, 3, st. ves., Lieut.-Com. C. O. D. Allingham, 1856, Coast of Africa

Archer, 13, sc. Capt. J. Bythesea, V.C. (1861) Coast of Africa

Ardent, 3, steam vessel, Capt. J. E. Parish, 1862, Woolwich

Argus, 6, steam ves. Com. L. J. Moore, 1860, China

Ariadne, 26, sc. Capt. E. W. Vansittart, 1846, North America and West Indies

Ariel, 9, sc. Com. W. C. Chapman, 1855, Cape of Good Hope

Asia, 84, Rear Admiral George Elliot, Capt. H. Broadhead, 1855, Portsmouth

Bacchante, 51, sc. Capt. D. McL. Mackenzie, 1859, Pacific

Barracouta, 6, st. ves. Com G. J. Malcolm, 1859, North America and West Indies

Barrosa, 21, sc., Captain W. M. Dowell, 1856, East Indies and China

Black Prince, 40, sc. Capt. J. F. B. Wainwright, (1853) Channel Squadron

Blenheim, 60, sc. Capt. Lord F. H. Kerr, 1852, Coast Guard, Milford

Bloodhound, 3, st. ves. Lieut.-Com. J. E. Stokes, 1856, Coast of Africa (passage home)

Boscawen, 20, Com. H. Campion, 1855, Southampton Training Ship

Brilliant, 16, Com. Grey Skipwith, 1848, Naval Reserve Drill Ship, Dundee

Brisk, 16, sc. Capt. J. P. Luce, 1852, West Coast of Africa

Britannia, 8, Cadet Training Ship, Captain R. A. Powell, C.B., 1855, Portland

Buzzard, st. ves., 6, Com. T. H. M. Martin, 1858, North America and West Indies

Cambridge, gunnery Ship, Capt. C. J. F. Ewart, C.B., 1855, Devonport.

Cameleon, 17, sc. Com. E. Hardinge, 1864, Pacific

Canopus, Naval Barrack, Capt. C. H. May, (1859) Devonport

Caradoc, sc., 2, Lieut.-Com. E. H Wilkinson, 1864, Mediterranean

Castor, 22, Com. J. Palmer, 1855, Naval Reserve Drill Ship, Shields

Centaur, 6, steam ves. Com. J. Z. Creasy (acting) 1862, China, ordered home

Challenger, 22, sc. J. J. Kennedy, C.B., 1864, North America and W. Indies

Chanticleer, 17, sc. Com. C. Stirling, 1864, Mediterranean

Charybdis, 21, sc. Capt. E. W. Turnour, 1857, Pacific

Clio, 22, sc. Captain T. Miller, 1855, Pacific. (Passage home.)

Cockatrice, 2, sc. Lieut. Com. R. M. Gillson (1865), Mediterranean

Colossus, 80, sc. Captain K. S. Sotheby, C.B., 1853, Coast Guard, Portland Roads

Columbine, 4, sc., Com. T. Le H. Ward, 1851, particular service

Coquette, 4, sc., Commander J. H. I. Alexander, 1860, East Indies and China

Cormorant, 4, sc. Com. C. M. Buckle (1860) East Indies and China

Cornwallis, 60, sc. Capt. J. N. Strange, 1854, Coast Guard, Hull

Cossack, 20, sc., Capt. W. R. Rolland, 1857, Mediterranean

Cumberland, 24, Capt. W. K. Hall, C.B., 1853, receiving ship, Sheerness

Curacoa, 22, Commodore Sir W. Wiseman, Bart., Australia

Curlew, 9, sc. Com. J. S. Hudson, 1861, S. E. Coast of America

Cygnet, 6, sc. Com. H. P. De Kantzow (1863) North America and West Indies

Dædalus, 16, Com. W. H. Fenwick, 1856, Naval Reserve Drill ship, Bristol

Dart, 5, sc. Com. F. W. Richards, (1860) Coast of Africa

Dasher, 2, st. ves., Com. P. De Saumarez, 1854, Channel Islands

Dauntless, 31, sc. Capt. J. B. Dickson, 1854, Coast Guard, Southampton

Dee, 2, st. Store Ship, Mas.-Com. G. Raymond, 1856, Woolwich

Defence, 16, sc. Capt. A. Phillimore, 1856, Channel Squadron

Desperate, 7, sc. Com. A. T. Thrupp, 1858, North America and West Indies

Devastation, 6, screw, Com. J. W. Pike, 1860, Pacific

Doterel, 2, sc. gunboat, Lieut. Com. W. F. Johnson, 1865, South America

Dromedary, sc. store-ship, Mast.-Com. A. Brown, (1854), particular service

Duke of Wellington, 131, Capt. J. Seccombe, 1859, Portsmouth

Eagle, 50, Commander J. W. Whyte, 1855, Naval Reserve Drill Ship, Liverpool

Eclipse, 4, sc., Com. R. C. Mayne, 1861, Australia

Edgar, 71, sc. Rr. Adml. S. C. Dacres, C.B., Capt. G. T. P. Hornby, 1862, Channel Squadron

Edinburgh, 60, sc. Captain C. F. Schomberg, 1851 Coast Guard, Queen's Ferry, N.B.

Egmont, receiving ship, Capt. F. A. B. Craufurd, 1854, Rio de Janeiro

Emerald, 35, sc. Captain A. Cumming, 1854 Channel Squadron

Enchantress, 1, st. Admiralty Yacht, Staff-Com. J. R. Pedley, 1862, Portsmouth

Encounter, 14, sc. Captain R. Dew, C.B., 1856, East Indies and China, (ordered home)

Esk, 21, Capt. J. F. C. Hamilton, 1855, Australia

Espoir, 5, sc. Com. S. Douglas, 1856, C. of Africa

Euryalus, 35, sc. Vice Adml A. L. Kuper, C.B., Captain J. J. S. Josling, 1861, China

Excellent, gunnery ship, Capt. A. C. Key, C.B., 1860, Portsmouth

Fairy, sc. yacht, tender to Victoria and Albert Portsmouth, Mast.-Com. D. M. Welch, 1844

Firefly, 6, st. ves. Com. A. L. Mansell, 1855, Mediterranean

Fisgard, 42, Commodore Sir. F. W. E. Nicolson, Bart. C.B. Woolwich

Flamer, sc. gunboat, Lieut. Com. G. S. Bosanquet, 1855, China

Formidable, 26, Vice-Adml. Sir G. R. Lambert, K.C.B., Capt. J. Fulford, Sheerness

Forte, 39, sc. Rear Admiral R. L. Warren, Capt. A. Mellersh, 1856, S.E. Coast of America

Forward, 2, sc. Lieut. Com. the Hon. H. D. Lascelles, 1855, Pacific

Fox, sc. store-ship, Staff-Com. J. O. Pullen, (1865) particular service

Foxhound, 4, sc. Com. W. H. Anderson, 1858, Mediterranean

Galatea, 26, sc. Cap. R. Maguire, 1856, North America, and West Indies

Geyser, 6, st. ves. Com. M. R. Pechell, (1856), particular service

Gorgon, 6, st. ves. Com. J. C Wilson, 1861, Cape of Good Hope. ordered home

Grappler, 2, sc. Lieut. Com. B. H. Verney, 1858, Pacific

Grasshopper, sc. gunboat, Lt. Com. F. W. Bennett, 1854, East Indies and China

Greyhound, 17, sc. Com. H. D. Hickley, 1858, North America and West Indies

Griffon, 5, sc. Com. J. L. Perry, 1858, Coast of Africa

Handy, 1, st. ves., Lieut. Com. W. D. M. Dolben, 1859, Coast of Africa

Hardy, 3, sc. gunbt, Lieut. Com. H. J F. Campbell, 1855, East Indies and China

Harrier, 17, sc. Com. F. W. Sullivan, 1859, Australia

Hastings, 60, sc. Rear-Admiral Sir L. T. Jones, K.C.B., Capt. C. F. A. Shadwell, C.B., 1855, Queenstown

Havock, 2, sc. gunbt, Lieut. Com. G. Poole, 1855, East Indies and China

Hawke, 60, sc. Capt. E. Codd, 1851, Coast Guard Queenstown

Hecate, 6, st. vessel, Capt. G. H. Richards, 1854, passage home,

Hesper, 4, sc. store ship, Mast, Com. A. F. Borer, 1854, East Indies and China

Hibernia, rec. ship, Rear Adm. H. T. Austin, C.B., Com. R. B. Harvey, 1859, Malta

Himalaya, 6, sc. troop ship, Captain E. Lacy, (1863), Portsmouth

Hogue, 60, sc. Captain A. Farquhar, 1849, Coast Guard, Greenock

Hornet, 17, sc. Com. J. Dayman, 1856, East Indies

Hydra, 1, st. ves., Lieut. G. R. Wilkinson, 1854, Woolwich

Immortalité, 35, sc. Capt. G. Hancock, 1855, North America and West Indies

Implacable, 94, Com. S. B. Dolling, 1856, Training Ship, Devonport

Impregnable, 78, Capt. P. S. Tremlett (1863) Training Ship, Devonport

Indus, Rear Admiral T. M. C. Symonds. C.B., Capt. W. Edmonstone, C.B., 1866, Devonport

Industry, 3, sc. store ship, Mast. Com. E. C. T. Yonel, 1860, particular service

Insolent, 2, sc. gunbt. Lieut. Com. G. Parsons, 1854, East Indies and China

Investigator, 2, st. ves. Lieut. Com. ———— Coast of Africa

Jackal, 4, st. vessel, Lieut. Com. H. McDyer 1855, Coast of Scotland

Janus, 4, sc. Com. W. J. H. Grubbe (1861) Coast of Africa

Jason, 21, sc. Capt. E. P. B. Von Donop, 1855, North America, W. Indies

Landrail, 5, sc. Com. W. Arthur, 1861, N. America and West Indies

Leander, 39, sc. Commodore T. Harvey, Pacific

Lizard, 3, st. ves. Lieut.-Com. H. J. Challis, 1854, Coast of Scotland

Lee, 5, sc. Lieut. Com. P. R. Sharpe, 1854, Coast of Africa

Leopard, 18, st. vessel, Capt. C. T. Leckie, 1858, East Indies and China

Leven, 1, screw gun vessel, Lt. Com. H. P. Knevitt (1855) East Indies and China

Liffey, 30, sc. Captain G. Parker, 1854, Mediterranean

Lily, 4, sc., Com. H. Harvey, 1857, North America and West Indies

Liverpool, 35, sc., Capt. R. Lambert, 1856, Channel Squadron

Meander, 10, Cap. F. L Barnard, 1855, Ascension

Magicienne, 16, st. ves. Capt. W. Armytage, 1856, Mediterranean

Majestic, 80, sc. Capt. E. A. Inglefield, 1853, Coast guard, Rock Ferry, Liverpool

Malacca, 17, st. ves. Cap. G. J. Napier, (1856), Mediterranean

Manilla, sc. Mast. Com. H. W. Burnett, 1856, East Indies and China

Marlborough, 131, sc. Vice Adml. R. Smart, K H., Captain C. Fellowes, 1856, Mediterranean

Medea, 6, st ves. Com. D'Arcy S. Preston, (1860) North America and West Indies

Medina, 4, st. ves. Capt. T. A. B. Spratt, C.B. 1855, Mediterranean

Medusa, 2, st. ves. Mas.-Com. J. H. Allard, 1851, particular service

Messene, 60, Captain G. Wodehouse, 1854, Mediterranean.

Megaera, 6, sc. Com. E. Madden, (1858) particular service

Miranda, 15, sc. Capt. R. Jenkins, 1857, Australia

Mullet, 5, sc. Com. C. H. Simpson 1860, Coast of Africa

Mutine, 17, sc. Com. W. Graham, 1858, Pacific.

Naiad, 6, store ship, Mas. Com. G. Reid, 1850, Callao

Narcissus, 30 sc. Rear Adm. Sir B. W. Walker, Bart., K.C.B., Capt. J. G. Bickford, (1860) Cape of Good Hope

Nereus, 6, store depot. Staff Com. C. R. P. Forbes, 1863, Valparaiso

Nile, 78, sc. Vice-Adml. Sir A. Milne, K.C.B., Capt. E. K. Barnard, 1859, North America and West Indies

Nimble, 5, sc. Com. J. D'Arcy, 1854, North America and West Indies

Odin, 16, steam vessel, Commodore Lord J. Hay, C.B. 1854, East Indies, passage home

Orestes, 21, sc. Capt. A. H. Gardiner, 1854, Cape of Good Hope

Orontes, 8, sc., troop ship, Capt. H. W. Hire, 1862, Portsmouth

Orlando, 46, sc. Capt. G. G. Randolph, , 1854 Mediterranean

Osborne, st. vessel, Staff Com. G. H. K. Bower, 1863, Portsmouth

Osprey, sc., 4, Com. A. J. Innes, 1861, East Indies and China

Pandora, 5, sc. Com. W. F. Ruxton, 1861, Coast of Africa

Pantaloon, 11, sc. Com. F. Purvis, (1860), East Indies.

Pearl, 21, sc. Capt. J. Borlase, C.B. 1856, East Indies and China

Pelican, 17, sc. Com. P. Brock, 1859, Mediterranean.

Pembroke, 60, Commodore A. P. Ryder, 1849, C.B., Capt. J. O. Johnson, 1856, Coast Guard Harwich

Perseus, 17, sc., Com. A. J. Kingston, 1860, China

Petrel, 11, sc. Com. G. W. Watson, 1858, North America and West Indies

Phaeton, 39, sc. Capt. E. Tatham, 1854, North America and West Indies

Philomel, 8, sc. Com. L. Wildman, (1866) Coast of Africa

Phœbe, 35, sc., Captain T. D. A. Fortescue, 1857, Mediterranean.

Pigmy, 3, st. v. Master Com. W. W. Vine, 1861 Portsmouth.

Pioneer, 6, sc Com. F. C. B. Robinson (acting), Australia, passage home

Plover, 5, sc. Com. the Hon A. L. Corry, 1859, North America and West Indies

President, 50, Com W. Mould, 1855, Naval Reserve Drill Ship, London.

Princess Charlotte, 12, Captain M. S. Nolloth, 1854, Hong Kong

Procris, 2, Capt. E. Ommanney, 1846, Lieut. Com. Hon J. B Vivian, 1856, Gibraltar.

Psyche, 2, st. vessel, Lieut.-Com. R. Sterne 1854, Mediterranean

Pylades, 21, sc. Capt A. W. A. Hood, North America and West Indies

Queen, 74, sc. Captain C. F. Hillyar, 1852, Mediterranean

Racehorse, 4, sc. Com. C. R. F. Boxer, 1860, China

Racoon, 22, sc. Capt. Count Gleichen, (1859), particular service

Ranger, 5, Com. H. R. Wratislaw, 1858, West Coast of Africa

Rapid, 11, sc. Com. C. T. Jago (1860) C. of Africa

Rattler, 17, sc. Com. E. H Howard, 1857, East Indies and China

Rattlesnake, 21, sc. Commodore A. P. E Wilmot, C.B. Coast of Africa

Resistance, 16, sc. Capt. W. C. Chamberlain, 1856, Channel Squadron

Revenge, 73, sc. Rr -Ad. H. R. Yelverton, C B., Capt. Hon. F. A. Foley, 1860, Mediterranean

Rifleman, 8, sur -ves. Mast. Commander J. W. Reed, 1857, China Seas

Rinaldo, 17, sc. Com. J. A R. Dunlop, 1860, 1858, North America and West Indies

Ringdove, 4, sc. Com. R. A. O. Brown, 1857, East Indies and China

Rosario, 11, sc. Com. H. D. Grant, 1859, North America and West Indies

Royal Adelaide, 26, Vice-Adml. Sir H. Stewart, K.C B Capt. C. Vesey, 1860, Devonport

Royal Oak, 34, sc Capt. F. A. Campbell, 1854, Channel Squadron

Russell, 60, sc. Capt. S. Grenfell, (1850) Coast Guard Falmouth

Satellite, 21, sc. Capt S. S. L. Crofton, 1856, S. E Coast of America

Saturn, Captain W Loring, C.B., 1848, Pembroke

Scout, 21, sc. Capt. J. Corbett, 1857, East Indies and China, ordered home

Scringapatam, Receiving Ship, Capt. J. H. Cockburn, 1850, Cape of Good Hope

Severn, 35, sc. Commodore F. B. Montrésor, East Indies

Shannon, 35, sc. Capt. O. J. Jones, (1855) N. America and West Indies

Sheldrake, 2, sc. gunboat, Lieut.-Com. John Nott, 1854, S. E. Coast of America

Shearwater, 11, sc. Com. R. G. Douglas, 1860, Pacific.

Slaney, 2, sc. gunboat, Lieut.-Com. W. F. Lee, 1855, East Indies and China

Sparrow, 5, sc. Com. Hon. E. G. L. Cochrane, 1860, C of Africa.

Spider, 2, sc. gunboat, Lieut. Com. E. A. T. Stubbs, 1854, South America

St. George, 84, sc. Capt. the Hon. F. Egerton, 1855, Mediterranean

Staunch, 1, sc., Lieut.-Com. J. S. Keats 1856, China

St. Vincent, 26, Com. M. Lowther, 1859, Portsmouth

Steady, 5, sc. Com. Fred Harvey, 1861, North America and West Indies

Stromboli, 6, sc. Com. A. R. Henry, 1857, S.E Coast of America

Styx, 6, sc. Com. the Hon. W. J. Ward, 1858, North America and West Indies

Supply, 2 sc. store ship, Mast. Com. C. Bawden, 1849, particular service

Surprise, 4, sc. Com. W. H. Whyte, 1858, Mediterranean

Sutlej, 35, sc., Rear-Adml. J. Kingcome, Captain M. Connolly, 1858, Pacific

Swallow, 9, sur. ves. Mast. Com. E. Wilds, 1855, East Indies

Tartar, 20, sc. Capt. J. M. Hayes, 1855, Pacific

Terror, 16, Capt. F. H. H. Glasse, C B. 1844, Bermuda

Topaze, 39, sc. Commodore the Hon. J. W. S. Spencer, (1854) Pacific

Torch, 5, sc. Com. F. H. Smith, 1858, Coast of Africa

Trafalgar, 70, sc. Capt. T. H. Mason, 1849, Mediterranean.

Tribune, 23, sc. Capt. Viscount Gilford, 1859 Pacific

Trident, 6, st. Com. C. J. Balfour, 1859, Gibraltar

Trincomalee, 16, Com. T. Heard, (1850) Naval Reserve drill Ship, Hartlepool

Triton, sc , 3, Lieut.-Com. E. F. Kerby, 1854, S E. Coast of America

Valorous, 16, st. ves., Capt. C C. Forsyth, 1857, Cape of Good Hope

Vesuvius, 6, sc. Capt. R. V. Hamilton, 1862, North America and West Indies

Victoria and Albert, steam yacht, Capt. H.S.H. Prince Leiningen, (1860,) Portsmouth

Victory, 12, Vice Adml. Sir Michael Seymour, G C B. Captain Francis Scott, C B , (1848) Portsmouth

Vigilant, 4, sc., Com. W. R. Hobson, 1859, East Indies and China

Vindictive, store ship, Mas.-Com. W. F. Lew, 1857, Fernando Po

Virago, 6, st ves. Com. W. G. H. Johnstone, 185 particular service

Vivid, 2, st. v. Staff Com. H. W. Allen, 1863, particular service

Vulcan, 6, sc. troop ship, Capt. A. C. Strode. 1863 East Indies and China, ordered home

Wanderer, 4, sc. Com. M. C. Seymour, 1859 Mediterranean

Warrior, 40, sc. Capt. the Hon. A. A. Cochrane, C B. 1854, Channel Squadron

Weazel, 2, sc gunboat, Lieut. Com. H. G. Hale, 1855, East Indies and China

Wellesley, 72, Captain E. G. Fanshawe, 1845, Chatham

Weser, 6, st. v Com. A. H. J. Johnstone, 1859, Mediterranean

Winchester, 12, Drill Ship for Naval Reserve, Com. C J. Balfour. 1846, Aberdeen

Wrangler, 4, sc. Com. H. H. Beamish, 1858, Coast of Africa

Wye, 2, sc. store-ship. Staff Com. V. G. Roberts, 1863, Sheerness

Zebra, 17, sc., Com. A. H. Hoskins, 1858, Coast of Africa

## STATIONS OF THE BRITISH ARMY.

(*Corrected up to 27th July*, 1863, *inclusive.*)

[Where two places are mentioned, the last-named is that at which the Depot is stationed.]

1st Life Guards—Regent's Park
2nd do.—Hyde Park
Royal Horse Guards—Aldershot
1st Dragoon Guards—Madras, Canterbury
2nd do.—Bengal, Canterbury
3rd do.—Bombay, Canterbury
4th do.—Curragh
5th do.—Curragh
6th do.—Aldershot
7th do.—Bengal, Canterbury
1st Dragoons—Birmingham
2nd do.—Birmingham
3rd Hussars—Piershill
4th do.—Newbridge
5th Lancers—Chichester, Canterbury
6th Dragoons—Bombay, Maidstone
7th Hussars—Bengal, Maidstone
8th do.—Bengal, Canterbury
9th Lancers—Brighton
10th Hussars—Newbridge
11th Hussars—Dublin
12th Lancers—Aldershot
13th Hussars—Aldershot
14th do.—Manchester
15th Hussars—Dublin
16th Lancers—York
17th do.—Madras, Maidstone
18th Hussars—Aldershot
19th do.—Bengal, Shorncliffe
20th do.—Bengal, Canterbury
21st do.—Bengal, Canterbury
Military Train (1st bat.)—Woolwich
Do. (2nd bat.)—Aldershot
Do. (3rd bat.)—Canada
Do. (4th bat.)—Woolwich
Do. (5th bat.)—Aldershot
Do. (6th bat.)—Curragh
Grenadier Guards (1st bat.)—Canada
Do. (2nd bat.)—Wellington Barracks
Do. (3rd bat.)—St. George's Barracks
Coldstream Guards (1st bat.)—Portman Street
Do. (2nd bat.)—Windsor
Scots Fus. Guards (1st bat.)—Aldershot
Fus. (2nd bat.)—Canada
1st Foot (1st.)—Madras, Colchester
Do. (2nd bat.)—Aldershot, Colchester
2nd do. (1st bat.)—Plymouth, Walmer
Do. (2nd bat.)—Corfu, Walmer
3rd do. (1st bat.)—Aldershot, Limerick
Do. (2nd bat.)—Gibraltar, Limerick
4th do. (1st bat.)—Bombay, Chatham
Do. (2nd bat.)—Corfu, Chatham
5th do. (1st bat.)—Shorncliffe, Colchester
Do. (2nd bat.)—Natal, Colchester
6th do. (1st bat.)—Aldershot, Colchester
Do. (2nd bat.)—Corfu, Colchester
7th do. (1st bat.)—Bengal, Walmer
Do. (2nd bat.)—Gibraltar, Walmer
8th do. (1st bat.)—Sheffield, Templemore
Do. (2nd bat.)—Gibraltar, Templemore
9th do. (1st bat.)—Cephalonia, Limerick
Do. (2nd bat.)—Corfu, Limerick
10th do. (1st bat.)—Dublin, Preston
Do. (2nd bat.)—Cape of Gd. Hope, Preston
11th do. (1st bat.)—Dublin, Fermoy
Do. (2nd bat.) C. of Good Hope, Fermoy
12th do. (1st bat.)—N. S. Wales, Chatham
Do. (2nd bat.)—Curragh, Chatham
13th do. (1st bat.)—Bengal, Fermoy
Do. (2nd bat.)—Mauritius, Fermoy
14th do. (1st bat.)—Jamaica, Fermoy.
Do. (2nd bat.)—New Zealand, Fermoy
15th do. (1st bat.)—N. Brunswick, Pembroke
15th do. (2nd bat.)—Malta, Pembroke

16th do. (1st bat.)—Canada, Templemore
Do. (2nd bat.)—Nova Scotia, Templemore
17th do. (1st bat.)—Canada, Limerick
Do. (2nd bat.) Nova Scotia, Limerick
18th do. (1st bat.)—Madras, Buttevant
Do. (2nd bat.)—New Zealand, Buttevant
19th do. (1st bat.)—Bengal, Chatham
Do. (2nd bat.)—Dublin, Chatham
20th do. (1st bat.)—Bengal, Chatham
Do. (2nd bat.)—Portsmouth, Chatham
21st do. (1st bat.)—Barbadoes, Birr
Do. (2nd bat.)—Madras, Birr
22nd do. (1st bat.)—Malta, Parkhurst
Do. (2nd bat.)—Malta, Parkhurst
23rd do. (1st bat.)—Bengal, Walmer
Do. (2nd bat.)—Malta, Walmer
24th do. (1st bat.)—Aldershot, Cork
Do. (2nd bat.)—Mauritius, Cork
25th do. (1st bat.)—Malta, Athlone
Do. (2nd bat.)—Edinburgh, Athlone
26th do.—Gosport, Belfast
27th do.—Bengal, Cork
28th do.—Bombay, Fermoy
29th do.— Curragh, Preston
30th do.—Canada, Parkhurst
31st do.—China, Chatham
32nd do.—Curragh, Preston
33rd do.—Bombay, Fermoy
34th do.—Bengal, Colchester
35th do.—Bengal, Chatham
36th do.—Dublin, Athlone
37th do.—Aldershot, Pembroke
38th do.—Bengal, Colchester
39th do.—Bermuda, Templemore
40th do.—New Zealand, Birr
41st do.—Glasgow, Preston
42nd do.—Bengal, Stirling
43rd do.—Bengal, Chatham.
44th do.—Bombay, Colchester
45th do.—Curragh, Parkhurst
46th do.—Bengal, Buttevant
47th do.—Canada, Athlone
48th do.—Bengal, Cork
49th do.—Manchester, Belfast
50th do.—Ceylon, Parkhurst
51st do.—Bengal, Chatham
52nd do.—Bengal, Chatham
53rd do.—Portsmouth, Birr
54th do.—Bengal, Colchester
55th do.—Portsmouth, Preston
56th do.—Bombay, Colchester
57th do.—New Zealand, Cork
58th do.—Dublin, Birr
59th do.—Aldershot, Preston
60th do. (1st bat.)—Tower, Winchester
Do. (2nd bat.)—Aldershot, Winchester
Do. (3rd bat.)—Madras, Winchester
Do. (4th bat.)—Canada, Winchester
61st do.—Jersey, Pembroke
62nd do.—Canada, Belfast
63rd do.—Canada, Belfast
64th do.—Aldershot, Colchester
65th do.—New Zealand, Birr
66th do.—Madras, Colchester
67th do.—China, Athlone
68th do.—Madras, Fermoy
69th do —Madras, Fermoy
70th do.—New Zealand, Colchester
71st do.—Bengal, Stirling
72nd do.—Bombay, Aberdeen
73rd do.—Aldershot, Colchester
74th do.—Madras, Perth
75th do.—Plymouth, Chatham
76th Foot—Aldershot, Belfast
77th Foot—Bengal, Chatham

78th do.—Dover, Aberdeen
79th do.—Bengal, Stirling
80th do.—ditto, Buttevant
81st do.—Bengal, Chatham
82nd do.—Bengal, Colchester
83rd do.—Shorncliff, Chatham
84th do.—Dublin, Pembroke
85th do.—Dover, Pembroke
86th do.—Curragh, Templemore
87th do.—Aldershot, Buttevant
88th do.—Bengal, Colchester
89th do.—Bengal, Fermoy
90th do.—Bengal, Colchester
91st do.—Madras, Chatham
92nd do.—Edinburgh, Stirling
93rd do.—Bengal, Aberdeen
94th do.—ditto, Chatham
95th do.—Bombay, Fermoy
96th do.—Cape, Belfast
97th do.—Bengal, Colchester
98th do.—Bengal, Colchester
99th do.—China, Cork
100th Foot—Gibraltar; Parkhurst

101st do.—Bengal, Chatham
102nd do.—Madras, Chatham
103rd do.—Bombay, Colchester
104th do.—Bengal, Parkhurst
105th do.—Madras, Pembroke
106th do.—Bombay, Birr
107th do.—Bengal, Fermoy
108th do.—Madras, Fermoy
109th do.—Bombay, Cork
Rifle Brigade (1st bat.)—Canada, Winchester.
Do. (2nd bat.)—Bengal, Winchester
Do. (3rd bat.)—Bengal, Winchester
Do. (4th bat.)—Malta Winchester
1st West India Regiment—Nassau
2nd do.—Bahamas
3rd do.—West Coast of Africa
4th do—Jamaica, for Africa
5th do —Jamaica
Ceylon Rifle Regiment—Ceylon
Cape Mounted Rifles—Cape of Good Hope
Royal Canadian Rifle Regiment—Canada
Royal Malta Fencible Artillery—Malta

## DEPOT BATTALIONS.

1st Depot Battalion—Chatham
2nd do —Chatham
3rd do.—Chatham
4th do.—Colchester
5th do.—Parkhurst
6th do.—Walmer
7th do.—Winchester
8th do.—Pembroke
9th do.—Colchester
10th do.—Colchester
11th do.—Preston
12th do.—Athlone
13th do.—Birr

14th Depot Battalion—Belfast
15th do.—Buttevant
16th do.—Templemore
17th do.—Limerick
18th do.—Fermoy
19th do.—Fermoy
20th do —Cork
22nd do.—Stirling
33rd do.—Aberdeen
Cavalry Depot—Maidstone
do.—Canterbury

## ARTILLERY AND ENGINEERS.

1st Hrs. Brig.—Woolwich
2nd Hrs. Brig.—Meerut
3rd Hrs. Brig.—Bangalore
4th Hrs. Brig.—Kirkee
5th Hrs. Brig.—Umballah
1st Brig.—Gibraltar
2nd Brig.—Dover
3rd Brig.—Malta and Corfu
4th Brig.—Aldershott
5th Brig.—Plymouth
6th Brig.—Portsmouth
7th Brig.—Montreal
8th Brig.—Dublin
9th Brig —Shorncliffe
10th Brig.—Canada
11th Brig.—Bengal
12th Brig.—Mauritius
13th Brig —Woolwich
14th Brig —Bengal
15th Brig.—Halifax N.S.
16th Brig.—Delhi
17th Brig.—Madras
18th Brig.—Kirkee
19th Brig.—Peshawur
20th Brig.—Kamptee
21st Brig.—Mhow
22nd Brig—Jullundur
23rd Brig.—Secunderabad
24th Brig —Mean Meer
25th Brig.—Agra
*Royal Engineers.*
A Troop Royal Engineer Train, Aldershott
1st Compy.—Devonport
2nd Compy.—Kensington
3rd Compy.—Gibraltar
4th Compy.—Halifax, N.S.

5th Compy.—Bermuda
6th Compy.—New Zealand
7th Compy.—Chatham
8th Compy.—China.
9th Compy.—Woolwich
10th Compy.—Aldershott
11th Compy.—Mauritius
12th Compy.—Cape
13th Compy.—Dublin (survey)
14th Compy.—Dublin (survey)
15th Compy.—Canada
16th Compy.—Southton (survey)
17th Compy.—Curragh
18th Compy.—Canada
19th Compy.—Glasgow (survey)
20th Compy —Chatham.
21st Compy.—Mauritius.
22nd Compy.—Chatham
23rd Compy.—Shorncliffe
24th Compy.—Aldershott
25th Compy.—Cape
26th Compy.—Chatham
27th Compy.—Gibraltar
28th Compy.—Malta
29th Compy.—Corfu
30th Compy.—Corfu
31st Compy.—Malta
32nd Compy.—St. Helena
33rd Compy.—Gibraltar
34th Compy.—Bermuda
35th Compy.—Chatham
36th Compy.—Chatham
37th Compy.—Chatham
38th Compy.—Chatham
39th Compy.—Chatham
40th Compy.—Chatham

R R 2

# PROMOTIONS AND APPOINTMENTS.

## NAVY.

ADMIRALTY, June 24.
Royal Marine Light Infantry—
The followinging Gentlemen-Cadets
to be sec.-lieuts. :—Augustus Bury
Liardet, Philip Sidney, Henry Arm-
strong Peake, George Edw. Coates
Westbrook, Robert Evans Mont-
gomery, George Sanderson Walker,
Sydney Tyers, Henry Vere Barclay,
Herbert St. George Schomberg,
Augustus Frederick Blyth, Herbert
Bradley, William Tankerville Allen,
William Percy Winkworth.

July 3.—Royal Marine Light Infantry—First Lieut. Charles Bulkeley
Nurse to be capt., vice Lloyd, placed
on half-pay list; Sec. Lieut. Wil-
braham Evors Evelyn Morley to be
first lieut., vice Nurse; First Lieut.
Melville Suther to be quartermaster.

ADMIRALTY, July 3.
Admiral of the Blue Francis Erskine Loch has been appointed to
receive a pension of £160 a-year, as
provided by Her Majesty's Order in
Council of 25th June, 1851, vacant
by the death of Admiral the Hon.
Sir George Elliot, K.C.B.; and the
name of Admiral Loch has been
removed to the Reserved Half-pay
List accordingly, and in consequence
of this removal, the following promotions, to date the 25th ultimo,
have this day taken place :—

Vice-Admiral of the Red the Hon.
Henry John Rous to be adm. of the
Blue.

Vice-Admiral of the White Sir
Michael Seymour, G.C.B., to be vice-
adm. of the Red.

Vice-Admiral of the Blue Frederick Thomas Michell, C.B., to be vice-
adm. of the White.

Rear-Admiral of the Red the Hon.
George Grey to be vice-adm. of the
Blue.

Rear-Admiral of the White Sir
Alexander Milne, K.C.B., to be rear-
adm. of the Red.

Rear-Admiral of the Blue the Hon.
Joseph Denman to be rear-adm. of
the White.

Capt. Henry Lyster to be rear-
adm. of the Blue.

Retired Vice-Adms. Henry Theo-
dosius Browne Collier, Henry Stanhope, and John Townsend Coffin, to
be retired adms., but without increase
of pay.

PROMOTIONS.
Captains—John E. Mills (1829),
who was Master Attendant of Devon-
port Dockyard from Feb., 1851, until
June, 1858, to the rank of Retired
Captain, under Order in Council,
Feb., 28, 1855.

Paymasters—Julian A. Messum,
John G. Whiffin, and James M. Low-
cay to the second class; William E.
L. Veale, John Freshfield, and Henry
W. Alridge to third class; William
Evans, of the Wellesley.

To be Chief Engineer—Thomas
Lumley.

To be Engineers—P. Hutchinson
of the Himalaya; W. H. Bambury
of the Dart; John Rice of the Asia,
supernumerary; H. Benbow of the
Cornwallis; William Inglis (A) of
the Osprey; J. Jessop of the Black
Prince; William Ross (acting) of
Foxhound; John West, of the
Columbine; Mathew Barker, supernumerary in the Indus.

To be First-Class Assistant-Engineers—P. Bland and Alexander Reid
of the Cumberland; J Forrest (A) of
the Edinburgh, J. K. Keay of the
Himalaya; W. B. Trenwith of the
Megæra; E. Ramsay of the Sphinx;
and A. Shanks of the Asia, J. M'Graw
(acting) of the Centaur; A. M'Intyre
(acting) of the Rambler; T. Ritchie
(acting) of the Araidne; J. Finlay
(acting) of the Nimble, and T. M'Far-
lane (acting) of the Scout.

APPOINTMENTS.
Commanders—R. O. Leach to the
Liverpool; G. F. Cottam to the
Recruit, commissioned.

Secretary—George P. Martin to be Secretary to Sir G. Lambert.

Lieutenants—J. C. H. Tracy to the Russell; R. B. Cay to the Majestic; G. D. Morant to the Formidable; A. H. G. Richardson to the Edgar; Lord Arthur P. Clinton to the Revenge; A. A. S. Watts to the Liverpool; Thomas V. Williams and C. S. P. Woodruffe to the Excellent; J. P. Barnett to the Majestic; John Inglis to the Excellent; Richard Sheepshanks to the Stork; Edward Poulden to the Excellent; Robert S. Chisholme to the Asia; James M. Morris to the Recruit.

Masters—Thomas Dobbin to the Racehorse; R. M. Curry to the Recruit; Christopher Albert to the Pelorus.

Surgeons—James C. Walsh to the Pembroke; James Davidson, M.D., to the Revenge; W. Ross, M.D., to the Meeanee; Cecil Crunden to the Leander.

Paymasters—Richard Mundy (additional) to the Britannia; Joseph Singleton to the Saturn; Frederick Lima to the Hornet; William H. Richards to the Eagle; John Freshfield to the Dædalus.

Assistant-Surgeons—R. Atkinson to the Haulbowline Hospital; W. G. Ridings to the Formidable, for the Marines at Deal; Samuel Grose to the Dauntless; John A. Yule to the Cumberland; Thomas Cann to the Recruit; Alfred W. Whitley (acting) to the Geyser; Robert Humphreys to the Mæander; T. L. Bickford to the Fisgard; C. W. J. Sutherland to the Rifleman; James Hutchinson (acting) to the Euryalus; Richard F. Bridgford to the Cambridge; Charles L. Conningham to the Wye.

Second Masters—Samuel M. Spry to the Dasher; H. D. Shortt to the Wye; A. H. Otter to the Resistance; W. Horn to the Medusa.

Sub-Lieutenants—John Hayes to the Resistance; John Anderson to the Liverpool; Hugh S. Baillie to the Racoon.

Midshipmen—F. H. S. O'Brien to the Liverpool; George T. Temple to the Defence; Francis E. Haigh to the Liverpool; Julian A. Baker to the Royal Oak; William N. Madan to

the Edgar; John Giles and Henry B. B. Beresford to the Resistance; R. F. Hoskyn to the Emerald; Pierre G. Evans to the Black Prince; W. Hailstone and Charles E. W. Hutton to the Warrior.

Naval Cadets — Reginald O'B. Carey and Robert D. Bruce to the Emerald; Edward Goldney, Archibald K. Harence, and J. D. Deane to the Black Prince; Charles W. Dickinson and Francis S. Knowles to the Warrior; Lord Lewis Gordon and H. J. Knight to the Resistance; Thomas C. Heathcote, Clement Royds, and William A. B. Beccles, to the Liverpool; Alexander W. Ogilvy, James L. Hammet, and Horace H. Barnard to the Defence: Frederic S. Pelly, Edward J. Bawtree, and Frederic Maitland to the Royal Oak; Robert H. Davies, Ford E. W. Lambart, John Phelips, Henry B. C. Wynyard, and Charles J. Barlow to the Edgar.

Naval Cadets (nominated)—L. W. Matthews, Arthur N. Hayne, W. H. Somerset, R. Findlay, W. S. Taylor, Charles P. Streeten, and E. A. Richmond, James Erskine Russell, E. B. Tinling, Robert H. Stewart, Henry D. Barry and Frank Wyley.

Master's Assistants—F. H. Whitelock to the Orlando; W. E. Filmer to the Victory, as supernumerary; L. G. Stovin to the Edgar; Frederick E. Thomson to the Recruit; Harry J. Miller to the Dasher: W. Stainer to the Himalaya.

Assistant-Paymasters — T. Elliott (in charge) to the Wye; W. F. Nicholson to the Duke of Wellington; Herbert F. Roe (additional) to the Edgar; Edward S. M. Power (in charge) to the Recruit; Thomas H. Bowling to the Edgar.

Clerks—C. L. W. La Grange to the Victory; George Deveson to the Cumberland; Henry G. Barlow, John H. Cleverton, and Arthur Hodson, to be Secretary's clerks in the Formidable.

Assistant-Clerk—Charles J. Bolt to the Recruit.

Chief Engineers—J. J. Greathead to the Mars; Thomas Duncanson to the Conqueror; Richard Sleeman to the Sphinx.

Engineers—J. F. Channon to the

Fisgard, as supernumerary; W. R. Leeson (acting) to the Indus; W. Wynd to the Cumberland; William Robinson to the Wye; W. J. Warren to the Fisgard, as supernumerary; William Maxwell to the Asia, as supernumerary; J. P. Lloyd to the Indus, for the Ripple; Edward Taylor to the Indus, as supernumerary; Richard Biddle to the Himalaya; W. R. Leeson (acting) to the Fisgard, as supernumerary.

Assistant-Engineers—Valentine C. Friend to the Indus, for hospital treatment; Thomas Vickery to the Resistance; James D. Chater to the Cumberland, as supernumerary; W. N. Sennett to the Indus, as supernumerary; Thomas Young to the Industry; Robert Spiers to the Fisgard, as supernumerary; C· E. Elfindell to the Fisgard, as supernumerary; M. J. Shannon to the Asia, for hospital treatment; T

Stead to the Asia, as supernumerary; J. M. Brankston to the Osprey; H. F. Strugnell to the Asia, supernumerary; S. T. Wallis, (for hospital treatment) and J. W. E. Baron (as supernumerary) to the Asia; W. H. Sedgwick to the Himalaya; Richard Stevens to the Ajax; E. E. Williams to the Dee; A. H. Symes to the Fisgard (as supernumerary); W. B. Chewley to the Stork; T· Cross to the Defence.

## COAST-GUARD.

Chief Officers—Charles J. Didham to Kingston; F. T. Hamilton to Dunbar; Henry B. Davis to Worthing; John A. Wallinger to Blackrock.

## ROYAL NAVAL RESERVE.

To be Honorary Lieutenant—H. Morris.

# ARMY.

THE ARMY GAZETTE.

*₊* Where not otherwise specified, the following Commissions bear the current date.

WAR OFFICE, PALL MALL, June 23.

1st Regt. of Dragoon Guards—Ens. Reginald Chalmer, from the 19th Foot, to be cor., vice Edward Hoare Reeves, promoted.

2nd Dragoon Guards—Cornet Arthur Brett to be Instructor of Musketry, vice Cornet John Taylor Marshall, who has rejoined his troop—20th April.

3rd Dragoon Guards — Lieut. Arthur Charles Van Cortlandt to be capt., by purchase, vice Arundell Neave, who retires; Cornet Winship Percival Roche to be lieut., by purchase, vice Van Cortlandt; George Robert Hodgson, gent., to be cor., without purchase, vice Roche.

4th Dragoon Guards — John Fisken Halket, gent, to be cor., by purchase, vice Ringrose, promoted.

6th Dragoon Guards—James Dunlop, gent., to be cor., by purchase, vice Owen Phibbs, promoted.

1st Dragoons—The Hon. Cosby Godolphin Trench to be cor., by purchase, vice the Hon. Montague Henry Mostyn, promoted.

4th Hussars—John Lambert Swale, gent., to be cor., by purchase, vice Harry Youl, promoted.

8th Hussars—Lieut. Richard William Palliser to be capt., by purchase, vice Esdaill Lovell Lovell, who retires; Cor. Frederick Helyar to be lieut., by purchase, vice Palliser.

12th Lancers—William Henry Buttanshaw, gent., late Lieut. 5th Bengal European Regiment to be paymaster, vice Roberts, whose services have been dispensed with.

13th Hussars — Joseph Mills gent., to be cor, by purchase, vice Edward Charles Starkey, promoted.

14th Hussars—James Crum, gent., to be cor., by purchase, vice James Colquhoun Revell Reade, who has retired.

15th Hussars—Lieut. David Ricardo to be capt., by purchase, vice Phineas Bury, who retires; Cor. David Maxwell to be lieut. by purchase, vice Ricardo; Robert Belford Wallis Wilson, gent., to be cor., by purchase, vice Maxwell.

18th Hussars—Lieut. Townley Patten Hume Macartney Filgate to be capt., by purchase, vice James Clarke Hicks, who retires; Cor. Charles John Fletcher to be lieut., by purchase, vice Filgate; William Macalpine Leny, gent, to be cor., by purchase, vice Fletcher.

Royal Regiment of Artillery—Lieut. George Agnew Goldingham to be sec.-capt., vice Henry Leenwin Dempster, who retires upon half-pay—21st May.

Royal Engineers — Lieut.-Col. Richard Strachey to be col., vice Stephen Pott, who retires—31st Dec., 1862; Lieut.-Col. Samuel Edgar Owen Ludlow to be col., vice Charles Edward Faber who retires—7th April; Capt. David George Robinson to be lieut.-col., vice Strachey—31st Dec., 1862; Capt. and Brevet-Major John Cumming Anderson to be lieut.-col., vice Ludlow—7th April; Sec. Capt. Frederick Sherwood Taylor to be capt., vice Robinson—31st Dec., 1862; Sec. Capt. John Mullins to be capt., vice Brevet-Major Anderson — 7th April; Lieut. George Newmarch to be sec. capt., vice Taylor—31st Dec., 1862.

Military Train — Ens. Fergus McKenzie to be lieut., without purchase, vice Henry Clarke, deceased—28th April.

Grenadier Guards—Lieut. and Capt. Francis Wheler, Viscount Hood, to be capt. and lieut.-col. by purchase, vice Edward Henry Cooper, who retires; Ens. and

Lieut. the Hon. William Sholto Douglas Home to be lieut. and capt., by purchase, vice Viscount Hood; Ens. and Lieut. Charles James Herbert to be lieut. and capt., by purchase, vice Sudeley Charles George, Lord Sudeley, who retires; Geo. Ernest Shelley, gent., to be ens. and lieut., by purchase, vice the Hon. W. S. D. Home; the Hon. Richard Maitland Westenra Dawson to be ens. and lieut., by purchase, vice Herbert—24th June.

1st Regiment of Foot—Capt. John Binnie Mackenzie, from the 19th Foot, to be capt., vice Onslow, who exchanges.

2nd Foot—Henry Barter, gent., to be ens., by purchase, vice Robert Carr Dunscombe, who retires.

5th Foot—Capt. and Brev.-Maj. Arthur Scott to be maj., by purchase, vice John Swaine Hogge, who retires; Lieut. John Rice Newbolt to be capt., by purchase, vice Brev.-Maj. Scott; Ens. Thos. Tarleton to be lieut., by purchase, vice Newbolt; Edward Harmsworth Ruddach, gent., to be ens., by purchase, vice Tarleton; Wm. Henry Major, gent., to be ens., by purchase, vice John Igglesden Troup, who retires—24th June.

17th Foot—Lieut. Samuel Bradburne to be capt., without purchase, vice Frederick Archibald Macreigght, deceased—15th May; Ens. William Frederick Woods to be lieut., without purchase, vice Bradburne — 15th May; James Mark Brooke, gent., to be ens., by purchase, vice Woods.

19th Foot—Capt. Geo. Onslow, from the 1st Foot, to be capt., vice Mackenzie, who exchanges; Walter St. James Young, gent., to be ens., by purchase, vice Reginald Chalmer, transferred to the 1st Dragoon Guards.

22nd Foot—Lieut. William Busfeild to be capt., by purchase, vice Robert Conway Dobbs Ellis, who retires; Ens. Edward Straton to be lieut., by purchase, vice Busfeild; Richard Charles Hare, gent., to be ens., by purchase, vice Straton.

28th Foot — Capt. Frederick Edward Medhurst, from half-pay, late 43rd Foot, to be capt., vice John William Preston, seconded on being appointed District Inspector of Musketry.

34th Foot — Ens. Henry E. Sharpe to be lieut., without purchase, vice John Francis Wyse, promoted—3rd March; Ens. John Christopher Cowslade, from 83rd Foot, to be ens., vice Sharpe; Lieut. George Malcolm to be adjt., vice Lieut. John Francis Wyse, promoted.

37th Foot—Ens. John Everard Whitting to be lieut., without purchase, vice Richard Bunn, promoted to an Unattached Company, without purchase; Paymaster, with the hon. rank of capt., Thos. Smith, from 25th Foot, to be paymaster, vice paymaster, with the hon. rank of Capt., Raynsford Taylor, who resigns.

49th Foot—Henry Board Williams, gent., to be ens., by purchase, vice Barne, promoted.

53rd Foot—Capt. Robert St. John, from the 72nd Foot, to be capt., vice Thomas Chas. Ffrench, who exchanges.

60th Foot — Ens. the Hon. Walter Courtenay Pepys to be lieut., by purchase, vice James Forbes, who retires; Edmund Lomax Fraser, gent., to be ens., by purchase, vice the Hon. Walter Courtenay Pepys; Henry Richard Ponsonby Lindesay, gent., to be ens., by purchase, vice Edward Burr, who retires—24th June.

72nd Foot—Capt. Thos. Chas. Ffrench, from the 53rd Foot, to be capt., vice St. John, who exchanges.

75th Foot—Capt. and Brevet-Lieut.-Col. William Knox Orme, from half-pay, late 10th Foot, to be capt., vice Capt. and Brevet-Lieut.-Col William Brookes, who retires upon half-pay.

82nd Foot—Ens. Chas. Neville to be lieut., without purchase, vice Henry Abigail Ellis, deceased—27th May.

83rd Foot—Lieut. William H. Ivimy to be capt., by purchase, vice William Minhear, who retires.

Ens. Charles Hay Tollemache to be lieut., by purchase, vice Ivimy; John Christopher Cowslade, gent., to be ens, by purchase, vice Tollemache.

90th Foot—Lieut. Randall Ironside Ward to be Instructor of Musketry, vice Lieut. Charles Dawson Barwell, promoted—4th March.

95th Foot—Ens. H. Aldridge, from the 84th Foot, to be ens., in succession to Lieut. Charles James Holbrook, deceased.

The restoration to full-pay of Capt. Frederick Edward Medhurst, from half-pay, late 43rd Foot, vice Crealock, seconded, on appointment as District Inspector of Musketry, as stated in the *Gazette* of the 20th Feb., last, has been cancelled, the latter officer having resigned the District Inspectorship.

102nd Foot—Ens. John Hampden Waller to be lieut., vice Clement Headington Dale, who resigns.

2nd West India Regiment— Charles Siegfried Tobias-Ternau, gent., late Lieut. and Adjt, 1st Light Infantry, British German Legion, to be paymaster, vice John Craven Mansergh, appointed to the Royal Artillery.

5th West India Regt.—Lieut.-Col. William Forbes Macbean, from St. Helena Regiment, to be lieut.-col.; Maj. and Brev.-Col. Henry Gahan, from St. Helena Regt., to be lieut.-col., without purchase; Maj. Thos. Cochrane, from Gold Coast Artillery Corps, to be maj.; Capt. Robert Alexander Loudon, from St. Helena Regt., to be maj., without purchase.

To be Captains—

Caps. Joseph Brownell, from Gold Coast Artillery Corps; John Henry Prenderville, from St. Helena Regt.; Henry Tayler, from St. Helena Regt.; John Baldwin Hainault Rainier, from St. Helena Regt.; Thomas G. Danger, from Gold Coast Artillery Corps; Edwin Hewett, from Gold Coast Artillery Corps; Henry John Fane, from St. Helena Regt.; John James Mathew, from Gold Coast Artillery

Corps; Gisborne Horner, from Gold Coast Artillery Corps.

To be Lieutenants—

Lieut. and Adjt. John McNamee, from St. Helena Regt.; Lieuts. Adolphus William Campbell, from St. Helena Regt.; John Lysaght Hewson, from St. Helena Regt.; William Russell Nash, from St. Helena Regt.; James Thomson, from Gold Coast Artillery Corps; Anthony Edmond Donelan, from St. Helena Regt; Robert John Stewart, from Gold Coast Artillery Corps; Albert Sharp, from Gold Coast Artillery Corps; Lieut. and Adjt. Thomas Davies, from Gold Coast Artillery Corps; Lieuts. Francis Charles Gavegan, from Gold Coast Artillery Corps; Geo. Vautier Lambe, from St. Helena Regiment; John Dudley Edward Crosse, from Gold Coast Artillery Corps.

To be Ensigns—

Ens. Thomas England, from St. Helena Regt.; Thomas Storrar Smith, from St. Helena Regt.; George Henry Evans, from St. Helena Regt.; Robertson Gilchrist Marshall, from Gold Coast Artillery Corps; Thos. Haffield Brien, from Gold Coast Corps; David Dempster Chadwick, from St. Helena Regt.; Robert Knapp Barrow, from Gold Coast Artillery Corps; Quartermaster John Hobson Wright, from the St. Helena Regt., to be quartermaster.

Royal Canadian Rifle Regt.— Major Kenneth Mackenzie Moffatt to be lieut.-col. by purchase, vice Brevet-Col William Henry Bradford, who retires upon half-pay— 12th May; Capt. Francis Gordon Hibbert to be maj., by purchase, vice Moffat—12th May; Lieut. Edward Whyte to be capt., by purchase, vice Hibbert — 12th May; Ens. Thos. Henry Selwyn Donovan to be lieut., by purchase, vice Whyte—12th May.

MEDICAL DEPARTMENT.

Assist.-Surg. John Wood, from the Royal Artillery, to be staff assist.-surg., vice William James Mullan, placed upon half-pay.

UNATTACHED.

Lieut. George Gibson, from the

## BENGAL STAFF CORPS.

### ADMISSION.

To be Major—
Capt. (Brevet-Lieut.-Col.) Crawford Trotter Chamberlain, of the late 28th nat. in.—18th Feb., 1863.

To be Captain—
Capt Alexander Paterson, of the late 2nd European Infantry—1st May, 1858.

### PROMOTIONS.

To be Lieutenant-Colonel—
Maj. (Brevet-Col.) William Edw. Mulcaster—4th April.

To be Major—
Capt. Henry Boileau Adolphus Poulton—7th April.

To be Captain—
Lieut. Henry Chad Cattley—20th March.

### ALTERATIONS OF RANK.

The undermentioned officers will take rank from the dates specified :—Lieut.-Col. William Richardson, from 25th March, 1861 ; Maj. Wm. Domett Morgan, from 25th Feb., 1861 ; Maj. Henry Mills, from 19th Oct., 1861 ; Maj. Benjamin Parrott, from 27th July, 1861 ; Capt. John Crawford Millar, from 9th May, 1861 ; Capt. Toovey Archibald Corbett, from 16th Jan., 1862 ; Capt. Chas. Allan McDougall, from the 2nd Feb., 1862.

The promotion of Capt. John Smith to the rank of Major as announced in the *Gazette* of 2nd Dec., 1862, has been cancelled.

The promotion of Lieut. John Arthur Henry Moore to the rank of Capt., from 18th Feb., 1861, as announced in the *Gazette* of 2nd Dec., 1862, has been cancelled.

## BENGAL ARMY.

Late 72nd nat. in.—Lieut. Harry Hammond Lyster, V.C., to be capt., in succession to Ford, retired—23rd Dec, 1862.

General List of Infantry officers —Ens. Robert Charnley Squire Charles Tytler to be lieut, in succession to Corfield, late 9th nat. in.. deceased—25th Jan.; James Cook to be lieut., vice Augus, resigned—28th Jan.

### ALTERATIONS OF RANK.

The undermentioned officers to rank from the dates specified :— Lieuts. Claude Stewart Morrison, from the 15th Dec., 1862 ; Frederick William Glasfurd, from the 18th Dec., 1862 ; Percy Wyndham Smith, from the 23rd Dec., 1862.

## MADRAS STAFF CORPS.

The admission of the undermentioned Officers to the Madras Staff Corps, as announced in the *London Gazette* of 24th Feb , 1863, has been cancelled :—Lieuts. Frederick Gadsden, 5th nat. in.; Wheatley Robertson, 5th nat. in.; Geo. Tyndall, 1st nat. in.; H. Glover Puckle, 8th nat. in.; Duncan McNeill, 26th nat. in.; Alexander Cook, 32nd nat. in.

## MADRAS ARMY.

3rd Regt. nat. in.—Capt. (Brev.-Maj.) Robert Jones to be maj , and Lieut. (Brev.-Capt.) Samuel Crawford Montgomerie to be capt., in succession to Keating, deceased—23rd March.

50th Regt. nat. in.—Lieut. John Duval to be capt., vice Keating, retired—1st Oct., 1861.

General List of Infantry officers —Ens. Robert Hunter to be lieut., in succession to Keating, 3rd nat. in., deceased—23rd March.

## BOMBAY ARMY.

### ALTERATIONS OF RANK.

General List of Infantry Officers Lieuts. Evlyn Gawler Sturt to take rank from 24th Jan.; Edw. Robert Reay to take rank from 31st Jan.

### MEDICAL OFFICERS.

Assist.-Surg. John Henry Wilmot, M.D., A.B., to be surg., vice Grierson, deceased—7th Jan.

### ALTERATIONS OF RANK.

Surgs. John Grant Nicolson, M.D., to take rank from 18th Dec., 1862; Robert Millar, M.D., to take rank from 1st Jan.

DOWNING STREET, June 26.

The Queen has been pleased to appoint Sir Charles Henry Darling, K.C.B., (now Capt.-Gen. and Governor-in-Chief in and over the Island of Jamaica and the Territories depending thereon\ \ \

Governor and Commander-in-Chief in and over the Colony of Victoria.

## THE MILITIA GAZETTE.

WAR OFFICE, PALL MALL, June 23.

2nd Regiment (Light Infantry) of West York Militia—Clervaux Darley Chaytor, gent., to be lieut., vice Whitaker, promoted.

1st West Regiment of Yorkshire Yeomanry Cavalry—Cornet John Foster to be lieut., vice St. Leger, deceased.

West Somerset Regiment of Yeomanry Cavalry—Francis John Helyar, gent., to be lieut., vice Pitman, promoted; Charles Cæsar Welman, late lieut. 49th Regiment, to be cor., vice Bernard, promoted.

Shropshire Militia—Col. Richard Frederick Hill to be hon. col., on resigning his commission as col.

West Essex Militia—Francis Lovell to be assist-surg., vice Gilson, promoted.

Memorandum—Her Majesty has been pleased to accept the resignation of the commission held by Lieut. Albert Robson Burkill in the Essex Rifles Militia.

2nd Regiment of Royal Cheshire Militia—Philip Whiteway, gent., to be lieut., vice Wilkin, resigned.

Cambridgeshire Militia—Lieut. Arthur Harris Rees to be capt., vice Bendyshe, resigned.

Memorandum—Her Majesty has been graciously pleased to accept the resignation of the commission held by Lieut. Sir Edward Filmer, Bart., in the East Kent Yeomanry Cavalry.

East Kent Mounted Rifles Yeomanry Cavalry—Cornet Augustus Saville Lumley to be lieut., vice Filmer, resigned; Robert Alured Denne, gent., to be cor, vice Lumley, promoted.

1st Devon Regiment of Militia— Henry Walrond to be super. lieut.

2nd or South Devon Regiment of Militia—Maj. the Hon. John Buller Yarde Buller to be lieut.-col., vice Lord Churston, resigned.

Memorandum—Argyll and Bute Artillery Militia—Her Majesty has been graciously pleased to accept the resignation of the commission

held by Capt. George A. R. in the above corps.

Argyll and Bute Artillery —George Patrick, gent., to lieut.

WAR OFFICE, PALL MALL, J.

1st Regiment of Royal G. Militia—Lieut. Thomas E. Marshall to be capt, vice D. deceased; Francis John S. gent., to be lieut., vice Mr. promoted.

Memorandum—Her Majesty been graciously pleased to a the resignation of the comm held by Cornet Herbert D. the Royal East Kent M. Rifles Yeomanry Cavalry.

Essex Rifles Militia—Per. Curling to be lieut., vice G. resigned.

6th Regiment of Royal L. shire Militia—William B. Midwood, gent., to be assist-s. vice Frederick Foulkes, resig.

Memorandum—Her Majesty been graciously pleased to a. the resignation of the comm. held by Cor. George The. Robert Preston in the Du. Lancaster's Own Yeomanry Ca. ry.

## THE VOLUNTEER GAZETTE

WAR OFFICE, PALL MALL, Jun.

2nd West Riding of Yorksh. Artillery Volunteer Corps—S. phen Lancelot Koe, Esq., to capt.

4th West Riding of York-hir Artillery Volunteer Corps—Arnold Parker, gent., to be sec. lieut.

1st West Riding of Yorkshir Rifle Volunteer Corps—Thom. Shepherd Noble, gent., to be super. lieut.

3rd West Riding of Yorkshire Rifle Volunteer Corps—Assist.-Surg. John Beach to be surg. vice McMichan, resigned; George Newstead, gent., to be assist.-surg., vice Beach, promoted.

39th West Riding of Yorkshire Rifle Volunteer Corps—John Bairstow Sharp, gent., to be ens.

Memoranda—Her Majesty has been graciously pleased to accept

the resignation of the commissions held by the following gentlemen:

3rd West Riding of Yorkshire Rifle Volunteer Corps—Ens. Wm. Henry Ramsden; Surg. John Little McMichan.

39th West Riding of Yorkshire Rifle Volunteer Corps—Ens. Geo. Henry Townend.

Memorandum—3rd London Rifle Volunteer Corps—Her Majesty has been graciously pleased to accept the resignation of the commissions held by Ens. Arthur Richards and Assist.-Surg. Joseph Reid in the above corps.

Memorandum—4th London Rifle Volunteer Corps—Her Majesty has been graciously pleased to accept the resignation of the commission held by Adjt. Charles John Hampton in the above corps.

London Rifle Volunteer Brigade —Mr. Sidney Chater, M.R.C.S., to be assist.-surg.

19th Somersetshire Rifle Volunteer Corps—Ens. Thomas Walter Swayne to be capt., vice Hood, resigned.

2nd Lancashire Light Horse Volunteer Corps—Frederick Annesley Bretherton, gent., to be lieut.

1st Manchester or 6th Lancashire Rifle Volunteer Corps—Ens. Alfred King Pearce to be lieut.

24th Lancashire Rifle Volunteer Corps—William Moseley Mellor, Esq., to be capt.

33rd Lancashire Rifle Volunteer Corps—Francis Marris Jackson, gent., to be lieut.

3rd Manchester or 40th Lancashire Rifle Volunteer Corps—Geo. Whitehead, gent., to be ens.

46th Lancashire Rifle Volunteer Corps—Ens. Henry Payne to be lieut.

2nd Orkney Artillery Volunteer Corps—James Cathie Scarth, Esq., to be capt.; Mr. John Paul to be first lieut.; Mr. William Harvey to be sec. lieut.

4th Orkney Artillery Volunteer Corps—John Stanger, Esq., to be capt.; Mr. Alexander Robertson to be first lieut.; Mr. John D. Turner to be sec. lieut.

Memoranda—Her Majesty has been graciously pleased to accept the resignation of the commissions held by the following officers, viz:—

1st Inverness-shire Artillery Volunteer Corps—First Lieut. Robt. Carruthers.

3rd Inverness-shire Rifle Volunteer Corps—Capt. George Grant Mackay.

3rd Inverness-shire Rifle Volunteer Corps—Robert Carruthers to be capt., vice Mackay, resigned.

8th Company of Herefordshire Rifle Volunteers—Richard James Hereford, Esq., late capt. 73rd Regiment, to be lieut, vice Fredk. Bodenham, Esq., resigned; Fredk. Bodenham, Esq., to be ens., vice James Phillips, Esq,, resigned.

Memorandum—Her Majesty has been graciously pleased to accept the resignation of the commission held by Capt. Frederic Morris in the 7th Kent Rifle Volunteer Corps. Also, the commission held by Lieut. John William Finch in the 42nd Kent Rifle Volunteer Corps.

42nd Kent Rifle Volunteer Corps —Ens. Philip Simpson to be lieut., vice Finch, resigned; Alfd. Monckton, gent., to be ens., vice Simpson, promoted.

2nd Company of Wigtounshire Rifle Volunteers—Samuel Taylor, gent., to be ens., vice David Shaw, resigned.

Inns of Court Rifle Volunteer Corps—Springall Thompson to be ens., vice Murray, resigned.

Memoranda — The Queen has been graciously pleased to accept the resignation of the commissions held by the following officers, viz.:—

St. George's Rifle Volunteer Corps—Captain John Chichester Knox.

Inns of Court Rifle Volunteer Corps—Ens. William Powell Murray.

29th Middlesex Rifle Volunteer Corps—Capt. William Henry Absolon.

40th Middlesex Rifle Volunteer Corps—Capt. Edward Letchworth.

1st or Exeter and South Devon Rifle Volunteer Corps—Walter Charles Edward Show to be capt.;

Ens. Henry Walrend to be capt.; Ens. George Frederick Truscott to be lieut.; Ens. Charles Allin Rodway to be lieut.

1st City of Edinburgh Artillery Volunteer Corps — First Lieut. John Spence to be capt., vice Ballantyne, resigned; William F. Vallance to be sec. lieut.

1st City of Edinburgh Rifle Volunteer Corps—George Thomas Kinnear to be lieut., vice Black, resigned; George Fowler to be ens., vice Millons, resigned; Archibald McKinlay to be ens., vice Lamb, resigned; Alexander Orrock to be ens., vice Hill, resigned.

2nd Derbyshire Rifle Volunteer Corps—George John Warren, Lord Vernon, to be capt.-commandt, vice Vernon, resigned; Lieut. Chas. Edward Boothby to be capt., vice Coke, resigned; Ens. William Cox to be lieut., vice Broadhurst, resigned.

Memorandum — Henry Bourchier Osborne Savile, Maj.-Commandt. of the 1st Gloucestershire Artillery Volunteer Corps, is entitled to rank in the General Service from the 13th of Sept., 1859, the date of the commission he held in the City of Bristol Rifle Volunteer Corps.

Memorandum—Her Majesty has been graciously pleased to accept the resignation of the commission held by Hon. Assist.-Surg. Wm. Macdonald, M.D., in the 2nd Company of the Dumbartonshire Rifle Volunteer Corps.

Memorandum—Her Majesty has been graciously pleased to accept the resignation of the commission held by Lieut. Robert Kennedy in the 4th Company of Dumfriesshire Rifle Volunteer Corps.

Memorandum—Her Majesty has been graciously pleased to accept the resignation of the commission held by First Lieut. Edmund Hannary Watts in the 3rd Northumberland Volunteer Corps.

Memorandum—Her Majesty has been graciously pleased to accept the resignation of the commissions held by Surg. George Carr in the 1st Aberdeenshire Rifle Volunteer Corps; Lieut. Charles Mackie and

Ens. David Connon i. ⋅ ⋅ Aberdeenshire Rifle \. ⋅ Corps.

Memorandum—Her M. ⋅ ⋅ been graciously plea⋅⋅l ⋅ ⋅ the resignation of ti⋅ ⋅ ⋅⋅ held by Lieut. Patr⋅⋅ ⋅⋅ Morrison in the 1st S⋅⋅⋅⋅ Rifle Volunteer Corp⋅.

---

WAR OFFICE, PALL MALL ⋅⋅.

14th Somersetshire Rifl⋅ ⋅ ⋅ teer Corps—Duncan Willi⋅⋅⋅ ⋅⋅ Skrine, gent., to be en⋅⋅ ⋅⋅ M. Skrine, promoted.

St. Georges Rifle \. ⋅⋅ Corps—Lieut. William H⋅⋅⋅ to be capt., vice Knox. ⋅⋅⋅ Ensign Reginald Thi⋅th⋅⋅⋅ Cocks to be lieut., vice H⋅⋅⋅⋅

20th Middlesex Rifle V⋅⋅⋅ Corps—Ens. John Fran⋅⋅ ⋅ wick to be lieut., vice B⋅⋅ resigned.

Memorandum—Her Maj⋅⋅⋅ ⋅ been graciously pleased to ⋅⋅ the resignation of the com⋅⋅ ⋅ held by Lieut. John Ward ⋅⋅ stone in the 1st Cheshire A⋅⋅⋅ Volunteer Corps.

Memorandum—Her Maje⋅⋅ ⋅ been graciously pleased to ⋅⋅⋅ the resignation of the com⋅ ⋅ held by First Lieut. Jam⋅⋅ ⋅ burner in the 1st Cheshire Eng⋅ Volunteer Corps.

Memorandum—Her Maje⋅⋅⋅⋅ been graciously pleased to ⋅⋅⋅ the resignation of the com⋅⋅ ⋅ held by Ens. John Downing F⋅⋅ in the 6th Cheshire Rifle Volu⋅⋅ Corps.

6th Cheshire Rifle Volur⋅ Corps — Henry Wat⋅on J⋅⋅ gent., to be ens., vice F⋅⋅ resigned.

1st Brecknockshire Rifle V⋅⋅ teer Corps—William Rhy⋅ Br⋅⋅ Powel, Esq., to be capt.-comma⋅⋅

1st Hampshire Engineer V⋅⋅ teers—Sec. Lieut. Frederick H⋅ Read Sawyer to be first lieut., ⋅ Buchan, promoted; William Cl⋅ Fitch to be sec. lieut., vice Saw⋅ promoted.

1st Hampshire Rifle Volunt. —Lieut. Thomas Burne⋅t W⋅ ham to be capt., vice Fau⋅⋅ resigned; Ens. Henry Sand

Simonds to be lieut., vice Woodham, promoted; Frederick Isaac Warner to be ens., vice Simonds, promoted.

16th Hampshire Rifle Volunteers —William Benson to be ens., vice Blackmore, promoted.

Memorandum—1st Hampshire Rifle Volunteers—Her Majesty has been graciously pleased to approve of Capt. William Barrow Simonds bearing the designation of capt.-commandt.

5th Company of the Stirlingshire Rifle Volunteer Corps—Robert Service, gent., to be ens, vice Fisher, resigned.

1st Kent Rifle Volunteer Corps —William Haynes, the younger, gent., to be ens., vice Brennan, resigned.

Memorandum—2nd Lincolnshire Artillery Volunteer Corps—Her Majesty has been graciously pleased to accept the resignation of the commission held by Capt. Frank Long.

Memorandum—3rd Lincolnshire Rifle Volunteer Corps—Her Majesty has been graciously pleased to accept the resignation of the commission held by Lieut. James William Jeans.

1st Administrative Battalion of Lincolnshire Rifle Volunteers— Maj. Weston Cracroft Amcotts to be lieut.-col., vice the Earl of Yarborough, resigned.

11th Lincolnshire Rifle Volunteer Corps—The Reverend George Urquhart to be hon. chap., vice the Rev. George Jeans, deceased.

2nd Company of Banffshire Rifle Volunteers (Aberlour) — George Riddoch to be lieut., vice Hurry, resigned; John McKerron to be ens., vice Riddoch, promoted.

3rd Company of Banffshire Rifle Volunteers (Keith) — Malcolm Stewart to be capt., vice Gordon, resigned.

7th Lancashire Artillery Volunteer Corps—John McGaffin, gent., to be sec. lieut.

Memorandum—The 71st Lancashire Rifle Volunteer Corps having been struck out of the records of the War Office, will henceforth cease to hold any number or designation in the Volunteer Force, and Her Majesty has been graciously pleased to approve of the services of Lieutenants Innes Macpherson and William James Audsley and Ens. John Milligan in that Corps, being dispensed with.

Her Majesty has been graciously pleased to accept the resignation of the commissions held by the following officers, viz.:

Maj. John Hornby in the 2nd Lancashire Rifle Volunteer Corps.

Capt. William George Ainslie in the 37th A Lancashire Rifle Volunteer Corps, and

Lieut. Myles Kennedy in the 52nd Lancashire Rifle Volunteer Corps.

7th Northamptonshire Rifle Volunteer Corps—Lieut. George Hodson Burnham to be capt., vice Henry Minshull Stockdale, resigned.

Memorandum—Her Majesty has been graciously pleased to accept the resignation of the commission held by Capt. Alexander Bell in the 1st Forfarshire Rifle Volunteer Corps.

Memorandum—Her Majesty has been graciously pleased to accept the resignation of the commission held by Ens. John Joseph Walmesley in the 2nd Cinque Ports Rifle Volunteer Corps.

Memorandum—Her Majesty has been graciously pleased to accept the resignation of the commission held by Capt. Henry Williams Pemberton in the 2nd Cambridgeshire Mounted Rifle Volunteer Corps.

## THE ARMY GAZETTE.

*⁎* Where not otherwise specified, the following commissions bear the current date.

WAR OFFICE, PALL MALL, June 30.

99th Regiment of Foot—Maj.-Gen. John Napper Jackson, from the 3rd West India Regiment, to be col., vice Gen. Sir John Hanbury, K.C.B., deceased—8th June.

3rd West India Regiment—Maj.-Gen. Maurice Barlow to be col., vice Maj.-Gen. John Napper Jackson, transferred to the colonelcy of the 99th Regiment—8th June.

2nd Regiment of Life Guards— Vet. Surg. Thornton Hart, from the 2nd Dragoons, to be vet. surg., vice John Legrew, who retires upon half-pay.

2nd Dragoons—Act. Vet. Surg. Andrew G. Ross to be vet. surg., vice Thornton Hart, transferred to the 2nd Life Guards—16th May, 1862.

3rd Hussars—Albert Praed Halifax, gent., to be cor., by purchase, vice Dodgson Hamilton Thompson, transferred to the 13th Foot.

5th Lancers—Act. Vet. Surg. Edward Stanley to be vet. surg., vice William C. Lord, transferred to the Cavalry Depot, Canterbury —24th June, 1862.

7th Hussars—Cor. Henry Augustus Bushman to be lieut., by purchase, vice Charles H. Baillie, who retires; William Steuart Lillingston, gent., to be cor., by purchase, vice Bushman.

9th Lancers—Francis Henry, gent., to be cor., by purchase, vice Thos. Albin Saunders, promoted; the Hon. Oliver George Powlett Montagu to be cor., by purchase, vice William Henry Lawrence, promoted—1st July.

13th Hussars—Thomas Edward Stopford Hickman, gent., to be cor., by purchase, vice Higford Higford, who retires.

19th Hussars—Ensign Joseph Schuyler Albert Bruff, from Madras General List, to be cor.—20th December, 1860.

20th Hussars—Ens. David Carruthers Budd, from Madras General List, to be cor.—8th June, 1860; Ens. Henry Jopp Beattie, from Madras General List, to be cor.— 19th December, 1860; Cor. Charles Bailey, from Bengal General List, to be cor.—16th November, 1861.

21st Hussars—Ens. Robert Carr Andrew, from Madras General List, to be cor.—12th July, 1860; Ens. Joseph William Minchin Cotton, from Madras General List, to be cor.—20th December, 1860; Cor. Thomas Deane, from Madras General List, to be cor.—4th March, 1862.

Royal Artillery—Lieut.-Col. and Brev.-Col. Frank Turner, C.B., on the Super. List, to be col.—10th March; Lieut.-Col. Henry Alex. Carleton, C.B., to be col., vice Francis Claude Burnett, retired upon full-pay—10th March; Capt. William Bainbrigge Marshall to be lieut.-col., vice Carleton—10th March; Sec. Capt. William Alex. Ross to be capt., vice Marshall— 10th March; Sec. Capt. Thomas Carlisle Crowe to be capt., vice Charles Clarke, removed to the Super. List—10th March; Lieut. Horace Seymour Kerr Pechell to be sec. capt., vice Crowe—10th March; Lieut. James Sconce to be sec. capt., vice Ross—3rd April; Lieut. Edmund Staveley to be sec. capt., vice Charles Donnethorne Bevan, deceased—9th June; the promotion of Sec. Capt. James Cecil Grove Price has been antedated to the 10th March.

Royal Engineers—Sec. Capt. Lionel Charles Barber, from halfpay, to be sec. capt., vice Brev.-Maj. Charles George Gordon, placed on the Seconded List—16th May; Lieut. Lewis Gower Stewart has been permitted to resign his commission; the services of Lieut. William Gustavus Temple Stace have been dispensed with.

6th Foot—Ens. Augustus Wm. Whitworth, from the 100th Foot, to be ens., vice Alfred Teevan, promoted.

7th Foot—Valentine John Augustus Browne, gent., to be ens., by purchase. vice Moore, transferred to the 20th Foot; the exchange between Lieut. Vincent Upton Langworthy, of the 7th Foot, and Lieut. Joseph Dooley, of the 100th Foot, which appeared in the *Gazette* of the 20th February, has been cancelled.

8th Foot—Lieut. James Seager Wheeley to be capt., by purchase, vice Alfred Downie Corfield, who retires; Ens. William Willoughby Egerton to be lieut., by purchase, vice Wheeley; Berkeley Augustus Fonblanque, gent., to be ens., without purchase, vice Egerton.

11th Foot—Hampden Denny, gent., to be ens., by purchase, vice George William Westropp, who retires.

12th Foot—Lieut. Henry J. Mac-Donnell to be adjt., vice George Gibson, promoted to an Unattached Company, without purchase.

14th Foot—Capt. Robert Wm. Jenkins, from half-pay, late 8th Hussars, to be capt., vice William John Coen, who reverts to half-pay.

16th Foot—Capt. and Brev.-Maj. Charles Armstrong to be maj., without purchase, vice Maj. and Brev.-Lieut.-Col. John Willet Payne Audain, who retires upon full-pay; Lieut. Charles Wynn Isdell to be capt., without purchase, vice Brev.-Maj. Armstrong; Ens. Richard Wood Robinson to be lieut., without purchase, vice Isdell; Ens. Robert Rainier McQueen, from the 44th Foot, to be ens., vice Robinson.

19th Foot—Maj. Henry de Renzy Pigott, from the 83rd Foot, to be maj., vice Bates, who exchanges.

20th Foot—Lieut. Samuel Johnstone to be capt., by purchase, vice Charles Frederick Houghton, who retires; Ens. Frederick Watkins Barlow to be lieut., by purchase, vice Johnstone; Ensign Stewart Abercrombie Wroughton to be lieut., by purchase, vice Charles A. Vernon, who retires; Ens. Thomas Ottiwell Moore, from the 7th Foot, to be ens., vice Wroughton; John Hugh Ford, gent., to be ens., by purchase, vice Barlow.

21st Foot—Lieut. Francis Wm. Hamilton to be capt., by purchase, vice Robert Beattie Henderson, who retires—1st July; Lieut. Jas. Henry Patrickson to be capt., by purchase, vice Augustus Breedon, who retires—1st July; Ens. and Adjt. James Ferguson to be lieut., by purchase, vice Edward Thomas Bainbridge, promoted; Ens. Fredk. Packman to be lieut., without purchase—1st July; Ens. Henry Beresford Nangle to be lieut., by purchase, vice Hamilton—1st July; Ens. James Whitton to be lieut., by purchase, vice Patrickson—1st July; Samuel Francis Ward, gent., to be ens., by purchase, vice Ferguson; Thomas Capel Rose, gent., to be ens., by purchase, vice Nangle —1st July; Lieut. Frederick Geo.

Jackson to be adjt., vice Lieut. Robert Cook, promoted.

23rd Foot—Gent.-Cadet Fredk. Stringer, from the Royal Military College, to be ens., without purchase, vice George Pepper Lowry, whose transfer from the 100th Foot, which appeared in the *Gazette* of 12th instant, has been cancelled.

24th Foot—Gent.-Cadet Edward Henry Randolph, from the Royal Military College, to be ens., without purchase, vice George James Gordon, promoted.

31st Foot—Maj. and Brev.-Lieut.-Col. Robert John Eagar to be lieut.-col., without purchase, vice Brev.-Col. Frederick Spence, C.B., who retires upon full-pay; Capt. and Brev.-Maj. George Walter Baldwin to be maj., without purchase, vice Brev.-Lieut.-Col. Eagar; Lieut. Thomas Christian Rycroft to be capt., without purchase, vice Brev.-Maj. Baldwin; Ens. Francis William Henry Davies Butler to be lieut., without purchase, vice Rycroft.

36th Foot—Ens. Thomas Enraght Percy Tyrwhitt to be lieut., by purchase, vice George Cotton Dumergue, who retires; William Hamilton Marriott, gent., to be ens., by purchase, vice Tyrwhitt.

39th Foot—George Charles Dawson Bampfield, gent., to be ens., without purchase, vice Henry French Cotton, transferred to the 92nd Foot,

41st Foot — Sydney Hooper, gent., to be ens., by purchase, vice Thomas Horner Pearson, transferred to the 43rd Foot.

42nd Foot—Lieut. Edward Orlando Van Haldane, from half-pay, 14th Hussars, to be lieut., vice William Wood, promoted to an Unattached Company, without purchase; Lieut. James Edmund Christie to be adjt., vice Lieut. William Wood, promoted to an Unattached Company, without purchase—4th May.

43rd Foot—Ens. Coll McLeod to be lieut., by purchase, vice Evelyn Arthur Rich, who retires; Ens. Thomas Horner Pearson, from the 41st Foot, to be ens., vice McLeod.

47th Foot—Lieut. William Carnegy de Balinhard to be instructor of musketry, vice Lieut. Ernest Peake Newman, promoted—1st June.

50th Foot—Lieut. Charles Augustus Fitzgerald Creagh to be capt., without purchase, vice Alfred John Lane, deceased—6th May; Ens. Richard Oliffe Richmond to be lieut., without purchase, vice Creagh—6th May.

53rd Foot—Lieut. Robert Holt Truell to be capt., by purchase, vice William Henry Campion, who retires; Ens. Henry Douglas Rooke to be lieut., by purchase, vice Truell; John Guillum Scott, gent., to be ens., by purchase, vice Rooke.

60th Foot—Lieut. Kennett Gregg Henderson to be capt., by purchase, vice William Spicer Cookworthy, who retires; Ens. Francis William Robins to be lieut., by purchase, vice Henderson; John Bartlett Stradling, gent., to be ens., by purchase, vice Robins.

67th Foot—Capt. Charles B. Knowles, from half-pay, late 77th Foot, to be capt., vice Brev.-Maj. Henry Crofton, who retires upon temporary half-pay.

74th Foot—Capt. William Wood, from half-pay, late 42nd Foot, to be capt., vice the Hon. John Baptiste Joseph Dormer, seconded on being appointed District Inspector of Musketry.

75th Foot—Lieut. Frederick Cornwall to be capt., by purchase, vice Brev.-Lieut.-Col. William Knox Orme, who retires; Ens. Robert John Fitzgerald Day to be lieut., by purchase, vice Cornwall; Joseph Napoleon Fitz-Mathew, gent., to be ens., by purchase, vice Oscar Vernède, who retires; Raymond William Parr. gent., to be ens., by purchase, vice Day—1st July.

83rd Foot—Maj. Robert Bates, from the 19th Foot, to be maj., vice Pigott, who exchanges.

84th Foot—Gent.-Cadet Reginald William Peckitt, from the Royal Military College, to be ens, without purchase, vice Henry Aldridge, transferred to the 95th Foot.

85th Foot—Lieut. Finch White to be instructor of musketry, vice

Lieut. George Henry Stace, who resigns the appointment—18th June.

88th Foot—Capt. John Edwin Dickson Hill to revert to half-pay, Capt and Brev.-Maj. Joshua Grant Crosse, who was seconded on 20th February, 1863, on appointment as district inspector of musketry, resuming his former position as regimental capt.

92nd Foot—Ens. Henry French Cotton, from the 39th Foot, to be ens., vice Walter Sherwill Stanhope Troup, who retires.

94th Foot—Lieut. Charles Butler to be capt., by purchase, vice Osmond de Lancey Priaulx, who retires; Ens. Percival Richards to be lieut., by purchase, vice Butler; Gent.-Cadet George Robinson, from the Royal Military College, to be ens., by purchase, vice Richards

95th Foot—Ens. John French Jordan to be lieut., by purchase, vice Albert Jones, who retires; John Cuthbert Leckie, gent., to be ens, by purchase, vice Jordan.

97th Foot—Ens. Madoc Davies to be lieut., by purchase, vice Robt. Gray, who retires; Joseph Henry Jameson, gent., to be ens., by purchase, vice Davies.

100th Foot—The exchange between Lieut. Joseph Dooley, of the 100th Foot. and Lieut. Vincent Upton Langworthy, of the 7th Foot, which appeared in the *Gazette* of the 20th Feb., 1863, has been cancelled.

101st Foot—To be Ensigns—Ensigns Albert Lloyd, from Madras General List—7th June, 1861; Algernon Robert Sanderson from Madras General List—8th June, 1861; George Segundo Sewell, from Bengal General List—11th July, 1861; William Henry Browne from Bengal General List—20 October, 1861.

103rd Foot—To be Ensigns—Ensigns John Galway, from Bombay General List—27th Sept., 1860; Thomas Price, from Madras General List—7th June, 1861; Edmond George Powys Wood, from Madras General List—8th June, 1861; Andrew Harry Spencer Neill, from

Madras General List—20th Aug., 1861; Edmund Leopold Clarke, from Bengal General List—2nd Jan., 1862.

104th Foot—Lieut. Sir Atwell King Lake, Bart., to be capt., vice Francis Ingram Conway-Gordon, who retires; Ens. Robert Campbell Richardson to be lieut., vice Sir Atwell King Lake. To be Ensigns —Ensigns Lestock Walters Iredell, from Madras General List—4th Oct., 1860; William Henry Curtis Smith, from Madras General List —19th Dec., 1860; Vincent Chas. Edward Parker, from Bengal General List—8th June, 1861; Theodore Augustus Tharp, from Madras General List—8th June, 1861; Arthur Leycester Wynter, from Madras General List—20th Aug., 1861; Brodrick Hudleston, from Bengal General List—4th Dec., 1861.

106th Foot—To be Ensigns— Ensigns James Winslow, from Madras General List—20th Nov., 1860; Edmund Rogers Coker, from Madras General List—8th June, 1861; Henry Bailey, from Bengal General List—2nd Oct., 1861; Guy Golding Bird, from Madras General List—4th Jan., 1862.

107th Foot—To be Ensigns— Ensigns Edward Thorpe Rogers, from Madras General List—12th June, 1860; William Morgan Playfair, from Madras General List— 19th December, 1860; John Geo. Montague De Lair Bean, from Madras General List—19th Dec., 1860; Frederick William Nicolay, from Madras General List—8th June, 1861; Walter Cave, from Bombay General List—8th June, 1861; George William Beresford, from Bengal General List—26th Oct , 1861; Alexander Innes Shepherd, from Bengal General List— 20th December, 1861.

109th Foot—To be Ensigns— Ensigns Alexander Hayes, from Madras General List—7th June, 1861; Alfred Hercules Mayhew, from Madras General List—8th June, 1861; William Holden Webb, from Bombay General List—8th June, 1861; Richard Tabuteau Mayne, from Bengal General List

—2nd Jan., 1862; Arnold Dashwood Strettell, from Bengal General List—4th March, 1862.

### STAFF.

Lieut.-Col. and Brev.-Col. John Miller Adye, C.B., Royal Artillery, to be deputy-adjt. general to the Royal Artillery serving in the East Indies, vice Lieut.-Col. G. Moir, C.B., who resigns the appointment—23rd June.

Lieut.-Col. Henry Lynedoch Gardiner, Royal Artillery, now serving as assist.-adjt.-gen. to the Royal Artillery at Head-Quarters, in the room of Brev.-Col. Edwin Wodehouse, C.B., whose period of service has expired—1st July.

### MEDICAL DEPARTMENT.

Staff Surg. Luke Barron, M.D., having completed 20 years' full pay service, to be staff surg.-maj., under the provisions of the Royal Warrant of 1st October, 1858—7th May.

Staff Assist.-Surg. Geo. Calvert to be staff surg., vice Curtiss Martin, appointed to the 2nd West India Regiment—18th June, 1862.

### VETERINARY DEPARTMENT.

Michael Francis Healy, gent., to be act. vet.-surg , vice Daniel Maclean, promoted.

Charles Percivall, gent., to be act. vet.-surg., vice Andrew Galbraith Ross, promoted.

### BREVET.

The undermentioned officers having completed the qualifying period of service in the rank of lieut.-col., under the provisions of the Royal Warrant of 14th Oct., 1858, to be Colonels:—

Maj. and Brev.-Lieut.-Col. Colin Frederick Campbell, 46th Foot— 24th Jan.

Lieut.-Col. Henry Aimé Ouvry, C.B., half-pay, 9th Lancers, Assist.-Quartermaster-Gen. at Ceylon— 26th March.

Lieut.-Col. William Payn, C.B., 72nd Foot—22nd April.

Lieut.-Col. the Hon. Augustus George Charles Chichester, 77th Foot—16th June.

Col. Francis Claude Burnett, on the Retired Full-pay List, Royal Artillery, to be maj.-gen., the rank being honorary only—10th March.

Lieut.-Col. and Brev.-Col. Fredk. Spence, C.B., retired full-pay, 31st Foot, to have the honorary rank of maj.-gen.

Maj. and Brev.-Lieut.-Col. John Willett Payne Audain, retired full-pay, 16th Foot, to have the hon. rank of col.

Maj. Felix Augustus Victor Thurburn, retired full-pay, Bengal Staff Corps, to have the hon. rank of lieut.-col.

Deputy Inspector-Gen. of Hospitals Cornelius Clarke Linlon, retired on full-pay from Her Majesty's Indian Military Forces, to have the hon. rank of inspector-gen. of hospitals.

Deputy Inspector-Gen. John Forbes, retired on full-pay from Her Majesty's Indian Military Forces, to have the hon. rank of inspector-gen. of hospitals.

Surg.-Maj. Charles Morehead, retired on full-pay from Her Majesty's Indian Military Forces, to have the hon. rank of deputy inspector-gen. of hospitals.

Paymaster, with the hon. rank of Maj., Charles Scarlin Naylor, upon half-pay, late of the Invalid Depôt, Yarmouth, to have the hon. rank of lieut.-col.—1st June.

Paymaster Norborne Gilpin Smith, 17th Foot, to have the hon. rank of capt.—14th May.

Paymaster Augustus Bolle de Lasalle, 20th Foot, to have the hon. rank of capt.—18th May.

Paymaster James George, 92nd Foot, to have the hon. rank of capt.—21st May.

The undermentioned promotions to take place in her Majesty's Indian Military Forces, consequent on the death of Lieut.-Gen. Robert Blackall, Bengal Infantry, on the 20th April:—

Maj.-Gen. Howard Dowker, Madras Infantry, to be lieut.-gen.—21st April.

Col. George Burney, Bengal Infantry, to be maj.-gen.—21st April.

The undermentioned officers to have the local rank of lieut.-col.:—

Capt. Lewis Pelby, of the Bombay Staff, whilst filling the appointment of resident in the Persian Gulf.

Capt. Herbert Frederick Disbrowe, of the Bombay Staff Corps, whilst acting as British agent at Muscat.

Capt. Robert Lyon Playfair, of the Madras Artillery, whilst acting as British agent at Zanzibar.

———

THE VOLUNTEER GAZETTE.
WAR OFFICE, PALL MALL, June 30.

1st Shropshire Artillery Volunteer Corps—Edward Burd, M.D., to be assist.-surg.; Joseph Bayley to be hon.-assist.-surg.

19th Renfrewshire Rifle Volunteer Corps—James Wilson, gent., to be ens., vice Irvine, resigned.

Queen's (Westminster) Rifle Volunteer Corps—Capt. Joseph Wm. Bushby to be maj., vice Loch, resigned; Lieut. James Sherwood Westmacott to be capt., vice Bushby, promoted.

Memorandum—Queen's (Westminster) Rifle Volunteer Corps—The Queen has been graciously pleased to accept the resignation of the Commissions held by the following Officers; viz.: Major Henry Brougham Loch, C.B.; Capt. Herbert Henry Walford.

Memorandum—37th Middlesex Rifle Volunteer Corps—The Queen has been graciously pleased to accept the resignation of the Commission held by the following officer; viz.: Capt. Edward Sayer.

7th West Riding of Yorkshire Rifle Volunteers—Robert Gunter, Esq., late Capt. 4th Dragoon Guards, to be maj.

25th West Riding of Yorkshire Rifle Volunteers — Ens. Jasper Leavens White to be lieut., vice Baker, resigned; Arthur Robson White, gent., to be ens., vice J. L. White, promoted.

Memorandum—Her Majesty has been graciously pleased to accept the resignation of the commission held by Capt. H. Jeffreys Farrar in the 37th Kent Rifle Volunteer Corps.

12th Kent Rifle Volunteer Corps —Edward Stainton Hall, gent., to be lieut., vice Rashleigh, resigned;

William Shadbolt, gent., to be ens., vice Butler, resigned; Flaxman Spurrell, Esq., M.D., to be hon.-assist.-surg., vice Tippetts, resigned.

37th Kent Rifle Volunteer Corps —The Hon. William Archer Amherst (commonly called Lord Viscount Holmesdale) to be capt., vice Farrar, resigned; Henry Jeffreys Farrar, gent., to be lieut., vice Whitford, deceased.

[The following Appointment is substituted for that which appeared in the *Gazette* of the 5th inst. :]

23rd Norfolk Rifle Volunteer Corps—The Rev. Edward Charles King Bearcroft to be honorary chaplain.

Memorandum—Her Majesty has been graciously pleased to accept the resignation of the Commission held by First Lieut. William Hichens in the 11th Cornwall Artillery Volunteer Corps.

11th Cornwall Artillery Volunteer Corps—Sec. Lieut. William Cade to be first lieut.; Robert Snaith Hichens to be sec.-lieut.

Memorandum—1st Berwick-on-Tweed Artillery Volunteer Corps —Her Majesty has been graciously pleased to approve of Capt. Thos. Allan bearing the designation of Capt.-com.

Memorandum—3rd Argyllshire Rifle Volunteers—Her Majesty has been graciously pleased to accept the resignation of the Commission held by Assist.-Surg. John Pirie in the above corps.

———

WAR OFFICE, PALL MALL, July 3.

7th Lancashire Artillery Volunteer Corps—First Lieut. George Sinclair Robertson to be capt.

12th Lancashire Artillery Volunteer Corps—First Lieut. Robert Anderson, to be capt., Sec. Lieut. Robertson Fernie to be first lieut.; Sec. Lieut. Thomas Barnes Clarke to be first lieut.; Sec. Lieut. Thomas Couldrey to be first lieut.

2nd Lancashire Rifle Volunteer Corps—Capt. Thomas Lund to be maj.

37th A. Lancashire Rifle Volun-

teer Corps—Myles Kennedy, Esq., to be capt.

52nd Lancashire Rifle Volunteer Corps—John Henry Augustus Schneider, gent., to be lieut.

64th Lancashire Rifle Volunteer Corps—Capt. Peter Sylvester Bidwill to be maj.; Lieut. Thomas Feild to be capt.; Edmond Joseph Hore, Esq., to be capt.; Ens. John Frederick O'Donnell to be lieut.; Assist.-Surg. Daniel Walter Parsons to be surg.

80th Lancashire Rifle Volunteer Corps—Henry John Simpson, gent., to be lieut.

Memorandum—The Queen has been graciously pleased to accept the resignation of the Commissions held by the following Officers, viz.: Lieut. Roland Davies in the 1st Manchester or 6th Lancashire Rifle Volunteer Corps; and Capt. William Thomas Blacklock, in the 80th Lancashire Rifle Volunteer Corps.

26th Somersetshire Rifle Volunteer Corps—Washington Lafayette Winterbotham, gent., M.B., to be assist.-surg.

34th Cheshire Rifle Volunteer Corps—Fitzroy Somerset Cochrane, gent, to be ens., vice Hewitt, resigned.

South Middlesex Rifle Volunteer Corps—Hon. Assist.-Surg. Wm. Burke Ryan, M.D., to be assist.-surg.

48th Middlesex Rifle Volunteer Corps—James Henry Worthy to be ens.

Memorandum—29th Middlesex Rifle Volunteer Corps—Her Majesty has been pleased to signify her pleasure that Lieut. George Forbes Upward be removed from the Commission which he holds in this corps.

1st Newcastle-upon-Tyne Artillery Volunteers—Major Henry Christian Allhusen to be lieut.-col.; First Lieut. Hugh Clayton Armstrong to be capt.; First Lieut. Hugh Clayton Armstrong to be capt.; First Lieut. William George Woods to be capt.; Sec. Lieut. Ralph Hume Tweddell to be first lieut.; Sec. Lieut. Wm. Charles Ponsford to be first lieut.;

Super.-Lieut. Richard White to be first-lieut.; Charles Albert Schlesinger, gent, to be first lieut.; Matthew Wheatley Anderson, gent., to be sec.-lieut.

8th Northumberland Rifle Volunteer Corps—Lieut. R. L. Latimer to be capt.

Memorandum—The Queen has been graciously pleased to accept the resignation of the commission held by Capt. Henry Walker Kerrich in the 14th Company of Surrey Rifle Volunteers.

14th Company of Surrey Rifle Volunteers—Geo. Henry Cazalet, Esq., late Capt. 33rd Foot, to be capt., vice Kerrich, resigned.

Wiltshire Rifle Volunteers—1st Company—Wm. Pinckney, Esq., to be captain.

5th Company—William Anstie, gent., to be ens.

6th Company—The Rev. Richard Rowley to be honorary chaplain.

Memorandum—Her Majesty has been graciously pleased to accept the resignation of the commissions held by Capt. Ambrose Denis Hussey, Lieut. Edw. Dean Fisher, and Ens. Charles Brown in the 1st Wiltshire Rifle Volunteer Corps; and Capt. Charles Henry Sainsbury Pickwick in the 9th Wiltshire Rifle Volunteer Corps.

Memorandum—Her Majesty's acceptance of the resignation of the Commission held by Hon. Assist.-Surg. Oliver Calley Maurice in the 17th Wilts Rifle Volunteer Corps has been cancelled.

1st Renfrewshire Rifle Volunteer Corps—James Bruce Miller, gent., to be ens., vice Black, resigned.

9th Derbyshire Rifle Volunteer Corps—Edward Ward Fox, Esq., to be lieut., vice Thornhill, resigned.

Memorandum—Her Majesty has been graciously pleased to accept the resignation of Lieut. William Pole Thornhill in the 9th Derbyshire Rifle Volunteers.

[The following Appointment is substituted for that which appeared in the *Gazette* of the 23rd ult.]

2nd Derbyshire Rifle Volunteer Corps—Geo. John Warren, Lord Vernon, to be capt., vice Vernon, resigned.

Memorandum—Her Majesty has been graciously pleased to approve of Captain Lord Vernon bearing the title of Capt.-Comt. of this Corps.

3rd Administrative Battalion of Durham Rifle Volunteers—James George Echalaz, Esq., late Capt. 55th Foot, to be adjt., from the 1st of April.

Memorandum — Adjt. James George Echalaz, of the 3rd Administrative Battalion of Durham Rifle Volunteers, to serve with the rank of Capt.

1st Lancashire Engineer Volunteer Corps — Richard D'Oyley Fletcher, Esq., to be adjt., from the 14th of April.

---

## THE ARMY GAZETTE.

War Office, Pall Mall, July 10.

*₊* Where not otherwise specified, the following Commissions bear the current date.

1st Regiment of Dragoons—Lieut. Julius Tottenham, from the 60th Foot, to be lieut. vice Croft, who exchanges.

9th Lancers — Lieut. William Macnaghton Erskine to be capt. by purchase, vice Samuel Ashton Pretor, who retires; Cor. Perceval Clark to be lieut. by purchase, vice Erskine.

15th Hussars — Cor. William Macalpine Leny, from the 18th Hussars, to be cor. vice Martin Farrington, deceased.

16th Lancers — Lieut. Richard Fielding Morrison to be capt. by purchase, vice David Barclay, who retires; Cor. Hans Sloane-Stanley to be lieut. by purchase, vice Morrison; Augustus Croft Dobree, gent. to be cor. by purchase, vice Sloane-Stanley; Jemmett Charles Duke, gent. to be cor. by purchase, vice Henry Mitchell Jones, transferred to the 1st Dragoon Guards.

Royal Artillery—Lieut.-Col. and Brev.-Col. Thomas Beckett Fielding Marriott to be col. vice Edward Walter Crofton, C.B. deceased—27th June; Capt. and Brev.-Maj.

John Lindredge Elgee to be lieut.-col. vice Brev.-Col. Marriott—27th June; Sec. Capt. Albert Henry Wilmot Williams to be capt. vice Brev.-Lieut.-Col. John Davenport Shakespear, placed upon half-pay —19th June; Sec. Capt. William Smyth Maynard Wolfe to be capt. vice Brev.-Maj. Elgee—27th June; Lieut. Wallace Gilmour to be sec. capt. vice Williams—19th June; Lieut. Robert Preston Lewis Welch to be sec. capt. vice Wolfe—27th June.

Royal Engineers—Capt. Charles Edward Dawson Hill to be lieut.-col. vice Ouchterlony, deceased—30th April; Sec. Capt. Joseph Gore Ryves to be capt. vice Hill—30th April: Lieut. John Ord Halsted to be sec. capt. vice Balgrave, deceased — 22nd March; Lieut. Harry North Dalrymple Prendergast to be sec. capt. vice Mullens, promoted—7th April; Lieut. Frederick Augustus Howes to be sec. capt vice Ryves—30th April.

Scots Fusilier Guards—Maj. and Brev.-Col. John Hamilton Elphinstone Dalrymple to be lieut.-col. without purchase, vice Brev.-Col. Francis Seymour, C.B. who retires upon half-pay; Capt. and Lieut.-Col. and Brev. - Col. Frederick Charles Arthur Stephenson, C.B. to be maj. without purchase, vice Brev.-Col. Dalrymple; Lieut. and Capt. David Hunter Blair to be capt. and lieut.-col. by purchase, vice Brev.-Col. Stephenson; Ens. and Lieut. Henry Farquharson to be lieut. and capt. by purchase, vice Blair; Ens. George Gosling, from the 26th Foot, to be ens. and lieut. by purchase, vice Farquharson.

15th Regiment of Foot—Lieut. Robert Coupe to be capt. without purchase, vice Walter Goodwin Hrwkins, deceased — 29th May; Ens. Francis Walker Cary to be lieut. without purchase, vice Coupe —29th May.

19th Foot—Lieut. Charles James Forbes Smith has been permitted to take and use the surname of Forbes in addition to and after that of Smith.

25th Foot—Robert Stein For-

long, Esq. late Capt. 2nd Dragoons, to be paymaster, vice Thomas Smith, appointed to the 37th Foot.

27th Foot—Maj. Barclay Thomas to be lieut. col. by purchase, vice Herman Stapylton, who retires; Capt. James Henry Creagh to be maj. by purchase, vice Thomas; Lieut. George Stewart White to be capt. by purchase, vice Creagh; Ens. Cecil John Foot to be lieut. by purchase, vice White; James Walton Powell Buxton, gent. to be ens. by purchase, vice Foot.

35th Foot—Lieut. Mars Mourier Pohle to be capt. by purchase, vice M. Villiers Sankey Morton, who retires; Ens. James Johnston Twining to be lieut. by purchase, vice Pohle; Thomas Astley Maberly, gent. to be ens. by purchase, vice Twining.

36th Foot—Sur. Arthur Bell, from the 76th Foot, to be surg. vice Surg.-Maj. James Jopp, M.D. who exchanges.

37th Foot—Richard John Frederick Edgcumbe, gent. to be ens. by purchase, vice John Everard Whitting, promoted.

43rd Foot — James Thomas O'Brien, gent. to be ens. by purchase, vice Robert Barclay Allardice, transferred to the 93rd Foot.

46th Foot—Lieut. Peter Shuttleworth, from the 69th Foot, to be lieut. vice Kentish, who exchanges.

60th Foot—Lieut. James Henry Herbert Croft, from the 1st Dragoons, to be lieut. vice Tottenham, who exchanges.

69th Foot — Capt. and Brev.-Maj. George Richard Browne, from the 88th Foot, to be capt. vice Cahill, who exchanges; Lieut. Allan Joshua Kentish, from the 46th Foot, to be lieut. vice Shuttleworth, who exchanges.

70th Foot—Surg. George Cunningham Meikleham, M.D. having completed twenty years' full-pay service, to be surg.-maj. under the provisions of the Royal Warrant of the 1st October, 1858—16th June.

76th Foot—Surg.-Maj. James Jopp, M.D. from the 36th Foot, to be surg. vice Arthur Bell, who exchanges.

81st Foot—Robert Chas. Nicholetts, gent. to be ens. by purchase, vice Thomas Rogers, appointed quartermaster.

88th Foot—Capt. Patrick Cahill, from the 59th Foot, to be capt. vice Brev.-Maj. Browne, who exchanges.

93rd Foot—Ens. Edward Boase to be lieut. by purchase, vice R. K. A. Dick Cunyngham, who retires; Ens. Robert Barclay Allardice, from the 43rd Foot, to be ens. vice Boase.

Rifle Brigade — Ens. Charles Fairfield to be lieut. without purchase, vice F. William Ramsbottom, deceased, 27th June.

5th West India Regiment—The date of Capt. Prendeville's transfer from St. Helena Regiment is 1863, not 1860, as stated in *Gazette* of 23rd ultimo.

MEDICAL DEPARTMENT.

Staff-Assistant-Surgeon Henry Sacheveral Edward Schroeder, M.D. to be staff-surg. vice Augustus Morphew, appointed to the 1st West India Regiment—2nd December, 1862.

BREVET.

Capt. Augustus Hotham, half-pay unattached, to be maj.—23rd November, 1841.

Capt. and Brev.-Maj. Augustus Hotham, half-pay unattached, to be lieut.-col.—11th November, 1851.

Paymaster Mark Teversham, 16th Foot, to have the honorary rank of capt.—10th April.

The undermentioned officers, whose retirement on full-pay appeared in the *Gazette* of the 23rd June, to have the hanorary rank of maj.-gen :—

Col. Stephen Pott, Royal Engineers—31st December, 1862.

Col. Charles Edward Faber, Royal Engineers—7th April.

The undermentioned First Class Schoolmasters, to be superintending schoolmasters with the relative rank of Ens. under the provisions of the Royal Warrant of 10th May :—Joseph Barnes, John Newsom, John Little, John Grant.

Memorandum—Captain Augustus Hotham, half-pay unattached, has been permitted to retire from the Service by the sale of his Commission, under the conditions o the Horse Guards' Circular Memorandum of the 15th February, 1861.

## THE MILITIA GAZETTE.

WAR OFFICE, PALL MALL, July 3.

7th Regiment of Lancashire Militia — Lieut. John George Cooke to be capt.

90th, or Stirlingshire, &c., Highland Borderers Light Infantry Regiment of Militia—Lieut. Edgeworth Horrocks to be capt. vice Cullen, resigned.

Royal Glamorgan Light Infantry Militia — Vaughan Hanning Lee, Esq. to be capt.

WAR OFFICE, PALL MALL, July 7.

Essex Rifles Militia—Lieut. William Roberts Knobel to be capt. vice Swann, resigned; James Henry Morrell to be capt. vice Davies, resigned.

WAR OFFICE, PALL MALL, July 10.

3rd or Royal Westminster Light Infantry Regiment of Middlesex Militia—William Hewgill Kitchen to be lieut. vice Chapman, promoted; Edmund Waller to be lieut. vice McEwen resigned.

Royal Glamorgan Artillery Militia—John Heyworth, gent. to be lient.

East and North York Artillery Militia—George Sutton, Esq. to be capt. vice Grimston, promoted.

1st Royal Lanarkshire Militia—John Sommerville Marshall, gent. to be assist.-surg. vice Holt, resigned.

2nd Royal Lanarkshire Militia—Lieut. William Lefroy to be capt. vice Alston, promoted.

Queen's Own Royal Regiment of Glasgow and Lower Ward of Lanarkshire Yeomanry Cavalry—James Stirling Stirling Stuart, Esq. to be capt. vice James Merry, resigned.

King's Own Light Infantry Regiment of Militia — Edward Francis Hart, gent. to be lieut.

## THE VOLUNTEER GAZETTE.

WAR OFFICE, PALL MALL, July 7.

6th Company Shropshire Rifle

Volunteers—Robert H. Anstice, Esq., to be lieut.

3rd Dorsetshire Rifle Volunteer Corps—John Francis Hodges, jun., gent., to be ens., vice Devenish, resigned.

3rd Berwickshire Rifle Volunteer Corps—Ens. James Martin to be lieut.; Hilton Middleton to be ens.

7th Berwickshire Rifle Volunteer Corps—Robert Nicholson Slight to be lieut.; James Taylor Marshall to be ens.

Memorandum—Her Majesty has been graciously pleased to accept the resignation of the commission held by Lieut. David H. Somerville in the 3rd Berwickshire Rifle Volunteer Corps.

Memorandum—The 7th Berwickshire Rifle Volunteer Corps has been united to the 1st Administrative Battalion of Berwickshire Rifle Volunteers.

1st Gloucestershire Artillery Volunteer Corps—John Strachey Hare, gent., to be sec. lieut., vice Daubney, resigned.

16th Gloucestershire Rifle Volunteer Corps—Francis Robert Jarrat, gent., to be ens., vice Baker, promoted.

Memorandum—Her Majesty has been graciously pleased to accept the resignation of the commissions held by Lieut. Charles Sandeman and Ens. William Morphew in the 8th Kent Rifle Volunteers.

7th Kent Rifle Volunteer Corps—William Frederick Portlock Dadson, late Capt. Royal Marines, to be capt., vice Morris, resigned.

8th Kent Rifle Volunteer Corps—Ens. George William Paine to be lieut, vice Drake, resigned; Henry James Brown, gent., to be ens. vice Morphew, resigned.

37th Middlesex Rifle Volunteer Corps—Lieut. Richard Butt to be capt, vice Sayer, resigned.

5th Sussex Rifle Volunteer Corps—Lieut. William Austen Pearless to be capt., vice Wells, resigned; Ens. John Cuthbert Stenning to be lieut., vice Pearless, promoted; William Rudge to be ens., vice Stenning, promoted.

1st Manchester or 6th Lanca-

shire Rifle Volunteer Corps—Thomas Tebbutt Crompton, gent., to be lieut.

8th Lancashire Rifle Volunteer Corps—Ens. John Richard Hutchinson to be lieut.; Samuel Walker, gent.; to be ens.; Edward Scott, gent., to be ens.; Thomas Bridge Bott, Esq., M.D., to be surg.

Memoranda—Her Majesty has been graciously pleased to accept the resignation of the Commissions held by the following Officers: viz.: Capt. Samuel Sandbach Parker in the Liverpool Rifle Volunteer Brigade or 5th Lancashire Rifle Volunteer Corps; and Majs. Frank Ashton and Edw. Stanley Heywood in the 1st Manchester or 6th Lancashire Rifle Volunteer Corps.

3rd North Riding of Yorkshire Artillery Volunteer Corps—The .Rev. William Keys to be hon. chap.

Memorandum—The 11th Renfrewshire Rifle Volunteer Corps has been incorporated in the 10th Renfrewshire Rifle Volunteer Corps.

10th Renfrewshire Rifle Volunteer Corps—Lieut. Thomas Ballantyne to be capt., vice Grieve, resigned; Ens. John Erskine to be lieut., vice Ballantyne, promoted; Ens. John Kincaid to be lieut., vice Rennie, resigned; Chas. McDonald, gent., to be ens., vice Erskine, promoted; John Mailer, gent., to be ens., vice Kincaid, promoted.

2nd Essex Artillery Volunteers—The Rev. William Henry Richards to be hon. chap.

[The following Appointment is substituted for that which appeared in the *Gazette* of the 26th ult.:]

1st Brecknockshire Rifle Volunteer Corps—Wm. Rhys Brychan Powel, Esq., to be capt.

Memorandum—Her Majesty has been graciously pleased to approve of Capt William Rhys Brychan Powel bearing the designation of Capt.-Com. of the 1st Brecknockshire Rifle Volunteer Corps.

Memorandum—Her Majesty has been graciously pleased to accept the resignation of the commissions held by Capt. Thomas Calthorpe Webster and Capt. Wynne Albert Bankes in the 3rd Cambridgeshire Rifle Volunteer Corps; and also of the Commission held by Adjt. Charles Stanhope Smelt in the 1st Administrative Battalion of Cambridgeshire Rifle Volunteers.

WAR OFFICE, PALL MALL, July 10.
9th Tower Hamlets Rifle Volunteer Corps—John Frederick Shaw, gent., to be ens.

Memorandum—The 12th Tower Hamlets Rifle Volunteer Corps has been united to the 1st Administrative Battalion of Tower Hamlets Rifle Volunteers.

1st Sussex Artillery Volunteer Corps—Dr. Samuel Barker to be sec. assist.-surg.

12th or Carron Company of the Stirlingshire Rifle Volunteer Corps.—James Eason, gent., to be ens.

1st Flintshire Rifle Volunteer Corps—Humphrey Edward Owen, gent., to be ens.

Memorandum—3rd Perthshire Rifle Volunteer Corps—Her Majesty has been graciously pleased to accept the resignation of the commission held by Capt. Charles Cholmeley Hale.

3rd Perthshire Rifle Volunteer Corps—Lieut. Charles McDiarmid to be capt.; Ens. Chas. Stewart to be lieut.

Memorandum — 8th Isle of Wight Rifle Volunteers — The Queen has been graciously pleased to accept the resignation of the Commission held by Lieut. Benjamin Temple Cotton in the above corps.

8th Isle of Wight Rifle Volunteers—William Charles Plumley to be lieut., vice Cotton, resigned.

Memorandum — 2nd Cornwall Rifle Volunteer Corps—Her Majesty has been graciously pleased to accept the resignation of the Commission held in this corps by Hon. Assist.-Surg. Philip Vincent.

1st Administrative Battalion of Cornwall Rifle Volunteers—Philip Vincent to be surg.

1st Forfarshire Rifle Volunteer Corps—Lieut. William Kerr to be capt., vice Bell, resigned; Ens. Robert Overend Parker to be lieut., vice Kerr, promoted; James Rankin, gent., to be ens., vice Chalmers, resigned.

2nd Berwickshire Artillery Volunteer Corps—Andrew Oliver to be sec. lieut.

Dumfries-shire Rifle Volunteer Corps, 4th Company—George Dalziel, promoted. 5th Company—Rev. James Monilaws to be hon. chap.

Memoranda—1st Administrative Battalion of Inverness-shire Rifle Volunteers — Adjt. Charles R. Fraser to serve with the rank of Capt., from the 23rd July, 1860.

1st Administrative Battalion of East York Rifle Volunteers—10th Corps (Hedon)—Her Majesty has been graciously pleased to accept the resignation of the commission held by Lieut. Arthur Iveson and Ens. Robert Charles Metcalfe.

Memorandum—Her Majesty has been graciously pleased to accept the resignation of the commissions held by the following officers, viz:—Sec. Lieut. Edward Dreossi in the 11th Lancashire Artillery Volunteer Corps, and Capt. Edward Lees, Lieut. John Kershaw, and Lieut. John Howard in the 23rd Lancashire Rifle Volunteer Corps.

## THE ARMY GAZETTE.
*⁎* Where not otherwise specified, the following commissions bear the current date.

INDIA OFFICE, July 13.
Her Majesty has been graciously pleased to appoint Lieut.-Col. R. Lyon Playfair, of the Royal Madras Artillery, to be Her Majesty's Consul at Zanzibar; and Lieut. Col. Herbert Frederick Disbrowe, of the Bombay Staff Corps, to be Her Majesty's Consul at Muscat.

ST. JAMES'S PALACE, June 23.
The Queen has been pleased to appoint Lieut.-Col. Wm. McCall, Unattached, to be Clerk of the Cheque of Her Majesty's Honble. Corps of Gentlemen-at-Arms, vice Cargill, retired. This appointment to date from 11th June.

War Office, Pall Mall, July 17.

6th Regiment of Dragoon Guards—Lieut. William Wallace Graham to be adjt., vice Lieut. Gair, who resigns the appointment.

14th Hussars—Capt. F. Pemberton Campbell, from 83rd Foot, to be Capt., vice Mackenzie, who exchanges.

Royal Artillery—The undermentioned Gentlemen Cadets to be lieuts.:—Sisson Cooper Pratt, vice Price, promoted—24th June; W. Henry Frederick Sorell, vice Carey, promoted—24th June; F. Brinkley vice Goldingham, promoted—24th June; Alexander Walter Ferrier, vice Dyce, promoted—24th June; Samuel Stephen Bomford, vice Sconce, promoted—24th June; F. Lowry Graves, vice Layton, deceased—24th June; Gilbert Sidney Parry, vice Staveley, promoted—25th June; Francis William James Barker. vice Pechell, promoted—24th June; Henry John Rawle, vice Gilmour, promoted — 24th June; Charles Anglesea Empson, vice Welsh, promoted—27th June; Serjeant-Major Rueben Butler to be riding master, vice J. Everett, appointed Adjt. of the Depot, Royal Horse Artillery—1st July.

Royal Engineers—The undermentioned Gentlemen Cadets to be lieuts., with temporary rank:—Herbert Paget Knocker, vice Newmarch, promoted—24th June; H. Pincke Lee, vice Sandford, promoted—24th June; John Noble Mainwaring, vice Barber, resigned —24th June; Killingworth Richard Todd, vice Hasted, promoted—24th June; Francis Quintin Edmondes, vice Prendergast, promoted—24th June; William Fitz Henry Spaight, vice Jackson, removed from the army by the sentence of a general court martial—24th June; Charles Birkbeck, vice Howes promoted —24th June; William Sinclair Smith Bissett, vice Stewart, resigned—30th June; William H. Coaker, vice Stace, whose services have been dispensed with—30th June.

Military Train—Sidney Francis Austin, gent., to be ens., without purchase, vice McKenzie, promoted·

1st Regiment of Foot—Lieut. Herbert Small Janvrin, from the 64th Foot, to be lieut., vice Aglen, who exchanges.

7th Foot—Capt. James H. Patrickson, from the 21st Foot, to be capt., vice Saunders, who exchanges.

7th Foot—Gentleman Cadet T. John Raymond Mallock, from the Royal Military College, to be ens., without purchase, vice Richard S. Hall, promoted.

11th Foot—Serj.-Maj. W. Mullins to be quart.-mast., vice Daniel Deacon, deceased.

12th Foot—Lieut. John S. Richardson to be capt., by purchase, vice Edward Herrick, who retires.

15th Foot—Gentleman Cadet H. Laurence Dundas, from the Royal Military College, to be ens., without purchase, vice Lloyd Fenton, transferred to the 44th Foot; Gent. Charles William Beverley McKenzie, from the Royal Military College, to be ens., without purchase, vice Francis Walter Cary, promoted.

19th Foot—Lieut. Francis E. Biddulph to be capt., by purchase, vice John Gibsone, who retires; Ens. William Joseph Lynch to be lieut, by purchase, vice Biddulph; Gent. Cadet Alfred James Paterson, from the Royal Military College, to be ens., without purchase, vice Lynch.

20th Foot—Maj. Alexander H. Cobbe, from the 87th Foot, to be maj., vice Lyons, who exchanges.

21st Foot—Capt. Aubrey W. O. Saunders, from the 6th Foot, to be capt., vice Patrickson, who exchanges; Gent. Cadet Francis W. Hutton, from the Royal Military College, to be ens., without purchase, vice Whitton, promoted.

24th Foot—Gent. Cadet Charles Erskine, from the Royal Military College, to be ens., without purchase, vice Albert Frank Adams, promoted.

35th Foot—Lieut. Robert J. G. Grant to be capt., without purchase, vice Brev.-Maj. William R. Goate, deceased — 22nd March;

Ens. Frederick Bowdler Gipps to be lieut., without purchase, vice Grant—22nd March ; Gent. Cadet William Paul Barry Brereton, from the Royal Military College, to be ens., without purchase, vice Gipps.

36th Foot—Lieut. Redmond B. C. Daubeny, from the 69th Foot, to be lieut., vice Bond, who exchanges.

44th Foot—Gent. Cadet William Liston Dalrymple from the Royal Military College, to be ens., without purchase, vice R. R. McQueen, transferred to the 16th Foot.

50th Foot—Gent. Cadet Thomas Waring, from the Royal Military College, to be ens., without purchase, vice Richmond, promoted.

The second Christian name of Capt. Creagh is *Augustine*, not *Augustus*, as stated in the *Gazette* of the 30th June, 1863.

52nd Foot—Lieut. R. W. Ellis to be capt., by purchase, vice W. James Stopford, who retires ; Ens. Henry Frederick Barker to be lieut., by purchase, vice Ellis ; Ens. Francis Edward Dowler to be lieut. by purchase, vice Henry Richard Beattie, who retires ; Ens. Robert William Blackwood, from the 96th Foot, to be ens., vice Barker ; Gent. Cadet W. A. F. Blakeney, from the Royal Military College to be ens., without purchase, vice Dowler.

59th Foot—Lieut. Launcelot C. Brown to be capt., by purchase, vice Charles Hotham, who retires ; Ens Patrick Chalmers to be lieut , by purchase, vice Brown ; James George Bruce, gent., to be ens., by purchase, vice Chalmers.

60th Foot—Lieut. William H. Moseley, to be adjt., vice Lieut. James Arthur Morrah, promoted ; Lieut. Astley Fellowes Terry to be adjt., vice Lieut. James Forbes, who has retired.

64th Foot—Lieut. Artemas T. Aglen, from the 1st Foot to be lieut., vice Janvrin, who exchanges ; Ens. John Gee to be lieut., by purchase, vice Arthur R. Alston, who retires ; Robert Barlow Manning, gent., to be ens., by purchase, vice Gee.

69th Foot—Lieut. E. S. Bond from the 36th Foot, to be lieut., vice Daubeny, who exchanges.

82nd Foot—Gent. Cadet James Bird Hutchinson, from the Royal Military College, to be ens, without purchase, vice Charles Neville, promoted.

83rd Foot—Capt. Lawrence Mackenzie, from the 14th Hussars, to be capt., receiving a portion of the former difference between Cavalry and Infantry, vice Campbell, who exchanges ; Gent. Cadet Raymond Oliver De Montmorency, from the Royal Military College, to be ens , without purchase, in succession to Lieut. Brymer, deceased.

87th Foot—Maj. Thomas Casey Lyons, from the 20th Foot, to be maj., vice Cobbe, who exchanges.

96th Foot—Gent. William Newbigging, from the Royal Military College, to be ens., by purchase, vice Robert William Blackwood, transferred to the 52nd Foot.

104th Foot—Gent. Cadet Stanley Napier Roberts, from the Royal Military College, to be ens., vice Robert Campbell Richardson, promoted.

109th Foot—The name of the Ens. transferred from the Madras General List is *Hoyes*, not *Hayes*, as stated in the *Gazette* of 30th June,

UNATTACHED.

The promotion of Brev.-Col. C. Rochfort Scott to an unattached Majority, which appeared in the *Gazette* of 2nd July, 1861, to bear date 17th April, 1857, the date of his appointment as Lieutenant-Governor of the Royal Military College, Sandhurst, the ante-date not to carry back pay.

BREVET.

Captain Henry Chad Cattley, Bengal Staff Corps, to be maj.—21st March.

Paymaster with the honorary rank of capt., Francis William Fellows, 8th Foot, to have the honorary rank of Major—3rd June.

Paymaster John Christopher V. Minnett, 14th Foot, to have the honorary rank of Capt —19th Mar.

Paymaster Robert C. Streatfeild, 60th Foot, to have the honorary rank of Captain— 8th June.

The name of Captain Lewis

*Pelly* was erroneously spelt *Pelby* in *Gazette* of 30th ult., on being granted the local rank of Lieut.-Colonel.

THE MILITIA GAZETTE.
WAR OFFICE, PALL MALL, July 14.

Argyll and Bute Artillery Militia—Charles MacQuarrie, gent, late First Lieut. Argyll and Bute Artillery Militia, to be quartermaster.

Stirlingshire, &c., Militia or Highland Borderers—Walter H. Erskine to be capt., vice John Crawfurd Tait, resigned.

Memorandum—Her Majesty has been graciously pleased to accept the resignation of the Commission held by Maj. Geo. Francis Stuart in the 2nd Regt. of Royal Cheshire Militia.

WAR OFFICE, PALL MALL, July 17,

East and North Yorkshire Artillery Militia—Yarborough Geo. Lloyd, gent., to be first lieut.

90th or Stirlingshire and Dunbartonshire, &c., Regt. of N.B. Militia—(Highland Borderers)—Arthur Archibald Deane Weigale, gent., to be lieut., vice Geo. Scott, resigned.

Royal London Militia—Lieut. George Thomas Oldfield to be capt., vice James Bunce Curling, deceased; Lieut. Thomas Waterman the younger to be capt., vice Augustus Henry Garland, resigned.

1st Regt. of Royal Surrey Militia—Lieut. Augustus Barrington Godbold to be capt., vice Boulcott, resigned.

THE VOLUNTEER GAZETTE.
WAR OFFICE, PALL MALL, July 14.

1st Bute Artillery Volunteer Corps—First Lieut. Charles Fellowes Maclachlan to be capt.; Sec. Lieut John MacKirdy to be first lieut., vice Maclachlan, promoted; Hon. Assist.-Surg. William Paterson, M.D., to be assist.-surg.

Memorandum—Her Majesty has been graciously pleased to approve of Capt. Christopher Domvile Savage to be capt.-comt. of the 1st Bute Artillery Volunteer Corps.

7th Company of Leicestershire Rifle Volunteers — John Bohun Chandler Fox, gent., to be ens.

3rd Durham Rifle Volunteer Corps—Ens. John Marsters to be lieut.; Ens. Henry Dixon to be lieut.; William Lewis Dobinson to be ens.; Charles Holloway Reed to be ens.; Robert Taylor to be ens.

1st Administrative Battalion of East York Rifle Volunteers, 10th Corps (Hedon)—Arthur Iveson, Jun , Esq., to be lieut., vice Iveson, resigned; Godfrey Richard Park, Esq., to be ens., vice Metcalfe, resigned.

Isle of Man Rifle Volunteer Corps—William Douglas Scott to be major commanding the several Volunteer Corps in the Isle of Man, vice Paynton Pigott S. Conant, resigned.

3rd Isle of Man Rifle Volunteer Corps—Lieut. John Aspinall to be capt., vice Hall, resigned; Walter C. Lucas to be lieut., vice Aspinall, promoted; John Kneale to be ens., vice Nicholson, resigned.

Memorandum — 2nd Lincolnshire Rifle Volunteer Corps—Her Majesty has been graciously pleased to accept the resignation of the Commission held by Capt. William Henry Smyth.

1st Administrative Battalion Lincolnshire Rifle Volunteers—Wm. Henry Smith, Esq., to be maj., vice Amcotts, promoted.

2nd Lincolnshire Artillery Volunteers—First Lieut. James Edwards to be capt., vice Long, resigned; Sec. Lieut. James Reed to be first lieut., vice Edwards, promoted; Edward Bannister, gent., to be sec. lieut., vice Reed, promoted.

3rd Lincolnshire Rifle Volunteer Corps — Hugh Arthur Henry Cholmeley, Esq., to be capt., vice Parker, resigned.

15th Lincolnshire Rifle Volunteer Corps—Henry Lamden, gent., to be hon. assist.-surg., vice Bromley, deceased.

Memorandum—Her Majesty has been graciously pleased to accept the resignation of the Commissions held by Capt. Anthony B. Pike and

Sec. Lieut. Edward J. Miller in the 14th Kent Artillery Volunteer Corps.

12th Kent Artillery Volunteer Corps—Thomas Edward Fraser Seabrook, Esq. M.D. to be hon. assist.-surg. vice Martin, deceased.

Memorandum—Her Majesty has been graciously pleased to accept the resignation of the Commission held by Hon. Chap. the Rev. Alexander Webster in the 3rd Cumberland Rifle Volunteer Corps.

10th Cumberland Rifle Volunteers — Alfred Hodgetts to be lieut.

2nd West Riding of Yorkshire Engineer Volunteer Corps — Laurence Walker, gent. to be super. lieut.

1st Administrative Battalion of West Riding of Yorkshire Rifle Volunteers—William Dalla Husband, Esq. to be surg. vice Paley, resigned.

4th West Riding of Yorkshire Rifle Volunteer Corps — Lieut. Francis Robert Sowerby to be capt. vice Sutcliffe, resigned; Ens. Mark Henry Drury to be lieut.; John Edwards Hill, gent. to be ens. vice Sunderland, deceased; Henry Akroyd Ridgway, gent. to be ens. vice Edgar, promoted; John Emmett, gent. to be ens. vice Drury, promoted.

7th West Riding of Yorkshire Rifle Volunteer Corps—Ens. William Walter Lupton to be lieut. vice Smeeton, deceased.

39th West Riding of Yorkshire Rifle Volunteer Corps — Richard Edwin Ruffe, gent. to be hon. assist.-surg.

Memoranda—Her Majesty has been graciously pleased to accept the resignation of the Commissions held by the following officers:

3rd West Riding of Yorkshire Rifle Volunteer Corps — Ensign Joseph Smith.

4th West Riding of Yorkshire Rifle Volunteer Corps—Capt. John Crossley Sutcliffe.

Memorandum — The 1st West Riding of Yorkshire Engineer Volunteer Corps has been attached to the 2nd West Riding of Yorkshire Engineer Volunteer Corps for administrative purposes.

Memorandum — The 35th and 39th West Riding of Yorkshire Rifle Volunteer Corps have been attached to the 3rd West Riding of Yorkshire Vol. Corps for administrative purposes.

13th Worcestershire Rifle Volunteer Corps — Francis Knipe, gent. to be ens. vice Gustard, promoted.

Staffordshire Rifle Volunteers—1st Administrative Battalion, 37th Corps—The Rev. George Mather, M.A. to be hon. chap.; Titus Deville, Esq. M.D. to be hon. assist.-surg.

2nd Administrative Battalion, 25th Corps — Ens. Joseph Jones Heath to be capt.

3rd Administrative Battalion, 18th Corps—Lieut. Joseph Pearson to be capt. vice Mathews, resigned.

20th Corps—Ens. Edwin Luther Bullock to be lieut. vice Hooper, resigned; Henry Jesson, gent. to be ens. vice Bullock, promoted.

4th Administrative Battalion, 5th Corps—Ens. Bernard Peard Walker to be lieut. vice Clark, resigned; J. E. Underhill, gent. to be ens. vice Walker, promoted.

11th Corps—William Roberts, gent. to be ens. vice Ward, resigned.

12th Corps — Edward Gibbs, Esq. to be capt. vice Bagnall, resigned; John Edmund Fellows to be ens. vice Best, resigned.

29th Corps—John Lister Murcott, gent. to be lieut. vice Gibbs, resigned; Walter Gibbs, gent. to be ens. vice Lewis, resigned.

[The following Appointment is substituted for that which appeared in the Gazette of the 12th May last.]

6th Staffordshire Rifle Volunteer Corps—John Ward, gent. to be ens. vice Ford, resigned.

Memorandum—Her Majesty has been graciously pleased to accept the resignation of the Commission held by Ens. William Bailley Partridge in the 5th Monmouthshire Rifle Volunteer Corps.

Memorandum—Her Majesty has been graciously pleased to accept the resignation of the Commission held by Sec. Lieut. William Clark in the 1st Forfarshire. Artillery Volunteer Corps.

Memorandum—The 77th Lancashire Rifle Volunteer Corps having been struck out of the records of the War Office, will henceforth cease to hold any number or designation in the Volunteer Force, and the services of Capt. John Knight and Lieut. James Hallows in that Corps have accordingly been dispensed with by Her Majesty.

Memorandum—Her Majesty has been graciously pleased to accept the resignation of the Commission held by Ens. Jacob Wilson Fair in the 29th Lancashire Rifle Volunteer Corps.

---

WAR OFFICE, PALL MALL, July 17.

34th West Riding of Yorkshire (Saddleworth) Rifle Volunteer Corps—Capt. Francis Frederick Whitehead to be maj.; Lieut. Joshua Hirst to be capt.; Lieut. Thomas Wrigley to capt; Ens. George Frederick Buckley to be lieut; Ens. Arthur Hirst to be lieut; John Edward Dowse, gent., to be ens.; Charles Kershaw Hilton, gent., to be ens.; Assist.-Surg. Beckett Bradbury to be surg.

Memorandum—Her Majesty has been graciously pleased to accept the resignation of the commissions held by Capt. John Wells and Ens. Thomas Clough in the 28th West Riding of Yorkshire Rifle Volunteer Corps.

7th Northamptonshire Rifle Volunteer Corps—Richard William Sherwood, gent., to be lieut, vice George Hodson Burnham, promoted; William Alfred Rubbra, gent., to be ens., vice William Wake Clarke, resigned.

Memorandum—Her Majesty has been graciously pleased to accept the resignation of the commission held by Lieut. W. H. Lanyon in the 21st Cornwall Rifle Volunteer Corps.

21st Cornwall Rifle Volunteer Corps—Ens. George Appleby Jenkins to be lieut.

Linlithgow Company or 1st Linlithgowshire Rifle Volunteers—Dr. Robert Spence to be assist.-surg., vice Gilmour, promoted.

14th Kent Artillery Volunteer Corps—First Lieut. Edward Montague Browne to be capt., vice Chaplain, resigned; First Lieut. Andrew Purvis to be capt., vice Pike, resigned; Sec. Lieut. George Tomlinson to be first lieut., vice Browne, promoted; Sec. Lieut. Joseph Prowse to be first lieut., vice Purvis, promoted.

1st Middlesex Artillery Volunteer Corps—Super. Sec. Lieut. John Wilson Pillans to be sec. lieut.; William Compton Smith to be super. sec. lieut., vice Pillans, promoted.

Queen's (Westminster) Rifle Volunteer Corps—William Frederick Higgins to be lieut., vice Westmacott, promoted.

36th Middlesex Rifle Volunteer Corps—Jonathan Potter to be ens.

1st Sussex Rifle Volunteer Corps —A George Field to be surg.; the Rev H. H. Wyatt to be hon. chap.

23rd Norfolk Rifle Volunteer Corps—George William Mills to be ens.

2nd Hampshire Artillery Volunteer Corps—Sec. Lieut. Timothy White to be first lieut., vice Houghton, resigned; Sec. Lieut. Andrew Lockie to be first lieut., vice Besant, resigned.

1st Derbyshire Mounted Rifle Volunteer Corps—Mr. Geo. Bower Thorpe to be hon. assist.-surg.; Mr. James Martin to be hon. vet.-surg.

Retford or 2nd Nottinghamshire Rifle Volunteer Corps—John Dick Atkins Burnaby, gent., to be ens.

Memorandum—5th Warwickshire (Stratford-on-Avon) Rifle Volunteer Corps—Her Majesty has been graciously pleased to accept the resignation of the commission held by Ens. W. H. Hunt.

Memorandum—2nd Midlothian Artillery Volunteer Corps—Her Majesty has been graciously pleased to accept the resignation of the commission held by Capt. Leybourne Watson in this corps.

Memorandum—4th Forfarshire Artillery Volunteer Corps—Her

Majesty has been graciously pleased to accept the resignation of the commission held by Capt. Henry Gourlay in the above corps.

Memorandum—Her Majesty has been graciously pleased to accept the resignation of the commission held by Ens. Gerald Upcher in the 3rd Cambridgshire Rifle Volunteer Corps.

Memorandum—The 49th Lancashire Rifle Volunteer Corps has been attached to the 9th Lancashire Rifle Volunteer Corps for Administrative purposes.

Memorandum—Her Majesty has been graciously pleased to accept the resignation of the commission held by Ens. Charles Henry Taylor in the 11th Lancashire Rifle Volunteer Corps.

# COLBURN'S

# UNITED SERVICE MAGAZINE

AND

## NAVAL AND MILITARY JOURNAL.

No. CCCCXXVI.—MAY, 1864.

## CONTENTS.

LONDON:

## HURST AND BLACKETT, PUBLISHERS,

SUCCESSORS TO HENRY COLBURN,

13, GREAT MARLBOROUGH STREET.

SOLD ALSO BY BELL AND BRADFUTE, EDINBURGH; M'GLASHAN AND GILL,

DUBLIN; AND ALL BOOKSELLERS.

## NEW PUBLICATIONS.

**Court and Society from Elizabeth to Anne.** Edited from the Papers at Kimbolton. By the DUKE OF MANCHESTER. SECOND EDITION REVISED. 2 vols. 8vo. with Portraits. 30s.

*From the Times.*—"These volumes are sure to excite curiosity. A great deal of interesting matter is here collected, from sources which are not within everybody's reach. The light now thrown on the story of Queen Catherine will interest every reader."

*From the Post.*—"The public are indebted to the noble author for many important documents otherwise inaccessible, as well as for the lively, picturesque, and piquant sketches of Court and Society which render his work powerfully attractive to the general reader."

*From the Daily News.*—"The merits of the Duke of Manchester's work are numerous. The substance of the book is new; it ranges over by far the most interesting and important period of our history: it combines, in its notice of men and things, infinite variety; and the author has the command of a good style—graceful, free, and graphic."

**William Shakspeare.** By VICTOR HUGO. Authorized English Edition. 1 vol. 8vo. 12s. (Just Ready.)

**Reminiscences of the Opera.** By BENJAMIN LUMLEY, Twenty Years Director of Her Majesty's Theatre. 1 vol. 8vo. 15s. (In May.)

**My Life and Recollections.** By the Hon. GRANTLEY F. BERKELEY. 2 vols. 8vo. with Portrait. 30s. (Just ready.)

**The Life of the Rev. Edward Irving.** Illustrated by HIS JOURNAL and CORRESPONDENCE. By MRS. OLIPHANT. THIRD AND CHEAPER EDITION REVISED. 1 vol. with Portrait 9s. bound.

**Memoirs of Queen Hortense, Mother of Napoleon III.** NEW and CHEAPER EDITION, 1 vol. with Portrait, 6s.

**A Personal Narrative of Thirteen Years' Service among** THE WILD TRIBES OF KHONDISTAN, FOR THE SUPPRESSION OF HUMAN SACRIFICE. By MAJOR-GENERAL JOHN CAMPBELL, C.B. 1 vol. with Illustrations. 14s.

**A Young Artist's Life.** 1 vol. crown 8vo. 10s. 6d.

**Memoirs of Jane Cameron, Female Convict.** By A PRISON MATRON. Author of "Female Life in Prison." 2 vols. 21s.

**The Destiny of Nations, as Indicated in Prophecy.** By the Rev. JOHN CUMMING, D.D. 1 vol. 7s. 6d.

**Travels and Adventures of an Officer's Wife in India, China,** AND NEW ZEALAND. By MRS. MUTER, Wife of LIEUT.-COLONEL D. D. MUTER, 13th (Prince Albert's) Light Infantry. 2 vols. 21s.

**Travels on Horseback in Mantchu Tartary:** being a Summer's Ride beyond the GREAT WALL OF CHINA. By GEORGE FLEMING, Military Train. Royal 8vo. with Map and 50 Illustrations. Handsomely bound.

**Cheap Edition of "Les Miserables."** By VICTOR HUGO. Authorized English Translation. Illustrated by Millais. 5s. bound, forming the New Volume of HURST AND BLACKETT'S STANDARD LIBRARY OF POPULAR MODERN WORKS.

## THE NEW AND POPULAR NOVELS.

**Janita's Cross.** By the Author of "St. Olaves." 3 vols.

**Adela Cathcart.** By GEORGE MACDONALD, M.A. Author of "David Elginbrod," &c. 3 vols.

**Dr. Jacob.** By the Author of "John and I." 3 vols.
"There is much freshness and originality about this book."—Saturday Review.

**My Stepfather's Home.** By LADY BLAKE. 3 vols.

**Barbara's History.** By AMELIA B. EDWARDS. SECOND EDITION.
"It is not often that we light upon a new novel of so much merit and interest as 'Barbara's History.' It is a very graceful and charming book which the world will like."—Times.

**Rathlynn.** By the Author of "The Saxon in Ireland." 3 v.

**Peculiar.** A TALE OF THE GREAT TRANSITION. EDITED BY WILLIAM HOWITT. 3 vols.

*John Greswold.* By the Author of "Paul Ferroll." 2 vols. (In May.)

*Not Dead Yet.* By J. C. JEAFFRESON, Author of "Live it Down," &c. 3 vols. (In May.)

# COLBURN'S
# UNITED SERVICE MAGAZINE.

## RE-ENLISTMENT OF TIME-EXPIRED MEN.

The question of standing armies can hardly be called a question of this century. Our wildest economists, the staunchest adherents of our Manchester school, will scarcely proclaim the doctrines of the seventeenth century on this point. In their opinion a standing army is a standing nuisance; but its removal at present is about as probable as the abolition of the income tax, or the payment of our national debt. Every succeeding Spring we have the usual discussion on the Army estimates, the usual proposition to reduce the army by 10,000 men, and the usual multiplicity of questions, characterised, we regret to say, as much by want of information on the points they moot, as by praiseworthy zeal on the part of the inquirers. It would be unfair to say, that the military element is not represented in our House of Commons, but it is no disparagement to our parliamentary colonels to say, that however great the opportunity they have of calling the public attention to army matters, the very position that gives them that opportunity, prevents them from being fully cognisant of the grievances they wish to expose. This state of feeling about the army is re-produced on a grander scale among the nation at large. The British public cannot be said to be up in military matters. They know that they have an army, but they don't see much of it; they deem it a somewhat expensive luxury, and though pretty well convinced that it is anything but a perfect machine, have very little idea of its defects and grievances.

The national welfare of the soldier, his moral and physical improvement, and the efficiency of the army in general, are questions that cannot but gain by being brought more prominently before public opinion. We plead guilty to a certain degree of professional vanity, but while we maintain that certain matters are beyond the cognisance of the uninitiated, we think that others must benefit by the light thrown on them, from whatever quarter it comes.

At present our ideas of efficiency are generally connected, perhaps too closely, in the head of that unhappy mortal—the tax payer, with the idea of an immediate expenditure of £ s. d. Our military system somewhat resembles the style of life of a man, who having an income of £10,000, lives at the rate of £100,000 a year for the first three months, and then breaks up his household, and retires with his housekeeper to a cottage in the corner of his park. By some misfortune we get involved in war ; nothing is too dear for us, we lavish money in a hundred ways ; subsidise any number of foreign legions, and do not grudge the expense, whether profitable or not.   Do we revert to peace again, there is nothing but reduction talked about, and to save an outlay of a few thousands, we lay ourselves open to an expenditure of some millions.

It would be absurd to deny that a great deal has been done for the army since the Crimean War, but we can scarcely allow that the problem of efficiency has been solved.   It is an unquestionable fact, that we have not yet military resources in proportion to the population, wealth, and what has hitherto been the political position of these isles.   Far be it from us to wish to bring England to the position of a continental military power.   Those countries have, to recruit their armies, the immense resource of the conscription, and it has been, and we hope long will be the boast of our country, that she is wealthy enough, not to throw such a burden on the shoulders of her poorer classes.   A great and immediate danger would alone justify such a measure.   What we mean is, that at the present moment, should we be obliged to send an army into the field, we have scarcely 30,000 men available for that object, and that great difficulty would be found in keeping up their numbers.   In time of need we cannot recruit our forces fast enough, and in time of peace we cannot keep the men we have already.   The truth is, the service is not popular enough.   It has risen, we believe, in public opinion during the last few years, but still our soldiers are not respected and looked up to as they should be.   Our men, after serving ten or twelve years, and having had time, as we should think, to get attached to the service, leave it in vast numbers, and prefer the immediate advantages of a civil life to the ulterior but solid bonus of a pension.   We have seen men, the very day they completed their limited service, shave off their moustache, and buy a seedy suit of plain clothes.   We wish to call the reader's attention more particularly to this latter question, the one of limited enlistment, and must plead the importance of the subject as an excuse for the prolixity of our arguments.

Let us try and examine this question in all its phases, and in doing so let us suit ourselves to the spirit of the age, and attempt to look upon it in purely a financial light.   What is the value of the article we wish to secure ?   What is the price we offer for it ?   Is that price sufficient ?   If not, what ought we to give ?   And could that increased price, whatever it is, be paid without bringing on the country an increase of expenditure, for which it would not be prepared.   These are the points we wish to bring before the public, and the problems we will attempt to solve.

Everybody who has had the slightest thing to do with the army, knows that while it takes two or three years for a cavalry soldier, and four or five for an artilleryman to learn his work thoroughly, a real disciplined soldier, whatever corps he belongs to, cannot be made under two or even three years. We may safely assert, that in the total term of twenty-one years' service, the best are from the fifth to the seventeenth, or thereabouts. A man when he has completed ten years' service, is, so to speak, in the very prime of his usefulness. The mere fact of his having served so long in our ranks, proves that he has fulfilled certain conditions of health and good behaviour, which we can only expect in a certain proportion of the men who join our army. He has been under examination, as it were, for ten long years. We can form a fair estimate of his merits and demerits; and if we take him into our service again, we admit that he has passed the ordeal successfully. But why enlarge on such a theme? We think everybody will allow us to take for granted his superiority in points of character and discipline, but as regards his more advanced age, will he not be considered inferior to his younger comrade? Few of these ten years' men will be under twenty-eight, and the greater part will vary from twenty-eight to thirty-six. Now according to the sanitary report for 1861, the mortality among the great bulk of the British Army serving at home, in the Mediterranean, North America, West Indies, Cape, Mauritius, New Zealand, Australia, Madras, and Bombay, showed the following progressive rate according to age:—

| | |
|---|---|
| under 20 . . . . | 4·3 per 1,000. |
| 20-24 . . . . | 9·16 |
| 25-29 . . . . | 13·46 |
| 30-34 . . . . | 19·38 |
| over 40 . . . . | 28·67 |

From this it would appear, that were we to take our ten years' men into the service again, we must expect a greater mortality among them than among the recruits, who otherwise would have to fill their places. These returns are of course for a year of peace. Let us turn to the report on the sanitary condition of the army in the Crimea, and we shall find a very different result. The mortality from disease alone in the East during the period ending March 1855 and so including the time of the greatest exposure and hardships is given as follows:

| | |
|---|---|
| under 21. | 34 per 100 |
| 21 to 25 | 27.5 ,, |
| 25 „ 30 | 23 |
| 30 „ 35 | 27 |
| 35 „ 40 | 43 |
| 40 and upwards | 68 .. |

During the whole of the war it was

| | |
|---|---|
| under 21 | 29 per 100 |
| 21 to 25 | 22 ,, |
| 25 „ 30 | 21 |
| 34 „ 35 | 27 |
| 35 „ 40 | 47 .. |
| 40 and upwards | 44 ,, |

B 2

In considering these returns, we must remember, that the great bulk of the young soldiers came out in the spring and summer of '55, when the great hardships were over and when the army generally was incomparably healthier than during the preceding twelve months. The returns were procured from some regiments, who had formed part of the expeditionary force from the beginning and perhaps the numbers in the ages above 35 were too limited, to ensure very accurate results. We have also before us a report furnished by the surgeon of the Scots Fusilier Guards, by which it appears, that of the soldiers, who left home with the head-quarters of the battalion 44.100 died during the campaign; out of a draft of younger soldiers, who joined in July 1854 49.100 died; while out of a second lot of very young recruits, who arrived in the Crimea in November 1854, 68 3.100 were lost. A third arrival composed of older materials, which disembarked in December 1854 under more favourable conditions, probably when the Guards were moved to Balaklava, only showed a mortality of 26 6.100. Judging from these facts and from the universal complaints of the regimental surgeons as to the physical inefficiency of the recruits, who were sent out in the winter of 1854, the authors of the report above cited, come to the conclusion, that 25 to 30 is the best age for the soldier of an army in the field, and that next to this period come the years immediately preceding and immediately following it. We may safely say, therefore, that while under ordinary circumstances amongst soldiers as amongst the civil population at large, the rate of mortality increases with age, when we come to the exposure and hardships of a campaign, the fully developed man has much greater powers of resistance than his younger comrade. In the soldier we wish to re-enlist, we have therefore better average character, greater experience in the work and drill of the service, more pliancy to discipline and more endurance, than we can expect to find in the recruit who would have to fill his place.

What price do we offer for this article, the superiority of which we have attempted to prove? Exactly the same as for the inferior one. We give the same to the recruit on whom we have not spent a shilling, and to the old soldier on whose education and improvement we have expended a considerable sum. The recruit and the ten years' soldier are alike tempted to enlist by a bounty varying from £1 to £3 and a free kit differing in value according to the corps; the only advantage the latter possesses, is that should his kit be in good order, in lieu of a fresh one, he receives an allowance in money of £2 to £5. In fact the only inducements the ten years' man has to re-enlist, are the immediate bonus of a bounty of some £3 to £6, and the less remote prospect of pension at the end of his service. The pay given to the recruit of two days and to the old soldier of ten years' service is exactly the same; good conduct pay, which is supposed to be a reward for long service combined with good behaviour, is subject to so many conditions and so much affected by the interior economy and mode of punishment in different regiments, that it is anything but a certainty even for the generally well behaved man to obtain it. We will venture to say, that not half the men, who have completed their first term of service and who would be allowed to re-enlist, are in the receipt of the extra pay their service would entitle them to. In point of pay therefore, to a large proportion of our old soldiers, a second term of service offers no advantages; the prospect of pension- is too distant, we are afraid, to have much weight with a young man of 28 or 30, who scarcely knows whether he will live to enjoy it; there remains but the bounty, the attractions of which will depend very much on the position and feelings of the recipient. The recruit and the old soldier are placed in very different circumstances; the one is often starving, generally in difficulties of some sort or other, is perhaps attracted by the pomp and circumstance of war and is utterly unacquainted with the dark side of the picture; the other on the contrary is not in want, has had his illusions dispelled long ago, and is quite familiar with all the drawbacks of a military existence. The wish for change, which in one case may impel the recruit towards the service, will act with exactly opposite effect on the old soldier. And yet to these two men we offer the very same bait and one too, which is not calculated to have the same influence on the experienced man as on his rawer comrade. The old soldier, however anxious he may be to obtain so large a sum as the bounty offered, knows right well its real value and how long it will last him. The decision he has to make is not a hurried one and is in no way influenced by the flesh pots of a recruiting tavern, but one, that he has long matured and probably often discussed before the prejudiced and grumbling audience of a barrack room. Can we wonder at the results obtained hitherto? The proportion of ten years' men re-enlisting has diminished from nearly ⅔ of the whole as it was at first, to, we are informed less than half, and of these a large number change their regiments and so deprive us of one of the great advantages their re-enlistment would give. This year, in '65, '67, and '68 a large proportion of our soldiers will have completed their first term of service, and we are afraid that the greater the number entitled to their discharge, the greater will be the proportion of men who will leave our ranks. Discontent is a very contagious disease, as the sad experience of the white Mutiny in India ought not to tell us in vain.

We have now reached the most difficult point in our task; it is comparatively easy to point out the faults in our present system; they are far too evident not to strike the eye of even the superficial observer. We have now to find a remedy, and in the course of our search for it we must steer clear of that reef, so dangerous to all army reformers, increased expenditure. It is possible, that

in course of years, the army may reach that utopian state, when
desertion will be unknown, and when every time-expired man will
be only too glad to re-enter our ranks. At present, however, we
are afraid the service has not sufficient charms in itself to dispense
with some extraordinary inducements. Hitherto we have appealed
to the soldier's love of money and of the immediate pleasures it
procures; were we to attack his vanity and acquisitiveness combined,
would there not be a greater chance of success? Could not we
substitute a small increase of pay for the large bounty we give
at present? The latter is a mere premium to drunkenness and
immorality, the former would present a solid and durable advantage
and considerably improve the social as well as the financial position
of the old soldier, by putting him on a superior footing to the
recruit. And here we would meet the objection, that soldiers are
too short sighted not to prefer the immediate possession of a certain sum of money to the enjoyment of a far greater sum, scattered
in small daily fragments over a certain number of years. We maintain on the contrary, that most men will prefer the latter method,
simply from the knowledge, which however improvident, they cannot help having, that in the first case they can obtain but a very
temporary advantage, while in the other the results will last them
as long as they are in the army. After all, anybody who has seen
our soldiers at the important operation of signing accounts, will
allow that he is quite capable of calculating the difference between
say 2d. a day for 9 or 10 years and £4 or £5 down. Finally, what
better proof do we require of the non-success of the present bounty
system and its want of attraction for the old soldier, than the fact
that a great many men leave their regiments and re-enlist afterwards
in another corps, for what is necessarily a much smaller pecuniary
advantage. We do not say, that a higher rate of bounty would
not produce results, but we firmly believe these results could
be obtained in the way we have proposed, with more profit to
the receiver and with more credit to the giver. Let us picture to
ourselves the scenes so prejudicial to good order and discipline,
that might be enacted were some 50 or 60 men of the same regiment to become entitled to and receive a large bounty of £5 or £6 on
the same day. Could we punish the offenders for falling into the
very temptations we have purposely exposed them to? The feeling
to which we would appeal, instead of coming under the head of
one of the grossest kinds of acquisitiveness, will deserve the better
and nobler name of "desire to improve one's condition." Vanity
in its different shades is also far less objectionable, and this we
would satisfy or at least attempt to do so, by giving our veteran
a few little advantages, to which surely his superior worth would
entitle him. Why should the old soldier, for instance, be subjected
to exactly the same course and amount of drill as his younger
comrade? Why should he be annoyed by a weekly inspection of
necessaries? Why should he not have some extra indulgences

in the matter of leave? and above all why should he not carry on his uniform some distinguishing mark, showing that he is serving his second term of service? We may depend upon it, our old soldier would be quite sensible of these little distinctions. His position would be envied by his younger companions in arms and from this feeling of envy, that of higher estimation would be inseparable.

What we would suggest, would be something of this sort. At present we believe, the soldier on re-enlisting receives on an average about £5. 5s. 0d.; we would leave him a small bounty of say £2. This and his travelling allowance of £1 would give him the means of enjoying his two months furlough; there is no doubt, one of the great reasons that prevent the soldier from re-enlisting is his love of change, and this natural feeling we must try to satisfy to the best of our power. The remaining sum of £3. 5s. we would abolish, and substitute for it an increase of pay of 2d. per diem, to be granted only on immediate re-enlistment in the same corps or regiment, and liable to forfeiture only on conviction of certain offences by a court-martial. It is needless to remark on the benefit such an increase would be to the soldier, when we consider that the daily sum irrespective of conduct pay, he has to spend, varies from 2½d. to 4d. according to the different branches of the army. Good conduct pay as it exists, at present, we would not interfere with. Finally we cannot help thinking, that were the first term of service made 12 years for the whole army, as it is at present for the Artillery and Cavalry, that alone would be productive of good results on the re-enlistment question. The soldier would then have served more than half his time, and the thoughts of pension might have a little more weight than under the present circumstances. The expense of additional pay would be diminished, and we should avoid the difficulty that a different term of service in the various branches of the army must throw in our way, were we to grant this boon to the re-enlisted soldier.

We have now to consider the financial question, and we venture to assert that the proposed improvement, instead of causing increased expenditure, will in the long run be productive of considerable saving to the public. It will be first necessary to arrive at the number of men who could be re-enlisted, and so might become entitled to increased pay. We find that during the last 15 years ('47—'61 inclusive) between 290,000 and 300,000 men have joined our ranks, thus showing a yearly average of 20,000 recruits, and we may assume that this supply would be sufficient to keep our forces at their present strength, provided of course we obtain a fair proportion of re-enlistments. It appears by the returns furnished to the Commission appointed in 1859 to inquire into the system of recruiting the Army, and in which the history of the recruit through his first two years' service was traced, that out of 1000 recruits who had joined between the 1st January and 31st Decem-

ber, 1858—by the end of 1859, 153 had deserted, 16 had purchased their discharge, 26 had died or been invalided, and 8 had
disappeared from various causes; this period gives of course an
average service of 18 months to each recruit, calculating on this
basis, we find that at the end of two years the original number of
1000 will be reduced to 753. From other returns presented to
the same Board, we gather that the annual rate of desertion between
two and five years' service is 6·7 per thousand, and between five
and ten years' service not quite 3· per 1000. According to the
sanitory report for 1861, out of 200,886 effective men in 1861,
3786 died and 6127 were discharged as invalids, making an
average of 49·3 per 1000 for both these causes. Continuing our
calculations on the basis furnished by these fresh data, we find
our 753 men reduced at the end of their third year of service to
about 710, and so on allowing something for discharge by purchase
and other casualties we arrive at the approximate number of 480
after ten and of 430 after twelve years' service. We cannot pretend to very great accuracy in these figures, we have not been
able to take into account the age of the recruit, which may vary
from sixteen to thirty, and so affect the mortality; we must bear in
mind, that the returns upon which our calculations are based, are
those of years of peace, and in so long a lapse of time as twelve
years it would be wise to take into account the losses some period,
however short, of war might cause to our forces. We think,
however, the result obtained will be accurate enough for our purpose.

Making some allowance for the chance of colonial wars, and
deducting the number of men, who would be pronounced medically
unfit, and those who would be rejected on the score of character,
we may reduce our 480 to 400, and our 430 to 360. Of these,
we must expect a certain number to take their discharge, however attractive we make the service to them. Let us suppose we have
350 ten years' men, or 320 twelve years' men, fit and willing to
re-enlist.

Assuming nine years to be adopted for the second term of
service of the whole army, and following our re-enlisted soldier,
as we have done the recruit, through this period, we find that our
320 men would be reduced at the close of their thirteenth year to
about 306; the decrease would continue yearly on a slightly increasing scale, the rate of mortality and invaliding being greater
among these men than among the younger soldiers, whilst the
casualties from desertion and discharge by purchase will be much
reduced. This number of 306 at the end of the thirteenth year
would represent a mean of 313 serving during that year; continuing our calculation year by year, adding up the successive averages
obtained and dividing the sum by nine, the total period of service,
we shall obtain the average number of old soldiers in our ranks.
This figure, 246 will give us the mean between the 313 men we

shall have to pay in the first year, and the greatly reduced proportion who will accomplish the last year of their second term of service. We will reduce this number 10 per cent to allow for the chances of war, colonial or otherwise, and so have for remainder 221. If out of the original 1000 (reduced as we have seen at the beginning of their second term of service to 320), we shall have to pay a yearly average of 221, out of the original 20,000 we shall have to pay $20 \times 221$ or 4420. The second year we work our scheme we shall have an increased number receiving extra pay, as in addition to the number left of our original batch, we shall have a fresh complement of 6400 men re-enlisting, and this number will steadily increase every successive year, till the end of the ninth year, at the close of which our expenditure will be relieved by the discharge of what will be left of our first batch of re-engaged men. The annual expense will then cease to increase and become a steady figure. When therefore, our scheme has been at work for 9 years, the yearly average of old soldiers we shall have to pay will be $4420 \times 9 = 39,780$, or in round numbers 40,000. The expense of additional pay to 40,000 men at twopence a day will be £121,666 8s. a year, from which we have to deduct the part of the present bounty we propose to abolish. The sum given to men re-enlisting as bounty and allowance in lieu of kit has varied from upwards of £7 to the mounted man, to about £4 10s to the infantry soldier. We will take a mean of £5 5s., and so suppose an immediate saving of £3 5s. per reenlisted man, which we balance against the expence of additional pay.

| | |
|---|---:|
| Increased pay of 40,000 at 2d. per diem. . . | £121,666 |
| Saving on bounty £3 5s. for 6,400 men. . . | 20,800 |
| Remains | £100,866 |

We will now proceed to investigate the comparative expense of enlisting 6,400 recruits, and of re-enlisting 6,400 old soldiers. Both these men receive the same bounty and kit, or value of kit. The travelling allowance of £1 is given to the old soldier whether he re-enlists or takes his discharge. We need therefore take no account of these items. The following expenditure applies to the recruit alone :—

| | £ | s. | d. |
|---|---:|---:|---:|
| 1. Recruiting expenses on 6,400 recruits at £2 | 12,800 | | |
| 2. Recruiting fees averaging £1 5s. . . | 8,000 | | |
| 3. Loss on 425 deserters out of the above, say £6 | 2,350 | | |
| 4. Recruiting expenses, and recruiting fees on 425 recruits to replace them, £3 5s . | 1,381 | 5 | |
| 5. Bounty and kit to same, average £4 5s . | 1,806 | 5 | |
| 6. Proportion of expenses to recover deserters . | 1,000 | | |
| 7. Clothing of 425 recruits, (122 artillery, cavalry, and engineers, at £3, 303 infantry at £2) . . . . . | 872 | | |

| | | | | |
|---|---|---|---:|---:|
| 8. Expense of marking necessaries and knapsack, say 2s for 6,825 recruits . . . | | | 692 | 10 |
| 9. Loss on 245 recruits who desert between being finally approved and joining corps, average loss £3 15s . . . . | | | 911 | 5 |
| 10. Bringing home 3,650 old soldiers at £20 | | 73,000 | | |
| 11. Travelling expenses of 6,400 discharged old soldiers at 15s per man . . . . | | 4,800 | | |
| 12. Taking out 3,650 recruits in place of others at £12 . . . . . . | | 43,800 | | |
| 13. Levy money on 173 Horse Artillerymen at £61 2s 6d . . . . . . | | 10,561 | 12 | 6 |
| Ditto | 889 Artillerymen at £37 4s | 33,070 | 16 | |
| Ditto | 601 Cavalry at £31 13s 11d | 19,049 | 4 | |
| Ditto | 4,609 Infantry at £18 1s . | 83,192 | 9 | |
| Ditto | 128 Engineers at £50 . | 6,700 | | |

Total    £304,287   6   6

To this it would be fair to add the loss on the 6,400 recruits by desertion during the second year of their service.

| | | |
|---|---:|---:|
| Loss on 325 deserters belonging to the preceding year, calculated as above at £6 . . | 1,950 | |
| 325 recruits to replace them, all expenses included . . . . . . | 3,213 | |

Total    £309,450   6   6

We will suppose that under the present conditions about one third of these 6,400 would re-enlist in their own regiments, and so realise for us a proportional part of the economies we have just exposed. The remainder who take their discharge, and re-enlist subsequently into another regiment, cause us the same expense as an ordinary recruit.

Deduct one-third of £309,450 6s 6d . . £103,800 2 2

Remains    £206,300   4   4

It may be necessary to explain as concisely as possible a few of the items mentioned above. 1. About two-thirds of the recruits raised are enlisted by recruiting parties detached from regiments and corps; the expense of each recruit raised in this manner was shown before the Committee on the recruiting question, to be about £3. There are of course certain expenses on the men raised by pensioners; £2 will therefore not be too high an estimate for the whole. 2. The recruiting fees for head-quarter recruits are less, while those paid on a district recruit for the line, are slightly more than what we have given. 6. The item for desertion is one-sixth of the yearly charge in the Estimates on that head, and is less than the proportion the number of 6,400 bears to 20,000, the annual gross total of men enlisted. It would be as well to remark, that the rate of desertion among the old soldiers is so small, that it is not worth while noticing. 8. The charge for marking necessaries is not included in the compensation given to old soldiers. 10. The number of 3,650 represents the proportion out of 6,400 on foreign service. The cost of bringing home a soldier from, and taking him out to India, is stated in the Report on the organization of the Indian forces, to be £25 and £14 respectively. When it is considered that the great bulk of our men on foreign service are in India, and our other Eastern colonies, to which the cost of conveyance will be still heavier, £20 and £12 will not be thought too high estimates of the expense. 11. This item is the cost of the soldier's removal to his home from the place of discharge, if in the British Isles, or from the port of disembarkation, if arrived from abroad. 13. These are the prices charged to the Indian Government for every man of each arm landed in India, and may be called the cost of the education of the soldier, varying of course in amount according to the importance and complexity of the duties he has to learn.

The enormous difference above shown we might increase by sundry other items, the exact amount of which, however, it would be difficult to arrive at. For instance, the infantry recruit who enlists in September, receives the same clothing that is served out in April to the soldier in the ranks. In the case of the artillery recruit, this privilege is extended as far as the end of December. Both these men receive their yearly clothing again in April of the following year; it therefore only has to last in the one case six, and in the other four months; and evidently represents a greater value to the owner after the lapse of that time, than the clothing issued to the old soldier, and which has been in wear twelve months. We may be said to give to the recruit who enlists within the periods above mentioned, half and two-thirds of the value of his clothing; that is to say, £1 6s in one case, and £2 7s in the other. Again, we might remark, that the re-enlistment of old soldiers would tend to reduce the expenses connected with the administration of martial law. They would give a much smaller per centage of courts-martial and subsequent imprisonments. Let us confine ourselves to the balance-sheet we have just made out, and to the conclusions we can draw from it. 6,400 enlisted recruits cost £309,450 more than 6,400 re-enlisted soldiers, and so to enlist a recruit costs about £47 14s more than to re-enlist an old soldier.

If such is the state of the case, one cannot but wonder why it has been, and how long it will be allowed to continue. One would suppose that on mere grounds of economy, putting efficiency quite out of the question, we would try to secure the largest number of old soldiers we could. Perhaps, hitherto, it has been thought that the ten years' men would re-enlist in any case; the less we gave them, the greater the economy. That theory has evidently broken down. If we wish to realize any economy at all, we must risk a little more; let us invest a little more capital in the re-enlistment question; it will bring us in interest at an enormous rate. According to our scheme, the yearly expense of increased pay to the old soldiers would be £100,066. If we deduct this sum from £206,300, at which we estimated the cost of replacing the men who won't continue to serve, (at all events in their own regiments,) we shall still have a yearly saving on this score of £105,434.

There is one serious objection however, we must foresee, and do battle with to the best of our ability. If you increase the numbers of the re-enlisted men, we shall be told you will also increase the number of pensioners and the amount paid to them. This of course is perfectly true. We think, however, that the additional amount added to the pension list, will by no means equal the economies realized by increased re-enlistment. The number of men discharged to pension is exceedingly small; out of our 6,400 re-engaged men, how many would be left at the expiration of their twenty-one years' service? In a period of nine or ten years, we must take into consideration the chances of war, and we have shown in an earlier part of this paper, what sad havocs its fatigues and exposure produce among the ranks of our army. The number of men discharged to pension for disability or length of service in 1860 was 1519 and in 1861, 2835; we find on the other hand, the number of recruits raised in 1839 (the year corresponding to 1860 and anterior to the passing of the Limited Enlistment Act) was 21,197, while in 1840 it was only 15,960. We may conclude from these figures, that the per centage of men, who perform the whole of their service and obtain pension, is very small, disability probably furnishes a much greater quota than length of service alone. However large will be the proportion of men who will re-engage, if we offer them better terms, it is clear their number will never equal that of the soldiers who would have been serving under the old rules of the continuous service; and even the increase that has been made to our forces during the last few years will not cause the pension list to swell to the amount of former times, or even to retain its present large proportions.

Before we dismiss our financial statement from our mind, we had better glance at some difficulties that will be experienced in the execution of our scheme. At present we have two different periods of service, for which we have proposed to substitute one uniform term of 12 years. During the first ten years after this change, we should still have to deal with men enlisted under the present circumstances i.e. for ten years. Would it be advisable to give them an increase of pay on re-enlistment or only after 12 years, as we would do to their brethren of the Cavalry and Artillery? In the former case we should have an increase of expense, and perhaps cause some ill feeling between the different branches of the army; in the latter case we might not have the results, that could be expected from an immediate increase. At all events, however, the evil would be but a temporary one. Would we extend the advantages of increased pay to the re-enlisted men we have already; and to the few long service men who are still in our ranks? These measures would cause a slight increase of expense and one which would be met by no corresponding economy. It would however diminish every year, and cease altogether at the latest in ten years' time. These questions are perfectly open, and we have mentioned them more from a wish to prove that they have not been unnoticed, than from a fear of the difficulties they might give rise to.

There is but one consideration, we have yet to touch upon. How do the facts we have disclosed, bear upon the question of recruiting? and what influence may the discharge of so many of our time expired men have on the population from which we obtain our raw material? We are afraid a very unfavourable one. When we send away 10,000 men who won't re-enlist, we spread them over the country to denounce our system and to throw discredit on it, if not by their words, at all events by the fact of their refusing to abide by it any longer. It is not only 10,000 we lose, but perhaps double or treble their number we prevent from entering our ranks. We have spoken above of the efficiency of our army, of the difficulty there has been and would be in recruiting it in time of war, and we may be told that all we have said on the desirability of retaining the ten years' men in our ranks, has very little bearing on these important questions. These soldiers would not be allowed to leave in time of war, and would be obliged to serve at least two years beyond the expiration of their present service. In time of peace their departure cannot have the same importance. We can only answer, that to have efficiency in time of war, we must begin by having it in time of peace, and precisely what we complain of, is not the want of exertion in time of war, but the shortsightedness of some of our measures in time of peace. Supposing that notwithstanding our wishes and endeavours for peace, we are obliged to take part in a European or American struggle at the end of this or at the beginning of next year, we shall assuredly not promote the efficiency of our army for that period, by allowing some 10 or 12,000 old soldiers to take their discharge this year without making the slightest efforts to retain them. The fewer calls we make on our very limited recruiting field, the more resources will it have left for us. The refuse article will always be there at our disposal, but the longer we put off employing it the better. By retaining its old soldiers, this country, should it be involved in war, will have a more efficient army to begin with and a less exhausted population to recruit it from.

While we seem to think it a matter of indifference, whether our ranks are completed by old soldiers or raw recruits, the French, taught by their experience in the Crimea, are aiming at increasing largely the number of veterans in their service. The sum of from

£80 to £100 paid as exemption money by the conscript, who does not wish to serve, goes almost in its totality to the old soldier, who is re-enlisted to fill his place. He receives a part of the sum in the shape of bounty at the beginning, the remainder on the expiration of his time, and in addition to those advantages, his daily pay is slightly increased. When we consider the difference in the resources which the two countries have at their disposal to recruit their army, we must be struck by the different estimation in which old soldiers are held by them. As matters stand with us at present, we may well ask ourselves the question whether we really wish to keep our old soldiers in the ranks. There are two courses open for our choice. We can adopt a system of short service, abolish our pension list altogether, increase the pay of the soldier and so obtain a better article. Should we, on the contrary, wish to abide by our present system of long service and aim at re-enlisting the time-expired man, we must make up our minds to hold out some solid inducement to him. Partial remedies will be of little avail. The evil is great and must be stopped by some radical measure. The scheme we have suggested, has the merit of not increasing, at all events materially, our expenditure; if applied according to our method, the increase of expense will always be proportional to the economy effected. We cannot claim for it the distinction of novelty, for since our attention has been turned to this subject we have been glad to find that we are following in the steps of some of the most distinguished officers of our army.

We trust that the labour bestowed upon these pages, and the researches they have necessitated will not be useless, and that the reader, however little persuaded he may be of the efficacy of our proposal, will be convinced of the truth of the considerations we have urged. Our aim will have been accomplished, if we have succeeded in establishing these facts:

1. Our old soldier is more efficient and therefore worth more than the recruit.

2. He has, in consequence, a right to expect more than the latter, and so more than we give him at present.

3. He is not satisfied with the way we treat him, and if we intend to keep him in our service, we must do something more for him.

4. We could afford to give him an increase of pay without increasing the expenditure, as by re-engaging him a considerable saving is effected.

Let us conclude by hoping that this question will meet with the attention it deserves, and that some abler and more experienced writer will undertake the difficult task of presenting it to the public in a manner worthy of its importance. By so doing he will deserve well of his country, and give us an opportunity of proving that there are some exceptions to our general rule of penny wise and pound foolish.   •

Books quoted.—Statistical, Sanitory, and Medical Report for the year 1861. Army Estimates, 1864–65. Papers relating to the future organisation of Her Majesty's European Forces serving in India, 1860. Report of the Commissioners appointed to inquire into the present system of Recruiting in the Army, together with the Minutes of Evidence. Clothing Regulations, 1861, etc., etc.

# OSWALD HASTINGS,

### OR THE ADVENTURES OF A QUEEN'S AIDE-DE-CAMP.

## By W. W. KNOLLYS.

Oswald Hastings, the hero of the following pages, is the son of a clergyman holding the important but badly paid living of Puddlecombe, a little country town in the county of ——. The Rev. Francis Hastings, was the descendant and representative of an old family which had once been rich, but had through combined carelessness and extravagance sunk lower and lower, till on the death of Mr. Hastings' father, the family property was found to be so involved that the executors were compelled to sell it. After satisfying every claim, they were only able to hand over a poor hundred pounds per annum to the late possessor's only son, the father of our hero. He had at that time just been installed in the family living of Puddlecombe, which brought him in another £120 a year, and with the usual improvidence of poor clergymen forthwith married a pretty penniless girl who was only destined to brighten his poverty for some twelve years. Like most clergymen's wives, however, she was extremely prolific, and in her short wedded life contrived to present her husband with no less than eight little pledges to that fortune which ever proved herself so unkind to him. In the course of the next sixteen years, calamity on calamity heaped themselves on Mr. Hastings' head. One after the other of his children sank into an early grave, he himself lost his health from anxiety and overwork, and that his cup might be completely filled, a short time before the date at which this story commenced, he lost by the failure of a bank the whole of his private income. £120 a year was, with the utmost economy, barely sufficient to provide the simplest food and the plainest clothing for himself and his family, but could not defray the expenses of education. His eldest son John was, it is true, off his hands, and indeed in a position to have helped his father had he chosen to do so; but John was one of those selfish people who never help any one, save those who do not require assistance. He had, at an early age, been articled to a solicitor in London, and shown so much capacity and shrewdness, that his master who had made a fortune and wished for leisure to enjoy it, took him into partnership. Nor did his good luck end here; he found as much favour in the eyes of the solicitor's only daughter as he had in those of the solicitor himself; and soon he became son-in-law as well as partner.  So long as his father asked for no assistance, John was most dutiful in his conduct, most regular in the somewhat formal letters in which he engrossed his sentiments—feeling he had none.  Indeed, when occasionally business took Mr. Hastings to London, he was always received with the most conventional affection at the luncheon table of his prosperous son's house in Russell Square.  Mrs. John Hastings, to do her justice, was not behind her husband in decorum of behaviour, and always welcomed the old man with a hospitality which shone in their well polished plate, if it did not come warm from the heart.  She was one of those people whose eyes glitter but never sparkle; the light which came from them resembled the reflection of the sun on ice, more than anything else.  She was rich, all her friends were rich, her father never cultivated any who were not so unless they could be useful to him, and she had never seen anything of poverty except in the persons of street-beggars.  She was therefore apt to associate respectability and worth with wealth, and to despise poverty in a proportionate degree.  One thing, however, saved Mr. Hastings from her contempt, which was the fact that he was a clergyman, and, ex-officio, a gentleman.  She looked on him as a creditable appendage, and to a certain extent was induced to forgive him for being poor, so long as he did not ask for anything more expensive than an occasional luncheon.  The smooth and decent toleration of this outside-show couple towards Mr. Hastings, soon changed into civil but very decided alienation when the crash came which shattered his little fortune so completely.  Their first thought was not "what can we do to help him," but "how can we best resist any claims he may make on us."  Mrs. John Hastings suggested that it would be better to anticipate them by writing a letter of condolence, in which should be inserted a regret that owing to Mrs. John's delicate state of health—she was only delicate because she considered illness to be a mark of her position, she had heard fine ladies were never strong—they could not ask Edith—the parson's only daughter—to come and stay with them, "that as to any pecuniary assistance they were very sorry, but with a young family growing up they were obliged to save all they could."  Now we may remark that the young family here alluded to, only consisted of one little child, little more than a year old, and another in prospect.  The letter was accordingly written in this strain and certainly effected its object, for henceforth Mr. Hastings never mentioned his circumstances to his heartless son, and indeed seldom wrote to him at all.  John more moved by his father's uncomplaining silence then he would have been by the most piteous appeal, comforted himself and stifled his conscience by the reflection that things could not have turned out so badly after all, or an attempt would _certainly_ have been made to change his resolution, and as to the money it was his wife's, and only held by him in trust for her, and their family, consequently that he would not be justified in giving any of it to his father.

Mr. Hastings was not without comfort in his distress. Apart from the consolations of religion, his only daughter Edith, a tall, beautiful brunette of sixteen, and his second son, Oswald, vied with each other in trying to make their father forget his misfortunes. Oswald had hitherto been studying at the Puddlecombe Grammar School, but his father could no longer afford to keep him there, and he was accordingly brought home. Ill health, acting on a naturally procrastinating and timid disposition, had prevented Mr. Hastings from deciding as to what Oswald's future profession should be, and now, shrinking under the weight of his misfortunes, he possessed even less courage than formerly, to look into that future which had for long years brought him nothing but evil. Oswald was more sanguine. In his childhood he had once got hold of the "Camp and Court of Buonaparte," and from that moment he had decided on being a soldier. An officer, if he could by some, as yet, unexplained means obtain a commission, but if not, he would enlist, and, like Ney, Marmont, and Massena, win his way to fame and fortune. His hopes had been, at one time, high.

A few months before, while walking out in a lane near Hastings House, the old family property above mentioned, he had heard a great uproar, and immediately afterwards seen a young girl, accompanied by a middle-aged lady, running towards him in an agony of terror. A second glance showed that they were pursued by a dog, whose foaming mouth, and short, sharp, unnatural bark at once proclaimed him mad. The girl, evidently a young lady, from her dress, was, he thought, the most perfect embodiment of female loveliness he had ever beheld. Her straw hat had fallen off, and her golden hair hung dishevelled over a face which, though blanched with terror, was still exceedingly beautiful. She was so frightened that she did not look where she was going, and just as she came within ten yards of him, she stumbled over a stone and fell. The governess, her companion, at the same moment, sank exhausted at the side of the road, a little behind the girl. The dog, however, took no heed of the former, as she did not lie in his path, but rushed straight at the prostrate figure before him. Her doom seemed fixed, for, though she had got up again directly, she made no effort to stir, but stood as if paralyzed. At that conjuncture Oswald reached the spot, and having, with great presence of mind, taken off his coat, cast it over the animal just as he was about to spring on her. Seizing the dog by the throat with both his hands, he endeavoured to strangle him. The brute, powerful by nature, was rendered still stronger by madness, and, notwithstanding the protection afforded by the coat, bit Oswald's right wrist severely before the crowd, which was following in pursuit, could help him to kill it. As soon as this was accomplished, he turned towards

the girl he had saved, and who he ascertained was the only daughter of the present owner of Hastings Hall.   That gentleman had
only lately returned from a lengthened trip on the Continent, which
accounted for Oswald's ignorance of the person whom he had so
gallantly saved.   She was too much frightened to be able, for some
minutes, to do anything but sob hysterically.   The governess was
more voluble both in her terror and her gratitude, throwing her
arms round Oswald's neck, she gave him a shower of kisses which
somewhat disconcerted the receiver, and which he would gladly have
exchanged for one smile from her younger companion.

When the latter had somewhat recovered, Oswald accompanied
her to her home, and reaped an ample reward for his services in
the few but earnest words in which she expressed her thanks.
What the tongue left unsaid, was supplied by the eyes—beautiful
eyes, too, blue and large, yet not of that melting liquid sort, which
suggest water on the brain, and look as if they had been picked out
of a jelly, but bright, sparkling eyes, which only betrayed their tenderness when looked deeply into ; changeable, too, were they, now
almost violet, now of a stone-grey colour.   As to the rest of her
charms we shall not weary the reader with a horse-dealer sort of
description of them, but merely say that she was a ver sunny-looking girl, sixteen years old, with golden hair, goody complexion,
rather full figure, and tolerably regular features.   Oswald, little
accustomed to ladies society, thought he had miraculously lighted
on an angel.   This made him so shy, that when Ellen, for that was
the girl's name, said he had saved her life, Oswald looked as if she
had accused him of picking her pocket.

Fortunately, neither handsome lads, nor pretty girls require to
talk much, in order to please, at the first interview.   Afterwards it
is different, but the first time, it is only necessary that they should
be very good-looking and seem quite unconscious of that fact.

Oswald said to himself that he accompanied her to the park gates
because she was still frightened, but in reality he took that trouble
because she was pretty and looked kindly at him.   He would repeat
to himself, most energetically—why, it is difficult to understand
unless it was that he had suspicions as to the truth of his assertion
—that he only went out of common politeness.   It was impossible
to allow a lady, who had gone through such a great and recent
danger, to return home without the escort of a gentleman.   How
could he delude himself with such sophistry ?   He knew very well
that a similar politeness to an ugly old woman would have been a
great tax on his good-nature.   The fact is, that the politeness of
which we are so proud is, in nine cases out of ten, called forth by
charms, and not sex.   Oswald did not reason, however, he only felt
in love, for he was very young—his age not being more than seventeen, though he looked older.   After her first thanks, Ellen was as
shy as himself, but the causes were different.   He knew he was in
love with her, and felt, in consequence, twice the man he had been

half an hour before.  She did not know anything, save that a perfect little bit of romance had just taken place, of which she was the
heroine, and felt that it was very nice walking with the hero, said
hero being, fortunately, good-looking.  In the case of the boy, it
was feeling with knowledge, and in that of the girl, feeling without
it.  The one loved the object which called out the feeling, the other
enjoyed the feeling without thinking about the cause of its existence.
But a truce to moralizing.

On reaching the park gates, Oswald turned to go away, in spite
of all Ellen's entreaties that he would come in and receive her
father's thanks.  This offer he declined with more haughtiness than
politeness, for he was a lad that lived much in the past, and he
could not forget that his own ancestors had once dwelt in the
splendid mansion now inhabited by Mr. Kirkman, the retired stock-
broker, whose only child Ellen was.  The girl looked pained at his
words, and Oswald hastened to make partial amends for them by
saying, getting very red as he did so,

"I live close by, so I dare say I shall often meet you out
walking."

"If you won't come in, at all events, you will tell me your name
—will you not?—that a a may call on you, to thank you for your
kindness and courage."P P

"My name is Oswald Hastings; but I do not want to be thanked.
I would do what I did to-day for anyone; and that I should have
been of any service to you, is quite sufficient pleasure to me without
any thanks.  Good-bye, Miss Kirkman."

As he said this, he held out his hand to her, and then, for the
first time, saw he was bleeding rather copiously from the dog's bite,
and began to feel considerable pain.  Excitement had prevented
him from  discovering that he was hurt sooner.  At the sight
of the blood, both Ellen and Madame Perier, the governess, utter
exclamations of terror, and the latter gave such a shriek that the
lodge-keeper hurried out to see what was the matter.

"Ah Mr. Hastings," said Ellen, "why did you not tell us you
were hurt?  How selfish of us not to think of it before!  Does not
it pain you much?  Here let me bind it up for you.  Madame come
and help me?"

So saying, she began with trembling hands to pull up the
sleeve of his coat, and wrap her handkerchief round the wounded
wrist, turning almost as pale while so employed, as she had been
when awaiting the apparently inevitable attack of the rabid dog a
quarter of an hour before.  Madame Perier came to her assistance,
and being of a romantic turn, called to mind the story of Eleanor
of Castille and proceeded to suck the wound with such energy,
that her face became smeared all over with blood.  The sight
tickled Oswald's fancy so strongly, that, in spite of the pain he
was suffering, he burst out laughing.  This,  which somewhat

reassured Ellen, only alarmed Madame Perier, who exclaimed with
horror in every feature.

"*Oh mon Dieu*, the brave young man I have fear that he has
already got the hydrophobie. He laugh now, on the spot he will
bark. Oh, that villain dog!"

Full of dread of this catastrophe, she applied her mouth so
strongly to Oswald's wrist, that in her agitation she nearly made
her teeth meet. He did not laugh now, but making a wry face,
shook her off saying rather gruffly, "Nonsense, I shall be all right
directl ."

He had hardly uttered these words, when a sudden faintness
came over him, and he fell to the ground insensible, dragging
down the enthusiastic little French woman, who had in vain endeavoured to support him.

The lodgekeeper, seizing Oswald under the arms, dragged him
into the cottage, Ellen and Madame Perier followed, the latter
suggesting every sort of absurd remedy, such as bleeding with a
pen-knife—she had once seen a man in a fit thus bled—burnt
feathers, slapping his hands, &c., and saying every now and then
"Ah what misfortune! Such a fine boy! The horrid country that
it is! All for my sake too! He will die! He will go mad! Holy
Mary, blessed mother of Jesus save him! May the ten thousand
virgins intercede for him! Don't go near him my dear, he may
bite you," till at last old Hodgson, the lodgekeeper, told her to
"hold her furrin clack," for the lad would do well enough if she
would only leave him alone.

Ellen paid little attention to what the governess said, but though
frightened to death, had the presence of mind to send off a little
boy for a doctor, whilst she herself ran up to the house for
assistance. On her return with her father, and a couple of footmen
carrying a hurdle, she found Oswald recovering from his swoon,
and Madame Perier cautiously holding a glass of water near him
in order, as she explained herself, to ascertain whether he had gone
mad or not. A little later the doctor entered, and after touching
the wounds with caustic, prescribed an emetic at night, and a couple
of pills in the morning. He was a country practitioner of the old
school, and treated almost every ailment from a sprained ankle to a
fever with the same remedies. Mr. Kirkman pressed Oswald to
come up to the house and rest, but Oswald fearing lest his father
should be anxious at his absence declined the invitation, and
accepted the doctor's offer of a seat in his gig. Before his
departure Mr. Kirkman thanked him warmly for the service he
had rendered him, and promised to call next morning, and see
how he was getting on, Madame Perier insisted on kissing him.
She declared she was desolated at what had happened and called
him her Bayard. Ellen said little, but pressed his hand timidly,
and blushing deeply gave him a look of thanks, which made him
*think* himself the most fortunate fellow living. She forgot to ask

for the handkerchief with which she had bound up his wrist, and
he took good care to take it away with him. It is needless
to say that it became a precious relic in his eyes, and for that night
at all events was placed beneath his pillow.

In compliance with the anxiety which we trust our readers will
feel as to the danger experienced by Oswald in having been bitten
by a dog which was undoubtedly mad, we may assure them that
Madame Perier's fear as to his becoming rabid, was perfectly
groundless. It is true that nearly an hour elapsed before his
wounds were attended to, but the fact of the bites having been
inflicted through thick cloth, the copious discharge of blood which
washed out the poison, and the free use of caustic, saved him
from that dreadful malady—hydrophobia.

True to his word, next morning, Mr. Kirkman and his wife in
their best attire, and in a very gaudy carriage, " For," said Mrs.
Kirkman, " it will be only a proper attention to the young man to
let him see it's not a nobody's daughter he has saved," drove up to
the rectory. They really were very grateful to Oswald, but at the
some time not sorry for an opportunity of expressing their obligations grandly; and Mrs Kirkman, at all events, looked forward
with some pleasure to the idea of charming the Hastings, with her
affability. She was terribly disappointed as to the effect of her
imposing appearance. Oswald, who wore his arm in a sling, but
was otherwise little the worse for his wounds, was rather stiff and
silent, while Mr. Hastings and Edith were as provokingly at their
ease as if their visitors had been the curate, or the local
solicitor. They did not seem to notice Mrs. Kirkman's splendid dress, or the magnificent bracelets which she wore, and
treated Oswald's deed of chivalry as merely an act of gallant humanity,
instead of what it really was, a service which he had had the
honour of rendering the richest man in the county. There was no
flutter, no running up-stairs to dress, no hurrying work under the
sofa. On the contrary, when the Kirkmans entered, Edith quietly
laid down on an occasional table the shirt she was making for her
brother, while the rector merely shut up the blotting-book, on
which he was writing his next Sunday's sermon, and both rose to greet
their visitors with dignified unembarrassed courtesy. Mr. Kirkman's
pomposity and Mrs. Kirkman's obtrusive affability, alike glanced
harmlessly from the armour of self-respect with which the Hastings
were clothed. After a stiff twenty minutes, during which the
visitors felt that they, who had meant to be so patronising to the
poor parson, had been, they knew not how, kept down to a most
unpleasantly low level, they departed. As they were saying good-bye,
Mr. Kirkman, who though vulgar was not a bad-hearted man,
invited the whole party to come and dine with him that day
week, the Rector would have excused himself, but Mr. Kirkman
was so pressing that a refusal was impossible; Mrs. Kirkman fancied
the evident hesitation to accept their hospitality proceeded from

humility, for she was not a woman to benefit by any lesson that was not positively bawled in her ears and added to Edith.

"You need not be shy, my dear, about meeting any grand folks, for we sha'nt have any one there, we shall be quite *eng putite committee*, as madame says."

It may here be observed that the good lady's acquaintance with the French language, her knowledge of which she was very fond of displaying, did not extend to pronunciation.

After their departure, a debate ensued in the family circle as to whether after all the Rector should not write and decline the invitation. We have said he was naturally indolent, and misfortune had rendered him averse to mixing with strangers. He was therefore in favour of a refusal. Edith said little, but rather advised acceptance, for she thought a change would rouse her father from the apathy which was daily growing on him. Oswald protested he did not care about it, but yet painted very strongly the rudeness of refusing so hearty an invitation. The fact was, that he would have dined with old Nick himself, if Ellen had been Belzebub's daughter. At last the question was decided, much to Oswald's ill-concealed relief in the affirmative.

On the night of the important dinner, Mr Kirkman took an opportunity when the ladies had left the drawing-room, of reiterating his thanks. Oswald, whose heart was with Ellen in the drawing-room, was very absent, and paid little attention to the broker's gratitude. Indeed he hardly knew what he was about, so engrossed was his mind with the thought of the fair girl who had sat next him at dinner. Indeed, if he had been asked what he had been eating and drinking, he would probably have said "Ellen." Her image had never been absent from his mind all the week, and in every ring of the bell he had fancied he could detect her hand. Day after day had he wandered about the neighbourhood of the park in the hopes of seeing her, but without success. This circumstance appeared inexplicable to him, but arose from Mrs. Kirkman having forbidden her to walk outside the gates for fear of other mad dogs; for Mrs. Kirkman wishing to be thought a fine lady, cultivated her nerves, which afforded a handsome annuity to the village doctor. It must not be supposed from this, that Ellen had been so ungrateful as not to have visited the Hastings. One day she had obtained permission to take the carriage and go with Madame Perier to call on Edith. Unfortunately the latter was out, and Oswald had only the poor satisfaction of catching a moment's glimpse of his lady-love, as she put her head out of the carriage window to ask if Miss Hastings was at home, and of hearing her make eager enquiries about his own health.

But to return to our sheep, Mr. Kirkman, as we have said, took the opportunity afforded by the ladies of thanking Oswald for having saved his daughter's life. His gratitude was heartily, though pompously expressed, and he concluded by asking what *Oswald's intentions* were as to a career.

"What do you intend to do, young man. You are old enough to be thinking about an occupation, and if I can be of any use to you, I shall feel bound to do what I can."

"Thank you," said Oswald, whose pride was hurt by the word 'bound,' "you are very kind but I don't consider you are bound at all. I only did for Miss Kirkman what I should have been glad to do for any one."

"That's right my boy, I like to see you modest about it. But John Kirkman never allows a service to go unpaid, it's not his way, balance both sides of the ledger, my boy, that's my motto, and I don't fancy you the less for not wishing to be rewarded." Oswald flushed up to the roots of his hair at this coarse, yet not ill meant speech, and was about to answer somewhat angrily, when his father who was afraid of what might be said, and did not see why his son's prospects should be injured by taking offence at what was probably only fault of manner, here took up the conversation, and said,

"My son is very anxious to go into the army, but unfortunately I am unable to get him a commission."

"Be a soldier. Well, I'm sorry for that. I hate soldiers, they are a dissolute profitless set of fellows, and give themselves great airs, though they are generally a parcel of paupers. Why I could buy up a score of them as easy as I could crack this walnut. You had much better put your son into an office, I could get him a clerkship directly, I dare say."

"Well, I think that would be the best thing for him. I am not very fond of the army myself. Young officers are so wild, and extravagant that I should tremble for the temptations to which Oswald would be exposed were he to become a soldier, but he is determined to be nothing else."

"You had much better be a clerk, young man," said Mr. Kirkman, turning to Oswald, "there's no knowing what you might rise to, if you are only careful and industrious, you might even be Lord Mayor of London some day; and as to money, which is the great thing after all, look at the number of our richest bankers and merchants who have begun by being merely clerks. There's Mr. Maybanks, the Head of Trouts and Co. the celebrated banking firm. He was nothing but a mere clerk in the office at starting. As for soldiers they are a set of empty-headed fools who never come to any good. They live on the taxes which we, hard-working men of business, pay for their keep, and much they do for it too. Nothing but wear red coats and swagger about country towns, flogging a poor soldier now and then to show they have some power. A parcel of drones, I can't see the use of them at all."

"I think," replied Oswald, "that there is something more than mere money, and I would far sooner be a poor General who had won a victory than the richest merchant in London."

"Well, well, there's no use arguing with boys, and if you must

be a soldier, why you deserve a good turn at my hands, and I'll
do what I can to help you. I suppose you can't afford to buy a
commission. . Ah! I thought not, so I'll get our member to see
if he can't persuade the Duke to give you one for nothing; but
you'll repent it, mark my words if you don't."

Mr. Hastings thanked him for his offer, and Oswald, though
chafing at Mr. Kirkman's manner, knew that he intended to be
kind and likewise expressed his gratitude. Another reason for
consenting to lay himself under an obligation, was the thought of
Ellen. To offend her father would involve his rarely seeing her,
while it was only as a successful soldier that he could discover a
chance of winning her hand.

Months passed away, during which Oswald waited eagerly for
the result of Mr. Kirkman's efforts to obtain him a commission.
In the interval he occasionally met Ellen in her walks, the governess' duenna instinct being somewhat counteracted by admiration
for the "brave young man who save my life." Madame Perier was
also possessed by an infatuated idea that her "Bayard," as she
called him, was attracted by her own mature charms, instead of
admiration for her charge. It was most amusing to see the oglings
she directed towards him, and to witness the painful endeavours
she made to blush through her rouge on his approach. At last
she awoke to a conviction of the true state of affairs when her
rage was boundless and ridiculous. She upbraided Ellen for her
disgraceful conduct. She reviled Oswald to her, she declared
that men were ever inconstant and never to be trusted. She
called him a *girouette*,* "what you call a cock weather." She
swore that she would avenge his perfidy on the whole sex and
punish men by never speaking to them again—she was fifty at the
least—and wound up by, in a moment of wrath and forgetfulness,
tearing her hair—she had once been on the stage—till it being only
a front came off bodily in her hands to her great discomfiture, and
Ellen's extreme amusement.

After this outbreak of feminine rage, Oswald never found an
opportunity of meeting Ellen in her walks; but enjoyed some
amends for the deprivation in the constant visits to the park which
he was at that time enabled to pay without attracting attention.
Mrs. Kirkman happened to hear that the Duchess of Kingsberry
was about to get up some private theatricals, and as she was very
anxious to ape her betters, she determined to have some too. Now
Oswald was excessively fond of the drama, and had, when at school,
acted several times with great success. Mrs. Kirkman, having
ascertained this fact, eagerly enlisted his services, and the consequence was that Oswald was brought very much into contact with
them. Madame Perier ventured one day to hint at the danger of
having a young man constantly about the house, but was at once
rebuked by Mrs. Kirkman's indignant remark, that she was con-

* Weathercock.

vinced that he was too sensible to dream of the presumption of
thinking of her daughter. Besides, she observed, they were both
so young that the idea was ridiculous.

"I can see as far through a brick wall, Madarme, as most people,
and when I want your advice I shall ask for it." There is nothing
affords such opportunities for love-making as private theatricals,
particularly where the mother piques herself on her penetration,
is too proud to suspect danger, and is troubled with nerves. Frequent rehearsals, continual consultations about dress, and perpetually hearing each other say their parts, render it impossible for
the most zealous Cerberus to prevent flirtation, and the task becomes much more difficult when both parties are seriously in love
with each other. It had come to this, silently, gradually, but not
less surely in the months which had elapsed since Ellen had first
found that great want of a young girl's heart, a hero. They had
neither of them spoken of their love, but it had beamed from their
eyes, it had thrilled from their finger's ends, and was not less acknowledged because unexpressed. At last, one day even expression
was no longer wanting. Oswald had gone into the temporary
theatre one evening to see that everything was prepared for the
dress rehearsal which was to take place that night, and was just
about to depart, when Ellen entered to look for a bracelet she
fancied she might have dropped there. He assisted her in the
search, and as they were both stooping down to see if by chance
it was under a sofa, he felt her silky hair touch his cheek. It
would have been difficult for a man to have exercised self-control
under such circumstances, for a fresh-hearted, impetuous youth,
like Oswald, it was impossible. Without a word of preface he
seized her hand, and said,

"Dear Ellen, I love you so. I cannot help telling you of it.
I know I am poor and without position, but we are both young,
and please God, if I become a soldier, I will win such honour and
fame that you shall not be ashamed of me. Pray do say you love
me; Nelly, dear Nelly I know you do. I can see it in your face,
but let me hear you say you do."

Ellen blushed painfully, and replied,

"I don't know Oswald. I never thought about it. I know I
like to be with you and talk with you, and I always feel dull when
you are away."

"Thanks, darling; then you do love me, I am sure you do.
Please say so my own."

"Well then," whispered Ellen, "I think I do. I know I
always pray for you, when I say my prayers at night."

"Dear, dear girl, you have made me so happy, and you shall
never be sorry for what you have said. With your love to spur
me on, I feel certain I shall be a great man."

With that he put his arm round her waist, and was just about
to give her a — when to their dismay Madame Perier, who from

. the dark part of the room had been watching their proceedings, rushed forward, exclaiming,

"Mademoiselle, what inconvenance is this. Making the love to a young man without your papa and mamma's permission, I expire from shame. Such is not the conduct of young ladies brought up as it is necessary.* Come away directly, and see how your mamma will regard it. As for you, sir, it resembles you the perfidy."

So saying, she hurried Ellen off bathed in tears to Mrs. Kirkman, to whom she related all that had taken place. That lady could no longer refuse to believe Madame's assertions, which were fully borne out by Ellen's tears and silence.

No people are so selfish as valetudinarians, and her first thought was for herself and not for her daughter.

"Oh dear, oh dear! Was ever mother so plagued. Have you no regard for my health. Ellen, you naughty wicked girl! I am sure this will give me another attack, but you don't care, you hussey! you wouldn't mind if it killed me, and I feel certain you will bring me to my grave some day with your bad conduct. What intolerable presumption. A beggarly parson's son to think of my daughter. It is quite shocking, oh I feel so ill, why don't you send for the doctor, Madarme; but none of you care anything about me, unfeeling creatures! Such ingratitude too of the brat! after my having been so kind to him, taking notice of his low family, and introducing him to society in our house. The wretch! Madarme, go and tell Mr. Kirkman I want him. Really Ellen in my weak state of health, it is positively barbarous of you to behave so."

It may be mentioned that notwithstanding her weak state of health Mrs. Kirkman, had managed to get through two glasses of porter and the best half of a chicken that day at luncheon.

Ellen did not say a word in self-defence all this time, beyond repeating,

"I could not help it mamma. I really couldn't. He saved my life, and I am so fond of him. It's not his fault, so don't scold him please."

"Not his fault, indeed; but it is his fault, and yours, and Madarme's too, for that matter. She should have kept a better look out, but it's always the case with them foriners you never can trust them."

Mr. Kirkman now entered the room, and his anger when he heard what was the matter though not so noisy as his wife was quite as strong. The scene ended by Ellen being sent to her room, and Mr. Kirkman going in search of Oswald whom he found still in the theatre, thinking with mingled feelings of delight, and dismay over what the last half hour had brought forth. Mr. Kirkman's face when he entered, prepared him for the words which followed. He determined for Ellen's sake to do all he could to appease her father's wrath, but this resolution was soon swept away by the feelings of wounded pride, aroused by the language used towards him.

* We presume Madame meant *comme il faut*.

" So, young gentleman, I hear you have been silly and insolent enough to make love to my daughter. Now I'll have you to understand that she's meat for your betters. I haven't made all my fortune to throw it away on the wife of a rare penniless boy like you ; the son of a trumpery parson with nothing but a miserable £100 a year or so to live on. And you're going to be a soldier too. I should like to know how you could keep a wife tramping about as you will be from place to place, and from Canada to India. I suppose you intend your wife to ride on the top of a baggage waggon and do her own washing. Pooh, boy ! When you are old enough to marry, you should look out for somebody in your own rank of life, and not try to entrap an heiress like my daughter. 1 tell you I would sooner see her married to a carcass butcher than a soldier, who is only after all a butcher with a red coat and kills men instead of bullocks. You ungrateful young rascal ; is this all the return you make for my kindness to you and your designing father? Let me never see you enter this door again."

Oswald had been on the point of breaking in a dozen times during this tirade, but he muttered to himself the magic word Ellen, and biting his lips, held his tongue till Mr. Kirkman was out of breath. Then, though white as a sheet from anger, he quietly replied,

" If you were not Ellen's father I would make you repent having spoken as you have of me and my father. I *do* love your daughter, and she loves me, but my father knows nothing about it. As for your money, I only wish you were as poor as I am, for then my chance of marrying Ellen would be better than it is now. I am penniless as you say, and have no position ; but a firm determination can do a great deal, and you will see that I will some day obtain such a position that you will feel yourself honoured by being connected with me. As for coming inside your doors again, you needn't be afraid of that ; but I tell you plainly that till Ellen tells me herself that she no longer loves me, I will never give her up. I only ask one favour of you ; that is, don't be harsh with her, poor girl, for the fault, if there is any, is all mine."

" I shan't ask your permission to do what I choose with my own daughter, and as for you, you ungrateful boy, I had intended to use my interest for you, but if you did do me a service once, you have made up for it now, so never expect anything from me again."

" I neither expect, nor will I receive anything from you," said Oswald, who at once left the house to think bitterly of the sweetness of the cup which had been snatched from his lips, ere he had done more than merely taste it.

(*To be continued.*)

## OUTLINE OF THE JENA CAMPAIGN.

In the month of September, 1806, the hatred of the French by the Prussians knew no bounds. For the last six months this feeling had been fanned by the duplicity of Napoleon in the affair of Hanover, and by the formation of the Confederation of the Rhine, as well as by the contempt he had shown for Prussia; at, last, on the receipt of intelligence at Berlin that the overtures of Napoleon to Russia and England had failed, the flame broke out. An ultimatum was despatched on October 1st to Paris, pressing for an answer by the 8th. Napoleon answered by crossing the Saale, and war was declared.

The time chosen by Prussia for commencing hostilities was most inopportune. She had just succeeded in making an alliance with England and Russia, but no material help could be expected from either for some time; whilst Austria, prostrated by Austerlitz, and perhaps justly angry at Prussia for deserting her in that campaign, had resolved to remain neutral.

At this time Napoleon's army, delayed in its march back from Austria, by various pretences, long after the time stipulated in the treaty of Presburg, was still in Germany. It was quartered in the valley of Maine, and consisted of six *corps-d'armée* with the Imperial Guard, and the reserve cavalry under Murat.

| No. of Corps. | General. | Strength. | Head-Quarters. |
|---|---|---|---|
| 1 | Bernadotte | 20,000 | Lichtenfelds. |
| 3 | Davoust | 27,000 | Bamberg. |
| 4 | Soult | 32,000 | Amberg. |
| 5 | Lannes | 22,000 | Schweinfurt. |
| 6 | Ney | 20,000 | Nuremberg. |
| 7 | Augereau | 17,000 | Wurtzburg. |
| Imp. Guard | Bessières | 20,000 | Wurtzburg. |
| Cavalry | Murat | 32,000 | Wurtzburg & Kronach. |
| | Total | 190,000. | |

All these were troops inured to war, well practised in the art of campaigning, with perfect confidence in their generals; and, owing to a long series of successes, never dreaming of defeat.

The Prussian army was neither so numerous nor so well-disciplined as that of the French. Engaged in none of the wars which had been devastating Europe for the last fourteen years, they had had no real practice in the field, and their generals, soldiers of the previous century, had not studied, or, at least, not taken to heart, the new method of warfare introduced by the French Revolution and perfected by Napoleon; but relying on their old system —which in the days of Frederick the Great was the best in Europe —they had no fear for the result, and only longed to try, at last, their strength with the enemy.

They were divided into two grand armies; one under the Duke of Brunswick, and the other under the Prince of Hohenlohe.

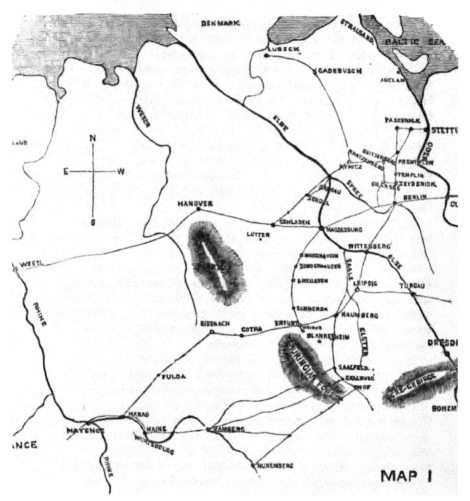

MAP I

### Duke of Brunswick's Army.

Advanced Guard, under Duke of Weimar
   on the Saale :  .    .    .  . 10,000
Main Army, at Magdebourg .   .  . 66,000
General Ruchel, on Hessian Frontier  . 17,000——93,000.

### Prince Hohenlohe's Army.

Prussians and Saxons, in Saxony  .  . 50,000
Reserve, at Magdebourg    .    . 15,000
Garrisons  .    .    .    .    . 25,000——90,000.

Grand Total    .  . 183,000.

The theatre of war that we have to take into consideration is bounded on the east by the Oder, on the north by the Baltic and

Denmark, on the west by Holland and the Rhine, and on the south by the Maine and the Bohemian mountain ranges of the Erz-Gebirge and the Reisen-Gebirge.  It is traversed in a south-east to north-west direction by two large rivers, the Weser and the Elbe, which are separated from each other by the Hartz mountains, and receive innumerable tributaries from either side.

Three great roads cross the country from west to east; being the principal lines of communication between France and Prussia. Of these, the first crosses the Rhine at Wesel, and leads on Berlin through Hanover and Magdebourg.  The second quits what was then France at Mayence, and goes to East Prussia through Hanau, Fulda, Erfurt, Naumberg, Leipsic, &c.  The third, branching off from the second at Hanau, follows the course of the Maine through Wurtzburg and Bamberg, and enters the valley of the Saale through the Thuringian Forest by three passes, viz., Saalfeld, Saalburg, and Hof.

The northern part of this country is a vast sandy plain covered with forests, morasses, and lakes, but with good communications; and, although of a very unfruitful soil, well cultivated.  On the south the Reisen-Gebirge and the Erz-Gebirge, which separate Bohemia from Silesia and Saxony respectively, send out a few low spurs, but from the west of the Erz-Gebirge runs, in a north-westerly direction, the more important chain of the Thuringian Forest.  This part of the country is generally covered with forests; the roads are bad, and the defiles numerous.

Napoleon always took, if possible, the initiative; it was in the attack that his genius and energy had the greatest play, and he knew well that it best suited the temperament of the French.

Of the three roads we have mentioned that lead from France to Prussia the first and second offered no particular advantages; on the contrary, they would at once have shown his intention, and the distance of the first put it out of the question.  But the third, by the defiles of the Thuringian Forest, and on which his armies were encamped, turned both the Saale and the Elster, cut the enemy off from Dresden, and interposed between him and the advancing Russians, who were as yet only on the Niemen.  Napoleon accordingly chose this as his line of operation.

We have seen that the Prussian army was inferior to the French in numbers, discipline, experience, and generals; their proper policy would, therefore, have been to have acted on the defensive, and hope, by delaying the critical struggle, to equal in time their adversaries on all these points.  This, too, would have allowed the Russians to come up to their aid, when they might unite, take the offensive, and hope with their superior numbers, to drive Napoleon across the Rhine.

Under these circumstances, it seems that the Prussians should have taken up a position behind the Elbe; where, supported by the fortresses of Magdebourg, Wittenberg, Torgau, and Dresden, which close all the principal roads on Berlin, they might hold Napoleon at bay; waste his strength and spoil the *morale* of his troops by making him undertake long and dreary sieges; and afterwards, by using the Oder, with its fortresses, as a second line of defence, draw him further from his base of operations and towards the Russians.

But to do this would be to abandon a large part of Prussia and Saxony to the enemy without a struggle, and would oblige the Elector of Hesse-Cassel to join the French with his 50,000 men, instead of remaining neutral, as at present. Saxony, too, consented to join Prussia only on condition of her frontier being covered. These considerations, together with the enthusiasm, not unmixed with vanity, the consequence, as it always is, of ignorance, which filled the breast of every Prussian, from the king to the peasant, made them determine to take the offensive; and almost the only thought that arose in their minds was immediate collision with the French.

Prince Hohenlohe's plan was to divide the army into two corps. The left, commanded by himself, was to march through the defiles of the Thuringian Forest, and turn the French right; while the right, under the Duke of Brunswick, was to advance by Gotha, and try to turn their left. It seems that the chief reason for proposing this plan was that he considered that his rank and position entitled him to a separate command; but the Prussians, infatuated as they were, could not help seeing the folly of attempting with inferior forces to outflank the French on both sides at once.

The Duke of Brunswick originally wished to take up a defensive position in the Thuringian Forest; but as no one supported him, it was finally resolved that the left, under Hohenlohe, should advance by Jena and Saalfeld: the right, under the king and the Duke of Brunswick, by Gotha and Eisenach; that they should unite on the 12th of October, on the other side of the Thuringian Forest, attack the centre of the French, and cut it in two.

The principal reasons given for this plan were—first, that it would put an end to the hesitation of the Elector of Hesse-Cassel; and, secondly, the mistaken notion that it would cut off Napoleon's communications with France, whereas even if deprived of the valley of the Maine, he would always have that of the Danube open to him. In compliance with these views, the right was marched to Erfurt and Weimar, with Ruchel's corps as an advance guard at Eisenach; the left to Blankenheim, covered by 10,000 men under Tauenzein at Schleitz.

But before they could advance any further, Napoleon was upon them. On the 8th of October his army crossed the frontier in three columns. On the right Ney and Soult advanced from Bareith to Hof. In the centre Bernadotte, Davoust, Murat, and the Imperial Guard marched from Bamberg towards Schleitz; and on the left Lannes and Augereau, after making a feint in the direction of Gotha, countermarched towards Saalfeld by Grafenthal.

The Prussians fell back to Schleitz.

On the 9th the French crossed the Saale.  Soult passed Hof,

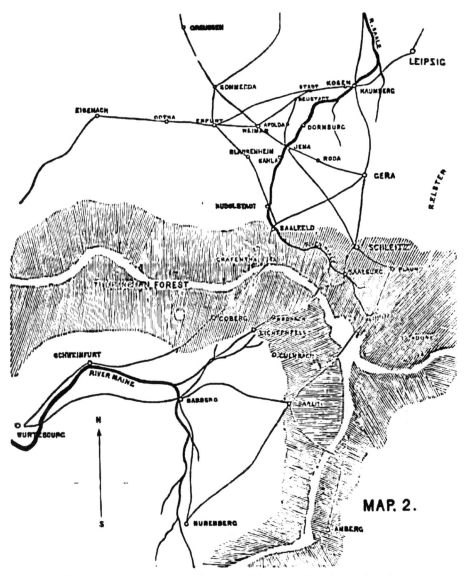

MAP. 2.

and Bernadotte attacked and took Schleitz.   The next day Lannes
defeated at Saalfeld a detachment of Prussians under Prince Louis,
who was killed.

The Prussians, on hearing of the advance of the French, concentrated about Weimar.  The choice of Weimar on their right
as the place of concentration, was perhaps owing to the feint made
by Augereau on Gotha; but whatever the reasons might have been
it was a fatal mistake, as it uncovered the capital, and allowed Napo-

leon to seize their lines of communication. The proper place
would have been about Gera : and Napoleon consequently expected
to find Hohenlohe there, while the Duke of Brunswick would attack his left. But on both these points he was soon undeceived,
for on the next day Lannes and Ney moved to Auna ; Soult and
Murat to Gera ; and on the 12th he heard that the Duke of Brunswick was approaching the Saale.

There are three bridges over the Saale, at Naumberg, at Dornburg, and at Jena. If, therefore, Napoleon could take possession
of them all, he would cut the enemy off from their base, which they
could only regain by making a long circuit by Magdebourg, and
with this object in view, he made the following dispositions. Davoust, Bernadotte, and Murat were sent to Naumberg, while some
of Murat's cavalry advanced to Leipsic and seized the gates of the
city. Soult, Augereau, and Ney between Jena and Gera. Lannes
to Jena. Thus changing front to the left by bringing his right
forward.

On the same day, Prince Hohenlohe was on the road from Jena
to Wiemar, and the Duke of Brunswick at Weimar.

The French army, therefore, concentrated between the Saale and
the Elster, cut the Saxons off from Dresden, and the Prussians from
the direct road to Berlin, while, at the same time, its own communications with France were secure by the valleys of the Maine
and the Danube. If they were forced at Naumberg their communications would not be touched ; but if they were forced at Jena,
the consequences would be more serious. It was, therefore, at this
point that Napoleon massed the greater part of his troops.

The plan formed by the Duke of Brunswick under these circumstances, was to try to reach Magdebourg by the shortest possible
route, namely by the left bank of the Saale. He accordingly
marched on the 13th in five divisions with three miles interval between each, leaving Hohenlohe to guard the passages of Jena, and
Dornburg, and to follow him next day. He proposed also to leave
three divisions opposite Naumberg to guard the defile of Kosen,
and to protect his right flank as he passed. He then meant to
wait for Hohenlohe and march together by the left bank of the
Saale to Magdebourg. And this was perhaps the best thing he
could have done. If Schmettau had afterwards shewn more energy
in taking Kosen, and if Hohenlohe had shewn more vigilance on
the evening of the 13th, and if he had on the 14th retired fighting
towards Magdebourg, the Prussian army might have been saved.
But we are anticipating.

On looking at the position of the two armies, we see that Napoleon, by the direction of his march alone, and without fighting any
action, has compelled his adversary to quit a large part of his territory in order to regain his lost communications. But he did not
mean to rest satisfied with this success, his object was the utter
annihilation of his enemy.

At Jena the river Saale runs in a deep channel.  On its left bank, opposite Jena, the heights of the Landgrafenberg rise up and command an extensive view of the country round Weimar, upon which Hohenlohe's army reposed.  Several ravines lead from the river up the sides of the heights, along the principal of which runs the road from Jena to Weimar.  This road, before it reaches the summit, winds round a hill called for this reason the Schnecke, and which was occupied by the Prussians.  Napoleon, thinking this too strong to be taken without much loss, ordered Lannes to send skirmishers up the other ravines, and to dislodge the enemy from the Landgrafenberg, which was done.  He then followed, and from the top had a full view of Hohenlohe's camp.  The Duke of Brunswick, marching towards Auerstadt, was hid by the undulations of the ground, so Napoleon thought that the whole Prussian army was before him, and laid his plans accordingly.  The main body was to attack on the next day from the Landgrafenberg, while Davoust and Bernadotte were to operate from Naumberg on their rear.

As Napoleon was the strongest, he could afford to make a detachment ; but, if he had known the real state of the case, he would most likely have sent Soult to reinforce Davoust at Naumberg, and would have also gone there himself, as that was now the decisive point.  For if the French should receive a check at Jena, it would be of no consequence ; but, if the Duke of Brunswick were successful at Auerstadt, the Prussians would regain their communications, and a large part of the fruits of the present position of the two armies would be lost to the French.

By great exertions Napoleon succeeded in making the road up the Landgrafenberg practicable for artillery ; and during the night of the 13th, the corps of Lannes, and the Imperial Guard reached the summit.

Hohenlohe, thinking that Napoleon had gone to Dresden, and that Lannes and Augereau would attack him from the Thuringian forest, had drawn up his army parallel to the road from Jena to Weimar, with his left resting on the Schnecke, and thus exposed to the attacks of the French.  A small ridge hid Lannes from the Prussians, yet Prince Hohenlohe—or rather Tauenzein, who commanded the left division—appears to have been very inactive, for if he had sent out as he ought to have done, cavalry patrols, they must have discovered that the French were operating in force by the right bank of the Saale, and not by the Thuringian forest.  In fact, Napoleon's seizure of the Landgrafenberg was extremely rash, and it was only this inactivity of the enemy which enabled him to succeed.  Sheltered, however, by the friendly ridge, and by the care he took to avoid fighting, Napoleon gave his orders for a decisive attack on the next day unsuspected.

Davoust was to advance from Naumberg, and Bernadotte from Dornburg, to act on the Prussian rear.  Murat, who had collected the heavy cavalry at Dornburg, was to move up to Jena, cross the ascended, while Augereau was to move one division, with his cavalry and artillery, up the Weimar road, and the other up a small ravine on the right of it.

Napoleon's army was 100,000 strong. Hohenlohe's 50,000, and Ruchel, who was at Weimar, had 18,000 thus making the Prussian army 68,000 strong.

At daybreak on the 14th of October, Napoleon advanced to the attack. A thick fog covered the ground, which lasted for several hours, and hid the movements from the Prussians. Lannes' division, divided into two brigades under Gazan and Suchet, carried the villages of Closwitz and Kospoda, and drove Tauenzein back in disorder with the loss of 20 guns. At nine o'clock the fog cleared up, but by this time, Napoleon had gained space enough for his troops to deploy upon, and the critical moment for him was over. Augereau had formed upon the left of Gazan. Soult on the right of Suchet, facing a little to the right towards General Holzendorf.

D 2

who had been detached to Nerkwitz to observe the passage at Dornburg. The Imperial Guard was on the slopes of the Landgrafenberg, and Ney was just passing through Jena. Napoleon now halted.

Hohenlohe, aware of his danger, changed front to his left in good order, and sent word to Ruchel to come up as fast as possible.

Ney then advanced between Lannes and Augereau, and attacked and carried a battery which was playing on his men. The Prussian cavalry charged him and broke the French horse, but the infantry, forming into squares, drove them back. Napoleon sent Lannes to support him, and the Prussians retired.

Ney again advanced and carried the village of Vierzehn-Heiligen, in the centre of the Prussian position, while Augereau took Isserstadt on their right; but on their left the Prussian cavalry made several successful charges, and succeeded in taking some guns. Hohenlohe, for a short time, thought that he might gain a victory, and directed Ruchel, who was coming to his assistance, to retake Vierzehn-Heiligen. But before he could arrive Soult had repulsed Holzendorf, and had wheeled round to his left, the whole line then advanced, and the Prussians, outflanked on either side, were driven back in confusion. Ruchel coming up, met the stream of fugitives, and was forced back with them. Napoleon threw Murat's cavalry upon the mass, and the rout was complete. The Saxons were the only part of the Prussian army that retained any order; and they were soon surrounded and compelled to surrender. Soult advanced so rapidly that he cut off most of the Prussian right wing, and made them prisoners, while the rest were totally dispersed.

In this battle the French were so much superior, that after they had got room to deploy, the defeat of the Prussians was certain. Hohenlohe's great faults were allowing Napoleon to get that room, and bringing up his troops by detachments, so that each was overwhelmed in its turn.

At the same time that Hohenlohe was fighting Napoleon at Jena, Davoust was engaged with the whole of the Duke of Brunswick's force at Auerstadt. The Duke of Brunswick had marched, as we have said, from the camp at Weimar on the 13th, in five divisions, left in front, with three miles interval between each; Blucher commanded the advanced guard, then came the third division under General Schmettau, then the second division under Wortensleben, then the first division under the Prince of Orange, and lastly the reserve, consisting of two corps under Arnim and Kuhnheim.

The road from Naumberg to Weimar crosses the Saale at Kosen, and then ascends through a defile to the plateau of the Sonnenberg. The importance of this defile is evident. If held by the Prussians it would prevent their being molested by Davoust during their march; but if held by Davoust, he would be able at any time to attack them.

At midnight on the 13th, the first and second divisions, and the

reserve were at Auerstadt, while Schmettau was only six miles from
the defile of Kosen.  Informed by some prisoners that the French
had possession of Naumberg, the Duke of Brunswick ordered
Schmettau to take possession of the defile at once; but he, thinking that the next morning would be time enough, did not move,
and the opportunity was lost, for next morning it was in possession
of the French.

At six a.m. on the morning of the 14th, Davoust received a despatch from Napoleon, ordering him to cross the Saale, and march
upon Apolda.  It also added "if the Prince of Pontecorvo (Bernadotte) is with you, you may move together; but the Emperor hopes
that he will be already in the position assigned him at Dornburg."
Bernadotte interpreting the order to mean that Napoleon wished
him at Dornburg, marched there accordingly.  This is certainly the
meaning that most people would have attached to the order; but,
as things turned out, by marching to Dornburg he was never engaged at all, and Davoust, being left to himself, ran great risks of
being overwhelmed by the Duke of Brunswick; consequently, he
was severely reprimanded by Napoleon, who never allowed that he
had made a mistake.

The country on the left bank of the Saale, opposite to Naumberg,
is very hilly with several villages scattered here and there over it.
The Saale is not fordable, and the only good road which traverses
the country is the one from Naumberg to Apolda, through Kosen
and Auerstadt.

Davoust left Naumberg in three divisions.  Gudin, leading, passed
the bridge at Kosen at six a.m., followed by Morand and Friant.
The Prussians had also begun their march thinking that Schmettau
had secured their right flank.

The Prussians were 66,000 strong and the French but 26,000.

The same fog which hung over the field of Jena prevailed here
also, and hid the strength and movements of the hostile armies
from one another.  At eight a.m. Davoust's advanced guard met
the Prussians.  The king, who was with the Duke of Brunswick,
ordered Blucher to drive off the French, while Davoust supported
his advanced guard with the whole of Gudin's division.  Blucher
charged and was repulsed with a battery of horse artillery; nothing
daunted he charged again, but was again repulsed with the loss of
another battery.  Gudin now advanced to Hassenhausen, while
Wortensleben deployed on the right of Eckartsberg.  Blucher went
round to the left of the French and charged again, but Gudin
forming his division into squares, repulsed him as before.

If at this time Schmettau had supported Blucher, and charged
Gudin's squares with his infantry, the French would in all pro-
bability have been driven off, but he remained quite passive, and
Blucher's cavalry alone could effect nothing.

Morand now came up on the left of Gudin, towards the Sonnenberg, and was attacked by Prince William of Orange, but repulsed

him. Friant moved up and took Speilberg, and outflanked the
Prussian left, while part of the division of the Prince of Orange

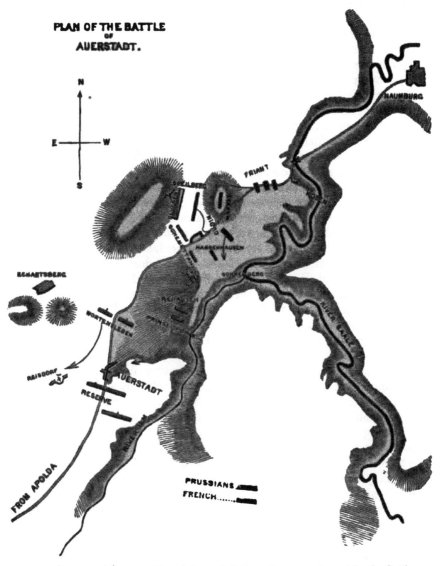

PLAN OF THE BATTLE
of
AUERSTADT.

came into position on the right of Schmettau, and outflanked the
French left.

Morand pressed forward to the heights of the Sonnenberg, which
commanded the field of battle. The King, sensible of the danger,
tried to drive him back, but after a desperate struggle, was defeated;
and the Sonnenberg, together with the village of Rehausen fell into
the hands of the French. At the same time Gudin's division over-
bore the Prussian left, and the king, outflanked on both sides, retired.

Schmettau retired by Eckartsberg, the Prince of Orange by Auerstadt, and Wortensleben by Reisdorf. Friant attacked and carried Eckartsberg, and the Prussians retired covered by Blucher. Davoust, having lost more than a third of his men, could not follow, and bivouacked on the field.

The Prussians retired in good order, until when approaching Apolda they saw the fires of Bernadotte's corps on the heights; then breaking and turning to the right they quitted the road, and presently falling in with the fugitives from Jena, the panic became universal; guns, waggons, &c., were abandoned, and the whole army fled across the fields in the utmost confusion.

The causes which led to the defeat of the Prussians by less than half their number of French were—first, they began the fight too soon; secondly, their cavalry attacked the French infantry without being supported; thirdly, two-fifths of the Prussians were held in reserve, and seem scarcely to have been engaged at all, consequently the French were always superior to them on the field of battle; and fourthly, the advantage of ground was with the French.

Unfortunately for the Prussians, their four principal generals, viz.: the Duke of Brunswick, Marshal Mollendorf, General Schmettau, and General Ruchel had been killed; and the soldiers, left without leaders, wandered over the country in all directions. Six thousand took refuge in Erfurt. The king arrived on the 16th at Sonderhausen, gave Hohenlohe the command of all the troops that he could collect, and named Magdebourg as the rallying point.

Napoleon had thus succeeded in defeating his enemy; it now remained that he should follow him up closely, and prevent his making head again; and that he should try to cut him off from Berlin and the Oder. With these objects in view, he made the following dispositions. Bernadotte to march to Neustadt, Davoust to return to Naumberg, Soult to move to Buttelstadt near Weimar, where the greatest number of the fugitives were collected, Murat and Ney to march on Erfurt, Lannes and Augereau to take up a position in advance of Weimar, thus illustrating his maxim of "close to strike, open like a fan to pursue." He also now established his communications with France by the main road through Erfurt, Fulda, and Mayence. Afterwards, as the campaign advanced, he also made use of the road by Wesel and Hanover.

Napoleon thus divided his army into two parts; one, composed of the divisions of Ney, Soult, and Murat, was to pursue the enemy to Magdebourg; the other, composed of the divisions of Bernadotte, Davoust, Lannes, Augereau and the guard, was to cross the Elbe, march on Berlin, and seize the fortresses on the Oder. For the sake of clearness we will follow in turn each of these two grand divisions, beginning with the first.

On October 15th, Soult reached Greussen, and came up with Blucher, who was escorting the grand artillery park, and the div-

sion of Kalkreuth.  Blucher moved off towards Hesse, leaving Kalkreuth to cover his retreat.  Soult attacked Kalkreuth, defeated
him, and following came up with him again on the 16th at Nord-
hausen, defeated him again and took 20 guns and 3,000 men.  The
Prussian division dispersed.  Soult arrived at Magdebourg on the
21st.

Erfurt capitulated, with 15,000 prisoners, on the evening of the
15th, and Ney and Murat followed Soult to Magdebourg.

We will now follow the second grand division of Napoleon's
army.

Bernadotte came up with Prince Eugene, who commanded the
reserve at Halle on the 17th, and after an obstinate fight defeated
him.  Prince Eugene retired to Magdebourg.

Davoust marched to Leipsic on the 18th, and to Wittenberg on
the 20th.  On the same day Lannes arrived at Dessau.  Davoust
marched to Berlin on the 26th.

Napoleon, seeing that Magdebourg might be made a trap, in which
to catch all single fugitives, ordered Murat to scour the country
round, while Ney was not to complete the investment.

Hohenlohe left Magdebourg with 1,600 infantry, 6 regiments of
cavalry, and 64 guns, and marched for Stettin; but arriving at
Spandau on the 16th, he found that it had capitulated to Murat
that very day; he was therefore obliged to go back and try to
reach Locknitz by Gransee and Zeydenick.  Napoleon sent Murat
and Lannes to cut him off from Zeydenick, by the direct road from
Berlin.  The Prussians finding themselves anticipated fell back to
Gransee.

Hohenlohe waited here for three hours in hopes that Blucher,
who having marched by Hesse and Hanover was also trying to
reach the Oder, would come up; but seeing nothing of him he set
out for Boitzenberg, which he reached on the 27th.  But the
French following caught him again at Prentslow, and Hohenlohe
surrendered.  Two of his corps, however, escaped; one was over-
taken by the French cavalry at Passewalk, and was compelled to
capitulate; the other reached Stettin on the 28th, but was refused
admittance by the governor.  They moved northwards, but were
surrounded at Anclam on the 29th, and made prisoners.  Stettin
capitulated when summoned on the evening of the 28th.

Meanwhile the Duke of Saxe-Weimar, who had commanded the
advanced guard in the Thuringian Forest, and consequently had
not been engaged at all, marched, with 1,300 men, by Lutter, and
reached Stendal on the 25th.  Feigning to attack the troops in-
vesting Magdebourg, he turned sharp to the north, and crossed
the Elbe at Tangermunde, on the 26th, and marched to Kyritz,
where he halted one day.  He then marched to Kratzenberg where,
on the 29th, he was joined by Blucher, who took the command.
Blucher had marched to Boitzenberg on the 28th, but hearing that
Hohenlohe had surrendered, he had retraced his steps to Kratzenberg.

Blucher's force now amounted to 24,000 men and 60 guns; and with it he proposed to raise the siege of Magdebourg, and supporting himself on that fortress and on Hameln, to maintain a position in rear of Napoleon's army. But Napoleon sent three divisions after him. Bernadotte and Murat were to cut him off from Stralsund and Rostock, while Soult was to interpose between him and the Elbe. Blucher finding the French too strong for him, resolved to fall back upon Lubeck, which he entered on the evening of the 5th of November, but was driven out the next day by the French and retired to Ratkau on the very border of Germany, where he was compelled to surrender.

Custrin capitulated to Davoust on the 31st of October, and Magdebourg with 22,000 prisoners on the 8th of November.

This campaign shows the fatal consequences of allowing the enemy to seize your communications. Napoleon never showed greater genius than in the plan of the campaign, or greater energy than in the pursuit of the broken army. He detected at once the vital point, and showed as much boldness as skill in striking at it. His troops, once through the Thuringian Forest, and the bridges of the Saale seized, the fate of the campaign was sealed; but it required great genius and untiring energy to make the most of it. The Prussians, too slow and too much divided, never had a chance. Annihilated at Jena, and with four of their generals killed, they had no one to rally them. Prince Eugene with the reserve, was their last stay; and if, instead of fighting in a bad position at Halle, he had retired behind the Elbe, and taken up a position from Magdebourg to Wittenberg, he might have maintained himself there until the remainder, with the exception of those that had taken refuge in Erfurt, rallied behind him, and then retreated on the Oder. If he had even gained a victory it would only have delayed his retreat for a day, and would have cost the Prussians more men than it was worth; but defeated, their last hope was gone, and the powerful kingdom of Prussia fell to pieces in four weeks, as if under the spell of a magician.

---

# THE SOLDIER'S WHY AND BECAUSE; OR, THE THEORETICAL PRINCIPLES OF DRILL; AND THE CHIEF BATTALION MOVEMENTS EXEMPLIFIED IN BATTLE.

### BY LIEUTENANT A. STEINMETZ.

#### SECTION III. THE PRINCIPLES OF SKIRMISHING DRILL.[*]

I. Light infantry drill, skirmishing, and tactical mobility are commutable terms. The army which shall become most efficient in this respect will be the worthiest to wield the modern rifle.

[*] The chief sources of this section are the French *Ecole des Tirailleurs*, and General Renard's *Considérations sur la Tactique*, &c.—Dumaine, Paris.

There has been light infantry, with its appropriate tactics, in all times. The Greeks had their *psilites*; the Romans their *velites*, slingers, and archers. In the Middle Ages light infantry was represented by the "adventurers," archers, &c.; later, by the *arquebusiers* and the "*enfans perdus*" or "Devil's Own" of the day; under Louis XIV, by the *dragons*, the *mousquetaires*, and *partisans*. Under the Empire, and at the Camp of Boulogne, each division of infantry in the French army had a regiment of light infantry, just as at present it has a battalion of Foot Chasseurs; and each battalion had, as at present, a company of *Voltigeurs*.

The distinction of light from heavy infantry no longer exists in the British army, excepting in name. Formally, light infantry was absolutely necessary, because the infantry of the line, being heavily armed, could not fight at a distance on account of its peculiar armament; but now-a-days, the soldier with his rifle can fight at a distance as well as at close quarters; and it is thought unnecessary to have two sorts of infantry. Nevertheless, if it be useless to have two distinct sorts of infantry, one of which shall be specially qualified as light infantry, it would be advisable to have men in small numbers, furnished with the most improved weapons, designed and set apart for special service. All nations have recognised this necessity, especially the French, where *Chasseurs à pied* are, to all intents and purposes, light infantry of the best material; and, apparently reverting to the old regulation, they have incorporated ten battalions of these Foot Chasseurs with their regiments of the line; and it appears that our recent Ordnance Select Committee are of opinion that a partial employment of arms of precision— such as the modern small bore rifles, so superior to all others when accurately made, "would be attended with advantage, and is not inexpedient."*

Whether these rifles should be allotted to special regiments, like the French Chasseurs, or distributed amongst marksmen of known skill and coolness, is a question for higher authorities to decide; in either case there must be two kinds of ammunition in store and in the field; but in the former, one ammunition only in a regiment.

II. The services which may be rendered by this sort of infantry are sometimes of the utmost importance. Thus, in 1799, in the campaign of Switzerland the Archduke Charles, by his skilful manœuvres, had so far succeeded that he was on the point of cutting off Massena's army near Zurich; but to reach that position it was necessary to effect the passage of the Aar. The Austrians endeavoured to force the passage, which was defended by Ney's

---

* It appears, however, that in the recent trial of rifles for the Rifle Association, Mr. Whitworth's large bores—the same calibre as the Enfield's—bore away the palm. We are certainly not surprised at this result, and believe that the bore of the Enfield is capable of being made as efficient as any smaller bore, and that it is far more appropriate in a military weapon.

division on the opposite bank.  With this object they concentrated an enormous mass of artillery, whose incessant fire protected the construction of a bridge which they were throwing over the river. Of course, they had committed an important error in not previously occupying the opposite bank ; but they were pressed for time —it was necessary to expedite the passage—they had no time for that precaution ; nor, indeed, as will presently appear, could they ever have anticipated the final opposition to their well-planned operation.  The French troops gave way under the fire of the Austrian artillery.  On retiring, however, they left the Swiss Carabiniers, dispersed with their arms of precision, and concealed in the ruins, or behind hedges and rocks.  These expert riflemen gave fire with admirable accuracy, decimated the Austrians, and made such havoc in their ranks that the latter were compelled to give up the construction of the bridge, and the Archduke's movement became a failure.  This is the most remarkable instance in the old wars, in which soldiers dispersed with arms of precision, utterly frustrated the most important movements and decided the victory.

Another remarkable instance has but recently occurred in the present Sleswig-Holstein War.  For their success at Büffel Köppel, which resulted in the evacuation of the outlying ground, the Prussians were indebted to the superior qualities of their breech-loader, the Zündnadel rifle.  Firing about three times as fast as the Danes, who are armed with the ordinary Minié, they availed themselves of the intervals between the successive salvos of the enemy to pour shot upon shot into him whilst loading.  The Danes retired rapidly, leaving several men in the hands of the enemy, and carrying off a number of wounded.  A similar result will infallibly ensue on all occasions when the hostile regiments are equal in point of numbers.

III. Skirmishers are detached only in the presence of the enemy. They begin the battle and prepare the engagement of the masses. If they necessarily decide nothing, it will be found in future battles that their "beginning" will really be "half the battle."

It is impossible to devote too much attention to the development of their drill.  In its influence on the whole army it may be deemed the prime element of that manœuvring mobility which will prepare victory in future battles.

The French began this tactical innovation, and they have certainly brought it to something like perfection.

Fighting in skirmishing order was the startling characteristic of the French Revolutinary Armies.  That method of the Republican War has been attributed to chance, to the necessities of the case— with the raw, enthusiastic, undisciplined levies fighting for national existence.  German writers put forth the opinion, and it has been adopted even by French writers who, it seems, did not give themselves the trouble to investigate the origin of this remarkable innovation in the method of war.  Chance, at all events, had nothing to do with it. Skirmishing, with reserves in support, and bayonet-charges with columns of battalions were not the result of a fortuitous inspiration, nor of the enthusiastic impetuosity which animated the Volunteers of that epoch, and impelled them to rush forward in disarray. On the contrary, that mode of fighting formed part of a system of tactics whose methods had, for twenty years previously, been meditated by all the most experienced military men of France. The Marshal de Broglie, the conqueror of Sunderhausen and of Bergen, was their most decided advocate, and he had put them in practice at the camps of Metz and Vaussieux. They were the salient characteristics of the *perpendicular order of battle*, which was destined to crush those armies that persisted in the ancient linear order. This method of war had but two kinds of fire,—by volleys and by files or at random; but the advocates of the perpendicular system had observed, during the Seven Years' War, the slight effect of those volleys and shots at random, and they eagerly accepted the principles diametrically opposed as professed by Menil-Durand and Joly de Maizeroy, and which Marshal de Broglie had put into practice, with perfect success, at the camps of Metz and Vaussieux.

IV. This method inculcated that in battle the fire of the line should be only the exception; that it should be used only in the defensive, behind works and obstacles on the ground; and to execute it the columns were deployed in three ranks. It was held that the only efficient fire in battle was that of trained soldiers taking good aim, furnished with good arms, and, especially, free in all their movements; in a word, it was decided that the fire of skirmishers should supersede that of the line.

The fire of skirmishers was to be incessant; their curtain should cover the line of the columns both in the advance-march and in retreat; and, moreover, this curtain of skirmishers had the advantage of masking the movements of the line from the enemy.

When the masses deployed to fire volleys all along the line, the skirmishers unmasked the front of the battalions and filed to the rear like the Roman Velites. When the double columns advanced to charge, the skirmishers filled the intervals between the columns, in order to protect the flanks, and to continue the fire as long as possible.

On the field of battle all the movements, changes of front or direction, retreats, &c., were under the protection of the skirmishers. In manœuvring marches the skirmishers equally surrounded the column, reconnoitred for them, protected them. They scouted the coverts, the heights, seized the defiles or other positions favourable to the march, and kept the enemy's scouts at a distance. They were supported by battalions in column.

The tacticians of the French school did not believe that these important services of skirmishers could be performed by companies drawn from the line—which they deemed it necessary to preserve intact; but it was, nevertheless, a settled point that the battalion, whether deployed or in column, needed a proper flankment. Accordingly, they designated for this special service the company of Grenadiers and a company of Chasseurs, with which each battalion was provided. All the movements were to be performed at the double.

V. Such was the original conception of this important improvement in tactics; Augereau and Masséna adopted, and improved them. The bands of skirmishers were supported by strong columns which threatened the enemy in front, whilst the skirmishers operated on his flanks, which they turned. Under the Empire the continuance of this system gave these troops more mobility than was possessed by the other continental armies; hence their success; and bands of skirmishers will always be the best tactical formation for young troops without much training, but brave and enthusiastic; although to secure its most perfect results, the best training and steadiest discipline are imperatively required  In 1814, at Fontainebleau, Bianchi's Austrian column met a French division commanded by Alix. The latter was composed of young soldiers, and inferior in numbers. Alix instantly extended a brigade in skirmishing order, overlapping the head of the Austrian column. In vain the Austrians endeavoured to oppose them with their skirmishers; they were forced to retreat in disorder, leaving a crowd of prisoners.

VI. But however useful in certain cases, it must always be remembered that it is not free from this most serious inconvenience, namely, the difficulty of rallying such scattered bands in the event of their being routed by the enemy's cavalry. At the present day such a mode of attack would only be adopted in the following circumstances, namely: when the ground is so broken that the infantry can advance neither deployed nor in column—when a battalion, a regiment, a brigade, or even a division, may be launched in great bands of skirmishers, penetrating everywhere, taking advantage of shelter, and making their fire converge on one and the same point, until they seize the desired position. But the utmost bravery is absolutely necessary in the troops for such action; and it is certain that the French skirmishers of 1813 never equalled those of 1793.*

VII. The general advantages of skirmishers are—1, That their fire is very formidable and ruinous to troops in line; 2, their front is greatly extended—a French company of Voltigeurs covering a battalion; 3, their march is easy, they pass over all kinds of ground, and the most broken is precisely that which is most favourable to their operations. Skirmishers are certainly not adapted for the shock of battle; nevertheless, the French skirmishers are diligently trained to use their bayonets individually against cavalry.

The Voltigeurs cover the front and the manœuvres of their re-

* Vial, *Cours d'Art et d'Hist. Milit.*, and *Art et Hist. Milit.—Anon.*

spective battalions. The Foot-Chasseurs have a special destination;
they are considered as both light infantry and as a very portable
artillery—in fact, a hand artillery. They fight the enemy's artillery
at long range. They appui the flanks of the line. Finally, they
may be employed, with their powerful weapon, to make an opening
in the enemy's line with their concentrated and simultaneous fire.
They are armed with the best French military rifle, whose bullet
weighs nearly 200 grains more than that of the Enfield. They are
well-trained in musketry. They practice all their manœuvres at
the double; and it is a fine sight to see them wheel into line—the
column advancing at the double, or *pas de course*, or run. They
seem to have attained the perfection of tactical mobility.

VIII. This modern light infantry of the French, which includes
the *Turcos* and the Zouaves—is an institution suggested by their
difficulties with the Arabs in Algeria. It was a contrivance designed to meet the imperative requirements of desultory warfare.
In this matter the contrast between England and the French, is
somewhat striking. In the north-west of India, England has a
district very similar in its military features to Algeria. The climate
is nearly the same; so is the nature of the ground; and so is the
border population. Frequent forays and hostile encounters occur
there; and that district has formed some of the best men in
the British service. But that these long and highly instructive encounters should not have had any lasting influence upon the mode
in which all kinds of light service are carried on in the British
army—that, after more than twenty years of fighting with Affghans
and Beloochees, that part of the service should have been found so
defective that French examples had to be hurriedly imitated, in
order to bring the infantry, in this respect, into a state of efficiency—
is indeed very strange and incomprehensible. The French Chasseurs
were the occasion of introducing many new and important improvements:—1, The new system of dress and accoutrements, the tunic,
the light shako, the waist-belts instead of the cross-belt; 2, the
*rifle* and the *science of its use*, in fact, the modern *school of musketry*; 3, the prolonged application of the "double" in field-evo-
lutions; 4, the bayonet exercise; 5, gymnastics in the physical
training of the soldier; 6, the modern system of *skirmishing* in
its totality. If we condescend to be candid, asks an intelligent
and patriotic writer, for how much of all this—so far as it really
exists in the British Army—are we not indebted to the French?
There is certainly still plenty of room for improvement. Why should
not the North Western frontier of India form the troops employed
there into a corps capable of doing for the English army what the
Chasseurs and Zouaves have done for the French? The real practice
ground for skirmishers is before the enemy; and here the French
had a splendid school for their light infantry in the fearfully broken
ground of Algeria, defended by the Kabyles—the bravest, most
tenacious and most wary skirmishers the world ever saw. Here

it was that the French developed in the highest degree that instinct for extended fighting, and taking advantage of cover, which they have shown in every war since 1792; and here the Zouaves especially turned to the best account the lessons given to them by the natives, and served as models for the whole army. Generally a chain of skirmishers is supposed to advance in something like a deployed line, crowding together, perhaps, on points offering good cover, and thinning where they have to pass open ground; occupying the enemy's skirmishers in front, only now and then taking advantage of a hedge or so, to put in a little flank fire, and, withal, not expected, nor even attempting to do much besides occupying their opponents. Not so the Zouaves. With them, extended order means the independent action of *small groups*, subordinate to a common object, the attempt at seizing advantages as soon as they offer, the chance of getting near the enemy's masses, and disturbing them by a well-sustained fire; and, in small engagements, the possibility of deciding them without calling in the masses at all. With the Zouaves, surprise and ambush are the very essence of skirmishing. They do not use cover merely to open fire from a comparatively sheltered position; they chiefly use it to creep, unseen, close up to the enemy's skirmishers, jump up suddenly, and drive them away in disorder. They use it to get on the flanks of their opponents, and there to appear unexpectedly in a thick swarm, cutting off part of their line, or to form an ambush, into which they entice the hostile skirmishers, if following too quick upon their simulated retreat. In decisive actions, such artifices will be applicable in the many pauses occurring between the great efforts to bring on decision or the crisis of battle; but in petty warfare, in the war of detachments and outposts, in collecting information respecting the enemy, or securing the rest of their own army, such qualities are of the highest importance. What the Zouaves are, only one example will suffice to show. In outpost duty, in all armies the rule is that, especially at night, the sentries must not sit, nor much less lie down, and they are to fire as soon as the enemy approaches, in order to alarm the pickets. The Zouaves manage the thing differently. "At night," writes the Duke d'Aumale, describing a camp of Zouaves, "at night, even the solitary Zouave placed on the brow of yonder hill, and overlooking the plain beyond, has been drawn in. You see no videttes; but wait till the officer goes his rounds, and you will find him speaking to a Zouave who is lying flat on the ground, just behind the brow of the hill, and watchful of everything. You see yonder group of bushes. I should not be at all surprised if, on examination, you were to find there ensconced a few couples of Zouaves. In case a Bedouin should creep up into these bushes to espy what is going on in the camp, the Zouaves will not fire, but despatch him quietly with the bayonet, just in order to shut the trap."
What are soldiers who have learnt, then, out-post duty in peace

garrisons only, and who cannot be trusted to keep awake except when standing or walking—to men trained in a war of ruse and stratagem, against Bedouins and Kabyles? With all these deviations from the prescribed system, the Zouaves have been surprised only once by their wary enemies.*

IX. The drill of these French corps is a model of skirmishing. Nothing more simple, succinct, and to the purpose, can be desired than their diminutive drill-book, entitled *Ecole des Tirailleurs*, of which a good portion consists of "observations," explanations, in fact, enlisting the *intelligence* of the soldier into a thorough appreciation of the purpose of his movements. They form in groups of two, four, or eight; the group of four being called *camarades de combat*—a skirmishing brotherhood, or fighting comrades, who rally together, regulating their fire in halves. This is the basis of the whole system. They are taught to consider themselves as so many groups, and are left to their own discretion in rallying. The nearest group and the shortest way constitute the rule. These groups are, as it were, intermediate links between single skirmishers, and the whole body of skirmishers. Whoever saw or did skirmishing, knows the value of this; especially in the rallying to resist cavalry or foragers. There is very little question as to the right or the left as immovable points; but right is right, and left is left, with regard to the direction in which the movement is to take place. The great innovation is the grouping in fours, which forms the manoeuvring unit, and the idea is carried out in the entire system.†

X. The general principles of skirmishing are as follows:—

1. The movements of a troop of skirmishers should be subjected to rules which furnish its leader with the means of directing it according to his plans, and with the utmost celerity in the execution.

2. These movements should not be executed with the same order or harmony as those of a troop in close order, because that regularity would only tend uselessly to retard the execution.

3. A troop of skirmishers charged with the scouting of a corps, should subordinate its movements to those of the corps, so as constantly to cover it.

4. A skirmishing troop must always have a reserve, whose strength and composition vary according to circumstances.

5. If this troop is sufficiently near the principal corps to be supported by it, a small reserve will suffice for each company, destined to fill up the gaps, to carry cartridges to the line, to relieve the fatigued skirmishers, and to serve as a rallying point.

---

* The foregoing account is from an admirable pamphlet entitled, "Essays addressed to Volunteers." Smith and Son, London.

† I am indebted for this short summary of the French skirmishing, to a military correspondent of the *Times*, who suggested that the *Ecole des Tirailleurs* would be worth translating and study, if only on the part of the Volunteers. The following pages will give the pith of the entire system, omitting, as much as possible, all that *is already adopted* in our drill.

6. If the principal corps is at too great a distance, another reserve, besides those of the companies, will be required, composed of whole companies, destined to support and reinforce the parts of the line which may be sharply attacked. This reserve should be strong enough to be able to relieve at least half of the companies deployed as skirmishers.

7. The reserves should be posted in rear of the centre of the line of skirmishers; those of the companies at one hundred and fifty paces; and the principal reserve at four hundred paces. Of course this rule is not invariable. Whilst keeping always in position to succour the line, the reserve must, as much as possible, take post so as to aid each other, and to take advantage of all the accidents of the ground, in order to conceal themselves from the enemy, and avoid his fire.

8. The movements of skirmishers must be at the quick or the double; the run should only be used in cases of absolute necessity.

9. In all movements, skirmishers carry their arm as most convenient to themselves.

10. The officers and non-commissioned officers regulate the rate of the skirmishers in rapid movements, urge them to husband their strength, to keep cool and collected, and see that they avail themselves of all the advantages of the ground. It is only by this continual superintendence of all the officers, that a line of skirmishers can secure good results.

XI. The great feature of the French skirmishing drill, is the accurate order of its training—the whole being divided into five distinct parts, collectively involving all the requirements of skirmishing.   PART I.

1. Deploying to the front.
2. Deploying by the flank.
3. Extending.
4. Closing.
5. Relieving skirmishers.

### PART II.

1. Advancing.
2. Retiring.
3. Changing direction.
4. Marching by the flank.

### PART III.

1. Firing at the halt.
2. Firing on the march.

### PART IV.

1. Rallying.
2. Forming column for marching in all directions.
3. The Assembly or closing on the reserve and centre.

### PART V.

1. Deploying a battalion in skirmishing order.
2. Rallying the battalion deployed in skirmishing order.

In the four first parts the movements are supposed to be executed by a company deployed in skirmishing order, on an extent of space equal to the front of a battalion. In the fifth part, each company of the battalion being deployed in skirmishing order, is supposed to occupy a space of one hundred paces. From these two examples may be deduced the rules for every case, whatever may be the strength of the troop, and the extent of ground which it should cover.

XII. *Deploying.* The company deploys to the front when it is in rear of the line on which the skirmishers must be established; it deploys by the flank when it is already on that line. For deployment the company is told off in sub-divisions and sections, and in groups of four men, called *camarades de combat*, who take care always to remember each other. The leader sees that the files forming the centre of the sections and sub-divisions are designated in the usual way.

A company may be deployed on any group—the right, the left, or the centre. In this way the skirmishers may be advanced with the utmost possible celerity to the ground which they are to occupy.

A line of skirmishers should be, as much as possible, in alignment; but to obtain this regularity, we must not neglect to avail ourselves of all the advantages presented by the ground to cover the troops.

The space between the skirmishers depends upon the extent of the ground they have to cover; but the fire will not be sufficiently kept up if the groups of four are separated by more than forty paces. The distance between the men of a group is in general, five paces.

The space to be occupied to cover a battalion, comprises the front of a battalion, *plus* the half of the intervals separating it from the neighbouring battalions. When the front of a line, whose wings are not appuyed, must be covered with skirmishers, it will be necessary either to send skirmishers to the flanks, or give the cordon of skirmishers greater extent than that of the line, in order to oppose the movement of the enemy's skirmishers, who might endeavour to disturb the flanks.

XIII. *Deploying to the front.* A company at the halt, or on the march, may be deployed to the front, on the left group of the first sub-division, and the second sub-division kept in reserve. The following are the commands and movements :—

1. First Sub-division—*Skirmish.*
2. On the left group—twenty paces—*Extend.*
3. Quick, (or Double,)—*March.*

At the first command, the sub-lieutenant and the serjeant-major take post rapidly two paces in rear of the centre of their respective sections—the sub-lieutenant to the right, the serjeant to the left ; the *fourrier** advances one pace in front of the centre of the first

* The word "fourrier" means "quartermaster," but he is merely a serjeant.

sub-division, and takes post between the two sections in the front rank as soon as the movement commences. The fourth serjeant posts himself on the left of the first rank man, as soon as he can pass. The captain points out the spot towards which this serjeant is to march. The lieutenant posts himself in front of the centre of the second sub-division, and gives the word of command :—

*Second sub-division*—to the rear—*March.* Thereupon the second sub-division marches to the rear, so as to disengage or unmask by three paces, the flank of the first sub-division. Its leader then halts it; the second serjeant posts himself on the left flank, and the third on the right flank.

At the word *March,* the left group, led by the fourth serjeant, advances towards the point indicated. All the other groups of four, bringing well forward their left shoulder, advance at the double diagonally, so as to gain to the right the space of twenty paces, which must separate each of them from the neighbouring one on the left. When the second group has advanced in a line with the first, and twenty paces from it, it front-turns, conforms to the rate and direction of the first, and constantly keeps twenty paces from it, and on the same alignment.

The third group and all the others act precisely in the same manner, and arrive successively on the line. The right guide leads up the last group.

The left guide having reached the point on which the left of the line is to be appuyed, the captain halts the skirmishers; the men composing each group of four instantly extend five paces from each other, to the right and left of the first rank man of the even file of the group; the men of the rear rank to the left of their file-leaders. Those that lag behind get into the line as quickly as possible.

If during the deployment, the line is disquieted by the enemy's fire, the captain may extend the groups as soon as they get their distances.

The line being formed, the serjeants on the right, on the left, and at the centre of the sub-divisions, take post ten paces in rear of the line, opposite to the right, the left, and the centre. The leaders of sections promptly rectify any irregularities that may be apparent, and take post twenty-five or thirty paces in rear of the centre of their sections; each of them has with him two skirmishers

---

The places of officers, &c., in the French regulations are as follows :—The captain on the right of his company, the lieutenant two paces in rear of the centre of the second sub-division; the sub-lieutenant two paces in rear of the second sub-division, on the left of the lieutenant; the first serjeant in rear of the captain. This serjeant, called "the non-commissioned officer of replacement," is the right guide of his company in the manœuvres. The third serjeant, in rear of the left of the second sub-division; the fourth serjeant in rear of the left of the first sub-division; the fourrier in rear of the first sub-division on the right of the lieutenant. In the eight companies of each battalion, the second serjeant is on the left of the front rank of the battalion. The corporals are posted in the front and rear ranks, on the right and left of each sub-division, according to their size.

taken from the section; the leader of the section also has near him a drummer or bugler, to repeat the bugle-calls of the captain. The group opposite the direction of the deployment, furnishes the two skirmishers who march with the leaders of the sections. When deploying on the centre, the left group of the first section is taken.

The skirmishers are especially habituated to find shelter behind all the obstacles presented by the ground; if necessary, they lie down to avoid the enemy's fire; the correctness of the alignment must be sacrificed for this important advantage.

The moment the deployment of the first subdivision begins, the lieutenant leads the subdivision of reserve, by the shortest way and as quickly as possible, to about 150 paces in rear of the centre of the line; and keeps it there, unless otherwise ordered. The reserve conforms to all the movements of the line; this rule is general.

The captain directs the whole of the movement, and takes post about 80 paces in rear of the centre of the line. He has near him a drummer or bugler, and four men taken from the reserve.

Deployments on the right or centre of the subdivision take place by the same words of command, only substituting "right" or "centre" for "left." The deployment on the right or on the centre is performed in accordance with the same principles; in the latter case, the centre of the subdivision is indicated by the first group of four men of the second section; the third serjeant (*fourrier*) posted on the right of that group, is the guide of the section during the deployment.

Whatever may be the nature of the deployment, on the right, the left, or the centre, the *camarades de combat* or fighting comrades always extend five paces from the front-rank man of the even-file.

When the company has to deploy in skirmishing order at a distance so near the corps which it has to cover, that a reserve becomes useless, the movement is executed in the same manner; the senior serjeant commanding the fourth section, and another serjeant the second; a third serjeant acting as guide of the centre. The supernumerary rank is posted 10 paces in rear of the line, opposite their places in line. The lieutenant has near him a drummer or bugler, the other remaining with the captain.

XIV. Deployment by the flanks is executed in a similar manner as to the posts of officers and serjeants, &c.

In deploying by the right flank from the halt, the words of command, are as follows:—

    1. Second subdivision—*Skirmish.*
    2. By the right flank, 20 paces—*Extend.*
    3. Quick (or double)—*March.*

In deploying from the centre, the words of command are:—

    1. Second subdivision—*Skirmish.*
    2. By the right and left flank, 20 paces—*Extend.*
    3. Quick (or double)—*March.*

All these movements are clearly figured in the French drill-book before mentioned.

In other respects the movement is similar to that described.

The captain may deploy the company on any group whatever; in this case the serjeant designated to occupy the centre, p sts himself at the indicated group, and the deployment proceeds as before detailed.

XV. The superintendence of the officers over a line of skirmishers cannot be too active. In battle the officers do not use the rifle. Such is the inculcation of the French regulations, and that of ours is the same; but Marshal Bugeaud, the distinguished French leader, is of a different opinion. He thinks that all the officers should be armed with a two-shot revolver rifle. Thus, he says, in a regiment of four battalions, there would be ninety-six armed officers, or one hundred and ninety-two more shots to fire on some important occasion or crisis, for he does·not mean that the officers should fire as soon or as often as the soldiers. "The effect of these hundred and ninety-two shots well aimed and fired at close quarters, will be incalculable. These shots will certainly bring down the leaders of the enemy, for officers who are good shots and are cool and collected will select these victims. What an immense superiority over our opponents! This superiority will result not only from the shots of the rifles, but also from the *morale*, which will be much greater in officers armed with good rifles, than with those who have only their swords for defence, which makes them dread a *mêlée*. I admit," adds the enthusiastic veteran of the African war, "that carrying a rifle may be rather troublesome to officers on the march; but we soon get used to carrying the rifle. I carried a very heavy one throughout all the campaigns of Spain. But even if the thing be fatiguing, what is that compared with victory, or the disgrace and disaster of being vanquished?"*

During fire, the officers and non-commissioned officers must see to the maintenance of order and silence. They must prevent the skirmishers from imprudently straggling, urge them to be calm and cool, and not to fire until they distinctly see the object to be hit. The skirmishers must use their utmost intelligence to profit by all the shelter of the ground, to conceal themselves from the enemy and avoid his fire. It often happens that the intervals are momentarily lost when a shelter is occupied in common by several neighbouring men; but at the proper time for quitting it, they should quickly re-establish the line by taking up the regulated intervals.

* The two-shot revolver carbine is best suited to an officer. It might be slung like the revolver-pistol, with which we manage to march very comfortably. Doubtless it will be objected that the officer must attend to his troop, and has not to fire: but, in practice, a man has also to attend to his life; and his coolness and courage are sustained just in proportion to his certainty that he has a weapon on which he can depend in the hour of peril. As fighting in skirmishing order will certainly be more developed in future wars, the carbine will become much more useful than it could be at the epoch when Marshal Bugeaud suggested its adoption.

As the death of the leader of a troop may cause disorder in its ranks, the marksmen should be recommended to direct their attention and aim to the enemy's leaders.

---

# EXPERIMENTS AT SHOEBURYNESS,

*In order to decide whether the Armstrong or Whitworth*
*"Principle" be preferable for Artillery.*

In our numbers for February and March last (pp. 159—174 and 326—345 inclusive) we explained at great length the distinguishing features of the Armstrong and Whitworth guns, [in the article headed "Improvements in Small Arms and Artillery,"] and we endeavoured to make it as plain as possible how it had happened that the Government had been led to adopt the Armstrong "principle" in preference to any of its rivals. We will therefore in this place merely remind our readers that the Armstrong guns were selected in 1858, because there was at that time an urgent necessity for some improvement on the old smooth-bored guns and the "Armstrongs" were already *an established fact ;* that is to say, several *had been made* by their inventor, and having been tried, were found to be most wonderful in their performances, while Mr. Whitworth had not then even thought of making any guns at all. Circumstances, as we explained at length, soon afterwards turned his attention to *rifled small arms* and thence to artillery, and *in the course of his experiments* he produced both small arms and great guns, which, in many respects at least, are superior to their rivals, especially in the larger calibres and for the Naval service. As for the Whitworth rifle, there is no doubt of its immense superiority to the Enfield, and it will probably, at some future period, supersede it if the Prussian "needle gun" or some other breech-loading rifle should not, in the meantime be found preferable. The Whitworth "principle" however, which mainly consists in the very quick turn or "twist" in the rifling, may be combined with the breech-loading and "needle" mode of firing. In our opinion, it is not desirable that the private soldier should be enabled to fire away quickly, merely for the sake of getting rid of his ammunition without seeing the object at which he fires, and without taking aim. But that is beside the present question.

No sooner had the Government selected the Armstrong gun for public service and manufactured as many as the time allowed, than, of course first one Member of Parliament got up and then another, and session after session, and one after another proceeded to "interrogate," as the French say, or "interpellate" the Secretary at War (or for war) as to why he had chosen Armstrong and not Whitworth for his model? At last the "interpellations" in the

House and the growlings of "thundering Jove" (which claim to be the voice of the nation) grew so frequent that the authorities have come to the determination to "reconsider the whole question," and to decide, if possible, whether they had better, for the future, go on manufacturing "Armstrong" guns [either breech-loaders or "shunt guns,"] or adopt the Whitworth model, either as it is or with such modifications as may be agreed on; and if they had happened to adopt Whitworth's "principle" at first, they would probably now be asked to try his rival. The question is a wide one and will take long to decide; in addition to which, if it should be considered advisable, on the whole, to make any radical change in the system, the misfortune is that poor John Bull [or the nation] will have so many thousand more "obsolete" guns on hand, in addition to the many thousand old iron smooth bores already encumbering the arsenals, forts and dockyards in all directions.   It is not advisable to have two totally opposite kinds of weapon in use at once, if it be possible to avoid it.   One of the two must either be *better* than the other, *or there is no use in changing.*   The Armstrong gun *is a good gun* up to a certain calibre and shoots well.   There is no doubt about that; only some artillery officers, who ought to be good judges, say that it is "too good" for rough work, by which they mean that it is too finely and curiously made, consequently more expensive than necessary, and that a sufficiently good gun for all *ordinary* purposes and which would shoot as straight, might, perhaps, be adopted.   After all that is said about the cost of the Armstrong guns however, they are no dearer, weight for weight, than brass ones were; and the Whitworth guns as well as any others, when of large calibre, such as 5½, 6 and more inches bore, will probably not be made any cheaper.   The brass guns could not be made under from £180 to £200 per ton, so that one of the fine old brass 24-pounders or 32-pounders (if they had such) which the Spaniards used to put in their Santa Trinidads and galleons and men-of-war in the last century, and which could not weigh less than 2½ or 3 tons, would now be worth four or five hundred pounds sterling a piece.   There are still some such to be seen at Cadiz, St Sebastian and other fortresses, as well as brass 13 inch mortars, and very good shots could be made with them, as the writer of these lines can testify from personal experience; but brass guns were given up in England long ago, merely on account of their costliness when it was found they could be replaced by cast iron ones which "answered all the purpose."   The iron ones however *did not* answer *all* the purpose as they were supposed to do, because if the shot fitted the cast iron gun too tightly, so as to make it go straight, the gun was sure to burst, and therefore the shot was made to fit loosely and *would not go direct to its mark.*   But now that the world has discovered that if a thing is to be done at all it had better be well done or let alone, and consequently none but "rifled" artillery and small arms

can be used, we must revert to the costly system of brass, or its
substitute *wrought* iron, which is found, as it appears, to be even
better. "*Hinc illæ lacrymæ.*" Our great neighbour improves
his artillery, and one fine day, when least expected, he "smashes
up" his opponent as if he were made of glass, and forthwith all
Europe and America, of course, as well as all the world, must
do likewise or be swallowed up too, like frogs before a stork.
One great lady takes it into her head to revive the obsolete and
absurdly hideous fashion of blowing out her skirt with steel or
whalebone hoops and straightway all the women in Europe (and
even the Caffre and Hottentot women in the Colonies) must do
likewise or look "out of fashion." But to return to our sheep.
The Whitworth "principle" consists, as we have said, in the first
place in a very quick turn or twist in the rifling of the barrel (one
turn in 20 inches in his small arms, the bore of which is less than
half an inch, whereas the Enfield rifle has only the proportion of one
turn to six feet and a half of length, with a bore of nearly six-
tenths of an inch diameter); secondly in using elongated projectiles hexagonally shaped instead of circular or cylindrical shot; and
thirdly the whole gun, in the case of artillery, is "composite" or
"built up" with hoops of homogeneous iron (a kind of soft steel)
forced cold over a forged tube of the same metal; the whole being
formed into a perfect mass which is turned and polished outside,
and rifled hexagonally within. Sir William Armstrong's guns, on
the other hand, are made of wrought iron bars *twisted* into a barrel,
and also strengthened on the outside with cylinders, fixed on while
red hot. Both of the two are made to be breech-loaders, and Mr.
Whitworth's guns at present are both one and the other in the
same piece; but Sir William Armstrong's gun, proper, cannot be
loaded by the muzzle. While the "Armstrong" *per se*, is essentially a breech-loader, that maker has also perfected his "Shunt
gun," which is only a muzzle-loader. There are therefore now
three kinds on trial; Sir William Armstrong's breech-loader, his
muzzle-loader, or shunt gun, and Mr. Whitworth's gun, which is
both and either. It is of course to be understood that all of them
can be made of any calibre desired, from the size of a rifle, under
half an inch bore, up to 13 or 15-inch guns, which would propel
a steel cylindrical or hexagonal shot or shell, weighing from 600 to
1000 pounds.

Having premised this, it will be necessary for us to give the
reports of the experiments now making at Shoeburyness, day by
day, as far as we can obtain them. The guns first used are
called 12-pounders, but it is not said whether they have the calibre
of the old guns of that name, which fired a spherical shot about four
inches and two-fifths in diameter, or whether they carry an elongated
projectile weighing only 12 lbs., in which case their bore would be
much less. We shall, however, state further in the sequel, and those
readers who desire to refresh their memories, are referred to our

former article on the subject, or to Sir **J. E. Tennent's** " Story of the Guns."

The series of Experiments commenced at Shoeburyness on the 4th of April. Sir William Armstrong was represented by one of his 12-pounder field guns, weighing 8 cwt 1 qrs. 6lbs with a length of 7 feet and charge of 1¼ lbs. of powder and one turn in 9 feet, 6 inches of length in the rifle:—also by a 12-pounder " shunt gun," or muzzle-loader, weighing 8 cwt. 3 qrs. 27 lbs., (length not stated) charge 1¾ lbs. of powder, and the rifling in the same proportion as his other gun, viz., 1 turn in 9 feet 6 inches. The reader, will therefore see that the Armstrong guns have not so much as one complete turn or twist of the rifle grooves in their whole length; but are in fact what were usually known in the olden time, probably as ⅔ or ¾ turn rifles.

Mr. Whitworth had one gun in the field only, but which is both muzzle and breech-loader or either, as may be preferred. It is only 6 feet, 8 inches in length, weighs 10 cwt., has a charge of 1¾ lbs. of powder and in the report before us it is stated to have *one inch* of turn in 55 inches, but which we apprehend must be a mistake, for 1 turn in 55 inches; as the very principle of the Whitworth rifle (see Sir **J. E.** Tennent's Story of the Guns, p. 51), is said to consist in a turn in the spiral *four times greater than* the Enfield rifle; whereas 1 *inch of turn* in 55 inches would scarcely be more than the Enfield rifles or Armstrong guns have. We must therefore leave this for the present in abeyance. The first day's firing seems to have been merely preliminary, and the particulars were not allowed to be taken down by the reporters of the Press. It appears, however, that in general, the *recoil* of the Whitworth gun was less than that of the Armstrong breech-loader, which may be accounted for in the first place by its being more than 1½ cwt. *heavier,* and the breech-loading lead-covered shot of the Armstrong gun in question fitting much tighter, and having to *force its own way* into the rifling of the bore and cut its own grooves in its lead wrapper; but the shunt gun also, in general, recoiled, on this occasion, sometimes more and sometimes less than either the breech-loading Armstrong, or the Whitworth. Much also depends on the weight of the respective projectiles, which is not stated. In fact, the whole report of the first day's firing is "nil" to the public, as yet. It is only allowed to transpire that "judging from the eye," the shunt gun had the longest range, but the worst line, and the breech-loading Armstrong, now used in the service, much the same as the Whitworth gun.

The next day (5th of April) we make out that in five rounds at 200 yards the breech-loading Armstrong put 5 shots in a space of 21 inches by 21. The Armstrong shunt gun, 5 shots in 19 by 17 inches, and the Whitworth, 5 shots in 8¼ by 9 inches, or almost all in the same hole, and that the Bull's eye! But after all 200 yards is nothing and we have done as much, *at that distance,* with a smooth bore. At 300 yards the Armstrong breech-loader put its shot all in a space of 25 inches from the Bull's eye, and the shunt gun all in a space of 22 inches from the Bull's eye, while the Whitworth, as before, put every shot in the same hole, and that *the Bull's eye.*

At 400 yards the breech-loading Armstrong scattered its shots from 5 to 34 inches from the centre of the Bull's eye; the shots of the shunt gun are said to have been "little scattered and well together," and those of the Whitworth from 5 to 22 inches from the centre of the Bull's eye. On this occasion, at the 400 yards, the practice of the shunt gun is said to have been really good, and that of the Whitworth really bad; which shows that many circumstances must occasionally intervene to interrupt the harmony of the best regulated affairs. Until the actual Practice Reports are given, with elevations and results entire, no judgment can be formed.

On the 6th, the following notes are given, as the results of the third day's firing, at 500 yards :—

Breech-loading Armstrong, nearest shot to centre of Bull's eye,

|  |  |  |  |
|---|---|---|---|
|  |  |  | 9 inches. |
| „ | „ | furthest | 40 inches. |
| Shunt gun, | „ | nearest shot | 8 inches. |
| „ | „ | furthest „ | 24 inches. |
| Whitworth, | one shot in the Bull's eye. |  |  |
| „ | furthest shot from centre of Bull's eye 31 inches. |  |  |

At 600 yards, breech-loading Armstrong, nearest to centre of Bull's eye,            20 inches.

    „        three shots in a line, wide.

Shunt gun,    nearest shot,  12 inches;  furthest, 36 inches.
Whitworth,        „    „    20 inches ;    „    30 inches.
        "all well in line but wide" (by this we presume that the direction was good, but the shots struck, some above and others below the cross line.)

At 700 yards, breech-loading Armstrong, nearest to centre of Bull's eye,  .    .    .    30 inches;  furthest, 54 inches.
Shunt gun,        nearest 12 inches;  furthest, 36 inches. not much scattered.

Whitworth, two misses,  „    12 inches; the three shots in a triangular form above the Bull's eye.

The muzzle Armstrong (shunt) is not fired with "lubricating" wads, but the Whitworth and the breech-loading Armstrong gun use them and are also sponged out, without dipping the sponge in water. Armstrong breech-loader was not sponged out at all, but the lubricating wad is intended to supersede the necessity for sponging, in breech-loaders.

The fourth day's firing was on the 7th of April, and is stated as follows: At 1300 yards (first round) breech-loading Armstrong knocked the wooden target down by a shot which struck 2 feet to

the right at the bottom of the target ; distant from the Bull's eye,
7½ inches. A shot of this kind counts 7½ the wrong way and is
recorded as a miss. Shunt gun, Armstrong, shot in line but struck
the ground seven yards short of the target.

Whitworth, shot in line but struck 2 yards short of the target.
Same range, (1300 yards) second round.

Breech-loading Armstrong, target knocked down as before, but
this time by the concussion of the shot in striking the ground in
front, and in the ricochet the target was struck, but not penetrated,
recorded again as a miss.

Shunt gun, shot struck the ground at a distance to the right.

Whitworth, 2 feet above Bull's eye, to the right.

These two rounds are said to have been only "preliminary," and
not counted.

At 900 yards. Breech-loading Armstrong, nearest 12 inches;
      "         "      "    furthest 48 inches
The practice good and the best of the three guns.

Shunt, (Armstrong) nearest 10 inches ;   2 separate misses.

Whitworth, nearest 12 inches ; furthest 7½ inch graze at the
bottom, counted as a miss.

At 800 yards, breech-loading Armstrong, nearest 20 inches;
      "         "      "    furthest 48 inches.
Shunt, (Armstrong) nearest 9 inches ; furthest 42 inches.
Whitworth,  .  . nearest 17 inches ; furthest 48 inches.
Shot less scattered than with the breech-loader.

The fifth day of the Experiments was chiefly occupied in ascertaining the ranges due to various elevations of the 12-pounders,
and there is not any thing made public which is worth recording.
When the experiments are concluded and the committee shall have
made their report, we shall no doubt have sufficient data given us
to be satisfied that their decision, whatever it may be, is made with
good reasons and on just grounds. It appears, however, to have
been discovered in the course of the experiments, that by some
accident, the "sighting" of the Whitworth gun, which was done at
Woolwich, gave *four minutes and a half* more elevation to it than
was intended, and consequently Mr. Whitworth's piece appeared
to range farther at the *same* elevation than the others did, when
in fact it had 4½ minutes *more* than they had. This is indeed little
more than the fifteenth part of a degree, but in such close competition it is of consequence and the deductions had to be made accordingly. It appears from the reports before us that the Armstrong
shunt gun (muzzle-loader) in point of fact ranges as far with the
same elevation in most cases as the Whitworth gun, and has consequently as flat a trajectory. The non-professional reader is reminded
that the latter expression means that the shot is *not higher above the
level ground*, in the highest part of its flight, than another:—the
"Trajectory" being the line described in the air by the projectile.
As regards the term "Pounder" we have ascertained from authority,

since commencing to write these lines, that the present 12-pounders as well as the other rifled guns, actually fire an elongated shot of the weight by which they are indicated, and are consequently much smaller in the bore than the old guns of the same designations. The rifled 12-pounder has only a bore of 3 inches in diameter, instead of *more* than four and a half (4·023), which the old 12-pounder had.   A gun of 7-inch bore is now called a 110-pounder, but a smooth-bored gun of the same calibre only carried a spherical solid cast-iron shot, 42 lbs. weight, and was called a 42-pounder, and so on.   In future, however, it is intended to designate all the larger guns in the service by their calibres ; as 7-inch guns for instance, instead of 110-pounder, and 5½-inch instead of 70-pounder.   We have also been assured at the fountain head of information for all such matters, that we were correct in our surmise on the subject, and that the Whitworth rifled 12-pounder now firing at Shoebury-ness, has *one entire turn* of the rifling in the length of 55 inches, which in a 12-pounder of 3-inch calibre is 9 inches and 42 hundredths and not *one inch* in 55 inches, as was erroneously printed in the newspaper reports of the first day's firing.   The rifled Armstrong breech-loading gun for field service, [now under experiment] which only weighs 8 cwt. 1 qr. 6 lbs., and carries a 12-lb. shot, which is fifty times more efficient and destructive than any round shot, shell or spherical case shot ever invented is actually lighter by one third than one of the old smooth-bored brass 9-pounders, as these weighed 13½ cwt ! Though only called "medium" guns. the old brass 12-pounders made for field service weighed 18 cwt, and were too heavy for any but "position" guns.   The Horse Artillery had to drag the brass "nines" at a gallop, over all kinds of ground and therefore any of the new rifled 12-pounders are a vast improvement and not more expensive, as we have already said.

It appears by the reports before us, that on the fifth day of experiments, the practice consisted in firing twenty rounds of shot and five of common shell, with five of Shrapnel shell, from the Whitworth (muzzle or breech-loader), and five of segment shell from the Armstrong breech and muzzle loaders.   The rounds were all fired at two degrees of elevation, and the time of flight is stated as follows :

Breech-loading Armstrong  .   .   .   8.575 seconds (segment shell).
Muzzle-loading Armstrong (shunt)   8.366   ,,       ,,       ,,
Whitworth muzzle-loader*  .   .   .   8.525   ,,    (Shrapnel shell).

Fifth day's firing continued (at embrasures of field-works) at 900 yards :

Breech-loading Armstrong, segment and common shell;  65 target marks ; five gunners killed.

Muzzle-loading Armstrong, 20 target marks ; one gunner killed.

Whitworth gun, 58 target marks ; three gunners killed.

* By calling the Whitworth gun a "muzzle loader" on some occasions, we presume that it is in those cases loaded by the muzzle, but it is both one and the other at *pleasure*.

The breech-loader and the Armstrong gun are said to have damaged the embrasures against which they fired more than the Whitworth.  This probably arises from the segment shells being more effective than those fired from the Whitworth gun.

On the sixth day's firing, it is stated that the guns, which had been taken to the marshes for practice at the field-works the day before, were placed in position at 700 yards, and the *programme* was, five rounds of shot, and five of segment shell from the Armstrong guns, and five of Shrapnel from the Whitworth.  By "Shrapnel" shell, the reader must understand case shot, or musket bullets placed in a rather thin iron case, with bursting powder, and a fuse of the proper length, so called from its inventor, the late General Shrapnel, of the Royal Artillery.  It was afterwards called "spherical case shot," to distinguish it from cylindrical case shot, which was only in a tin canister, and ranged a very short distance, but in the Whitworth gun it is of course made elongated and hexagonal to fit the bore.  Sir William Armstrong's "segment" shell has been fully described in our former article ("Improvements in Small Arms and Artillery"); and though the reports from the ground say that segment shells *cannot* be fired from the Whitworth gun, we do not see the reason why they could not be made to fit that gun as well as the Armstrongs, nor if so, why Mr. Whitworth has chosen Shrapnel shell instead, as he must have also made the latter on purpose.  The old spherical case, or Shrapnel, could not fit his gun or answer the purpose.  This point is therefore reserved for future explanation.  The results given are as follows:

Sixth day's firing.  For firing at the three embrasures of the field-works, in continuation of Friday's, the fifth day's firing, the breech-loading Armstrong, for the first round, was laid at one degree twelve minutes; the Armstrong muzzle-loader, for the first round, at one degree nine minutes; and the Whitworth at one degree four minutes.  All the rounds that followed were at various elevations and deflections; the committee still acting on the recent resolution to allow the competitors to fire their guns as they please.

At 700 yards.

Breech-loading Armstrong, with segment, 48 pieces through the rear targets; 14 pieces lodged; 3 pieces glanced; 2 gunners killed.

Armstrong muzzle-loader, with segment, 26 pieces through the rear targets; 2 pieces lodged; 3 pieces glanced; 2 gunners killed.

Whitworth, with Shrapnel, 14 pieces through the rear targets; 1 piece lodged; 1 piece glanced; and *no* gunner killed.

At 700 yards (again).

Breech-loading Armstrong, with common shell, 17 pieces through the rear targets; 1 piece lodged; 8 pieces glanced; 1 gunner killed.

Muzzle-loading Armstrong, with common shell; 1 piece through the rear target; none lodged; none glanced; 1 gunner killed.

Whitworth muzzle-loader, with common shell, 14 pieces through the rear targets; 5 pieces lodged; 5 pieces glanced; 5 gunners killed.

The five rounds of solid shot did little more than obtain the range. "The embrasures of the breech-loading Armstrong and muzzle-loading Armstrong suffered much more damage than the Whitworth muzzle embrasure." We do not see what difference it can make in the damage or explosion whether the charge is put in at the breech or the muzzle, since the Whitworth gun is loaded either way; we merely copy the report as it is before us at present. It is said that, "Sergeant Major Jones's gabions stood fire much better than the sheet-iron ones *in the embrasure of the Armstrong muzzle gun,* and there were few, if any, gabion fragments strewed about." By this last expression, we infer that the guns fired *at* the embrasures, and not that they were placed in a battery and fired *through them,* which the wording of the last paragra h of the report, viz.: "the embrasures *of the* breech-loading Armstrong, &c.," seemed to imply. The report continues, "At the 700 yards the field-works were untenable, assuming that the enemy within them had been as unserviceable as the three worn-out mounted 32-pounders. But it almost seems that the earth-work practice is the least satisfactory that the guns can make, because it is not easy to fix the damage sustained by the earth-works where previous damage is not made good, and because a shell bursting in the embrasure may show nothing on the target. Still, earth-work practice could not properly have been omitted from the programme." After the firing at 700 yards, the guns were moved forward to the 600 yards range, and an experiment was made to ascertain which of the guns would do most damage to an "abbatis" by firing at it. By "abbatis" (or abattis) is meant an artificial obstacle to the attack or advance of troops, made either by felling trees and pointing their branches where they lie, if in a wood, or cutting the tops off and fixing them in the ground, so as to form a sort of "chevaux de frize," or hedge, which troops cannot pass in any regular order. They are a very formidable obstacle where a sufficient quantity of trees fit for the purpose can be had. The result is given as follows, charges as usual, and with segment shells for the Armstrongs and Shrapnel for the Whitworth:

Breech-loading Armstrong, with segment shell, the abattis was opened sufficiently to allow troops to pass with ease.

Muzzle-loading Armstrong, with segment, the same result.

Whitworth gun, with Shrapnel, the abattis was practically un-injured. (This, in our opinion, only shows that the Whitworth gun must adopt the segment shells, or *shut up*).

Common shell firing was then tried, and, results given below:

Breech-loading Armstrong, with common shell, results nil.

| Muzzle-loading ditto | ditto | ditto |
| Whitworth gun | ditto | ditto |

It appears, therefore, that in the segment shell, from whatever gun it can be properly fired, Sir William Armstrong has given us the power to destroy stockades, and *pahs* in New Zealand, or

elsewhere, by direct fire, in a very few rounds, which the common
shells and round shot were unable to do.  The reader has only to
recollect that the Armstrong segment shell (or *shot* when not used
as a shell) is formed of segments, bound together by a thin coating
of lead run outside of them, and having the charge for bursting in
the core, or hollow central axis of the cylinder, while the common
shells, or Shrapnel, have the bursting powder in a little bag in one
part of the shell only.  The segment shells, as we have said in our
former article, are the most destructive projectile yet invented, for
general purposes; but they will not answer against thick armour
plates, as they would shiver on the outside, though they penetrate
a great thickness of timber with ease.*

Eighth day's firing.  This is said to have been for length of
range, " beginning at three degrees, and ending with all the rounds
at four degrees.  At each elevation there are twenty rounds of solid
shot, five of common shell, and five of segment, or Shrapnel.  To
all appearance, from the battery, the Whitworth and the Armstrong
muzzle-loaders ploughed up the wet sand on the same spot, while
the service breech-loading Armstrong fell about 100 yards short."
But as this gun has a quarter of a pound less powder than the
others, and is made to fire solid shot, this may account for the
difference.  We do not understand why the Armstrong service
breech-loader, which is intended *never to fire anything but its own
segment shot,* which are made into shells merely by putting in the
bursting powder and fuze, should be made to fire solid shot, unless
it be to ascertain whether, with a smaller charge, it can also, in case
of necessity, throw a solid shot as far as the other two kinds
of gun.

As regards the error of four and a half minutes in the sighting
of Whitworth's gun, the following corrected elevations are given to
show how it competes with the Armstrong muzzle or shunt gun :

At 300 yards, Whitworth  .  .  21 minutes, (12-pounder).
  ,,        Armstrong shunt  22    ,,        ,,
At 500 yards, Whitworth  .  .  38    ,,
  ,,        Armstrong shunt  38    ,,
But at 200 yards, Whitworth would only require  .  5 min. elev.
  ,,        Armstrong shunt would require  .  13    ,,
And at 400 yards Whitworth would have  .  .  24    ,,
  ,,        Armstrong shunt  .  .  .  32    ,,

It is deduced from the course of the experiments hitherto, that, on
the whole, the trajectory of the Armstrong shunt-gun, 12-pounder, is
as good as that of the Whitworth gun.  It was found that at this
period (after seven days firing) the vent of the Whitworth gun was
somewhat choked, and required a new vent-plug to be screwed in,
which was done by permission, on the admission of Mr. Whitworth
that, to that extent, he admitted its present inferiority, as the

* Story of the Guns pp. 114—117, "at 1000 yards it pierced a bulk of elm
3 feet thick!"

Armstrongs could have gone on perfectly well without being repaired in any way. As one gun was allowed to be new vented, the other two were, of course, also admitted to the same indulgence. If Mr. Whitworth's gun is to compete with the others, he will require to make his vent-pieces equally durable, of course. As Mr. Whitworth's men, in new venting his gun, also took the liberty to clean it and put a new sight and breech-ring to it, the Armstrong guns were also ordered to be cleaned, and the new sight and breech-ring were removed from the Whitworth gun.

As far as we can see, it is generally admitted by those best able to form an opinion at present, that the Armstrong guns have at least fully maintained their position, as far as 12-pounders and field service are concerned.

Ninth day's firing. The Armstrong breech-loader (or one of them) now under experiment, differs in some slight degree from the service gun in use, and seems to have been intended to compete with the other guns in firing solid shot; but it would appear that the alterations, trifling as they may be, are not *improvements*, as the practice from this gun with solid shot is decidedly inferior to that of its rivals. The Armstrong segment shot or shell, as we have said, is the most destructive projectile ever yet invented, and had better be let alone. Why seek to gild refined gold or paint the lily? and as regards the determined "set," which appears to have been made by many naval officers against the Armstrong breech-loaders for sea service, it is stated to be a positive fact, that in one man-of-war, at all events, at Kagosima, the gunners or crew who had to fire them, had never had a day's practice with their Armstrong guns with shot or shell, or even blank cartridges; other ships had fired only a few rounds of service charges: others again, only a few of blank cartridges. It is obvious therefore, that to send ships to engage an enemy, under a hot fire, with guns of which the men who were to work them really knew nothing, was an act of great rashness, and if the men in the heat and hurry of action mismanaged the guns, and did not place or screw up the vent-pieces properly, that is not the fault of the guns, but of those who mismanage them. At any rate we shall have a good substitute for them in either the Armstrong shunt gun, which is a muzzle-loader, or in Whitworth's guns, which may be made simple muzzle-loaders, if naval men prefer them. We need not fear that the British Navy may be obliged to be content with the old smooth bored 8 and 10-inch guns and now give, as far as our reports detail it, the ninth day's proceedings.

At 3 degrees of elevation the Whitworth muzzle-gun
ranges    .    .    .    .    .    . 1600 yards.
At 3 degrees of elevation, the Armstrong muzzle-loader
ranges    .    .    .    .    .    . 1600
At 4 degrees of elevation the Armstrong breech-loader
ranges    .    .    .    .    .    . 1700

At 4 degrees of elevation the Whitworth muzzle-loader
   ranges  .    .    .    .    .    . 1900 yards
At 4 degrees of elevation the Armstrong muzzle-loader
   ranges  .    .    .    .    .    . 1900  ,
     Average of both muzzle-loaders .    . 1930  ,
       ,,        ,,   breech-loaders .    .    . 1750  ,
At 5 degrees Armstrong breech-loader ranges .   . 2000  ,
     ,,   Whitworth muzzle-loader  ,,    . 2000  ,
     ,,   Armstrong muzzle-loader  ,,    . 2000  ,
     Average of both muzzle-loaders .    . 2200  ,,
       ,,        ,,   breech-loaders .    .    . 2000  ,,

Trials for accuracy, breech-loading Armstrong was slightly behind
the others.

The Whitworth muzzle-loader and the Armstrong muzzle-loaders
were both equal.

The accuracy of the ranges, having been questioned by Mr.
Whitworth, the final result remains to be decided. Sir William
Armstrong protests that even if the Whitworth gun should prove
to carry "solid" shot a few yards further than his guns, it is of
no consequence, because solid shot would be of no use at extreme
ranges, and is not used with field guns at such distances. Nevertheless, for the sake of comparison and experiment, the trials are
to be continued up to ten degrees. At the shortest ranges the
Whitworth guns made the best practice, then the shunt gun, and
now it appears the Whitworth has the advantage. As from 5 to 10
degrees, there is the same margin as from point blank up to 5
degrees, it is possible the shunt gun may in the end come up to
the Whitworth. As for the breech-loading Armstrong it must be
recollected that its charge is a quarter of a pound of powder less than
either of the others, which is a vast deal in $1\frac{3}{4}$ lbs., being a seventh
part less, and this alone must prevent its ranging so far at high
elevation, if that be of any consequence. As far as field service
goes, the Armstrong breech-loader is a good gun, as we have all
along maintained, and the majority of artillery officers who are conversant with them allow. It is intended that the 12-pounders shall
be tried in firing at brick walls as well as at stockades, and in rapid
firing to test the endurance of each. The brick walls are three
bricks in thickness (2 feet, 3 inches), and there is little doubt but
the Armstrong segment shells will prove as destructive to these and
the stockades as they were against the *abattis*. We learn that the
Armstrong guns were neither new vented nor require it, and that
it was only the Whitworth gun which availed itself (if we may use
the expression) of that indulgence or must have ceased firing.
The Armstrongs as yet require nothing but a fair field and no favour.
The whole of these field guns are to be tested in every possible or
"impossible" way. They are to be overturned in muddy ditches,
left all night in limbo, and then taken up for immediate use ; they
are to be tried at all ranges and elevations, and finally loaded with

increasing charges to see how far their endurance will hold out. Of course, in this final act they must be fired by electric wire by a man under cover of a bomb-proof shelter. It seems that the Whitworth hexagonal shot, when it strikes the ground *bores its way* and is apt to deflect very much to one side, and not only that but it screws itself up at a very high angle out of the ground and flies right up into the air with a "whirring" noise far over the parapet at which it is fired, and over the heads of any people who would be inside the fort, so that it is not available for *enfilading* or *ricochet* fire, as the others are, and the old smooth-bored guns with spherical shot are. It is very possible therefore, that if, after every thing else has been tried, and in case the Whitworth gun *should be preferred* on all *other accounts,* that it might be necessary to have "enfilading" guns for siege purposes separate from guns for direct firing; which would be a great drawback. It is evident, therefore, that many items have to be taken into account before making out the balance in favour of the guns under trial. Field guns are not siege guns, but they are often required to enfilade field works and if a shot strikes a few yards short and then goes straight on at a low angle, it is very destructive to troops in column at long ranges or in line, as well as to ammunition waggons, &c., behind the line; if on the contrary, it flies up to the moon on touching the ground a little too short of the enemy, it might as well have been fired into the air at once, or not at all. This peculiarity alone would seem to put the Whitworth gun, under present circumstances, behind the others, as a field gun. We do not pretend to prejudge the question, which is in able and impartial hands and will be, doubtless, carefully weighed and decided.

In firing at the embrasures, all the guns really made such accurate practice, that their shots went clean through the interior openings, in general, without doing so much damage to the cheeks of the embrasures as if they struck them. But they might, when necessary, be fired against the cheeks, if the object were to destroy them, or at the merlons if preferred. It is no fault in any gun to be mathematically true to its object. The time-fuzes were accurately bored, and exploded where intended, just in front of the embrasures, the fragments doing great damage to the "dummies," which represented the gunners behind the parapets. It appears that the gabions made of iron bands, instead of twigs, are very dangerous to the men behind them, for, when struck by a shot, the fragments and pieces of iron band are sent in all directions with great violence, and are even worse than the grape or case shot and fragments of segment shells; cutting and wounding like iron hail, just as the splinters on board ship inflicted more wounds than the shot which caused them. In coast batteries, firing at ships, on the other hand, Mr. Whitworth's hexagonal shot has an advantage in striking short, as it has been proved, on a former occasion, that it screwed its way *in the water,* instead of being turned upwards as it is by the too solid ground of the earth, and pierced the ship's side below her armour, which no round shot could do.

It seems that the practised and expert artillery gunners made much better practice than the civilians employed by the makers, either Whitworth or Armstrong, and that when the latter were allowed to fire their own guns, they made *very wild practice indeed.* Then "Big Will," Sir William Armstrong's 13 inch gun, weighing 22 tons, was fired with 70 lbs of powder only, instead of 90 lbs as before, and with a shot of 612 lbs, made of steel, against a box target, having an outer plate of 6½ inches of solid iron, backed with 24 inches of teak, lined with an inner skin of 1 inch iron, making 7½ inches of iron in all, and 24 inches of teak; but the range was only 200 yards. But the experiment, as all knew before, was superfluous, for the shot, of course, went not only right through and through everything, but knocked the target *all to smash,* so that it could not have been used again, if wished to continue the useless experiment. In fact, the very best 6½ inch iron plate that can be made, backed by 24 inches of teak, offers no more resistance to "Big Will" than an old paper hat-box; and if such guns are mounted in our coast batteries, and well directed, no iron-plated ship can remain exposed for a minute to their fire, any more than our celebrated "wooden walls" dared to face the casemated granite forts of Cronstadt.

In our next number we will continue to follow the experiments, but time and space now warn us to conclude, as proofs require to be corrected and our days of April are numbered.

P.S.—At the last moment allowed us (to be in time for publication) we observe, that on Monday the 18th of April the contest was continued for destructive effect, and on Tuesday the 19th for rapid and continuous effect. The brick walls were 28½ inches thick, and well and solidly built, such as are usual for loop-holed walls at the gorges of permanent works, and other situations where not required to support earth behind them. The firing began at 1100 yards, and Mr. Whitworth's gun had to commence. The target was 14 feet wide, and 8½ feet high; but it seems that out of 15 shots it was only hit 6 times directly, and once after a ricochet, 8 missing altogether; but nevertheless the wall was very much ill-treated, and nearly demolished, by only these six shots. Sir William Armstrong's shunt-gun hit its wall (same dimensions and range) 14 times out of the 15 allowed. All the shot and shell which struck went clean through, and the whole wall was so dilapidated, ricketty, and full of holes, that a very few more shots would have brought it down. As far as the walls were concerned, it was considered that Mr. Whitworth's was as much damaged as the other. The wooden targets placed behind showed, however, that the Armstrong projectiles were much more effective, as Sir William's target was splintered into great holes, and seamed in all directions, by the fragments of the segment shells, while the common shells and Shrapnel from the Whitworth gun had done very little damage. The few pieces that had reached it were from the common shells, and no bullet marks of the Shrapnel could be observed. It is evident, therefore, that if the Whitworth gun be ever adopted, it must take to the segment shells of the Armstrong pattern for general use.

In the continuous firing, though the Armstrong breech-loader did very well, the shunt-gun was preferred, as it seemed the screw of the breech-loader, in such cases, is liable to get stiff and fouled. Mr. Whitworth fired 200 rounds in 72 minutes, Sir William Armstrong's breech-loader in 81 minutes, and the shunt-gun in 82 minutes. But on another occasion, an officer at Shoeburyness fired 100 rounds from the common service breech-loader in 24 minutes, *and made good practice with it at every shot.* At the end of 200 rounds all the guns were so hot that it was impossible to touch them. In this state they were ordered to fire eight shots at small bull's-eyes at 300 yards, in which competition the Armstrong breech-loader and Mr. Whitworth's made equally good practice, but neither of them remarkably well. The shunt-gun, however, put all its shot in a space of about 15 inches square, and it is said that its superiority in this contest was undeniable. Impressions are to be taken of the interior of all the guns to see how they stand the firing. It is finally stated that the Whitworth gun was, on the occasion formerly mentioned, cleaned *by permission* and not without authority, and that the same was given to the Armstrongs. The contest of the 12-pounders will now be soon brought to an end, and then that of the larger calibres will commence.

(*To be continued.*)

## CURIOSITIES OF NAVAL LITERATURE.

### THE WHISTLE.

" The mere animal sense of the ear, so to speak, has often a quick sense of apprehension, when the mind is too much absorbed to notice ordinary sounds. The sailor will sleep calmly through the roar and tumult of the wildest storm, but the first sound of the boatswain's *whistle* will at once arouse him."—*Darien,* ii. 103.

In our degenerate days, the " pipe," or " call," or " whistle," is attached chiefly, if not exclusively, to the office of the boatswain and his mates; but in the " good old times," the kings, both of England and Scotland, wore the whistle as a symbol of maritime sovereignty. Thus, when James V. made a tour of inspection of his coasts, sending a precept at the end of May, 1539, to Dumbarton, that boats and ships, well victualled, might be sent to the isles to meet him there, he ordered his working goldsmith, Mossman, to convert 4½ ounces of gold of the mine into one *quhissel,* which *whistle* was at that time the emblem of supreme command in naval affairs; it was to have " ane dragon" enamelled thereon, and weigh the weight he ordered, "unicorn weight." " The whistle was delivered to the king the penult* day of July. The workmanship cost £10 4s.

And from a dispatch of M. de Bapaumes, Ambassador to the Queen of France, we learn that, " on Thursday, November 1st, King Henry VIII, gave a magnificent entertainment on board a new vessel which was to be christened by his sister; it was a large ship of 207 guns, with accommodation for nearly a thousand troops; the monarch himself acted as galley-master, appearing in the costume of a sailor, made in cloth of gold of frize, and *wearing a golden whistle*, the response to which when he blew it, was melodious music from a band of trumpets and clarions." By the bye, we rather suspect that the ladies of the court looked on their young boatswain sovereign with eyes gleaming with admiration. " Mass was performed on board by the Bishop of Durham, and then the king led forward his royal sister, who gave the vessel the name of *La Pucelle Marie.*"†

The condescension of the same monarch towards one of his naval officers was graciously manifested when, before quitting the flagship, the " Great Harry," at Spithead, he " toke his chayne from his necke, with a *greate whistle of gold* pendante to the same, and did put it aboute the necke of Sir George Carewe, gevinge hyme also therewith many good and comfortable wordes."‡ This incident, which will be hereafter referred to, occurred in the month of July 1545.

Descending from the sovereign to his subjects, we remark that at the reception of Anne of Cleves, the bride elect of Henry VIII, at Calais, A.D. 1539, " the Earl of Southampton, as the Lord Admiral of England, was dressed in a coat of purple velvet cut on cloth of gold, and tied with great aiglettes, and trefoils of gold to the number of four hundred, and baldrick wise *he wore a chain at which hung a whistle of gold* set with rich stones of great value." We are also told that, " in this company were thirty gentlemen of the king's household very richly appareled with great and massy chains, Sir Francis Bryan and Sir Thomas Seymour's chains were of especial value and straunge fashion. The Lord Admiral had also a number of gentlemen in blue velvet and crimson satin, and his yeomen in damask of the same colours.§ The mariners of his ship, wore satin of Bruges."

After this theatrical pageant, we need not have been surprised if the boatswain, or rather the Lord Admiral, had " piped all hands," and passed the word to

* Agnes Strickland's Queens of Scotland. i. 355.
† Addit. MS. ii. 718. Lives of the Princesses of England, by Mary Anne Everett Green, v. iii.
‡ Account of the loss of the " Mary Rose," in the Life of Sir Peter Carew.—Archæologia, xxviii. 110.
§ Agnes Strickland's Lives of the Queens of England, iv. 331.

> "  .  .  .  .  . Strew the deck
> With lavender, and sprinkle liquid sweets,
> That no rude savour maritime invade
> The nose of nice nobility."

Be it remembered that although this gorgeous display of naval-millinery was got up to welcome the gentle lady whom the king delighted to honour, England's future queen, the chivalric lover's future—"Flemish mare !"—"tell it not in Gath, publish it not in the streets of Askelon ;" yet this gold and jewellery, this damask, velvet, and satin, really did encumber the limbs of the Lord Admiral and his naval suite.  The fact seems absurd, and it was absurd ; but we can almost match the absurdity in our days, for not to dwell on the "Bumble" family in all the pomp of Beadledom ; or powdered "Jeames" in scarlet plush ; or Knights of the Bath in crimson sarcenet ; look at one of our present admirals ·in full dress, and we ask whether Mambrino's helmet itself could surpass in discomfort his lace-bound hat ?  Why its very name is droll —"cocked-hat !"  And then those masses of gold bullion, called "epaulettes ;" and the uncomfortable looking coat and "continuations," all refulgent with barbaric gold.  The whole affair is unseemly and grotesque ; and we trust the time is not far distant when a uniform will be introduced into the navy characterised by simplicity and good taste.

But suppose that for a short time we return to Calais, and while there let us gaze on that noble Lord Admiral, his officers and mariners, "deck'd out in all their bravery."  The whole scene seems like a dream ; and the masquerade finery appears to be far less suited for the ship's-company of an English man-of-war, than for the crew of Cleopatra's barge, the "petty officers" of which wore petticoats ; being as Plutarch tells us, "Maids of most distinguished beauty, who habited, like the Nereids and Graces, assisted in the steerage and conduct of the vessel ;" while the "able-seamen" were "boys who, like painted Cupids, stood fanning her on each side the sofa."  The reader will call to mind how exquisitely and faithfully Shakespeare has paraphrased and poetized Plutarch's description of this voyage.*  And whilst rendering merit to whom merit is due, let us not forget the obligation of the navy to that philosopher who made the important discovery that, "there is a natural, an alliterative, and perhaps chemical affinity between petty officers, and petty coats."†

Let us now introduce to the reader another Lord Admiral, one whose name is deservedly cherished by his countrymen, we mean the brave Sir Edward Howard ; and for the better understanding of what follows, it must be borne in mind that the Earl of Surrey's sons, Sir Edward and Sir Thomas Howard, were ordered with two of the king's—Henry VIII.—ships, to look out for the famous

* Antony and Cleopatra, Act ii. Scene ii.  Plutarch, Life of Antony.
† The Letter Bag of the Great Western.

Andrew Barton, who had under his command two vessels, the Scottish "Lion," and the "Little Jenny," sailing under Letters of Marque, granted by James IV. of Scotland, brother-in-law to our Henry VIII.  And also that, during the cruise, Sir Thomas served under his younger brother Edward, on account of the greater naval skill and experience of the latter.  Further it may be well to remind our readers that Edward Howard—whose death we shall presently allude to—was succeeded in the office of Lord Admiral by his brother Thomas; that the said Thomas was generally called by the old historians Lord Howard; that he was created Earl of Surrey in his father's life time, after the title of Duke of Norfolk was restored to the old Earl (A.D. 1514); and lastly, that the aforesaid Thomas was father of the poetical Earl of Surrey.

To return to our story.  We all know the aspiration of the poet,

> " Oh! that the Lord the gift would gie us,
>     To see oursels as others see us !"

Now in the present case, Sir Andrew Barton did not see himself as his opponents—the Howards—saw him, that is to say as a pirate, but rather as a regularly commissioned Admiral.  It must, however, be remembered that the title of Admiral was, in those days, rather vaguely assumed, even as sometimes that of Captain is now. Let us not, therefore, dwell too severely on nice distinctions, because, to speak the truth, it was sometimes difficult to discriminate between a real pirate and a bona-fide Admiral; and, indeed, it is greatly to be feared that both offices were too frequently united in one and the same person.  Be this as it may, so far was Barton from acknowledging any inferiority to his adversaries, that he expresses astonishment at their presumption and want of manners in not doing homage to the flag—Saint Andrew's Cross—under which he sailed; thus when at last the English fell in with Barton, in the Downs, June, 1511,

> " .   .   .   They stirred neither top, nor mast ;
>     Stoutly they pressed Sir Andrew by.
> ' What English churles are yonder,' he sayd,
>     ' That can so little curtesy ?
>
> " ' Now by the roode, three years and more
>     I have been admirall over the sea ;
> And never an English, nor Fortingall,*
>     Without my leave can pass this way.' "

Verily such a defiance, if true, was enough to rouse the blood of all the Howards!  "English churls" forsooth! but in the action which ensued, poor Barton fell mortally wounded by an archer who " smote Sir Andrew to the heart."  Alas! we "come to bury Cæsar not to praise him ;" still less to find fault with him.  So let us pardon the brave old man's prejudices, which, perhaps, blinded him to the fact that his courtly adversaries were not so accustomed

---

* Percy Reliques of Ancient Poetry.

to the sea as he was, and therefore had not equal opportunities for learning good manners; it being, of course, understood that the real school for politeness is the ship. "How should he know how to behave, he never was at sea?" wrote Lord Nelson to his friend Davison, in allusion to Admiral Sir John Orde.

Returning to the death of Barton, we observe that, his last words were an encouragement to his companions;

"' Fight on, my men,' Sir Andrew
    'A little I'me hurt, but yet not slaine;
I'le but lye downe and bleede awhile,
And then I'le rise and fight againe.
' Fight on, my men,' Sir Andrew sayes,
    'And never flinch before the foe;
And stand fast by Saint Andrewe's crosse
Untill you heare my *whistle* blowe.'

" They never heard his *whistle* blowe,
    Which made their hearts waxe sore adread;
Then Horseley sayd, ' aboard, my lord,
    For well I wott Sir Andrew's dead.' "

So died Sir Andrew Barton, one of the most eminent seamen of the age; and his death was not the only calamity which resulted from this battle, for the "Little Jenny" was sunk, owing to the skill of Peter Simon, "the ablest gunner in all the realm,"

" And he lette goe his great gunnes shot,
    Soe well he settled itt with his cc,
The first sight that Sir Andrew sawe,
    He see his pinnace sunk in the sea."

Worse than this, the Scottish "Lion" was captured, and worse than all, national indignation being aroused, the fatal field of Flodden was ere long covered with the dead bodies of King James IV, his nobles, and adherents. And then a nation did indeed mourn! (A.D. 1513).

But further, previous to this naval fight, England, properly speaking, only possessed one royal ship, the "Great Harry" built in 1504. Before this, it was customary for the sovereign, when he wanted ships, to hire or to press them from merchants, so that the capture of the Scottish "Lion" was an important fact, were it only that the English navy was thereby doubled; thus Sir Edward Howard says to Henry VIII.,

" Sir Andrewe's shipp I bring with mee;
    A braver shipp was never none.
Now hath your grace two shipps of war,
    Before in England was but one."

It seems that this exploit of the two Howards, laid the foundation of Sir Edward's fortune; for on April 7, 1512, Henry VIII. constituted him, according to Dugdale, Admiral of England, Wales, &c.

The new Lord Admiral did not long enjoy his promotion, for he lost his life in the service of his country in the following year. He retained the confidence and affection of his royal master, to whom, shortly before his death, he wrote a long and interesting letter on the condition and qualities of the ships composing the fleet under his command, which thus quaintly concludes: " I remit al thys to the order off your most noble Grace, whom I pray God preserve from al adversite, and send yow as much victory off your enemys as ever had any off your noble ancetry.   Written in the Mary Roose by your most bounden subject, and your poor Admirall, Edward Howard."*

To understand the cause of his death, it is necessary to allude to a " tirrible fight" which took place in the year 1512, between the English fleet of " five and twentie faire ships," and the French " navy of nine and thirtie ships," at " the Bay of Brittaine." Now, in those days lived one Sir Thomas Knevet, the King's Master of the Horse, who so well conducted the manœuvres of cavalry, that his " Grace" concluded he must be equally qualified to direct the evolutions of ships, and therefore appointed him to the command of the " Regent," one of the finest vessels composing the present fleet.   And with respect to the French fleet, the principal ship " was a great carrack, called the ' Cordelyer,'† which the Queen of France had lately built at an immense expence," and she —the ship not the Queen—was commanded by " a valiant sea captain named Primaugay,"‡ alias " Primauget," alias " Porsmauget."   So perplexing was the name to our English seamen, that they re-christened the brave Frenchman, Sir Pierce Morgan.

It appears that in this action the " Regent" and the " Cordelier" engaged each other, and the attention of both fleets became, at length, concentrated in the " bloody combat" which took place between these two ocean gladiators.   They closed and " grappled;"— " in conclusion, the Englishmen entred the carrack, which when a gunner saw he desperately set fire on the gunpowder," and both ships, containing together sixteen hundred men, were blown up. On this, " the rest of the fleets separated in consternation, as if by mutual consent, without further fighting."   We are here reminded of that terrible scene at the battle of the Nile, when the L'Orient was scattered aloft in a shower of fire, and each awe-struck fleet ceased firing !

The death of his friend Sir Thomas Knevet, who was blown up in the Regent, greatly distressed the Lord Admiral, and he " made his vow to God, that he would never more see the King in the face, till he had revenged the death of the noble and valiant knight."§

* MS. Cotton. Calig. D. vi. fol. 101. Orig.   Printed in Sir H. Ellis's Letters, i. 217.
† Baker's Chronicles.
‡ Monstrelet's Chronicles. xii. 147.
§ Wolsey's Letters to Fox, &c., &c.   Lingard's Hist. of England, vi. 17. 18.

Accordingly, in April of the following year, 1513, we find Sir
Edward blockading the harbour of Brest, within which the French
fleet were lying at anchor, and, owing to the shallowness of the
water, secure from attack.

But besides the main fleet of the French situated as above, there
was a detachment of six gallies lately arrived from Marseilles under
the command of Pregent, otherwise called by the chroniclers Prior
John.

These gallies were moored far up the Bay of Conquet, between
two rocks bristling with cannon, and the gallant Admiral resolved
on cutting them out. Taking two gallies and four boats, he sailed
into the bay, and succeeded with seventeen seamen in boarding
from his own galley that of the French commander. But unfortunately the gallies soon sheared asunder, and overpowered by
numbers, the brave Lord Admiral, with his not less brave followers,
was driven overboard and drowned; "the just issue," says sour
old Baker, "of his headstrong enterprise." Thus fell the great
Lord Admiral, Sir Edward Howard, on the 25th April, 1513, a
martyr to his oft-repeated maxim, that "no Admiral was good
for anything, that was not brave even to a degree of madness!"[*]
Even in death he thought with grateful affection of his Royal Master, to whom " in his sailor-like will he left his *whistle*, the in-
signia of his command;" but his untimely end prevented the
return of the cherished emblem to the King. He could do no
more, and so, " just before he sunk, he threw *his whistle* into the
sea,"[†] thus preventing, as far as he was able, its desecration by
falling into the hands of the enemy.

In continuing our subject, we request attention to an interesting
ceremony, wherein it would almost seem that Henry VIII. regularly invested Sir George Carew, Captain of the 'Mary Rose,' with
*the whistle* on appointing him to the office of Vice-Admiral. Now
the brother of Sir George was Sir Peter Carew, an eye-witness of
the ceremony, as well as of the loss of the "Mary Rose," concerning all which his biographer[‡] has left us a vivid description.
These Carews, three of whom held commands in the fleet, were
good men and true. At the funeral[§] of Sir Peter, Sir Henry
Sidney, "the Lord Deputie, when he saw his corpes putt into the
grave, sayde, ' Here lyeth nowe in his laste reste a mooste worthye
and a noble gentle knyght, whose faithe to his prynce was never
yet stayned, his troth to his countrie never spotted, and his
valyentnes in service never daunted. A better subjecte the prince
never had.' "[||]

To proceed : after an account of an engagement between the

* Hume, Hist. of England, iii. 87.
† Agnes Strickland's Lives of the Queens of England, iv. 99.
‡ The Lyffe of Sir Peter Carewe, by John Vowell, alias Hooker, Archæologia.
xxviii. 96.
§ 15th Dec. 1575. Ibid.
|| Ibid, p. 145.

English and French fleets, our authority informs us that, "not long after the seas being waxed calm, and the weather very fair, the French galleys, having wind and weather at will, they would also needs range and scour the seas; and finding them clear, and the English Navy to be laid up in harbour, they came along all the south coast of England, even unto the Isle of Wight, where some of them landed, and did much harm; and some of them came unto the haven of Portesmouth, and then rowed up and down; there being never a ship at that instant in that readiness, nor any such wind to serve, if they had been in readiness to impeach them. The King, who upon the news hereof was come to Portesmouth, fretted, and *his teeth stood on an edge,* to see the bravery of his enemies, to come so near his nose, and he not able to encounter with them; wherefore immediately the beacons were set on fire throughout the whole coast, and forthwith such was the resort of the people, as were sufficient to guard the land from the entering of the Frenchmen; likewise commandments were sent out for all the King's ships, and the other ships of war, which were at London and Queenborow, or elsewhere, that they should with all speed possible make haste and come to Portesmouth." &c., &c. "The King as soon as his whole fleet was come together, willeth them to set all things in order, and to go to the seas; which things being done, and every ship cross-sailed and every Captain knowing his charge, it was the King's pleasure to appoint Sir George Carewe to be Vice Admiral of that journey, and had appointed unto him a ship named the Marye Rose, which was as fine a ship, as strong, and as well appointed, as none better in the realm. And at their departure the King dined aboard with the Lord Admiral Vicount Lisle in his ship name the Great Henry, and was there served by the Lord Admiral Sir George Carewe, this gentleman Peter Carewe, and their uncle Sir Gawen Carewe, and with such others only as were appointed to that voyage and service. The King being at dinner, willed some one to go up to the top, and see whether he could see anything at the seas. The word was no sooner spoken, but that Peter Carewe was as forward, and forthwith climbeth up to the top of the ship, and there sitting the King asked of him what news?—who told him that he had sight of three or four ships, but as he thought they were merchants; but it was not long but he had ascryed a great number, and then he cried out to the King' that there was as he thought, a fleet of men-of-war. The king supposing them to be the French men-of-war, as they were indeed, willed the board to be taken up, and every man to go to his ship, as also a long-boat to come and carry him on land. And first he hath secret talke with the Lord Admiral, and then he hath the like with Sir George Carewe, and at his departure from him, took *his chain from his neck, with a great whistle of gold pendant to the same, and did put it about the neck of the said Sir George Carewe,* giving him also therewith many good and com-

fortable words.   The King then took his boat, and rowe: to the
land; and every other captain went to his ship appointedd to him.
Sir George Carewe being entered into his ship, commanded every
man to take his place, and the sails to be hoysted; but the same
was no sooner done, but that the Marye Rose began to heel, that
is, to lean on the one side.   Sir Gawen Carewe being then in his
own ship, and seeing the same, called for the master of his ship,
and told him thereof, and asked him what it meant? who answered,
that if she did heel, s e was like to be cast away.   Then the said
Sir Gawen, passing by the Marye Rose, called out to Sir George
Carewe, asking him how he did? who answered, that he had a
sort of knaves whom he could not rule.   And it was not long after
but that the said Marye Rose, thus heeling more and more, was
drowned, with seven hundred men which were in her, whereof very
few escaped.   It chanced unto this gentleman, as the common
proverb is, ' the more cooks, the worst potage.'   He had in this
ship one hundred mariners, the worst of them being able to be a
master in the best ship within the realm, and they so maligned
and disdained one the other, that refusing to do that which they
should do, were careless to do that they ought to do; and so
contending in envy, perished in forwardness.   The King this
meanwhile stood on the land, and saw this tragedy, as also the
lady, the wife to Sir George Carewe, who with that sight fell into
swooning, the King being oppressed with sorrow on every side,
comforted her, and thanked God for the other, hoping that of a
hard beginning there would follow a better ending.   And notwithstanding this loss, the service appointed went forward as soon
as wind and weather would serve, and the residue of the fleet,
being about the number of one hundred and five sails, took the
seas.   The Frenchmen perceiving the same, like as a sort of sheep
running into the fold, they shifted away, and got them into their
harbours, thinking it better to lie there in a safe skin, than to
encounter with them of whom they should little win."

We may naturally feel surprised at the loss of the Marye Rose, but
perhaps the wonder was that other ships did not follow her example;
—indeed the Great Harry had nearly undergone the same fate—
which Sir Walter Raleigh says,* " was occasioned by a little sway in
casting the Mary Rose about, her ports being within sixteen inches
of the water;" whereas we think that nine feet should be about
the minimum height of ports of first class ships.

But not only was the Marye Rose and her gallant commander
' drowned,' but the beautiful *whistle* given scarcely an hour before
by the King to Sir George Carewe was ' drowned' also.   There it
lies at the bottom of the sea at Spithead, and if our divers fail in
restoring it to us, we trust that as a pious lobster picked up the
crucifix of Xavier from its ocean bed, brought it on shore, and
reverently laid it at the Saint's feet—so some other well-disposed

* Invention of shipping.

member of the crustacea family may find the *whistle* of Sir
George Carewe, and carefully deposit it on Southsea beach, from
whence we hope to see the precious relic conveyed to one of our
national museums.

Having traced the official possession of the *whistle* to the
Sovereign, the Lord Admiral and the Captain, we remark, that on
the gradual establishment of a Royal Navy, it is natural to suppose
that the respective duties of the various officers were more clearly
defined, and then the Master became par excellence *the* executive
officer, and so, conjointly with the Captain was adorned with the
*whistle;* thus in "The Tempest," the Boatswain says, "Heigh,
my hearts; cheerly, cheerly, my hearts, yare, yare; take in the
topsail : tend to the *Master's whistle."*    So also Sydney, as quoted
by Dr. Johnson, observes that "the masters and pilots were so
astonished, that they knew not how to direct, and if they knew
they could scarcely, when they directed, hear their own *whistle."*
And Sir William Monson in his Naval Tracts says, "all this while
the ship lay upon the lee ; and seeing it was in vain to expect my
return, the *master* called with the *whistle* to fill the sails." And
again, "as the *master* commands the tackling of the ship, the
hoising or striking of the yard, the taking in or putting out the
sails, upon the blowing of the *master's whistle,* the boatswain takes
it with his, and sets the sailors with courage to do their work."
Here it appears that the *whistle* still belonged to the master, but
that his authority was in some sort delegated to the boatswain, by
whom it, the whistle, was also worn.    And in Hackluyt's account
of the action  between an English merchant vessel the 'Three Half-
moons,' and eight Turkish gallies, A.D. 1563, the *whistle* is appropriated to the boatswain ; "chiefly the boatswain shewed himself valiant above the rest; for he fared amongst the Turks like
a wood lion, for there was none of them that either could or durst
stand in his face, till at last there came a shot from the Turks,
which brake his *whistle* assunder and smote him on the breast, so
that he fell downe, bidding them farewell, and be of good comfort,
encouraging them likewise to winne praise by death, rather than
to live captives in misery and shame."

When—we were going to say in an evil hour—the captain and
master surrendered the *whistle* to the exclusive use of the boatswain, we know not.  It was probably when lieutenants were
introduced into the service, and when the arrangements concerning
the relative rank and duty of masters and lieutenants were first
adopted ; arrangements which some think are so unfortunately
purpetuated at the present time.    However this may be, the
*whistle* was established as the prerogative of the boatswain's office
long before 5th December 1675, on which date Teonge in his
Diary tells us that, "Last night our boatswaine died very suddenly,
and this afternoone I buryed him in the Greek's church-yard. He
was nobly buryed, and like a souldyer.  He had a neate coffin,

which was covered over with one of the King's jacks, and his boarson's *sylver whistle* and chaine layed on the top, *to shew his office,* betweene two pistolls crost with a hanger drawne."

Moreover, the *whistle* was formerly used in foreign as well as in the English service, thus Evelyn says in his Memoirs, 7th October, 1644, at Marseilles, "We went to visite the gallys, being about twenty-five; the captain of the Galley Royal gave us most courteous entertainment in his cabine, the slaves in the interim, playing both loud and soft musiq very rarely. Then he showed us how he commanded their motions with a nod and his *whistle,* making them row out."

And after Captain Jaques Cartier on his arrival in Canada, "in the yeere of our Lord 1535, had *touched* diverse diseased men, some blinde, some lame and impotent, and some so old that the haire of their eye-lids came downe and covered their cheekes," first, however reciting "the Gospel of Saint John, that is to say in the beginning was the word," and then, "praying to God that it would please him to open the hearts of this poore people, and to make them know his holy word, and that they might receive baptisme and christendome, and that done, taking a service booke in his hand, and with a loud voyce reading all the passion of Christ word by word;"—then it was that these poor heathens, in gratitude for this sailor missionary's kindness, "tooke the chayne of our Captaine's *whistle* which was of silver, and showed us that such stuffe came from the river," to which they pointed. A strange congregation this! "This poore people kept silence, and were marvellously attentive." On their dismissal, "the captaine commanded trumpets and other musicall instruments to be sounded, which when they heard they were very merie."[*] And well might they have been merry, had they comprehended the good tidings of great joy which had been just proclaimed to them!

But it may be asked whether the ancients used the *whistle* to their Navy? Of course they did, a young midshipman is apt in reply; how else could duty be possibly carried on? How were they to lower a cask of pork, or salute the captain when going over the side, or belay the main-sheet without piping the whistle?

We confess that the little we know on the subject seems to controvert the idea that a *whistle* was used in the Biremes and Triremes of the Ancients, for "he who had command over the rowers was called Hortator and Pausarius, or Portisculus, which was also the name of the staff or *mallet* with which he excited or retarded them. He did this also with his voice in a musical tone, that the rowers might keep time."[†]

"One ready stands to sing a marine song
To the brisk seamen as they row along,
Whose lively strains a constant movement keep,
To show when every oar should brush the deep;

[*] Hackluyt, iii. 222.
[†] Adam's Rom. Antiq.

And as each stroke falls on the sounding main,
He cheers their labours with an answering strain."
We are further told that
"Against the mast the tuneful Orpheus stands,
Plays to the wearied rowers, and commands
The thoughts of toil away."
And also that,
"His notes direct how every oar should strike,
How they should order keep."*

These ancient practices are hardly extinct in our time, thus;
"The boats on the Ganges are paddled sometimes by forty men.
The paddlers are directed by a man who stands up, and sometimes
makes use of a branch of a plant to regulate their motions, using
much gesticulation, and telling his story to excite either laughter
or exertion."†

But without troubling ourselves about the Naval routine of
the Ancients, we observe that in early times the Spaniards used
the *whistle* on board their ships, for in "the valiant fight performed
in the St. of Gibraltar, by the Centurion of London against five
Spanish gallies, in the month of April 1591," being becalmed,
"they saw sundry gallies make towards them, in very valiant and
courageous sort, the chiefe leaders and souldiers in those gallies
bravely apparalled in silke coates, with their silver *whistles* about
their neckes, and great plumes of feathers in their hattes."

Nothing daunted the Centurion, "who before their coming
had prepared for them and intended to give them so soure a welcome as they might; and thereupon having prepared their close-
fights and all things in a readinesse, they called upon God, on
whom onely they trusted, and having made their prayers, and
cheered up one another, to fight so long as life endured, they
beganne to discharge their great ordnance upon the gallies."  On
the other hand the "Centurion was fired five several times, with
wilde-fire and other provision," and, "in every of the gallies there
were about 200 souldiers, who together with the shot, spoiled,
rent and battered the Centurion very sore through her maine
maste, and slew foure of the men in the saide shippe, besides ten
other persons hurt, by meanes of splinters which the Spaniards
shotte: yea in the ende when their provision was almost spent,
they were constrained to shoote at them hammers, and the chaines
from their slaves, and yet God bee thanked, they received no more
damage, but by spoyling and over-wearying of the Spaniards, the
Englishmen constrained them to ungrapple themselves, and get
them going; and sure if there had bene any other fresh shippe or
succour to have relieved and assisted the Centurion, they had
slaine, suncke, or taken all those gallies and their souldiers."

Our interest in this "sore and deadly fight," has almost caused

* Potter's Grecian Antiq. ii. 150.
† Nav. Chron. ii. 63.

us to forget that, "the trumpet of the Centurion sounded foorth the deadly points of warre, and encouraged them to fight manfully against their adversaries; on the contrary part, there was no warlike musicke in the Spanish gallies, but onely their *whistles of silver*, which they sounded foorth to their owne contentment."[*]

But the earliest notice which occurs to us of the use of the *whistle* at sea is contained in the following lines:—

"One with a *whistle* haug'd about his necke,
    Showes by the sounde which cord must be vndone,
And straight the ship-boy readie at a becke,
    Vnto the tops with nimble sleight doth runne."[†]

Now Ariosto was born in the year 1474, and according to Sir John Harrington he commenced the "Orlando" when he was thirty years of age. We cannot therefore greatly err if we suppose that the above passage was written, and that therefore the *whistle* was used at sea as early as the year 1504; indeed it must have been used earlier than this period, provided that the following notice in the inventory of the jewels of James III of Scotland, namely, "Item, a *Quhissill* of gold,"[‡] referred to a *Naval* whistle; bearing in mind that the above-named king was murdered in the year 1488.

Was it an accidental coincidence that Shakespeare as well as Ariosto should refer to the effect of the *whistle* in arousing the energy of the ship-boy?

"————————behold
Upon the hempen tackle ship-boys climbing;
Hear the shrill *whistle*, which doth order give
To sounds confus'd."

This again reminds us of another passage:

"One with his *whistle's* sound, the want of speech
Supplies, and gives the needful charge to each."[§]

We remark further that Falconer defines "call (sifflet du maître d'équipage) a sort of *whistle* or pipe, of silver or brass, used by the boatswain and his mates to summon the sailors to their duty, and direct them in the different employments of the ship."

"It is sounded to various strains, adapted to the different exercises, as hoisting, heaving, lowering, veering away, belaying, letting go a tackle &c., and the piping of it is as attentively observed by sailors, as the beat of the drum to march, retreat, rally, charge, &c., is obeyed by soldiers."[||]

We may be surprised that so simple an instrument as the whistle has—so to speak—such capability for expressing so many ideas. But we see the same varieties of command conveyed to soldiers through the different notes of the bugle; and more singular still

* Hackluyt ii. 164.
† Orlando Furioso, book xviii.
‡ Tytler, History of Scotland, iv. 351.
§ Orlando Furioso, book xviii.
|| Falconer's Marine Dictionary.

the half civilised Maroons—who proved such formidable enemies to our regular troops—"had a particular call upon the horn for each individual by which he was summoned from a distance, as easily as he would have been spoken to by name had he been near."* And we are told that Robert Bruce "winds his horn in so masterly a way, that Sir James Douglas instantly pronounces that blast to be noone but the King's."† Indeed the Scotch appear to have been famed for the noise if not for the melody of their horns, for when defeated by Edward I. they rushed down upon the Earl of Surrey, "blowing their horns, which according to the expression of a contemporary historian, ' made a noise enough to have startled hell itself.' "‡

Hitherto we have alluded to the *whistle* as connected with the naval service; but it seems that civic dignitaries occasionally assume the whistle as an emblem of authority for, "at the great Cobb Ale of Lyme Regis, a feast kept up for many days of each Whitsuntide for the maintenance of the Cobb or harbour there, the Mayor presided. A silver *whistle* and chain were given to the borough for the use of the Mayor to be worn at this great feast."§

Not only so, but in olden times our learned judges opined that the purity of the ermine was not sullied, nor the gravity of the wig‖ diminished by the companionship of the boatswain's *whistle;* for " the reviewer of Mr. Foss's Vols. V. and VI. of the Judges of England in the January number of the Gentleman's Magazine, (1858), suggests that he should give some account of the first use, and ultimate disuse of the boatswain's *whistles* which he says are " suspended from the necks of the judges, (Coke for example) of this period."¶ And who among landsmen could with greater propriety be adorned with the *whistle* than this venerable judge? To whom the naval supremacy of old England was so dear, and who in the quaint language lately quoted in the House of Commons** declared that "the King of England's Navy doth excell the shipping of all other foreign kings and princes; for if you respect beautiful statelinesse, or stately beauty, they are so many large and spacious kingly and princely palaces. If you regard strength and defence, they are so many moving impregnable castles and barbicans, and were termed of old the walls of the Realm. When our English Navy is among the ships of other nations, it is like lions *inter pecora campi,* and like a falcon *inter phasianos, perdices, et alia volatilia timida cæli.*"

* History of the Maroons, by K. C. Dallas, i. 89.
† Tytler's Hist. of Scotland, ii. 339.
‡ Tytler's Scottish Worthies, i 159.
§ Notes and Queries. 2nd Ser. v. 21. 24 Ap. 1858
‖ Are we guilty of an anachronism, in assuming that the wig was then worn on the judicial bench?
¶ Notes and Queries 2nd Series, No. 115. 13 March, 1858, p. 213.
** Speech of Mr. C. Clifford on the Navy Estimates, Times, 26th February, 1864.

## MILITARY ENGINEERING OF THE ANCIENTS.

### (*Continued.*)

In No. 415 of the old *Spectator*, which number was given to the world on the 26th of June, 1712, there is to be found the following remark, from Addison's pen: "The Wall of China is one of those Eastern Pieces of Magnificence which makes a Figure even in the Map of the world, although an Account of it would have been thought Fabulous were not the Wall itself still extant."

During the century and a half which have elapsed since the above sentence was written, much has been learned in Europe respecting the origin and construction of this great work of antiquity, in consequence of an increased freedom of intercourse with the descendants of its builders. It has been thus ascertained that the object of the Great Wall was to check the invasions, from the north, of the hordes of Mongol Tartars; that it was constructed during the Sin dynasty, about 250 years before the Christian era, and that it was completed in the reign of the Emperor Chin Chee Kwong. It is, however, a disputed point, among those well qualified to judge, whether this great fortification was the result of voluntary or of enforced labour; for it has been argued, with some show of probability, that, from internal evidence, "the Great Wall of China seems far more likely to have been the cherished desire of the people than the odd fancy of a cruel king—a noble effort towards self-preservation rather than a monstrous freak of tyranny." This argument is to be found at length in Mr. Fleming's interesting work, "Travels on Horseback in Mantcbu Tartary."

It is said that the wall was built in ten years by many millions of labourers, forming the population of the small feudal states in the north of China, and that at least 200,000 lives were sacrificed to the severity of the labour. It extends from east to west, along the frontiers of three provinces, over about nineteen degrees of longitude. Its total length has been computed to be 1400 miles, and Mr. Barrow, the historiographer to Lord Macartney's embassy in 1793, considered, as the result of calculation, that a far greater quantity of materials was employed in its construction than in that of all the houses in both England and Scotland. But his premises may be distrusted. Assuming the number of houses to be 1,800,000, with 2,000 cubic feet of masonry apiece, he evidently supposed that the Great Wall, from the westernmost point of Kan Suh up to the Lia-tong Gulf, had the same strong profile that he saw it possessing in the neighbourhood of Pekin—the only part of it that he had an opportunity of examining.

In the same manner, nearly all who have visited this great work are too apt to conceive they are rightly describing *ex pede*

*Herculem.* They either exaggerate its importance, or deride its inutility, according to their judgment of that particular portion of the wall to which they may have happened to have had access. Hence a diversity of opinion among those who, with equal powers of judgment, generalise too rapidly from insufficient and varying data. A mistaken view of a subject must inevitably be taken by those who deduce the whole from a part, and this axiom is especially obvious in the tangible physical case of the Great Wall of China. It is proposed, therefore, to state now, in order, different travellers' accounts of the dimensions and other details of different parts of this long line of defence. From these will be inferred the variable nature of the profile of a most interesting specimen of the Military Engineering of the Ancients—a work of defensive fortification which ranks as one of the great wonders of the world, and which has withstood the ravages of time for upwards of 2,100 years!

To commence at the east end of the wall, and to accept once more the pleasant guidance of Mr. Fleming, we find that, at the town of Shan-hai Kwan on the Gulf of Lian-tong, the height of the wall averages 35 feet, including five or six feet for a crenelated parapet on the north side. The main rampart is 20 or 25 feet thick. The towers, which are from 150 to 200 yards apart from centre to centre, are 10 feet higher than the walls, and are built 30 or 40 feet square at the base. Both towers and walls are at this place admirably constructed to resist the attacks of enemies and time. Upon a solid granite base, six or eight feet high, there rests an earthen rampart, well rammed, and revetted on both sides by countersloping walls of brickwork. This brickwork is remarkably good. The courses are regular, the joints are well pointed, and the bricks are set in a firm white lime mortar, of an extremely tenacious description. Each brick measures nine inches in length, four-and-a-half in width, and two-and-a-half in thickness. They appear to be made of a light sandy clay, and are of a characteristic bluish gray, or dark slate colour.

Should the reader care to see a brick from the Great Wall of China, he may do so without much trouble, by visiting the Royal United Service Institution in Whitehall Yard, where there is deposited a specimen, taken (as its label states) from Chii-fung-kwan, on the 23rd March, 1861, by Mr. Fonblanque, Assistant Commissary-General. This brick measures fourteen inches in length, it is six-and-three-quarter inches wide, and two-and-a-half thick. It has a bluish gray colour, appears to have been well burnt, rings well on being struck, and the fractures show a close homogeneous texture. Pulverized rock appears to have been mixed with the clay, in the same manner that we now use sand. Altogether the brick is a good brick, and speaks well for the Chinese workmanship two thousand years ago.

Journeying westward from the above mentioned town of Shan-hai Kwan, the traveller finds the Great Wall ascending the mountains, and reducing the dimensions of its profile. The wall itself is often but eight feet thick, the towers that flank it but eight feet high. In many places the wall has been worn down to the level of the country; in others it is rudely built of rubble or of loose stones. According to the statement of an engineer officer who accompanied Lord Macartney's embassy, in 1793, the wall near Pekin is built of earth and brick to a height of 20 feet, and rests upon a stone base projecting two feet beyond the brickwork, and of the same height of two feet. The rampart is composed of well-rammed earth, revetted on both sides with brickwork, and its terreplein is covered with square tiles; the thickness being 25 feet at base, and 23 feet at the level of the platform. The towers, which are 37 feet high, are square, and their walls have a batter outwards—the side of the square being 40 feet at the base, and 30 feet at the top. The thickness of the parapet wall is only eighteen inches.

And thus, with varying proportions, usually respectable, but sometimes contemptible, journeys on from east to west, up hill and down dale, the wonderful "Ten Thousand Lee Old Wall," as the Chinese call it, (the lee being equivalent to about one third of an English mile). The euphonious name, in its native tongue, is Wan Li Tchang Sing.

Here and there, offshoots from the Great Wall encircle, at right angles to it, some neighbouring town or village, as, for example, the pass and town of Lo-wan Eu, which is distant six or seven miles from the city of Sunwha, and lies about a hundred miles west of the above mentioned Shan-hai Kwan. At this point, the wall measures about seventeen feet ten inches in height, though occasionally, where the parapet is highest, it exceeds eighteen feet six inches. Its thickness is only thirteen feet, and the height of the parapet five feet four inches. The towers are thirty-one feet three inches high, and twenty-eight feet one inch thick. The parapet is embrasured or crenelated, and the merlons are loop-holed; and the towers, too, are pierced for the discharge of some projectile.

Captain Parish, of the Royal Engineers, who accompanied Lord Macartney in his mission to Pekin, in 1793, remarks that the soles of the embrasures of the Great Wall were pierced with small holes, similar to those used in Europe for the reception of the swivels of wall pieces. He says further, that, "The holes appear to be part of the original construction of the wall, and it seems difficult to assign to them any other purpose than that of resistance to the recoil of fire-arms." From the inference which it seems intended should be drawn from this sentence, there may be deduced, *en passant*, an opinion concerning the date of the invention of gunpowder, which is much at variance with our preconceived and usually accepted ideas on the subject. But, as

it is proposed to discuss this question, in all its bearings, on some
future opportunity, it will not be advisable to continue a fanciful
speculation on the subject on the present occasion, especially since
our inquiries have been hitherto restricted to the discussion of the
defensive, and not the offensive, military engineering of the
ancients.

*Revenons à nos moutons.* At Lo-wan Eu, the wall, for the
most part, is constructed of brick, with rubble-work in the centre;
but further away it is composed almost wholly of stone, in fact,
whatever materials were closest at hand would appear to have been
made use of; thus, wherever granite abounds, the wall consists of
large, shapeless masses of granite, worked only on the outside.
The towers, however, appear to have been nearly always built of
brick, resting upon broad foundations of hewn stone, and the
central intervals between them vary, in different places, from a
hundred and fifty to three hundred yards. There is, of course, a
strong guard-house at Lo-wan Eu, as there is at all of the important
gateways and passes traversed by the Great Wall.

These guard-houses are very numerous in China, the rule being
that there shall be one of them at every half league, on all the
great roads. They are always whitewashed, whatever be the
material, wood or earth, of which they are constructed. Near
each guard-house, or barrack, is a square tower, which serves in
time of war for giving signals, at night-time, by means of fire-
works, thus forming what we used in England before the invention
of telegraphy, a system of semaphore towers. With reference to
these towers, the French missionary, M. Huc, relates that in the
year 780 B.C., the Emperor Yeou Wang, the thirteenth of the
Tcheou dynasty, was weak enough one night to yield to the absurd
request of his wife, and to order the alarm signal fire-works to be
displayed. The Empress' request was prompted partly by a wish
for amusement at the expense of the Chinese soldiers, and partly
by a desire to ascertain whether these fire-work signals would
really, as they professed, summon the troops to the defence of the
capital, Pekin. As the messages passed on, from province to
province, the governors despatched in turn their military mandarins
and forces to the rescue of the city. When the soldiers learned,
on their arrival, that they had been called together for the capricious
amusement of a silly woman, they returned home full of indignation; and when, shortly afterwards, the Tartars made an actual
invasion upon the empire, and advanced with rapidity to the very
walls of the capital, the Emperor gave the alarm in grave earnest,
but not a man stirred throughout the empire, thinking that this
time the Empress was again amusing herself. The consequence
was, that, as the cry of "wolf" had been raised once too often,
the wolf at last actually got into the fold, for the Tartars captured
the city of Pekin, and massacred the royal family. As for the
authenticity of this story, all that can be said is *se non vero è ben*

*trovato*, and that we have read something like it in the pages of
Æsop.

M. Huc somewhat ridicules Mr. Barrow's description of the
grand and imposing Great Wall of China.   He says that he has
crossed it at fifteen different places, and that on several occasions
he travelled for whole days on roads parallel to it.   At many
places he found it consisting, not of the strong double-turreted
rampart which exists towards Pekin; but of a low wall of brickwork,
earth, and sometimes even merely of flint stones roughly piled up.
As to the foundation wall, described by Mr. Barrow as composed
of large masses of freestone cemented together, the French traveller
asserts that he never discovered the slightest trace of any such
work.   It is obvious, however, that the Emperor, acting as
engineer, said to have been Thsin Hoang Ti, would fortify with
especial care the vicinity of the capital, as being the point to
which the Tartar hordes would be most likely to advance.   It
is natural further to conceive, that the mandarins charged with
the execution of the Emperor's plan, would faithfully discharge
their duty by perfecting the works immediately under the
Emperor's eye, and would content themselves with erecting a
less powerful defence at those remote points of the empire where
the Tartars were little to be feared, as, for example, the position of
the Ortous and Alechan mountains.

The pig-tailed Chinese of the present day, testify by their
appearance to the inability of their ancestors' fortification to
resist the raids of the lawless tribes residing on the borders of the
old empire.   But we should not, on this account alone, condemn
the presumption of the idea, or the manner in which it was
carried out.   The same principle, under the same circumstances,
was put into effect four hundred years later by the Roman
governors of Britain; that is to say, by distinguished generals
of a nation who exalted military science into a virtue, by men
who believed, and acted in believing that "in summo imperatore
quatuor hæ virtutes inesse debent, virtus, auctoritas, felicitas,
*scientia rei militaris.*"   But in the case of the Great Wall of
China, though the engineers of all ages have condemned it as
a fortification, though there is no great amount of skill, and
but little of ingenuity displayed in its construction, yet we cannot
refuse a certain tribute of admiration to the energy and perseverance
of its builders, who have left behind them an extraordinary monument of the masonic art, to take rank as the chief of the seven
great wonders of the world.   And in reference to its comparatively
low powers of resistance to the advance of the dreaded invaders,
it is well to remember the following remarks of Gibbon, truisms
though they be: The military art has been altogether changed
since their time by the invention of gunpowder, which now enables
man to command the two most powerful agents of nature, air and
fire.   Mathematics, chemistry, mechanics, and architecture, have

been applied to the service of war; and the adverse parties now oppose to each other the most elaborate modes of attack and of defence.  Historians may indignantly observe that the preparations of a siege would found and maintain a flourishing colony, yet we cannot be displeased that the subversion of a city should be a work of cost and difficulty; or that an industrious people should be protected by those arts which should always be taught to accompany the progress of military virtue.  Cannon and fortifications now form an impregnable barrier against the Tartar horse; and Europe is secure from any future irruption of barbarians; since, before they can conquer, they must cease to be barbarous.  Their gradual advances in the science of war would always be accompanied, as we may learn from the example of Russia, with a proportionable improvement in the arts of peace and civil policy; and they themselves must deserve a place among the polished nations whom they subdue.

Gibbon's allusion to the Great Wall of China is couched in almost identically the same words as those employed by Addison in the quotation standing at the head of this article.  Built, as he says, to protect the frontiers of the empire against the inroads of the Huns, this stupendous work, which holds a conspicuous place in the map of the world, has *never* contributed to the safety of an unwarlike people.  But, as if in contradiction to this assertion, Dr. Stanley (in his "Sinai and Palestine") speaks of the Great Wall which *still* defends the Chinese Empire against the Mongolian tribes, from whom the civilization of Northern Asia has experienced the same reverses as that of Southern Asia from the Arabs.  Such opposite conclusions do great minds deduce from precisely the same premises!  And it has therefore been thought advisable to state here in detail the *pros* and the *cons* of each branch of the subject now under consideration, and these not propounded, in a mixed form, as the original ideas of any one individual, but as the separate results of thoughtful investigation on the part of those well qualified to offer an opinion, of men generally recognized as great and trustworthy authorities.

After the above description of the Great Wall of China, it is proposed to offer some slight account of the defensive walls erected by the Romans, with similar object, in their province of Britain. It will be recollected that Rome owed her most extensive and permanent conquests in this country to Cneius Julius Agricola, the father-in-law of the historian Tacitus.  Under Agricola, in the year 78, A.D, a frontier was established to the lands, acquired by these conquests, by the erection of a line of works between the Friths of Clyde and Forth—a distance of forty miles—while the districts within that line were rendered secure by the establishment of camps and fortresses, wherever the condition of the tribes seemed to require the presence of any armed force among them. A double line of forts was built by Ostorius Scapula along the

Avon and Severn, and a second wall, from the Solway Frith to the mouth of the Tyne, was erected under Hadrian, A.D. 121; forty years later, in the reign of Antoninus Pius, the propætor Lollius Urbicus connected Agricola's military stations, or detached forts, between the Friths of Clyde and Forth, by a turf rampart built upon foundations of stone. This Wall of Antoninus (as it was called) a short distance beyond the modern cities of Edinburgh and Glasgow, was fixed as the northern limit of the Roman province. Finally, the Emperor Septimus Severus, after chastising the Caledonians, A.D., 209, erected his celebrated rampart nearly parallel to Hadrian's, from the east coast, near Tynemouth, to the Solway Frith—a distance of about seventy-four miles. The vestiges of this great work are still visible in some places. It was twelve feet high, eight feet thick, and had battlemented parapets four feet high. The defence and manning of this wall was provided for by means of eighteen stations, four miles apart (each accommodating 600 men), eighty-one castles, less than a mile apart (each garrisoned by 100 men), and three hundred and thirty turrets, or watch-towers (each containing a few men). The total garrison requisite for the defence of the wall may thus be taken as about 13,000 men.

It is needless to point out how these military walls failed to stop the inroads of the Picts and Scots. Similar in object to the Great Wall of China, they were similarly inefficacious in checking the advance of the wild hordes they were built to repel. And, in glancing backwards through the history of the art of fortification —with that acuteness of perception which (we flatter ourselves) is acquired by experience—we find it a source of wonder that there have actually occurred so many attempts at defence by extensive lines of wall, which are now universally admitted to be both faulty in principal, and useless in practice. Thus, the Emperor Hadrian, in addition to his wall between the Solway and Tyne, built several on the threatened frontiers of Germany. In previous numbers we have described the Sidd Nimrúd, (or Parapet of Nimrod), which stands—seventy miles long—on the Babylonian plain; and the Egyptian Gisr el Agoos, which is about a hundred and seventy miles long. At the beginning of the sixth century, the mountains of Caucasus were covered by the so-called "rampart of Gog and Magog," built by Cabades and his son Chosroes. Huge stones, seven feet thick and twenty-one feet long, were laid together, like Cyclopean masonry, without mortar or metal cramps, and formed a wall 300 miles long, running from the shores of Derbend over the hills and through the valleys of Daghestan and Georgia Then the Emperor Justinian constructed long walls in the Crimea for the protection of the Goths, with whom he had entered into alliance, and besides these, he built (as Gibbon relates) a strong wall across the straits of Thermopylæ, which seemed to protect, but which had so often betrayed the safety of Greece.

From the edge of the sea-shore, through the forests and valleys, and as far as the summit of the Thessalian mountains, a strong rampart was carried, which occupied every available entrance, and was garrisoned by a force of 2,000 men.

According to Strabo (vii, iv, 6), Ansander built a wall across the Isthmus of the Chersonese, near the Palus Mœotis. This wall was 45 miles long, and was flanked by towers about 2,000 yards apart. Remains of it are still to be seen. Again, Anastasius built a wall 160 miles long, from the Propontis to the Euxine.

Nor must be forgotten the Celtic lines of wall, erected in this country long before the Roman occupation—such as, for instance, the three British dykes across the Langton Wold in the East Riding which extend from Malton (Derventio) to the Humber at Cave; and the "Gryme's Dyke" in Hertfordshire, which runs from Berkhampstead to Wendover and Missenden, having been built apparently as a means of defence against the invading Belgæ.

A very curious system of defence, adopted by the early inhabitants of Britain, is to be found in the detached "vitrified forts" (as they are called), of which the ruins are to be seen in the shires of Perth, Forfar, Kincardine, Aberdeen, Banff, Moray, Inverness, Ross, Cromarty, Argyle, Bute, Berwick, and Galloway. These forts are about fifty in number, but Dr. Hibbert has also found vitrified remains at Elsness in Sanday, one of the Orkneys. They consist of solid masses of a glassy structure, somewhat resembling volcanic lava, or the refuse of a furnace. Some are round, some elliptical; whilst others are square or of parallelogram plan. Their walls vary in thickness from two or three up to twenty feet, and in height from four to twelve feet. A few of them are approached by regular causeways or ramps and many are furnished with wells. They were first noticed and described in 1773 by Mr. Williams, a mineral surveyor, who suggests, as a possible explanation of their origin, that the early inhabitants of the country, unacquainted with the use of mortar, may have discovered that some rocks, which resist the action of fire, become fusible when subjected to a high temperature in contact with certain others. It is unnecessary to pursue a fruitless inquiry into the exact origin of these curious works, for the date of their construction, and the nationality of their builders, are still matters of speculation among skilled antiquaries.

Nor can we boast a greater knowledge concerning the dates and authors of the British hill-forts, or the Irish *dunes*—the chief of the former being the fortress of the White Caterthun overlooking the Scottish valley of Strathmore, the most important of the latter being the Rath Keltair at Downpatrick, and Rath Righ of Tara Hill, in the county of Meath, which is said by tradition to have been the ancient seat of the Irish kings. These earthen *raths* or *dunes* are mostly circular; and they are generally found together, in pairs. They abound in the level districts of Ireland, as well as on heights where stone is not readily accessible: and in the different localities where they are found they derive their peculiar character from the peculiar features of the country they defend.

One more instance may be adduced of an early British fort, viz., that of Cair (the Castle) Conan, in St. Breage, Cornwall. This fort, which is situate upon Tregoning Hill, about six hundred feet above the sea, measures one hundred and six yards by ninety-two, but its form is irregular, being adapted to the contour of the hill. It has two parapets and ditches, the latter being in both cases about eighteen feet wide. The outer parapet is formed of earth and is twelve feet high, but the inner, which is fifteen feet high, has its exterior slope (at an angle of 40°) faced with rude rubble masonry. This is a peculiarity which deserves attention, since it is almost the solitary instance—as far as the writer knows— of this mode of construction. Another point worthy of remark, in considering the design of this work, is its difference in plan from these usually met with, which are mostly circular. Sir Gardner Wilkinson says, in a paper upon "Cair Brea," read at the Royal Institution of Cornwall:—"it is a mistake to suppose that all British camps are round: the circular form was the one preferred if the ground was suited to it; a perfect rectangular encampment may at once be pronounced not British, but by far the greater number of British camps were of irregular form—according to their position and the shape of the hill, with a general inclination to curved lines wherever they could be judiciously introduced."

Similar to, but far more magnificent than, these ancient British fortifications, are the remains of the earthworks in the Mississippi Valley, of which a most interesting account is given in Dr. Wilson's "Pre-historic Man." Constructed at some remote period by the predecessors of the red man, they abound particularly in the state of Ohio, where their number exceeds 11,000. Some of these mounds served for fortifications, some for temples, and others for sepulture; but it is only with the first of these that we have to deal on the present occasion. Dr. Wilson states that they stretch away from the upper waters of the Ohio to the westward of Lake Erie, and thence along Lake Michigan, nearly to the Copper Regions of Lake Superior. Through Wisconsin, Iowa, and the Nebraska territory, they have been traced extending towards the Rocky Mountains; while, on the South, their area is bounded by the shores of the Gulf of Florida and the Mexican territory, where they seem gradually to lose their distinctive character, and pass into the great *teocallis* of a higher developed Mexican architecture. The unknown people by whom they were constructed, judging by the form of several skulls dug out of the burial-places, were of the Mexican or Toltecan race. They were at all events of a race far different from the comparatively modern Red Indian, and it has been justly noticed, as worthy of special remark, that the sites selected for the cities and

settlements of European immigrants are often those which
are chiefly favoured by the "mound-builders," which can rarely be
said of the Indian settlements.  These earthworks were almost all
confined to fertile valleys or alluvial plains, and Sir Charles Lyell
shows that some were so ancient that rivers have had time, since
their construction, to encroach upon the lower terraces which support
them, and again to recede for the distance of nearly a mile,
after having undermined and destroyed a part of the works.
Some are overgrown by trees having 800 rings of annual growth,
and these trees (according to General Harrison) would not
have sprouted for several thousands of years after the works were
forsaken.

But as to the date of these fortifications, it is impossible even to
hazard a guess.  In Lyell's "Antiquity of Man" an attempt is made
to show that the delta of the Mississippi indicates an antiquity of
no less than a hundred thousand years, and that the implement-
containing beds of the Somme valley are at least as ancient.  But
this idea, of course, is not applicable to the huge earthworks
which swarm in the valleys of the Ohio and its tributaries.
It is clear, at all events, that they owed their origin to a settled
agricultural population, who must have made considerable progress
in civilisation, and who must have been in that respect far superior
to the so-called aborigines of America, the Red Indians.

Waiving the question of exact date of construction, the remains
of fortifications of such remote antiquity must possess great
interest, with reference to the subject of this article—the military
engineering of the ancients—and we therefore propose to subjoin
some accounts of the principal of these great forts, as described
in Dr. Wilson's book.

Fort Hill, Ohio, occupies the summit of a detached hill,
elevated about five hundred feet above the bed of Bush Creek,
which flows round two sides of it, close to its precipitous slope.
Along the whole edge of the hill a ditch has been excavated,
and the earth from it has been formed into a parapet whose
height varies from six to fifteen feet.  In its whole extent, the
parapet measures eight thousand, two hundred and twenty-
four feet, or upwards of one and a-half miles in length, and it
encloses an area of forty-eight acres, which is now overgrown by
gigantic forest trees of great age.  Here and there openings occur
in the walls, at points where the rock is so steep as to make
access impossible: it may therefore be concluded that these
openings communicated with towers to flank the walls.  The
ditch has been excavated, partly in earth, and partly in sandstone
rock—in some places to a depth of twenty feet.  Large ponds or
artificial reservoirs for water have been made within the inclosure,
and at the southern point, where the natural area of this stronghold contracts into a narrow and nearly insulated projection
terminating in a bold bluff, it rises to a height of thirty feet above

the bottom of the ditch, and has its own special reservoirs, as if here was the citadel or keep of the fortress.  At this point there appear strong traces of the action of fire upon the rocks and stones, but whether this be remote or recent, is is impossible to say. Fort Hill then was evidently no temporary retreat of some nomad horde, but a military work of great magnitude, which, even with all the appliances of modern engineering skill, would involve the protracted operations of a numerous body of labourers, and when completed must have required a no less numerous garrison for its defence.  And this may be taken as an example of these remarkable military earthworks, though they necessarily differ greatly in detail from their ingenious adaptation to their varying sites.

The "Fort Ancient," built upon two nearly detached terraces, rises with precipitous banks twenty-three feet above the Little Miami River, Ohio, and consists of earthen ramparts, measuring at the most accessible points eighteen or twenty feet high, and extending altogether to a length little short of four miles, besides numerous detached outworks, which add materially to its defensive power.  Professor Locke, of Cincinnati, surveyed "Fort Ancient" with a numerous staff of assistants, and reported that its parapets contained about 628,000 cubic yards of earth.  He also expressed his astonishment " to see a work, simply of earth, after braving the storms of thousands of years, still so entire and well marked." The parapets are formed of clay nearly impervious to water and, at numerous points, they are revetted by large quantities of water-worn stones, seemingly taken from the bed of the river Little Miami.  "Fort Ancient" has also been carefully examined by the Messrs. Squier and Davis, who remark " A review of this magnificent monument cannot fail to impress us with admiration of the skill which selected, and the industry which secured this position. Under a military system, such as we feel warranted in ascribing to the people by whom this work was constructed, it must have been impregnable.  In every point of view it is certainly one of the most interesting remains of antiquity which the continent affords."

Another class of defensive works—assumed, with much probability, to mark the sites of fortified towns—is adduced by Dr. Wilson as a further proof of the settled character of the ancient population of America.  One of these fortifications, called "Clark's Work," on the north fork of Point Creek, in the Scioto valley, is rectangular in plan, and within its ramparts, which inclose an area of 127 acres, there are numerous sacrificial mounds and symmetrical earthworks, which appear to have been designed for religious or civic purposes.  In this, as in some other examples, a stream has been turned from its original course into an entirely new channel, in order to admit of the completed circuit of the work ; and within its inclosures many very interesting relics have been dug up.  "The amount of labour," Mr. Squier remarks, "expended in the construction of this work in view of the imperfect means at the command of the builders, is immense. The embankments measure together nearly three miles in length; and a careful computation shows that, including mounds, not less than three million cubic feet of earth were used in their composition." Though this is less than a quarter of the amount of excavations necessary to form the ditches, &c., of a modern fort, it is evident that large numbers must have been employed in the construction of such extensive mural defences as "Clark's work," and that the garrisons requisite for such great strongholds must have been proportionately large. Sir Charles Lyell mentions that the solid contents of one mound alone are estimated at twenty millions of cubic feet, so that four of them would be more than equal in bulk to the Great Pyramid of Egypt.

Most of these fortifications in the Mississipi valley are constructed of earth, but in some few cases the walls of the inclosures consist of stone, rudely piled together, without mortar or cement, and due apparently to special local facilities which led to the substitution of the one material for the other. The embankments and ditches of the different works vary in strength, as is natural, according to the peculiar features of the ground upon which they are situated; but, after such a long lapse of time, it is obviously impossible to form any clear opinions concerning the profile of these works. With reference to their plan, it is curious to observe that they consist, for the most part, of regular geometrical figures. One, for instance, has for its ground-plan a regular ellipse, whose major axis is 1150 feet; another is circular, with diameter of 917 feet; a third is square, with side of 1080 feet; whilst a fourth is octagonal, and measures 950 feet across. It is almost impossible to conceive how such works could have been so accurately laid out on the ground, without the use of the theodolite, and various mathematical instruments, upon the invention of which we moderns are so apt to pride ourselves. It is evident that the "mound-builders" must have been well acquainted with the principles of geodesy, that they must have had some means of measuring angles, and must have also employed some recognised standard of lineal measurement.

Such are the curious fortifications of an unknown "pre-historic" people; and they seem to bear out the writer's assertion, that the subject of this article, while interesting to the soldier, is also instructive to the ordinary student of the world's history.

The circular trace, that they seem to have adopted for so many of their works, is found in many other ancient fortifications. Layard mentions that the walls of the old Assyrian city, Al Hather, were flanked by numerous towers, but form almost a complete circle, in the centre of which rises the palace, fort, or keep. This work dates, probably, from the reign of one of the Sassanian kings of Persia, certainly not prior to the Arsacian dynasty, who commmenced their sway about 150 B.C. The reader, however, might be deluged *usque ad nauseam* with instances of the employment of the circular trace in ancient fortifications. It is very curious, therefore, to notice that the walls of the old Peruvian capital Cuzco, the "Holy City," were nearly all *en tenaille*, and that the re-entering angles were right-angles, so contrived that every part should be seen, and as perfectly flanked as in the best European fortresses of the present day. "It is not' a little singular," Mr. Fergusson remarks, in his *Handbook of Architecture*, "that this perfection should have been reached by a rude people in Southern America, while it escaped the Greeks and Romans, as well as the mediæval Engineers." One part, however, of the city Cuzco was protected by two semicircular walls, as Mr. Prescott records in his "Conquest of Peru." The diameter of this semicircle was about 400 yards long, the same length as that of the other side of the city, which was protected by rectilineal walls, though the precipitous character of the ground was of itself almost sufficient for its defence. It is no wonder, then, that even the experienced soldier Pizarro, when he came within sight of the city in 1527, should have expressed his astonishment at the strength of its fortifications, and the labour expended upon its construction. The walls were built of polygonal blocks of limestone, carefully fitted together, without any mortar or cement, and so exactly were they adjusted that the blade of a knife could not be inserted between the joints. · According to Mr. Prescott, some of these blocks were thirty-eight feet long, eighteen feet wide, and six feet thick; they were brought from a distance of from four to fifteen leagues, and twenty thousand men were employed upon the work for fifty years! Other authorities make a more moderate estimate of the size of the stones, viz.: eight or ten feet long, by about half as much in width and depth, the weight of each being from fifteen to twenty tons. They are piled upon one another in three successive terraces, and are arranged with a degree of skill nowhere else to be met with in any work of fortification anterior to the invention of gunpowder. The citadel, or keep, consisted of three towers detached from one another, so that each should be capable of independent defence. Humboldt states that simplicity, symmetry, and solidity, are the three features which constitute the distinguishing characteristics of all Peruvian edifices. Certainly the last of these characteristics is to be found in the Walls of Cuzco, whose remains, to the present day, excite the admiration of the traveller.

One more ancient Peruvian fortification should be noticed, according to the description given of it in the "Pre-historic Man." This work, of which the ruins are still to be seen, stood upon the desert of Atacama, near the base of the Andes. The buildings are all small, and nearly of uniform size, each consisting of a single apartment. The walls are constructed of irregular blocks of granite cemented together, and the front walls are pierced with loop-holes, both near the floor and about five feet above it.  The floors are of cement, and are on a level with the top of the wall of the building in front.  We see, therefore, in the ancient defences of Peru, a development of the *fausse-braye*, or *cavalier*, principle of obtaining several tiers of fire ; in addition to the perfect flank defence of the walls procured by the above described *tenaille* lines at Cuzco, and these are tokens of an advanced knowledge of the art of fortification, which, there is very little doubt, was not possessed by the contemporary Engineers of Europe.

## SIR JOSEPH THACKWELL AND SADOOLAPORE.

[It is no new thing to find writers on general history, no doubt unintentionally, unjust to particular individuals, and when those individuals belong to the United Services it becomes our duty to rectify the matter, as far as the materials are at our command. In this spirit we print the following communication, which has reference to an implied reflection on the gallant Sir Joseph Thackwell, whilst serving against the Sikhs.]

Mr. Edwin Arnold, M.A., of Oxford, has recently published a work, entitled "The Marquis of Dalhousie's Administration of British India."  When describing the action of Sadoolapore on the 3rd December, 1848, he says, "Thackwell's guns, however, after two hours' fighting, completely subdued the Sikh fire, and the Infantry, Native and Europeans, were desirous to advance." Now, this is a great exaggeration! The truth is that the Infantry, who after deployment into line, had thrown themselves upon the ground in pursuance of orders, betrayed their impatience of their recumbent position in a very unequivocal manner.  It is not true that any officers or soldiers in the detachment urged General Thackwell to attack the Sikh position on the evening of the 3rd December.  This was the invention of some disordered mind!

The Sikh Army, moving out of their entrenchments, occupied three fortified villages and high plantations of sugar cane, affording a strong position, and awaited the approach of Thackwell's detachment.  Sir Joseph was on his march towards the Sikh position, bent upon an immediate assault, when he received peremptory orders from Lord Gough to halt until he was reinforced by Godby's Brigade, which had been dispatched to the ford of Ghurre Kere Puttun.  He had advanced very close to the three above-mentioned villages, leaving the village of Sadoolapore in his rear, when he halted according to orders.  He had not been long halted when the Sikhs opened fire upon him.  Godby's Brigade which found it impossible to pass the river Chenab without boats, did not join Thackwell until the morning of the 4th.  In the middle of the

night of the 3rd, the Sikh Army deserted their position and retired
to the river Jhelum, withdrawing their guns.

The British detachment, which was not half of Lord Gough's
army, inflicted great loss upon the Sikhs; but, the lateness of the
day and the prospect of having to attack the intrenched position
afterwards, induced Sir Joseph to defer his assault upon the Sikh
position until the morning of the 4th December   The ground in
Thackwell's front was not well known to him, never having been
carefully explored, for which, however, he was not responsible.
He did not know how far the intrenchments were from the villages.
When Lord Gough directed Thackwell to halt until reinforced,
he expressed the opinion that he was too weak to encounter Shere
Sing without an accession to his strength, and that if he immediately attacked the enemy, he would in all probability be *écrasé*.

I am confident that if the Sikhs had not retreated to the Jhelum
in the night, they would have been vigorously attacked on the
morning of the 4th of December.

A wing of Infantry and two Ressalahs of Cavalry were detached to protect the ferry at Ghurree kee Putton over which
Godby's Brigade were striving to cross.

A Calcutta Magazine published in August, 1849, says in reference to Sadoolapore, " It must be remembered that the days
were then very short and his instructions not to engage without
Godby (modified afterwards when too late) determined Sir Joseph
not to follow up his success that night.  When, as it is now
known, the whole Sikh army was in his front, it was most fortunate that he did not advance."

A notification published by the Government of India on the 31st
January, 1849, runs thus, "His Lordship begs to congratulate
the Commander-in-Chief on  the success of the measures which he
adopted for effecting the passage of the Chenab and  to convey to
him the assurance of his satisfaction with, and his best thanks
for the judicious arrangements by which he was enabled, with
comparatively little loss, to carry into execution his plans for the
passage of that difficult river, and for compelling the retreat of
the Sikh army from the formidable position which they occupied
on its further bank, after they had been engaged, and beaten back
by the forces under Major-General Sir Joseph Thackwell.  The
Governor-General offers his best thanks to Major-General Sir
Joseph Thackwell for his successful direction of the force under
his command, and for the dispositions by which he compelled the
enemy to retire, and ultimately to quit the ground he had occupied."

Lord Gough in a Despatch to the Governor-General, dated
December 10th 1848, writes, "I can only repeat the warm approval I have already expressed of the conduct of the Major-General and of every officer and man under his command."

It is not right that people should hastily condemn Sir Joseph for not pressing his advantage.  It should be remembered that he was recommended for a Brevet majority for his gallantry in the Peninsula, and that he received several wounds, losing his left arm, and had two horses shot under him at the Battle of Waterloo before he gave up the command of his squadron of the 15th King's Hussars.  His conduct at Sobraon, also, in 1846, was not that of a *lâche !*

---

## FOREIGN SUMMARY.

Paris, April 25.

There are a great variety of rumours current with respect to the objects of Lord Clarendon's mission ; but as they cannot all be true, and they all claim to be based on the authority of this or that person who might be supposed to know, I do not think it worth while to repeat any of them.  That his lordship met with a cordial reception from the Emperor is certain, and that in the event of his superseding Earl Russell in the Foreign Office, his communications would be received with a favourable bias on the part of the French Government, is hardly less so.  It seems probable that the chief object of his mission with regard to the Duchies was to determine what should be done in the event of Denmark and the German Powers rejecting the propositions that would be made to settle the future of Schleswig Holstein at the Conference.  The question of the Conference was undoubtedly the special object of his mission, but it may be presumed that it extended generally to removing by personal explanation any feeling of soreness that might remain in the Emperor's mind on account of the refusal of England to join the Congress he proposed, and to bring about a thoroughly cordial understanding.  There is not a potentate living more open to representations made in this spirit, or so willing to respond by adopting them ; and certainly there is not another on the continent who is so thoroughly aware of what a British Government can do, and how far it must yield to the desire of the nation.  The ridiculous statements that have been circulated in England with respect to his making it a condition precedent to the accordance of his good graces to the Palmerston Ministry, that Garibaldi should be got out of the country, must have caused him some humiliation, probably not lessened by Lord Clarendon having thought proper to rise in the House of Lords for the purpose of denying the assertions made by Messrs. Cobden and Bright's Paper.  If there is any truth at all in the assertion that pressure was put on the British Government to induce them to get Garibaldi out of England, it certainly was not by France.  I do not believe either that Lord Palmerston and his colleagues, or any other English government,

* Sir Joseph's force consisted of three British regiments, the 3rd Light Dragoons, the 24th and 61st regiments and native corps.

would submit to anything resembling dictation from any power on earth; but it is easy to imagine that the desire to propitiate Austria more especially, and to make matters run smoothly at the Conference, would make them glad to see him depart.

That a glance at the totals inscribed in the French Budget for the Army and Navy, is enough to alarm any tax payer, cannot be denied, and I am quite sure that nothing will tend to attach Frenchmen to England, and overcome the foolish prejudice against us which is entertained by the majority of them, than to see that a good understanding between the Emperor and our Government, is followed by an immediate reduction in the amount as a consequence. The amount by which it is reduced is almost equally divided between the two branches of the service. The vote for the Army is reduced by £100,000, and that for the Navy, £96,000. This is the first fruits of Lord Clarendon's mission, and augurs well for the future, even if we had not the encouraging assurance contained in the Emperor's letter to M. Fould, that the hopes of peace were daily becoming stronger. I have more than once stated that the Frenc nation no longer desires war on account of the glory to be gained by it. In the report on the Budget this is expressed in strong terms. It is not in this place that I can go into details on the subject of the increase of French commerce, but to account for the evident desire for peace, I may say that it has developed itself, even within the last twelve months, in an extraordinary degree. In addition to the knowledge of this increase, and that it is principally of a kind which a war would almost annihilate, it is probable that most of them have seen a statement, first published in the *Pays*, of the cost to France of recent wars. The Crimean war is said to have cost her £53,920,000; the Italian, £13,800,000; the China and Cochin-China, £6,640,000; the occupation of Rome, £2,000,000; the expedition to Syria, £680,000; the war in Kabylia, £440,000; advances in virtue of the treaty of Zurich, £1,560,000; discounts and advances £2,000,000; extraordinary works on account of these wars, £31,480,000; making a total of nearly £111,000,000.

*La France*, in an article on the Navy, asserts that not only is the credit of inventing iron-clads due to the present Emperor, but that the French Navy is stronger in these vessels than England. The same assertion, probably derived from this source, was made in the House of Commons. I cannot believe that this is true. The Admiralty, however, must be aware of the truth as regards this statement. The French paper is mysterious, and does not go into details, but there is no necessity for shrouding the question in mystery. I am assured on excellent authority, that the French Government and ours interchange information regarding these matters.

Just nine years ago, the law regarding substitutes came into force; and the manner in which it has worked has been altogether satisfactory. Previous to this time, there were numerous agents who undertook, in consideration of a certain sum, to provide substitutes for those conscripts who did not wish to serve. Some few of these agents may have been honest men, who somehow found a profit in carrying on the business, but a great many of them were very much like the crimps who used to abound about Wapping. Having picked up a man who usually had a very good, or rather a very bad reason for entering the army, he advanced him money at an usurious interest, or made him drunk, and debited him with advances which he had never received; so that generally the unfortunate substitute found himself on joining the regiment, without a penny. Not unfrequently the agent received the money, and decamped, without troubling about the substitutes at all. In short, there was all the rascality perpetrated which cunning could devise. By the new law, the Government undertook to accept a certain sum in lieu of personal service; and the sums received on this account were amalgamated in a fund which was employed in procuring substitutes. The advantage of this arrangement to the person paying, being, that he was certain of not being called upon to pay twice; and to the Government, that instead of having to accept any ruffian to whom there was no objection on physical grounds, it was able by the offer of a liberal bounty, to induce men to re-enlist; thus procuring trained men of good character, hardened by service, and far better able to withstand the hardships of campaigning than the newly joined conscripts. Here are some figures which will prove more forcibly than words, how well the law has worked. On the first day of this year the French Army contained 298,904 men who had served four years, 70,006 who had served from eight to fourteen years, 21,449 from fourteen to twenty years, and 11,313 upwards of twenty years. The increase in the number of veterans in the army, has led to a corresponding decrease in the mortality. So recently as 1859, the mortality was $1\frac{1}{2}$ per cent; in 1860, $1\frac{1}{2}$; in 1861 it was rather less, and in 1862 it was diminished to 0·90. At the same time that the health of the Army has increased, so also has the morality. It was said that the adoption of the new law, for reasons which space will not allow me to go into, would entail a burden on the state. Experience has proved the contrary. The bounty has been increased, and the soldier instead of having to serve thirty years before being entitled to a pension, has now only twenty-five years to serve.

In the last summary, mention was made of a review of the juvenile portion of the army by the Emperor, at which the Prince Imperial was present, wearing the uniform of the 1st regiment of grenadiers, and carrying his little knapsack like the rest of the youngsters. To military men some further details respecting these very young soldiers, will not be without interest. Altogether they number 5572; 571 belonging to the imperial guard, 4877 to the line, and the remainder to different foreign corps. They are fed, clothed, and educated by the State up to the age of eighteen, when they have the choice of entering the service in the ordinary way, or of quitting the regiment.  At fourteen years of age they are sent to the military workshop, or to an office, or they are added to the band of musicians.  Those attached to the regiments of the line wear a very simple and inexpensive costume, but an exception is made in the case of those belonging to the Imperial Guard; they are clothed and armed like the soldiers themselves.

The Spahis and Turcos are going to Algeria, the latter to be replaced in Paris by a battalion of the 2nd regiment of the same arm of the service, and the former by a select corps composed of the sons of Arab chiefs.  Some of those already stationed here who have shown themselves apt in cultivating gardens, &c., are to be sent to the model farm at Grignon before being sent back to Algeria, and a portion of the Turcos are to remain in Paris for the present, to initiate the new comers into the routine of duty in the capital.

Waterloo seems to be better remembered in France than in England.  The other day one of the Paris journals repeated a statement made ten months ago that the French ambassador in London had been present at a dinner given on the anniversary of Waterloo.  The 'Moniteur' contradicted this, but, notwithstanding, Baron Gros seemed to think the matter of so much importance, that he wrote to the editor to explain that the banquet in question was that given regularly every year by the Lord Mayor to the Queen's ministers, and that it was given on the 17th and not on the 18th of June.  If it had been given on the latter day, though the coincidence would have been entirely fortuitous, he would have felt himself obliged to refuse the invitation for fear of misrepresentation. A relic of the same memorable battle has been sent to the Prussian minister for war within the last few days, if the Rhenish gazette tells the truth, to be disposed of in aid of the wounded soldiers' fund.  It is a silver plate, weighing about half a pound, which was picked up on the road to Gemappes on the 18th of June, 1815. It is engraved with the arms of the first Napoleon, and the minister, thinking it would fetch a great deal more than its intrinsic value, on account of its historical interest, has announced that he will receive tenders for it to the 1st of May, on which day it will be adjudged to the highest bidder.

The Parisians are to be gratified by the sight of another embassy from Japan.  The ambassadors from that strange and distant country were saluted on landing at Marseilles with the usual number of guns, and a squadron of hussars was in waiting to escort them to the hotel that had been prepared for them, the road being kept by troops who presented arms as they passed along.

There is no doubt that communication between France and Italy will be facilitated by the tunnelling of Mount Cenis, and that this tunnel will eventually be completed, but the obstacles to be surmounted are far greater than was generally anticipated. The perforation is being made on the French and Italian side simultaneously, but such is the hardness of the rock that the average progress made in twenty-four hours is only nine-tenths of a metre. It is estimated that it will be fourteen years before this tunnel, begun six years since, will be completed. The cost is £160 the metre, and for the three leagues the total cost will be at least £4,400,000.

From Cochin-China the French government has received satisfactory news. Things are very quiet there, and the natives who have been enlisted in the French service are remarkably docile and well-conducted. The number of these is 2500, including a small body of cavalry. The works undertaken for the improvement of Saigon were to be commenced shortly, and the expenditure on this account in the present year would, it was estimated be £40,000. The young King of Cambodia has been presented by the chief of Admiral de la Grandiere's staff, with a uniform superbly ornamented with gold lace.

Very few Jews, I imagine, serve in the English army, but the case as regards the continental armies is very different. The French army includes a considerable number, some of them holding high rank, but a greater number is probably to be found in the Austrian army. L'Europe, a Frankfort journal, says that there are upwards of twelve thousand serving in that army, six hundred of whom are non-commissioned officers, surgeons, &c., two are majors, four captains in the cavalry, four in the infantry, fifteen lieutenants and thirty-four subs.

The convention concluded between France and Mexico contains eighteen articles, the principal points of which may be summed up very briefly. The French troops in Mexico are to be reduced with the least possible delay to 25,000, including the foreign legion, and they are to be still further reduced in proportion as the native army is organised. The foreign legion in the service of France to remain in Mexico six years after all the French troops are withdrawn, but at the expense of the Mexican government, which will have the power of shortening this term. In all the garrisoned towns where there are French and Mexican troops, the French commanders will have the supreme command, and the same in the case of combined expeditions; but they must not interfere in any of the administrative departments. So long as the requirements of the army of occupation render it necessary to send a service of transports from France to Vera Cruz every alternate month; the voyage there and back is to be paid for by Mexico at the rate of £16,000 on each occasion. To cover the expenses of the expedition to the 1st of July, 1864, Mexico is to pay France £10,800,000; so long as it remains a debt it will be charged with interest at the rate of 3 per cent. After the date mentioned, the entire cost of the army of occupation will have to be borne by Mexico; and this is fixed at £40 per man per annum, payable on the last day of every month. Shares in the new loan to the amount of £2,640,000 are to be handed over to France at once on account of the expenses of the expedition; and a yearl sum of £1,000,000 on the accounts above mentioned and in the indemnification of the claims of French subjects, whose grievances caused the expedition to be undertaken. Mexican prisoners are to be set at liberty directly the Emperor Maxmillian sets foot in Mexico.

The Mexican Deputies are said to be well-content with their reception at Miramar by the Archduke Maximillian, now the Emperor of Mexico. The address was delivered by M. Guttierez d'Estrada in French, but was responded to by the Emperor in the Spanish language, very much to the gratification of the deputation. While this ceremony was taking place at Miramar, the Bishop of Trieste, assisted by other clerical functionaries, were performing a Te Deum at the cathedral; it is to be presumed out of gratitude at the anticipation of the restoration of order and the influence of their church in a country, from whence both had almost disappeared. In the evening the Emperor gave a dinner, at which he appeared for the first time in the uniform of a Mexican lieutenant-general, decorated with the order of the Virgin of Guadaloupe and the National Order of Mexico. Ambassadors have been dispatched to different countries to notify his acceptance of the crown.

The 6,000 men who are to form the Foreign Legion which the Emperor Maximillian. is authorised by his brother to raise in Austria for service in Mexico are to be divided thus: three battalions of infantry, one regiment of hussars, one of hulans, a company of pioneers, a company of engineers, and a battery of artillery. There will be no difficulty in getting experienced officers to command these volunteers, as those who quit the Austrian service for this purpose can return to it at any time within six years, and the deficiency of volunteers, if any, can easily be made up by taking them from other German States. The uniform of the troops is thus described. The infantry are to have a blue woollen blouse, loose, like those worn by sailors, the collar of which can either be fastened under the chin or turned down, the necktie to be worn in the way most agreeable to the soldier. The pantaloons are to be madder-coloured, with gaiters reaching nearly to the knee, the hat of felt or beaver, and surmounted by an eagle's feather. They will be armed with a carbine having a sword bayonet affixed. The black leather knapsack is to be lined with waterproof canvas; the cartouche box and the bayonet will be suspended from the waist belt, which will be attached by means of braces to the straps of the knapsack. The cavalry are to be armed with a sabre and revolver, the hulans with lances without pennons. The men are to be recruited from among those not on active service and the reserve. The terms offered are a bounty of 25 florins for privates and 50 florins for non-commissioned officers. At the expiration of six years' service they will have the option of continuing to serve or of retiring with an allotment of about sixteen acres of land, the tools and other necessaries requisite for cultivating it, and a house. Thus, after many delays and much irritation among the parties principally concerned, the Mexican affair is settled for the present. I say for the present, because the vote of the American House of Representatives not to recognise a monarchy in Mexico may, when the civil war in that country is ended, lead to a pretext being found for a war in which Mexico would be powerless to resist, notwithstanding that the Senate has rejected the resolution. That the new emperor is not blind to this possibility is evident from the obstinacy with which he refused to abandon his reversionary rights to the throne of Austria. There is no doubt that the Emperor Napoleon knew and approved of the claims made by the Emperor Maximillian, and there is very little that the pressure of France was brought to bear to bring about the somewhat tardy settlement of the question. The Emperor of France was very much irritated, and there is very good authority for believing that he did at last send a telegraphic despatch to Miramar announcing that if the matter was not settled within a few hours, he would avail himself of the right given to him to name a member of his family to ascend the Mexican throne and send him there immediately.

There are rumours afloat that Austria intends to occupy the marshes on behalf of the Papal Government, in accordance with engagements entered into by a treaty at Gaeta in 1849. As such a proceeding would involve a war with Italy it may safely be assumed to be without foundation. Nevertheless the rumours of an approaching war between these two powers become more frequent, and a good deal of quiet agitation is going on in favour of the exiled princes which is entirely owing to a belief in the imminence of a war. That Austria would be ready, and even glad to enter into a contest with Italy there is good reason to believe, but then Italy must be the aggressor, or there would be the fear that France would lend her her assistance. By the way I may as well mention in this place that it was by a typographical error that I was made to say in the last summary in speaking of Italy that it was a power which *awes* France so much ; what I wrote was, which *owes* France so much.

From Austria there are the usual accounts of disaffection in her provinces. In Galicia, Hungary and Venice the agitators are carrying on their work, and in the former province the prisons must be pretty numerous to contain all the individuals that have been arrested. There is no doubt that the energetic measures adopted by the Austrian Government there have assisted Russia very materially in extinguishing the embers of the revolution in Poland. Notwithstanding that her finances have in no way improved, Austria has increased the number of troops on a war footing very considerably. The motive for this is principally from the apprehension that Italy will not be long before she invades Venetia on some pretext or other, and also because certain discoveries made in Hungary with respect to a proposed insurrection there proved it to be organized on a serious scale.  The seizure of muskets in that country, even though there were not quite so many as 5000, was still large enough to show this, because the inference may fairly be drawn that this only represents a much larger number which the authorities have not been able to discover.

The Austrians are not at all reconciled to the Schleswig-Holstein campaign, or rather they are not reconciled to the cost of it, for it is not to be supposed their sympathies are with the Danes, or that feelings of humanity have anything to do with it.  Their discontent on this subject is heightened by the recent success of the Prussians at Dybböl, which almost eclipse the exploits of their own soldiers. The reception which Garibaldi has met with in England must have been gall and wormwood to the government and army more especially, and is anything but gratifying to the nation.  Probably the building, the name of which is best known in Austria is Barclay and Perkins' Brewery, and the desire which Garibaldi expressed to visit that establishment, and the comparisons that have been made between the reception given to him there, and that given to General Haynau must have caused great annoyance.

Whatever may have been the difficulties between the Emperor and his brother Maximillian with respect to the reversionary claims of the latter to the Austrian throne, and the ill-feeling engendered between them by the dispute, it did not survive the moment of separation.  When they stood on the platform together, recollections of former days when they played together without a thought of the future, no doubt softened their hearts, and at the last moment, when the signal for the train to start had been given, the two brothers threw their arms round each other and remained in this attitude for some seconds, and there were tears in the eyes of both when they parted, and Heaven only knows what grief in their hearts, for both have serious reason to look anxiously to the future.  It was an evil day for Austria when she linked her fortunes with Prussia in the intervention in the Duchies; she has incurred a large expenditure, has been carried far beyond her original intention, and the return she expects to derive from Prussia under certain circumstances will bind her to follow the policy of that power at the Conference, even though it may be anything but conducive to Austrian interests.

It is curious to see how completely Prussia, as a nation, has been eclipsed by the action of her army,  Nobody hears or cares what the government has been doing in the meantime.  Whether the liberals have been making progress, or the reactionists have been gaining ground is equally a matter of indifference to foreigners ; their undivided attention has been given to the exploits of her army before Dybböl.

Of Spain we habitually hear very little.  It is asserted by their newspapers, that revolutionary agents in league with those who are acting in other parts of the continent, are busy in Spain and

Portugal. There have been some ministerial changes, and these have been accompanied by indications of a desire on the part of the higher classes to take steps for the recovery of the commercial credit of the country abroad. The betrothal of the Count de Paris to the daughter of the Duke of Montpensier, has no political significance now that Spain has so little weight in European affairs. If she possessed the power she formerly did, it would have excited much commotion among foreign diplomatists; the sympathies of the queen naturally leading her to desire to see her kinsfolk on the throne of France, to say nothing of the satisfaction it would give her as a woman, to humiliate her former subject.

Notwithstanding the assertion that things are looking bad for the Dominicans, the Spaniards have little cause to rejoice. According to a statement in a Spanish newspaper, the losses of the army have been 12,000; but nine-tenths of these were from maladies from which they speedily recovered on being removed to a healthier climate. The strength of the army does not exceed 9,000 altogether, and it is pretty certain that a great many of these are on the sick list. In fact, the state of affairs on the island is very critical. The autumn will not begin for some months, and the Spanish Government is over sanguine in saying that the campaign they intend to open then will be a decisive one; unless, indeed, they mean to intimate that in the event of their not being victorious, they will withdraw from the island altogether; and I do not suppose they mean that.

The Lutnick and Bronenossetz, the two new iron-sides, were not launched without a serious hitch as regards the former. They are sister vessels, the dimensions of both are 201 feet in length, 46 in width, and rather less than 12 in depth. The motive power of the engines is only 160 horses each; but the applause which greeted the descent of the Warrior into the water was trifling compared with that exhibited by the Russians at the sight of the two first iron-cased vessels afloat which had been entirely built in Russia. As regards the strength of the army, the annual report furnished to the Emperor states it to be 1,135,670, thus divided: Infantry, 694,511; other arms, 114,159; and a force of 127,000 very closely resembling the Irish constabulary in the duties it has to perform. There is also a reserve force of 200,000. With such an army, even supposing that these figures are exaggerated, it is not surprising that the financial difficulties of the empire are so great as to compel her to come into the foreign market for a new loan. There have been no serious encounters during the past month between the Polish insurgents and the Russians, and there is little doubt that the individuals arrested in Poland, who were seized in the act of levying contributions on behalf of the National Committee, were merely sharpers, who abused the name of the committee to collect money for their own benefit. One serious drain of men and money is probably closed by the defeat of the Circassians, who seem at last to have given up all intention of continuing their resistance. They are now emigrating to Turkey in multitudes, which is apparently just what the Russian Government desires. The sending of so many steamers by the Porte, to bring away the foreign officers who have been serving with the Circassians, is not likely to have been done without previous arrangement with the Russian Ambassador at Constantinople. It would not be fair to blame the present Emperor of Russia for what has been done in Circassia. The policy which has been pursued towards that country was begun before he succeeded to the throne, and many reasons may be assigned why he could not abandon it.

In the event of another war in the Crimea, it will be useful for our navy to be aware that the Russian charts of the Gulf of Odessa will contain not only the various rocks and shallows to be avoided, but also the direction of the currents. To ascertain this, every captain leaving the port of Odessa is supplied with bottles hermetically closed, which they are to throw overboard on reaching the open sea. Each of these bottles contain a note in Russian, English, French, and Italian, requesting the finder to return it to the captain of the port of Odessa, with a statement of the precise locality in which it was found.

---

# THE INVASION OF DENMARK AND THE POLITICAL CRISIS.

### THE CONFERENCE.

Have we arrived at the last scene of the sanguinary drama which is being performed in the North of Europe; or, when the curtain drops, will it suddenly rise again, and the spectator be startled by the display of all the armies in Europe drawn up in battle array, with bayonets bristling, lighted matches in the hands of artillerymen, and a naval back-ground of iron-clads, with the flags of England and of France floating from the main? Who can say? The Conference which, whilst we are writing, is sitting in deliberation to settle the Danish Question, and, if possible, satisfy all parties, and preserve the peace of Europe, has no easy task to perform. It is scarcely with feelings of a friendly nature that the representatives meet at this Conference. The Danish Commissioners must still cast a thought towards the burning happy homes of their slaughtered countrymen; the Austrian and Prussian Ministers are flushed with the consciousness of victory, and superior strength. Baron de Beust has perhaps the most difficult task of all; he represents all the minor States of Germany, the Slesvig-Holstein element, and is not only opposed to the Danish view of the settlement of this question, but is, moreover, in antagonism to the two great German Powers. Under these circumstances, the attitude

which England and France will assume, is that which will regulate
the result. England has given her sympathy unmistakeably to
Denmark, but no material aid ; let her, now that the moment of
deliberation has arrived, come forward and insist on the strength
of the Treaty of London, of which she is a signatary, that the
integrity of the Danish Monarchy shall be guaranteed, and that
meantime bloodshed shall be put a stop to in Jutland.

The mission of Lord Clarendon to Paris is no secret. Its object
was to come to an understanding with the Government of the
Emperor of the French as to the line of policy to be followed at the
Conference.

The question as to whether the Duchies shall remain attached to
the Crown of Denmark, either by a real, or by what is termed a
"personal" union, is of no vital importance to the interests of
Europe ; but all the States are equally interested that the peace of
the world shall not be disturbed for so secondary a question. If
the war is carried on in Jutland, the peace of Europe runs the risk
of being broken. Moreover, it sounds oddly in our civilized century
that the roar of cannon should still be heard whilst the plenipotentiaries of the principal Powers are assembled for pacific negotiations.

We believe we are correctly stating the views of the Emperor of
the French, when we say that he has given his adhesion to the
Conference on the strict understanding that an armistice shall be at
once declared. This motion will be brought forward at the opening
of the Conference, and should it be declined, it is impossible to
foresee the result.

The principal object of the mission entrusted to Lord Clarendon
to the French Emperor, was to establish between the two Western
Powers a preliminary understanding, with a view to impress upon
the members of the Conference a line of conduct likely to lead to a
practical solution.

As things now stand, the object was not so much to concert a
common programme for the settlement of the Dano-German quarrel,
as to obtain by common action a suspension of hostilities ; so that
the Conference might meet with a spirit of conciliation and moderation, without which no result can be expected. We are happy to
state, that as far as England and France are concerned, a perfect
understanding has been arrived at. Lord Clarendon has returned
to England, after having made a formal engagement in the name of
his Government, to support energetically the demand of an armistice, which the Prince de la Tour d'Auvergne, the French plenipotentiary, brings forward in the very first sitting of the Conference.
In other words, England and France have mutually bound themselves to act in concert against such Power or Powers as should
decline the proposed armistice.

Prussia got wind of this, and hence her desperate efforts to carry
Dybböl before the Conference met. She has succeeded in this, and
is now eager to push forward the siege of Fredericia. The delay in
the meeting of the Conference, which was originally fixed for the

20th of April, and postponed purposely by the German representatives, is, to say the least of it, a very un-diplomatic act in the courteous sense of the term; but the object was clear: to gain more time to achieve, if possible, another victory over the Danes. Public opinion has already expressed itself strongly on this point, and it will only tend to strengthen the determination of the two Western Powers in that praiseworthy resolution to inaugurate diplomatic negotiations by a suspension of hostilities. The delay of Baron de Beust's arrival in London, is attributed to the intrigues of the Court of Berlin; and the excuse of the Austrian and Prussian representatives for not attending the Conference on the 20th, was that the German Confederation was not represented. The Conference met, nevertheless, under the presidency of Earl Russell. The representatives of England, France, Russia, and Sweden, simply noted the absence of the German Commissioners, and adjourned to the 25th. No allusion was made in this preliminary sitting to the armistice, in consequence of that absence. It will be proposed under the condition of *uti possidetis*, unless Denmark should consent to evacuate Alsen, in which case Austria and Prussia would withdraw their troops from Jutland.

Such is the political position of parties at the moment we write.

The question very naturally arises: " why did not England and France come forward sooner and have thus prevented all the bloodshed which has taken place?" The answer to this is ready at hand. The Mexican Question hampered the action of the French Emperor. The Archduke Maximillian still lingered at Miramar, doubts arose as to his acceptance of the Imperial Crown and angry words passed to and fro. This question is now, happily, settled, and the Emperor feels that he is himself again. The French troops in Mexico are to be reduced as soon as possible to 25,000 men, including the foreign legion, which will consist of 8,000 men. This legion will remain in Mexico six years after the withdrawal of the French troops, and form part of the Mexican army as long as the Mexican government should deem it advisable. The transport service between France and Vera Cruz, is to be paid by Mexico. Moreover, the Mexican government engages to pay the expenses of the French expedition which amount to 270 millions of francs, and the cost of every French soldier is fixed at 1000 francs per annum, as long as they are in the service of Mexico.

This having been duly agreed upon and signed, France can now complacently turn her thoughts towards Europe.

The representatives at the Conference for the settlement of the Dano-German Question are,

For *England*: Earl Russell and Lord Clarendon.

*France*: Prince de la Tour d'Auvergne, French Ambassador at London.

*Austria*: Count Apponyi, the Austrian Ambassador, and Privycouncillor Biegeleben,

*Prussia* : Count Bernstorff, the Prussian Ambassador, and Privy councillor Balan, formerly Prussian Ambassador at Copenhagen.

*The German Confederation* : Baron de Beust, Minister of Foreign Affairs for Saxony.

*Russia* : Baron Brunow, the Russian Ambassador, and Councillor Ewers.

*Sweden* : General Wachtmeister.

*Denmark* : M. de Bille, the Danish Ambassador; M. de Quaade, Minister of Foreign Affairs; and Councillor Krieger.

The instructions given to the Austrian and Prussian representatives are, we believe, to bring forward the following propositions as a basis for deliberation:

" Integrity of the Danish Monarchy; Political and Administrative Autonomy of the Duchies; Maintenance of their Union in one single State (*nexus socialis*), and Rendsburg to be made a German Federal Fortress as a guarantee of the autonomy and indivisibility of the Duchies.

The Frankfort Diet, on the other hand, has given the following instructions to Baron de Beust :

" 1. To exert all his efforts to assure the recognition of the rights of the Germanic Confederation, and of the Duchies of Holstein, of Slesvig, and of Lauenburg, and especially to obtain the greatest possible independence for these latter.

" 2. To avoid as much as possible all dissension between the German Plenipotentiaries at the Conference, to concert preliminarily with the representatives of Austria and of Prussia, whenever any important deliberation is to be brought forward, the representatives of the said Powers being equally invited to follow the same example under analogous circumstances."

Bavaria proposed as an amendment, that the Duke of Augustenburg should be recognized as Duke of Slesvig-Holstein as an independent Duchy, to be separated for ever from Denmark. This was rejected by the Diet. Popular feeling runs high in Germany. The following declarations proposed by a Committe of thirty-six delegates from the various German Diets, have been forwarded to Baron de Beust :

" The actual right and manifest will of the people require the separation of the Duchies of Slesvig-Holstein from Denmark.

" The actual right and manifest will of the people summon the Prince of Augustenburg to the throne of the inseparably united Duchies.

" If this right be disputed, it does not come within the scope of the Conference of the Powers to arrive at a decision, which appertains solely to the people, and to its representatives.

" We protest in the name of the nation against every arrangement as to the future of the Duchies, without or against their consent, and we reserve at present and for the future the right of Germany, and the wish of the inhabitants of Slesvig-Holstein."

This impotent declaration though it may tie the hands of M. de Beust cannot have any effect upon the Conference. The question remains between France and England on one side and Austria and Prussia on the other.

Conflicting elements are at work. An armistice and the maintenance in full force of the Treaty of London of 1852, which guarantees the integrity of the Danish Monarchy form the bases upon which the Conference meets.

## THE WAR.

Dybböl has fallen, after a gallant resistance, and a fearful loss of human life on both sides. It will be remembered that, after the abandonment of the Danewerke, the Danes entrenched themselves on the Dybböl heights, there determined to make a stand, which they did so effectually that the Prussian commander, Field-Marshal Wrangel, found it necessary to have recourse to regular siege-works, to bring up his heavy guns, open trenches, and send for reinforcements. It was, however, evidently only a question of time. That Dybböl must eventually fall was clear to every observer, if the Danes did not receive material aid. Their little army, harrassed and worn out by continual duties, could not stand for ever against the overwhelming numbers of the enemy. The cowardly act of the bombardment of Sonderborg did not daunt them. They stood to their guns and awaited the onslaught of the Prussians. For two months the Prussians had been raining shot and shell into the works, and the final assault was ordered to take place on the 18th of April. The Danish batteries Nos. 1 and 2 had been demolished; batteries 3 and 4, the latter the key of the position, were in a bad state, and the Danes would have been justified in abandoning their works and retreating to Alsen. This they did not do. The official returns of the loss on the Prussian side has not yet been published, but report says that 60 officers fell, and more than 1000 men. The loss of the Danes has been very heavy. The following is the official report of the Danish Minister of War, issued at Copenhagen on the 19th, the day after the assault:

"After a severe bombardment last night, which was continued at daybreak with even greater violence, the works were almost entirely dismantled. The redoubts 4, 5, and 6 having been taken, the position of the left wing became untenable, and a retreat commenced. At this period the attack was so furious that the reserves from the barracks were unable to make head against it, and the retreat continued with considerable loss. The right wing accomplished their retreat with least loss comparatively, but were still severely cut up. The force occupying the *tête-de-pont* held that work until the retreating brigades had taken up a position on the

island of Alsen, although the extraordinarily violent fire of the
enemy had dismounted the guns, which fell into his hands.  About
100 killed, and from 700 to 800 wounded, were brought over to
Alsen."

We regret to say that Major Rosen and General Du Plat are
dead.  The following is the official account given by the Prussian
commander:

"Prisoners: 44 officers, 3,145 men; killed: 22 officers, 480
men; wounded, in our hospital: 21 officers, 580 men.  Among
the officers taken are two commanders of regiments, Dreyer and
Falkensjold.  Among the officers killed are: 1 general, 3 commanders of regiments, Du Plat, Bernstorff, and Lessen, and 1 major
on the staff of the commander-in-chief, Von Rosen.  Of these, 20
dead bodies have been delivered up to the Danes, and 2 were buried
in the trenches.  In addition to these, several dead bodies, which
lay in different spots, were to-day buried separately at the *tête-de-
pont* and other places.  Many of the enemy must have been drowned
in the Sound, and the fire from our batteries must have caused some
loss on the Island of Alsen.  On a moderate calculation the hostile
loss may be estimated at 100 officers and 4,500 men.  According
to official advices received here to-day, about 100 killed and 800
wounded were conveyed to Alsen, in addition to the above, thereby
making the total loss of the enemy about 5,500 men."

This is a heavy list, if correct, and a dark cloud of mourning lays
like a pall over the once happy land of Denmark.  The King of
Prussia has been to the head-quarters of his army to congratulate
Field-Marshal Wrangel and his troops upon this victory.  Truly a
heavy responsibility for so much misery must fall upon the royal
mind at the view of so much slaughter.  The following account of
the attack is from an eye-witness:

"We awaited the attack at daybreak, but in vain, although the
fire became much more violent between four and six o'clock.  The
ground trembled for miles around, the windows rattled; fifty
shells per minute were showered upon our men, upon the works,
and upon the buildings in the neighbourhood.  After six the fire
abated, and the attack was made at ten.  Strong hostile columns
pressed forward against the works out of the rifle-pits, only a few
hundred paces distant, formerly ours, but now held by the enemy.
The regiments forming the first line upon the left wing, the 2nd
and 22nd, were outflanked after a short contest and forced to
surrender, after Colonel Lasson, the chief of the brigade, had fallen.
Isolated shots only were able to be fired from the works and the
field-batteries posted between them.  As far as I am aware, no fire
was given from the intrenchment in the rear, and when the 8th
Brigade, 9th and 20th Regiments, which had only arrived a few
days previously, advanced from its position in reserve, the Prussian
flag was already to be seen on the Forts 4 and 5.  The men
nevertheless went forward with steady courage under a violent

fire; they succeeded in repulsing the enemy, and even in recovering
a portion of the works, but were ultimately compelled to withdraw
by the hail of bullets from the storming parties and the fire of the
field-batteries planted upon the heights.

"The 3rd Brigade (16th and 17th Regiments) was posted on
the first line of the right wing, and succeeded in holding that
position for some time after the left wing had retreated, but was
then forced to succumb. The retreat never for a moment degenerated into flight; and wherever regiments or detachments were
not cut off by the enemy, the distance to the tête de pont was traversed in good order. The garrison at that point consisted of the
3rd and 18th Regiments (2nd Brigade). The powerful fire of the
enemy, which had been directed upon this position from the heights,
had dismounted the guns and now raked the bridges, shells meanwhile falling into Sonderborg, the lower part of which was again in
flames. The regiments retreated across the bridges into Alsen,
where the Guards had already taken up a position in the neighbourhood of the Castle, while the garrison of the tête de pont
engaged in a fresh and violent contest with the storming parties of
the enemy. Our guns in the Church Battery fired upon the
attacking columns with great effect; and the Rolf Krake, which
steamed three times into the Vemmingbond under a heavy fire, sent
her deadly projectiles into the enemy's ranks, causing confusion
and loss. When further resistance became useless, the garrison
also retreated from the tête de pont, the bridges were disconnected,
and the safety of the remaining portion of the army was secured.
The cannonade, however, continued all the afternoon. During
the engagement the powder mazagine of the Mill Battery was
blown up, and many doubtless fell at this point. One brave fellow,
however, must have survived, for all the guns of the battery were
fired after the hollow roll of the explosion had died away. Their
charge was too precious to be lost."

The following account of the attack has been published at the
Prussian head-quarters :

"The Prussian assault upon Forts No. 1 to No. 6 took place
simultaneously in six columns at ten o'clock this morning. The
Prussian flag waved above all the six forts by a quarter past ten.
At 11 Forts No. 7, 8, 9, and the newly-constructed works in
rear of the first series were stormed, and Fort No. 10 capitulated.
At half-past twelve the two strong works at the tête-de-pont were
carried. One of the bridges across the Alsen Sound was disconnected by the enemy ; the other was destroyed by the fire of our
artillery. The enemy was then entirely dislodged from his strong
position, and confined to Alsen.

"The attack upon Forts No. 1 to No. 6 was carried out by the
Prussian infantry amid loud cheers, without firing a shot, under
the most violent hostile small-arm and grape fire. The Rolf Krake
made her appearance when the forts were already carried and

afforded cover to the troops, but the Prussian batteries soon compelled her retreat.

"The loss of the Prussian troops cannot yet be stated with even approximate certainty. Between 3,000 and 4,000 Danish prisoners, many of whom are officers, have been brought in. Fifty to eighty guns were captured in the works, as well as a large number of flags.

"Immediately after the *tête-de-pont* was stormed, orders were given that the greater part of the troops and of the artillery should leave for Jutland to besiege Fredericia and occupy the entire province."

The Conference will, it is to be hoped, put a stop to the advance further into Jutland.

Another official (Prussian) account gives the following details:

"His Royal Highness the Crown Prince and the Field-Marshal (von Wrangel) witnessed the first part of the attack from the height near the Gammelsmark battery, the second portion from the Spitzberg, and the termination from a position further in advance, upon the Sonderborg-road. Two Staff officers were attached to each of the six storming parties to bring the Crown Prince and the Field-Marshal early reports of the progress of the attack.

"The storming parties were stationed at daybreak in the approaches and parallels, the reserves under cover in their rear, while all the batteries kept up an extremely violent fire upon the forts. One brigade was posted at the Sandberg, in order, according as circumstances might require, either to cross on pontoons and in boats to Alsen, or to divert the enemy's attention by a demonstration in that direction.

"With the stroke of ten all the batteries in the front ceased fire, and all six storming columns broke out under loud cheers simultaneously from the foremost parallel. The enemy met them with a violent fire from small arms and grape, but nothing was able to arrest the impetuosity of the attacking force, which hurried on without firing a shot. By twelve the entire line of forts, together with the *têtes-de-pont*, were in our hands.

"The Danish man-of-war Skjold, carrying eighty-four guns, lay off the shore, but did not attempt to take part in the engagement. Our loss cannot yet be ascertained. That of the enemy is apparently much greater. Two Danish Generals were left dead on the field; 3,000, to 4,000 prisoners, many being officers, and two regimental commanders have been brought in; 50 to 80 guns, with numbers of colours, have been taken. The brigade at the Sandberg was unable to cross, owing to the opposite shore being too strongly occupied, but its object was attained by a diversion of the enemy's force being caused.

General von Raven has undergone amputation. The son of General von Roon the Minister of War is amongst the wounded. According to the latest advices the Prussians were advancing on Horsen.

The remnant of the Danish army still holds its ground in Alsen, and the Prussian batteries are being brought up to drive them from that stronghold also.

The siege of Fredericia seems to have come to a standstill. The sudden inactivity of the Austrians is still wrapped in mystery. The story of the mutiny of the Hungarians, though denied, has not been satisfactorily cleared up. Reports of serious dissensions between the Austrian and Prussian Commanders are still rife. That an ill-feeling exists there can be no doubt.

Let us renew the expression of the hope that the Conference now sitting will put an end to this unjustifiable and unchristian war.

---

## A TRIP TO TENERIFFE.

Why the faculty have never recommended Teneriffe as a refugium for consumptive patients has always been a moot point. Its temperature is more equable and its atmosphere more invigorating than that of its more favoured Portuguese rival, while the scenery in the neighbourhood of Oratava is unquestionably finer and the sources of enjoyment more varied and interesting. Perhaps the known comforts of hotel life in Madeira are deemed superior to "roughing it" in Teneriffe. Perhaps the society of Funchal is considered more attractive, or the voyage less irksome, or the expense limited to the published tariff—or there may be inducements of another kind.

The presence of an Empress may make the Island fashionable, or Islington may wish to meet Belgravia—to meet on such terms of communion as misfortune sometimes brings in its train; since all rendezvous on the same sad errand. There is, however, another reason—less known it may be, but no less potent—a reason which takes the shape of an insect renowned for its strength above that of all creation—so notorious for its hostility inveterate and insatiable—so active in its attacks upon passive mankind! Unjust would be the accounts of Teneriffe without due mention of this omni-present incolant; for sooner can the eye forget its seeing and the hand its skill, than that the recollection of our first night in the Fonda del Oratava should be obliterated from the memory. Yet the spotless sheets and native worked coverlet seemed not to harbour aught that could drive sleep from the wearied eyelids and madden the disturbed occupant of the couch into frenzied gambols round the room! enough of this—for it is here when in the language of the poet.

" Great fleas have bigger fleas upon their backs to bite 'em,
    And little fleas have lesser fleas, and so ad infinitum—"

Sweeping indeed must be the reform of hotel abuse in this particular before invalids can dare venture a residence in the Valley of Oratava. The Spaniard has no idea of comfort for himself, much less has he sympathy for the well-being of others. Give him his greasy soup and the half-soddened meat from which it was expressed, with a full garnish of vegetables, and he is content. He will eat and be full. He will puff his cigar over the dessert and desire no more. If at a table-d'hôte he will arise and go forth. Post-prandial conversation has no charms for him. The business between himself and the landlord has been concluded satisfactorily and if he return to sleep, it will be at the hour of rest. The big, cheerless coffee-room will be unfrequented by him. He retires to what slumber he can get for his money, and in all conscience *that* is little enough. In Oratava the charge is a dollar a-day for board and lodging, and even this is considered exorbitant, only to be tolerated because the Villa is the resort of fashion and wealth in the summer months. There is a Spanish hotel in Santa Cruz, a few doors from Richardson's, in which the landlord professes to board and lodge his patrons for three shillings a-day; and yet there have, been grumblers.

Why therefore should any native proprietor venture an outlay on an establishment for chance foreign visitors? Why should he astonish his domestics by insisting on thorough cleanliness, when filth is unnoticed or not taken into account?

Such at any rate were the excuses which Signor Antonio of the Villa hotel pleaded when we upbraided him with want of consideration for our comfort—nor was he altogether proof against our appeals.

War was proclaimed against the household, and to the consternation of the oldest inhabitant, the mansion was scrubbed from top to bottom, thereby rousing every small demon from its lair, and to our discomfiture in turn producing the undesired effect of adding four-fold to the nightly annoyance! Efforts to suit our English fastidiousness in matters culinary resulted in equal failure, and we were fain to fall back on the ancient regimen in every respect.

No—our hopes lie not in the Spanish proprietor, but in the enterprising English speculator. Mr. Richardson has promised to place a branch establishment in this beautiful region, and by attention, no doubt cleanliness will overcome the only drawback to ease and convalescent quietude which is at present unattainable. We are inclined to advocate still more—why should not our government establish a sanitarium in Oratava? House rent is ridiculously cheap. The most commodious mansion in the place, with garden and stabling attached, does not exceed £40 a year, while the rental of the generality of houses averages half that amount. Year by year departmental officers both civil and military are invalided from the West coast of Africa to this Island. In fact, the rule in favour of the latter is that two months leave of absence on medical certificate is granted every two years and allowed to reckon as Coast Service. From the

manifest advantages of this warrant, it is true the executive officers
are at present precluded.

The writer having by the merest chance escaped death in the
Gambia, and wishing to recruit the health shattered by five years
recurrent fevers, had to obtain private leave of absence and pay
his own way, while one who did not belong to the tabooed class
was invalided thither at the public expense. This is however
beside the question.

At present the efficiency of the Coast Garrisons is greatly impaired by continual invaliding of officers to England, who would
otherwise regain strength here in a few months—nay, more—the
equable invigorating climate of Teneriffe would no doubt have
greater renovating effect than even six months absenteeism in England. A military sanitarium in Oratava, or a tour of Mediterranean
service for our Zouave battalions, is therefore the only feasible
method of solving what must soon become a difficult problem.

The chief object of interest to sight-seers in the Villa is the
celebrated old tree "whose trunk was hollow when *Alonso del
Lugo* and his conquistadores in 1493 established Spanish authority
here, and turned the bark into a chapel for holy mass, after it
had served Druidical purposes amongst Guanche tribes for ages."*

It stands in the garden of the Marquis of Sansal almost hidden
from view by dense circumambient foliage; fitting retreat for its
decaying age. The wildest theories have been started respecting
its time of life which has been determined by naturalists as ante-
diluvian or even "at a period coeval with the advent of man."

The height of the Dragon-tree (as this ancient guardian of
the Hesperides is named) is about 60 feet and its circumference
at the base close upon 50 feet. The trunk rears itself gnarled
and branchless to about 15 feet, and terminates in a bunch of
trees, as it were, which entwining their roots round the inner
rind of the parent stem, sprout upwards with clustering plume-
like foliage. The flowers throughout the garden are indeed
wonderful specimens of the giant growth in this congenial climate.
Tree fuchsias and camillas, monstrous dahlias, mimosas and
geraniums, and other floræ too numerous to mention. Yet not
to them, nor even to the noblest monarch of the forest is the
stranger asked to direct his attention, but to a slender cabbage
palm of considerable altitude, to which in its rarity the gardener
proudly points and claims respect; so true it is that human nature
is insatiable and ever grasping at a shadow!

The cathedral of Oratava is the finest in the Island and the
natives are justly proud of it. With less meretricious ornament
there is a decaying grandeur about the building irresistibly fas-
cinating. The interior is dimly lighted from above, except in
parts where with considerable judgment a window has been more
recently inserted to throw a gleam of light across a painting. In

* Professor Piazzi Smyth.

this church there is an original of Murillo; but even *his* Virgin and Child, had less charms for us than a wonderful old picture which at first glance seemed but a daub of black paint. A few moments study, however, brought out the subject clear and defined: an old monk engaged in a translation of the bible, the table upon which he wrote seeming to stand out from the canvass.

Two angels exquisitely carved in the purest white marble, invite the devotee with outspread wings to the massive silver altar, and soft weird-like music issuing the while from an organ placed out of sight falls upon the ear with solemn effect, and fills the mind with an holy awe. Say not that the religion of the Roman is empty, fanciful, grotesque and meaningless! Every rite performed—every mystery veiled—every genuflexion enjoined, appeals earnestly to the senses of the ignorant many, and to the refined tastes of the few, and although we may deprecate the cunning of a church which can curtail a commandment to suit its own views, we must acknowledge and admire the untiring devotion of its members of every class who, under all circumstances and at all times, are ever mindful of their religious duties. Throughout the Island, at varying distances, the traveller comes suddenly upon curious erections which some writers with little reverence and less descriptive powers have compared to giraffe menageries. They are called "Golgothas," and are simply walled enclosures of a large crucifix, opposite which every Spaniard doffs his sombrero and bows the knee as he passes. Then again at every cross-road, at every spot of danger or local interest, in the crater-bed of a volcano, or on the summit of an eruption, in the Plaza or the Almeda, on the walls of houses, in every chamber and even on the roof top—the great emblem of our salvation meets the eye at every turn.

Incomplete as must be any account of Teneriffe without the description of an ascent of the Peak, we are compelled by force of circumstances to take the same distant view of the mountain which in reality fell to our lot. To the "Alpine Club" and such climbers of the world's crags, it will not seem strange that the Peak which has been accomplished by our boy-prince and even by ladies, should be inaccessible at certain periods. Towards the fall of the year, winter sets in on the mountain with violent snow storms, which completely choke up the few known paths to the summit.

But even if the tourist succeed in tempting a guide to accompany him, the intensity of the cold and rarity of the atmosphere would be dangerous in the extreme. Enthusiasts have made, or attempted to make, the ascent in the winter months, but such adventurers have been glad enough to beat a hasty retreat down the snow-clad heights into the genial atmosphere of Oratava:

"For there may be snow on the mountain-top
   While there's heat in the valley below."

As in some sort consolation-stakes for the disappointment of not scrambling up the rocks of "Alta Vista," or looking down into the sulphurous crater of the utmost peak, we projected a trip to a small town built at the very base of the mountain, and named euphoniously "Icod de los vinos." Mounted on hardy mountain ponies, which, for cat-like feats, would be invaluable in the Alhambra of Leicester Square, we rode down the three miles of precipitous pavement which conducts to Puerto, whence the road lay along the coast to our destination.

In Humboldt's time, little remained untold respecting the Port of Oratava, much less is there now, when the place has degenerated into a nonentity—its trade stagnant, and its dangerous harbour unfrequented; yet its pretty squares and streets, its beautiful quintas and royal gardens, merit a less premature end than that predestined for them by Professor Smyth, in the future lava streams from the terrible peak. As we journeyed along, we could not but be struck by the volcanic nature of the earth's surface—great boulders lying loosely about, deep gullies, evidently crater-beds at the remote time when the mighty volcano belched its hidden fires and curious lineal indentations in the rocks, which some geologists would fain ascribe to the action of glaciers. More attractive, however, than the lava-formed substratum, is the rich alluvial-deposit terraced along the slopes of the mountain into cochineal plantations. Alas! for the past glories of the vine. Here, for miles around, extend fields of that unsightly though most important usurper, the cactus, interspersed here and there with patches of potatoe and corn crops. In 1829, the rain came down in torrents, sweeping before it the vineyards of the valley, or rather, scarping the soil in its headlong descent. At Puerto there was great distress and consternation, for it was believed to be the work of a waterspout; but the theory of Dr. Smyth seems the correct one, i.e., that the surcharged soil of the peak was forced to overflow by an unusually heavy discharge of the clouds, which was not felt or even seen in the lower districts.

The vine disease succeeded this deluge, and the fruit withered and dried. Meantime, a speculating gentleman introduced the insect which bids fair to rival in return profits every other product of the colonies, and although at first looked upon with distrust, if not contempt, a few short years turned the scale in its favour, and a virtue was made of the necessity which prompted the introduction of cochineal from Honduras.

As the name implies, the district in the neighbourhood of Icod was once celebrated for its grapes. In fact, at a still remoter period, this portion of the island was alone known to traders, and the port, if not the capital of the island, was Guarachico, a town distant about four miles, and which stands to Icod in the same relation as Santa Cruz to Laguna, and Puerto to the Villa del Oratava.

Built under its towering shadow, nothing could exceed the moon-lit peak as seen from Icod. One felt as if the craggy ribs of the mountain were within grasp, while the keen wind, purified in its career over the region of snow, awakened the senses to a full appreciation of these healthy Highlands. Day-light opened up fresh beauties to the eye, rich cultivation spreading away on all sides, the quaint old houses of the townspeople and the strange costumes of the peasantry who flocked into the narrow streets with baskets of luscious fruit, all charming to a degree.

Our lilliputian landlady was most attentive to our comforts, and deserves what Trollope would call "an innkeeper's immortality." She extemporised wonderful dishes for our consumption, which were flanked by a few bottles of choice old native wine, presented to us by the Alcalde of the City, who also favoured us with his company, while we discussed its merits.

Next morning we descended the hill-side into impoverished but beautifully situated Guarachico.

The prevailing silence which is remarkable in most Spanish towns was here intensified so to speak, no sound but the sad sea waves broke the supernatural stillness, and under such mournful influence our recollections travelled back to that awful time when the lava-stream from the Peak rushed impetuously over the cliff that overhangs the town, and lodged incontinently in the bay. Having bathed in the narrowed channel we returned to Icod en route for Oratava. It were vain to describe the wonderful steeps we accomplished on our way; but whether along the ledge of a precipice or down the wall-like abruptness of the bridle-path at many points, or holding on by the ears to prevent slipping over the saddle in an ascent, we had equal confidence in our sure-footed animals, and reached Puerto unwearied, and with sharpened appetite for the Irish hospitality that awaited our arrival.

It has often been said that immigrants become more naturalized by an act of franchise than the very natives of the country which they have adopted. *Americanior Americanis* has passed into a proverb. It is not so with the Irish of Teneriffe. Generations may have passed since the first persecuted exiles settled in the Island, and still the national characteristics remain intact. In Puerto so many old Irish families took refuge that for a time it almost lost its Spanish character. Even jealousy of foreign landed interest was kept in abeyance, and the authorities presented the settlers with a few acres to be used as a burial ground.

In the cathedral is also a recess which coronated by the harp of old Ireland is easily recognised as the "Capilla de St. Patrick," Here we found a remarkable old slab bearing the following interesting epitaph.

" *D. D. Bernadri Walsh alias Valois— Waterfordiensis in Hibernia, in portu Orotaviensi Insulæ Nivariæ vulgo Theneriffe nuper defuncti A.D.* 1713."

A scion of this noble house is mentioned by Southey in his life of Nelson, as the brave youth who tore the shirt off his back to bandage the wounds of an English sailor during the disastrous attack on Santa Cruz—of two other descendants, one is a present Alcalde, and the other a Marquis of a district in the Island.

We have spoken of Irish hospitality in the port, but it would be as invidious, as ungenerous to pass over unmentioned Spanish urbanity and kindness in the Villa of Oratava.

A young gentleman, (Don Senor E——S——) attached himself to our party, and through his intervention nothing could be more exhilarating than the round of gaiety which greeted us on all sides; nothing could be more delightful than the manner in which we were treated at these reunions.

Oh! those happy nights—can they ever be forgotten? Where ceremony dispensed with, we were met most cordially and allowed to reciprocate kindly feelings unreservedly, albeit in the strangest of patois! Oh! for those pretty little flirtation scenes of the cotillon, those delicious polkas and the graceful Havanera. Sublunary delights are few, but among the recollections of the past will ever remain the pleasant hours spent in the company of the bright eyed senoritas of Oratava.

Having received a "*Billete de presentacion*" to a grand ball in the Casino at Santa Cruz, we returned to the metropolis to avail ourselves of the opportunity of becoming better acquainted with the citizens. The community we left behind is a little world in itself. Once the barrier of formal introduction passed we felt at home with all.

Sociability is natural because most families are related, and the usual strictness of Spanish life is there unheeded. Their rules of *etiquette* are those of the "Hill" in the *Strange Story*, and the Marquesa de F——, is the social Mrs. Poyntz. Different far did we find it at Santa Cruz as seen at the ball. Society arrived late, and exacted all due observances. The stiff-brocaded matrons jealously overlooked the performances of their daughters, who in flowing amplitudes were much more mindful of an *appearance* than the mazes of the dance. Government officials and officers of the garrison looked prim and uncomfortable under the eye of their captain-general, and an air of restraint pervaded all except the English portion of the company. Under such circumstances, enjoyment is difficult, yet the affair was regarded as a decided success. During the winter months these balls are of frequent occurrence, and serve as an attraction to the residents throughout the Island. Those indeed who are able to afford it, possess houses in the three chief towns, and while they pass the summer months in Laguna, return to winter at Santa Cruz; yet we have often wondered how the owners of the "Pino" can bring themselves to *relinquish* their charming abodes for temporary discomfort elsewhere. It is a remarkable fact, that Teneriffe festivities are ever

attended with exceeding great noise.  From early dawn on a gala
day the bells of the different churches ring forth loud and continuous, not without a degree of melody to those who appreciate
such music; while great guns are fired at morn, and noon, and
night from a saluting battery consisting of 24 brass pieces.  Then,
too, these commemoration days are of frequent occurrence, and
the strangest events furnish excuse for extra performances.

The announcement of the fact that Her Most Christian Majesty
had arrived at that consummation so devoutly to be wished and so
important for the continuance of her regal line, was celebrated by
the usual salvo of bells and guns!  The troops were also ordered
to appear in full dress for three days, and everybody congratulated
everybody that no revolution need be expected for some time to
come; perhaps even the embryo prince might some day raise
Spain to its proper position as a first class power.  And why
should she not be a first class power we repeat?  the day must
come when Spanish diplomatists will open their mouths in the
Councils of Europe, but as yet we fear it is far distant.

Improvement in every department is manifest and encouraging,
and if only ability be brought to equal increasing resource a
great future awaits their enterprise.  Yet it is a pity that under
such circumstances a remote dependency like a province in St.
Domingo should be able to resist successfully and even to defeat
her armies.

Sad indeed will be the day for the white man's authority
in Niggerdom when any portion of that race gain the ascendant,
for what is now pretentious arrogance would become abnormal
usurpation.

Week after week transports arrived with troops *en route* to Hayti
—unfortunate men doomed to die in the mountain passes of that
unhealthy Island.  We were present at a general inspection of
the regiment in garrison, and could not help admiring the steadiness and soldier-like appearance of the beardless boys, who in
march and movement exhibited well-drilled qualities.  That such
troops will in the end be successful against rabble niggers cannot
be doubted, but we could wish the white man's supremacy
established without much unnecessary display of power.  If they
take example by our short and decisive policy in the present
Maori struggle, they will send their best man to quench the fire in
its earliest stage lest a general conflagration should ensue.

Much has been said and written of late on the destiny of the
African.  Exploration has accomplished wonders in the interior of
that mighty continent.  In America, freedom sounds her loud
peon, and in the West India Islands, as in our settlements on the
West African Coast, the black man is fast rising in the scale of
social progress.  The civilising effects of education and missionary
labour are fain to produce immediate results, and enthusiasts look
to the accomplishment of an oft-quoted prophesy soon to be

fulfilled. But we ask are they fit for self-government? Are they worthy to be welcomed as men and brothers into the family of nations? Is it better that they should stand alone tottering and ridiculed, or continue allegiance supported, and utilized? Before the reader decides the question for himself, we would recommend the perusal of two books written in sportive or sarcastic vein, but containing great truths. We mean "*The West Indies*," and "*Wanderings on the West Coast of Africa*," which in our opinion exhaust the subject. Nor are any two men more competent to judge even on passing observation of results than our worthy friends Mr. A. Trollope and Captain Burton.

While we moralize, the signal-bell of the English Mail Steamer warns us that we must be up and away, and leaving behind the salubrious climate of the Fortunate Islands once more tend our course to pestilential Gambia.        E. R.

## EDITOR'S PORTFOLIO;

### OR,

## NAVAL AND MILITARY REGISTER.

On the 7th of last month, a Meeting was held at Willis' Rooms, St. James, on the subject of a proposed School for the Daughters of Officers of the Army; an institution which all who know anything about the subject, must admit to be one of great importance, and for which the aid of the public may be very fairly expected. H.R.H. the Duke of Cambridge took the chair, and there was a large and influential attendance. From a report that was read by the Rev. S. Jenner, (Hon. Secretary,) it appeared that the want of an institution of the kind had attracted the attention of several philanthropic individuals of high standing, both civil and military, who accordingly formed themselves into a provisional committee a few months since, and privately collected subscriptions in aid of so useful a project. In a short time their efforts were crowned with such success, that they were enabled to purchase on very advantageous terms a building situated near Bath, and known as the Lansdowne Training College. This building, which originally cost £14,000, was bought by the Committee for less than a quarter of that sum, and can, it seems, be rendered serviceable for the accommodation of about one hundred and twenty inmates, at an outlay of about £5,000. It has eight acres of ground attached to it, and its situation is most healthy. In order to bring the matter before the nation in a form befitting its importance, the Duke of Cambridge, as head of the army, was solicited to preside over a Meeting, at which the objects of the Institution could be laid before the public; and His Royal Highness had promptly complied with that request.

The Royal Duke, on taking the chair, remarked, that "The claims of the daughters of military men on the benevolence of the nation, to assist them in obtaining a proper education, were so well founded, that very few words from him in their favour would suffice. In fact, all that the meeting would have to decide, would be the manner in which these wants could best be met. In a country like this, such institutions were sorely needed, so little help being rendered by the Government to members of the Naval and Military Services. A building having already been obtained in the neighbourhood of Bath, with funds collected privately, at a price much below its actual value, only a small sum would be needed to render it serviceable for the purposes intended; and an income of £2,000 or £3,000 a year, would, for the present, be sufficient to set it going."

A vote of thanks was moved by Sir R. Dacres to his Royal Highness, for having presided over the meeting, and seconded by General Ashburnham, who said the debt of gratitude they owed to the civilians on the committee was a large one; in fact, the institution owed its origin to them. The motion having been carried by acclamation, his Royal Highness, in returning thanks, said that he quite agreed with Sir John Fergusson, that, although the religious instruction should be carried out on Church of England principles, still if parents belonging to other denominations were willing to abide by this rule, their children should not be excluded.

The School is now, therefore, fairly before the public, and we cannot allow ourselves to doubt that the appeal will be liberally responded to. Contributions may be paid to any banker, or army agent.

---

The Conference to settle the Dano-German conflict with a view to the maintenance of the peace of Europe, has commenced its sittings at London, under the presidency of Earl Russell. Lord Clarendon has succeeded in establishing a good understanding between the Governments of England and of France, and the first motion will be the suspension of hostilities pending the Conference.

Dybböl has fallen. The Danes still hold out at Alsen. The Prussians are pushing forward their batteries, and threaten to occupy the whole of Jutland. It is however to be hoped that all further hostilities will be put a stop to by the " Conference."

---

One of the most recent telegrams from New York, left that

remarkable body, the Army of the Potomac, "preparing for an early forward movement;" but three days later we learn that a "destructive storm" has interrupted its communications with Washington, and though, of course, it has been "largely reinforced," the "early forward movement" seems to have been adjourned *sine die*. But then "active preparations are being made for a campaign in the south-west;" only unluckily it is the Confederates who are taking the initiative, and invading Kentucky. These are not very hopeful signs for the Federal cause, and "gold at 189," shows what Wall Street thinks of them. General Grant is reported as busily engaged in removing officers of all ranks, and a glance at the Army list will show what good grounds he has for that course.

———

As we noticed last month, the Volunteer Easter Monday Review was held on new ground this year, somewhat to the discomfort of mere sightseers, who of course could not find as ample accommodation at Guildford as they had been used to at Brighton; but all else regarded the change as an improvement. Sir John Pennefather says in his Report to the Adjutant-General: "The site selected was, in my judgment, well adapted for the purpose, having in view the numbers engaged—being a dry, undulating heath, sufficiently spacious to manœuvre over, affording ridges for positions—the surface so far broken as to fairly test the efficiency of the several corps, without to any extent impeding the movements—with brushwood and detached plantations all round, affording excellent opportunities for skirmishing." The troops present numbered 16,033, with twenty-four guns, which were divided into an attacking and a defending force, and their manœuvres occupied about two hours and a half. Some of the difficulties of real service were experienced in the effort to drag the guns into position along narrow winding lanes, in a sandy soil; but they were surmounted, and all passed off most satisfactorily, except that an unfortunate clergyman lost his life, in great measure from his own recklessness. The crowd was too great for the ground to be properly kept, and the reverend gentleman got so close to the troops, that he received a mortal wound from a ramrod accidentally discharged. One or two of the Volunteers also sustained some injury from falls; but all who are *competent* to judge, were quite agreed that more real instruction *was imparted* on that one day, than all the Brighton "military promenades" had afforded.   Such being the case, we shall look to a yearly change of scene.

Sir John Pennefather's Report speaks as favourably of the Volunteers as their real friends could desire; and he concludes with a piece of sound advice, such as might be expected from so distinguished an officer, and which cannot be too often repeated, if these auxiliaries to our regular forces are ever to become as efficient as they might be.

" It affords me," he says, " the utmost gratification to state that my report of the Volunteers must be most favourable.  Those engaged on the 28th instant, seemed animated by one and the same spirit, to perform their duties as soldiers to the best of their ability.  The corps are composed of fine, active, intelligent men, well dressed, their appointments well put on, their arms generally in good order, their step is alert and active, they skirmish well, and keep up an excellent sustained fire.  But the battalions require more steady drill in order to render their movements more collected, more handy, and more self-possessed as compact bodies, in the hurry, noise, and confusion unavoidable in real action.  And whilst I consider the force in a state of efficiency most creditable to the officers and Volunteers, and most valuable as a defensive force, I recommend more steady company and battalion drill, and that the corps should be brigaded as often as convenient, and the brigades commanded by the same brigadiers."

That this plain speaking proceeds from full consideration, and is mingled with a sincere desire to give all the commendation that can honestly be bestowed, is quite evident from the postscript of the gallant General's Report, which says:—"I should also report that the detachment of Light Horse of the Honourable Artillery Company, which worked under Major-General Rumley with the Horse Artillery, turned out very well, and manœuvred steadily and quickly.  The corps is well appointed, well mounted, and the men ride well."

Such commendation will no doubt have its effect, and we shall look to see it given to many corps next year, for of course all will labour hard to win it.

———

Our metropolis has of late been in a state of excitement through the visit of Garibaldi. As stated by himself, his object was to return thanks to his English friends for kindness lavished on him, particularly after the affair of Aspromonte, but the ardour of some of his partisans very far outran this, and probably no European Government but our own could have safely refrained from interference with them. Among other studiously offensive things, the admiration that they expressed for Mazzini, induced Garibaldi to utter praises of that individual which many of his friends must regret.

Garibaldi's health being obviously but indifferent when he arrived, the week of comparative quiet that he was allowed to enjoy in the Isle of Wight, was no doubt of benefit to him; but no amount of strength and good-will could carry him unharmed through such a round of fatigue and excitement, as his admirers, high and low, prepared for him in London, besides inviting him to visit every considerable provincial town. He stood the entry to London, the bestowal of the freedom of the city, a number of fashionable assemblies, where he was an undoubted "lion;" two appearances at the Crystal Palace, and deputations without end. But his real friends saw when he had had enough, and more than enough of all this, and persuaded him to withdraw after a three weeks' ovation, such as has seldom been accorded to any one in this country. His so-called "working men" admirers however, were furious at the abridgment of their Saturnalia; particularly as he whom they claimed as exclusively their own, had been patronized by Dukes and Duchesses, Premiers and Chancellors of the Exchequer, and even after he had left London, they met on Primrose Hill "to protest against the manner in which he had been hurried away from England;" but were dispersed by the police.

———

A paper was read at the Royal United Service Insitution, in Whitehall Yard, on Monday the 18th of April, 1864, at 8.30 P.M., by Lieutenant-Colonel H. M. Synge, R.E., Colonel St. Leger Alcock in the Chair. "On the Constructive Service of the Army, or, Military Work by Military Means: being suggestions towards better efficiency in the design, superintendence, and execution of the works and buildings, necessary to the maintenance and for the duties of the Army; at the same time augmenting the combatant force and lessening the estimates." Among the members and visitors present were Viscount Ranelaigh, General Crawford, Colonel the Hon. Crichton Stuart, M.P., the Hon. Colonel Bernard, M.P., Sir H. Verney, Bart., M.P., Sir Edward Synge, Bart., Colonel Chapman, D.A.G.R.E., Professor Tyndall, Majors Ewart, Leahy, R.E., &c., &c.

The following is a summary of the Paper:

1. Premliminary maxims. Truisms, that fighting power is the essence and object of all armies, and the proper aim of army arrangements. The application of this principle to the subject, would result in an increase of the combatant force, and in economy, by doing military work by military means; effect on number and

efficiency. The combination of structural and combatant functions is the perfect attainment of the end in view; if practicable?

The aspects of the question of this practicability are:

1stly. From the military point of view. The effect upon the soldier of employment on military works. (*a*) Personally. (*b*) In discipline. (*c*) In pay.

2ndly. From the constructive point of view. The value of military labour in getting work done.

All arguments were drawn from fact, precedent, or close analogy:

As to the soldiers efficiency. His healthfulness, suppleness, intelligence, and resource would be improved, and whilst habits of discipline and sufficiency of drill were provided for, the tendency to be amenable to discipline would be fostered and encouraged.

One great question as to his increased pay, was, what will he do with it? The increase would not in itself be an evil, but a good. Inducement to its right use was needed and at hand, in affording the soldier greater liberties of marriage, throwing on himself the consequent expenses. Opinions against the soldiers having working pay, had their weight as to authority; but they were inapplicable to the case in hand. There were greater objections to the present course of debarring the soldier from work, and from marriage; and there would be benefits to the service by the course proposed, as well as to the soldier.

The question from the constructive point of view was the value of military labour in getting work done; one of relative cost and of sufficient workmanship, and of the necessity for skilled labour in modern warfare. Comparisons of cost were then instituted, and the authorities referred to, and showed savings on *execution* by military means.

The gradual expansion of the existing military features might be effected without injury to any existing civil interest, with a diminution of expenditure consequent thereon. Simple forms for the record of work, and of military superintendence and execution, with explanations, were afforded. The lecturer then dwelt on the peculiar value of the principles on which the above suggestions were based, from the circumstances of Great Britain, and concluded with an anticipative reply to objections formed on partial misapprehension of the scope of the suggestions submitted. The application he intended was, that constructive services were properly the duty of the Army, and formed an invaluable military school.

The Chairman said Colonel Synge had modestly laid claim to no originality; but he was the first to offer a solution to two of the great difficulties of the day with respect to the Army, namely, the question of marriage, and of limited service. With respect to military works by military means, it had been well said that the pick-axe as well as the sword was the ensign of Roman conquest. The greatest military power that ever existed employed the soldier in time of peace in what we should consider civil works; and thereby rendered him sounder, hardier, and healthier in time of war.

Sir Harry Verney, Bart., M.P., said one great object of the present day was to raise the moral status of the Army, and he hoped the time would come when the soldier would be enabled to return to his native village a better member of society, having learned a trade, and able to earn a respectable livelihood, and thereby holding out an inducement and an example to young men themselves to enter the service. The subject was one of great importance, because, owing to the high rate of wages paid in all occupations, it was said that the character of the men who entered the army was not so good as it was some years ago. With regard to the expense of military work, it had been stated that a target was constructed in Jamaica, some thirty years ago, at a cost of three dollars by soldiers, and the repair of it alone was estimated at £200. It showed the importance of employing the men, and he believed that the more they were employed, the more popular the service would become.

Lord Ranelagh agreed with Sir Harry Verney as to the importance of teaching the men a trade, but he could not see any chance of employing them on military works. He should like Colonel Synge to illustrate what he meant by military works, for in his paper he seemed to go beyond the digging of trenches and the throwing up of batteries.

Major Leahy, R.E. stated, that at the present moment, military labour was exclusively employed upon the new fortifications at Portland, and upon military works at Dover, and at another important station; that a large work, estimated to cost £80,000 by contract, had been taken over by the Department, and a very large saving would be effected by employing the military upon this work.

Major Ewart, R.E., thought a comparison could not fairly be instituted between the French and the English soldier. In the French service, raised by conscription, artists of all kinds could be employed at a small remuneration, whereas we had to go into the open market and engage labour at the ordinary wages. He might mention that he had carried on the whole repair of a camp in this country by military labour.

General Crawford thought the employment of soldiers on military works perfectly feasible; but he dissented from the views of Colonel Synge on the question of marriage. They were enlisted only for ten years, and would be able to marry with greater advantage afterwards.

Major Leahy stated, that in the Belgian army the men were enlisted for two years. They had been employed upon the fortifications at Antwerp; and in the winter they were taught trades, which in the summer they put into practice. In our service, with enlistment for ten years, there would be no difficulty in extending the system of military labour, and, as a means of carrying it out, he agreed with Colonel Synge that military superintendence was essential.

Colonel Synge, in reply, expressed regret that the financial view of the question had not been taken up. With regard to the question of the soldier's marriage, he was at one time prejudiced against it, but it appeared to him, that marriage offered the complete solution of the question of the soldier's work wages, and of his re-enlistment or his useful discharge, he might say it was the key-stone of the arch. With respect to the training of officers, he wanted to bring before them that constructive duties ought to be the training-school of those officers who are to be the fighting men. He had been asked what were military works. His reply was that everything required by an army, whether for its main-tenance or for the purpose of its duties was a military work. The soldier might be likened to something like a snail, who carried his house about on his back. The man best to supply all his wants would be the most efficient soldier, and in his opinion, victory attended efficiency rather than only numbers.

Colonel Synge stated that he had been informed that works in Canada had been carried out by military means at one-fifth the expense that they would otherwise have cost, and in further proof of the easy feasibility of training under skilled labour, he referred to the excellent work performed in past years by convicts in Ireland under the simple stimulus of an additional quantity of food. Skilled work performed by young convicts trained in prison had elicited the marked approval of the late Sir James Graham.

The Chairman conveyed to Colonel Synge the thanks of the Meeting for his admirable Paper.

---

# CRITICAL  NOTICES.

ADELA CATHCART. By George Macdonald, M.A., Author of "David Elginbrod," &c., 3 vols.

Mr. Macdonald's former works have given ample proof of the versa-tility of his talents, but here they are turned to a somewhat unusual account, for he has devoted himself to constructing, not one novel, but something like a dozen, every one of which shews the hand of a master. The story of Adela Cathcart, the nominal heroine, is simple enough, as befits what is the mere string to bind the different tales to-gether. She is the only daughter of a retired Colonel, and at the open-ing of the tale she is seen nearly wearied to death by the perverse attention of an empty-headed cousin, who, aided by his scheming mother, seeks her dower rather than herself. Mr. John Smith, an old bachelor friend of her father, comes to pass the Christmas, and is alarmed at seeing his so-called niece pining away of ennui. To rouse and interest her, he devises a club of story writers, and her cure is effected, partly by listening to their various well-told tales, and, in some small measure by an attachment that thereby grows up between Adela and one of the number. The curate and his wife, the schoolmaster and his wife, and the doctor, all bear their part, and each is made to sketch his or her own character in a way alike natural and pleasing.

One great charm will be found in several graceful poetical pieces which are insterspersed among the stories.

It would demand more space than we can spare to analyse the various tales, and where all are so good, we have some hesitation in declaring a preference for any one in particular. But we must own to viewing with special favour "The Light Princess," and "The Shadows," and "The Curate's Story." Others may be equally gratified with "The Broken Swords," or "My Uncle Peter," and the teller of "The Child's Holiday," well deserves to succeed in carrying off the heiress—for that is the end at which the Doctor eventually arrives.

MY STEPFATHER'S HOME. By Lady Blake. 3 vols.

Original in design, and most clever in execution, "My Stepfather's Home" is by far the best novel that we have seen for many a day. We do not recollect to have met with Lady Blake as a novelist before; but if this work is indeed her first production, it is a most remarkable one. The style is lively, the conversation natural, and the incidents such as may be observed in every-day life, but told in a manner that enchains the reader's attention from beginning to end. As the merest outline of the plot, we may remark that Mrs. Seaford, a young widow lady, with one little girl, marries Mr. Rivers, a clergyman, who has a ward, Mabel Clifton, and on Mabel's character and conduct the whole story depends. Jessie Seaford is the narrator of all that relates to her Stepfather's Home, and most admirably does she discharge her task. She gives the most natural picture in the world of her child-like, jealous anger at her mother's marriage, of her wounded feelings at seeing Mabel always preferred to herself by her stepfather, and of the rivalry between them when they both mix in the world. Earnest, unselfish love is seen in the case of Jessie, and much heartlessness in that of Mabel, but eventually she improves, and at last she is happily married, though not to any one of the numerous admirers who have been hanging on her every look; but who is the favoured individual we do not feel at liberty to state.

## NAVAL OBITUARY.

Vice-Admiral William Richardson (on the Retired List C.) died at Stockwell Crescent, Surry, on the 8th of April, in his 80th year. The gallant Admiral had seen much service, and was the son of Mr. W. Richardson, a Medical Officer at Haslar Hospital, and nephew of Rear-Admiral Raggett. He entered the Navy in 1794, and was for a short period on board the Alfred shortly before she was engaged in Lord Howe's action of 1st June. On the 6th of November 1796 he joined, as midshipman, the Prince George bearing the flag of Rear-Admiral Parker, under whom he took part in the action off Cape St. Vincent 14th February 1797. During the next six years he was employed off Cadiz, in the Channel, West Indies and Mediterranean. in the Boston, Formidable, Queen Charlotte, Barfleur, Téméraire, Calcutta, Dreadnought and Victory, bearing the flags of Admirals Sir C. Thompson, J. H. Whitshed, Hon. W. Cornwallis, and Lord Nelson. By the latter nobleman he was presented, on October 5, 1803, with his first commission as Acting Lieutenant of the Termagant to which ship he was confirmed on April 30, 1804. After taking part in the Expedition to Copenhagen in 1807, as Lieutenant of the Goshawk, he was appointed in May 1808, First Lieutenant of the Bombay, in which capacity he served also in the Rodney, America, and Menelaus, Captains Cuming, Sir Josias Rowley, Sir E. O. King, and Sir Peter Parker, all in the Mediterranean, where he came into frequent contact with the enemy's fleet and batteries near Toulon. While first of the America he commanded with credit the boats of that ship, the Leviathan, and the Eclair at the capture of a large number of merchant vessels which had taken shelter under the batteries at Languelia. In this dashing enterprise the British lost 16 men killed and 20 wounded. Mr. Richardson's next appointment was to the Médusa in June 1813, and in February of the following year he removed to the York, in which ship a portion of the Peninsula army was conveyed to Quebec. He next served in the Caledonia, bearing the flag of Sir Graham Moore, then in the Rochfort, Captain Sir A. Dickson, and after completing more than nine years as First Lieutenant of several line of battle ships, he was advanced, in December 1818, to the rank of Commander. He was one of the first Commanders selected by the Duke of Clarence to the post of Second-Captain in a line of battle ship, and as such was employed in the Windsor Castle, under Sir E. D. King, from May 1827 to May 1828. In 1835 he was appointed to the command of the Clio, in which ship he was actively engaged in protecting the merchants carrying on the gun trade at Portendik on the Coast of Africa, as well as in assisting the Royalists on the Coasts of Catalonia and Valencia. For these services he was promoted to post rank in June 1838, and was created a knight of Isabella the Catholic. Captain Richardson held the out-pension of Greenwich Hospital until advanced to the rank of Rear-Admiral in September 1857, and he attained the rank of Vice-Admiral on 9th February 1864. For many years he acted as Honorary Secretary at Gosport of the Royal Naval Benevolent Society, and was an active member of the Committee of the Old Naval Club of 1765. Vice-Admiral Richardson married in 1816 the daughter of Mr. Richard White, and niece of Admiral George McKinley, by whom he had a daughter and two sons, the elder of whom died a few weeks after resigning the command of the Pluto on the Coast of Africa, and the younger is one of the Senior Clerks attached to the Transport Department of the Admiralty.

---

Admiral Hugh Patton died on the 18th March, at his chambers, 90 Cockspur Street. The deceased officer, who had attained the age of 73 years, was first cousin of the present Vice-Admiral Robert Patton, R.N. He entered the Navy in October, 1804, as a first-class boy on board the Puissant, 74, at Portsmouth; and becoming attached, shortly afterwards, to the Bellerophon, 74, fought, as midshipman of that ship, at the battle of Trafalgar. At the commencement of 1806 he joined the Niobe, 40, and assisted at the capture of the Nearque, 16; and after further serving on the Jamaica station was promoted to lieutenant February 1, 1811. As lieutenant he served on the Irish station and at Portsmouth; and shared in a yard-arm-and-yard-arm conflict, of upwards of a hour, with the French frigate Etoile, 40, which terminated in a drawn battle. He was advanced to commander December 6, 1813, and after three years' command of the Alban, 12, obtained post rank August 12, 1819. He was appointed to the Rattlesnake, 28, fitting for the West Indies, in November, 1823, and to the Isis, 50, at Jamaica, in September, 1825, whence he returned in 1827. He accepted the retirement October 1, 1846, became rear-admiral January 19, 1852, vice-admiral September 10, 1857, and admiral April 27, 1863.

---

# STATIONS OF THE ROYAL NAVY IN COMMISSION.

*(Corrected to 26th April.)*

*With the Dates of Commission of the officers in Command.*

Aboukir, 86, sc, Commodore P. Cracroft, C.B., 1854, Jamaica

Acorn, Hosp. Ship, Mast.-Com. H. Hutchings, 1861, Shanghae

Active, 90, Training Ship, for Naval Reserve, Com. T. Heard, 1860, Sunderland

Adventure, 9, sc. troop ship, Capt. C. L. Waddilove, 1862, particular service

Alecto, 3, st. ves., Com. W. H. Blake, 1860, S.E. Coast of America.

Alert, 17, sc. Com. H. C. Majendie, 1864, Pacific.

Algerine, 1, sc. gunboat, Lieut.-Com. A. R. Blane, 1856, China.

Antelope, 3, st. ves., Lieut.-Com. C. O. D. Allingham, 1856, Coast of Africa

Archer, 13, sc. Capt. F. Marten, (1861) Coast of Africa

Argus, 6, steam ves. Com. J. Moresby. 1856, China

Ariel, 9, sc. Com. W. C. Chapman, 1855, Cape of Good Hope

Asia, 84, Rear Admiral George Elliot, Capt. H. Caldwell, C.B., 1853, Portsmouth

Aurora, 35, sc. Capt. Sir F. L. McClintock, Kt., 1854, Channel Squadron

Bacchante, 39, sc. Capt. D. McL. Mackenzie, 1859, Pacific

Barracouta, 6, st. ves. Com. J. D'Arcy, 1863, North America and West Indies

Barrosa, 21, sc., Captain W. M. Dowell, 1858, East Indies and China

Black Prince, 41, sc. Capt. J. F. B. Wainwright, (1855) Channel Squadron,

Blenheim, 60, sc. Capt. P. H. Mason, 1849, Coast Guard, Milford

Bombay, 67, sc., Capt. C. A. Campbell, 1863, Sheerness.

Boscawen, 70, Com. G. S. Nares, 1862, Southampton Training Ship

Brilliant, 16, Com. Grey Skipwith, 1848, Naval Reserve Drill Ship, Dundee

Britannia, 8, Cadet Training Ship, Captain R. A. Powell, C.B., 1855, Dartmouth

Buzzard, st. ves., 6, Com. T. H. M. Martin, 1859, North America and West Indies

Bulldog, 6, st. ves., Capt. C. Wake, 1859, North America and West Indies

Cambridge, gunnery Ship, Capt. C. J. F. Ewart, C.B., 1855, Devonport

Cameleon, 17, sc. Com. T. M. Jones, 1859, Pacific

Canopus, Naval Barrack, Capt. C. H. May, (1859) Devonport

Caradoc, sc., 2, Lieut.-Com. E. H. Wilkinson, 1856, Mediterranean

Castor, 22, Com. J. Palmer, 1855, Naval Reserve Drill Ship, Shields

Centaur, 6, steam ves. Com. J. Z. Creasy, 1864, China, passage home

Challenger, 22, sc. J. J. Kennedy, C.B., 1856, North America and W. Indies

Chanticleer, 17, sc. Com. E. F. Risk, 1856, Mediterranean

Charybdis, 21, sc. Capt. E. W. Turnour, 1857, Pacific

Cockatrice, 2, sc. Lieut. Com. R. M. Gillson (1855), Mediterranean

Colossus, 80, sc. Captain E. Codd, 1857, Coast Guard, Portland

Columbine, 4, sc., Com. T. Le H. Ward, 1861 Pacific

Conqueror, 70, sc., Capt. W. G. Luard, 1857, Japan

Coquette, 4, sc., Commander A. G. R. Roe, 1863, East Indies and China

Cormorant, 4, sc. Lieut.-Com. G. Peele, (1855) East Indies and China

Cornwallis, 60, sc. Capt. J. N. Strange, 1854, Coast Guard, Hull

Cossack, 20, sc., Capt. W. R. Rolland, 1857, Mediterranean

Cumberland, 24, Capt. W. K. Hall, C.B., 1853, receiving ship, Sheerness

Curacoa, 23, Commodore Sir W. Wiseman, Bart., C.B. Australia

Curlew, 9, sc. Com. J. S. Hudson, 1861, S. E. Coast of America

Cygnet, 5, sc. Com. W. S. De Kantzow (1863) North America and West Indies

Dædalus, 16, Com. W. H. Fenwick, 1856, Naval Reserve Drill ship, Bristol

Dart, 5, sc. Com. F. W. Richards, (1860) Coast of Africa

Dasher, 2, st. ves., Com. P. De Sausmarez, 1854 Channel Islands

Dauntless, 31, sc. Capt. J. B. Dickson, 1854, Coast Guard, Southampton

Dee, 1, st. Store Ship, Mas.-Com. G. Raymond, 1858, particular service

Defence, 16, sc. Capt. A. Phillimore, 1856, Channel Squadron

Devastation, 6, screw, Com. J. W. Pike, 1860, Pacific

Doterel, 2, sc. gunboat, Lieut. Com. W. F. Johnson, 1855, South America

Dromedary, sc. store-ship, Mast.-Com. A. Brown, (1864), particular service

Duke of Wellington, 131, Capt. J. Seccombe, 1859, Portsmouth

Duncan, 81, sc. Vice-Adm. Sir James Hope, K.C.B., Capt. R. Gibson, 1863, N. America and West Indies

Eagle, 50, Commander W. E. Fisher, 1856, Naval Reserve Drill Ship, Liverpool

Eclipse, 4, sc., Capt. R. C. Mayne, 1864, Australia

Edgar, 71, sc. Rr. Adml. S. C. Dacres, C.B., Capt. G. T. P. Hornby, 1862, Channel Squadron

Egmont, receiving ship, Capt. F. A. B. Craufurd, 1856, Rio de Janeiro

Enchantress, 1, st. Admiralty Yacht, Staff-Com. J. E. Petley, 1863, Portsmouth

Encounter, 14, sc. Captain R. Dew, CB., 1856, East Indies and China, (ordered home)

Esk, 21, Capt. J. P. C. Hamilton, 1858, Australia

Espoir, 5, sc. Com. S. Douglas, 1858, C. of Africa ordered home

Euryalus, 35, sc. Vice Adml Sir A. L. Kuper, K.C.B., Capt J. H. Alexander, 1863, China

Excellent, gunnery ship, Capt. A. C. Key, C.B., 1860, Portsmouth

Fairy, sc. yacht, tender to Victoria and Albert Staff-Com. D. N. Welch, 1863, Portsmouth

Falcon, 17, sc. Com. G. H. Parkin, (1858,) Australia.

Firefly, 5, st. ves. Lieut.-Com. G. R. Wilkinson, 1854, Mediterranean

Fisgard, 42, Commodore. H. Dunlop, C.B., Woolwich

Flamer, 2, sc. gunboat, Lieut. Com.T. S. Gooch, 1854, China

Formidable, 26, Vice Admiral Sir C. Talbot, K.C.B., Capt. J. Fulford, 1846, Sheerness

Forte, 39, sc. Rear Admiral R. L. Warren, Capt. A. Mellersh, 1864, S.E. C of America

Forward, 2, sc. Lieut. Com. the Hon. H. D. Lascelles, 1855, Pacific

Fox, sc. store-ship, Staff-Com. J. C. Pullen, (1863) particular service

Foxhound, 4. sc. Com. W. H. Anderson, 1859, Mediterranean

Galatea, 26, sc. Cap. R. Maguire, 1855, Devonport

Geyser, 6, st. ves. Com. A. T. Thrupp, (1858), particular service.

Gibraltar, 81, sc. Capt. J. C. Prevost, 1854, Mediterranean

Gladiator, 6, st. ves., Capt F. H. Shortt, 1858, particular service.

Grappler, 2, sc. Lieut. Com. E. H. Yerney, 1856, Pacific

Grasshopper, sc. gunboat, Lt. Com. F. W. Bennett, 1854, East Indies and China

Greyhound, 17, sc. Com. H. R. Wratislaw, 1864, North America and West Indies

Griffon, 6, sc. Com. J. L. Perry, 1858, C. of Africa.

Handy, 1, st. ves., Lieut. Com. R. P. Mowtray, 1862, Coast of Africa

Hardy, 2, sc. gunbt, Lieut. Com. H. J. F. Campbell, 1855, East Indies and China

Harrier, 17, sc. Com. E. Hay, 1858, Australia

Hastings, 50. sc. Rear-Admiral Sir L. T. Jones, K.C.B., Capt. C. F. A. Shadwell, C.B., 1853, Queenstown

Havock, 2. sc. gunbt, Lieut. Barclay, 1849, East Indies and China

Hawke, 60, sc. Capt. E. Heathcote, 1853, Coast Guard, Queenstown

Hector, 34, sc., Capt. Preedy, C.B., 1855, Channel Squadron

Hesper, 4, sc. store ship, Mast. Com. A. F. Boxer, 1854, East Indies and China

Hibernia, rec. ship, Rear Adm. H. T. Austin, C.B., Com. R. B. Harvey, 1859, Malta

Himalaya, 6, sc. troop ship, Captain E. Lacy, (1862), Devonport

Hogue, 60, sc. Captain A. Farquhar, 1849, Coast Guard, Greenock

Hornet, 17, sc. Com. the Hon. R. Hare, acting, East Indies

Hydra, 1, st. ves., Com. A. L. Mansell, 1855, Mediterranean

Icarus, 11, sc. Com. H. T. Boger (acting) Mediterranean.

Immortalité, 35, sc. Capt. G. Hancock, 1855, North America and West Indies

Implacable, 24, Com. S. B. Dolling, 1856, Training Ship, Devonport

Impregnable, 78, Capt. F. S. Tremlett (1863) Training Ship, Devonport

Indus, Rear Admiral T. M. C. Symonds. C.B., Capt. W. Edmonstone, C.B., 1863, Devonport

Industry, 2. sc. store ship, Mast. Com. E. C. T. Youcl, 1850, particular service

Insolent, 2, sc. gunbt. Lieut. Com. G. T. Nicolas, 1856, East Indies and China

Investigator, 2, st. ves. Lieut. Com. ————, Coast of Africa

Irresistable, 68, Capt. J. B. Dickson, 1854, Southampton.

Jackall, 4, st. ves., Lieut.-Com. H. M. N. Dyer, 1855, Scotch Fisheries.

Jaseur, 3, sc. Com. W. J. H. Grubbe (1861) Coast of Africa

Jason, 21, sc. Capt. E. P. B. Von Donop, 1855, North America, W. Indies

Leander, 39, sc. Commodore T. Harvey, Pacific

Lizard, 3, st. ves. Lieut.-Com. H. J. Challis, 1854, Coast of Scotland

Lee, 5, sc. Lieut. Com. C. E. Foot, 1861, tender to Rattlesnake, Coast of Africa

Leopard, 18, st. vessel, Capt. C. T. Leckie, 1858, East Indies and China

Leven, 1, screw gun vessel, Lt. Com. H. P. Knevitt (1855) East Indies and China

Liffey, 39, sc. Captain G. Parker, 1854 Mediterranean

Lily. 4, sc., Com. A. C. F. Heneage, 1857, North America and West Indies

Liverpool, 35, sc., Capt. R. Lambert, 1855, North America and West Indies

Lyra, 9. sc., Com. R. A. Parr, 1861, Cape of Good Hope

Mæander, 10, Capt. J. G. Bickford, (1860) Ascension

Magicienne, 16, st. ves. Capt. W. Armytage, 1860, Mediterranean

Majestic, 80, sc. Capt. J. A. Paynter 1854, Coast guard, Rock Ferry, Liverpool

Manilla, sc. Mast. Com. H. W. Burnett, 1856, East Indies and China

Marlborough, 131, sc. Vice Adml. R. Smart, K.H., Captain C. Fellowes, 1848, Mediterranean

Medea, 6, st. ves. Com. D'Arcy S. Preston, (1860) North America and West Indies

Medusa, 2, st. ves. Mas.-Com. J. H. Allard, 1861, particular service

Mecanee, 60, Captain G. Wodehouse, 1854, Mediterranean.

Miranda, 15, sc. Capt. R. Jenkins, 1857, Australia

Mullet, 5, sc. Com. C. H. Simpson 1860, Coast of Africa

Naiad, 6, store ship, Mas. Com. G. Reid, 1850, Callao

Narcissus, 39 sc. Rear Adm. Sir B. W. Walker, Bart., K.C.B., Cape of Good Hope.

Nereus, 6, store depôt. Staff Com. C. R. P. Forbes, 1863, Valparaiso

Nimble, 5, tender to Nile, 1854, North America and West Indies

Orestes, 21, sc. Capt. A. H. Gardner, 1866, Cape of Good Hope

Orontes, 2, sc., troop ship, Capt. H. W. Hire, 1862, particular service

Orlando, 46, sc. Capt. G. G. Randolph, 1864 Mediterranean

Osborne, st. yacht, Staff Com. G. H. K. Bower, 1863, Portsmouth

Osprey, sc., 4, Com. A. J. Innes, 1861, East Indies and China

Pandora, 5, sc. Com. W. F. Ruxton, 1861, Coast of Africa

Pantaloon, 11, sc. Com. F. Purvis, (1860), East Indies.

Pearl, 21, sc. Capt. J. Borlase, C.B. 1855, East Indies and China (ordered home)

Pelican, 17. sc. Com. H. W. Comber, 1857, Mediterranean.

Pelorus, 21, sc. Capt. H. Boys, 1857, East Indies and China

Pembroke, 60, Commodore A. P. Ryder, 1848, C.B., Capt. J. O. Johnson, 1856, Coast Guard Harwich

Perseus, 17, sc., Com. A. J. Kingston, 1860, China

Peterel, 11, sc. Com. E. Madden, 1858, North America and West Indies

Phaeton, 39, sc. Capt. G. Le G. Bowyear, 1856, North America and West Indies

Philomel, 5, sc. Com. L. Wildman, (1858) Coast of Africa

Phœbe, 35, sc., Captain T. D. A. Fortescue, 1857, Mediterranean.

Pigmy, 3, st. v. Master Com. W. W. Vine, 1861 Portsmouth.

Plover, 5, sc. Com. the Hon. A. L. Corry, 1859, North America and West Indies

President, 16, Com. W. Mould, 1855, Naval Reserve Drill Ship, London.

Prince Consort, 35, sc., Capt. G. O. Willes, C.B. 1856, Channel Squadron

Princess Charlotte, 12, Captain M. S. Nolloth, 1856, Hong Kong

Princess Royal, 73. sc. Rear-Adm. G. St. V. King, C.B., Capt. W. G Jones, 1861, Cape of Good Hope and East Indies

Procris, 2, Capt. E. Ommanney, 1845, Lieut. Com. Hon J. B. Vivian, 1856, Gibraltar

Psyche, 2, st. vessel, Lieut.-Com. R. Hearne, 1854, Mediterranean

Pylades, 21, sc. Capt. A. W. A. Hood, North
America and West Indies

Racehorse, 4, sc. Com. C. R. F. Bozer, 1860,
China

Raccoon, 22, ss. Capt. Count Gleichen, (1859),
particular service

Ranger, 5, sc. Com. W. E. Gordon, 1861, Coast
of Africa

Rapid, 11, sc. Com. C. T. Jago (1860) C. of Africa

Rattler, 17, sc. Com. J. M. Webb, 1854, East
Indies and China

Rattlesnake, 21, sc. Commodore A. P. E Wilmot,
C.B. Coast of Africa

Research, 4, ss. Capt. A. Wilmhurst, 1861,
Devonport

Resistance, 16, ss. Capt. W. C. Chamberlain,
1856, Mediterranean

Revenge, 73, sc. Rr.-Ad. R. B. Yelverton, C.B.,
Capt. Hon. F. A. Foley, 1860, Mediterranean

Rifleman, 8, sur.-ves. Com. J. Ward, 1858,
China Seas

Rinaldo, 17, sc. Com. J. A R. Dunlop, 1860,
1862, North America and West Indies

Ringdove, 4, sc. Com. R. A. O. Brown, 1857,
East Indies and China (ordered home)

Rosario, 11, sc. Com. H. D. Grant, 1859,
North America and West Indies

Royal Adelaide, 26, Adml. Sir C. H. Fremantle, K.C.B. Capt. F. B. F. Seymour, C.B.
1854, Devonport

Royal Oak, 35, sc. Capt. F. A. Campbell, 1864,
Mediterranean

Royalist, 11, sc. Com. E. J. Pollard, (1861)
N. America and West Indies

Royal George, 78, sc. Capt. M. de Courcy 1862,
Coastguard Kingstown, Dublin.

Salamander, 4, st. ves. Com. the Hon. J
Carnegie, 1861, Australia

Satellite, 21, sc. Capt. S. S. L. Crofton, 1856,
S. E. Coast of America

Saturn, Captain W. Loring, C.B., 1848, Pembroke

Scylla, 21, sc. Capt. R. W. Courtenay, 1859,
East Indies and China.

Seringapatam, Receiving Ship, Capt. J. H. Cockburn, 1850, Cape of Good Hope

Severn, 35, sc. Commodore F. B. Montrésor,
East Indies

Shannon, 35, sc. Capt. O. J. Jones, (1855) N.
America and West Indies

Sheldrake, 2, sc. gunboat, Lieut.-Com. John
Nott, 1854, S. E. Coast of America

Shearwater, 11, sc. Com. R. G. Douglas, 1860,
Pacific.

Slaney, 3, sc. gunboat, Lieut.-Com. W. F. Lee,
1855, East Indies and China

Snipe, 5, sc. Com. A. H. W. Battiscombe, 1861,
Coast of Africa

Sparrow, 5, sc. Com. Hon. E. G. L. Cochrane,
1860, C. of Africa

Speedwell, 5, sc. Com. C. F. Cottam, 1861,
Coast of Africa

Spider, 2, sc. gunboat, Lieut. Com. E. A. T·
Stubbs, 1854, South America

St. George, 84, sc. Capt. S. Grenfell, 1860,
Coast Guard, Falmouth

Staunch, 1, sc., Lieut.-Com. J. S. Keats 1854,
China

St. Vincent, 26, Com. S. J. Greville, 1860, Portsmouth

Steady, 5, sc. Cap. Fred Harvey, 1861, North
America and West Indies

Stromboli, 6, ss. Com. A. Phillips, 1860, S.E.
Coast of America

Styx, 6, sc. Com. the Hon. W. J. Ward, 1858,
North America and West Indies

Supply, 2 sc. store ship, Mast. Com. C. Bowden,
1849, particular service

Surprise, 4, sc. Com. W. H. Whyte, 1856, Mediterranean

Sutlej, 35, sc., Vice-Adml. J. Kingcome, Captain T. P. Coode, 1862, Pacific

Swallow, 9, sur. ves. Mast. Com. E. Wilde, 1855,
East Indies

Tamar, 3, sc. troop ship, Capt. F. H. Stirling,
1860, West Indies

Tartar, 20, sc. Capt. J. M. Hayes, 1858,
Japan

Terror, 16, Capt. F. H. H. Glasse, C.M. 1844,
Bermuda

Trafalgar, 70, sc. Capt. C. F. Schomberg,
1851, Coast Guard, Queen's Ferry, N.B.

Tribune, 23, sc. Capt. Viscount Gifford, 1859
Pacific

Trident, 3, st. Com. C. J. Balfour, 1859,
Mediterranean

Trincomalee, 16, Com. E. Field, (1860) Nava,
Reserve drill Ship, Hartlepool

Triton, sc., 3, Lieut.-Com. ———
S.E. Coast of America

Valorous, 16, st. ves., Capt. C. C. Forsyth, 1857,
Cape of Good Hope

Vesuvius, 6, sc. Capt. R. V. Hamilton, 1862,
North America and West Indies

Victoria and Albert, steam yacht, Capt. H.S.H.
Prince Leiningen, K.C.B. (1860,) Portsmouth

Victory, 12, Vice Adml. Sir Michael Seymour,
G.C.B. Captain Francis Scott, C.B., (1845)
Portsmouth

Vigilant, 4, sc., Com. W. R. Hobson, 1859,
East Indies and China

Vindictive, store ship, Mas.-Com. W. F. Lew,
1857, Fernando Po

Virago, 6, st. ves. Com. W. G. H. Johnstone, 1856
North America and West Indies

Vivid, 2, st. v. Staff Com. H. W. Allen, 1863,
particular service.

Vulcan, 6, sc. troop ship, Capt. A. C. Strode, 1863
East Indies and China, ordered home

Wanderer, 4, sc. Com. M. C. Seymour, 1859,
Mediterranean

Warrior, 40, sc. Capt. the Hon. A. A. Cochrane,
C.B. 1864, Channel Squadron

Wasp, 13, sc. Capt. W. Bowden (1861) East
Indies and China

Wessel, 2, sc. gunboat, Lieut. Com. H. G.
Hale, 1855, East Indies and China

Wellesley, 72, Captain W. H. Stewart, C.B.
1854, Chatham

Weser, 6, st. v. Com. A. H. J. Johnstone, 1859,
Mediterranean

Winchester, 13, Drill Ship for Naval Reserve,
Com. C. J. Balfour, 1848, Aberdeen

Wye, 3, sc. store-ship. Staff Com. V. G. Roberts,
1863, particular service

Zebra, 17, sc., Com. C. J. Lindsay, 1861, Coast
of Africa

# STATIONS OF THE BRITISH ARMY.

### (Corrected up to 28th April, 1864, inclusive.)

[Where two places are mentioned, the last-named is that at which the Depot i stationed.

1st Life Guards—Hyde Park
2nd do.—Windsor
Royal Horse Guards—Regent's Park
1st Dragoon Guards—Madras, Canterbury
2nd do.—Bengal, Canterbury
3rd do.—Bombay, Canterbury
4th do.—Dundalk
5th do.—Cahir
6th do.—Aldershot
7th do.—Bengal, Canterbury
1st Dragoons—Aldershot
2nd do.—Birmingham
3rd Hussars—Manchester
4th do.—Dublin
5th Lancers—Bengal, Canterbury
6th Dragoons—Bombay, Maidstone
7th Hussars—Bengal, Maidstone
8th do.—Bengal, Canterbury on passage home
9th Lancers—Dublin
10th Hussars—Dublin
11th Hussars—Dublin
12th Lancers—Hounslow
13th Hussars—Aldershot
14th do.—Aldershot
15th Hussars—Edinburgh
16th Lancers—York
17th do.—Madras, Maidstoe
18th Hussars—Norwich
19th do.—Bengal, Shorncliffe
20th do.—Bengal, Canterbury
21st do.—Bengal, Maidstone
Military Train (1st bat.)—Woolwich
Do. (2nd bat.)—Aldershot
Do. (3rd bat.)—Canada
Do. (4th bat.)—New Zealand
Do. (5th bat.)—Aldershot
Do. (6th bat.)—Curragh
Grenadier Guards (1st bat.)—Canada
Do. (2nd bat.)—St. George's Barracks
Do. (3rd bat.)—Chelsea
Coldstream Guards (1st bat.)—Windsor
Do. (2nd bat.)—Wellington Barracks
Scots Fus. Guards (1st bat.)—Chelsea Barracks
Fus. (2nd bat.)—Canada
1st Foot (1st.)—Madras, Colchester
Do. (2nd bat.)—Portsmouth, Colchester
2nd do. (1st bat.)—Devonport, Walmer
Do. (2nd bat)—Gibraltar, Walmer
3rd do. (1st bat.)—Aldershot, Limerick
Do. (2nd bat.)—Gibraltar, Limerick
4th do. (1st bat.)—Bombay, Chatham
Do. (2nd bat.)—Corfu, Chatham
5th do. (1st bat.)—Shorncliffe, Colchester
Do. (2nd bat.)—Natal, Colchester
6th do. (1st bat.)—Aldershot, Colchester
Do. (2nd bat.)—Jamaica, Colchester
7th do. (1st bat.)—Bengal, Walmer
Do. (2nd bat.)—Malta, Walmer
8th do. (1st bat.)—Sheffield, Templemore
Do. (2nd bat.)—Malta, Templemore
9th do. (1st bat.)—Cephalonia, Limerick
Do. (2nd bat.)—Corfu, Limerick
10th do. (1st bat.)—Killkenny, Preston
Do. (2nd bat.)—Cape of Gd. Hope, Preston
11th do (1st bat.)—Dublin, Fermoy
Do. (2nd bat.) C. of Good Hope, Fermoy
12th do. (1st bat.)—New Zealand, Chatham
Do. (2nd bat.)—Dublin, Chatham
13th do. (1st bat.)—Bengal, Fermoy on passage home
Do. (2nd bat.)—Mauritius, Fermoy
14th do. (1st bat.)—Jamaica, Fermoy.
Do. (2nd bat.)—New Zealand, Fermoy
15th do. (1st bat.)—N. Brunswick, Pembroke
15th do. (2nd bat.)—Gibraltar, Pembroke

16th do. (1st bat.)—Canada, Templemo
Do. (2nd bat.)—Nova Scotia, Templem
17th do. (1st bat.)—Canada, Limerick
Do. (2nd bat.) Nova Scotia, Limerick
18th do. (1st bat.)—Madras, Buttevan
Do. (2nd bat.)—New Zealand, Butteva
19th do. (1st bat.)—Bengal, Chatham
Do. (2nd bat.)—Birmah, Chatham
20th do. (1st bat)—Bengal, Chatham
Do. (2nd bat.)—Honghong, Chatham
21st do. (1st bat.)—Barbadoes, Birr
Do. (2nd bat.)—Madras, Birr
22nd do. (1st bat.)—Malta, Parkhurst
Do. (2nd bat.)—Malta, Parkhurst
23rd do. (1st bat.)—Bengal, Walmer
Do. (2nd bat.)—Gibraltar, Walmer
24th do. (1st bat.)—Shorncliffe, Cork
Do. (2nd bat.)—Mauritius, Cork
25th do. (1st bat.)—Malta, Athlone
Do. (2nd bat.)—Ceylon, Athlone
26th do.—, Portsmouth, Belfast
27th do.—Bengal, Cork
28th do.—Bombay, Fermoy
29th do.—Dublin, Preston
30th do.—Canada, Parkhurst
31st do.—Plymouth, Chatham
32nd do.—Dublin, Preston
33rd do.—Bombay, Fermoy
34th do.—Bengal, Colchester
35th do.—Bengal, Chatham
36th do.—Bengal, Mullingar
37th do.—Aldershot, Pembroke
38th do.—Bengal, Colchester
39th do.—Bermuda, Templemore
40th do.—New Zealand, Birr
41st do.—Curragh, Preston
42nd do.—Bengal, Sterling
43rd do.—New Zealand, Chatham.
44th do.—Bombay, Colchester
45th do.—Curragh, Parkhurst
46th do.—Bengal, Buttevant
47th do.—Canada, Athlone
48th do.—Bengal, Cork
49th do.—Manchester, Belfast
50th do.—New Zealand, Parkhurst
51st do.—Bengal, Chatham
52nd do.—Bengal, Chatham
53rd do.—Portsmouth, Birr
54th do.—Bengal, Colchester
55th do.—Madras, Preston
56th do.—Bombay, Colchester
57th do.—New Zealand, Cork
58th do.—Newry, Birr
59th do.—Aldershot, Preston
60th do. (1st bat.)—Tower, Winchester
Do. (2nd bat.)—Aldershot, Winchester
Do. (3rd bat.)—Birmah, Winchester
Do. (4th bat.)—Canada, Winchester
61st do.—Jersey, Pembroke
62nd do.—Canada, Belfast
63rd do.—Canada, Belfast
64th do.—Gosport, Colchester
65th do.—New Zealand, Birr
66th do.—Madras, Colchester
67th do.—China, Athlone
68th do.—New Zealand, Fermoy
69th do.—Madras, Fermoy
70th do.—New Zealand, Colchester
71st do.—Bengal, Stirling
72nd do.—Bombay, Aberdeen
73rd do.—Aldershot, Colchester
74th do.—Madras, Perth, on passage home
75th do.—Aldershot, Chatham
76th Foot—Madras, Belfast
77th Foot—Bengal, Chatham

78th do.—Dover, Aberdeen
79th do.—Bengal, Stirling
80th do.—ditto, Buttevant
81st do.—Bengal, Chatham
82nd do.—Bengal, Colchester
83rd do.—Aldershot, Chatham
84th do.—Curragh, Pembroke
85th do.—Dover, Pembroke
86th do.—Dublin, Templemore
87th do.—Aldershot, Buttevant
88th do.—Bengal, Colchester
89th do.—Bengal, Fermoy
90th do.—Bengal, Colchester
91st do.—Bengal, Chatham
92nd do.—Edinburgh, Stirling
93rd do.—Bengal, Aberdeen
94th do.—ditto, Chatham
95th do.—Bombay, Fermoy
96th do.—Cape, Belfast
97th do.—Bengal, Colchester
98th do.—Bengal, Colchester
99th do.—China, Cork
100th Foot—Malta; Parkhurst

101st do.—Bengal, Chatham
102nd do.—Madras, Chatham
103rd do.—Bombay, Colchester
104th do.—Bengal, Parkhurst
105th do.—Madras, Pembroke
106th do.—Bombay, Birr
107th do.—Bengal, Fermoy
108th do.—Madras, Fermoy
109th do.—Bombay, Cork
Rifle Brigade (1st bat.)—Canada, Winchester.
Do. (2nd bat.)—Bengal, Winchester
Do. (3rd bat.)—Bengal, Winchester
Do. (4th bat.)—Gibraltar. Winchester
1st West India Regiment—Bahamas
2nd do.—Barbadoes
3rd do.—Sierra Leone
4th do—Cape Coast Castle
5th do —Jamaica
Ceylon Rifle Regiment—Ceylon
Cape Mounted Rifles—Cape of Good Hope
Royal Canadian Rifle Regiment—Canada
Royal Malta Fencible Artillery—Malta

---

# DEPOT BATTALIONS.

1st Depot Battalion—Chatham
2nd do.—Chatham
3rd do.—Chatham
4th do.—Colchester
5th do.—Parkhurst
6th do.—Walmer
7th do.—Winchester
8th do.—Pembroke
9th do.—Colchester
10th do.—Colchester
11th do.—Preston
12th do.—Athlone
13th do.—Birr

14th Depot Battalion—Belfast
15th do.—Buttevant
16th do.—Templemore
17th do.—Limerick
18th do.—Fermoy
19th do.—Fermoy
20th do.—Cork
22nd do.—Stirling
23rd do.—Aberdeen
Cavalry Depot—Maidstone
     do.—Canterbury

# PROMOTIONS AND APPOINTMENTS.

## NAVY.

PROMOTIONS.

To be Lieutenant—Sub-Lieut. T. J. Macnamara.

To be Surgeons — Assistant-Surgeons Charles Morton and William Dickson Smyth, M.D.

To be First-Class Assistant-Engineers—Horace H. Small, of the Phaeton; John Lesson, of the Indus; Thomas G. Pumnett, of the Warrior; Thomas J. Warburton, of the Hector; John R. Harvey, of the Rosario; Joseph Tapp, of the Jason; Thomas Hatton of the Trident; Everden Wimshurst, of the Bacchante.

APPOINTMENTS.

Rear-Admiral — Hon. Charles G. J. B. Elliot, C.B., to be Commander-in-Chief on the south-east coast of America, vice Rear-Admiral Richard L. Warren, whose period of service has expired.

Captains—J. A. Paynter to the Majestic, vice Inglefield, whose period of service has expired; T. H. Mason to the Blenheim, vice Lord F. H Kerr, whose period of service has expired; W. Crispin to be one of Her Majesty's Naval Aide-Camps, vice Forbes, promoted; C. A. Campbell to the Bombay.

Commanders—T. C. Forbes to Formidable, vice Triscott, whose period of service has expired; Alexander B. Usborne (staff) to the Fisgard, for surveying service; W. Arthur to the Excellent; Wm. Dawson to the Achilles.

Lieutenants—Charles J. Brownrigg to be flag-lieutenant to Vice-Admiral Sir Charles Talbot, K.C.B., Commander-in-Chief at Sheerness; James Buchanan and Henry J. Carr to the Bombay; W. F. M. Molyneux to the Research; H. A. Monteith to the Defence; M. A. Hare to the St.

George; J. F. Prowse to the Hawke; C. W. Beaumont, F. A. Jackson, F. A. Jackson, F. W. B . Jones, H. S. Baillie, and R. P. W. Powney, to the Marlborough; Hon. A. F. Wood to the Excellent; John S. Eaton to the Fisgard; Henry Hand to the Himalaya; Frederick Parke to the Dauntless; Leicester Chantrey Keppel to the Indus; C. H. Hawkins to the Research.

Masters—John W. Reed to the Fisgard, additional; James H. Lawrence to the Irresistable, for the Coast Guard; George Robinson and James H. Kerr, to the Duncan, for the surveying service; Benjamin Sydney Jackson to the Sealark; W. G. Aldrick to the Blenheim; James B. Haines to the Brisk; Charles Ricketts to the Clio.

Secretaries — Paymaster Stephen H. Moore to be secretary to Rear-Admiral Hon. C. Elliot; John E. Sullivan to be secretary to Admiral Super. Austin, at Malta.

Surgeons — Thomas Stratton, M.D., (staff), to the Canobus; Wm. M. Gordon, M.D., to the Victory, additional; Lowry J. Monteith to the Cumberland.

Paymasters—Edw. D. Herbert to the Egmont; G. W. O. Simmonds to the Resistance; James D. Gilpin to the Bombay; Stewart Watson to the St. George; Edwin Jago to the Cossack; James E. G. Simonds to the Blenheim; Wm. G. Parmeter to the Majestic.

Sub-Lieutenant — William B. Wilkinson to the Prince Consort; Edward F. Keppel to the Bombay.

Assistant-Surgeons — Edward Dunn, M.D., to the Wye; Henry Fagan, M.D., to the Victory; Frederick Piercy to the Royal Adelaide; Robert Purves to the Dasher; Garland W. L. Harrison to the Victory; Joseph May to the Blenheim; John S. Dobbyn to the Colossus; Charles Strickland to the Supply; Charles J. Fennell to the Wellesley.

Midshipmen — Edmund F. Jeffreys to the Aurora; Cyril Corbet and George L. W. Adair to the Prince Consort; John H. Broom and Francis Powell to the Black Prince; James M. Bance to the Aurora; James L. Heane to the Gladiator; Philip B. Aitkins, Thomas S. Hoghton, Francis H. N. Harvey, S. Bridger, Henry P. T. Skinner, Robert C. Gorst, James C. C. Dennis, Edmund S. Poe, Charles V. Strange, Richard G. Day, and Charles E. Morison, to the Bombay; Baldwin W. Walker to the Orlando; Thomas E. Sullivan to the Hector: Francis R. B. Kemp to the Edgar.

Naval Cadets—Thomas H. S. Robertson, Digby H. Hamilton, Douglas E. D. Curry, and Charles Stephenson, to the Bombay; H. J. Wodehouse and William G. Eden to the Revenge; Francis C. B. B. Simpson to the Liffey; H. F. Haszard to the Duncan; Wm. N. Atkinson to the Hector; Alfred A. Sims to the Edgar; Henry C. S. Wright, Anthony M. Hammond, Somerset A. Hungerford, Herbert Horner, and Charles Reeve, to the Duncan; Gilbert E. Cornwall to the Prince Consort; William H. M. Daniel, John L. E. de Watteville, John B. Hemming, and Wm. R. Cooksey, to the Black Prince; Richard W. O. Voysey, Edward P. Tomkinson, George H. Bruce, and Alfred G. Waller, to the Warrior; Edward P. Brooks, Arthur H. Baker, Philip A. Parsons, and William B. Ponsford, to the Hector; Charles R. Dawes and Herbert K. Heyland, to the Defence; John D. Aubertin to the Aurora; Octavius Greig to the Gladiator.

Naval Cadets (nominated)—H. Smiles, Stephen C. Kemble, Augustus Brocklebank, W. M. C. Maturin, Charles W. Aylmer, Geo. Walmisley, Joseph Alleyne, Fredk. *Bell,* Archibald W. Cavage, Arthur *G. Cuthbert,* Henry C. Dawson, *Philip A. C. De Crespigny,* Arthur

Dove, Charles S. Elton, Reginald B. Fulford, George K. Gordon, Martin A. Hammill, Wm. P. L. Heyland, Edwin A. Hobson, Walter H. Maher, the Hon. Basil Napier, Michael P. O'Callaghan, Charles G. Robinson, George H. C. Stapleton, Ferdinand F. Tupper, and Frank C. Younghusband, Henry Trafford, H. A. Ogle, Thomas Hadley, Richard H. Solly, James H. Galloway, and Henry P. Routh.

Master's Assistants—Geo. Hole, Charles Heyward, and Robert M. Bryant, to the Bombay; Edward R. Connor to the Bann.

Assistant-Paymasters—Edward W. Golden to the Duke of Wellington; Walmsley A. Dangerfield to the Geyser; Ebenezer F. Nicholson and Thomas Marsh to the Bombay; John Prebble to the Hector; Frederick Hyndman to the Victory, additional; John Willcocks to the Adventure; W. C. Devereux (in charge) to the Seringapatam; Charles H. J. Collings, H. M. Harrison, and Charles H. Drew, to the Bombay; E. F. Nicholson to the Formidable; John Hide and R. J. Sweetman to the Rattlesnake.

Clerks—A. H. Grey to the Wellesley; Arthur Hodgson to the Bombay.

Assistant-Clerks—George Jackson and F. H. Trollope to the Bombay; Frank N. Burney to the Formidable; E. A. Lang and John B. Sams (additional) to the Bombay; Frank E. Croome, Thomas W. Hall, and Henry Stubbs, of the Fisgard, for Somerset House; John P. M'P. King to the Royal George.

Chief Engineers—Robert James Hay to the Bombay; James Coade to the Bristol; Wm. B. Stephens (acting) to the Archer; Charles R. Chamberlain to the Scout; Richard L. Canney to the Himalaya; Thos. H. Symons to the Forth.

Engineers—George T. Blundal to the Sutlej; David Robb to the Stork; John James to the Erne; Edward M. Avoy to the Bombay; George Lucas to the Majestic; William Rowley (A) to the Ætna; James Vercoe to the Sanddy; E. Eckersley and James T. Page to the Euryalus, for disposal; Thomas Brindley to the Tortoise; G. H. Loxdale to the Lark.

Assistant-Engineers — Thomas Pringle (for tenders), and Fredk. Holden to the Colossus; William Chase, Ebenezer Bennet, John Pickles, Angus M'Intyre, George F. Greaves, Samuel H. Trentham, Robert Pattison, and William T. Power, to the Euryalus (additional) for disposal; John Balas to the Research; James Graham, Charles Thompson, Robert Hetherington, Robert Roberts, and Charles Wakeman to the Bombay; Robert Wingfield (first-class) to the Dauntless.

First-Class Assistant-Engineers —James K. Keay to the Indus; Job Annable to the Himalaya; Valentine Horne to the Caledonia; Joseph Knight to the Bombay, William Bryant to the Hogue (for tender); C. Lund, J. Crawford, and L. P. Lewis (supernumeraries) to the Fisgard.

Second-Class Assistant-Engineers—Ivie A. Couper to the Himalaya; J. Preeble to the Hector.

---

## ROYAL MARINES.

ADMIRALTY, April 5.
Royal Marine Artillery—First Lieut. and Adjt. Robert Woolcombe to be capt., dated 1st inst., vice Seale, placed on half-pay; Sec. Lieut. John Layland Needham to be first. lieut. dated 1st inst.

---

ADMIRALTY, April 8.
Royal Marine Artillery—First Lieut. Henry Ives de Kantzow to be adjt., vice Woolcombe, promoted—6th April.

---

## COAST GUARD.

Inspecting Chief Officer—Henry Harper (staff commander) from Blue Hill to Seafield.

Chief Officers—Robert B. Graham (staff commander), to Sheephaven; James H. Lawrence (master), from St. Margaret's Bay to Townsend; Joseph Cutajar, from South Sea to St. Margaret's Bay.

---

## ROYAL NAVAL RESERVE.

To be Lieutenants — William Broadfoot, William Richards.

To be Honorary Lieutenant—George William Pierrepoint Bentinck, M.P.

## ARMY.

THE ARMY GAZETTE.

*₊* Where not otherwise specified, the following Commissions bear the current date.

WAR OFFICE, PALL MALL, March 22.

6th Regt. of Dragoons—Thomas John Newnham, Gent, to be cornet, by purchase, vice William Thomas Skinner Snell, who retires.

15th Hussars—Surg. William Godfrey Watt, having completed 20 years' full-pay service, to be surg-maj., under the Royal Warrant of 1st October, 1858—1st March.

Royal Artillery—Lieut-Col. and Brevet-Col. George Augustus Frederick De Rinzy to be col. vice Burke Cuppage, removed as a General Officer—1st March: Capt. and Brev-Lieut-Col. Phillip Gosset Pipon to be lieut-col., vice De Rinzy—1st March; Second Capt. John Kelly to be capt., vice Pipon—1st March; Lieut. William Dobree Carey to be second capt., vice Kelly—1st March; Gent-Cadet Edward Albert Ollivant to be lieut., vice Carey; Gent-Cadet Walter Reginald Fox to be lieut., vice Archibald William Montgomerie, who resigns; Gent-Cadet John Graham Stone to be lieut., vice Palmer Boyd, summarily dismissed the Service.

Royal Engineers — Lieut-Col. William Frederick Marriott (Staff Corps) to be col., vice Burke who retires upon full pay—27th Feb.; Capt. and Brevet-Major James Thomas Walker to be lieut-col., vice Marriott—27th Feb.; Second Capt. David Thomson to be capt., vice Brevet-Major Walker—27th Feb.; Lieut. Frederick Colvin Mytton to be second capt., vice Thomson—27th Feb; Gent-Cadet Walter Park Jones to be lieut., with temporary rank, vice Mytton.

2nd Regiment of Foot—Lieut. Arthur Wellesley Gosset to be capt., by purchase, vice John Chalmers, who retires; Ensign Charles William Davie to be lieut., by purchase, vice Gosset; Ensign

Robert Bleazy to be lieut., by purchase, vice Frederick Blake, who retires; Gent-Cadet Augustus Frederick F. Adams, from the Royal Military College, to be ensign, by purchase, vice Davie, John Paton Lawrie to be ensign; by purchase, vice Bleazy.

5th Foot — Ensign Francis Goldie Taubman to be lieut., by purchase, vice Robert Hull, who retires; Gent-Cadet William Straston Saunders, from the Royal Military College, to be ensign, by purchase, vice Taubman.

9th Foot—Lieut. Spencer Field to be capt., by purchase, vice George Spaight, who retires; Ensign James Edward McDonnell to be lieut., by purchase, vice Field; Gent-Cadet Alexander George William Malet, from the Royal Military College, to be ensign, by purchase, vice MacDonnell.

12th Foot — Captain William Thomas Baker, from the 85th Foot, to be capt., vice Morland, who exchanges.

13th Foot—Gent-Cadet Charles Moore, from the Royal Military College, to be ensign, by purchase, vice Robert Warren, promoted.

15th Foot — Edmund Charles Elliston, Gent., to be ensign, by purchase, vice William Francis Maitland Kirwan, transferred to the 78th Foot.

16th Foot — Lieut. Thomas Russell to be capt., by purchase, vice Graves Chamney Swan Lombard, who retires; Ensign Reginald Laurence Herbert Curteis to be lieut., by purchase, vice Russell; Mallcott Sydney Richardson, Gent., to be ensign, by purchase, vice Curteis.

21st Foot—Gent-Cadet William Lowther Ernle Money-Kyrle, from the Royal Military College, to be ensign, by purchase, vice Cecil Lloyd, transferred to the 28th Foot

23rd Foot—Lieut. Alan Graham to be capt., by purchase, vice

Philip Henry Knight, who retires; Ens. Robert Frederick Williamson to be lieut, by purchase, vice Graham; Gent-Cadet William Phibbs, from the Royal Military College, to be ens., by purchase, vice Williamson.

24th Foot—Colour-serg. William Hughes, from the 12th Foot, to be ens., by purchase, vice Percival Trosse Fortescue, who retires.

25th Foot — Surgeon Robert Browne, having completed 20 years' full-pay service, to be surg-maj., under the Royal Warrant of 1st October, 1858—1st March.

28th Foot—Ens. Cecil Lloyd, from the 21st Foot, to be ens., vice Edward Agincourt Brind, transferred to the 88th Foot.

32nd Foot—Lieut. Samuel Black Noble to be capt., by purchase, vice Edward Augustus Thurlow Cunyngham, who retires; Ens., Frederick Nassau Golding to be lieut., by purchase, vice Noble: Gent-Cadet Mathew William Lyster, from the Royal Military College. to be ens., by purchase, vice Golding.

40th Foot—Gent-Cadet George Frankling, from the Royal Military College, to be ens., without purchase, vice Andrew Ducrow, died of wounds.

53rd Foot—Lieut. James Malley, from the 92nd Foot, to be lieut., vice Leslie, who exchanges—23rd March.

78th Foot—Lieut. Thomas Owen Silvester Davies to be capt., by purchase, vice Brev-Lieut-Col. Laurence Pleydell Bouverie, who retires; Ens. Colin Mackensie to be lieut., by purchase, vice Davies; Ens. William Francis Maitland Kirwan, from the 15th Foot, to be ens., vice Mackensie.

85th Foot—Capt. George Morland, from the 12th Foot, to be capt., vice Baker, who exchanges.

86th Foot—Capt. Francis Pike, from the 91st Foot, to be capt., vice Fry, who exchanges.

88th Foot—Ens. William Scott Richardson to be lieut., by purchase, vice John Beveridge Gladwin Jebb, who retires; Ens. Edw.

Agincourt Brind, from the 28th Foot, to be ens., vice Richardson.

89th Foot.—Capt. Henry W. Somerville Carew, from half-pay late 29th Foot, to be capt., vice William Drage, who retires upon temporary half-pay.

91st Foot—Capt. John William Fry, from the 86th Foot, to be capt., vice Pike, who exchanges.

92nd Foot—Ens. Charles Callaway Ross to be lieut., by purchase, vice Cockburn McBarnett, who retires; Lieut. William Norman Leslie, from the 53rd Foot, to be lieut., vice Malley, who exchanges —23rd March; Gent-Cadet Henry Vesey Brook, from the Royal Military College, to be ens., by purchase, vice Ross.

96th Foot — Lieut. Frederick John Josselyn to be capt., by purchase, vice William Duff Pereira, who retires; Ens. Charles Polliott Powell to be lieut., by purchase, vice Josselyn; Gent-Cadet John Carter O'Neal, from the Royal Military College, to be ens., by purchase, vice Powell; Lieut. Dennis Du Moulin Gunton to be adjutant, vice Lieut. F. J. Josselyn, promoted.

104th Foot — Lieut. Thomas Alexander Hunter to be capt., vice Sir Atwell King Lake, Bart., who retires — 2nd January; Ensign Lestock Walters Iredell to be lieut, vice Hunter—2nd January; Gent-Cadet Sydney Byng, from the Royal Military College, to be ens., vice Iredell; the name of the Paymaster appointed in the *Gasette* of the 1st inst., is Richard Richardson, late ens. Her Majesty's Indian Forces, and not Lieut. Robert Campbell Richardson, as then stated.

107th Foot—Gent-Cadet Robert Jocelyn Waller, from the Royal Military College, to be ens., vice Joseph Ralph Edward John Royle, promoted.

108th Foot—Gent-Cadet Vincent Lewis Mathias, from the Royal Military College, to be ens., vice Augustus Erskine, promoted; Richard Bainbridge Mitchell, Gent., late Her Majesty's Indian Forces, to be Paymaster.

109th Foot—Ens. Donald Wm. Mackinnon to be lieut., vice Henry Charles Holland Hastings, who resigns; Gent-Cadet Charles Andrew Cathcart, from the Royal Military College, to be ens., vice Mackinnon.

Rifle Brigade—Lieut. FitzRoy Stephen to be capt., by purchase, vice Charles William Earle, who retires; Ens. Alexander Stuart Harington to be lieut., by purchase, vice Stephen; Walter Frederick Cavendish, Gent., to be ens., by purchase, vice Harington.

1st West India Regiment—Ens. Ralph Henry Potts to be lieut., by purchase, vice John Blaksley, promoted, by purchase, in the 4th West India Regiment; Charles Henry Wilson Lock, Gent., to be ens., by purchase, vice Christian Branford Stewart, promoted.

Cape Mounted Riflemen—Capt. and Brev. Maj. T. Hare to be maj. without purchase, vice Brev. Col. J. Armstrong, placed upon half-pay on appointment as Col. on the Staff; Lieut. E. A. Lynar to be capt., without purchase, vice Brev. Maj. Hare; Ens. C. J. N. Hallewell to be lieut., without purchase, vice Lynar.

### STAFF.

Lieut-Col. and Brev-Col. K. D. Mackenzie, C.B., half-pay, late 92nd Foot, to be deputy-adjt.-gen. in Ireland, vice Brev. Col. F. P. Haines, appointed to the command of a brigade.

### UNATTACHED.

Maj. and Brev. Lieut.-Col. E. G. Hallewell, half-pay, unattached, to be lieut.-col., without purchase; Capt. and Brev.-Col. J. F. Du Vernet, half-pay Royal African Corps (Staff Officer of Pensioners), to be maj., without purchase; Capt. and Brev. Lieut.-Col. W. Brooks, half-pay, late 75th Foot, Town Maj., Dublin, to be maj., without purchase; Lieut. H. W. S. Carew, from 29th Foot, to be capt., without purchase.

### BREVET.

Col., with the temporary rank of *Maj.-Gen.*, B. Cuppage, Royal *Artillery, to be maj.-gen.*, vice B. *Willis, who retires* upon full-pay;

Col. J. H. Burke, retired full-pay, Royal Engineers, to be maj.-gen., the rank being honorary only. The honorary rank of Lieut-Col. granted to Maj. J. H. Brooks, late 19th Hussars, on retirement, in *Gazette* of 26th ult., has been cancelled, in consequence of that officer not having retired on a pension, as stated in the *Gazette.* Capt. J. Hudson, Bengal Staff Corps, to be maj.; Capt. G. R. Westmacott, Bengal Staff Corps, to be maj.; Capt F. H. M. Sitwell, Bengal Staff Corps, to be maj. The Christian name of Serjt.-Maj. (with local rank of Ens.) Brown, of the Royal Artillery, is Brice, not Bryce. as stated in *Gazette* of March 17, 1863.

In consequence of the promotion of Maj.-Gen. Cuppage, the under-mentioned officers on the retired full-pay list of the Royal Artillery, who stood before him on the effective list at the time of their retirement, to be promoted as follows:—Col. A. Macbean to be maj.-gen; Col. R. L. Garstin to be maj.-gen.

### MEMORANDUM.

Maj. and Brev.-Col. J. F. Du Vernet half-pay, late Staff Officer of Pensioners, has been permitted to retire from the service by the sale of his commission, under the conditions of the Horse Guards Circular, Memorandum of Feb. 15, 1861.

---

## THE MILITIA GAZETTE.

WAR OFFICE, PALL MALL, March 22.

Royal London Militia — Wm. St. Aubyn, Capt. 6th Tower Hamlets Rifle Volunteers, to be lieut., vice Daniel Harrox Bennett, promoted; Robert Rankin Hutchinson, Capt. 4th Tower Hamlets Rifle Volunteers, to be lieut., vice George Thomas Oldfield, promoted; Richard Wilson Love, gent., to be lieut., vice Thomas Waterman the younger, promoted.

Northamptonshire and Rutland Militia—Deniel Lenton, Esq., to be assist.-surg.

West Kent Light Infantry Militia—Capt. Thomas Montagu

Martin Weller to be maj., vice Robinson, resigned.

4th or Royal South Middlesex Regt. of Militia—Thomas Provis Wickham to be lieut., vice Underwood, resigned.

Memorandum—1st King's Own Staffordshire Militia—The Queen has been graciously pleased to accept the resignation of the Commissions held by Capt. Sidney Leveson Lane and Lieut. George William Moore.

WAR OFFICE, PALL MALL, March 25.

Light Infantry Battalion of the Royal Sussex Militia—John Aldridge, late Major 21st Foot, to be maj., vice Gage, promoted.

Dorset Regt. of Militia—Amelius Morland Smith, gent., to be lieut., vice Brown, promoted.

West Kent Light Infantry Militia—Lieut. Markland Barnard to be capt., vice Monypenny, promoted.

Isle of Wight Artillery Militia—Henry Farnell, gent., to be first lieut., vice Young, resigned.

Edinburgh Artillery Militia—Robert Legat, gent., to be lieut., vice Macgeorge, resigned.

Artillery Regt. of Royal Lancashire Militia—Her Majesty has been graciously pleased to accept the resignation of the commission held by Maj. Benjamin Remington Williams.

2nd Regt. of the Duke of Lancaster's Own Militia—Her Majesty has been graciously pleased to accept the resignation of the commission held by Lieut. Robert George Wynne Wrench.

THE VOLUNTEER GAZETTE.

WAR OFFICE, PALL MALL, March 22.

4th Administrative Battalion of Staffordshire Rifle Volunteers—Walter Blake Burke to be adjt., from the 3rd March, 1864.

1st London Artillery Volunteer Corps—Capt.-Comt. John Richard Lambert Walmisley, late Capt. Hon. Artillery Company, to be maj.-comt.

3rd London Rifle Volunteer Corps—Ens. Alexander Crossman to be lieut.; Edwin Barnett, gent.,

to be ens.; Charles Butterfield Gray, gent., to be ens.; Dr. Joseph Henderson, M.R.C.S., to be assist.-surg.

19th Middlesex Rifle Volunteer Corps—Ens. Charles Fowler to be lieut., vice Preston, resigned.

London Irish Rifle Volunteer Corps—Robert Bedford Hitchcock to be ens.; Richard Farmer Chattock to be ens.

44th Middlesex Rifle Volunteer Corps—William Wykes Ladell to be capt., vice Paine, resigned.

4th Staffordshire Rifle Volunteer Corps—Lieut. John Edward Newman to be capt., vice Dowell, deceased.

16th Staffordshire Rifle Volunteer Corps—William Hargreaves, gent., to be ens, vice Mayer, deceased; George Barnes, gent., to be hon. assist.-surg., vice Turner, deceased.

4th Renfrewshire Rifle Volunteer Corps—Robert Galt, gent., to be lieut., vice Guy, resigned.

1st Flintshire Rifle Volunteer Corps—Robert Platt, gent., to be hon. assist.-surg., vice Jones, resigned.

2nd Essex Artillery Volunteer Corps—George Alfred Jolly to be first lieut.

6th Essex Rifle Volunteer Corps—Lieut. Octavius Bawtree to be capt., vice Bishop, resigned; Ens. James Samuel Cooke to be lieut., vice Bawtree, promoted; Ens. Arthur Thomas Osborne to be lieut.; Horace George Egerton Green to be ens., vice Cooke, promoted; Alexander Miller White to be ens., vice Osborne, promoted.

1st Sussex Artillery Volunteer Corps—James Hannington to be sec. lieut.; Henry Tester to be sec. lieut.; Thomas Lainson to be sec. lieut.; William Robert Wood to be sec. lieut.; Wm. Henry Mason to be sec. lieut.

2nd Manchester or 33rd Lancashire Rifle Volunteer Corps—James Henry Deakin, Esq., to be hon. col.; Maj. William Willmott Mawson to be lieut.-col.; Capt. John Porteus to be Super. maj.;

Lieut. Edward Jackson to be capt., vice Fisher, resigned.

3rd Cambridgeshire **Rifle** Volunteer Corps—George **Frederick** Long Dashwood to be ens., vice Clare, resigned; Henry Howard France to be ens., vice Hoare, resigned.

---

WAR OFFICE, PALL MALL, March 25.

4th Administrative Brigade of Lancashire Artillery Volunteers—Adjt. Anthony Humphrey Hamilton Whitehead—late of the 21st Lancashire Artillery Volunteer Corps, to be adjt, from the 15th Oct., 1863.

12th Sussex Rifle Volunteer Corps—William Henry Stone to be capt, vice Osmond, resigned; Frederick James Smith to be ens., vice Smith, resigned.

3rd Administrative Battalion of Somersetshire Rifle Volunteers—John Nicholls, Esq., Hon. Assist.-Surg., of the 10th Somersetshire Rifle Volunteer Corps, to be surg.; Edward Horatio Walker Swete, gent., hon. assist.-surg., in the 27th Somersetshire Rifle Volunteer Corps, to be assist.-surg.

20th Lincolnshire Rifle Volunteer Corps—Ens. Charles William Goodson to be lieut., vice Sharpley, resigned; Douglas Stockdale, gent., to be ens., vice Goodson, promoted.

4th Argyllshire Artillery Volunteer Corps—John Mackeller to be hon. assist.-surg.

1st Administrative Battalion of Durham Rifle Volunteers—Capt. John Joicey to be maj.

Memorandum—This officer is permitted to retain his commission in the 10th Durham Rifle Volunteer Corps.

11th Durham Rifle Volunteer Corps—Lieut. Thomas Hunter Murray to be capt., vice Reid, resigned; Ens. Robert French Gibson to be lieut., vice Murray, promoted; Thomas Henry Shipperdson to be ens., vice Gibson, promoted.

1st Lanarkshire Artillery Volunteer Corps—Sec. Lieut. James Martin to be first lieut., vice J. D. Kirkwood, promoted; Henry Wallach, gent., to be sec. lieut., vice Martin, promoted.

2nd Administrative Battalion of Lanarkshire Rifle Volunteers—Assist.-Surg. Robert Perry, M.D., to be surg., vice R. T. Corbett, resigned.

3rd Lanarkshire Rifle Volunteer Corps—Arthur Barff, Esq., to be capt., vice Peter Fulton, resigned; John Ross, M.D., to be assist.-surg.; William Wotherspoon, gent., to be assist.-surg.

4th Lanarkshire Rifle Volunteer Corps—Robert Granger, gent., to be ens., vice J. D. Johnston, promoted.

5th Lanarkshire Rifle Volunteer Corps—Ens. David Guthrie to be lieut., vice G. J. Morrison, resigned; Assist.-Surg. Alexander Patterson, M.D., to be surg., vice J. Drummond, resigned.

19th Lanarkshire Rifle Volunteer Corps—John Walker, Esq., to be capt, vice T. Steven, resigned; William Macfarlane Miller, gent., to be ens., vice W. C. Crawford, promoted.

25th Lanarkshire Rifle Volunteer Corps—Iver Myhlenphort, gent., to be lieut., vice McKendrick, resigned.

96th Lanarkshire Rifle Volunteer Corps—Alexander Hope Pattison, gent., from 30th Lanarkshire Rifle Volunteer Corps, to be ens, vice Graham, resigned.

The following Appointment is substituted for that which appeared in the *Gazette* of the 23rd ult.:

5th Lanarkshire Rifle Volunteer Corps—Ens. George Strathern to be lieut., vice Alexander Fyfe, resigned.

1st London Artillery Volunteer Corps—First Lieut. Ferdinand Vigors to be capt.; First Lieut. John Spencer Price to be capt.; Sec. Lieut. Charles Strudwick to be capt.; Thomas Henry Maudsley the younger, esq., to be capt.; Sec. Lieut. Frederick John Padley to be first lieut.; Hermann Curtis to be first lieut; George Gammon Adams to be first lieut.; Francis Horatio Pryce to be first lieut.; Frederick Arthur Lake to be sec. lieut.; Samuel Neale Driver, to be sec. lieut.; Richard Deeton Hughes to be sec. lieut.

1st Middlesex Engineer Volunteer Corps—Sec. Lieut. John Collins Boys to be first lieut., vice Parkinson. resigned; Sec. Lieut. John Budd Phear to be first lieut., vice Wyatt, resigned.

19th Middlesex Rifle Volunteer Corps—Capt. John Stewart Oxley to be maj, vice Hughes, promoted.

17th Renfrewshire Rifle Volunteer Corps—Lieut. John Harvey to be capt., vice Harvey, resigned; Thomas Orr, gent, to be lieut., vice Harvey, promoted; Andrew Glen, gent., to be ens, vice McNab, resigned

1st City of Edinburgh Artillery Volunteer Corps—Lieut William Elgin to be capt., vice Henry Harrison, resigned.

1st City of Edinburgh Rifle Volunteer Corps—Ens. T. C. Hanna to be lieut., vice Ogilvie, promoted; Ens. Archibald McKinlay to be lieut., vice Douglas, resigned; John McIntosh to be ens., vice Hanna, promoted.

Memorandum—For John E. Stewart, read John C. Stewart, to be ens., vice Mitchell, promoted.

2nd Administrative Battalion of Forfarshire Rifle Volunteers—Robert Thomas, Esq., to be maj.

1st Norfolk Rifle Volunteer Corps—Frederick Sayers Brown to be ens., vice Keith, promoted.

Memorandum-- The 2nd, 62nd and 81st Lancashire Rifle Volunteer Corps have been united in an Administrative Battalion, which will be numbered as the 8th in the County of Lancaster.

---

## THE ARMY GAZETTE.

*₌* Where not otherwise specified, the following Commissions bear the current date.

WAR OFFICE, PALL MALL, March 29.

5th Regt. of Dragoon Guards—Capt. Richard Fielding Morrison, from the 7th Foot. to be capt., vice Colvin, who exchanges; Cor. Richard James Streatfeild to be lieut., by purchase, vice Thomas Booth, who retires; George Os-borne Springfield, gent., to be cor., by purchase, vice Streatfeild.

1st Dragoons—Lieut. William Lawrence Twentyman to be capt., by purchase, vice Richard Molesworth, who retires; Cor. Allan Maclean to be lieut., by purchase, vice Twentyman.

14th Hussars — Cor. George Staunton Lynch-Staunton to be lieut, by purchase, vice Charles Alexander Price Talbot, who retires; the Hon. John St. Vincent Saumarez to be cor., by purchase, vice Lynch-Staunton.

17th Lancers — Cor. Joseph Devonsher Jackson to be lieut., by purchase, vice William Sandys Browne, who retires; Edward Stanley Obré, gent., to be cor., by purchase, vice Jackson.

Royal Artillery—Surg. James Macmillan Scott Fogo, having completed 20 years' full-pay service, to be surg.-maj., under the Royal Warrant of the 1st Oct., 1858—5th March.

1st Regt. of Foot—Ens. Hutchison Posnett to be lieut.. by purchase, vice Alexander Bruce Tulloch, promoted by purchase, in the 96th Foot; Ens. Arthur Fishe, from the 15th Foot, to be ens., vice Posnett.

2nd Foot — Bernard Arthur Beale, gent., to be ens., by purchase, vice Henry William Thompson, who retires.

3rd Foot—Ens. Henry Drinkrow Harrison to be lieut., by purchase, vice William Pitt Butts, who retires; Henry Brian Buchanan, gent., to be ens., by purchase, vice Harrison.

4th Foot—Lieut. Stephen Weston Bent to be capt., by purchase, vice James Constable, who retires; Ens. John Edmund Sinclair to be lieut, by purchase, vice Bent; Ens. John Thomas Carruthers, from the 78th Foot, to be ens., vice Sinclair.

7th Foot—Capt. William Butterworth Colvin, from the 5th Dragoon Guards, to be capt., vice Morrison, who exchanges.

8th Foot—Lieut. John William Hughes to be capt., by purchase, vice William Raymond Ximenes,

L 2

who retires; Ens. Marmaduke Stourton to be lieut., by purchase, vice Hughes; Robert Garnett, gent., to be ens., by purchase, vice Stourton.

9th Foot — Reginald Heber Blunt, gent., to be ens., by purchase, vice Malet, transferred to the 39th Foot.

15th Foot — Edward James Singleton, gent., to be ens., by purchase, vice Arthur Fishe, transferred to the 1st Foot.

23rd Foot—Capt. the Hon. Savage Mostyn to be maj., without purchase, vice Brev. Lieut.-Col. James Gubbins, made Supernumerary on appointment as Assist.-Adjt.-Gen. at Malta; Lt. John Keat S. Henderson to be capt., without purchase, vice the Hon. Savage Mostyn; Ens. Geo. Wildes to be lieut., without purchase, vice Henderson.

27th Foot—Lieut. Aiskew Clay to be adjt., vice Robert B. R. Glasgow, who resigns that appointment—27th Jan.

34th Foot—Ens. Joseph Edw. Savill to be lieut., without purchase, vice Rupert Inglis Cochrane, deceased—26th Jan.; Evelyn Arthur Rich, gent., to be ens., by purchase, vice Savill.

39th Foot—Ens. Henry Fredk. Gaubert, to be lieut., by purchase, vice Thomas R. Gosselin, who retires; Ens. Alexander Geo. Wm. Malet, from 9th Foot, to be ens., vice Gaubert.

50th Foot—Lieut. William H. Barker to be adjt., vice Lieut. Edmund Leach, who resigns that appointment.

52nd Foot—Lieut. Charles Keyworth to be capt., by purchase, vice Alexander Hope Graves, who retires; Ens. Henry Lyttleton Powys to be lieut, by purchase, vice Keyworth; Ens. Metcalfe Studholme Brownrigg, from 83rd Foot, to be ens., vice Powys.

58th Foot—Lieut. Charles Edw. Foster, to be capt., by purchase, vice Henry Turner, who retires; Ens. Richard Pearson Crozier to *be lieut.*, by purchase, vice Foster; *William Fryer* Daniel Dickinson,

gent., to be ens., by purchase, vice Crozier.

60th Foot—The Christian names of Assist.-Surg. Young, appointed on the 5th May, 1854, are *Adam Graham*, not *Grahams*, as then stated.

76th Foot—Capt. James Nicholas Colthurst, from 83rd Foot, to be capt., vice O'Connor, who exchanges.

78th Foot—Ronald Mackintosh, gent., to be ens., by purchase, vice John Thomas Carruthers, transferred to 4th Foot.

83rd Foot—Capt. Luke Edw. O'Connor, from 76th Foot, to be capt., vice Colthurst, who exchanges; Edward Arthur Butler, gent., to be ens., by purchase, vice Metcalfe Studholme Brownrigg, transferred to 52nd Foot.

96th Foot—Lieut. Alexander Bruce Tulloch, from 1st Foot, to be capt., by purchase, vice Fredk. Henniker, who retires.

105th Foot—Alexander Davidson, gent., late Riding Master in Her Majesty's Indian Military Forces, to be paymaster.

2nd West India Regt.—Lieut.-Col. Thomas Hardwick Smith has been permitted to retire from the Service by the sale of his commission.

3rd West India Regt.—Capt. and Brev.-Maj. James Leith, from half-pay, late 2nd Dragoons, to be capt., vice Matthew Smith Blyth, who retires upon temporary half-pay; Lieut. John Francis Henry Harrison to be capt., by purchase, vice Brev.-Maj. Leith, who retires; Lieut. Edw. Douglas Jones to be adjt., vice Lieut. John Moore, who resigns the appointment.

### MEDICAL DEPARTMENT.

Staff Surg. John Wm. Mostyn, M.D., having completed twenty years' full-pay service, to be staff surg.-maj. under the Royal Warrant of 1st Oct., 1858—8th March.

Assist.-Surg. Henry Knagga, from the Cape Mounted Riflemen, to be staff assist.-surg., vice John Macartney, deceased—28th March.

The second Christian name of Assist.-Surg. Edward J. Boulton, transferred from the 2nd West

India Regt. to the staff, on 28th July, 1863, is *Joseph*, not *James*, as then stated.

To be Staff Assist.-Surgs. from 30th Sept., 1863, such antedate not to carry pay prior to 7th Feb., 1864:—Robert William Troup, M.B., William Raymond Kynsey, gent.; Robert William Lawless, gent., James Forbes Beattie, M.D.; Robert James Blair Cunynghame, M.D.; Alexander Thomson, M.D.; Alexander Turner, M.D.; Alexander Francis Preston, M.B.; Richard William Forsayeth, gent.; John Phillippes De Gorrequer Delmege, M.D.; Charles Mac-Donogh Cuffe, gent.; Valesius Skipton Gouldsbury, M.D.; John Alexander Shaw, M.D.; Charles Haines, gent.; Forbes Dick, M.D.; Hopetoun Currie Collier, gent.; John Edward Barker, M.B.; Joseph Ridge Greenhill, gent.; Hubert Rothwell Greene, gent., Robert Henry Bolton, gent.; Henry Morris, gent.; Philip Patterson Lyons, M.B.; Edmund Hunt Condon, M.D.; James Barker, gent.; James Barry, M.D.; Charles Alfred Atkins, gent.; William Patrick Smith, gent.; George Fearon, gent.; Christopher J. Weir, M. B.; Francis Howard, M.D.; Frederick Joseph Byrne, gent., William Elgee, gent.; Thos. White, M B

MILITARY STORE DEPARTMENT.

Deputy Assist.-Superintendent of Stores J. M. Lloyd has been permitted to resign his commission—15th Jan.

BREVET.

The undermentioned promotions to take place consequent on the death of Maj.-Gen. Edw. Harvey, on 11th March, 1864:—

Brev.-Col. Mark Kerr Atherley, Lieut.-Col., on half-pay, late 92nd Foot, to be maj.-gen.—12th March.

Maj. Richard O. Francis Steward, upon half.pay, Unattached, to be lieut.-col.—12th March.

Capt. Frederick William Craven Ord, Royal Artillery, to be maj.—12th March.

The undermentioned Officers having completed the qualifying service in the rank of Lieut.-Col.,

under the Royal Warrant of 1st Oct., 1858, to be cols. :—

Lieut.-Col. Neville Hill Shute, 64th Foot—30th Aug., 1863.

Maj. and Brev. Lieut.-Col. Andrew Browne, C.B., 44th Foot—13th Oct., 1863.

Lieut.-Col. Thomas Lightfoot, C.B., 84th Foot—4th April.

The commission as Brev.-Col. of Lieut.-Col. William Hope, C.B., 71st Foot, to be antedated to 26th 1862, he having on 25th of that month completed five years qualifying service.

———

WHITEHALL, April 1.

The Queen has been pleased to constitute and appoint Maj.-Gen. Charles Rochefort Scott to be Lieut.-governor of the Island of Guernsey.

———

WAR OFFICE, PALL MALL, April 1.
ROYAL MILITARY ASYLUM.

Lieut.-Col. and Brev.-Col. John Yorke, C.B., half-pay unattached, to be comt., vice Brev.-Col. Crutchley, promoted.

———

THE MILITIA GAZETTE.

WAR OFFICE, PALL MALL, March 29.

2nd Somerset Regt. of Militia—William Dickinson, gent., to be lieut., vice E. B. Ricketts, resigned.

4th Regt. of West York Militia—Bryan Stapleton, Esq., to be capt., vice Hare, promoted.

Shropshire Regt. of Militia—Lieut. Richard Altamont Smythe to be capt., vice Thos. Matthews, resigned.

Memorandum—Her Majesty has been graciously pleased to approve of Capt. Thomas Matthews retaining his rank and wearing his uniform, in consideration of his services in the above regt.

Montgomeryshire Yeomanry Cavalry—Walter Clapton Wingfield, gent., to be lieut., vice Lomax, resigned; Thos. Walley, gent., to be vet.-surg., vice Jenks, resigned.

———

WAR OFFICE, PALL MALL, April 1.

Northamptonshire and Rutland

Militia — Edward Moncton the younger, Esq., to be lieut.

North Somerset Regt. of Yeomanry Cavalry—Charles Clement Tudway, gent. to be cor., vice Mynors, promoted.

Duke of Lancaster's Own Regt. of Yeomanry Cavalry—The Right Hon. Arthur Edw. Holland Grey, Viscount Grey de Wilton, M.P., to be capt., vice Egerton, resigned; Edward Stanley Heywood, gent., to be lieut., vice Fazakerley, promoted.

[The following appointment is substituted for that which appeared in the *Gazette* of the 22nd ult.:]

Northamptonshire and Rutland Militia — Daniel Seaton to be assist.-surg.

---

## THE VOLUNTEER GAZETTE.

War Office, Pall Mall, March 29.

1st Administrative Battalion of Fifeshire Rifle Volunteers—Robt. Bethune to be adjt., from the 4th March, 1864.

London Rifle Volunteer Brigade —Francis Cotton, jun., to be ens.; Abraham Rhodes to be ens.; Thos. Jeremy Thomas to be ens.

Memorandum — The 1st (late 2nd) Merionethshire Rifle Volunteer Corps has been united to the 1st Administrative Battalion of Montgomeryshire Rifle Volunteers.

Memorandum—The 5th Montgomeryshire Rifle Volunteer Corps will henceforth be designated the 4th Montgomeryshire Rifle Volunteer Corps.

1st Aberdeenshire Artillery Volunteer Corps—First Lieut. James Morrison to be capt., vice James Abruthnot, resigned.

1st Administrative Brigade of West Riding of Yorkshire Artillery Volunteers—Maj. Geo. Wood to be lieut.-col.; William Marshall Selwyn, Esq., to be maj., vice Wood, promoted.

6th West Riding of Yorkshire Rifle Volunteer Corps—Maj. Thos. Brooke to be maj., vice Crosland, who retires.

15th Perthshire Rifle Volunteer Corps—Lieut. James Smitton to be capt., vice Grove, resigned; Ens. Alexander George Reid to be lieut., vice Smitton, promoted; Samuel Hally, gent., to be ens. vice Reid, promoted.

1st North Riding of Yorkshire Artillery Volunteer Corps—Robt. Frederick Ellis to be sec. lieut.

6th Renfrewshire Rifle Volunteer Corps—Ens. Archibald Coats to be lieut., vice Clark, resigned; William Murray, gent., to be ens., vice Coats, promoted.

---

War Office, Pall Mall, April 1.

9th Sussex Rifle Volunteer Corps—Edwin Henry to be ens., vice Upfold, resigned.

23rd Kent Rifle Volunteer Corps —Richard John Streatfeild to be ens., vice Waldo, resigned.

2nd Warwickshire Rifle Volunteer Corps—Charles Bill, gent., to be ens., vice Rotherham, resigned.

1st Clackmannanshire Rifle Volunteer Corps—Ens. Robert Buchanan to be lieut., vice John Bald Harvey, resigned; James Lambert to be ens., vice Robert Buchanan, promoted.

2nd Clackmannanshire Rifle Volunteer Corps—Wm. Snowdowne to be lieut., vice Robert Walker, resigned; Alexander McLaren to be ens., vice John Vicars, resigned.

5th Leicestershire Rifle Volunteer Corps—Joseph Goddard, gent., to be ens., vice Luck, resigned.

2nd Durham Artillery Volunteer Corps—Maj. the Right Hon. Earl Vaue to be lieut.-col.; Capt. Peter Campbell Mann to be maj.; First Lieut. William Dakers to be capt.; First Lieut. Robert Thorman to be capt.; Sec. Lieut. George William Elliott to be first lieut.; Sec. Lieut. Robert Keate Alves Ellis to be first lieut.

10th Durham Rifle Volunteer Corps—George Septimus Thompson, gent., to be hon. assist.-surg. vice Watson, resigned.

19th Durham Rifle Volunteer Corps—Mark Child, Esq., to be capt., vice Jaffrey, resigned; Ens. George Elgie to be lieut., vice Barr, resigned; William Richardson to be ens., vice Elgie, promoted; Geo.

Moore to be hon. assist.-surg., vice Simpson, resigned.

7th Cumberland Rifle Volunteer Corps—Ens. Septimus Bourne to be capt., vice Lamport, resigned; Charles Lamport to be ens., vice Bourne, promoted.

1st Manchester or 6th Lancashire Rifle Volunteer Corps—Lt. Alfred King Pearce to be capt., vice Walter Bousfield Westhead, promoted.

2nd Manchester or 33rd Lancashire Rifle Volunteer Corps—Wm. Clarence Matthews, gent., to be hon. assist.-surg.

3rd Manchester or 40th Lancashire Rifle Volunteer Corps—Ens. Samuel Moore to be lieut., vice Shaw, resigned.

47th Lancashire Rifle Volunteer Corps—Alfred Booth, gent., to be hon. quart.-mast.

[The following appointment is substituted for that which appeared in the *Gazette* of the 15th ult :—] William John Gant, esq., to be hon. capt. in the Cadet Corps, which is attached to the 4th Cinque Ports Artillery Volunteer Corps.

[The following appointment is substituted for that which appeared in the *Gazette* of the 25th ult. :—] 12th Sussex Rifle Volunteer Corps—Frederick James Quick to be ens., vice Smith, resigned.

---

THE ARMY GAZETTE.

\*\*\* Where not otherwise specified, the following Commissions bear the current date.

WAR OFFICE. PALL MALL, April 5.

6th Regiment of Dragoon Guards —Capt. Courtenay William Bruce to be maj., by purchase, vice Thos. Bott, who retires; Lieut. John Fryer to be capt., by purchase, vice Bruce; Cornet Cecil Edward Martyn to be lieut., by purchase, vice Fryer; Sydney Charles Du Vernet, Gent., to be cornet, by purchase, vice Martyn.

13th Hussars — Lieut. George Croft Huddleston to be capt., by purchase, vice Francis James King, who retires; Cornet Joseph Bonham Clay to be lieut., by purchase, vice Huddleston.

3rd Regiment of Foot—Capt. Charles Edgar Gibson, from 49th Foot, to be capt., vice Huyshe, who exchanges.

6th Foot—Capt. Spencer Field, from 9th Foot, to be capt., vice Stillman, who exchanges.

7th Foot—Ens. Henry Francis Keane Penrose to be lieut., by purchase, vice Francis Johnston Murray, who retires; Ens. Hugh Massy Barton, from the 67th Foot, to be ens , vice Penrose.

9th Foot—Capt. James Stillman, from 6th Foot, to be capt , vice Field, who exchanges; Cyril Rippingall Jackson, Gent., to be ens., by purchase, vice Samuel Goodman, who retires.

24th Foot — Lieut.-Col. and Brev.-Col. Thomas Ross, from half-pay, late Particular-Service, to be lieut.-col., vice the Hon. Daniel Greville Finch, who retires upon temporary half-pay.

25th Foot — Capt. Theodore Gordon, from 92nd Foot, to be capt., vice St. Leger, who exchanges; Duncan William Cork, Gent, to be ens., by purchase, vice Henry Hartley prior. transferred to 100th Foot.

32nd Foot—The names of the Gent.-Cadet appointed to an Ensigncy, in the *Gazette* of 22nd March, 1864, are Matthew William Lister and not Matthew William Lyster, as then stated.

47th Foot—Ens. John Larpent Utterton to be lieut., by purchase, vice Richard Parker Hawkes, who retires; Edward Montagu Manning, Gent, to be ens., by purchase, vice Utterton.

79th Foot—Capt. Alfred George Huyshe, from 3rd Foot, to be capt., vice Gibson, who exchanges.

60th Foot — Gent.-Cadet the Hon. Augustus William Charles Ellis, from the Royal Military College, to be ens., by purchase, vice Gerald Henry Talbot, who retires.

61st Foot — Lieut. Harry Hutchinson Augustus Stewart, from the 92nd Foot, to be lieut., vice Dashwood, who exchangee.

67th Foot—Gent.-Cadet Hugh Massy Barton, from the Royal

Military College, to be ens., without purchase, vice William Mascall Kenrick, promoted; Philip Quirk, Gent., to be ens., by purchase, vice Hugh Massy Barton, transferred to the 7th Foot.

78th Foot — Lieut. Andrew Murray to be instructor of musketry, vice Lieut. Thomas Owen Silvester Davies, promoted—22nd March; Quartermaster Charles Skrine to be paymaster, vice Paymaster, with the honorary rank of Maj., Joseph Webster, who retires upon half-pay—1st April.

84th Foot—Capt. John Penton to be maj., by purchase, vice Cornelius Charles Rollestone, who retires; Lieut. Henry Latham Bownrigg to be capt., by purchase, vice Penton; Ens. Norcliffe Gilpin to be lieut., by purchase, vice Brownrigg; Charles Lionel Maitland Kirwan, Gent., to be ens., by purchase, vice Gilpin.

91st Foot—Lieut. Hubert Plunkett Burke to be capt., by purchase, vice John Charles Sweny, who retires; Ens. William Darling Caudwell to be lieut., by purchase, vice Burke; Charles James Thorburn, Gent., to be ens., by purchase, vice Caudwell.

92nd Foot — Captain Henry Hungerford St. Leger, from the 25th Foot, to be capt., vice Gordon, who exchanges; Lieut. Charles Francis Dashwood, from the 61st Foot, to be lieut., vice Steward, who exchanges.

98th Foot—Ens. Edw. Haughton to be lieut., by purchase, vice W. Henry Simmonds, who retires; Gent-Cadet Alexander Harley Hyslop, from the Royal Military College, to be ens., by purchase, vice Haughton.

99th Foot — Ens. Anthony Charles Montague Jellicoe to be lieut., without purchase, vice Henry Kinalian, deceased—29th Jan.; Gent.-Cadet Charles Robert Gibson, from the Royal Military College, to be ens., without purchase, vice Jellicoe.

100th Foot—Lieut. John Worthy Chaplin to be capt., by purchase, vice John Leo, who retires; Ens. Walter Hudson to be lieut., by

purchase, vice Chaplin; Ens. Henry Hartley Prior, from the 25th Foot, to be ens., vice Hudson.

105th Foot—Gent.-Cadet Hugh De la Motte Hervey, from the Royal Military College, to be ens., vice Henry Eastfield Wilkinson, deceased.

Rifle Brigade — Ens. Leopold Victor Swaine to be adjt., in succession to Lieut. George Roberts Noseley, appointed Paymaster.

4th West India Regiment— Thomas Aked, Gent., to be ens., by purchase, vice William Cairnes, promoted.

PURVEYORS' DEPARTMENT.

Purveyor's Clerk Arthur Bull to be deputy purveyor, vice George Washington Warwick, resigned.

BREVET.

Lieut.-Col. John Hinde, C.B., 8th Foot, having completed the qualifying service in the rank of Lieut.-Col., under the Royal Warrant of 14th October, 1858, to be col.—3rd Jan.

Paymaster (with the honorary rank of Maj.) Joseph Webster, retired on half-pay, late 78th Foot, to have the honorary rank of Lieut.-Col.—1st April.

Paymaster William Causabon Frend, 51st Foot, to have the honorary rank of Capt.—30th March, 1863.

---

THE MILITIA GAZETTE.

WAR OFFICE, PALL MALL, April 5.

East York Militia—James Sissons Cooper, Gent., late Lieut. and Instructor of Musketry Royal North Lincoln Militia, to be quartermaster, vice Woodlock, resigned.

Worcestershire Regiment of Militia—Charles Evan Macdougall, Esq., to be lieut., vice Willett, resigned.

South Hertfordshire Regiment of Yeomanry Cavalry — Lieut. Charles Townshend Murdoch to be Adjt.

Devon Militia Artillery—Lieut. William Hammet Beadon to be capt., vice Marshall, resigned.

---

War Office, Pall Mall, April 8.

Durham Artillery Regiment of Militia—Hubert Delme Radcliffe, Esq., to be lieut, vice Tidswell, resigned.

King's Own Light Infantry Regiment of Militia—Lieut.-Col. Alfred Plantagenet Frederick Charles Somerset to be maj., vice Parry, resigned; William Stewart Graham, Esq., to be capt.

Royal Monmouth Militia—John Augustus Metcalf to be lieut., vice Rhys Brychan Powel, resigned.

Artillery Regiment of Royal Lancashire Militia—Capt. William Walker to be maj., vice Benjamin Remington Williams, resigned; Lieut. Richard Alison Johnson to be capt., vice William Walker, promoted.

---

THE VOLUNTEER GAZETTE.

War Office, Pall Mall, April 5.

3rd London Rifle Volunteer Corps—Ens. William Webb Venn, jun., to be lieut.

1st Midlothian Rifle Volunteer Corps—Lieut. James Cochrane to be capt., vice Gillon, deceased; Ens. John James Lundy to be lieut., vice Cochrane, promoted; Thomas Mark Berry to be ens., vice Kidd, resigned.

5th Devonshire Artillery Volunteer Corps—Robert Lloyd to be second lieut., vice Downe, resigned.

12th Devonshire Artillery Volunteer Corps — First Lieut. Edwin Simpson to be capt., vice Peake, resigned (erroneously gazetted in March last as Edward Simpson).

17th Devonshire Rifle Volunteer Corps — Thomas Hunt Edmonds to be ens., vice Shairp, resigned.

4th Northamptonshire Rifle Volunteer Corps—Lieut. William Davis to be capt.; Ens. John Macquire to be lieut.. vice Wm. Davis, promoted; Ens. Joseph Muscott to be lieut.; Richard Phipps to be ens., vice John Macquire, promoted; Richard George Scriven to be ens., vice Joseph Muscott, promoted; Wm. *Percival to be assist.-surg.*

1st Middlesex Engineer Volunteer Corps—Tansley Witt to be second lieut., vice Boys, promoted.

16th Middlesex Rifle Volunteer Corps—Ens. Henry Bullock to be lieut., vice Watson, promoted, John Aitkens to be ens., vice Scantlebury, resigned.

London Irish Rifle Volunteer Corps—Ens. John O'Connor to be lieut.

48th Middlesex Rifle Volunteer Corps—Arthur Smith to be lieut.

[The following appointment is substituted for that which appeared in the *Gazette* of the 11th ultimo.]

8th Worcestershire Rifle Volunteer Corps—Arnold Crane Rogers to be ens., vice Danks, promoted.

---

War Office, Pall Mall, April 8.

12th Tower Hamlets Rifle Volunteer Corps—John Rünty, Gent., to be ens.

6th Ross-shire Celtic Rifle Volunteer Corps—Lieut. Fredk. Walton to be capt.

5th Berwickshire Rifle Volunteer Corps—Lieut. William Fairholme to be capt.; Ens. Robert Romanes to be lieut.

3rd Dumbartonshire Rifle Volunteer Corps—Lieut. Thomas Logan Stillie to be capt., vice Mathew Grey, resigned; James Sdeuard, Gent., to be lieut., vice Thomas Logan Stillie, promoted.

10th Dumbartonshire Rifle Volunteer Corps—Donald Patrick Stewart, Gent., to be capt., vice Alexander Brown Armour, resigned.

6th Cambridgeshire Rifle Volunteer Corps—George Samuel Hall to be ens., vice Harlock, deceased.

1st Brecknockshire Rifle Volunteer Corps—Lieut. John James Williams to be capt., vice Powel, deceased.

---

India Office, April 11.

Her Majesty has been pleased to approve of the undermentioned promotions and alterations of rank amongst the Officers of the Staff Corps, and of Her Majesty's Indian Military Forces:—

## BENGAL STAFF CORPS.

To be Majors — Capt. John Fendall—30th December, 1863; Edgar John Spilsbury — 16th Jan.; Toovey Archibald Corbett —16th Jan.; James Sebastian Lawlins—21st Jan.

## BENGAL ARMY.

### MEDICAL OFFICERS.

To be Surg.-Majs.—Surgs. John Fullarton Beatsen, B.A., M.D.— 16th Oct., 1863; Charles Hathaway, M.D.—1st Dec. 1863.

To be Surgs.—Assist.-Surgs. William Henry Adley, vice Faithfull, deceased—10th Sept., 1863; Edward John Vivian, vice Webb, deceased—16th Sept., 1863; James Alexander Caldwell Hutchinson, vice Lay, retired—16th Oct., 1863; John Barclay Scriven, vice Rind, deceased—18th Dec., 1863.

### ALTERATIONS OF RANK.

The undermentioned Officers to take rank from the dates specified —Surg. Frederick Corbyn, M.D., from 10th May, 1863; Charles Lowdell, from 25th May, 1863; John Hooper, from 28th May, 1863; David Young, M.D., F.R.C.S., from 10th June, 1863; Joseph Fayrer, M.D.. F.R.C.P., F.R.C.S., from the 28th July, 1863.

## MADRAS STAFF CORPS.

### ADMISSION.

To be Capt. — Second Capt. Malcolm Bandinel Sabin Lloyd, of the Royal (Madras) Artillery— 13th Sept., 1860.

To be Lieut. — Lieut. Hugh Christian Menzies, of the 31st Native Infantry—15th Nov., 1853.

### PROMOTIONS.

To be Lieut.-Cols. — Majs. Arthur Loftus Steele—21st Dec., 1863; George Harper Saxton— 11th Jan.

To be Majs.—Capts. Alexander Campbell McNeill — 8th Dec., 1863; Llewellyn Paxton — 8th Dec., 1863; Edward Winterton Dun—8th Dec., 1863; Richard Clarke Babington—9th Dec., 1863; Henry Ambrose Hare—9th Dec., 1863; James George Roche Furlong — 30th Dec., 1863; Henry Spurgin Rammell — 30th Dec., *1863; Henry Manning Elliott—1st Jan.*

To be Captains—Lieut. Hugh Christian Menzies—12 Dec., 1861; James Giberne Bell—13th Dec., 1863; Henry Annesley Justice— 13th Dec., 1863; Charles Sheridan Blackwood Walton—15th Dec., 1863; Edward Dumaresq Gompertz—20th Dec., 1863; Evelyn Medows Norie—3rd Jan

## MADRAS ARMY.

### PROMOTIONS.

2nd Regiment of Light Cavalry —Lieut. Charles Napier Cherry to be capt, vice Gongh (Staff Corps), resigned—31st Dec., 1863.

3rd Regiment Light Cavalry— Lieut. John Linsey Ferrers to be capt., vice Fellows, retired—27th Jan., 1863.

Infantry — Majs. (Brev-Lieut-Cols) William Taylor Money, from the 33th N.I, to be lieut.-col., vice Haly (108th Foot), retired—3rd Nov., 1863; William Henry Freese, from the 37th Grenadiers, to lieut-col., vice Fischer, deceased —8th Jan.

30th Regiment of Native Infantry — Capt. (Brev.-lieut.-col.) Alexander Stevenson Findlay to be maj., in succession to Haly (108th Foot), retired 3rd Nov., 1863.

37th Regiment Native Infantry (Grenadiers) — Lieut. Archibald George Douglas Logan, to be capt., in succession to Fischer, deceased —8th Jan.

General list of Infantry Officers —Ens. Henry Whyte to be lieut., in succession to Owen, 28th N.I. (105th Foot), retired—1st Nov., 1863; George Chamberlain Cooper to be lieut., vice White, General List, deceased—26th Nov., 1863; Charles Edward Lorraine Eastall to be lieut., vice Ouchterlony, late 2nd European Regiment (105th Foot), resigned—3rd Dec., 1863.

### ARMY RANK.

The undermentioned officers to have the rank of Captain by Brevet:—Lieutenants Dashwood Charles Gordon Shettell, of the 13th N.I.—9th Dec., 1863; William Henry Lawrence Fuller, of the 4th Regiment N.I.—20th Dec., 1863; Selwyn New, of the 33rd Regiment N.I.—27th Dec., 1863; Edward Cave, of the 7th Regiment N.I.—27th Dec., 1863.

ALTERATIONS OF RANK.

General List of Infantry Officers —The undermentioned officers to take rank from the dates specified: —Lieutenants Henry Thomas Harris Baker, from the 25th March, 1863; Shelley Leigh Hunt, from the 3rd April, 1863; John Hotham, from the 1st May, 1863; Augustus Frederick Wilkinson, from the 26th July, 1863; George Leckey, from the 29th Aug., 1863.

BOMBAY STAFF CORPS.

To be Lieut.-Col.—Maj. (Brev.-Col.) Robert Romer Younghusband, C.B.—27th Dec, 1862.

To be Major—Capt. John Ashburner—1st Jan.

BOMBAY ARMY.

Promotion—14th Regiment Native Infantry—Lieut. Charles Henry Hunter Forbes to be capt, vice Ford (Staff Corps), retired—30th Sept., 1863.

General List of Infantry Officers —Ens. Robert William Welsh Grunlan to be lieut., in succession to Gordon, 14th N.I., retired—30th Oct., 1863; Francis Thomas Ebden to be lieut., in succession to Harding, 2nd N.I. (Staff Corps), killed in action—7th Nov., 1863; James Fortnom Willoughby to be lieut, vice Greenland, transferred to 56th Foot—18th Nov., 1863.

Alteration of Rank—Lieut. Chas. Maxwell Ryves to take rank from 30th Sept., 1863.

Her Majesty has been pleased to permit the undermentioned officers to resign their commissions:— Capt. Robert Campbell Burn, of the Madras Staff Corps—1st June, 1863; Lieut. Percy Bloomfield Patten Gough, Madras Staff Corps— 31st Dec., 1863.

WAR OFFICE, PALL MALL, April 12.

Royal Regiment of Artillery— Maj.-Gen. Sir W. Brereton, K.C.B., to be col.-commandant. by augmentation.

Royal Horse Guards—Lieut. F. G. A. Fuller to be capt., by purchase, vice the Hon. G. R. C. Hill, who retires; Cor. G. E. Paget to be lieut., by purchase, vice Fuller;

T. W. L. Brooke, gent., to be cor by purchase, vice Paget.

4th Dragoon Guards—J. Chadwick, gent., to be cor , by purchase, vice T. Edwards, who retires.

2nd Dragoons—Quartermaster-Serjt. J. Ferguson to be quartermaster, vice T. H. M'Bean, deceased.

17th Lancers—Regimental Serjeant-Major J. Berryman to be quartermaster, vice W. Garland, deceased.

21st Hussars—Paymaster, with the honorary rank of capt., J. George, from 92nd Foot, to be paymaster, vice Hicks, who exchanges; Lieut. C. W. Thomas to be instructor of musketry.

Royal Artillery—Col., with the local rank of maj.-gen., John St. George, C.B., from the supernumerary list, to be col., by augmentation; Col. W. H. Askwith, from the supernumerary list, to be col., by augmentation; Capt. A. N. Scott, from the supernumerary list, to be lieut.-col., vice Baker, who retires upon full pay; Brev.-Col., with the temporary rank of Brigadier-Gen., J. H. Lefroy, from the supernumerary list, to be lieut.-col., augmentation; Brev.-Col. W. M. H. Dixon, from the supernumerary list, to be lieut.-col., by augmentation; Lieut. A G. Miller to be 2nd capt., vice A. J. H. Wynne, who has been permitted to resign his commission; Lieut. L. H. H. Parsons to be 2nd capt., vice Whinyates, appointed adjt.; Gent. Cadet R. H. Wallace to be lieut., vice C Kirkwood, who has been permitted to resign his commission; Gent. Cadet J. P. Ewing to be lieut., vice Brinkley, seconded; Gent. Cadet T. A. Kelsall to be lieut., vice Miller; Gent. Cadet J. M. Hunter to be lieut, vice Parsons; Gent. Cadet F. H. Taylor to be lieut., vice R B. Hewson, deceased; 2nd Capt. F. A. Whinyates to be adjt., by augmentation; Serjt.-Maj. John Fyfe to be quartermaster, vice Kirkham, who retires on half pay.

Coast Brigade of Artillery— Serjt.-Maj. W. Spall, Royal Artillery, to be lieut., vice W. Lee, removed to the half-pay list.

Royal Engineers—Serjt.-Maj. J. Jones to be quartermaster, vice Michael Bradford, who retires upon half-pay; the second Christian name of Lieut., with temporary rank, Dillon, is *Philip*, and not *Phipps*, as stated in *Gazette* of 8th ult.

Military Train—Ens. W. Leir to be lieut., by purchase, vice J. Pettigrew, who retires.

2nd Regiment of Foot—R. Lawrence, gent., to be ens., by purchase, vice H. M. Matthews, transferred to the 57th Foot.

7th Foot—Ens. M. J. Fawcett to be lieut., without purchase, vice A. Tibeaudo, deceased; Ens. G. B. Meares to be lieut., without purchase, vice Fawcett, whose promotion, without purchase, on 17th Nov., 1863, has been cancelled; Ens. W. Daly to be lieut., by purchase, vice Meares, whose promotion by purchase on 1st Dec., 1863, has been cancelled; A. J. M. Reade, gent., to be ens., without purchase, vice Daly.

12th Foot — Ens. W. H. B. Peters to be lieut., by purchase, vice D. Seymour, who retires; T. B. Gent to be ens., by purchase, vice Peters; Paymaster J. P. Kingsmill has been removed from the Army, Her Majesty having no further occasion for his services.

13th Foot—Lieut. G. H. A. Kinlock to be Instructor of Musketry, vice Lieut. A. G. Wynen, coming home to join the Staff College.

20th Foot—Capt. W. L. D. Meares to be maj., by purchase, vice Sir A. R. Warren, Bart., who retires; Lieut. J. Aldridge to be capt., by purchase, vice Meares; Ens. R. D'Arcy to be lieut., by purchase, vice Aldridge; Gent.-Cadet. A. P. Pinching, from Royal Military College, to be ens., by purchase. vice D'Arcy.

23rd Foot—T. L. Courtenay, gent., to be ens., by purchase, vice G. Wildes, promoted.

25th Foot—Henry C. Darley, gent., to be ens., by purchase, vice *Thomas Stanhope Gildea*, transferred to the 72nd Foot.

40th Foot—Ens. Percy Cartwright to be lieut., by purchase, vice George Hobbs, who retires; Edward Martin, gent., to be ens., by purchase, vice Cartwright.

50th Foot—Lieut. Edm. Leach to be capt., by purchase, vice Geo. William Bunbury, who retires; Ens. James Frank Rolleston to be lieut., by purchase, vice Leach; James Edward Doidge Taunton, gent., to be ens., by purchase, vice Rolleston.

57th Foot—Ens. Henry Miller Powell, to be lieut., by purchase, vice Henry Moseley Muttit, who retires; Ens. Henry Melvin Matthews, from the 2nd Foot, to be ens . vice Powell.

60th Foot — Ens. Benjamin Frend, from 105th Foot to be ens. vice Cecil Henry Paulet, deceased.

72nd Foot—Lieut. Charles M. Stockwell to be capt., by purchase, vice William D. Ogilvy Hay, who retires; Ens. Walter Frederick Kelsey to be lieut., by purchase, vice Stockwell; Ens. Thomas Stanhope Gildea, from 25th Foot, to be ens., vice Kelsey.

73rd Foot—Ens. Edward Beauchamp St. John to be lieut., by purchase, vice James Fergusson, who retires; the Hon. Algernon Richard Hartland Plunkett to be ens., by purchase, vice St. John.

92nd Foot—Paymaster James Clarke Hicks, from 21st Hussars, to be paymaster, vice Paymaster, with the hon. rank of Capt. J. George, who exchanges.

93rd Foot — Ens. Alexander Innes Shepherd, from the 107th Foot, to be ens., vice Raikes, who exchanges—1st Feb.

107th Foot—Ens. Edward Augustus Raikes, from 93rd Foot, to be ens., vice Shepherd, who exchanges—1st Feb.

1st West India Regt.—Fredk. Friend Ridley Terry, gent., to be ens., by purchase, vice Ralph Henry Potts, promoted.

DEPOT BATTALIONS.

Capt. William Vesey Munnings, 24th Foot, to be instructor of musketry, vice Capt. Montague Browne, 24th Foot, about to be appointed Staff Officer of Pensioners—1st April.

COMMISSARIAT DEPARTMENT.

Deputy Assistant-Commissary-Gen. Owen Edward Hayter has been permitted to resign his Commission—1sst April.

BREVET.

Lieut.-Col. Windham Charles Leopold Baker, retired full-pay, Royal Artillery, to be col., the rank being hon. only—8th March.

Quart.-mast. William Reuben Kirkman, upon half-pay, Royal Artillery, to be capt., the rank being hon. only.

Memorandum—The surname of Maj.-Gen. the Hon. Alexander Gordon is Hamilton Gordon, and not Gordon only, as hitherto described.

Memorandum—The Christian names of Capt. and Brev.-Lieut.-Col. Drummond Hay, upon half-pay, late 78th Foot, are Thomas Robert Hay, and not Thomas Robert only, as hitherto described.

---

WAR OFFICE, PALL MALL, April 15.

BREVET.

Sec. Capt. Henry Clement Swinnerton Dyer, Royal Artillery, to be maj.

COMMISSARIAT DEPARTMENT.

Acting Deputy Assist.-Commissary-Gen. William John Jortin Warneford to be deputy assist.-commissary-gen.

HONOURABLE ARTILLERY COMPANY OF LONDON.

Sec. Lieut. Edward Mease to be first lieut., vice Dawes, retired.

The Commission held by Capt. Frederick Riviere is renewed for a further period of five years from the 4th March.

---

THE MILITIA GAZETTE.

WAR OFFICE, PALL MALL, April 12.

Memorandum — West Kent Yeomanry Cavalry—Her Majesty has been graciously pleased to approve of the West Kent Yeomanry Cavalry being designated by the title of "Queen's Own West Kent Yeomanry Cavalry."

East Kent Regt. of Militia—Capt. Richard Daniel Pennefather

to be maj., vice Lieut.-Col. Dering, resigned.

3rd Regt. of the Duke of Lancaster's Own Militia—Lieut. Wm. Fitch Storey to be capt., vice James Ormsby, resigned.

4th or Duke of Lancaster's Own (Light Infantry) Regt. of Royal Lancashire Militia — Frederick Annesley Bretherton, gent., to be lieut.

3rd Regt. of the Duke of Lancaster's Own Militia—Her Majesty has been graciously pleased to accept the resignation of the commission held by Capt. James Ormsby.

2nd Somerset Regt. of Militia—David Macliver, gent., to be lieut., vice Salmon, resigned.

1st Regt. of King's Own Staffordshire Militia—Lieut. David Dowie to be capt., vice Lane, resigned; John R. B. Elwes, gent., to be lieut., vice Dowie, promoted.

2nd Regt. of King's Own Staffordshire Militia—The Hon. Henry Stuart Littleton to be supernumerary lieut.; Samuel Perks, gent., to be super. lieut.

Warwickshire Yeomanry Cavalry—George Wise, gent., to be cor., vice Mordaunt, promoted.

Perthshire Militia — Patrick Small, gent., to be lieut.; Thomas McDougall, gent., to be lieut.; George Muirhead, gent, to be lieut.

1st Derbyshire Militia—Assist.-Surg. Joseph German to be surg., vice Harwood, resigned.

Derbyshire Yeomanry Cavalry—Capt. Charles Colvile to be lt.-col.; Lieut. Sir Mylles Cave Brown Cave, Bart., to be maj.; Thomas William Evans, Esq., to be capt.; Edward Sacheverell Chandos Pole to be capt.; William Sale, Esq., to be cor.

Forfar and Kincardine Militia Artillery—Lieut. Charles Basil Fisher to be capt., vice Fothringham, deceased.

1st Troop of Suffolk Yeomanry Cavalry — Philip Bennet the younger, Esq., to be capt., vice Philip Bennet the elder, resigned.

---

WAR OFFICE, PALL MALL, April 15.

[The following appointment is substituted for that which appeared in the *Gazette* of the 5th inst :—]

East York Regt. of Militia— James Sisson Cooper, gent., late Lieut. and Instr. of Musketry, Royal North Lincoln Militia, to be quart -mast., vice Woodlock, resigned—1st March.

Flintshire Militia—Lieut. Chas. William Shackle to be capt., vice Clowes, resigned.

King's Own Light Infantry Regt. of Militia—Capt. Samuel James Remnant to be maj., vice Edwards, resigned.

Queen's Own Light Infantry Regt. of Tower Hamlets Militia— William Henry Stainthorpe, gent., to be lieut., vice Buchanan, resigned.

Edinburgh County Militia— James Craig, gent., to be lieut., vice Younger, resigned.

6th Regt. of West York Militia —Malcolm Potter Macqueen, Esq., late Capt. 91st Regt., to be capt., vice Swann, resigned.

Queen's Own Regt. of Oxfordshire Yeomanry Cavalry—Capt. Benjamin John Whippy, to be maj.; Lieut. Henry Lomax Gaskell to be capt., vice Whippy, promoted; Cor. Beville Ramsay to be lieut., vice Gaskell, promoted.

----

THE VOLUNTEER GAZETTE.

WAR OFFICE, PALL MALL, April 12.

Memorandum — 2nd Norfolk Rifle Volunteer Corps — Adjt. Frank Astley Cubitt to serve with the rank of Capt.

1st Norfolk Rifle Volunteer Corps—Lieut.-Col. George Black late 75th Foot, to be lieut.-col., vice Brett, resigned.

17th Somersetshire Rifle Volunteer Corps—Ens. Alfred Pope to be lieut., vice Simmons, resigned; Charles Milsom the younger, gent., to be ens , vice Pope, promoted.

1st Aberdeenshire Rifle Volunteer Corps—Lieut. Irvine Kempt, to be capt., vice William Esplin, *resigned*; Ens. James Haddon *Bower* to be *lieut.*, vice Kempt, *promoted*; William Esplin, jun.,

to be ens., vice Bower, promoted; Lieut. Richard Latter to be capt., vice Alexander Pirie Hogarth, resigned; Ens. Alexander Stephen to be lieut., vice Latter, promoted; Charles Frederick Runey to be ens., vice Stephen, promoted.

9th Dumbartonshire Rifle Volunteer Corps—George Colquhoun, gent., to be ens., vice Alexander MacNiven, resigned.

3rd Durham Artillery Volunteer Corps—Henry Wilson, to be capt.; Sec. Lieut. Joseph Logan Thompson to be first lieut.; Isaac Tweddell to be sec. lieut.; Joseph Richardson to be sec. lieut.

2nd Administrative Battalion of Monmouthshire Rifle Volunteers —The Rev. John Cleaves Llewellyn to be hon. chap., vice Davies, resigned.

3rd Staffordshire Rifle Volunteer Corps—James Bull, gent., to be lieut., vice Dimmock, promoted.

9th Staffordshire Rifle Volunteer Corps—Lieut. John Nash Peake to be capt., vice Adams, promoted.

1st Isle of Wight Rifle Volunteer Corps — Thomas Matthias Baker to be ens.

18th Glamorganshire Rifle Volunteer Corps—Ens. Hubert de Burgh Thomas to be lieut.; Robert Stewart, gent., to be ens., vice Thomas, promoted.

13th Perthshire Rifle Volunteer Corps—Lieut. Robert Pearson Wylie to be capt., vice Macdonald resigned; Ens. James McFarlane to be lieut., vice Wylie, promoted; James Baxter, gent., to be ens., vice MacFarlane, promoted.

8th Surrey Rifle Volunteer Corps—Henry John Tritton, gent., to be ens., vice Jones, promoted.

12th Surrey Rifle Volunteer Corps—Septimus Merriman, gent., to be ens., vice Thomas Laxmore Wilson, resigned.

22nd Surrey Rifle Volunteer Corps—Henry Townshend, gent., to be ens., vice Weston, promoted.

5th Banffshire Rifle Volunteer Corps—Richard Hector to be ens., vice McArthur, resigned.

5th Derbyshire Rifle Volunteer Corps—Howard Allport, gent., to be ens., vice Turner, resigned.

1st Herefordshire Rifle Volunteer Corps—Ens. Henry Child Beddoe, promoted.

10th Renfrewshire Rifle Volunteer Corps—Alexander Campbell, gent., to be ens., vice McDonald, resigned.

22nd Renfrewshire Rifle Volunteer Corps—Lieut. John Munsie to be capt., vice Darroch, resigned; Ens. Robert William Robertson to be lieut., vice Munsie, promoted.

[The following appointment is substituted for that which appeared in the *Gazette* of the 15th ult :—]

3rd Renfrewshire Rifle Volunteer Corps—Stewart Clarke to be capt., vice Coats, resigned.

[The following appointment is substituted for that which appeared in the *Gazette* of the 1st January last.]

19th Surrey (Lambeth) Rifle Volunteer Corps—Charles Henry Driver, gent., to be ens.

Memorandum—The 8th Stirlingshire Rifle Volunteer Corps having been struck out of the records of the War Office has ceased to hold any designation in the County Force.

---

WAR OFFICE, PALL MALL, April 15.

2nd Norfolk Rifle Volunteer Corps—Frank Astley Cubitt, Esq., late Capt. 5th Fusiliers, to be adjt., from 19th Feb.—27th Feb.

38th Middlesex Rifle Volunteer Corps—Edward Robert King Harman, formerly of Her Majesty's 60th Rifles, and late of the Prince of Wales' Royal Regt. of Longford Rifles, to be adjt., from the 17th Dec., 1863.

21st Durham Rifle Volunteer Corps — William Watson, jun., esq., to be lieut., vice Holmes, resigned.

16th Middlesex Rifle Volunteer Corps—James Robinson to be ens , vice Peake, promoted.

20th Middlesex Rifle Volunteer Corps—William Jordan to be ens., *vice* Bennetts, promoted.

Queen's (Westminster) Rifle Volunteer Corps—Ens. Chas. Stephenson to be capt., vice Elliott, resigned ; Ens. Louis Davidson to be lieut., vice Fowler, resigned.

29th Middlesex Rifle Volunteer Corps—Henry Chas. Lewis Bebb to be ens.

6th West Riding of Yorkshire Rifle Volunteer Corps—Rober Lowenthal to be ens.

28th West Riding of Yorkshire Rifle Volunteer Corps—William Cass to be lieut., vice Best, resigned; Charles Horsfall Denham to be ens., vice Clough, resigned.

22nd Kent Rifle Volunteer Corps—John Jaap to be lieut., vice Filmer, resigned.

1st Cinque Ports Rifle Volunteer Corps—Morris Dickinson, Esq., to be ens., vice John Charles Savery, resigned.

1st City of Edinburgh Artillery Volunteer Corps—Maj Thomas Bell to be lieut.-col., vice Welwood, resigned; Capt. John Boyd to be maj., vice Bell, promoted; Sec. Lieut. David Robertson to be first lieut., vice Spence, promoted; James Laing to be first lieut., vice Chalmers Izett Paton, resigned; George Hay to be sec.-lieut., vice Robertson, promoted; Andrew Syme to be sec. lieut., vice James Paton, resigned.

8th Lancashire Artillery Volunteer Corps—Capt Charles Inman to be maj.

1st Lancashire Engineer Volunteer Corps—Capt. Thos. Duncan to be maj ; Sec. Lieut. Alexander Duncanson to be first lieut., vice Kirby, resigned; Robert Bouverie Mullner, gent., to be first lieut., vice Beloe, promoted; Henry Newman, gent., to be sec. lieut., vice Lobley, promoted; Robert Armstrong Foley, gent., to be sec. lieut., vice Arundall, promoted.

2nd Lancashire Engineer Volunteer Corps—David Mitchell Lyon, gent., to be hon. assist.-surg.

1st Manchester, or 6th Lancashire Rifle Volunteer Corps—Ens. George Harding to Walmsley, resigned.

gent., to be ens., vice Harding, promoted.

8th Lancashire Rifle Volunteer Corps—William Ormerod Walker, gent., to be ens.

47th Lancashire Rifle Volunteer Corps—Abraham Hartley, gent, to be lieut., vice West, resigned.

6th Ayrshire Rifle Volunteer Corps—Andrew Wilson Faulds to be ens., vice Faulds, promoted.

7th Ayrshire Rifle Volunteer Corps—Robert Forester to be capt., vice Baird, resigned.

10th Glamorganshire Rifle Volunteer Corps—Ens. Daniel Rees to be lieut., vice Howard, resigned.

Oxford University Rifle Volunteer Corps—Ens. Leopold George Gordon Robbins to be lieut., vice Clive, promoted.

3rd Hampshire Artillery Volunteer Corps—Daniel Williams to be capt.; Sec. Lieut. Joseph Smart Watson to be first lieut.

2nd Administrative Battalion of Worcestershire Rifle Volunteers—John Slaney Pakington to be maj.

7th Lincolnshire Rifle Volunteer Corps—Lieut. John Wilby Preston to be capt., vice Hollway, resigned; Ens. George Walker to be lieut., vice Preston, promoted; Robt. Mackinder, gent., to be ens., vice Walker, promoted.

18th Lincolnshire Rifle Volunteer Corps—Tom Casswell, gent., to be ens., vice Cragg, promoted.

10th Staffordshire Rifle Volunteer Corps—Thomas William Minton, gent., to be ens., vice Adams, resigned.

Lightning Source UK Ltd.
Milton Keynes UK
UKHW011835281118
333023UK00011B/916/P

9 780266 610144